MEDIEVAL AND RENAISSANCE FAMAGUSTA

For Ara

Medieval and Renaissance Famagusta

Studies in Architecture, Art and History

Edited by Michael J. K. Walsh, Peter W. Edbury and
Nicholas S. H. Coureas

ASHGATE

Published by
Ashgate Publishing Limited
Wey Court East
Union Road
Farnham
Surrey GU9 7PT
England

Ashgate Publishing Company
Suite 420
101 Cherry Street
Burlington, VT 05401-4405
USA

www.ashgate.com

British Library Cataloguing in Publication Data
Medieval and Renaissance Famagusta: studies in
architecture, art and history.
1. Famagusta (Cyprus)–History. 2. Architecture,
Medieval–Cyprus–Famagusta. 3. Architecture,
Renaissance–Cyprus–Famagusta. 4. Architecture,
Medieval–Conservation and restoration–Cyprus–
Famagusta. 5. Architecture, Renaissance–Conservation and
Restoration–Cyprus–Famagusta.
I. Walsh, Michael J. K., 1968– . II. Edbury, P. W. (Peter W.). III. Coureas, Nicholas S. H.
956.9'3-dc23

Library of Congress Cataloging-in-Publication Data
Medieval and Renaissance Famagusta : Studies in Architecture, Art and
History / Edited by Michael J. K. Walsh, Peter W. Edbury and Nicholas S. H. Coureas
pages cm
Contributions in English and French.
Includes bibliographical references and index.
ISBN 978-1-4094-3557-0 (hardcover : alk. paper)
1. Art, Cypriot–Cyprus–Famagusta. 2. Art, Medieval–Cyprus--Famagusta. 3. Art,
Renaissance–Cyprus–Famagusta. 4. Architecture,
Medieval–Cyprus–Famagusta. 5. Architecture,
Renaissance–Cyprus–Famagusta. 6. Cultural
Property–Protection–Cyprus–Famagusta. 7. Famagusta (Cyprus)–Buildings,
structures, etc. 8. Famagusta (Cyprus)–History.
I. Walsh, Michael J. K., 1968– editor of compilation. II. Edbury, P. W. (Peter W.), editor of
compilation. III. Coureas, Nicholas S. H., editor of compilation.
N7290.C92F366 2012
709.5693–dc23

2012000955

ISBN 9781409435570 (hbk)

MIX
Paper from
responsible sources
FSC® C018575
FSC
www.fsc.org

Printed and bound in Great Britain by
MPG Books Group, UK

Contents

List of Figures *ix*
List of Plates *xv*
List of Tables *xvii*
Notes on Contributors *xix*
Foreword by Philippe Roux de Lusignan *xxv*
Preface by Nicola Coldstream *xxvii*
Acknowledgements *xxix*

Introduction – Famagusta: An Imperilled Cultural Mosaic in the Eastern Mediterranean 1
The Editors

Part I: History and Historiography

1 Camlet Manufacture, Trade in Cyprus and the Economy of Famagusta from the Thirteenth to the Late Fifteenth Century 15
David Jacoby

2 Famagusta and the Tradition of History Writing in Frankish Cyprus 43
Peter W. Edbury

3 Mythes et réalités de la présence templière à Famagouste 53
Pierre-Vincent Claverie

4 Taverns in Medieval Famagusta 65
Nicholas S. H. Coureas

Part II: Art and Architecture

5 St Nicholas in Famagusta: A New Approach to the Dating, Chronology and Sources of Architectural Language 75
Arne Franke

6 Notes on the Marginal Sculpture of the Cathedral of St Nicholas 93
Allan Langdale

7 Les Ordres mendiants à Famagouste: une référence spirituelle et architecturale 115
Thierry Soulard

8 The Holy Mother of God Armenian Church in Famagusta 133
Dickran Kouymjian

9 Gothic and Byzantine in the Monumental Arts of Famagusta: Diversity, Permeability and Power 147
Justine M. Andrews

10 Famagusta from a Latin Perspective: Venetian Heraldic Shields and Other Fragmentary Remains 167
Vincenzo Lucchese

11 The Military Architecture of Venetian Famagusta 187
Gianni Perbellini

Part III: Conservation

12 What Lies Beneath: A Contemporary Survey of the Surviving Frescoes of the Churches in the Syrian Quarter of Famagusta 199
Michael J. K. Walsh

13 Twentieth-Century Restorations to the Medieval and Renaissance Monuments of Famagusta 217
Ege Uluca Tümer

14 Monumental Buildings in the Revitalization Process of Historic Urban Quarters: The Case of the Walled City of Famagusta 235
Naciye Doratlı

15 An Inspection of Three of Famagusta's Churches 255
Paulo B. Lourenço and Luís F. Ramos

16 An Assessment of the Structural Fabric of the Church of Saints Peter and Paul: A Case Study in Historical Record and Structural Appraisal 265
George S. Ballard and Stephen W. Kemp

17 The Historic Walled City of Famagusta, 2008: A Report 275
Robert Silman and Kent Severson

Appendix I: Address delivered by Michael J. K. Walsh in Paris, 4 April 2008 291

Appendix II: Press Release 293

Appendix III: Chronology of Venetian Administration, for Dating the Coats of Arms of Famagusta 297

Appendix IV: Armenian Manuscript Colophons from Famagusta and Cyprus 301
Compiled by Dickran Kouymjian

Appendix V: Typed Notes by M[onica] Bardswell, February 1937 from Conway Library, Courtauld Institute 307
Reproduced by Dickran Kouymjian

Bibliography *311*
Index *331*

List of Figures

'Famagusta' (146 x 179mm), in Karl Baedeker, *Konstantinopel, Balkanstaaten, Kleinasien Archipel, Cypern: Handbuch Fur Reisende* (Leipzig, 1914) *xxx*

5.1 Design drawing of window tracery for the west-façade of Cologne Cathedral, detail of '*Riss* F' (reproduced in Steinmann, M., *Die Westfassade des Kölner Domes* (Cologne, [2003]), © Dombauarchiv Köln, M. Steinmann) 88
5.2 Window tracery of St Nicholas, nave, upper storey, north (photograph: Arne Franke) 89

6.1 Sculpture of winged figure on the north face of the south tower of St Nicholas (photograph: Allan Langdale) 96
6.2 Central portal of St Nicholas (photograph: Allan Langdale) 101
6.3 Boss of the *Agnus Dei* from one of the canopies of the central portal of St Nicholas (photograph: Allan Langdale) 102
6.4 Statue of an ecclesiast or saint, limestone, ht. 56 in. Kept in the 'Chimney Mansion' Museum, Famagusta (photograph: Michael Walsh) 103
6.5 A gargoyle water spout from St Nicholas (photograph: Allan Langdale) 106
6.6 Corbel figure from St Nicholas (photograph: Allan Langdale) 107
6.7 Corbel figure from St Nicholas (photograph: Allan Langdale) 107
6.8 Fragments of leonine animals on the canopies of the central portal jambs of St Nicholas (photograph: Allan Langdale) 108
6.9 Dragon near the canopies on the façade of St Nicholas (photograph: Allan Langdale) 108
6.10 Dragon figure from the façade of St Nicholas, south tower (photograph: Wilbert 'Skip' Norman) 109
6.11 Knight (?) figure from the façade of St Nicholas, north tower (photograph: Wilbert 'Skip' Norman) 111

6.12 Nude man suffering, from the façade of St Nicholas, south tower (photograph: Wilbert 'Skip' Norman) 111

6.13 Figure of a harpy (?), St Nicholas, east face, south tower (photograph: Allan Langdale) 112

7.1 Stephano Gibellino, *Gravure représentant le siège de Famagouste* (Brescia, 1571), cl. BNF, détail représentant la ville 116

7.2 Eglise des Franciscains, vue générale (photograph: Justine Andrews) 117

7.3 Eglise des Carmes, vue générale extérieure, flanc sud (photograph: Thierry Soulard) 119

7.4 Eglise Sainte-Anne, vue générale extérieure (photograph: Allan Langdale) 123

7.5 Eglise des Carmes, vue intérieure vers l'abside (photograph: Thomas Kaffenberger) 125

7.6 Cathédrale Saint-Nicolas, vue générale du flanc nord (photograph: Thierry Soulard) 127

7.7 Cathédrale Saint-Nicolas de Famagouste, élévation intérieure (photograph: Thierry Soulard) 131

8.1 Armenian Church with residents in 1974 (photograph: Dickran Kouymjian) 134

8.2 Detail from *Nativity* in 1974 (photograph: Dickran Kouymjian) 144

9.1 Cathedral of St Nicholas, detail of chevet (photograph: Thomas Kaffenberger) 151

9.2 Cathedral of St George of the Greeks, west façade (photograph: Wilbert 'Skip' Norman) 152

9.3 Church of SS Peter and Paul (photograph: Allan Langdale) 153

9.4 Church of SS Peter and Paul, interior (photograph: Allan Langdale) 154

9.5 Church of SS Peter and Paul, north door (photograph: Michael Walsh) 155

9.6 Nestorian Church (photograph: Justine Andrews) 157

10.1 Portal of Loggia Bembo, near Cathedral of St Nicholas (photograph: Vincenzo Lucchese) 171

10.2 Comparison with Bembo blazon, engraved by V. Coronelli (1706) (photomontage: Vincenzo Lucchese) and convolute shield of Bembo, walled above a window of Loggia Bembo (photograph: Vincenzo Lucchese) 172

10.3 Blazon within a *sannitico* shield (photograph: Vincenzo Lucchese) 173

10.4 Arch with mixtilineal undulation, in portal of House of Assemblies (photograph: Vincenzo Lucchese) 174

10.5 Portal capitals of Loggia Bembo (photograph: Vincenzo Lucchese) 175
10.6 Palace of Provveditore, with coat of arms of Giovanni Renier, Famagusta (photograph: Allan Langdale) 176
10.7 Comparison with Renier blazon, engraved by V. Coronelli (1706) (photomontage: Vincenzo Lucchese) 177
10.8 St George of the Greeks, Famagusta (photograph: Thomas Kaffenberger) 178
10.9 Structure of vaults, including amphorae or pitchers, St George of the Greeks (photograph: Vincenzo Lucchese) 181
10.10 Barbaro shield in Vaulted Chambers of Famagusta Castle. Comparison with blazon engraved by V. Coronelli (1706) (photomontage: Vincenzo Lucchese) 182
10.11 Loredan shield on right parastas of Famagusta Gate in Nicosia. Comparison with blazon engraved by V. Coronelli (1706) (photomontage: Vincenzo Lucchese) 183
10.12 Winged lion above main entrance of Othello's Tower, Famagusta. Comparison with lion of Piazzetta San Marco in Venice and a miniature (early 16th century) (photomontage: Vincenzo Lucchese) 184
10.13 Crouched lion, near Othello's Tower, comparison with that at portal of Venice Arsenal (photomontage: Vincenzo Lucchese) 185

11.1 The dynamics of power in the Mediterranean 1558–1570 188
11.2 The historic monuments of Famagusta 193

12.1 Aerial view of Famagusta, 1917 (photographer unknown) 200
12.2 The Syrian Quarter of Famagusta in the 1930s (photograph: Theophilus Mogabgab) 200
12.3 Mrs Monica Bardswell at work in the 1930s on St George of the Greeks (Conway Library, Courtauld Institute) 205
12.4 St Anne Church, frescoes of the south wall (photograph: Monica Bardswell, Conway Library, Courtauld Institute) 206
12.5 St Anne Church, detail of *The Descent from the Cross* (photograph: Monica Bardswell, Conway Library, Courtauld Institute) 207
12.6 St. Anne Church, interior 2008 (photograph: Wilbert 'Skip' Norman) 208
12.7 St Anne Church, *The Assumption* (photograph: Wilbert 'Skip' Norman) 209
12.8 Armenian Church, *Flagellation* and *Nativity* (photograph: Monica Bardswell, Conway Library, Courtauld Institute) 210
12.9 Armenian Church, *St George and the Dragon* (photograph: Monica Bardswell, Conway Library, Courtauld Institute) 211

12.10	St George of the Greeks, apse of south aisle (photograph: Monica Bardswell, Conway Library, Courtauld Institute)	212
12.11	St George of the Greeks, apse of south aisle (photograph: Monica Bardswell, Conway Library, Courtauld Institute)	213
12.12	St Mary of Carmel, *St George and Dragon* (photograph: Monica Bardswell, Conway Library, Courtauld Institute)	214
13.1	British period entrances in the curtain wall at the port (photograph: Ege Tümer)	219
13.2	The Genoese loggia, as identified by Enlart but today disappeared (C. Enlart, *Villes Mortes du Moyen Age* [Paris, 1920], p. 152)	220
13.3	Grave excavations in the Templars' Church, 1941 (Mogabgab Archive, unpublished)	225
13.4	Accidental discovery of Venetian fountain in 1947 (Mogabgab Archive, unpublished)	225
13.5	Land gate approaches, excavation and clearance, 1937 (Mogabgab Archive, unpublished)	226
13.6	SS Peter and Paul before opening of windows and doors, 1938 (Mogabgab Archive, unpublished)	227
13.7	Restoration of the city walls, 1939 (Mogabgab Archive, unpublished)	228
13.8	Bedestan Street in 1946 (Mogabgab Archive, unpublished)	229
14.1	Character areas for Famagusta (Naciye Doratlı)	242
15.1	St George of the Latins, stone deterioration (photographs: Lourenço and Ramos)	258
15.2	St George of the Latins, loose stone elements (photographs: Lourenço and Ramos)	258
15.3	St George of the Latins, corroded modern lintel (photographs: Lourenço and Ramos)	258
15.4	St George of the Latins, weakened buttressing through stone deterioration (photographs: Lourenço and Ramos)	259
15.5	St George of the Latins, earthquake damage and cracking (photographs: Lourenço and Ramos)	259
15.6	St George of the Greeks and St Symeon with problematic areas marked. Plan (Lourenço and Ramos)	260
15.7	The Carmelite Church with window tracery deterioration (photographs: Lourenço and Ramos)	260
15.8	The Carmelite Church with problematic areas marked (Lourenço and Ramos)	261
15.9	Test planning of St George of the Latins Church (photographs: Lourenço and Ramos)	261

15.10 Dynamic testing on St George of the Latins (Lourenço and Ramos) 262

17.1 Ashlar dimension stone, filled with a core of mortared rubble (photograph: Silman and Severson) 277
17.2 Wind and water erosion (photograph: Silman and Severson) 278
17.3 St George of the Latins, general view (photograph: Silman and Severson) 279
17.4 Eroded brackets on the apse of St Nicholas Cathedral (photograph: Silman and Severson) 280
17.5 Potential plaster loss in the Church of St Anne (photograph: Silman and Severson) 283
17.6 The erosion of previous restorations, St George of the Greeks (photograph: Silman and Severson) 286

List of Plates

The Plates are located between pages 194–195.

1 Façade of Cathedral of St Nicholas (photograph: Allan Langdale)
2 Corbel figure from Cathedral of St Nicholas (photograph: Allan Langdale)
3 Cathedral of St George of the Greeks (photograph: Thomas Kaffenberger)
4 Armenian Church (photograph: Wilbert 'Skip' Norman)
5 Historic graffiti in the Armenian Church, in Armenian, Ottoman, French, English and Italian (photograph: Michael Walsh)
6 Byzantine churches of SS Zoni and Nikolaos in the Greek Quarter (photograph: Michael Walsh)
7 Cathedral of St George of the Greeks, fresco of the Crucifixion (photograph: Thomas Kaffenberger)
8 Church of St Mary of Carmel, fresco of St Nicholas (right) (photograph: Thomas Kaffenberger)
9 SS Peter and Paul, Sinopia *The Forty Martyrs of Sebaste* (photograph: Allan Langdale)
10 Keystone in Loggia Bembo, comparison with Venetian coin (photomontage: Vincenzo Lucchese)
11 The frieze-pew, probably from Salamis, near Loggia Bembo. Comparison with a Roman mosaic in *House of Dionysos*, Paphos (photomontage: Vincenzo Lucchese)
12 Drawing of galleon beside halo of a saint, left apse, St George of the Greeks (photograph: Vincenzo Lucchese)
13 St Anne Church, painted fragment with scroll (photograph: Wilbert 'Skip' Norman)
14 St Symeon Church, inscription (photograph: Allan Langdale)
15 St Anne Church, *Four Saints* (photograph: Wilbert 'Skip' Norman)
16 Armenian Church, *Flagellation* (photograph: Wilbert 'Skip' Norman)
17 St Mary of Carmel, *Nepotian, Ursyn, and Apollyn* (photograph: Allan Langdale)
18 St Mary of Carmel, *St George and Dragon* (photograph: Wilbert 'Skip' Norman)
19 St Mary of Carmel, *The Sisters* (photograph: Allan Langdale)

20 SS Peter & Paul, section (photograph: Kemp & Ballard)
21 SS Peter & Paul, ceiling plan (photograph: Kemp & Ballard)
22 Recent vandalism of ship graffiti in St George of the Greeks (photograph: Silman & Severson)
23 Cleaning samples, St George of the Greeks (photograph: Silman & Severson)

List of Tables

13.1	Twentieth-century restorations on fortifications	222
13.2	Twentieth-century restorations on churches	223
13.3	Twentieth-century restorations on palace and environs	224
13.4	Distribution of restoration works on monuments through the years	230

Notes on Contributors

Justine M. Andrews is an Associate Professor in the Department of Art History at the University of New Mexico in Albuquerque (USA). Her research interests include the visual culture of Medieval Cyprus and the fourteenth-century Eastern Mediterranean, as well as Crusader Art. She held a Fulbright Research Fellowship in Cyprus in 2008.

George S. Ballard has some 40 years' specialist experience in the application of instrumentation and non-destructive testing to the structural investigation of engineered structures and their foundations. His early research work in field instrumentation for crustal movement and earthquake detection at Geodesy and Geophysics, University of Cambridge, UK, led to the formation of a private practice in geotechnical, geophysical and structural assessments. Particular expertise is in Concrete Technology, Repair Systems, Tunnel Construction Methods, and Historic Building Conservation. He is an external lecturer at the Universities of York and Greenwich.

Pierre-Vincent Claverie (Assemblée Nationale, Paris). Historian of the Latin East, has published approximately 40 studies over the last 15 years, including a PhD thesis on *L'Ordre du Temple en Terre Sainte et à Chypre au XIIIe siècle* (Nicosia, 2005, 3 vol.). His fieldwork deals with the military orders, the Latin church and relations with the Mongols during the Crusades. In 2010 he defended a habilitation thesis entitled *Honorius III et la question d'Orient (1216–1227),* which is currently at press. His current projects concern the composition of the Frankish clergy and the history of medieval Catalonia.

Nicola Coldstream is a historian of medieval architecture specializing in the interface of architecture and decoration. Her books include *The Decorated Style* (1994) and *Medieval Architecture* (2002) a prize-winning volume in The Oxford History of Art series.

Nicholas S. H. Coureas studied Ancient and Medieval History at the University of London and currently works as a Senior Researcher at the

Cyprus Research Centre in Nicosia, Cyprus. He has published several books on the history of Lusignan Cyprus, among them *Cyprus and the Crusades*, co-edited with J. Riley-Smith (Nicosia, 1995), *The Latin Church in Cyprus, 1195–1312* (Ashgate, 1997), *The Assizes of the Lusignan Kingdom of Cyprus* (Nicosia, 2002) and, most recently, *The Latin Church in Cyprus, 1313–1378* (Nicosia, 2010). He has also published various articles on the commercial, religious, cultural and strategic aspects of the history of Lusignan Cyprus and is a member of the Society for the Study of the Crusades and the Latin East.

Naciye Doratli holds a PhD in Architecture. She studied Urban Conservation at Eastern Mediterranean University and is now an instructor in the Faculty of Architecture there. She has many scientific publications in the field of urban conservation and revitalization, and chapters in scholarly edited books. She is the Director of EMU Center for Cyprus Studies, a member of the EMU Urban Design and Research Center, registered as an independent expert in the European Commission FP7 (Seventh Framework Programme) and a member of Europa Nostra Scientific Council.

Peter W. Edbury is Professor of Medieval History at Cardiff University where he has taught since 1977. He has written widely on the history of Cyprus and Latin Syria. His best known publications include *William of Tyre, Historian of the Latin East* (with John Gordon Rowe) (Cambridge University Press, 1988) and *The Kingdom of Cyprus and the Crusades, 1191–1374* (Cambridge University Press, 1991). More recently he has re-edited two major treatises on the law and custom of the High Court of Jerusalem and Cyprus: John of Ibelin, *Le Livre des Assises* (Brill, 2003), and Philip of Novara, *Le Livre de Forme de Plait* (Cyprus Research Centre, 2009). He is currently engaged in an ambitious project to re-edit the Old French Continuations of William of Tyre and the so-called *Chronique d'Ernoul et Bernard le Trésorier*. He and Nicholas Coureas are working on a translation of the *Chronique d'Amadi*.

Arne Franke studied in Munich, Venice and Perugia. He holds academic degrees in art history and journalism from the Ludwig-Maximilians-University, Munich. In his thesis he examined Gothic architecture in Cyprus and in particular the Cathedral of St Nicholas in Famagusta. His general fields of research include high Gothic art and the Italian Renaissance. Having worked as editor for an art historical journal he is continuing his research.

David Jacoby, Professor Emeritus, Department of History, The Hebrew University of Jerusalem, Israel, has taught Medieval History for 40 years. His research and publications focus on Byzantium and its former territories, the Crusader states of the Levant, Cyprus and Egypt, and cultural exchange between the West and the Eastern Mediterranean in the 9th–15th centuries. He is the author of the first study devoted to the economic history of Famagusta: 'The Rise of a New Emporium in the Eastern Mediterranean:

Famagusta in the Late Thirteenth Century', *Meletai kai hypomnemata*, 1 (1984), pp. 145–79, reproduced in D. Jacoby, *Studies on the Crusader States and on Venetian Expansion*, Northampton, 1989, no. VIII. Among his studies are: 'Trade and the Economy of Cyprus (1191–1489)', in Th. Papadopoullos, ed., *History of Cyprus*, IV/1, *The Medieval Kingdom, Venetian Rule*, Nicosia, 1995, pp. 387–454 [in Greek].

Stephen W. Kemp has over 40 years' experience in the engineering design, construction, investigation and repair of structures in all continents except Antarctica. After several years with Ove Arup he set up in partnership his own materials testing laboratory and specialized in instrumentation and computer analysis of materials and structures. He now runs his own engineering consultancy. Committed to considering structures from the principles of Newtonian physics he considers that the remediation of structures should be driven by observations and information from the story told by the structure itself.

Dickran Kouymjian, Berberian Endowed Professor of Armenian History & Art, emeritus, was founder and Director of the Armenian Studies Program, California State University, Fresno (1977–2008). He has taught at Columbia University; University of California, Berkeley; the American University Beirut; the American University Cairo; the American University Paris; Yerevan State University; University of Paris-INALCO (Director, Armenian Section 1988–91), and the Catholic University of Louvain. His publications include some 20 books and more than 250 articles. He is co-author of the massive *Album of Armenian Palaeography* (2002, Arm. trans. 2006). In 2008 he was elected to the Armenian National Academy of Sciences. In the same year he was offered a festschrift: *Between Paris and Fresno: Armenian Studies in Honor of Dickran Kouymjian*.

Allan Langdale has written several articles on Famagusta's churches and Venetian remains, including 'At the Edge of Empire: Venetian Architecture in Famagusta, Cyprus'. He also made a documentary film *The Stones of Famagusta: the Story of a Forgotten City* (2008), and has recently completed a guidebook to the archaeology and historical architecture of the region of northern Cyprus.

Paulo B. Lourenço is full Professor at the Department of Civil Engineering, University of Minho, Guimarães, Portugal. He is also Head of the Structural Group and Head of Institute of Sustainability and Innovation in Structural Engineering. He is editor of the *International Journal of Architectural Heritage: Conservation, Analysis and Restoration* and Coordinator of the International Erasmus Mundus Master in Structural Analysis of Monuments and Historical Constructions. His main research interests are masonry and timber, non-destructive testing, advanced experimental and numerical techniques, innovative strengthening techniques and earthquake engineering.

VINCENZO LUCCHESE, architect and honorary inspector of Monuments for the Italian Ministero dei Beni Culturali, is Professor of *rilievo* of historical architecture at the Università di Architettura di Venezia. For many years his scholarly interests have included the historical patrimony of the architecture and art of Venice and territories of the Levant, with particular focus on Greece, its islands and Cyprus.

GIANNI PERBELLINI is an architect, town and country planner, specialized in cultural heritage, conservation, and an expert in history of architecture and military architecture. He is the chairman of the Scientific Council of Europa Nostra and member of the Council of Italian ICOMOS. Since 1973 he has been a frequent visitor to Cyprus, about which, besides many publications regarding the island, he wrote in 1975 the inventory of its fortifications. In Cyprus he was counsellor during 1996–98 for the Paphos Port Authority for the building of the harbour and in 2012 for UNDP-PFF CY for the Famagusta Walls. Recently he edited two books about Cyprus published by Marco Polo System: *Famagusta in Cyprus* (in English and Italian) and *Cipro la dote di Venezia* (in Italian). In 2011 he was the chairman of the team that won the second prize for the redesign of the old GSP area in Nicosia.

LUÍS F. RAMOS is an Assistant Professor at the University of Minho, Portugal. He received his PhD degree from the University of Minho in 2007 with a study of damage identification of ancient masonry structures. His current research interests include non-destructive testing, damage identification, structural health monitoring, dynamic tests, sonic tests, earth constructions, finite element analysis and non-linear analysis of masonry constructions. He has been involved in several national and international specialized consultancy projects and research projects. He is author or co-author of more than 100 technical and scientific publications in the fields of masonry and ND testing.

KENT SEVERSON, a 1985 graduate of the New York University Institute of Fine Arts Conservation Center training program, has participated in archaeological fieldwork and other conservation projects in Turkey, Greece, Italy, Cyprus, Egypt and Argentina. For the past 13 years, when not in the field, he has worked as a conservator in private practice, in Boston, Massachusetts. He has served as visiting instructor at the Iraqi Institute for the Conservation of Antiquities and Heritage, Erbil, Iraq. He is now conservator at the Doris Duke Foundation for Islamic Art at Shangri La in Honolulu, Hawaii.

ROBERT SILMAN is the President of Robert Silman Associates, Structural Engineers, a 130-person firm with offices in New York, Washington, DC and Boston. The firm has participated in the study and restoration of hundreds of landmark buildings throughout the world including such icons as Fallingwater, Carnegie Hall, the US Supreme Court, four State Capitols, Ellis Island and New York City Hall. Robert Silman is the recipient of many professional awards from organizations such as the International Association of Bridge and Structural Engineering, American Institute of Architects, Structural Engineers Association of New York, New York Landmarks Conservancy, Municipal Arts Society, New York City Landmarks Preservation Commission, Historic Districts Council, Concrete Industry Board and Carpenters' Company. Published work has appeared in *Fallingwater* (Rizzoli, 2011), *Structural Engineering International, Scientific American, The Structural Engineer, Bulletin of the Association for Preservation Technology* and *Cultural Resources Management Journal (US National Park Service).*

Thierry Soulard travaille depuis une vingtaine d'années sur l'architecture gothique du sud de la France aux XIIIe et XIVe siècles, à la suite de sa thèse de PhD sur la cathédrale de Limoges en 1993. C'est ce qui l'a conduit à étudier depuis douze ans les constructions gothiques de Chypre et à participer à plusieurs colloques, revues et livres portant sur ce sujet, en particulier une importante collaboration à la publication de l'Académie des Inscriptions et Belles-Lettres, *L'art gothique en Chypre* , édité en 2006. Il s'est attaché particulièrement aux sources du gothique chypriote, en particulier issues de l'architecture gothique rayonnante, de celle des ordres mendiants et de celle des Etats latins de Terre Sainte. Parallèlement, il enseigne l'histoire de l'art médiéval à Paris.

Ege Uluca Tümer is an Assistant Professor in the Department of Architecture at İstanbul Kültür University, where she has been teaching since 1999. In 2006 she completed her PhD dissertation entitled 'Urban Transformation and Development of Famagusta Throughout History' which has since been accepted for publication by Eastern Mediterranean University in Famagusta. Since 1998 she has been a member of Europa Nostra and was one of the founders and Executive Committee members of its branch in Turkey. She is also a member of the ICOMOS National Committee of Turkey. She is currently a Fulbright visiting scholar at the University of Pennsylvania, Historic Preservation Program and working on a project entitled 'A Conservation and Site Management Model for Famagusta Walled City'.

Michael J. K. Walsh was, for nine years, employed at Eastern Mediterranean University in Famagusta. In this time he successfully nominated Famagusta for inclusion in the World Monuments Fund Watch List, brought the Global Heritage Fund to the same city, and in 2010 acted as team coordinator for the United Nations project 'Cultural Heritage Data Collection in the northern part of Cyprus'. He is the author of *This Cult of Violence* (Yale University Press, 2002), *Hanging a Rebel* (Lutterworth Press, 2008) and *Runaway Dreams* (Kennedy & Boyd, 2011); and editor of *A Dilemma of English Modernism* (University of Delaware Press, 2007) and *London, Modernism and 1914* (Cambridge University Press, 2010). He is currently Associate Chair (Research) and Associate Professor of Art History at the School of Art, Design and Media, Nanyang Technological University in Singapore.

Foreword

Philippe Roux de Lusignan

Le 19ème siècle a été pour l'histoire des Lusignans et de Chypre, un siècle de recherches et de découvertes historiques et mythologiques importantes. Les historiens du 20ème siècle ont approfondi et complété ces recherches. Aujourd'hui, grâce à tous les colloques internationaux qui sont organisés, les historiens travaillant sur la période médiévale de Chypre et réunissant leurs connaissances ont fait découvrir des éléments importants sur le plus long règne de l'histoire de Chypre, période des Lusignans.

Preface

Nicola Coldstream

The east coast of Cyprus has a hinterland that has long been redolent of urban civilization and religious cult. Trade and religion flourished from the Bronze Age at Enkomi, through the Classical, Roman and early Christian periods at Salamis-Constantia, to the middle ages at Famagusta. The medieval city of Famagusta is the subject of this book. Surrounded by the modern town and encased within its circuit of walls and bastions built by the Venetian rulers in the sixteenth century, the old city partly survives to this day. Churches – mostly ruined – and the remains of secular buildings are dotted among modern houses and shops. The surprise for the visitor is that most of them are not in local Byzantine styles but in the Gothic style used by contemporary builders in Western Europe. Standing proud of later structures and built of the beautiful golden local stone, these churches are set exotically among palm trees against a backdrop of the deep blue Mediterranean Sea. Cyprus does not represent the furthest reach of Gothic architecture, since the crusaders built it in the Holy Land. Yet the buildings of Famagusta are of exceptional quality, and, owing to long-lasting political circumstances, are largely unknown to all but a few specialists. In the past, neglect and isolation helped to preserve this fabled medieval city; but the passage of time has caused alarming deterioration in its fabric. Were Famagusta to decay irretrievably, an outstanding medieval site would be lost forever. This book aims to bring Famagusta and its plight to the attention of the world.

The foundation date of Famagusta (Turk: Gazimağusa; Gr: Ammochostos) is still not clear, but it existed as a harbour, perhaps fortified, before the Lusignan rulers took over Cyprus in 1192. Of French origins, this branch of the family was crusaders from Jerusalem. It was not until 1291, however, when the crusading port of Acre fell to the Mamluks, that Famagusta began to flourish and grow rich. Trading both locally with the Levant coast and Egypt, and much further afield as an *entrepôt* used by Muslim, Genoese, Venetian and Catalan merchants, Famagusta enjoyed an economic boom throughout the fourteenth century. It was in these years that most of the churches were built and decorated: the cathedral, monasteries, and private family chapels, representing many different Christian denominations. Famagusta succumbed to Genoese rule in 1373 and in 1474 was annexed by Venice along with the rest of Cyprus.

Then, after a lengthy and bloody Ottoman siege, Famagusta eventually fell to Mustafa Pasha in 1571. From then on the city has been a Turkish settlement, the Roman Catholic cathedral converted to a mosque (hence its survival), the Christian population removed to the suburb of Varosha. The port declined, not to be reopened until 1906 under British rule. After Cyprus gained independence in 1960 the old city was closed to Greek Cypriots. The events of 1974, when Famagusta was taken into the Turkish sector of the island, exacerbated matters. But now that there is more freedom of movement between the two sectors and a greater will to arrive at a political settlement, it seems a good time to draw attention to Famagusta's claims to recognition.

The buildings can be saved only through international effort and cooperation. Michael Walsh has been working hard to achieve this, and has gained the support of the United Nations Peacekeeping Force in Cyprus, together with several international cultural organizations, notably the World Monument Fund, ICOMOS (International Council on Monuments and Sites), and Europa Nostra. These non-governmental, apolitical organizations are devoted to the conservation and preservation of our artistic heritage all over the world, a heritage that is witness to our shared past.

This book brings together the work of scholars from many nations. As its chapters demonstrate, art and architecture are historical documents that can be set alongside the written record to reveal the history not only of the city itself but of the multicultural reach of medieval civilization. Famagusta was a city where people of many different cultures met and mingled. Culture clashed with culture; but each learned something of another's world view. Let the preservation of medieval Famagusta be a symbol of such creative harmonies.

Acknowledgements

The Paris conference, and this book which resulted from it, involved the work of many individuals whom the editors would like to thank here. First and foremost, His Excellency Ingemar Lindahl (Ambassador of Sweden) who patiently worked to build trust and cooperation between all of those involved. With the endorsement of Michael Møller (Special Representative of the Secretary-General and Chief of Mission of the United Nations Peace Keeping Force on Cyprus) other key players were subsequently attracted to the project, none more important than the Greek and Turkish Cypriot Mayors of Famagusta, Alexis Galanos and Oktay Kayalp. It was a leap of faith on their part to become publicly involved, and without their support it would have been impossible to achieve so much. Throughout the entire process Erkut Şahali and Halil Güven were also reliable and determined. Demitris Pierides was quick to understand the importance of the project and through him the Pierides Foundation, the Thetis Foundation and the Leventis Foundation all made important financial contributions to meet the substantial costs of the enterprise. Philippe Roux de Lusignan in Paris found us the perfect location for our meeting at the National Archive. The French Embassy in Nicosia and The Seven Pillars Trust made generous contributions towards publication costs which were most welcome.

Behind the scenes the editors would like to thank Dan Frodsham for his involvement in the project from beginning to end, and for his infectious enthusiasm for the material remains of Famagusta; Beatrice Perbellini for supplying the editors with an impressive working bibliography; Anber and Johann at Sidestreets for hosting event after event for Famagusta; and Aida Taskinbayev who spent many weeks preparating a scholarly archive relating to the city. On a personal note, Michael Walsh would like to thank his wife Gül for fully understanding the importance of the endeavour and for providing the academic support and encouragement necessary during a process that was, from time to time, far from easy.

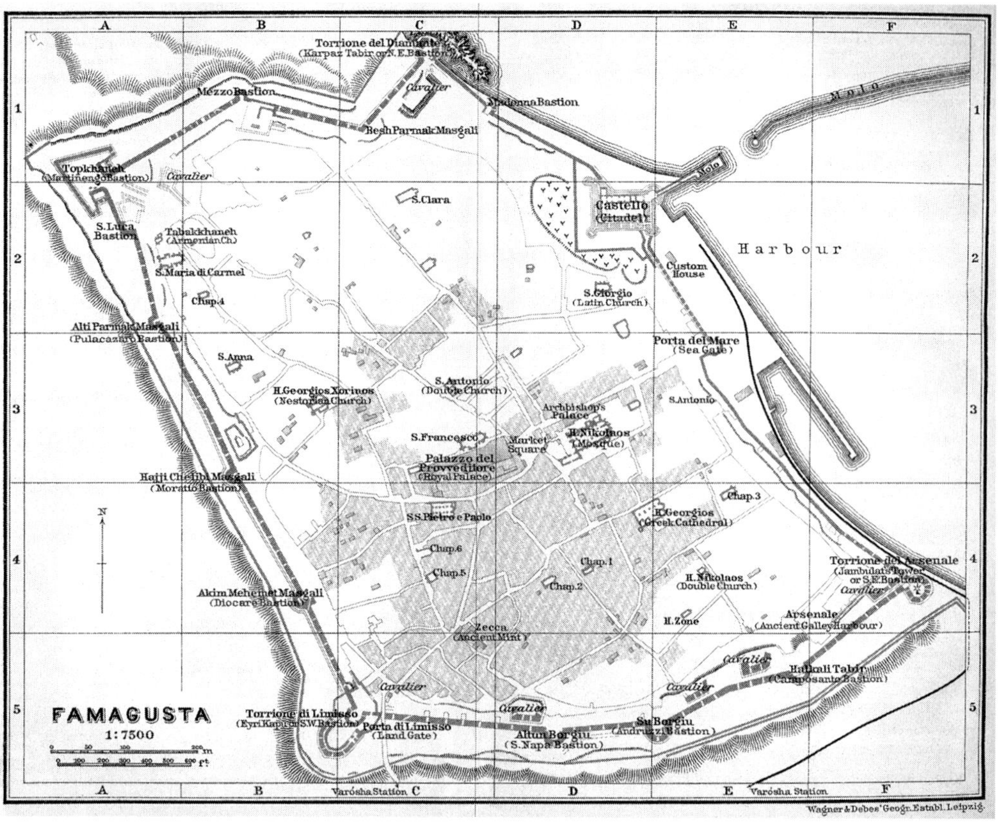

'Famagusta' (146 x 179mm), in Karl Baedeker, *Konstantinopel, Balkanstaaten, Kleinasien Archipel, Cypern: Handbuch Fur Reisende* (Leipzig, 1914)

Introduction
Famagusta: An Imperilled Cultural Mosaic in the Eastern Mediterranean

The Editors

Part I: Famagusta – The City
Peter W. Edbury

I well remember the thrill of my first visit to Famagusta. It was September 1971 and my wife and I had driven over in a hired car from Nicosia. Excitement and anticipation were palpable. And then there it was: the skyline dominated by the former catholic cathedral of St Nicholas flanked by other reminders of Famagusta's heyday, and in the foreground the massive bastions of the Venetian walls. Here was a place about which I had read, and which now exceeded all expectations.

In the middle ages, however, most visitors coming to Famagusta would have seen it first from the sea. Famagusta was, and is, a port. It owed its existence to its natural harbour, and in the course of time it would come to surpass the other ports of Cyprus and take its place as one of the leading commercial centres in the eastern Mediterranean. But in 1192, when the Lusignans took control of the island, there may not have been much there. The town was important enough to be chosen as the location of one of the four catholic bishoprics established in Cyprus in the 1190s, but the paucity of documentary and archaeological evidence from that era leaves little doubt that at that time Paphos, where ships from the West would make their first landfall, and Limassol, which was evidently the main port of call for ships sailing on to Syria, were of greater importance. Such traffic as used Famagusta would seem to have been either local shipping or ships making the comparatively short journey from places on the nearby coast of Syria.

All this was to change in the latter part of the thirteenth century. For much of that century the crusader-held ports of Syria and Palestine had enjoyed enormous prosperity, but from the 1260s onwards their security was undermined as the resurgent Egypt-based Mamluk sultanate set about a systematic conquest of the Christian territory. These campaigns were accompanied by a scorched-earth policy designed to ensure that there could be no recovery, and that included destroying the ports on the Levantine coast. At the same time the Italian maritime republics, whose ships dominated carrying trade, engaged in a series of wars among themselves which disrupted commerce and contributed to the weakness of the Christian position in the East. It was against this background that significant numbers of refugees from Syria arrived in Cyprus, bringing with them their skills and entrepreneurial expertise and adding to the available labour force. In 1289 the Muslims captured and destroyed Tripoli. Acre, Tyre, Beirut and the rest of Latin Syria followed in 1291. Among the many consequences of these developments was an abrupt change in the trade routes. Western merchants would henceforth trade in the Cilician-Armenian port of Ayas (Lajazzo, now Yumurtalık), in which case Famagusta was the most convenient port of call on the way, or they would trade in Famagusta itself, buying either Cypriot merchandise or merchandise shipped across from Syria by local merchants who were oblivious to the papal ban on trade with Mamluk ports. Famagusta's role as a centre for commerce was further stimulated by the fact that the Lusignan kings had come increasingly to use the facilities there as a base for naval activities against corsairs and against the surrounding Muslim-held lands.

If the end of the crusader presence on the coast of Syria and Palestine in 1291 marked the start of Famagusta's medieval heyday, the capture of the city by the Genoese in 1373 marked its end. Its twin role as a commercial hub and military base brought wealth in abundance. Some of that wealth was put to pious use, and a number of churches built at that time survive, at least in part. The cathedral of St Nicholas was under construction during the first three decades of the fourteenth century, and Saints Peter and Paul and Saint George of the Greeks would appear to be slightly later. The early years of the fourteenth century also witnessed the completion of the town walls, including the fortification of the harbour frontage.

This commercial prosperity depended on the regular arrival of merchant ships from the West, but as the fourteenth century drew on various problems became increasingly apparent. Prominent among the westerners were the Genoese; relations between them and the crown were frequently tense, and from time to time there were violent confrontations. The sack of Ayas in 1322 and its final conquest by the Muslims in 1337 damaged a major trade route. From the 1340s onwards Famagusta's position at the centre of trade in the eastern Mediterranean was further undermined by the relaxation of the papal prohibitions on western ships trading in Egypt and the other ports under Mamluk control. But if more ships were now bypassing Cyprus altogether, the total volume of trade itself would have shrunk appreciably as a consequence of the Black Death of 1347–48. Fewer producers and fewer consumers throughout the world of the Mediterranean and Near East inevitably meant less merchandise changing hands; that in turn meant less government revenue from commercial taxation, and thus less money to spend on defence and other requirements. It is against this background that we have to consider King Peter I's crusade, which in 1365 sacked Alexandria. Peter, who reigned from 1359–69, is often written off as an old-fashioned crusade idealist with a completely unrealistic dream of recovering Jerusalem for Christendom. However, behind the rhetoric of crusading, it would seem that he may in fact have been trying to re-establish the centrality of Cyprus in the trading networks in the eastern Mediterranean; certainly in the peace negotiations that followed the 1365 campaign it was commercial demands that feature most prominently. Whatever the truth, his military endeavours failed, and, although Famagusta doubtless profited during the 1360s from its position as his principal military base, Peter had clearly overstretched the resources of his island kingdom.

In 1369 Peter was murdered in a palace *coup* in Nicosia. The political infighting occasioned by this event coupled with the minority of his son and successor, Peter II, has to be seen alongside the deep resentment his war with the Mamluk sultanate had caused the Italian mercantile interests. The stage was set for the war with Genoa. Antagonisms stretched back as far as the 1290s if not beyond, but the actual *casus belli* was a riot at the coronation of Peter II in Famagusta in 1372 when a number of Genoese were killed. When Peter refused to consider compensation, the Genoese raised a substantial fleet. In 1373 their forces seized Famagusta by trickery and inflicted considerable damage on the island.

Famagusta remained under Genoese control until 1464, and although a much enfeebled Lusignan monarchy made occasional attempts to win it back, the kings often found themselves obliged to pay tribute to Genoa. Despite attempts to channel all the commerce of Cyprus through Famagusta, the town itself never regained its former prosperity. Indeed, Genoese occupation proved a disincentive for merchants from other maritime cities to go there. Just as the church building in the first half of the fourteenth century can be taken as an indicator of the level of prosperity at that time, so the lack of surviving monuments from the period of Genoese rule can be taken as a sign of economic stagnation.

In 1464 King James II, with the help of some Egyptian troops, was able to regain possession. Thereafter, and until the end of Venetian rule in 1571, Famagusta was administered separately from the rest of the island. In 1473–74 a dynastic crisis brought about by the failure of royal heirs resulted in the Venetians taking control in Cyprus, and their rule was formalized in 1489 with the abdication of James II's widow, Catherine Cornaro. Under Venice Famagusta's fortunes took a turn for the better. The population in the island as a whole was once again on the increase, and Venice invested heavily in the island's security as a bastion against the growing power of the Ottoman sultanate. The Venetians rebuilt and improved the walls of Famagusta, making them capable of withstanding artillery. They were to prove their effectiveness in the Ottoman siege, a siege of epic proportions which lasted from September 1570 until August 1571.

In the course of the last eight centuries Famagusta has undergone numerous changes of fortune. Against all the odds, the walls and several of the churches have survived virtually intact, and the ruins of many more buildings dating from the middle ages are also preserved. In 2008 I returned to Famagusta for the first time since 1971. It was just as impressive as I had remembered it. On this occasion I was able to admire the impressive interior of the church of Saints Peter and Paul for the first time, and also appreciate other details, such as the fine quality of some of the Venetian masonry in the walls, that had escaped my attention on my earlier visit. Famagusta is a most remarkable place; it is no surprise that its history and monuments are attracting ever more attention from scholars and conservationists.

Part II: Famagusta – The Project

Michael J. K. Walsh

To sit by the ruined monastery of St Francis at sunset, observing the west façade of St Nicholas cathedral recede through a spectrum of warm colours into darkness as the swallows circle the trees in the courtyard of the Palazzo del Provveditore, is to know something of the magic of Famagusta. The mystique is further enhanced through a juxtaposition of silhouetted palm trees, the sound of the *ezan*, and the scented sea breeze from the nearby Eastern Mediterranean – all of which seems inconsistent with the north European architecture which dominates the square. As darkness engulfs the great cathedral, lights illuminate the interiors and throw shadows through the rose window onto the parvis, causing the imagination to drift inexorably to another age, and to the sounds and ceremonies that used to take place behind those great doors centuries ago. The moon rises silently behind the mute belfries, then arches gracefully over the church of SS Peter and Paul, before disappearing again behind the Venetian walls.

Famagusta also possesses an unmistakably haunting quality, however, being the spectacular and abandoned stage-set on which great dramas were once played out by players now long gone. The dignity and tranquillity of the cityscape panorama is tempered by the knowledge that it was here the bloody death struggle took place between tens of thousands of men four and a half centuries ago. Every cut stone, every surviving painting, every traceried window, every graffitied name, is imbued with an importance, a gravitas, that makes the city and its port every bit as emotive as it is majestic. Famagusta may very well be matched in historical significance and cultural dignity by other medieval cities elsewhere, but it is surpassed by none.

This project was conceived in September 2002 through a genuine concern for the historic monuments, and surviving art, of Famagusta. The opening of the 'green line' between north and south Cyprus, and behind which Famagusta had been situated for almost three decades, the following year (2003) afforded some room for optimism, as did the progressive atmosphere in both communities leading up to the United Nations brokered Annan Plan in April 2004. It seemed that with a political solution to the 'Cyprus Problem', with reunification of the island, and with the entry of the new state into the European Union, Famagusta's fate would take a long-awaited kinder turn. In anticipation of the 2004 referendum, I delivered a lecture at the College Arts Association in Seattle, Washington, entitled *Cultural Welfare and Political Stalemate: The Case of Northern Cyprus* in which I highlighted some worrying facts concerning the future of Famagusta – with or without the reunification of the island. Whether submerged in a post-solution wave of commercial development and prosperity, or subjected to continued embargoes and neglect, the lack of any coherent Master Plan for the city and its heritage meant that either political eventuality came with its problems. Fortuitously, John Stubbs, Vice President of the New York based World Monuments Fund was present, and encouraged me to place the Cathedral of St Nicholas on the World Monuments Fund Watch List. With the failure of the Annan Plan several weeks after that speech was given, I decided to apply on behalf, not only of the Cathedral, but of the entire city, and every single structure within its walls. In New York in 2007, Famagusta was placed on the WMF Watch List of the world's 100 most endangered sites. In the inevitable wave of publicity which followed I emphasized that, far from being a politically controversial or divisive move, this concern might yet act as a positive element within a wider, long-term, process of reconciliation. On a more practical note, there was now a 'high-profile international platform which will act as a conduit through which specialized scholarship and expertise can be channelled in an attempt to protect, preserve and plan for the future of the historic town'.[1] The World Monuments Fund inspectors arrived soon afterwards and submitted a report entitled *The Historic Walled City of Famagusta,* which confirmed that safety was an immediate concern, as was the state of the remaining paintings in the walled city, and indeed the actual architectural structures themselves. The inspectors concluded their report: 'The scale of preserving the remaining historic elements of Famagusta is of such enormous proportions that one almost does not know where to begin.' It also warned 'until the current political situation is resolved, little can be done for most of the structures'. Later, scholars from the University of Minho arrived to further study structural damage, and to conduct dynamic identification and sonic tests, in relation to future earthquake activity. Their *Preliminary Report on the Inspection on Three Famagusta Churches,* if anything, allayed many of the fears that had brought them to Famagusta in the first place, though they too expressed great concern over safety, and the art, within the churches. Almost simultaneously a full USAID-sponsored investigation into the structural integrity of one of

---

[1] From my press release after the official announcement of the WMF status for Famagusta. This was certainly in keeping with the fundamental ideology of the *Famagusta Walled City Revitalization Plan,* financed by the EU, established by the United Nations Development Programme and Executed by UNOPS, which had appeared in the meantime (2006).

Famagusta's principal monuments resulted in the comprehensive report *SS Peter and Paul Famagusta: Measured Building Survey and Structural Assessment*.

To ensure that this growing momentum was not lost, a call was made for a scholarly meeting entitled *Medieval and Renaissance Famagusta: A Workshop for the Advanced Study of History, Art & Architecture in the Historic City*, the objectives of which were clear from the outset:

1. To emphasize and understand the rich historical and architectural heritage of the medieval port town of Famagusta between the years 1192–1571;
2. To appreciate the danger that it is facing on account of scholarly neglect and potential development;
3. To draw attention to the art and architecture of the city which are now in urgent need of international expertise.

Letters of support were forthcoming from the United Nations Chief of Mission in Cyprus (Michael Møller), the President of ICOMOS (Michael Petzet), the Vice-President of Europa Nostra (Costa Carras), while funding came from the offices of both the Greek Cypriot (Alexis Galanos) and Turkish Cypriot (Oktay Kayalp) mayors of Famagusta. Further substantial funding came from The Pierides, Leventis and Thetis Foundations. Under the guidance of the Ambassador of Sweden, His Excellency Ingemar Lindahl, a bi-communal 'Famagusta Committee' was also set up to steer the project through to fruition with maximum cooperation from both communities on the island. A neutral, yet appropriate, venue was organized by Philippe Roux de Lusignan, in Paris, and a date set for what was the most concentrated meeting yet convened on the subject of historic Famagusta. At this point Europa Nostra offered to ship the entire debate onto the premises of the European Commission, also in Paris, in order to maximize the impact of the considerable efforts already made by the organizers. In addition to keynote speeches, the powerful documentary film *The Stones of Famagusta: The Story of a Forgotten City* was screened courtesy of its makers Dan Frodsham and Allan Langdale, who were also present. At the end of the meeting, a Scientific Committee was set up by Europa Nostra and a public statement of intent made (see Appendix 2). Towards the end of 2008 I made a second trip to the World Monuments Fund headquarters in New York where it was suggested that, with time moving on, the heritage of Famagusta should not be made to wait for a solution to the 'Cyprus Problem'. In any case, no one present disputed the fact that continued neglect served to benefit no one, and agreed that Famagusta should receive the attention it so desperately deserves. Whether this would come through a combined effort by the World Monuments Fund and Europa Nostra, or whether the city could become a UNESCO World Heritage Site via a new designation system, it was agreed that the plight could be ignored no longer. As this goes to press, the American based Global Heritage Fund has also pledged substantial funding for the conservation of the Sea Gate, and in turn, future long-term planning for the historic city of Famagusta.

This book is the result of the efforts by scholars, ambassadors, politicians, sponsors, film-makers and so on, up to and including the year 2009. As the conference organizer and one of the editors of this publication, I would like to sign off, however, by reproducing the short statement I made at the European Commission to remind us that, however far we feel we have come, there is yet a long way to go until the cultural welfare of Famagusta is secure (Appendix 1).

Part III: Famagusta – The Collection

Nicholas S. H. Coureas

Although there have been numerous studies on the history and monuments of Medieval and Renaissance Famagusta scattered in various scholarly journals over the years, there has never been an entire book devoted specifically to the subject until now. These chapters, written by an international cast of scholars, form three distinct sections: History and historiography, art and architecture, and last but by no means least, conservation. The latter, in view of the slow but sure decay of the edifices, and especially the wall paintings of the medieval city, is not simply important but vital; it provided the impetus for the conference, the proceedings of which constitute this book. As Nicola Coldstream emphasizes in the preface, this book seeks to draw the world's attention to the fact that an outstanding medieval site will be lost if Famagusta's decay is not arrested.

Part I

David Jacoby's chapter presents comprehensively the role of Famagusta from the late thirteenth century onwards in the manufacture of camlets, rightly stressing that the city's function in manufacturing, and not simply exporting, these textiles has been overlooked thus far. He points out how settlers from Latin Syria introduced camlet production to Cyprus, discusses the types produced, their export destinations, the royal legislation and taxation of these camlets, and finally how Famagusta's production declined during the Genoese occupation and finally ended with the transfer of the dye plant from Famagusta to the capital Nicosia, so that under Venice production was centred in Nicosia, with Famagusta simply acting as an export outlet. Peter Edbury's chapter, examining Famagusta through the prism of the Cypriot chronicles, especially Amadi and Makhairas, shows how their more frequent allusions to the city from the late thirteenth century onwards reflects its growing importance at the time, not only as a commercial centre but also as a military base, with references to the arsenal and ship-building, and a political locus second in importance only to Nicosia. Discounting the idea that Famagusta was seen as part of the lost kingdom of Jerusalem, he argues that the kings' coronation there as kings of Jerusalem simply enabled them to acquire an international publicity. Makhairas' narrative vividly describes the Genoese pillage of Famagusta in 1373 but the narratives thereafter largely fall silent, thereby implying what Martoni's account of 1394 makes clear, the city's decline and decay.

Pierre Vincent Claverie's chapter discusses the Templars in Famagusta, observing that their commandery there was less important than those of Limassol, Gastria and Paphos. The architectural style of the so-called Temple church of St Anthony and the anonymous grave sites found there in 1941 furnish no proof that the Templar commandery was located there and Genoese notarial deeds of the late thirteenth and early fourteenth century suggests its location in the area of the *ruga Templi* in the southern part of the walled city, a question that archaeological excavations might resolve. These deeds also record the maritime activities of the Templars in Famagusta while the testimonies of Famagusta merchants in the *Processus Cypricus*, the extant proceedings of the Templar trial on Cyprus, vigorously refuted accusations that the Templars lacked piety. Part I concludes with my chapter on the taverns in Famagusta. Based largely on Genoese and Venetian notarial sources, the chapter points out their unconscious bias in failing for the most part to mention non-Latin tavern keepers, the location and distribution of the taverns, their customers and the types of food and drink consumed there. These sources, however, do show the active participation of women as tavern keepers and how it was a lucrative albeit socially not quite respectable profession.

Part II

Arne Franke's chapter on the Latin cathedral of St Nicholas opens the second section on the art and architecture of Famagusta. He argues that the cathedral's architecture shows mixed origins, partly French, partly from Cologne and the Rhineland, and partly Crusader from Latin Syria, making its character specifically Cypriot rather than deriving wholly or mainly from one tradition. He sees its patronage as stemming from the Latin clergy and people of Famagusta as opposed to the Lusignan crown, while seeing the chronology of its construction as consisting of four distinct phases spanning five decades, disagreeing thereby with Plagnieux and Soulard, who consider the cathedral finished by 1324. In his chapter on the marginal sculptures of the cathedral, Allan Langdale discusses their symbolism in a European as well as a Cypriot context, the history of their dismissal as unimportant by traditional art historians, an attitude going right back to St Bernard of Claivaux in the twelfth century, and their juxtaposition with official sculpture, the latter depicting biblical narratives while the former depicted more profane subjects. In doing so, however, it emphasized the concept and consequences of sin, and in his conclusion the author suggests that St Brigitte of Sweden may have castigated Famagusta's sinners with these sculptures as a backdrop. Dickran Kouymjian's chapter focuses on a surviving non-Latin church of Famagusta, dedicated to the Holy Mother of God. Juxtaposing papal letters and the colophons of Armenian manuscripts, he shows how the former point to an early fourteenth-century construction of the church while the latter indicate its possible existence as early as 1280, although the earliest specific reference to both the church and Famagusta dates from 1310–12. The colophons refer to the church as 'Green', a designation also found in the papal letters. From the late fourteenth to the early twentieth century the church was in disuse. Its frescoed walls are unusual for an Armenian church, most being without wall paintings, and in describing them the author remarks on elements deriving from fourteenth-century western art, concluding that they were painted, at least initially, by an Armenian artist from Cilicia in the early fourteenth century. In her chapter on the Gothic and Byzantine elements in the monumental arts of Famagusta Justine Andrews stresses that Cypriot art was both flexible and permeable. Its patrons, of varied confessional, ethnic and social origins like their target audiences, could regard and select Gothic, Byzantine and Latin Syrian artistic motifs as indicators of status and power rather than as identity markers, bringing to mind how wealthy modern-day Cypriots purchase Mercedes and BMW cars to project status rather than to identify politically or culturally with Germany. Turning to secular architecture, Gianni Perbellini's chapter on the military architecture of Venetian Famagusta shows that it was artillery developments securing the primacy of the infantry in wars within Europe and especially the Italian peninsula during the fifteenth and early sixteenth centuries more than the idea of resisting the Ottoman advance that impelled the adaptation of Venetian fortifications to firearms. He observes how Famagusta typologically reflects the whole transition period, from the medieval-type defences illustrated by the Genoese Othello tower to the state of the art Renaissance bulwarks embodied by the Martinengo bastion, which inspired fortifications throughout Europe and Spanish America down to the late nineteenth century. Vincenzo Lucchese's chapter, also focused on Venetian edifices in Famagusta and the heraldic devices found on them, highlights the utility of the lists of noble families recorded by the sixteenth-century writer Stephen de Lusignan for research purposes. He describes the Venetian buildings in the area of the cathedral of St Nicholas, with heraldic emblems of the Venetian Bembo family and architectural features reminiscent of the Sicilian Chiaromonte family, which in the later medieval and Renaissance periods had economic ties with Cyprus, drawing functional parallels between the Venetian loggia Bembo next to the cathedral with the corresponding loggia in the town of Nicosia in Sicily. Through the invocation of similar parallels between Venetian heraldic devices and sculptures in Famagusta and others corresponding to them in Venice itself he underlines the need for their restoration.

Part III

Part III on the conservation of Famagusta's architectural and artistic heritage commences with a survey of the extant murals by Michael Walsh. Recounting the restoration efforts undertaken to date he suggests that both the white paint and the cement covering murals in the church of St Anne can be removed to uncover the painted interior, mentioning Plagnieux and Soulard's caveat that the appropriate techniques must be employed. He observes that the waxing of the murals undertaken in 1938–39 by Monica Bardswell can facilitate the removal of overlying paint, especially in the Armenian Church, but warns that in unroofed churches such as St George of the Greeks murals survive only when located away from rain, wind and sun. Many murals in the Carmelite church, which Enlart described as perhaps the most interesting, have disappeared since his visit, and those remaining have greatly decayed since Bardswell's visit. Ege Tümer offers a comprehensive account of the British efforts to conserve medieval Famagusta between the years 1935–56. She assesses the quality of this work with reference to the Venice charter of 1964, highlighting important shortcomings, such as a lack of respect for the Ottoman heritage, the use of reinforced concrete, the restorations being generally indistinguishable from the original structures, thereby falsifying the artistic and historical evidence, and the fact that reconstruction where it occurred was not based on documents. Despite these faults, the work achieved saved many historic buildings from collapse. Looking to the future, Naciye Doratlı points out how conservation must take place not in isolation, but integrated within the wider perspective of urban planning. Assessing the EU-funded 2005 Revitalization Plan for the Walled City she endorses its tourism and culture-led emphasis while indicating that it did not take fully into account the symbiotic relationship between the walled city and the rest of the town. The settings as well as the monuments must be maintained, failing which the monuments will resemble 'mountains without foothills, Old Masters without frames'.

The two final chapters in this section record the findings derived from inspections and structural appraisals of individual churches. Lourenço and Ramos selected St George of the Latins, St George of the Greeks and the Carmelite Church for dynamic and sonic testing and preliminary diagnosis, forms of advanced non-destructive inspection. In the first church the inspection revealed severe stone deterioration resulting in inefficient buttresses, loose stones and a highly corroded concrete lintel over the main door. The second church did not differ significantly from its condition circa 1940 but its engravings and frescos need protection, while consolidation of the vault, the window tracery and the flying arch are also required. The third church, also in similar condition to that of circa 1940, shows voids in the masonry, severe stone deterioration around the bases of the western towers and protection needed for its frescos and engravings. The paper of Ballard and Kemp on the structural fabric of SS Peter and Paul likened the building to a house of cards, capable of surprising vertical loads but responding catastrophically to a sideways push. It recommends removal of the steel bar bents introduced under the British as well as the uppermost layers of render. A lightweight reinforced concrete slab could replace the render roof and provide tensile strength to control out of plane motion in the walls as well as bracing to prevent the entire nave from racking.

Five appendices follow the third Part, the first being Michael Walsh's address before the European Commission appealing for funds and expertise to arrest Famagusta's slow destruction; the second Europa Nostra's statement of intent to revive the city's unique cultural heritage in March 2008; and the third the preliminary report of the World Monuments Fund (WMF) inspectors, Robert Silman and Kent Severson, who paid a three day visit to Famagusta at the end of March 2008. The report affirms that Famagusta is a first rate historic site deserving WMF support and listing as a World Heritage Site, but stresses that the efforts to arrest the deterioration caused by natural forces are hampered by the current and ongoing political division of Cyprus. It observes that in the event of reunification the pressures of tourism and development will heighten the need to protect the medieval city. The sheer quantity of building fabric makes their preservation especially challenging, necessitating an overall preservation philosophy backed by strong political will.

Part I: History and Historiography

1

Camlet Manufacture, Trade in Cyprus and the Economy of Famagusta from the Thirteenth to the Late Fifteenth Century

David Jacoby

The economic rise of Famagusta began in the 1260s with the growing settlement of refugees from the coastal cities of the Crusader or Frankish Levant conquered by the Mamluk sultans of Egypt. Famagusta's commercial function expanded substantially after the fall of the Frankish states in 1291. The city became the main transit station for commercial exchanges between western ports on the one hand, Egypt and Syria on the other, and was inserted within the vast and complex commercial network of the Mediterranean. With varying fortunes the city maintained its function as major port in that framework from the late thirteenth century until 1489, when Venice imposed its direct rule over Cyprus.[1]

Famagusta's role in trade has drawn growing attention in the last 30 years or so. On the other hand, the city's function as manufacturing centre has been completely overlooked. The purpose of this chapter is to examine jointly these two facets of Famagusta's economy over some two centuries

[1] D. Jacoby, 'The Rise of a New Emporium in the Eastern Mediterranean: Famagusta in the Late Thirteenth Century', *Meletai kai hypomnemata* (Hidryma archiepiskopou Makariou III), 1 (1984): 145–79, repr. in D. Jacoby, *Studies on the Crusader States and on Venetian Expansion* (Northampton, 1989), no. VIII. For a more general overview of the Cypriot economy, see D. Jacoby, 'To emporio kai he oikonomia tes Kyprou (1191–1489)' (= 'Trade and the Economy of Cyprus (1191–1489)'), in Th. Papadopoullos (ed.), *Historia tes Kyprou*, vol. 4/1, *Mesaionikon Basileion, Enetokratia* (= *History of Cyprus*, vol. 4/1, *The Medieval Kingdom, Venetian Rule*) (Nicosia, 1995), 387–454 (in Greek). For a partially updated overview of the same topic in English, see D. Jacoby, 'The Venetians in Byzantine and Lusignan Cyprus: Trade, Settlement, and Politics', in Angel Nicolaou-Konnari (ed.), La Serenissima *and* la Nobilissima: *Venice in Cyprus and Cyprus in Venice* (Nicosia, 2009). See also N. Coureas, 'Economy', in A. Nicolaou-Konnari and C. Schabel (eds), *Cyprus. Society and Culture 1191–1374* (Leiden, 2005), 103–56. I have purposely limited the chronological range of this chapter to the Lusignan period.

by focusing upon the production and marketing of camlet, a woven fabric. Unlike other Mediterranean products, namely sugar and cotton, camlet has never been the subject of a thorough study, despite its growing diffusion from the thirteenth century onwards.[2] The origin of the name and the nature of camlets are disputed. Furthermore, in the absence of precise data regarding their fibres and weave, it is impossible to identify them among extant medieval textiles. It may seem paradoxical to deal with Famagusta from the thirteenth to the late fifteenth century by focusing upon an unidentified cloth, yet two reasons warrant that approach. Though fragmentary, the evidence regarding Cypriot camlets offers precious insights into Famagusta's economy and, more generally, into the evolution of the Cypriot economy.

'Camlet' appears in medieval sources under various Italian names as 'camelotto', 'clamelotto', 'ciambelotto', 'zambelotto', and the like, and their equivalents in other languages.[3] There is no consensus regarding the nature of Middle Eastern and Cypriot camlets before 1500. In the late thirteenth century Marco Polo regarded the textiles woven of white camel hair in Tangut, a Chinese province north of the Great Wall, as the most beautiful and best camlets in the world.[4] He must have encountered camlets in the Middle East on his way to inner Asia, at an earlier stage of his life, yet did not dwell upon their nature. A commentary to the *Biblia de Alba*, the Castilian translation of the Old Testament made in the first half of the fifteenth century, refers to camlets made in Syria from the hair of young goats.[5] Based on these and other sources, some consider that in the period covered by this chapter Eastern Mediterranean camlets were woven of camel hair, others that Angora goat hair or mohair was used, while still others suggest that a mixture of fibres occurred.

Strangely, none of the modern authors dealing in passing with camlets has faced the challenge posed by the 'lana da ciambellotti' or 'lana da fare ciambellotti', 'camlet wool'. The raw material from which Middle Eastern and Cypriot camlets were woven is mentioned by the fourteenth-century Francesco Balducci Pegolotti, an agent of the Florentine banking and trading company of the Bardi.[6] As in 'bambagia in lana', 'cotton wool', also cited by

---

2 The most recent treatments of sugar and cotton, including in Cyprus, are not entirely satisfactory for Cyprus. M. Ouerfelli, *Le sucre. Production, commercialisation et usages dans la Méditerranée médiévale* (Leiden, 2008); Jong-Kuk Nam, *Le commerce du coton en Méditerranée à la fin du Moyen Âge* (Leiden, 2007). My review of these studies will be published in the *Mediterranean Historical Review*, 25 (2010).

3 See K. Zangger, *Contribution à la terminologie des tissus en ancien français attestés dans des textes français, provençaux, italiens, espagnols, allemands et latins* (Bienne, 1945), 38–40. For Greek, see below, n. 88.

4 Marco Polo, *Il Milione*, ed. L.F. Benedetto (Florence, 1928), 60, chaps. 73–4: 'giambellot de poil de gamiaus', 'çamelloit de poil de gamans'.

5 Gloss to the book of *Exodus*, cited by J. Alfau de Solalinde, *Nomenclatura de los tejidos espanoles del siglo XIII* (*Anejos del Boletín de la Real Academia Espanola*, vol. 19) (Madrid, 1969), 68, n. 128. On camlets from goat hair in Asia Minor, see D. French, 'A Sixteenth Century English merchant in Ankara?', *Anatolian Studies*, 22 (1972): 242–3.

6 Francesco Balducci Pegolotti, *La pratica della mercatura*, ed. A. Evans (Cambridge Mass., 1936), 77, 85, 'camlet wool' in Famagusta; ibid., p. 34, in Constantinople where

Pegolotti, the term *lana* referred to fibres before spinning.[7] In November 1362 the Venetian Brancha Bagnese, a resident of Famagusta, owned five small sacks of 'lana de çambeloti' and 60 sacks of goat hair.[8] The names of the two fibre types and the distinction between them in the same inventory imply that neither ordinary sheep wool nor ordinary goat hair entered into Cypriot camlet weaves.[9] It is also noteworthy that the inventory does not directly refer to camel hair, although camels were used as pack animals in Cyprus.[10]

The nature of Middle Eastern and Cypriot camlets in the period covered here thus remains unknown. Nor can it be clarified by evidence regarding camlets produced in the West, since the term 'camlet', like other textile appellations, underwent a semantic evolution and was applied over the centuries to a variety of fabrics, the fibres and texture of which varied.[11] Camlet appears in some western documents as a serge woollen cloth of rather moderate quality. The tariff listing the goods taxed in Paris in the first half of the fourteenth century mentions 'camelot de Rains', an imitation camlet produced in Reims, among serge fabrics.[12] A Parisian inventory of 1438 lists a 'sarge vermeil de camelot', or 'red serge camlet'.[13] It has been suggested, therefore, that originally camlet had a serge weave.[14] There were also rough woollen textiles with cotton or

---

it presumably was on its way to manufacturing centres rather than imported for local production. For another testimony on 'camlet wool' in this city, see below, n. 111.

7 Pegolotti, *La pratica della mercatura*, p. 366.

8 C. Otten-Froux, 'Un notaire vénitien à Famagouste au XIVe siècle. Les actes de Simeone, prêtre de San Giacomo dell'Orio (1362–1371)', *Thesaurismata*, 33 (2003): 106–8, esp. p. 108, no. 183.

9 A western traveller asserted in 1575 that Cypriot camlets were woven of goat hair. Cited by V. Gay, *Glossaire archéologique du Moyen Âge et de la Renaissance*, texte revu par H. Stein (2 vols, Paris, 1887–1928), 1: 264. However, this testimony cannot be adduced for an earlier period.

10 Camels belonging to the Church of Famagusta are mentioned in a papal letter of 1328. C. Kaoulla and C. Schabel, 'The Inquisition against P. de Castro, Vicar of the Dominican Province of the Holy Land in Nicosia, Cyprus, 1330', *Archivum Fratrum Praedicatorum*, 77 (2007): 127–8. Also around 1340 in a version of the travel account of Ludolph of Sudheim: L. de Mas Latrie (ed.), *Histoire de l'île de Chypre sous le règne de la maison de Lusignan* (3 vols, Paris, 1852–61), 2: 215. Two 'chameliers', in charge of camels, testify in 1469. J. Richard, avec la collaboration de Th. Papadopoullos (eds), *Le livre des remembrances de la Secrète du royaume de Chypre (1468-1469)* (Sources et études de l'histoire de Chypre, vol. 10) (Nicosia, 1983), 145–7, nos. 232–3.

11 Incidentally, on the internet I have found a Chinese manufacturer advertising a '100 percent polyester camlet'.

12 L. Douët-d'Arcq, 'Tarif des marchandises qui se vendaient à Paris à la fin du XIIIe siècle', *Revue archéologique*, 9 (1852): 223. For the dating of the tariff, see R.-H. Bautier, 'La place de la draperie brabançonne et plus particulièrement bruxelloise dans l'industrie textile du Moyen Age', *Annales de la Société royale d'archéologie de Bruxelles, volume jubilaire* (Brussels, 1962), 35–6, esp. p. 36, n. 1, repr. in R.-H. Bautier, *Sur l'histoire économique de la France médiévale. La route, le fleuve, la foire* (London, 1991), no. X. A camlet of Reims is also listed in the inventory of King Ch. VI of France, compiled in 1387: L. Douët-d'Arcq (ed.), *Nouveau recueil de comptes de l'argenterie des rois de France* (Paris, 1874), 240. Serge was a twill weave with a diagonal rib pattern.

13 See Zangger, *Contribution à la terminologie des tissus*, p. 39.

14 F. Piponnier, 'À propos de textiles anciens, principalement médiévaux',

linen warp called 'tiretaine', apparently in camlet weave, two pieces of which measuring 14 arm-lengths each were recorded in France in 1267.[15] On the other hand, the 'chameletts' included among silk textiles in English royal accounts of the late fourteenth century were presumably western textiles woven of a mixture of silk and wool.[16] In the fifteenth century some western camlets were entirely made of silk.[17] It seems, therefore, that the nature of camlets varied from one region to the other and changed over time, the weavers mostly using fibres fairly abundant in their own region or imported raw materials.[18]

Despite the contradictory testimonies adduced so far, several factors point to the rank of Middle Eastern and Cypriot camlets in the hierarchy of medieval textiles. They were often listed together with silk fabrics.[19] They were coupled with them in garments, as in one sewn in 1239 for Count Alphonse of Poitiers.[20] Some of them were dyed with kermes, a high-quality and costly bright scarlet colourant only used otherwise for high-grade woollens and silk textiles.[21] Eastern Mediterranean camlets were fairly expensive, judging

---

Annales. Économies, Sociétés, Civilisations, 22 (1967): 872–3.

15 'Expensa in militia domini Philippi filii regis', in J.-D. Guigniaut et J.N. de Wailly (eds), *Recueil des Historiens des Gaules et de la France* (hereafter: *RHF*), vol. 21 (Paris, 1855), 394, 395: 'pro XIIII alnis tyretenae camelotae'. On 'tiretaine', see Gay, *Glossaire*, 2: 401.

16 L. Monnas, 'Silk Cloths Purchased for the Great Wardrobe of the Kings of England, 1325–1462', *Textile History*, 20 (1989): 286, considers them to be silk textiles. However, the purchase rolls mention this fabric as 'pann' s'ici vocat camalitz', 'a silk cloth called camelett'. This suggests that the cloth was not commonly known and that its inclusion among silk fabrics had to be explained.

17 Gay, *Glossaire*, 1: 262–3.

18 As suggested by W. Heyd, *Histoire du commerce du Levant au moyen-âge* (2 vols, Leipzig, 1885–86), 2: 703–5, and M. Lombard, *Les textiles dans le monde musulman, VII*^e^*–XII*^e^ *siècles* (Paris, 1978), 107–8, who deals with fabrics made respectively of camel and goat hair. The convoluted discussion of the issue by P.A., 'A Note on *Suf* or Camlet', *Bulletin of the American Institute for Iranian Art and Archaeology*, 5 (1938): 254–56, reaches the same conclusion without stating so. (I have been unable to identify this author).

19 Tariff of Barcelona, 1271, § 74, and tariff of Perpignan, 1284, §§ 58, 60, 61, 63 ('camelotz d'Outramar', thus from the Levant), 65; M. Gual Camarena, *Vocabolario del comercio medieval. Collección de aranceles aduaneros de la Corona de Aragón (Siglos XIII y XIV)* (Tarragona, 1968), pp. 131 and 144 respectively. See also below, n. 38.

20 'Itinera, dona et hernesia', in J.N. de Wailly and L.V. Delisle (eds), *RHF*, vol. 22 (Paris, 1865), 609. See also below, n. 35.

21 K.H. Schäfer (ed.), *Die Ausgaben der apostolischen Kammer unter Johann XXII. nebst den Jahresbilanzen von 1316-75 mit darstellender Einleitung* (Vatikanische Quellen zur Geschichte der päpstlichen Hof- und Finanzverwaltung) (2 vols., Paderborn, 1911), 2: 444: 'de cameloto de grana pro domino nostro', in 1324; p. 529: 'pro tinctura duo camelotorum de Suria in grana', in 1332. Both instances refer to Pope John XXII. On *grana* or kermes for woollens, see J.H. Munro, 'The Medieval Scarlet and the Economics of Sartorial Splendour', in N.B. Harte and K.G. Ponting (eds), *Cloth and Clothing in Medieval Europe: Essays in Memory of Professor E.M. Carus-Wilson* (Pasold Studies in Textile History, 2) (London, 1983), 13–69. For silk, see D. Jacoby, 'Silk in Western Byzantium before the Fourth Crusade', *Byzantinische Zeitschrift*, 84/85 (1991/1992): 483, repr. in D. Jacoby, *Trade, Commodities and Shipping in the Medieval Mediterranean* (Aldershot, 1997), no. VIII.

by their prices and the rates of taxation applied to them, in the same range as silks.[22] Finally, popes, kings, queens, and members of the nobility appear among the customers of these camlets.[23] In short, these fabrics were fine and fairly prestigious textiles in the period extending from the thirteenth to the late fifteenth century.

The production of camlets in Cyprus was closely related to their manufacture in the crusader or Frankish states of the Levant, and therefore it is fitting to consider the latter first. There is good reason to believe that the weaving of these fabrics in Tripoli, attested in the thirteenth century, had begun before the crusader conquest, like the manufacture of silken, cotton and linen fabrics produced in the Frankish states.[24] The production of all these textiles was largely geared to export. A black camlet from Tripoli is attested in Genoa in 1222.[25] The English royal chancery recorded four black camlets from Tripoli in 1235.[26] In 1241 Count Alphonse of Poitiers granted two camlets from this city to the nobleman Eustace of Neuville.[27] In 1253 King Louis IX of France, who was staying in Acre, entrusted the seneschal John of Joinville to buy in Tripoli 100 pieces of cloth in various colours, which he intended to offer to the Franciscan friars of his kingdom after returning home. However, it is unclear whether the cloth was 'camelot' or camelin, a woollen textile of rather poor quality.[28] Burchard of Mount Sion, who travelled across the Frankish Levant between 1280 and 1283, and the Arab historian Makrizi assert that 4,000 weavers, clearly an inflated figure, were engaged in the manufacturing of camlets and silk textiles in Tripoli.[29] Camlets from this city are attested

---

22 For some examples, see below, next note and n. 35.

23 See above, n. 21, and below, n. 74–5. Four pieces of camlet were bought in 1303 to sew a garment for King Jaime II of Aragon: Gual Camarena, *Vocabolario del comercio medieval*, p. 248. This must have been Levantine camlet, as implied by the rate of taxation cited in the tariffs mentioned above, nn. 12, 19. On camlets belonging to Count Eudes of Nevers in 1266, see below, n. 35.

24 D. Jacoby, 'The Economic Function of the Crusader States of the Levant: a New Approach', in S. Cavaciocchi (ed.), *Relazioni economiche tra Europa e mondo islamico. Secc. XIII–XVIII* (*Istituto Internazionale di Storia Economica 'F. Datini', Atti delle Settimane di Studi e altri convegni*, vol. 38) (Florence, 2007), 164, 174–5.

25 A. Ferretto (ed.), 'Liber magistri Salmonis (1222–1226)', *Atti della Società ligure di storia patria*, 36 (1906): 149–50, no. 398. The same document mentions a camlet coat adorned with 48 pearls.

26 *Dictionary of Medieval Latin from British Sources*, prepared by R.E. Latham (London, 1975), 248.

27 'Ea quae distributa fuerunt in milicia comitis pictavensis', in *RHF*, 22: 619.

28 Jean sire de Joinville, *Histoire de Saint Louis. Credo et lettre à Louis X*, ed. N. de Wailly (Paris, 1874), 328, § 99. The edited text mentions 'camelins' (see also pp. 328–30, §§ 600–602), whereas camlets appear in the corresponding versions of two other manuscripts. Camlets would have been too luxurious for the monks, since the king himself wore camelin: ibid., p. 20, § 36. On the other hand there is no evidence that Tripoli produced camelins. On these textiles, see Gay, *Glossaire*, 1: 261–2; Piponnier, 'À propos de textiles anciens', pp. 872–3.

29 J.C.M. Laurent (ed.), *Peregrinationes medii aevi quatuor: Burchardus de Monte Sion, Ricoldus de Monte Crucis, Odoricus de Foro Julii, Wilbrandus de Oldenborg* (Leipzig, 1864), 28; Taki-Eddin-Ahmed-Makrizi, *Histoire des sultans mamelouks de l'Égypte*, ed. and

in northern France in the early fourteenth century.[30] Twenty camlet pieces from Tripoli eaten up by worms were registered as having 'little value' in the inventory of King Philip V of France, compiled in 1317.[31] They had apparently been stored for a long time in the royal treasury. The production of camlets in Tripoli continued under Mamluk rule, as implied by the 'camelot de Tripe' listed in the Parisian tariff of the first half of the fourteenth century.[32] There may have been production centres other than Tripoli in the Frankish states, yet they are not documented.

By 1233 the volume of camlets exported from the Levant on Venetian ships had grown to the extent that Doge Giacomo Tiepolo included them in the list of commodities for which he fixed the freight charges to Venice. Camlets appear in the same context in the Venetian maritime statutes of 1255.[33] Acre was a major market for camlets, as for other textiles. In 1239 Emperor Frederick II ordered the purchase of woollens, linen or cotton buckram, silk fabrics known as sendals, as well as camlets in Acre.[34] In 1266, at the time of his death in that city, Count Eudes of Nevers owned several camlet garments, some black ones lined with red sendal, others blue lined with black sendal, and another lined with green sendal. The two camlet pieces sold after his death fetched 16 bezants, a fairly large sum. He had clearly purchased the camlet fabrics in Acre, like the 'tartar' silks in his possession.[35] Pegolotti refers to the sale of camlets in the section of his trade manual covering Acre in the pre-1291 period.[36] A Pisan trade manual compiled in 1278 mentions the sale of 'giamelotti d'Assira' by weight in Laiazzo, the main port of the Armenian kingdom of Cilicia. The reference is presumably to Syria.[37] 'Biauz camelos

trans. É. Quatremère (2 vols, Paris, 1837–45), 2/1, p. 103. For the dating of Burchard's pilgrimage and report, see A. Graboïs, 'Christian Pilgrims in the Thirteenth Century and the Kingdom of Jerusalem: Burchard of Mount Sion', in B.Z. Kedar, H.E. Mayer, R.C. Smail (eds), *Outremer. Studies in the History of the Crusading Kingdom of Jerusalem, presented to Joshua Prawer* (Jerusalem, 1982), 287–8.

30 J.-M. Richard, *Une petite nièce de Saint-Louis Mahaut, comtesse d'Artois et de Bourgogne (1302–1329). Étude sur la vie privée, les arts et l'industrie, en Artois et à Paris au commencement du XIVe siècle* (Paris, 1887), 174, 188.

31 Douët-d'Arcq, *Nouveau recueil*, p. 3.

32 Douët d'Arcq, 'Tarif des marchandises', p. 224.

33 R. Predelli e A. Sacerdoti (eds), *Gli statuti marittimi veneziani fino al 1255* (Venice, 1903), p. 73, § 2; p. 162, § CVIII.

34 J.L.A. de Huillard-Bréholles (ed.), *Historia diplomatica Frederici secundi* (6 vols, Paris, 1852–61), vol. 5/1: 586–7; new ed. by C. Carbonetti Venditelli, *Il Registro della cancellaria di Federico II del 1239–1240 (Istituto Storico Italiano per il Medio Evo, Fonti per la storia dell'Italia medievale, Antiquitates,* 19/1) (2 vols., Rome, 2002), 1: 279–80, no. 269.

35 A.-M. Chazaud (ed.), 'Inventaire et comptes de la succession d'Eudes, comte de Nevers (Acre 1266)', *Mémoires de la Société Nationale des Antiquaires de France* 32 (1871): 191, 194, 197, 199, 203. On his purchase of silks in Acre, see D. Jacoby, 'Silk Economics and Cross-Cultural Artistic Interaction: Byzantium, the Muslim World and the Christian West', *Dumbarton Oaks Papers*, 58 (2004): 231–2.

36 Pegolotti, *La pratica della mercatura*, p. 64.

37 R. Lopez and G. Airaldi, 'Il più antico manuale italiano di pratica della mercatura', in *Miscellanea di studi storici, 2* (Collana storica di fonti e studi diretta da

de Surie', 'pretty Syrian camlets', are coupled with various silk fabrics from Acre and Almeria (Spain) as luxuries in *Escanor*, a French Arthurian romance composed around 1280.[38] By 1290 the Genoese were importing to Egypt camlets, the origin of which is not stated.[39] In addition to Tripoli, one may envisage pieces shipped from Laiazzo and others woven in Cyprus. Syrian camlets were registered in the papal treasury in 1331 and 1332, yet we do not know since when they were kept there.[40]

It has been suggested that the earliest testimony regarding Cypriot camlets appears in an Arabic book attributed to Nizam al-Mulk, who served two Seljuk rulers, Alp Arslan and Malik, from 1059 to 1091.[41] According to this work, presents sent from Byzantium to one of the Seljuk rulers included some 'suf-i-Qubrusi', or 'Cypriot suf'.[42] However, the alleged equivalence of 'suf' and 'camlet' before the sixteenth century has not been convincingly proven, although 'suf' was later used in Asia Minor and Armenia for camlet.[43] Moreover, there is no evidence suggesting that Cyprus manufactured camlets before the thirteenth century. We may safely assume that their production was introduced into the island from the Frankish states of the Levant. A number of Arabic-speaking Oriental Christians or 'Syrians' settled in Cyprus in response to the appeal of Guy of Lusignan, shortly after the establishment of his rule over the island in 1192. Others were included among the refugees from the Levantine mainland reaching Cyprus in the course of the thirteenth century.[44] There were clearly camlet weavers among them, although we do not know when they arrived in the island. In any event, they are attested from the 1290s onwards, both in Nicosia and Famagusta.

Geo Pistarino, 38) (Genoa, 1983), p. 126, lines 3–4. The text has come down in a late transcription marred by numerous errors. Pegolotti, *La pratica della mercatura*, p. 59, also mentions the sale of camlets by weight in Laiazzo.

38 Girart d'Amiens, *Escanor: roman arthurien vers de la fin du XIIIe siècle*, ed. R. Trachsler (Geneva, 1994), 734, lines 17,899– 902.

39 As mentioned in the Genoese-Egyptian treaty of 1290: E. Pallavicino (ed.), *I Libri iurium della Repubblica di Genova*, 1/7 (Fonti per la storia della Liguria, XV; Pubblicazioni degli Archivi di Stato, Fonti, vol. 35) (Genoa, 2001), 78–83, esp. p. 80, no. 1,189: 'de iamellotis'.

40 P. Sella, *Glossario latino italiano: Stato della Chiesa – Veneto, Abruzzi* (City of the Vatican, 1944), 105 s.v. Camellotus, and above, n. 21.

41 H. Bowen, 'Nizām al- Mulk', *Encyclopaedia of Islam*, 2nd edn (12 vols., Leiden, 1960–2004), 8: 69–71.

42 D.N. Wilber and M. Minovi, 'Notes on the Rab'-i-Rashidi', *Bulletin of the American Institute for Iranian Art and Archaeology*, 5 (1938): 252, n. 10.

43 The equivalence of the two terms, without chronological distinctions, is argued by P.A., 'A Note on *Suf* or Camlet', pp. 254–5.

44 The immigration of Syrians following the appeal of 1192 is suggested by the reference to artisans and Arabic scribes mentioned in a passage translated by P.W. Edbury, *The Kingdom of Cyprus and the Crusades 1191–1374* (Cambridge, 1991), 16–17. See also J. Richard, 'Le peuplement latin et syrien en Chypre au XIIIe siècle', *Byzantinische Forschungen*, 7 (1979): 166–72, repr. in J. Richard, *Croisés, missionnaires et voyageurs. Les perspectives orientales du monde latin médiéval* (London, 1983), no. VII.

The destruction and depopulation caused by the Mamluk conquest in the coastal cities of the Levant substantially reduced or brought to an end the manufacturing and marketing of camlets in these cities, whether temporarily or definitively. These developments opened a niche in the camlet market. The raw materials entering in the camlets, as well as the skilled labour and the expertise required for their weaving and dyeing, were obviously available in Cyprus at that time. By the late 1290s the production and export of Cypriot camlets appears to have already been fairly substantial, to the extent that it prompted royal legislation, examined below. Incidentally, the political and demographic developments affecting Cyprus in the second half of the thirteenth century also induced large landholders to promote the cultivation of sugar cane and cotton with the help of Syrian refugees, who likewise transferred their expertise to the island.[45]

In the climate of economic crisis generated by the events of 1291 and by the massive influx of refugees from the mainland it was in the best interest of the Cypriot royal administration to guarantee the quality of locally-produced camlets, like that of other textiles, in order to further their marketing and export to the benefit of the local economy and the royal treasury. A royal decree of 1298 refers to the mandatory length and width of cloth pieces, in fact bolts, without citing measurements.[46] These appear in another decree, issued in 1305, which deals with two camlet types: 17 *bras* or arm-lengths for the length and one *bras* minus two fingers for the width of the first, unspecified type, and 14½ *bras* length and one *bras* width for black camlets.[47] Pegolotti confirms the production of long and short camlet bolts.[48] The decree of 1298 ordered these bolts to be inspected before sale by royal officers, who would affix a seal on to the cloth after ascertaining that their measurements conformed to the regulations. Cloth not submitted to inspection was to be cut into four pieces.[49] A royal tax of one denier per seal was mentioned in 1300 and 1305.[50]

In Nicosia the Genoese Oberto de Gavio entrusted his son-in-law Iohanes de Porta in September 1297 with the sale of camlets and ladanum, a resin used in herbal medicine and as a perfume ingredient, with a total value of 2,600 Cypriot white bezants. The share of the camlets in the amount is not stated and, therefore, it is impossible to determine their nature or number. Significantly, the goods were to be shipped exclusively to Laiazzo.[51] In view of the city's

---

45 Jacoby, 'The Economic Function of the Crusader States', pp. 189–90.

46 'Bans et ordonnances des rois de Chypre', in A.A. Beugnot (ed.), *Recueil des historiens des croisades, Lois* (2 vols, Paris, 1841–43), 2: 361, chap. X.

47 Ibid., p. 367, chap. XX. French 'bras' was rendered in Italian as 'braccio' in trade manuals. On Cypriot textile measurements, see below, Appendix. On black camlets produced in the Frankish Levant, see above, n. 26.

48 Pegolotti, *La pratica della mercatura*, p. 36, on camlets sold in Constantinople, undoubtedly of Cypriot origin. See below, n. 67.

49 'Bans et ordonnances des rois de Chypre', 2: 361–2, chaps X–XI.

50 Ibid., p. 365, chap. XV/1, and p. 367, chap. XX.

51 M. Balard (ed.), *Notai genovesi in Oltremare. Atti rogati a Cipro da Lamberto di Sambuceto (11 ottobre 1296– 23 giugno 1299)* (Collana storica di fonti e studi diretta da

role as transit station and Mediterranean outlet of one of the trans-Asian trade routes, it is clear that the Cypriot camlets were partly intended for the Mongol territories further east. The production of camlets in the Chinese province of Tangut, mentioned above, as well as in Tibet, both reported by Marco Polo in the 1290s, had been made possible by transfers of skilled labour, textile technology, or both from Asia Minor and the Middle East across the vast expanse of Mongol-ruled territories in the thirteenth century.[52] The volume or variety of camlet production in Mongol-ruled Asia was apparently not sufficient to meet the demand or the price of Cypriot camlets was particularly attractive. These factors account for the latter's diffusion in the region.

Several other transactions involving the shipping of Cypriot camlets are recorded in the early fourteenth century. On 10 October 1300 a camlet weaver residing in Nicosia, Iohanes son of Iosepe, a Syrian judging by the latter's name, concluded an agreement with representatives of the Peruzzi Company, a major Florentine banking and trading institution. On 4 March 1301, he was in Famagusta, where he received the substantial sum of 4,642 white bezants from the Peruzzi representatives. The nature of the contract between the weaver and the company is not stated. It is likely, however, that the Peruzzi, acting as entrepreneurs, had partly financed the activity of the weaver's workshop and that the sum paid was the remainder of the amount covering the price of all the delivered camlets. This sum alone would have bought around 190 pieces, according to a hypothetical calculation.[53] The delivery of a large number of camlets within less than five months suggests production in a workshop employing several weavers. Incidentally, two interpreters mediated between the parties at this occasion, which confirms the Syrian identity of the camlet weaver, an Arabic speaker not fluent in western languages who had presumably arrived in Cyprus within the preceding decades. One of the interpreters was Viviano de Ginnebaldo, whose fluency inArabic is attested in other transactions.[54]

Geo Pistarino, 39) (Genoa, 1983), 78–9, no. 63: 'implicatos in clamelotis [et] ladano'. The copulative *et* is missing in the edited text.

[52] Marco Polo, *Il Milione*, pp. 60, 112, respectively chaps 73–4 (see above, n. 4) and 117 (*gianbelot*). On cultural and technological transmission, see Th. T. Allsen, *Commodity and Exchange in the Mongol Empire. A Cultural History of Islamic Textiles* (Cambridge, 1997), 72–3.

[53] V. Polonio (ed.), *Notai genovesi in Oltremare. Atti rogati a Cipro da Lamberto di Sambuceto (3 luglio 1300–3 agosto 1301)* (Collana storica di fonti e studi diretta da Geo Pistarino, 31) (Genoa, 1982), 310–11, no. 262. The purpose of my hypothetical calculation is to assess, even approximately, the volume of the transaction. There are no data on prices and exchange rates for the late 1290s, a period of economic crisis and Cypriot coin debasement following the massive influx of refugees in 1291. Therefore I base my calculation upon the following factors: the earliest known camlet prices, from the 1390s, are six and eight ducats: see below, Appendix; in the 1330s one Venetian ducat was equivalent to 3½ Cypriot white bezants: Pegolotti, *La pratica della mercatura*, pp. 97–8. Thus the sum paid by the Peruzzi would have been 1,326 ducats, which at the rate of seven bezants a piece, would have bought some 190 camlets.

[54] Jacoby, 'The Rise of a New Emporium', pp. 174–6.

The second interpreter in the transaction, Iohanes de Porta, is already recorded as handling Cypriot camlets in 1297.[55] The Peruzzi also concluded with him an agreement in Nicosia and paid him the large sum of 6,385 white bezants in Famagusta, both operations occurring on the same days as in the previous instances. The reason for the payment to Iohanes de Porta is not stated.[56] However, in view of the latter's involvement in the camlet trade, it is likely that he had acted as middleman, collecting camlet bolts from weavers for delivery to exporters. A similar function is attested in Famagusta in the fourteenth century, as noted below.

Several transactions involving camlets were recorded in Famagusta around 1300. In March 1302 a local Syrian camlet weaver invested 250 white bezants in the trading venture of a Genoese about to travel to Cilician Armenia.[57] The will of a Pisan, dated 27 August 1300, mentions an unidentified short camlet garment.[58] In the following September a Genoese entrusted an unknown number of camlets to another Genoese in exchange for 20 Genoese pounds after their sale, with the provision that in case the bolts were shorter than prescribed, the two would share the resulting loss of income.[59] This clause is rather strange, since measurements should have been checked by a royal official, as stipulated in the decree of 1298.[60] The purchase of an unspecified number of camlets valued somewhat more than the previous batch, for sale in Genoa, is recorded later in September 1300.[61] A bolt of 'double camlet' is mentioned in the same month.[62] In November two Genoese merchants sent two bales of camlets to Genoa.[63] In February 1301 a bale of camlets was loaded on the Templar ship *Falcon* leaving Famagusta for Marseilles.[64] It is

---

55 See above, n. 51.

56 Polonio, *Notai genovesi*, pp. 312–13, no. 263.

57 R. Pavoni (ed.), *Notai genovesi in Oltremare. Atti rogati a Cipro da Lamberto di Sambuceto (Gennaio–Agosto 1302)* (Collana storica di fonti e studi diretta da Geo Pistarino, 49) (Genoa, 1987), 138–9, no. 110.

58 C. Desimoni, 'Actes passés à Famagouste de 1299 à 1301 devant le notaire génois Lamberto de Sambuceto', *Revue de l'Orient Latin*, 1 (1893): 60–61, no. 224: 'argodo (agodo?) clameloti curti'.

59 Ibid., p. 86, no. 262: 'plus curti quam debent esse de iure'.

60 See above, n. 46. It is possible, though, that the seal was only affixed to camlets sold for export, the rule attested in the late fifteenth century. See below, n. 140.

61 Desimoni, 'Actes passés à Famagouste', pp. 102–3, no. 298.

62 Polonio, *Notai genovesi*, p. 20, no. 18. On the possible meanings of 'double', see below, Appendix.

63 Polonio, *Notai genovesi*, pp. 144–6, no. 130: freight 'pro duabus tabulis clamelotorum'. C. Desimoni, 'Notes et observations sur actes du notaire génois Lamberto di Sambuceto', *Revue de l'Orient Latin*, 2 (1894): 218, explained 'tabula clameloti' as 'mesure ou quantité légale de la dite étoffe'. For the correct interpretation of *tabula* in this context, see a French text of 1461, 'balle ou tablette de mercerie', cited by Ch. du Fresne du Cange, *Glossarium ad scriptores mediae et infimae latinitatis* (10 vols, Paris, 1883–87), 8: 5, s.v. *tabula* 2. The use of *tabula* for 'bale' appears almost exclusively in connection with camlets.

64 Polonio, *Notai genovesi*, pp. 291–2, no. 246: 'in tablario uno clamelotorum'. 'Tablarium' is identical to 'tabula', on which see the previous note.

impossible to determine whether all the camlets mentioned above had been manufactured in Famagusta. Whatever the case, they were shipped from this city, which served as major maritime outlet for indigenous Cypriot products, in addition to its function as transit, storing and transshipment station for goods brought in from other countries. Italy was presumably the first destination of the Cypriot camlets exported by the Peruzzi, while Laiazzo, Genoa and Marseilles appear in other instances.

At first glance it would seem that an Arabic letter of Rashid al-Din provides further evidence regarding Cypriot camlet weaving in the same period. Apparently writing between 1295 and 1304, the vizier of Ghazan Khan, the Mongol ruler of Persia, instructed his own son, who was governor of Qinnasrin, a province of northern Syria, to send to Tabriz 50 camlet weavers from Antioch, Sis and Tarsus, 'not by force and compulsion, but by kindness and persuasion'. In addition, he was to request the king of Cyprus to send 20 more camlet weavers to Tabriz.[65] It has been convincingly argued that the letters ascribed to Rashid al-Din are spurious and were composed in the first half of the fifteenth century. Political and territorial elements support this view. Antioch was never in Mongol possession, and the province of Qinnasrin was only partly and briefly occupied by the Mongols.[66] One may add the puzzling anachronistic reference to Theophilus, son of Michael II, as king of Cyprus. The two Byzantine emperors bearing these names ruled in the first half of the ninth century, and the late author of the letter must have found their names in some old books.

An anonymous trade manual compiled around 1320 offers precious information regarding Cypriot camlets, their export and, indirectly, the function of Famagusta in their trading and shipping. The author of the manual listed the commodities merchants should take along for sale or barter to specific destinations, and the goods they may acquire there in exchange. He advised the transport of Cypriot camlets to numerous localities situated in a vast region extending from Egypt to the Mongol territories north of the Black Sea and to Central Asia, and specified the nature and approximate volume of camlets for each destination. His detailed recommendations warrant a close look. Beginning with southern destinations, they are as follows: in every colour, but mostly emerald-green, white, azure, and some pistachio or light green and yellow to Alexandria, Damietta and Cairo; large quantities in every colour to Beirut and Damascus; emerald-green, white, and pistachio-green to Tripoli; green, white and few pistachio-green to Laodicea (modern Latakia); mostly emerald-green, white and pistachio-green to Porto Bonello in the 'Gulf of Armenia', south of Alexandretta (modern Iskanderun); all colours, but in small quantities to Candelor (modern Alanya) and Satalia (modern Antalya),

[65] Letter partly translated by Wilber and Minovi, 'Notes on the Rab'-i-Rashidi': 248–52; see esp. p. 252 for the camlets.

[66] A.H. Morton, 'The letters of Rashid al-Din: Ilkhanid Fact or Timurid fiction?', in R. Amitai-Preiss and D.O. Morgan (eds), *The Mongol Empire and its Legacy* (Leiden, 1999), 172–4, 190–96.

on the southern coast of Asia Minor, and, without that restriction, to Phocea and Altoluogo/Theologo (ancient Ephesus) on the Aegean coast, in the Turkish emirate of Aydin; all kinds or types in large quantities to Constantinople; all colours, but especially emerald-green, turquoise blue, yellow, and light sky-blue to Caffa in the Crimea and Tana at the mouth of the Don river; all kinds to Saray, the capital of the Mongol Khanate of the Golden Horde on the Volga river; finally, without specification, to Urgenc in Turkestan.[67] Pegolotti mentions colour preferences for woollens in Satalia, namely light vermilion, yellow, pistachio-green, and in Altoluogo, namely light shades of sky-blue, turquoise, vermilion, pistachio-green, and emerald-green.[68] It is likely that the respective colour preferences for woollens were also valid for camlets in these two cities, for which the manual compiled around 1320 fails to provide such specific information.

The listing of Cypriot camlets in this manual reveals the amazingly broad and varied colour palette in which they were being dyed in the first half of the fourteenth century in response to a variegated demand, each market displaying the particular colour sensibilities of the region it supplied. Shades of blue and green were the most popular. It is noteworthy that black Cypriot camlets, mentioned in the royal regulation of 1305, are not cited in that context.[69] The manual does not specify where the Cypriot camlets were being manufactured, yet based upon later evidence there is good reason to believe that Famagusta was one of their major producers. The manual's lack of reference to other camlets implies that the Cypriot ones were in high demand and successfully competed with Middle Eastern camlets, thanks to their high quality, colours, attractive prices, or all these factors, since they were partly marketed in Cilician Armenia and Islamic countries producing these same textiles. A striking aspect of the manual's references to the Cypriot camlets is the broad geographic range and the complex web of bilateral commercial exchanges in which Famagusta was located around 1320. Since the manual's language is Italian, the advice given to Italian merchants regarding Egypt and Syria is especially noteworthy. It implies continuous intensive trade between Famagusta and these Mamluk territories, which conforms to numerous other sources documenting the pursuit of that traffic, despite the papal embargo on

---

[67] Excerpts edited by R.-H. Bautier, 'Les relations économiques des Occidentaux avec les pays d'Orient au Moyen Age. Points de vue et documents', in M. Mollat (ed.), *Sociétés et compagnies de commerce en Orient et dans l'Océan indien* (= Actes du Huitième colloque international d'histoire maritime, Beyrouth, 1966) (Paris, 1970), 313–14, 316–20, repr. in R.-H. Bautier, *Commerce méditerranéen et banquiers italiens au Moyen Age* (Aldershot, 1992), no. IV. The location of 'Porbonello', ibid., p. 318, in fact Porto Bonello, is provided by a thirteenth-century navigation manual: B.R. Motzo (ed.), *Il Compasso de Navegare. Opera italiana della metà del secolo XIII* (Cagliari, 1947), p. 60. The origin of the camlets is not specified with respect to Altoluogo, yet from the context it is clear that the manual implies Cypriot cloth.

[68] Pegolotti, *La pratica della mercatura*, pp. 58 and 55 respectively.

[69] On these camlets, see above, n. 47.

trade with these territories imposed shortly after the fall of the Frankish states in 1291.[70]

Pegolotti, who compiled his own manual in the 1330s, around a decade after the anonymous one, offers additional information regarding Cypriot camlets. He confirms that a seal guaranteeing standard quality and measurements was affixed to them, and stressed that the camlets sold in Satalia should bear that seal.[71] It follows that only Cypriot pieces reached this port, as suggested already by the manual of c. 1320. Pegolotti further specifies that the bolts of Cypriot camlets sold in Alexandria, Ramle, Acre, Beirut, Damascus, Tripoli and Latakia should measure 14 *bracci* or arm-lengths each.[72] He adds Venice to the destinations of Cypriot camlets, and records the freight charges for their shipping to this city on armed state galleys and private vessels, respectively at 2 per cent and 1.5 per cent of their value.[73] The fixing of the freight by the Venetian government implies large and regular shipments of Cypriot camlets and possibly others in transit from Famagusta to Venice.

It is likely that Cypriot camlets also reached other western ports, from which they were transferred to various destinations. We may safely assume that they were included among the numerous pieces listed in the fourteenth-century accounts of the popes, the kings of France, and members of the western nobility. In 1302 Raoul of Nesles, constable of France, owned six camlets in various colours with a total value of 30 pounds.[74] At her death in 1328 Queen Clémence, widow of King Louis X of France, possessed two pieces of camlet in two sections and three half pieces or bolts, all in ash colour, with an estimated value of 21 Parisian pounds.[75]

The marketing of Cypriot camlets in Laiazzo has already been mentioned. A camlet is listed in 1307 among goods forcefully taken by Venetians from this city.[76] The Venetian trade manual known as *Zibaldone da Canal*, completed in the 1320s at the latest, also refers to the camlet trade in Laiazzo. The origin of the cloth is not stated in the last two instances.[77] The treaty of 1333 between Venice and the Armenian kingdom provides additional evidence relevant for Cyprus, not found in earlier treaties between the two states or in other sources. It refers to the export of 'camlet wool', clearly to Cyprus. The raw material available then in the island appears to have been insufficient to meet

70 On the embargo and the limitations on its effectiveness, see Jacoby, 'The Venetians in Byzantine and Lusignan Cyprus', pp. 59–100.

71 Pegolotti, *La pratica della mercatura*, p. 58.

72 Ibid., pp. 69, 72, 90, 91, 102. The entry for Alexandria, ibid., p. 72, mentions 14 Cypriot *canne*, clearly a scribal slip.

73 Pegolotti, *La pratica della mercatura*, pp. 61, 144.

74 C. Dehaisnes (ed.), *Documents et extraits divers concernant l'histoire de l'art dans la Flandre, l'Artois et le Hainaut avant le XV*[e] *siècle* (2 vols, Lille, 1886), 1: 133.

75 Douët-d'Arcq, *Nouveau recueil*, p. 79. In this last instance the 'pieces' may have indicated bolts.

76 Mas Latrie, *Histoire de l'île de Chypre*, 3: 686.

77 A. Stussi (ed.), *Zibaldone da Canal. Manoscritto mercantile del sec. XIV* (Fonti per la storia di Venezia, Sez. V - Fondi vari) (Venezia, 1967), 109. Incidentally, the manual states that camlets are sold by the piece, thus contradicting other trade manuals.

the increasing demand of camlet weavers in Famagusta and Nicosia. At the same time Cypriot camlet weavers faced competition from Venetian weavers in the Armenian kingdom, as revealed by the same treaty of 1333.[78] These were most likely indigenous craftsmen enjoying Venetian nationality, rather than Venetian citizens, whose activity was financed by Venetian entrepreneurs.[79]

The relaxation of the papal embargo on trade with Egypt and Syria in 1344 led to the resumption of direct Western trade and shipping relations with these territories in the following year. This change in trade patterns reduced to some extent the function of Famagusta as warehouse and transshipment station for foreign goods. However, the loss of transit business was partly compensated by the growing share of indigenous export-oriented commodities passing through the city, among them camlets.[80]

Two notarial deeds of the 1360s drafted in Famagusta offer precious evidence regarding the city's camlet manufacture and trade. The will of the Venetian Lodovico Corner, from the parish of San Appolinario in Venice, drafted on 14 April 1363, confirms Famagusta's ongoing production of camlets in a wide range of colours. It records the purchase of several batches of camlets, some of which had still not been delivered. Georgius *çambeloterius*, the camlet weaver, owed 96 pieces, namely 11 light green, 11 dark brown, 20 green, 20 blue, ten red, seven yellow, six violet, seven light-blue, and four white. Georgius also owed eight pieces of 16 arm-lengths each, the colour of which is not stated. In addition, the priest Theodorus, who apparently acted as middleman collecting camlets from various weavers, owed 57 pieces, the remainder out of a consignment of 264 bolts, namely 28 sky-blue, 20 green, six olive-green, two vermilion, and one dark brown. Sand-coloured pieces are also mentioned.[81] It is noteworthy that many colours correspond to those mentioned in the trade manual of c. 1320, examined earlier. The large batches of camlets were clearly intended for export, yet there is no indication of their destination. The undelivered camlets suggest that Lodovico Corner had paid for them in advance. In other words, he had financed the operation of several workshops, whether directly or through an intermediary.

On 29 November 1363 a resident of Rhodes trading in Famagusta received a bale of 60 camlets belonging to Nicolò Venier as warranty for a loan of 103 ducats.[82] It is likely that these camlets, for which no colours are stated, had also been manufactured in Famagusta. A small hat covered with black

---

78 A. Sopracasa (ed.), *I trattati con il regno armeno di Cilicia* (Pacta veneta, vol. 8) (Rome, 2001), p. 111, § 7, and p. 110, § 3 respectively.

79 On Venetian nationality granted to indigenous inhabitants, as distinct from Venetian citizenship, see D. Jacoby, 'Citoyens, sujets et protégés de Venise et de Gênes en Chypre du XIIe au XVe siècle', *Byzantinische Forschungen*, 5 (1977): 159–88, repr. in D. Jacoby, *Recherches sur la Méditerranée orientale du XIIe au XVe siècle. Peuples, sociétés, économies* (London, 1979), no. VI.

80 Jacoby, 'The Venetians in Byzantine and Lusignan Cyprus', pp. 59–100.

81 Otten-Froux, 'Un notaire vénitien', pp. 52–3, no. 11.

82 Ibid., p. 76, no. 82: 'tabula çambelotorum'. On the meaning of *tabula*, see above, n. 63.

camlet, a colour absent from camlet exports, is listed in the inventory of goods belonging to Guy of Ibelin, bishop of Limassol, compiled after his death in 1367.[83] Ongoing camlet production in Famagusta in the years immediately preceding the conclusion of the treaty between Genoa and King Peter II on 21 October 1374 is indirectly attested by the contemporary operation of the royal dye-plant in the city and the collection of fees for the attachment of seals to camlets.[84]

Cypriot camlets continued to be exported in this period from Famagusta to various destinations, some of which are known. In 1355 a ship from Messina on its way from Rhodes to Constantinople was seized by Venetians in the Dardanelles. It carried a bale of 120 camlet bolts belonging to Raymond Serallier, a merchant from Montpellier identified as 'burgensis regis Cipri', thus a permanent resident of Cyprus. The camlets had been loaded on the vessel at Rhodes. They were thus clearly of Cypriot origin, while the other goods handled by the merchant's agent had been shipped from southern France.[85] In 1372 the widow of King Peter I of Cyprus, Eleanor of Aragon, sent camlets to Eleanor of Sicily, wife of King Pedro IV of Aragon.[86] Cypriot camlets were apparently appreciated in Sicily.[87]

Genoese forces temporarily occupied Nicosia and looted the city in 1373. Camlets, most likely manufactured in the city, were an important component of the booty they assembled.[88] In 1383 garments made respectively of blue,

[83] J. Richard, 'Guy d'Ibelin, O.P., évêque de Limassol et l'inventaire de ses biens (1367)', *Bulletin de correspondance hellénique*, 74 (1950): 114, repr. in J. Richard, *Les relations entre l'Orient et l'Occident au Moyen Âge. Études et documents* (London, 1977), no. V.

[84] Revenue from the operation of the dye-plant and the seals was granted by King P. II on 29 May 1374. See L. Balletto, 'Les Génois dans l'île de Chypre au bas moyen âge', in C. Mutafian (ed.), *Les Lusignans et l'Outre-Mer* (Actes du Colloque de Poitiers-Lusignan [20–24 October 1993]) (Poitiers, 1995), 31–2. The previous recipient of the grant was Simon of Montolif, mentioned in 1395 in a law-suit. Mas Latrie, *Histoire de l'île de Chypre*, 3: 781–3. He was presumably the royal chamberlain serving in 1360 and apparently identical with the individual bearing the same name listed among the Cypriot captives held by the Genoese in 1374: ibid., p. 781 n. 3; L. de Mas Latrie (ed.), 'Nouvelles preuves de l'histoire de l'île de Chypre sous le règne des princes de la maison de Lusignan', *Bibliothèque de l'École des Chartes*, 34 (1873): 80–84; Leontios Makhairas, *Khroniko tes Kyprou. Parallele diplomatike ekdose ton kheirographon*, eds M. Pieres and A. Nikolaou-Konnari (Peges kai meletes tes Kypriakes istorias, vol. 48) (Nicosia, 2003), 380.

[85] Heyd, *Histoire*, 1: 480–81, mistakenly includes the camlets among the latter. The documents regarding the seizure of the ship have been edited by L. de Mas Latrie, 'Commerce et expéditions militaires de la France et de Venise au moyen âge', in *Collection de documents inédits sur l'histoire de France*, vol. 37, *Mélanges historiques, Choix de documents*, vol. 3 (Paris, 1880), 121–34, 141–9; for the identification of the merchant, see pp. 121, 141, and for the 'tavula' or bale, pp. 123, 128.

[86] M.T. Ferrer i Mallol, 'La reina Leonor de Chipre y los Catalanes de su entorno', in D. Coulon, C. Otten-Froux, P. Pagès and D. Valérian (eds), *Chemins d'outre-mer. Études sur la Méditerranée médiévale offertes à M. Balard* (Byzantina Sorbonensia, vol. 20) (2 vols, Paris, 2004), 1: 313.

[87] For further evidence in this respect, see below.

[88] Makhairas, *Khroniko tes Kyprou*, p. 323, lines 20–25: 'tsamilottia' in ms. V.

black and red camlet and of three particular types of the cloth were taken on board a ship in Kyrenia, on the northern coast of Cyprus. This suggests that they had been woven in Nicosia, rather than in Famagusta.[89] The following year a vessel seized off the coast of Calabria carried personal goods belonging to the preceptor or commander of the Hospitallers in Cyprus, among them garments made respectively of black and striped camlet.[90] It is impossible to determine whether they originated in Famagusta or Nicosia.

The Genoese occupied Famagusta in 1373 and ruled the city until 1464. At first Famagusta's economy may have been boosted by the Genoese regulations favouring its operation, yet from the 1380s onward it suffered from increasing contraction. Ever more non-Genoese western merchants and ships engaging in long-distance trade sailed to Egypt and Syria without anchoring at Famagusta.[91] The local manufacture of camlets and their export nevertheless continued unabated. The customs records of Genoa for 1376 and 1377 list many vessels returning from Famagusta with one or several bales of camlets and the latter's shipment from Genoa to various destinations in the western Mediterranean.[92] In 1387 a Genoese merchant sent camlets from Famagusta to Venice.[93] Shortly before 1389 camlets and other goods belonging to Venetians were seized by the Genoese authorities of the city, yet released in the following year and shipped to Venice.[94] In the 1390s the Genoese government stated each year the freight charges for the transport of several types of camlets from Famagusta to Genoa, which suggests continuous production and sizeable exports. The camlets were divided into three groups: those manufactured in Nicosia or Famagusta worth more than 40 bezants or eight Venetian ducats; the same type of camlets from Nicosia costing between 30 and 40 bezants, equivalent to six and eight ducats respectively; finally, camlets *malaba*, which paid the lowest freight rate.[95] Nicolò de Martoni, who visited Famagusta in

---

89 The ship was seized off Rhodes and the request for reparations presented in Famagusta: L. Liagre-de Sturler (ed.), *Les relations commerciales entre Gênes, la Belgique et l'Outremont d'après les archives notariales génoises (1320-1400)* (Brussels-Rome, 1969), 548–55, esp. pp. 549–50, no. 411. Some garments were made of 'clameloti tortocii acanelati', 'torticii', and 'accamocati'. On these types, see below, Appendix.

90 The request for reparations was presented in Genoa in 1396. A. Roccatagliata, 'Aspetti di storia economica cipriota alla fine del Trecento', *La storia dei Genovesi*, 9 (1989): 389–91; edition ibid., pp. 409–19, no. 1, and for the camlets, pp. 412 and 416.

91 Jacoby, 'To emporio kai he oikonomia tes Kyprou', pp. 431–40; Jacoby, 'The Venetians in Byzantine and Lusignan Cyprus', pp. 59–100; M. Balard, 'Les Génois dans le royaume médiéval de Chypre', in M. Balard, *Les marchands italiens à Chypre* (Centre de Recherche Scientifique, Recueil de travaux, vol. 2) (Nicosia, 2007), 17–19, 78–81.

92 J. Day (ed.), *Les douanes de Gênes, 1376–1377* (Paris, 1963), 223, 307, 311, 328, 344, 349, and many other instances.

93 B. Cecchetti, *La vita dei Veneziani nel 1300. Le vesti* (Venice, 1886), repr. in B. Cecchetti, *La vita dei Veneziani nel 1300*, introduction by U. Stefanutti (Bologna, 1980), 51, n. 3.

94 Mas Latrie, *Histoire de l'île de Chypre*, 2: 402–3, and for the dates, p. 403, n. 3.

95 Ibid., 3: 774–7, esp. pp. 775–7, for 1391 and 1394: 'pro pecia clamelotorum torticiorum', 'pro pecia clemellotorum malaba'. Same freight charges in three documents relating to sailings from Famagusta to Genoa in 1391–94: S. Bliznyuk

1394, stressed the manufacture of a sizeable number of camlets in the city. He noted the employment of numerous women in the spinning of camlet wool, the main activity providing income to their families and sustaining the city's economy. The Genoese government sought to prevent women from leaving the city, fearing that they would be followed by men, a process that would accelerate Famagusta's demographic, economic, and urban decline.[96]

In 1398 Duke Louis II of Bourbon instructed his envoy to Cyprus, Bertrand Lesgare, to spend 200 ducats on camlets, some black and others dyed with kermes. The envoy bought in Nicosia 11 pieces for that sum, without specifying their colour or weave, and recorded his expenses for the attachment of official quality seals and the packing in four bales. In addition, he paid the customs dues of one ducat apiece in Famagusta. The detailed account for packing warrants our attention, since it reveals the nature of the bale called *tabula* or 'table', already encountered above, although the account uses the term for the container. The camlets were first packed in bocassin, a robust and cheap cotton cloth, further in oil-cloth to protect them from humidity during the maritime voyage, and, finally, the bale was bound with strings.[97] In 1404 King Ladislas of Naples, who had wedded Mary, sister of King Janus of Cyprus, expected the unpaid portion of his wife's dowry to include Cypriot camlets, in addition to sugar, bocassins, and spices.[98]

Cypriot camlets continued also to be widely appreciated in the Middle East. The Cretan Emmanuel Piloti, who resided in Alexandria from 1394–97 to 1416–19 and visited the city later, was well informed about trading in the eastern Mediterranean. He observed that a large number of Cypriot camlets providing substantial income were being exported, mostly to Alexandria, Cairo, Beirut and Damascus, and conveyed by caravan to Mecca.[99] Merchants

(ed.), *Die Genuesen auf Zypern, Ende 14. und im 15. Jahrhundert* (Studien und Texte zur Byzantinistik, herausgegeben von P. Schreiner, vol. 6) (Frankfurt am Main, 2005), 13, 21, 27, 44, 49, nos. 2–4, 6–7. On the types of camlets mentioned in these documents, their prices, and exchange rates, see below, Appendix.

96 L. Le Grand, 'Relation du pèlerinage à Jérusalem de Nicolas de Martoni, notaire italien (1394–1395)', *Revue de l'Orient latin*, 3 (1895): 628–9: 'mulieres que filant et procurant lanam pro zambellotis'. It is possible that Jewish women participated in the spinning. One of them, a new immigrant from Jerusalem, demanded in 1388 permission to return to that city. See two documents edited by B.Z. Kedar, 'Jerusalemite Jews in Genoese Famagusta, 1388', in B.Z. Kedar (ed.), *Jerusalem in the Middle Ages. Selected Papers* (Jerusalem, 1979), 204.

97 Mas Latrie, *Histoire de l'île de Chypre*, 2: 445–53, esp. pp. 447–8, 451–2: packing materials: 'Pour envelopper (...) baucassin (...), toille cirée et corde..., IIII tables à mettre les diz (= the said) chameloz'. On bocassin, see M. F. Mazzaoui, *The Italian Cotton Industry in the Later Middle Ages, 1100–1600* (Cambridge, 1981), 199, n. 8.

98 Mas Latrie, *Histoire de l'île de Chypre*, 2: 477–80, esp. p. 478.

99 P.-H. Dopp (ed.), *Traité d'Emmanuel Piloti sur le Passage en Terre Sainte (1420)* (Louvain-Paris, 1958), 108, 157–8. See D. Coulon, 'Du nouveau sur Emmanuel Piloti et son témoignage à la lumière de documents d'archives occidentaux', in Coulon, Otten-Froux, Pagès et Valérian, *Chemins d'outre-mer*, 1, 160, 169, for a new dating of Piloti's residence in Alexandria and of his manual, compiled between 1420 and 1438.

from Ancona sold camlets in Damascus in 1413 and 1419.[100] Pieces sent by the Venetian Lorenzo Soranzo from Nicosia were confiscated and sold in 1419 by the local authorities of Damascus.[101] In 1431 the Genoese ambassadors to Egypt were instructed to request payment for camlets delivered in 1426/27, most likely from Cyprus.[102] The following year Bertrandon de la Broquière, sent on a mission by Duke Philip the Good of Burgundy, witnessed the grant of six camlet bolts on behalf of King John II of Cyprus to the Karamanid ruler of Konya in Asia Minor.[103] In 1437 the Venetian Andrea Bernardin sent a large batch of 296½ pieces or bolts to Damascus.[104] A merchant from Zara who died in Damascus in 1461 owned a kermes-dyed camlet piece measuring 20 *pics* or arm-lengths.[105] Other camlets belonging to the Venetian consul in Damascus are listed in 1457 without stated origin, yet were presumably Cypriot. They were respectively dyed dark purple, black, bright pale yellow, and kermes-red.[106] The import of Cypriot camlets to Egypt in the first half of the fifteenth century may have been furthered by the contemporary decline of the corresponding local textile industries.[107] While not referring directly to camlets, Piloti provides a precious insight into this development by establishing a correlation between Alexandria's depopulation and the contraction in its production of silk and linen textiles.[108]

In 1433 a Genoese trading in Pera, the Genoese suburb of Constantinople, reported to his brother in Cyprus that camlet wool was unavailable.[109] This suggests that the island was importing camlet wool from Constantinople, as it

---

[100] E. Ashtor, 'Il commercio levantino di Ancona nel basso Medioevo', *Rivista Storica Italiana*, 88 (1976): 231.

[101] Ch. Verlinden, 'Marchands chrétiens et juifs dans l'État mamelouk au début du XVe siècle d'après un notaire vénitien', *Bulletin de l'Institut historique belge de Rome*, 51 (1981): 46.

[102] N. Iorga, 'Notes et extraits pour servir à l'histoire des croisades au XVe siècle', *Revue de l'Orient latin*, 6 (1898): 97.

[103] Ch. Schefer, *Le Voyage d'Outremer de Bertrandon de la Broquière, premier écuyer tranchant et conseiller de Philippe le Bon, duc de Bourgogne* (Paris, 1892), 111.

[104] S. Bliznyuk, 'Il commercio alla veneziana tra Cipro e Damasco', in Ch. A. Maltezou and P. Schreiner (eds), *Bisanzio, Venezia e il mondo franco-greco (XIII-XV secolo)* (Atti del Colloquio Internazionale organizzato nel centenario della nascita di Raymond – J. Loenertz o. p., Venezia, 1–2 dicembre 2000) (Venice, 2002), 349–63, esp. pp. 356–63, with prices.

[105] F. Bianchi and D. Howard, 'Life and Death in Damascus. The Material Culture of Venetians in the Syrian Capital in the Mid-Fifteenth Century', *Studi Veneziani*, N.S. 46 (2003): 266–8, esp. p. 268: 'petia I. zambeloti uchola'. The latter term appears to be a mispelling or a misreading for 'chocolo': see below, next note. The term was apparently derived from *coccus*, the cochineal insect or kermes yielding a red dye. The *pic* was identical to the *braccio*: see below, Appendix.

[106] Bianchi and Howard, 'Life and Death in Damascus', pp. 281–3. One of them was a 'zambeloto chocolo'.

[107] E. Ashtor, *Levant Trade in the Later Middle Ages* (Princeton, N.J., 1983), 200–206.

[108] Dopp, *Traité d'Emmanuel Piloti*, pp. 90–91.

[109] L.T. Belgrano (ed.), 'Prima serie di documenti riguardanti la colonia di Pera', *Atti della Società ligure di storia patria*, 13 (1877–84): 202.

apparently did in the 1330s when Pegolotti was compiling his trade manual.[110] Since we do not know the nature of camlet wool, it is impossible to determine its origin. At the same time Cypriot camlets were reaching Constantinople and the Black Sea. The Venetian merchant Giacomo Badoer, who operated in the Byzantine capital from September 1436 to early 1440, entrusted Antonio da Negroponte with the sale of two camlets, a white and a black one. The textiles had clearly been imported from Cyprus, like the sugar he handed over to that merchant, a resident of the Black Sea city of Trebizond returning home via Simisso.[111] Badoer also recorded a kermes-red camlet, which cannot be attributed to any specific region.[112]

The Egyptian raid of 1426 on Cyprus resulted in the capture of King Janus. In order to obtain his own release the king agreed in the following year to pay a substantial ransom, recognize Egyptian suzerainty over Cyprus, and deliver an annual tribute of 5,000 ducats to Sultan Barsbay and his successors.[113] At the time of his capture Janus had 2,000 ducats in cash, which were used for the purchase of camlets.[114] According to Arabic sources, the tribute was to be paid in 2,000 coloured camlets equivalent to 20,000 dinars, and the first instalment, in December 1427, consisted of 1,800 camlets in various colours and patterns.[115] However, the number of pieces in this delivery, the total value of which vastly exceeded the 5,000 ducats of the tribute, rather suggests a partial payment of the ransom.[116] The annual tribute was raised to 8,000 ducats before the death of King Janus in 1432.[117] In 1437 the Spanish nobleman Pero Tafur, who acted as ambassador on behalf of King John II, obtained from Sultan Barsbay that the value of the camlets delivered as tribute should be estimated at the price they commanded in Cairo, rather than at the price paid for them in Cyprus.[118] The difference was substantial. The camlets were valued 20 ducats apiece at the Egyptian court, whereas the Cypriot treasury paid only half that amount to the weavers of Nicosia, as stated by them in

---

[110] See above, n. 6.

[111] U. Dorini and T. Bertelè (eds), *Il libro dei conti di Giacomo Badoer (Costantinopoli, 1436–1440)* (Il Nuovo Ramusio, 3) (Rome, 1956), p. 88 line 32, p. 306 line 16, p. 307 line 29, and p. 334.

[112] Ibid., p. 457 line 18, and p. 604 line 13: 'zanbeloto chochola'.

[113] G. Hill, *A History of Cyprus* (4 vols, Cambridge, 1940–52), 2: 476–81, 488–9.

[114] Makhairas, *Khroniko tes Kyprou*, p. 459, lines 36–9, mss. O and R.

[115] M.M. Ziada, 'The Mamluk Conquest of Cyprus in the Fifteenth Century', *The Bulletin of the Faculty of Arts, Fouad I University* (Cairo), 2/1 (1934): 45, 49. On the value of the camlets, see below, Appendix.

[116] It is unclear how the value of the camlets was calculated. In any event, it was superior to 2¾ ducats a piece. See below, Appendix.

[117] And temporarily to 16,000 by James II, who ruled from 1464 to 1473: Tzorzes (M)poustrous (Georgios Bo(s)tr(y)nos e Boustronios, *Digesis Kronikas Kyprou*, ed. G. Kehayioglou (Peges kai meletes tes Kypriakes istorias, vol. 27) (Nicosia, 1997), 136. William Wey, who visited Cyprus in 1458, mistakenly mentions 10,000 ducats per year in 'chamelet': *The Itineraries of William Wey to Jerusalem, A.D. 1458 and A.D. 1462 and to Saint James of Compostella, A.D. 1456* (London, 1856), 78.

[118] M. Jiménez de La Espada (ed.), *Andanças é viajes de Pero Tafur por diversas partes del mundo avidos (1435–1439)* (Madrid, 1874), 83.

1489.[119] Tafur returned to Cyprus and, before leaving for Rhodes, King John II rewarded him with ten camlets for carrying out the mission in Egypt.[120] In 1453 the king sent 400 camlets to Cairo, which at the rate of 20 ducats apiece covered the entire amount of the annual tribute, to which he added 20 pieces of 40 *pics* or arm-lengths as present for the new sultan, al-Malik al-Ashraf Aynal. The latter enjoined the king to send him soft and delicate camlets.[121] In 1464 King James II the Bastard dispatched William Gonem, Latin archbishop of Cyprus, with 1,000 camlets to Cairo. The cloth must have been assembled in the royal treasury over several years.[122]

The assumption that the camlets delivered as tribute to Egypt were being woven in Nicosia is supported in various ways. The pilgrim Stephan von Gumpenberg, who visited the city in 1450, reported that camlet weaving was the main craft practised in the city.[123] The ongoing operation of the royal dye-plant in Nicosia also points in the same direction. Venice demanded in 1448 that the annual revenue yielded by the dyeing of camlets be restored to the Venetian bailo in the island, yet the plant was then leased to some Genoese merchants. The phrasing of the request suggests that there was a special section in the plant for camlets.[124] In 1449 a Genoese transferred his one-year lease of the dye-plant to another individual for no less than 3,640 Venetian ducats.[125] This sum implies a sizeable annual revenue and points to the prosperous state of the Cypriot luxury textile industry, in particular the production of camlets, in the island's territories under royal rule.

By 1467 there had apparently been a decline. King James II agreed that Venetians would be the first creditors to be reimbursed from the revenue of the plant, while complaining that its income had substantially decreased since the reign of his father.[126] In 1469 the official in charge of the dye-plant reported to the king the delivery of camlets measuring 40 *bras* or arm-lengths dyed with kermes in red and violet colours and others measuring 30 arm-lengths.[127] It is likely that the camlets which Cypriot merchants offered in 1486

---

[119] L. de Mas Latrie (ed.), 'Documents nouveaux servant de preuves à l'histoire de l'île de Chypre sous le règne de la maison de Lusignan', in *Collection de documents inédits sur l'histoire de France, Mélanges historiques, Choix de documents*, vol. 4 (Paris, 1882), 535, response of the Venetian Senate on 16 January 1490.

[120] Jiménez de La Espada, *Andanças é viajes de Pero Tafur*, p. 121.

[121] Letter of the sultan in 1456: Mas Latrie, *Histoire de l'île de Chypre*, 3: 73–5, esp. pp. 74–5: 'zambelloti molesini et fini'. The suggestion that these were perhaps camlets from Mosul (ibid., p. 889, s.v. Camelot) is groundless; see also below, Appendix.

[122] Mas Latrie, *Histoire*, 3: 129–30, continuation of p. 128, n. 1.

[123] Edition in *Reyssbuch dess Heiligen Lands* (Frankfurt, 1584), fol. 243v–245v.

[124] Senato, Deliberazioni, Mar, reg.3, fol. 62r: 'in possessionem et tenutam tinctorie clamilotorum civitatis Nicosie'; incomplete citation in Mas Latrie, 'Nouvelles preuves', *Bibliothèque de l'École des Chartes*, 35 (1874): 157.

[125] J. Heers, *Gênes au XVe siècle. Activité économique et problèmes sociaux* (Paris, 1961), p. 375.

[126] Mas Latrie, *Histoire de l'île de Chypre*, vol. 3, pp. 177–8.

[127] Richard, *Le livre des remembrances*, pp. 66–7, no. 141. The account also mentions 'tables, cordes et autres'. For these packing materials, see above, n. 97. For the price

near Larnaca to western merchants and pilgrims had been woven in Nicosia, since the manufacture of these fabrics had apparently ceased in Famagusta by that time.[128] In 1489 the camlet weavers of Nicosia and the inhabitants of Famagusta submitted to the Venetian government separate requests referring to the Nicosia plant, examined below.

Only a section of Nicosia's camlet production was delivered to Egypt. In 1460, in the course of the civil war opposing him to his sister Queen Charlotte, James (the future king) confiscated goods in several houses of the city, among them five bales of felt and 125 camlets.[129] Anton Audeth, member of the Cypriot social elite, stated in his will of 1453 that he stored 30 pieces measuring 30 *pics* in his house in Nicosia.[130] Some or all of these camlets were intended for sale, yet there is also evidence of private consumption in Nicosia in that period. Zacha, Anton Audeth's widow, owned a camlet garment in 1468.[131]

The royal treasury favoured the delivery of the Egyptian tribute in camlet bolts, rather than in other goods or cash, in view of the difference between purchase price in Cyprus and estimated value in Cairo.[132] However, shortly before the imposition of direct Venetian rule over the island in 1489 the annual tribute, which had entirely consisted in camlets, began to be mostly delivered in silken and woollen textiles, to which other goods were added. Dwindling production, implied by James II in 1467,[133] deficient quality of the camlets, dissatisfaction of the Egyptian court with the deliveries, or a combination of these factors account for that change.[134] Western visitors were nevertheless impressed by the local camlets. A pilgrim visiting Nicosia in 1480 claimed that the city produced many camlets, while another praised their quality.[135]

---

of these camlets, see below, Appendix. The dye-plant is also mentioned in passing in 1468: Richard, *Le livre des remembrances*, p. 93, no. 175.

128 As reported by Conrad von Grünemberg: J. Goldfriedrich und W. Fränzel, *Ritter Grünembergs Pilgerfahrt ins Heilige Land 1486*, Leipzig 1912, p. 60; this is a translation into modern German. The account's description of Cyprus is merely summarized in R. Röhricht and H. Meissner (eds), *Deutsche Pilgerreisen nach dem Heiligen Lande* (Berlin, 1880), 155.

129 Boustronios, *Digesis*, p. 106, lines 2–3. Note *tableV,*, a Greek version of *tabule* for bales, mentioned above. 'Tsamilotia apilota' were apparently non-felted camlets, in contrast to the felts mentioned earlier in the text. An incorrect translation of the passage by N. Coureas in George Boustronios, *A Narrative of the Chronicle of Cyprus 1456–1489* (Text and Studies in the History of Cyprus, vol. 51) (Nicosia, 2005), 101, § 64.

130 J. Richard, 'Une famille de "Vénitiens blancs" dans le royaume de Chypre au milieu du XVème siècle: les Audeth et la seigneurie du Marethasse', *Rivista di Studi bizantini e slavi*, 1 (1981) (= *Miscellanea Agostino Pertusi*, vol. 1): 122, no. VII.

131 Ibid., p. 128, no. X.

132 See above, n. 119.

133 See above, n. 128.

134 As illustrated by the instructions of 1489. See below, n. 136.

135 Santo Brasca, *Viaggio in Terrasanta, 1480, con l'itinerario di G. Capodilista*, ed. A.L. Momigliano Lepschy (Milan, 1966), 119, § 243; Ch. Schefer (ed.), *Voyage de la Saincte Cyté de Hierusalem* (Paris, 1882), 105. Somewhat later a third visitor mentioned the production of camlets, without specifying a location, in a way conveying that his readers were familiar with Cypriot camlets: Ambrosius Zeebout, *Tvoyage van Mher Joos*

The camlet weavers of Nicosia, who supplied their fabrics to the royal court, claimed that since they were unable to sell their cloth, they had ceased to practice their craft. This was clearly an overstatement. In 1489 they demanded that the tribute to Egypt, which Venice continued to pay in order to safeguard its commercial interests in the Mamluk territories, should exclusively consist of camlets. Venice responded positively to the request, provided the density of the weave was satisfactory, the camlets varied in colour, and their measurements conformed to the regulations of the camlet weavers. The reference to the latter's *matricula* or set of regulations suggests that the camlet weavers of Nicosia were organized in a guild.[136] In 1489 Balthasar Trevisan, first Venetian captain of Cyprus, had been instructed to deliver the annual tribute in high-quality goods and in as many camlets as available.[137] Despite these instructions and the positive response to the weavers of Nicosia, the Venetian government ordered in July 1490 the delivery of 6,000 ducats, the remainder of two instalments of the tribute, mostly in silken and woollen fabrics.[138] Time and again the sultans complained about the quality of the delivered goods. In 1498 Jeronimo Giustinian returned from Cairo with a letter from the sultan complaining that the goods sent were miserable and the camlets moth-eaten, an obvious overstatement.[139]

The camlet weavers of Nicosia presented yet another request in 1489. In the past, the royal seal had only been attached to camlets leaving Cyprus, the exporters paying the fee, which was collected by the customs in Famagusta. The reference to this city was obviously relevant only since its restoration to royal rule in 1464. No seal was affixed to cloth intended for personal use or sold in retail in the island. It is unclear whether this limitation was already implied in the royal decree of 1298 regarding the seals, or whether it had been introduced at some later date.[140] In any event, a new practice imposed by the Venetian administration in 1489 compelled the camlet weavers to notify every sale to the officer responsible for the operation of the royal dye-plant, who affixed the seal to the camlet and collected the fee, regardless of whether or not the cloth would be exported. In addition, the weavers complained that some merchants buying the cloth for export refused to reimburse the fee,

---

van Ghistele, ed. R.J.G.A.A. Gaspar (Hilversum, 1998), 279: Cyprus produces 'gulden laken, zijden laken ende cammelot'.

[136] Mas Latrie, 'Documents nouveaux', pp. 534–6; note ibid., p. 536, the reference to the number of threads and leases: 'dummodo laborentur boni et sufficientes cum quantitate filorum vel, ut dicunt, litiorum'. On the number of threads, see also below, Appendix. On the Venetian tribute policy, see B. Arbel, 'Venetian Cyprus and the Muslim Levant, 1473–1570', in N. Coureas and J. Riley-Smith (eds), *Cyprus and the Crusades* (Nicosia, 1995), 161–2, repr. in B. Arbel, *Cyprus, the Franks and Venice, 13th–16th Centuries* (Aldershot, 2000), no. XII.

[137] Mas Latrie, *Histoire de l'île de Chypre*, 3: 460, § 21.

[138] A.Ch. Aristeidou, *Anekdota engrapha tes Kypriakes istorias apo to archeo tes Venetias, vol. 1 (1474–1508)* (Pegai kai meletai tes Kypriakas istorias, vol 16) (Nicosia, 1990), 218–20, esp. p. 219, no. 22.

[139] Hill, *A History of Cyprus*, 3: 825–7.

[140] On this decree, see above, n. 46.

which originally they had paid. The Venetian government abolished the new practice and reinstated the old regulation existing in the Lusignan period.[141]

The manufacture of camlets in Famagusta was still of some importance in the 1450s, yet declined more steeply than in Nicosia in the following period. In 1453 Luca di Gavi declared in his will, drafted in Famagusta, having sent a camlet 'acamocatus' to Genoa. He owed Antonio Ribaldo, a resident of Famagusta, 80 bezants on account of his salary at the 'gabella' of the camlets, presumably the office collecting taxes on the export of camlets.[142] In 1459 Napoleone Lomellini, Genoese captain of Famagusta, was accused of having accepted a camlet of 40 *pics* length as bribe in order to favour one of the parties in a judicial case brought to his court.[143] The camlet's production in the city may be taken for granted. In 1480 a pilgrim noted that the bishop of Famagusta wore a garment made of grey camlet, most likely produced there.[144]

Camlet manufacture was obviously linked to the operation of the city's dye-plant. In 1456 a Jewish dyer undertook to work for two years at that plant. In 1491 the community of Famagusta acknowledged that the local manufacture of camlets and other textiles had been encouraged by the operation of the city's dye-plant at the time of Genoese rule, which ended in 1464, and in the reign of James II, which lasted until 1473. However, the dye-plant had since ceased to function and, as a result, the weavers of these fabrics had moved to Nicosia. The people of Famagusta complained about the decline of crafts in their city, which in turn led to the contraction of its population. They demanded, therefore, that those leasing the dye-plant in Nicosia be compelled to operate an additional one in their city, in order to enable the restoration of its textile manufacture.[145] The closure of the dye-plant after 1473 must have been prompted by the decline of textile manufacture in Famagusta, most likely the outcome of a long process caused by excessive Genoese taxation. The link

---

141 Mas Latrie, 'Documents nouveaux', pp. 535–6. The royal revenue accruing from the seals is also mentioned in 1395: Mas Latrie, *Histoire de l'île de Chypre*, 3: 781.

142 The relevant documents are edited by L. Balletto, *Piemontesi del Quattrocento nel Vicino Oriente* (Biblioteca della Società di Storia, Arte e Archeologia per le provincie di Alessandria e Asti, 26) (Alessandria, 1992), 107–13, esp. pp. 108, 110–11, nos. 7–8; on these two Genoese, see ibid., pp. 69–77. It appears that Luca di Gavi had leased the 'gabella' office and that Antonio Ribaldo had served there as his employee. Balletto fails to note this relationship between them.

143 The testimonies regarding the nature of the camlet differed: C. Otten-Froux, *Une enquête à Chypre au XVe siècle. Le* sindicamentum *de Napoleone Lomellini, capitaine génois de Famagouste (1459)* (Sources et études de l'histoire de Chypre, vol. 36) (Nicosia, 2000), 144 article 28: 'petiam unam clameloti (…) cogla'; p. 165: 'peciam unam clameloti cogli'; yet in p. 119 article 29: 'peciam unam clameloti torticii'. On these types, see below, Appendix.

144 Schefer, *Voyage de la Saincte Cyté de Hierusalem*, p. 107.

145 On the Jewish dyer, see Heers, *Gênes au XVe siècle*, p. 375, n. 10. His contract referred to woollens, yet the main point here is the activity of the dye-plant. For the petition of 1491, see Mas Latrie, *Histoire de l'île de Chypre*, 3: 490, § 12.

between demographic contraction, heavy taxation, and economic decline had already been stressed by the Genoese residents of the city in 1448.[146]

Camlet weaving was practised from the thirteenth century onward in Cyprus in two cities only: Nicosia, the seat of the royal court and the Cypriot social elite, and Famagusta, which developed into the island's major port, transit station, and outlet of indigenous products. The halt of camlet manufacture along the Levantine coast resulting from the Mamluk conquests opened new markets for Cypriot camlets and boosted their manufacture and export, promoted by western entrepreneurs. By 1300 Cyprus was already shipping its camlets to various destinations, both in the eastern and the western Mediterranean. The anonymous trade manual of c. 1320 reveals the impressive variety of colours in which they were produced and the broad geographic range of their distribution, which reached central Asia under Mongol rule.

The relaxation of the papal embargo on trade with Egypt and Syria in 1344 reduced Famagusta's function as transit station for foreign goods. The loss was partly compensated by the growing share of indigenous commodities in the city's trade and exports, partly fuelled by the ongoing production of camlets in a broad range of colours and in substantial volume. The Genoese rule over Famagusta further reduced the city's share in maritime trade and accelerated the contraction of its economy from the 1380s onward. In these circumstances local camlet production assumed increased importance in the framework of that economy, as observed by Nicolò de Martoni in 1394.

The restoration of royal authority over Famagusta in 1464 did not arrest the city's economic decline, which included the demise of its camlet manufacture after 1473. By contrast, Nicosia's camlet weavers benefited both from the city's function as seat of the Cypriot social elite and from the delivery of the annual Egyptian tribute, which ensured them a secure market for a section of their production. Camlet manufacture in Nicosia had nevertheless declined by 1489. The different course of camlet manufacture in the two cities in the second half of the fifteenth century partly illustrates the latter's diverging economic evolution in that period.

Cypriot camlets were fine and prestigious textiles. The absence of quantitative data prevents any assessment of the relative share of Famagusta and Nicosia in their production from the thirteenth to the late fifteenth century. Throughout that period Famagusta largely retained its position as outlet for the camlets of both cities. Cypriot camlets appear to have enjoyed broader diffusion in the East than in the West, where the growing consumption of silks in the upper ranks of society and western imitations reduced their marketing.[147] Camlets were not always common in the homes of Latin residents in Cyprus. A frequent formula in the wills of married men allocates to the testator's wife the right to retain all her clothes made of wool and linen

[146] Ibid., 3: 54–6, response of the Genoese government in January 1449.

[147] On western imitations, see above, nn. 12–15.

cloth, with the addition of silk cloth in affluent households.[148] Camlet never appears in that context.

The evidence illustrating the production, handling and diffusion of Cypriot camlets from the thirteenth to the late fifteenth century is fairly limited. While providing an insight into their nature and variety, it raises many complex and unresolved problems. It nevertheless reflects various aspects and stages in the function of Famagusta as manufacturing and trading centre and, more generally, the city's evolving role in the Cypriot economy.

Measurements, Weaves, and Prices of Cypriot Camlets

Trade manuals such as Pegolotti's compare Cypriot textile measurements with those of various cities, yet the estimates of these units differ according to the length ascribed to the *canna*. Desimoni states that the Genoese *canna* was 2.44776 metres long, and since 11 Genoese *canne* were equal to ten Cypriot short *canne*, the latter was 2.22 metres long.[149] Schilbach uses 2.336 metres for the Genoese *canna* and reaches 2.03 metres.[150] The Cypriot *canna* contained 3½ *bracci* or arm-lengths.[151] According to Desimoni, the *braccio* was thus 0.63484 metres long, while in Schilbach's view it would have measured 0.58 metre. For the sake of calculations, we may adopt here 0.60 metre as approximate length of the *braccio*. The *pic* or *picco*, from Greek *pekhys*, was a length unit used for textiles in Greek, Persian and other languages, as explained by Pegolotti: 'picco in grechesco e in persesco e in piu linguaggi (...). questi nomi vogliono dire misure con che si misura panni (...) a conto di lunghezze'. Hence 'piccoare, cioè misurare', meant 'to measure by the *pic*', with reference to woollens.[152] The Cypriot *pic* was an arm-length and thus identical to the island's *bras* or *braccio*.[153] The terms were similarly applied to camlets measuring 30 and 40 units.[154] The *pekhys* contained 28 *daktyloi* or 'fingers',[155] hence the latter measured c. 2 cm.

The mandatory camlet measurements stated in the royal decree of 1305 yield the following approximate results: c. 10.2 metres length and c. 0.56 metre width for the first type of camlets, 8.7 metres length and c. 0.60 metre

---

148 Otten-Froux, 'Un notaire vénitien', pp. 41–50, nos. 4, 6 and 8.

149 C. Desimoni, 'Observations sur les monnaies, les poids et les mesures cités dans les actes du notaire génois Lamberto di Sambuceto', *Revue de l'Orient Latin*, 3 (1895): 23. For the relation between the two *canne*, see Pegolotti, *La pratica della mercatura*, p. 98.

150 E. Schilbach, *Byzantinische Metrologie* (Handbuch des Altertumswissenschaft, vol. 12/4 = Byzantinisches Handbuch, vol. 4) (Munich, 1970), 43, 48–9. However, based on the *canne* of Florence and Venice he arrives at other results.

151 Pegolotti, *La pratica della mercatura*, pp. 77, 92, 101.

152 Pegolotti, *La pratica della mercatura*, pp. 18, 46.

153 Schilbach, *Byzantinische Metrologie*, p. 49, calculates the value of the same terms in Cypriot land measurements, yet these were not relevant for textiles.

154 See above, nn. 121, 127, 143.

155 See above, n. 150.

width for black camlets.[156] However, according to Pegolotti, the bolts of Cypriot camlets sold in various cities were to measure 14 arm-lengths or c. 8.4 metres.[157] In 1363 Georgius the camlet weaver owed eight pieces of 16 arm-lengths each, thus measuring c. 9.6 metres.[158] Later sources mention much longer bolts, of 30 or 40 *bras* or *pics*, thus measuring respectively c. 18 and c. 24 metres.[159] It follows that the camlet measurements cited in notarial deeds and trade manuals varied widely. Since they did not conform to the regulations issued in 1305, the latter must have been superseded by new regulations issued at an unknown date. The correspondence between Genoese Famagusta and Nicosia under royal rule with respect to the lengths of 30 and 40 *bras* or *pics*, attested in the 1450s, implies that these measurements had been imposed before the occupation of Famagusta by Genoa in 1373.[160] In 1490 the Venetian authorities referred to mandatory measurements, without stating them, in response to the request submitted by the camlet weavers of Nicosia.[161] There was a distinction between 'simple' and 'double' camlets.[162] 'Simple' may have designated mandatory measurements, while 'double' presumably referred to a bolt twice the prescribed length or width.[163]

As noted above, no camlets have been identified so far among extant medieval fabrics, yet documentary sources reveal that their weaves varied. The list of prescribed fees to middlemen handling camlets issued in 1372 in Barcelona distinguishes between pieces of one, two and four *fils* or threads, taxed eight, 12 and 16 *dineros* respectively.[164] It would seem that these definitions applied to the number of main warp threads in each dent of the reed. The more dents to the inch, the finer the reed and the greater the density of the weave, which accounts for the increase in price and in the middlemen's fee.[165] It has been suggested that *torticii* was related to *turcisi*, the colour turquoise.[166] Since the term appears more than once, a recurrent faulty

---

156 For the data, see above, n. 47.

157 See above, n. 72.

158 See above, n. 81.

159 See above, nn. 121, 127, 130, 143.

160 This is also suggested by the prices of 30 and 40 bezants for camlets from both cities in the Genoese regulations of the 1390s. See above, n. 91.

161 See above, n. 136.

162 'Simple': Richard, *Une petite nièce de Saint-Louis*, pp. 166, n. 1, 170, n. 4, 187, n. 1; B. Prost, *Inventaires mobiliers et extraits des comptes des ducs de Bourgogne, 1363–1477* (2 vols., Paris, 1902–13), vol. 1, no. 1,589, vol. 2, nos. 3, 199, 3,615; for 'double', see above, n. 62.

163 163 'Double' is used for silks in English royal accounts of the mid-fourteenth century with the meaning of double width and therefore more expensive. Monnas, 'Silk Cloths Purchased for the Great Wardrobe', pp. 288, 289–90.

164 Gual Camarena, *Vocabolario del comercio medieval*, p. 248.

165 For similar definitions in medieval silk weaving, see D. and M. King, 'Silk Weaves of Lucca in 1376', in I. Estham and M. Nockert (eds), *Opera Textilia Variorum Temporum, To honour Agnes Geijer on her Ninetieth Birthday 26th October 1988* (Stockholm, 1988), 69. The reed is a comb-like device on a loom separating the warp yarns. The dent is the space between two adjacent wires of the reed.

166 Richard, *Le livre des remembrances*, p. 173, n. 8.

transcription is excluded. Moreover, since *torticius* is associated with *cogla* or *cogli* and *malaba* in the description of camlet groups, these terms would have also been colours.[167] It is unlikely that camlets in two colours only were being sent to Genoa in the 1390s, a period in which Cypriot camlets in several colours were being exported. It seems, therefore, that the three terms stood for weave types. This suggestion is supported by additional varieties such as the 'clamelotus tortocius acanelatus', the nature of which is unclear, and the camlet 'accamocatus', presumably akin to a camoca weave or displaying the sheen of a camoca.[168] The striped camlets mentioned in 1384 reveal that camlets were not always plain and some were woven in more than one colour.[169] The quality of the cloth also varied according to the smoothness or coarseness of its surface, as suggested by the reference to soft and fine camlets, 'zambelloti molesini et fini'.[170]

The variations in weaves, measurements and qualities of camlet pieces account for the differing range of prices and freight charges mentioned above. In 1363 a bale of 60 camlets served in Famagusta as warranty for a loan of 103 ducats, yet we lack information regarding the camlets' measurements or nature.[171] The prices noted in Nicosia and Famagusta in the 1390s varied from below 30 to above 40 bezants apiece, these two sums presumably being the most common.[172] In 1398, according to the account of Bertrand Lesgare, envoy of Duke Louis II of Bourbon, three ducats were equal to 48 sous parisis, the exchange rate being one ducat for 16 sous parisis. This last sum was also equal to five Cypriot bezants.[173] Thus one ducat was worth five bezants, and the prices of 30 and 40 bezants equivalent to six and eight ducats respectively. Lesgare purchased 11 camlets for 200 ducats in 1398. These must have included many kermes-dyed pieces, which were sold at more than twice the price of various other camlets, as noted below. Even so, we cannot arrive at 200 ducats for 11 pieces unless we assume that Lesgare bought more expensive camlets or paid inflated prices. The prices registered in Nicosia in 1469 were 775 bezants for five kermes-dyed camlets of 40 *bras*, or 155 bezants a piece, and 1,200 bezants for 16 pieces of 30 *bras*, or 75 bezants a piece.[174] The rate of exchange recorded in 1468 in Nicosia was seven bezants to one ducat.[175] The price of the 16 pieces, 75 bezants, was somewhat more than ten ducats a piece. It thus conformed approximately to the amount of ten ducats paid for

---

167 See above, n. 95, 143, for citations.

168 See above, n. 89. Camoca was a costly figured silk, either monochrome or polychrome, sometimes brocaded with designs in gold thread, originally produced in China. See L. Monnas, 'Textiles for the Coronation of Edward III', *Textile History*, 32 (2001): 7–8.

169 See above, n. 90.

170 See above, n. 121.

171 See above, n. 82.

172 See above, n. 95.

173 Mas Latrie, *Histoire de l'île de Chypre*, 2: 450–51.

174 Richard, *Le livre des remembrances*, p. 66, no. 141.

175 Mas Latrie, *Histoire de l'île de Chypre*, 3: 220.

the camlets delivered as Cypriot tribute to the Egyptian court, a price stated by the weavers of Nicosia in 1489.[176] The five other camlets mentioned in 1469 were far more expensive, on account of their length and especially their costly kermes dye. From this last instance we may conclude that the Cypriot court refrained from delivering costly dyed camlets as tribute. The price of Cypriot camlets in ducats appears to have risen from the 1390s to the 1480s.

---

176 See above, n. 119.

Famagusta and the Tradition of History Writing in Frankish Cyprus

Peter W. Edbury

The work that goes under the name of the *Chronique d'Amadi* is an anonymous history of Cyprus in Venetian Italian which dates from the sixteenth century.[1] The man whose name is associated with this work, Francesco Amadi, was a Venetian *erudit* who died in 1566; he was the owner of the unique surviving manuscript, not the author. *Amadi*, as I shall refer to this work from now on, recounts the history of the crusades from the time of the First Crusade and the Lusignan regime in Cyprus to the year 1442. As a piece of literature it is singularly unimpressive – the style lacks polish, and the work is no more than a compilation in an Italian translation of earlier works which vary considerably in detail and interest. Anyone looking for a more sophisticated piece of Italian Renaissance historiography should turn instead to the *Historia overo Commentarii de Cipro* by Florio Bustrone, even though the content of that work would appear to be in large measure derived from *Amadi*.[2] It is, however, the rather artless approach to his materials characteristic of the *Amadi* compiler that appeals to historians of Lusignan Cyprus. Put simply, the fact that he lacked literary pretension would seem to indicate that he stayed close to his texts, and so, although in the form we have it, it is a 'late' source, the information it conveys inspires far greater confidence than, say, the writings of Francesco Amadi's contemporary, Etienne de Lusignan. What I should like to suggest is that *Amadi* best encapsulates the phrase used in my title, the tradition of history writing in Cyprus.

Some of *Amadi*'s sources have come down to us in the original French – this is generally true of the material before the closing years of the thirteenth century; other sources have not survived, and so *Amadi*, *faute de mieux*, becomes the best account we have for the period concerned – indeed, *Amadi*'s

[1] 'Chronique d'Amadi', in *Chroniques d'Amadi et de Strambaldi*, ed. R. de Mas Latrie (Paris, 1891, 1893), vol. 1.

[2] Florio Bustrone, 'Chronique de l'île de Chypre', ed. R. de Mas Latrie, *Collection de Documents inédits sur l'histoire de France: Mélanges historiques*, 5 (Paris, 1886), 1–531.

detailed narrative of events from the first quarter of the fourteenth century is of particular value. For the period from the mid-fourteenth century to the end *Amadi* is generally overshadowed by the fuller, yet related, Greek narratives of Leontios Makhairas and his Italian translator, Diomedes Strambali.

For the twelfth century and the opening years of the thirteenth the *Amadi* compiler used two sources: the Old French translation of William of Tyre and its continuations, and one of the collections of brief annals known to historians as the *Annales de Terre Sainte*. William's Latin text ended in the year 1184; at some point in the first three decades of the thirteenth century it was translated into French and then a continuation, adapted from another history which goes by the name of the *Chronique d'Ernoul et de Bernard le Trésorier*, was pasted on at the end to bring the story down to 1232. Recent examination of the manuscripts of these two works has led to the conclusion that none of the printed editions are satisfactory. The 1871 Mas Latrie edition of *Ernoul-Bernard* managed to conflate three different recensions in a way that makes it well-nigh impossible to tease out the different manuscript traditions or work out what was in the earliest version and what was added later.[3] The 1859 edition of the continuations in the *Receuil des historiens des croisades* chose to give prominence to a later version, the so-called Colbert-Fontainebleau continuation, which marks an important development of the earlier recensions;[4] anyone wishing to see what the original continuation as adapted from *Ernoul-Bernard* looked like would do well to go back to the 1729 edition by the Maurists, Martène and Durand, in volume five of the *Veterum Scriptorum et Monumentorum … Amplissima Collectio*. Sadly they chose to rely on a manuscript which comes low on the stemma.[5] The only modern edition of any part of the continuation is M.R. Morgan's text of the Lyon, Bibliothèque de la Ville, ms. 828 for the years 1184–97. Unfortunately she believed that this version represented the original version of this narrative, whereas in fact it comes at the end of a long line of recensions and so is actually the furthest removed from the original.[6]

The *Annales de Terre Sainte* survive in three French versions, two of which were published in 1884, while the third has only recently been brought to public attention.[7] In the early fourteenth century Marino Sanudo incorporated

---

3 *Chronique d'Ernoul et de Bernard le Trésorier*, ed. L. de Mas Latrie (Paris, 1871).

4 'L'estoire de Eracles empereur et la conqueste de la Terre d'Outremer', *R[ecueil des] h[istoriens des] c[roisades: Historiens] oc[cidentaux]*, 2 (Paris, 1859).

5 *Veterum Scriptorum et Monumentorum … Amplissima Collectio*, ed. E. Martène and U. Durand, 5 (Paris, 1729), 581–752. They employed Paris, BN, ms. fr. 9082 (Rome: 1295) (= *RHC Oc.*, ms. G).

6 *La continuation de Guillaume de Tyre (1184–1197)*, ed. M.R. Morgan (Paris, 1982). English translation: *The Conquest of Jerusalem and the Third Crusade*, trans. P.W. Edbury (Aldershot, 1996), 11–145. See P.W. Edbury, 'The Lyons *Eracles* and the Old French Continuations of William of Tyre' in *Montjoie: Studies in Crusade History in Honour of Hans Eberhard Mayer*, ed. B.Z. Kedar, J. Riley-Smith and R. Hiestand (Aldershot, 1997), 139–53.

7 'Annales de Terre Sainte', ed. R. Röhricht and G. Raynaud, *Archives de l'Orient latin*, 2 (1884), documents, pp. 427–61; 'A New Text of the Annales de Terre Sainte', ed. P.W. Edbury, in *In Laudem Hierolsolymitani: Studies in the Crusades and Medieval*

a translation of the *Annales* into Latin in his *Liber secretorum fidelium crucis*, and there is also a Spanish version.[8] Material from the *Annales* is included in the compendium known as *Les Gestes des Chiprois*[9] and also in the post 1240s sections of the Old French Continuations of William of Tyre, as well as in *Amadi*.

The *Amadi* compiler continued to use the *Annales de Terre Sainte* for the thirteenth century, and indeed there are annalistic entries in his work not known from any other earlier extant source. For the period from the early 1220s to 1242 he produced a translation of Philip of Novara's memoir of the war in Cyprus and the Latin East between the Ibelins and the adherents of Frederick II, evidently using a text of this narrative that differed at certain points from the extant French version.[10] After the mid 1240s he again relied on the *Annales de Terre Sainte* and, from the late 1250s, made increasing use of the narrative conventionally if misleadingly attributed to the 'Templar of Tyre'.[11] Whereas *Amadi* contains a full translation of Philip of Novara's text, the material from the 'Templar of Tyre' is often summarized, and, as there appears to be little or no use of the latter before the end of the 1250s, it is quite possible that the compiler was not working from a text such as the *Gestes des Chiprois* in which Philip of Novara and the 'Templar of Tyre' are juxtaposed, but knew of them separately.

A few snippets of information apart, before 1300 all the information to be found in *Amadi* can be found in Old French materials dating from much closer to the events. But as we come to the early fourteenth century we find that *Amadi* has a detailed narrative of the events of the years 1306–1310 when the lord of Tyre, Amaury of Lusignan, held power in Cyprus, that is clearly based on an Old French narrative, but one that does not survive. The decades that follow are treated extremely summarily, but with the accession of King Peter I in 1369 the narrative becomes far more detailed, and remains so until the end of the Genoese war of 1373–74. After that the information remains sparse except for the description of the Mamluk invasions of Cyprus of 1424–26. The narrative is uneven to say the least. At one extreme the material dealing with

---

Culture in Honour of Benjamin Z. Kedar, ed. I. Shagrir, R. Ellenblum and J. Riley-Smith (Aldershot, 2007), 145–61.

8 Marino Sanudo, 'Liber Secretorum fidelium crucis' in *Gesta Dei per Francos*, ed. J. Bongars (Hanau, 1611; reprinted Jerusalem, 1972), 206–32; 'Las cruzadas en la historiografía española de la época: traducción castellana de un redacción desconocida de los "Anales de Tierre Santa"', ed. A. Sánchez Candeira, *Hispania: Revista Española de Historia*, 20 (1960), 325–67.

9 For the full text, *RHC Documents arméniens*, 2 (Paris, 1906), 651–872. For modern editions of the sections by Philip of Novara and the Templar of Tyre, see below nn. 10 and 11.

10 Philip of Novara (Filippo da Novara), *Guerra di Federico II in Oriente (1223–1242)*, ed. and trans. S. Melani (Naples, 1994). English translation: *The Wars of Frederick the Second against the Ibelins in Syria and Cyprus by Philip of Novara*, trans. J. La Monte and M.J. Hubert (New York, 1936).

11 *Cronaca del Templare di Tiro (1243–1314)*, ed. and trans. L. Minervini (Naples, 2000); English translation: *The 'Templar of Tyre': Part III of the 'Deeds of the Cypriots'*, trans P. Crawford (Aldershot, 2003).

the years 1218–42, drawn from Philip of Novara's well-known account of the war in Cyprus against the Hohenstaufen, takes up 80 pages in the published edition while the account of the years 1306–10 occupies 150. By comparison the 35-year reign of King Hugh IV (1324–59) is dismissed in a mere eight pages and the period from the death of Peter II in 1382 to the eve of the Mamluk invasions in 1424 is covered in ten.

There are, however, important questions relating to the *Chronique d'Amadi* that have not been sufficiently addressed. Did the translator also assemble the compilation, or did the work previously exist in its entirety in French? An answer to that question might help decide further questions about the relationship of *Amadi* to another major narrative for medieval Cypriot history, the Greek-language *Recital concerning the Sweet Land of Cyprus* by Leontios Makhairas.[12] There is no doubt that the texts of their narratives from the mid-fourteenth century onwards are closely related. But precisely how awaits elucidation. The problem is compounded by uncertainty as to how far Leontios was the originator of the material his work contains. What we know of his career suggests that he was active between 1401 and the early 1430s.[13] That prompts various questions: to what extent was he the original author of the detailed narrative his work contains of the reign of Peter I (1359–69) and the Genoese war of 1373–74, or, given that his own personal memory cannot have extended to Peter's reign, did he simply adapt an existing history? Leontios's account is fuller than *Amadi*'s. *Amadi*'s account of the reign of Peter I could well be an abridgement of a more detailed narrative, but did the *Amadi* compiler derive his material from Leontios, or, bearing in mind that occasionally *Amadi* has particular pieces of information not present in the *Recital*, could *Amadi*'s narrative be closer to a lost near-contemporary account of these years that Leontios also utilized? And if so, was that account, like the other *Amadi* sources, written in French?

The principal narrative sources for Lusignan Cyprus come in a historiographical tradition that is uneven and, in large measure, derivative. Even Philip of Novara's memoirs of the years 1218–42, which survive in the original French and which can be seen as an ambitious work of literature,[14] are preserved in a form in which Philip's narrative has at some point been superimposed on a version of the *Annales de Terre Sainte*. *Amadi's* account of the political crisis of 1306–10 and Leontios Makhairas's account of the Genoese war of 1373–74 are impressive pieces of historical writing, even if they are translated and, to an unknown extent, adapted from lost originals. But for other periods we have scant information, and other sources can only

---

12 Leontios Makhairas, *Recital concerning the Sweet Land of Cyprus entitled 'Chronicle'*, ed. R.M. Dawkins (Oxford, 1932). The edition by M. Pieris and A. Nikolaou-Konnari (*Chroniko tis Kuprou* (Nicosia, 2003)) lacks an index or commentary: it is to be hoped that this omission will be rectified.

13 Leontios Makhairas, ed. Dawkins, 2: 14–21.

14 G.N. Bromily, 'Philippe de Novare: Another Epic Historian?', *Neophilologus*, 82 (1998), 527–41.

make good this deficiency in part: Chris Schabel's recent work on the reign of King Hugh IV shows what can be achieved.[15]

So what sort of evidence do these sources give for Famagusta? For the late twelfth century and the thirteenth, the answer is 'not very much'. Although Famagusta features in one near contemporary English source for the Crusaders' invasion of Cyprus in 1191,[16] the town is ignored by *Ernoul-Bernard* and the William of Tyre Continuations in their accounts. Only in the last recension of the Continuations, the so-called 'Lyon *Eracles*' which reached its final form in the 1240s at the earliest, does Famagusta find a passing mention in the description of the conquest.[17] This silence in the narratives persists until we come to the arrival of the emperor Frederick II in Cyprus in 1228. Philip of Novara and the anonymous author of this section of the Colbert-Fontainebleau continuation of William of Tyre provide accounts that to a significant extent corroborate and complement each other. The most dramatic event relating to Famagusta was the Ibelins' occupation of the town in May 1232, when their forces were able to gain entry from the direction of the harbour, having landed on the rocky islets that form its outer limit. Both narratives mention a tower – evidently the castle which guards the entrance to the harbour – but there is no mention of any other fortifications.[18] The harbour frontage was clearly not fortified at this date,[19] but the fact that the invaders chose to attack from that direction rather than landing on the coast nearby and taking the town from the rear may suggest that there was a perimeter wall. The castle was previously mentioned in one of the later English accounts of the 1191 conquest, and was apparently alluded to by the German visitor Wilbrand of Oldenburg, who was in Cyprus in 1211 and reported that Famagusta was 'not greatly fortified'.[20]

Most of the other references to Famagusta in the thirteenth century show it as a terminus for ships sailing between Cyprus and the Christian-held ports on the mainland.[21] This is no accident. All the evidence from before

---

15 C. Schabel, 'Hugh the Just: The Further Rehabilitation of King Hugh IV Lusignan of Cyprus', *Epeterida Kentrou Epistemonikon Erevnon*, 30 (2004), 123–52.

16 Ambroise, *The History of the Holy War: Ambroise's Estoire de la Guerre Sainte*, ed. M. Ailes and M. Barber (Woodbridge, 2003), 1: 30, 34.

17 *La continuation de Guillaume de Tyre*, pp. 118, 119.

18 'Eracles', pp. 399–400; Philip of Novara, pp. 172 ('tour dou port'), 176–80.

19 See further P.W. Edbury, 'Famagusta in 1300', in *Cyprus and the Crusades*, ed. N. Coureas and J. Riley-Smith (Nicosia, 1995), pp. 338–9.

20 Wilbrand of Oldenburg, 'Itinerarium Terrae Sanctae' in *Itinera Hierosolymitani Crucesignatorum*, ed. S. de Sandoli (Jerusalem, 1978–84), 3: 230; 'Itinerarium Peregrinorum et Gesta Regis Ricardi', ed. W. Stubbs, in *Chronicles and Memorials of the reign of Richard I* (London, 1864–65), 1: 199. This source, which for this section is dependant on Ambroise and would appear to date from c. 1220, here translates the latter's 'citié', a word chosen, so it would seem, to form a rhyme with 'verité', as 'castrum'.

21 'Eracles', pp. 368 (1228), 392 (1231), 433 (1247); Philip of Novara, pp. 98, 100 (1228), 152 (1231); *Templare di Tiro*, pp. 128 (1269), 212 (1291).

the late thirteenth century points to Paphos (before the earthquake of 1222) and Limassol as the normal ports of call for ships on the long-distance routes between western Europe and Latin Syria, the implication being that sea-borne trade in Famagusta was largely restricted to the more localized traffic with Syria and the surrounding areas.

It is only after the fall of the last major crusader ports in Syria – Tripoli in 1289; Tyre and Acre in 1291 – that we can discern a raising of Famagusta's profile as a centre for long-distance commerce. As is well known, other evidence, notably the registers of the Genoese notary Lamberto di Sambuceto, make this point in a manner that is far more persuasive.[22] But there is also a wealth of anecdotal evidence in the narrative materials, especially in *Amadi*'s detailed account of the years 1306–10. In 1294, in an early phase in the conflict that is usually known as the War of Curzola, we read of Venetian hostilities against Genoa in Cypriot waters. A Venetian fleet arrived at Limassol and inflicted considerable damage on Genoese property there, including the commune's tower. It then sailed to Salines and thence to Famagusta, where the royal castellan told the Genoese to flee as he could not guarantee their safety. (The narrator is careful to point out that, by the terms of their privileges, he was in fact obliged to defend them.) In fact the Venetians seem not to have entered Famagusta and sailed instead to the Cilician Armenian port of Ayas looking for Genoese ships. This episode implies a greater importance for Limassol where the Genoese had a tower – there is no evidence, so far as I am aware, for the Genoese or any other western mercantile commune having a fortified establishment in Famagusta – and also that Famagusta at that date was not readily defensible.[23] A passage interpolated into a fourteenth-century Venetian chronicle describes another incident in the same war when in 1297 a Venetian captain 'took a certain Genoese ship out from below the tower at Famagusta by taking down the chain in defiance of the Genoese and Cypriots and had it burnt before their very eyes'.[24] But the chief interest is the changing trade routes that the story indicates: with the loss of Latin Syria, the one significant port remaining in Christian hands on the mainland near Cyprus was the Cilician port of Ayas, and merchant ships from the West bound for Ayas would naturally sail round the southern coast of Cyprus, putting in at Famagusta on the way. There are a number of instances from the early years of the fourteenth century showing ships plying between Famagusta and Ayas,[25] and plenty of anecdotes to show that by the end of the first decade of the fourteenth century Famagusta was where the communities of western

---

22 There is a large literature. A fundamental study is D. Jacoby, 'The rise of a New Emporium in the Eastern Mediterranean: Famagusta in the Late Thirteenth Century', *Meletai kai Ipomnimata*, 1(1984), 145–79. See also the studies by M. Balard, now conveniently collected in his *Les marchands italiens à Chypre* (Nicosia, 2007).

23 *Templare di Tiro*, pp. 258–60; 'Amadi', p. 231.

24 Andrea Dandolo, 'Chronicon Venetum a pontificatu Santi Marci ad annum usque MCCCXXXIX', in *Rerum Italicarum Scriptores*, ed. L.A. Muratori (Milan, 1728), 12: 407. The interpolated passage is not included in the 1938 edition by E. Pastorello.

25 'Amadi', pp. 314–15, 323, 336, 352–3, 374, 377–9.

merchants were now concentrated.[26] What is more striking is the number of instances of people travelling between Cyprus and the West who made use of Famagusta. In an earlier period crusaders, including Richard the Lionheart in 1191, the emperor Frederick II in 1228 and Louis IX in 1248, had come ashore at Limassol. But by the early fourteenth century it was clearly normal to sail on to Famagusta, or, conversely, set off from there. Among prominent figures who did so were Hayton of Gorhigos in 1307, Eschiva of Ibelin, lady of Beirut, in 1309, the papal legate Raymond of Piis in 1310, Constance of Aragon, the bride of King Henry II, in 1317, John del Conte, archbishop of Nicosia in 1319, Constance of Aragon returning to the West in 1326, and Maria of Bourbon, the bride of Hugh IV's eldest son, in 1329.[27]

It is also clear from *Amadi* that early years of the fourteenth century witnessed major changes to Famagusta itself. There is mention of work on the walls which would seem to indicate that there was a major programme of fortification in progress the first decade of the century. We are told that work on the new cathedral began in April 1308, although allegedly progress was slowed by the peculation of the new bishop. It would also appear that there were improvements to the street plan; quite what this amounted to is not clear, but it would appear to have included the creation of the open space in front of the royal palace in the centre of the town.[28]

The improvements to the fortification were linked to another important development, the growing importance of Famagusta as a military and naval base. We might note that in 1308 the military equipment found in the Templar house in Limassol was sent to the royal stores in Famagusta, and in 1310 there is mention of the 'torre del arsinal'.[29] The use of Famagusta as a base for operations against the Muslims was not new in the fourteenth century: we are told that it had been the place of embarkation for the relief of Ascalon in 1247 and the relief of Acre in 1291, and no doubt it was used on other occasions before 1291 when Cypriot troops were sent to help defend Latin Syria.[30] In 1300 it was the point of departure for a major Cypriot-led expedition against Egypt comprising 16 galleys and a number of smaller vessels, and two years later Famagusta was intended as the base for the forces being prepared to relieve the Templars on Ruad.[31] A couple of anecdotes show that by 1308 Famagusta was where the armed galleys deployed by the Cypriot government were based, and in 1310, after the death of Amaury of Tyre and the seizure of Famagusta by a group of knights loyal to Henry II, it was pointed out to the remaining members of Amaury's party that, in gaining Famagusta, the royalists had acquired control of the whole of the kingdom's naval resources.[32]

26 *Templare di Tiro*, pp. 326, 332; 'Amadi', pp. 241, 255, 261, 395.
27 'Amadi', pp. 278–80, 296, 326, 398–9, 400, 403.
28 'Amadi', pp. 291, 326–7.
29 'Amadi', pp. 291, 326.
30 'Eracles', p. 433; *Templare di Tiro*, p. 212.
31 *Templare di Tiro*, p. 300; 'Amadi', pp. 236, 239.
32 'Amadi', pp. 272, 276, 343.

Amadi recounts in considerable detail the events of the summer of 1310 when Famagusta was held by a group of knights loyal to the king.[33] It was their actions that led to the restoration of Henry II, and it is likely that the narrative of the years 1306–10 was composed specifically by someone in their circle as a celebration of their achievement. It is not clear whether the Famagusta knights were men with fiefs in the vicinity, or whether they just happened to be in Famagusta for military or personal reasons at the time of Amaury's assassination. It might be noted that they were quick to secure the support of the leaders of the Italian communities, and that they took extra measures to defend Famagusta from attack.[34] There was now a distinct possibility that a full-scale civil war would break out between the royalist knights in Famagusta and the erstwhile supporters of Amaury of Tyre who held Nicosia. In the event war was avoided: the royalists were able to gather widespread support from knights elsewhere in the island, and, with the active help of the Hospitallers, they were able to stand firm while their opponents' position crumbled and a deal was agreed to secure the king's release from Armenia. It was this episode that signalled that Famagusta, besides having emerged as the principal international port and base for naval activities, could now claim a political importance that put it second only to Nicosia.

The political importance of Famagusta was given visible expression in 1324 when, on the accession of King Hugh IV, and after he had been crowned king of Cyprus in Nicosia, he was crowned in Famagusta as king of Jerusalem. The Lusignan claim to the crown of Jerusalem dated from 1269; Hugh III and Henry II had both been crowned in Tyre, but now, as *Amadi* explains, 'the vassals and the prelates had decided that, because they could not crown him in the city of Tyre because the Saracens held the land, there was no better place in Cyprus where they could crown him king of Jerusalem than Famagusta'.[35] Hugh's coronation as king of Jerusalem in Famagusta was to be repeated for both Peter I (1360)[36] and Peter II (1372).[37] I do not think there are any grounds for believing that Famagusta was in some special sense seen as a part of the kingdom of Jerusalem; rather the coronation there of three successive kings should be seen as the continuation of the celebrations surrounding the inauguration of each new reign and as an opportunity to publicize the Lusignans' credentials as heirs to the kingdom of Jerusalem before an international audience. It was a ceremonial occasion, accompanied by the appointment of favoured nobles to the titular offices of state – seneschal, constable, marshal and chamberlain of Jerusalem – which, so far as I can gather, honoured the recipient with a fine-sounding title, but carried no duties beyond that of assisting in the coronation ritual. Apropos the coronation of Peter II in 1372 *Amadi* – but not the normally more detailed Leontios Makhairas – noted that it was because the king of

33 'Amadi', pp. 333–79 *passim*.
34 'Amadi', pp. 334–5.
35 'Amadi', pp. 402–3.
36 Leontios Makhairas, ed. Dawkins, § 104; 'Amadi', p. 408.
37 Leontios Makhairas, ed. Dawkins, § 324; 'Amadi', p. 432.

Jerusalem was crowned in Famagusta that the seal of *commercium* and the silver coinage bear the arms of Jerusalem.[38]

The account of Peter I's reign shows Famagusta continuing to fulfil its role of the principal base for naval operations against the Muslims.[39] It was clearly the principal port for ships making for Egypt and Syria,[40] and also for Rhodes and Western Europe,[41] although in 1367 Peter embarked on his second voyage to the West from Paphos.[42] There is mention of the arsenal there and, on one occasion, of ship building.[43] In the description of the preparations to withstand the Genoese invasion of 1373 *Amadi* – but not Makhairas – reports the order to 'build and fortify the wall of the Famagusta arsenal and have it crenellated'.[44] What this would seem to indicate is that the arsenal, which presumably would have had dry dock facilities for laying up ships, was the weak point in the fortifications. It was at the southern end of the harbour, and the adjacent 'tower of the arsenal', which is also mentioned in the context of the fighting in 1373, formed the southeastern bastion of the town's defences.[45] Leontios Makhairas records that, shortly after their capture of Famagusta in 1373, the Genoese took steps to heighten the walls of Famagusta on the grounds that they were vulnerable to assailants using scaling ladders, and at the same time they tried to get the sea to fill the moat below the walls.[46]

Leontios Makhairas has a detailed and graphic account of the Genoese capture and pillage of Famagusta. He mentions in particular the ruining of the Lakha family – Nestorian merchants who had made their fortune in bringing merchandise from Syria and selling it to the westerners who were subject to a papal prohibition barring them from trading with the Muslims.[47] With Famagusta in Genoese hands, the narratives have little to say about the town except to describe the efforts of Peter II in particular to get it back. Shortly before the Genoese capture of Famagusta, the Cypriot government attempted to raise money by means of a forced loan. The figures given by Leontios Makhairas are suspect and quite possibly incomplete: the burgesses of Nicosia were to find 100,000 ducats, but no figure is given for their counterparts in Famagusta; the Jews of Nicosia had to find 70,000 ducats and those of Famagusta 30,000.[48] At the very least these figures imply that the Jewish community in Nicosia was larger and wealthier; whether they are indicative of the relative wealth of Nicosia and Famagusta as a whole is less clear.

---

38 'Amadi', p. 432.

39 Leontios Makhairas, ed. Dawkins, §§ 118, 127, 129, 134, 139, 145, 151–2, 173, 180, 186, 191, 194, 220–22, 285, 288, 295; 'Amadi', pp. 414–16.

40 Leontios Makhairas, ed. Dawkins, §§ 181–2, 185, 188, 193, 224, 298, 300, 301, 306, 309.

41 Leontios Makhairas, ed. Dawkins, §§ 108, 162, 174, 205; 'Amadi', p. 410.

42 Leontios Makhairas, ed. Dawkins, § 216.

43 Leontios Makhairas, ed. Dawkins, §§ 160, 177, 213, cf. 125.

44 'Amadi', p. 439.

45 Leontios Makhairas, ed. Dawkins, § 362.

46 Leontios Makhairas, ed. Dawkins, §§ 449–50.

47 Leontios Makhairas, ed. Dawkins, §§ 91–6, 452–3.

48 Leontios Makhairas, ed. Dawkins, § 397.

There are of course many other sources for the history of Famagusta besides these narratives, and restricting the discussion to the anecdotal evidence from the historical writings under consideration has meant disregarding much that is of fundamental importance. We have, for example, to turn to a pilgrim account, that of Nicolo da Martoni writing in the 1390s, for confirmation of what these narratives imply but do not actually say: that, after the Genoese occupation, Famagusta fell into ruinous decay.[49] The documentary evidence for trade and ecclesiastical affairs is extensive, as are the archives for the years of Genoese control. The evidence reviewed here can only tell us a limited amount, but what it does record is important. There is a certain amount of information on urban topography and fortifications; very little on urban society and *mentalités*.[50] Much has been written about Famagusta in its fourteenth-century commercial heyday; far less attention has been given to pre-1373 Famagusta as a base for military and naval endeavours, and it is perhaps the importance of that theme that emerges most clearly from this discussion.

---

49 'Relation de pèlerinage à Jérusalem de Nicolas de Martoni, notaire italien', ed. L. Le Grand, *Revue de l'Orient latin*, 3 (1895), 627–8.

50 Makhairas's remark (ed. Dawkins, § 482) to the effect that among the reasons that God allowed the Cypriots to lose Famagusta was His anger at the widespread sodomy there probably tells us more about the author than about prevailing sexual preferences.

3

Mythes et réalités de la présence templière à Famagouste

Pierre-Vincent Claverie

Parmi les mystères qui entourent l'histoire de Famagouste au Moyen Âge, une place de choix mérite d'être réservée à l'implantation des templiers dans la ville. L'histoire de l'Église latine de Chypre est un domaine de recherche fécond auquel chaque publication apporte son cortège de découvertes. Il a fallu ainsi attendre 2005 pour identifier deux évêques latins de Famagouste du milieu du XIIIe siècle, dont le second a été rapproché par Chris Schabel d'un abbé de Bellapaïs contemporain. Le cas de Georges de Famagouste, dont il s'agit présentement, donne un aperçu de la difficulté que rencontrent les chercheurs qui aspirent à cerner les contours du clergé latin de Chypre.[1]

Le patrimoine architectural de Famagouste ne comble pas toujours ces lacunes du fait de l'indigence chronique de son épigraphie. Une place d'honneur revient, parmi les innombrables sanctuaires de la ville, à l'église templière de Saint-Antoine, évoquée par plusieurs sources narratives. Ces dernières sont dominées pour le début du XIVe siècle par la figure exceptionnelle de la *Chronique d'Amadi*, qui perpétue le souvenir d'un récit consigné après le retour sur le trône d'Henri II de Lusignan.[2] Des sources narratives découle l'essentiel des informations disponibles sur la commanderie du Temple de Famagouste avant le déclenchement du procès de l'ordre, en 1307. Aussi cet essai n'aura-t-il pas d'autre ambition que de démonter un mythe historiographique tenace, avant d'évoquer l'activité de la commanderie de Famagouste à la veille de sa dévolution à l'Hôpital.[3]

---

1 P.-V. Claverie, E. et J.-P. Grélois, '*Apud Ciprum Nicossiam*: notes sur les relations cyprio-auvergnates au XIIIe siècle', *Επετηρίδα του Κέντρου Επιστημονικών Ερευνών*, 31 (2005): 39–71.

2 Voir plus largement sur la question P. Edbury, 'Famagusta and the Tradition of History Writing in Frankish Cyprus', *ici-même*. Ce récit affiche une concision extrême pour les années 1306–10.

3 J.-B. de Vaivre, 'Les églises jumelles de Famagouste', *Monuments et mémoires de la fondation Eugène Piot*, 82 (2003): 139–71.

Les prémices de l'implantation du Temple à Famagouste

Mais que savons-nous au fait de l'implantation des templiers dans la ville de Famagouste ? Les aléas de l'histoire chypriote réduisent nos connaissances à un flot de conjectures en raison de la disparition des archives centrales du Temple, concentrées à Nicosie après 1291. Les chroniques de Florion Bustron et de Francesco Amadi évaluent le patrimoine insulaire de l'ordre au début du XIVe siècle à une huitaine de villages, auxquels s'ajoutent plusieurs propriétés de Nicosie, Limassol, Paphos et Famagouste. Il n'est pas douteux que le Temple ait disposé de commanderies dans chacune de ces cités dès son acquisition de l'île en 1191.[4] Les frères du Temple se firent un devoir d'accueillir dans ces maisons, en 1229, les familles aristocratiques de l'île qui refusaient de reconnaître la tutelle de l'empereur Frédéric II. Leur garnison de Gastrie refusa d'ouvrir ses portes, trois ans plus tard, aux troupes du comte Gualtiero da Chieti qui venait d'essuyer un refus similaire à Famagouste.[5] L'importance de la commanderie de Famagouste dans la première moitié du XIIIe siècle reste une énigme, en l'absence de témoignages concrets de la part des sources normatives et diplomatiques chypriotes. Aucun retrait de la règle du Temple ne mentionne en effet son existence, à la différence des commanderies de Gastrie et de Paphos sous la maîtrise de Pierre de Montaigut (1219–32). Une bulle du pape Martin IV de 1282 révèle l'ampleur des relations tissées dans la seconde moitié du siècle par les commanderies chypriotes avec le couvent central d'Acre. Le souverain pontife accuse Hugues III de Lusignan dans cette lettre d'avoir compromis, par la mise sous séquestre des commanderies de l'île, le transfert de leurs revenus et productions à Acre, où l'ordre les entrepose pour son usage personnel ou plus exactement celui de la Terre sainte.[6] La commanderie de Famagouste ne paraît pas avoir rivalisé en importance lors de la *Querela Cypri* avec celles de Limassol, Paphos et Gastrie, qui focalisèrent la colère du roi. Il ne fait cependant guère de doute que la commanderie Saint-Antoine subit une commise en bonne et due forme jusqu'à la réconciliation de Guillaume de Beaujeu avec le roi Henri II en 1285. La question se pose dès lors de localiser précisément cette commanderie, pourvue comme à Limassol et Nicosie d'une chapelle du plus bel appareil. Cette problématique nous conduit à évoquer préalablement le statut des 'églises jumelles' de Famagouste qui a fait couler beaucoup d'encre.[7]

---

4 Florio Bustron, 'Chronique de l'île de Chypre', ed. R. de Mas Latrie, *Collection de Documents inédits sur l'histoire de France: Mélanges historiques*, 5 (Paris, 1886), pp. 170–71, 246–7; P.W. Edbury, 'The Templars in Cyprus', in M.C. Barber (ed.), *The Military Orders. Fighting for the Faith and Caring for the Sick* (Aldershot, 1994), p. 191, n. 7.

5 Philippe de Novare, *Guerra di Federico II in Oriente (1223-1242)*, ed. S. Melani (Naples, 1994), § 90, pp. 178, 180, § 100, p. 194.

6 H. de Curzon, *La règle du Temple publiée pour la société de l'histoire de France* (Paris, 1886), § 618–20, pp. 319–21; P.-V. Claverie, 'L'ordre du Temple au cœur d'une crise politique majeure: la *Querela Cypri* des années 1279-1285', *Le Moyen Age*, 104 (1998): 495–511.

7 Florio Bustron, 'Chronique', p. 116; *Chroniques d'Amadi et de Strambaldi*, ed.

La question des 'églises jumelles' de Famagouste

Le visiteur qui parcourt les ruines de Famagouste rencontre, au nord de la cathédrale Saint-Nicolas, deux édifices massifs, qui présentent une certaine parenté architecturale avec les sanctuaires libanais de Saint-Sauveur de Kubba et de Sainte-Catherine d'Enfé. Ces deux chapelles parallèles, séparées par un espace de trois mètres, comportent chacune une nef unique terminée par une abside.[8] Celle qui se trouve le plus au nord comporte trois travées, voûtées sur croisées d'ogives, qu'il serait légitime de dater en Occident du XIIIe siècle. L'archéologue Camille Enlart s'est proposé d'identifier en 1899 ce sanctuaire avec l'église Saint-Antoine de Famagouste, que des sources notariales génoises situent aux abords du port de la ville. Enlart a cru pouvoir attribuer la chapelle la plus méridionale aux hospitaliers, après avoir distingué dans son abside la représentation d'un portement de croix au-dessus d'une adoration liturgique de saint Sébastien. Cette peinture aujourd'hui effacée mettait en scène une théorie de religieux, vêtus de blancs, qu'il paraît difficile de rapprocher des frères de l'Hôpital. Jean-Bernard de Vaivre a relié, il y a quelques années, cette représentation aux épidémies de Peste qui ravagèrent l'île de Chypre à compter de 1348. Ce contexte l'a conduit à évoquer l'hypothèse d'une dévolution probable du sanctuaire à une congrégation italienne, qui pourrait n'avoir revêtu que le rang de confrérie. La fin du Moyen Âge vit en effet de nombreux tiers ordres fleurir dans les pays méditerranéens sur la base des Pénitents de Saint-Antoine-Abbé, institués par les dominicains de Gênes en 1306.[9]

L'érection d'un second sanctuaire a probablement été rendue nécessaire par l'allure étriquée de la première chapelle, qui ne compte qu'une travée sur voûtes d'arêtes de 10 mètres de long sur 8 de large. Quel crédit peut-on dès lors accorder à la croix pattée qui orne un des linteaux de la chapelle méridionale conformément à l'usage de l'ordre de l'Hôpital ? On a pu objecter récemment que l'emploi généralisé de cet emblème en Orient ôte toute pertinence à l'identification proposée jadis par Enlart.[10] La chapelle méridionale possède, quoi qu'il en soit, une guérite dotée de sept porte-bannières de pierre qui incite à lui prêter le rôle de campanile du sanctuaire septentrional. Cette association fréquente au sein des ordres militaires trouvait son expression au Moyen Âge à Nicosie, où l'Hôpital possédait un clocher à côté de son église. La situation n'évolua à Famagouste qu'au moment de l'érection au XVIe siècle du lourd clocher-arcade, qui surmonte la première travée de la chapelle nord.[11]

R. de Mas Latrie (2 vols, Paris, 1891–93), vol. 1, p. 214.

[8] J.-B. de Vaivre, 'Les églises jumelles', p. 140; Cliché n° 1.

[9] C. Enlart, *L'art gothique et la Renaissance en Chypre* (2 vols, Paris, 1899), vol. 2, pp. 372–6; J.-B. de Vaivre, 'Les églises jumelles', pp. 169–70; G.-G. Meersseman, 'Etudes sur les anciennes confréries dominicaines, I: Les confréries de saint Dominique', *Archivum Fratrum Praedicatorum*, 20 (1950): 5–113.

[10] Cliché n° 2.

[11] J.-B. de Vaivre, 'Les églises jumelles', pp. 151–4.

Les sépultures anonymes retrouvées en 1941 dans le chœur de la prétendue église templière démontrent que l'édifice n'avait manifestement aucune vocation militaire. Son style gothique avancé en fait indubitablement une construction du milieu du XIVe siècle, peu conciliable avec l'histoire du Temple. Aussi y-a-t-il de fortes probabilités pour que l'église Saint-Antoine ait fait les frais de sa dévolution aux hospitaliers, même si l'*oculus* de la chapelle actuelle présente des similarités avec celui de la chapelle moréote de Malvoisie, dévolue à l'ordre. Cette parenté repose en réalité sur la simultanéité des restaurations entreprises au niveau de ces deux sanctuaires au milieu du XXe siècle. Une série de clichés de 1896 et 1939 révèlent en effet l'obturation prolongée des ouvertures des églises jumelles de Famagouste à la suite de la destruction de leurs vitraux. L'appareillage actuel de leurs fenêtres remonte dans ces conditions à la campagne de restauration menée par les Britanniques après 1942.[12]

La localisation de la commanderie Saint-Antoine

L'étude des églises jumelles de Famagouste apporte peu de réponse, en soi, à la localisation de la commanderie Saint-Antoine. Les spéculations ont cependant fleuri au cours du temps sur les bâtiments susceptibles de correspondre à la maison du Temple de Famagouste. Yvette Carbonell-Lamothe s'est, par exemple, complu dans un essai sur les monuments gothiques de Chypre à identifier cette commanderie avec une maison forte, voisine des pseudo-églises du Temple et de l'Hôpital. Camille Enlart, lui-même, s'était interdit cette spéculation gratuite en 1899, en se contentant de décrire la remarquable cheminée que comporte cet édifice du XIIIe siècle.[13]

Si l'on suit le témoignage des sources diplomatiques, la maison du Temple de Famagouste trônait au milieu d'une rue du port à laquelle elle avait fini par donner son nom *(ruda* ou *ruga Templi).* Cet axe transversal abritait les maisons de nombreux négociants bolonais ou génois comme Domenico Albergati, Giovanni Balbo et Oddone del Sesto, dont la demeure jouxtait, pour le dernier, le mur de la commanderie fortifiée. Cette proximité se matérialisait par une fréquentation assidue de l'endroit par les notaires ligures, Lamberto di Sambuceto et Niccolò Binelli, qui y instrumentèrent six actes à la fin de l'année 1299.[14] L'absence de templiers dans les listes testimoniales de ces contrats révèle la liberté de manœuvre accordée aux Génois sous les voûtes

---

12 J.-B. de Vaivre,'Les églises jumelles', pp. 147–8; P.-V. Claverie, *L'ordre du Temple en Terre sainte et à Chypre au XIIIe siècle* (3 vols, Nicosie, 2005), vol. 1, p. 330.

13 Y. Carbonell-Lamothe, 'Les monuments gothiques des Lusignan', in Jacques Charles-Gaffiot (ed.), *La France aux Portes de l'Orient. Chypre, XIIe–XVe siècle* (Paris, 1991), p. 92; C. Enlart, *L'art gothique*, vol. 2, p. 631.

14 C. Desimoni, 'Actes passés à Famagouste de 1299 à 1301 par devant le notaire génois Lamberto di Sambuceto', *Archives de l'Orient latin*, 2 B (1884), n° XVII-XXII pp. 12–17, n° LV. p. 33, n° LX. pp. 35–6; R. Pavoni, *Notai Genovesi in Oltremare: Atti rogati a Cipro da Lamberto di Sambuceto (Gennaio-Agosto 1302)* (Gênes, 1987), n° 60. pp. 82–3.

du Temple au plus fort de l'hiver. Il est hautement probable, à l'aune de ces données, que la rue du Temple soit à rechercher dans la partie méridionale de la ville, bordant le rivage. Les nombreuses destructions opérées dans cette zone, où se dressent les ruines d'un hôpital dédié à Saint-Antoine, semblent avoir eu raison de sa clôture. Sa localisation pourrait être affinée à l'occasion du lancement d'une campagne de fouilles systématiques dans le secteur. La présence de nombreux Italiens dans les murs du Temple trouve son origine naturelle dans l'ampleur des activités navales développées par le Temple après la chute d'Acre.[15]

Les activités des templiers de Famagouste

Les archives du notaire génois, Lamberto di Sambuceto, permettent d'appréhender la complexité des montages financiers élaborés ou cautionnés par les templiers avant la diffusion des lettres de change. L'emploi de nationaux, comme l'avitailleur Pietro Alerio, débouchait sur la conclusion de contrats fructueux entre les Ligures et les patrons de nave templiers, qui se passaient de la caution juridique du commandeur de Famagouste. Les templiers avaient en effet toute licence de noliser leurs navires à des commerçants génois, comme Giacomo da Solaro, Giacomo Pico et Leonello da Vindergio, en empruntant au besoin de l'argent à des marchands catalans.[16] Famagouste était, de l'avis d'un pèlerin allemand des années 1270, le port le plus proche d'Acre et de Jaffa, que les navires pouvaient rallier en l'espace de trois jours et trois nuits. Une série d'actes passés en 1302 par le commandeur de la Sainte-Anne, Pierre Visien, nous révèle la nature ainsi que le volume des produits exportés en Europe à partir de ce nouvel emporium. La nef de Pierre Visien devait profiter du printemps pour gagner l'Occident avec une cargaison de 65 tonnes de cendres végétales et de coton en vertu de contrats négociés au mois de novembre précédent.[17]

Aussi opulente qu'elle pût être, la place de Famagouste ne se réduisait pas qu'à un lieu de commerce au début du XIVe siècle. Les ordres militaires tirèrent profit de sa localisation exceptionnelle dans leurs tractations diplomatiques avec les Mongols de Perse, qui avaient remporté en décembre 1299 une victoire décisive sur les forces mameloukes, regroupées en Syrie du Nord. Le commandeur du Temple, Pierre de Vares, nolisa à cette fin auprès d'un armateur génois, le 25 février 1300, une nef famagoustaine portant le vocable de saint Jean. Les archives de Lamberto di Sambuceto permettent de connaître la teneur exacte du contrat négocié entre les deux hommes. Le Saint-

---

15 P. Plagnieux et T. Soulard, 'Famagouste. L'Hôpital Saint-Antoine', in J.-B. de Vaivre et P. Plagnieux (ed.), *L'art gothique en Chypre* (Paris, 2006), pp. 248–50; Cliché n° 3.

16 R. Pavoni, *Notai Genovesi in Oltremare (1302)*, n° 155. pp. 184–5, n° 162. p. 192.

17 S. de Sandoli, *Itinera Hierosolymitana Crucesignatorum (saec. XII–XIII)* (4 vols, Jérusalem, 1978–84), vol. 3, pp. 23–4; R. Pavoni, *Notai Genovesi in Oltremare (1302)*, n° 104. pp. 132–3, n° 150. pp. 179–80.

Jean devait se tenir prêt, contre le versement de 2 000 besants sarracénats, à gagner la Syrie entre le mois de mars et la mi-juillet 1300 avec un équipage de 55 hommes. Son capitaine Pietro Rosso prit l'engagement d'effectuer, sous 1 000 florins d'astreinte, une halte dans le port de Limassol à l'aller comme au retour du voyage prévu à destination de Tortose, Tripoli, Tyr et Acre. L'acte instrumenté par Lamberto di Sambuceto indique que cette rotation devait se répéter au moins une fois entre la mi-mars et la mi-juillet 1300 dans le cadre du soutien logistique apporté à une hypothétique tête de pont asiatique. Les Latins entreprirent durant l'été une série de raids sur le littoral syro-égyptien avant de prendre possession de l'île de Rouad, située en face de la ville de Tortose.[18]

La suite des événements nous est connue par le registre de Lamberto di Sambuceto et le témoignage oculaire du comte catalan, Bernat Guillem d'Entença, qui accosta à Famagouste à la fin de l'automne 1300. Majordome, c'est-à-dire intendant d'Aragon en 1257, présent au siège de Murcie en 1273, le comte d'Entença arriva manifestement courbé par le poids de l'âge en Orient. Le célèbre armateur barcelonais, Bernat Marquet, affréta pour lui en compagnie d'un certain Sanç Pérez de Santmartí un navire, le Sant Nicolau, signalé à Famagouste vers le 13 décembre 1300. Le comte, qui n'était pas en mesure d'acquitter son passage, mit du temps à écouler la cargaison d'huile et de froment qu'il avait embarquée en vue d'assurer ses arrières. Il finit par convaincre, le 3 ou 4 janvier suivant, les templiers d'intervenir en sa faveur. Le commandeur de la voûte du Temple remit alors en fin de journée au patron de la nef 15 384 gros tournois censés couvrir les frais du voyage du comte, estimés à mille livres de Barcelone. Cette opération permit à Bernat Guillem d'Entença de rejoindre avec sa suite les couvents du Temple et de l'Hôpital, qui stationnaient depuis plusieurs mois sur l'île de Rouad. La présence à Famagouste du commandeur de la voûte du Temple témoigne de l'importance grandissante de cette base d'opérations, tournée vers 'les rivages enflammés' de la Syrie-Palestine. Les termes de l'accord de janvier 1301 témoignent également du standard international reconnu à la monnaie capétienne en Orient.[19]

Les efforts des templiers en vue de reprendre pied en Orient se heurtèrent, malgré la motivation de nombreux croisés, à une conjoncture défavorable. Le général Qutluq-shāh avertit les chrétiens au mois de février 1301 que l'Ilkhan Ghazan ne pourrait les rejoindre en raison de tempêtes de neige persistantes. À l'annonce de cette nouvelle, les 600 chevaliers cantonnés sur l'îlot de Rouad se retirèrent au début du mois d'avril, en abandonnant la défense de l'île aux templiers. Le maître de Catalogne et gonfalonier d'Espagne, Berenguer de Cardona, avait précédé ce repli général en rentrant à Barcelone dès le mois

18 C. Desimoni, 'Actes passés à Famagouste', n° LXXIV. pp. 42–3.

19 V. Polonio, *Notai Genovesi in Oltremare: Atti rogati a Cipro da Lamberto di Sambuceto (3 Luglio 1300–3 Agosto 1301)*, (Gênes, 1982), n° 166, pp. 193–5, n° 171, pp. 199–201; A. Fuess, Verbranntes Ufer. *Auswirkungen mamlukischer Seepolitik auf Beirut und die syro-palästinensische Küste (1250–1517)* (Leyde, 2001).

de mars. Nous savons grâce au minutier de Lamberto di Sambuceto qu'il avait envoyé, le 9 février 1301, l'ancien commandeur de Tortosa, Berenguer Gamir, négocier son passage sur la nef de Bernat Marquet contre 270 livres de Barcelone. Le navire partit de Famagouste, peu après le premier mars, pour s'arrêter à Limassol et y embarquer les deux commandeurs, ainsi que quatre autres chevaliers et 28 écuyers ou sergents. Bernat Marquet veilla à notifier préalablement ses bonnes intentions au commandeur du Temple de Famagouste, frère Julien de Saint-Georges, par un acte qui nous est parvenu. L'îlot de Rouad demeura aux mains des templiers jusqu'au débarquement soudain, le 26 septembre 1302, d'un corps d'armée mamelouk en provenance de Tripoli. La flotte chrétienne, qui appareilla de Famagouste à l'annonce de l'attaque égyptienne, ne put que constater les dégâts. La capture à Rouad de 120 chevaliers du Temple n'affecta cependant nullement leur image de marque au sein de la société famagoustaine.[20]

La dévotion des frères du Temple

La piété des templiers émerge avec force des actes du *Processus Cypricus*, instruit à partir de 1310 dans l'île d'Aphrodite. Parmi les dépositions rassemblées par les évêques de Limassol et de Famagouste, une place insigne revient à celle du trésorier de l'Église de Beyrouth, Pascal, qui confirme avoir vu trois membres de l'ordre communier le plus normalement du monde dans une église famagoustaine aux alentours de 1296. Le prieur dominicain de Nicosie, lui-même, rend grâce aux nombreuses aumônes effectuées par les frères du Temple à Nicosie et à Famagouste depuis son arrivée dans l'île en 1295.[21]

Cette admiration prend la forme d'une véritable ferveur chez le marchand famagoustain, André Boussat, qui appartient à une famille d'origine vénitienne, promise à un grand avenir. Un acte de Lamberto di Sambuceto du 9 août 1301 le présente comme un citoyen vénitien impliqué dans le commerce en direction de la Crète. Ses domaines d'activité semblent avoir tourné autour du négoce de toiles françaises, auquel se mêlaient des importations de fromage crétois aux côtés d'opérations de change traditionnelles. Une série d'actes d'octobre 1301 et d'avril 1302 en fait un exportateur de bois de construction et de céréales en direction de la Crète. Boussat ne renâcle pas à commercer avec des négociants génois, comme le révèle une minute du notaire Giovanni de

---

20 P.-V. Claverie, ' "*La cristiandat en mayor peril*" ou la perception de la question d'Orient dans la Catalogne de la fin du XIIIe siècle', *Les templiers en Pays catalan* (Canet, 1998), pp. 110–11; V. Polonio, *Notai Genovesi in Oltremare*, n°219, pp. 256–8, n° 258, pp. 305–6.

21 K. Schottmüller, *Der Untergang des Templer-Ordens* (2 vols, Berlin, 1887; réédition, New-York-Vaduz, 1970), vol. 2, pp. 393–9. Cf. A. Gilmour-Bryson, *The Trial of the Templars in Cyprus. A Complete English Edition* (Leyde, Boston et Cologne, 1998), pp. 431–41.

Rocha du mois de novembre 1309, le présentant comme un ancien débiteur du marchand Sorleone Cibo.[22]

Notre homme d'affaires repousse avec force dans sa déposition la quatre-vingt-treizième charge retenue contre le Temple, en témoignant des fréquentes distributions de pain et de monnaie opérées par les templiers à Acre, puis à Limassol, où il a longtemps résidé. Il reconnaît avoir entendu parler, quelque part, du serment imposé aux nouvelles recrues de l'ordre d'œuvrer en faveur de son accroissement matériel par des moyens néfastes. À propos d'informations annexes, il déclare avoir entendu les femmes de Famagouste rapporter des propos tendancieux sur les supposées transgressions sexuelles des templiers. Ces derniers auraient déclaré aux matrones qu'ils n'épargnaient que les femmes accomplies, en utilisant une double négation dans laquelle les historiens contemporains se sont empressés de distinguer une erreur de calame. Les templiers auraient voulu de la sorte choquer leur auditoire en affirmant qu'ils ne liaient commerce qu'avec des femmes mariées, ou en âge de l'être, si l'on omet le cadre d'une simple plaisanterie.[23]

Les interrogatoires du 4 mai 1310 mentionnent un second marchand originaire d'Acre en la personne du Famagoustain, Guy de Bandes. Ce personnage documenté par Lamberto di Sambuceto était capable de négocier d'importants contrats de commande en direction de l'Occident, en recourant à des mandataires pisans ou chypriotes. Il n'hésitait pas comme Boussat à exporter des matières aussi diverses que le coton, le poivre, des toiles de Reims ou tout autre textile prisé dans le bassin méditerranéen. Sa position estimée dans la société famagoustaine l'amenait à entériner nombre de contrats et à officier en tant que procureur pour des marchands engagés au loin. Son témoignage est l'un des plus favorables qui soit en faveur du Temple, dont il souligne la piété à Acre et Limassol, incompatible avec les différents outrages sacramentels reprochés à l'ordre.

À l'article 93 du formulaire de 1308, Guy oppose les distributions de pain, viandes et vêtements opérées par l'ordre en faveur des nécessiteux et des jeunes dames, ou veuves, dans le besoin. À l'accusation d'incurie proférée contre Jacques de Molay, il rétorque avoir toujours 'entendu que tout ce que le maître et le couvent de l'ordre faisaient et ordonnaient de bon et d'honnête était respecté et observé par l'ensemble de l'ordre'. Notre marchand conclut sa déposition en déclarant, comme la plupart des autres témoins, n'avoir rien à reprocher au grand commandeur de l'ordre dans le royaume de Chypre, Jacques de Dommarien.[24]

---

22 J. Richard, *Chypre sous les Lusignans. Documents chypriotes des archives du Vatican (XIVe et XVe siècles)* (Paris, 1962), pp. 123–8; N. Coureas, 'The role of the Templars and the Hospitallers in the movement of commodities involving Cyprus, 1291–1312', in P. Edbury et J. Phillips (ed.), *The Experience of Crusading* (2 vols, Cambridge, 2003), vol. 2, pp. 272–3.

23 J. Richard, *Chypre sous les Lusignans*, pp. 123–8; N. Coureas, 'The role of the Templars ', pp. 272–3; A. Gilmour-Bryson, *The Trial of the Templars in Cyprus*, p. 426, n. 68.

24 K. Schottmüller, *Der Untergang des Templer-Ordens*, vol. 2, p. 392. Cf. A. Gilmour-Bryson, *The Trial of the Templars in Cyprus*, pp. 429–30 ; N. Coureas, 'The role of the Templars', p. 273.

La même bienveillance se retrouve chez le frère du podestat génois de Chypre, Pasquale di Mar da Genova. Percivalle apparaît dans divers contrats instrumentés par le notaire Lamberto di Sambuceto en 1297–99, à l'occasion de l'achat d'un navire de 1100 besants blancs à son parent Lanfranco di Mar. Son statut éminent l'amène à entériner des quittances délivrées par le consul de Marseille à Famagouste, Hugues Raymond, en présence du consul de Gênes, ou à œuvrer en tant que procureur pour des concitoyens en déplacement. Percivalle apparaît dans pas moins de 27 actes instrumentés par Lamberto en s'alliant, au besoin, à des parents comme l'armateur Benedetto di Mar afin de commercer dans l'Égée et la mer Noire. C'est à ce titre qu'il pourrait avoir été interrogé le premier, en mai 1311, malgré son étonnement à l'égard des griefs reprochés au Temple, dont il ignorait l'existence avant le printemps 1308.

Percivalle tient, en effet, les templiers comme de fidèles adeptes de l'eucharistie et des saints sacrements pour les avoir vus célébrer des offices divins comme aucun autre ordre. Son admiration se fonde sur le témoignage du négociant Matteo Zaccaria, qui a passé de longues années de détention au Caire où il a côtoyé une quarantaine de captifs pris à Rouad il y a une dizaine d'années. Ces derniers ont préféré endurer les rigueurs de la captivité plutôt que de céder à l'appel de la richesse et de la liberté, que les mamelouks leur faisaient miroiter en cas d'apostasie. Percivalle déclare ne rien savoir des intentions d'enrichissement des templiers ou de leurs affidés, avec qui il ne paraît avoir eu aucun contact commercial.[25]

Le *Processus Cypricus* évoque, à côté de ces témoignages, la figure d'un certain frère, Gauvain de Raval, reçu à Famagouste en 1302 par Jacques de Molay en présence du commandeur de l'île, Raimbaud II de Caromb. Son patronyme inconnu en Orient pourrait renvoyer à une réception organisée dans la fièvre du 'passage particulier' de 1300, si deux indices ne plaidaient en faveur de son origine locale. Sa première déposition, d'une part, ne détaille aucun diocèse d'origine comme si celui-ci était désormais *in partibus*. Son second interrogatoire établit, en outre, sa présence à Acre avant 1291, où il fut le témoin de nombreuses aumônes templières. Tous ces éléments soulèvent la question du degré de corruption de son patronyme qui pourrait l'affilier aux Ravendel ou *Ravendal* de Maraclée.[26] Le Temple de Famagouste comprenait, au-delà de ces combattants, un grand nombre de laïcs rémunérés en raison de leurs compétences particulières.

---

[25] K. Schottmüller, *Der Untergang des Templer-Ordens*, vol. 2, pp. 160–61. Cf. A. Gilmour-Bryson, *The Trial of the Templars in Cyprus*, pp. 67–9 ; N. Coureas, 'The role of the Templars', pp. 269–70.

[26] A. Gilmour-Bryson, *The Trial of the Templars in Cyprus*, pp. 61, 142–3 et 373–4; J. Richard, 'Les comtes de Tripoli et leurs vassaux sous la dynastie antiochénienne', in P.W. Edbury (ed.), *Crusade and Settlement* (Cardiff, 1985), pp. 214, 222 n. 11; R. Röhricht, *Regesta regni Hierosolymitani (MXCVII-MCCXCI)* (2 vols., Innsbruck, 1893–1904), vol. 1, n° 1102, p. 287. Les Ravendel tiraient leur nom du fief édessain de Rāwandān sur lequel le vicaire du royaume de Jérusalem, Melior, n'avait plus que des droits théoriques.

Le personnel de la maison du Temple de Famagouste

Les minutiers génois nous renseignent sur la nature ainsi que l'ampleur du personnel de la commanderie de Famagouste. Les gages des scribes du Temple semblent ne pas avoir été négligeables au vu de l'exemple d'un certain Simon Mestre, engagé dans des exportations de coton en direction de la Vénétie. Sa notoriété l'amena à entériner au XIVe siècle divers contrats impliquant la commanderie locale du Temple à l'instar d'un autre scribe d'origine syrienne. Mansūr ibn Seymūn, dont il s'agit, apparaît en marge d'un prêt à intérêt passé en avril 1302 entre le commandant d'une nef templière et un marchand barcelonais, en partance pour Gênes. Ce réfugié d'Acre témoigne de la continuité de la politique orientale du Temple, en même temps que de la qualité de sa réorganisation navale. Notre personnage paraît en effet avoir rempli à bord de la Sainte-Anne le rôle de comptable et de notaire, chargé de rédiger les contrats d'engagement des différents membres de l'équipage.[27]

Les employés les plus estimés des templiers semblent avoir été les médecins ou 'physiciens', qui assurèrent la réputation de la maison de Limassol au début du XIVe siècle. Celle de Famagouste abritait à la même époque un médecin d'origine grecque qui avança au comte Bernat Guillem d'Entença, en décembre 1300, la somme appréciable de 16 350 gros tournois en échange d'une cargaison de 8 000 muids de blé. Le caractère privé de la quittance délivrée par son frère Thomas, le jour du déchargement de la cargaison, exclut toute association du Temple à cette transaction de gré à gré, malgré la suggestion d'Alain Demurger d'une implication du commandeur de la voûte de Limassol.[28]

L'acte établit en effet un contrat privé entre le comte, propriétaire d'une quantité de blé supérieure au prêt consenti, et les deux médecins appelés à le représenter sur la place de Famagouste. Thomas reconnaît à ce titre au comte un droit de regard sur le choix de ses acheteurs, avant de prendre livraison d'un second lot de 3 006 muids de froment et de trente jarres d'huile d'olive, pour lesquelles il réclame une commission de 229,5 besants blancs. Une quittance de janvier 1301 tend à indiquer que les deux frères ne tardèrent pas à écouler la majeure partie de cette cargaison auprès du Temple, après avoir réalisé de substantiels profits. Les 797 tonnes de blé échangées à cette occasion placent les frères Thomas et Théodore de Famagouste parmi les principaux hommes d'affaires de la ville.[29]

---

27 R. Pavoni, *Notai Genovesi in Oltremare: Atti rogati a Cipro da Lamberto di Sambuceto (6 Luglio–27 Ottobre 1301)* (Gênes, 1982), n° 206, pp. 247–8 ; V. Polonio, *Notai genovesi in Oltremare*, n° 258, pp. 305–6 ; Pavoni, *Notai Genovesi in Oltremare (1302)*, n° 150, pp. 179–80.

28 Ramon Llull, *Raimundi Lulli opera latina*, ed. H. Harada (Turnhout, 1980), vol. 8, p. 296; V. Polonio, *Notai genovesi in Oltremare*, n° 148, pp. 170–71 ; A. Demurger, *Jacques de Molay. Le crépuscule des templiers* (Paris, 2002), pp. 211–12, 288, 168.

29 N. Coureas, *The Latin Church in Cyprus, 1195–1312* (Aldershot, 1997), p. 133; V. Polonio, *Notai genovesi in Oltremare*, n° 166, pp. 193–5, n° 171, pp. 199–201; C. Desimoni, 'Observations sur les monnaies, les poids et les mesures cités dans les

Quatre autres instruments du minutier de Sambuceto mettent en exergue les activités bancaires d'un avitailleur ou *accatator* du Temple, employé à Famagouste à la même époque. Pietro Alieri ou Alerio y apparaît comme témoin ou bénéficiaire d'opérations financières aux côtés de compatriotes ou partenaires d'affaires, comme Oberto del Monte. Le regain des activités maritimes de l'ordre après la bataille de Homs suscita une vague d'embauches dont les notules de Sambuceto témoignent avec éloquence. L'ampleur du piratage sur les côtes chypriotes poussa le Temple à exiger des marins désireux de rejoindre ses rangs des cautions, gelées durant le déroulement des expéditions. Une quittance d'un mercier de Famagouste de juin 1301 permet de fixer le montant de ces fonds de garantie à 60 sous chypriotes par personne. Les marins recrutés paraissent avoir été majoritairement provençaux et catalans en raison de l'engagement préférentiel des Famagoustains 'de souche' dans la marine royale. La quittance d'Henri de Tyr souligne la brièveté de ce type de contrats passés le temps d'un voyage ou d'une expédition, arrêtée, en l'espèce, à huit semaines. Le dépositaire de la fidéjussion devait attendre la présentation d'une lettre du capitaine ou responsable de l'opération pour pouvoir restituer aux marins la somme gagée sous peine d'une amende double.[30]

Le développement des arsenaux de Famagouste contribua à faire de ce nouvel emporium une ville clé du royaume de Chypre au moment de l'usurpation du prince Amaury de Tyr. Le prince se conforma aux ordres de la papauté en internant les templiers de son royaume au printemps 1308 dans les casaux de Khirokitia et de Yermasoyia, voisins de Limassol. Des rumeurs d'évasion l'amenèrent à rassembler dans le casal royal de Lefkara les dignitaires du Temple, qui animaient la résistance comme le maréchal Aymon d'Oiselay et le grand commandeur, Jacques de Dommarien. Le régent de Chypre continua jusqu'à son assassinat, en juin 1310, à redouter un coup de main de ses adversaires contre le port de Famagouste. Aussi affecta-t-il les esclaves des templiers, théoriquement placés sous séquestre, à la fortification des murailles de la ville. La guerre civile, qui suivit son assassinat, remit la commanderie Saint-Antoine de Famagouste sur le devant de la scène.

Le capitaine Ague de Bethsan demanda aux chevaliers de Limassol et de Paphos de rallier le port de Famagouste avec les templiers internés dans le casal de Khirokitia. La *Chronique d'Amadi* précise que le maréchal du Temple, le commandeur de Pouille, le grand commandeur, Jacques de Dommarien, le turcoplier et le drapier de l'ordre furent assignés à résidence dans la commanderie de Famagouste à des fins préventives. Les partisans du roi Henri II craignaient une alliance objective entre les templiers et le connétable Aimery, qui entendait prendre la succession de son frère Amaury. Ces craintes

actes du notaire génois Lamberto di Sambuceto', *Revue de l'Orient latin*, 3 (1895): 24.

30 C. Desimoni, 'Actes passés à Famagouste de 1299 à 1301 par devant le notaire génois Lamberto di Sambuceto', *Archives de l'Orient latin*, 2 B (1884), n° LXXVI-LXXVIII, pp. 44–5; C. Desimoni, 'Actes passés à Famagouste de 1299 à 1301 par devant le notaire génois Lamberto di Sambuceto', *Revue de l'Orient latin*, 1 (1893), n° CCCVI, pp. 106–7; V. Polonio, *Notai genovesi in Oltremare*, n° 413, pp. 493–4; A. Demurger, *Jacques de Molay*, p. 178.

furent vérifiées, dans le cas d'Aymon d'Oiselay, à l'occasion d'une nouvelle tentative de soulèvement en 1311. Ses coreligionnaires optèrent pour la voie de la sagesse, en se détournant du métier des armes avant la dévolution de la commanderie Saint-Antoine de Famagouste aux johannites.[31]

[31] *Chroniques d'Amadi et de Strambaldi*, vol. 1, p. 360; Florio Bustron, 'Chronique', p. 219.

Taverns in Medieval Famagusta

Nicholas S. H. Coureas

As one would expect, the port city of Famagusta, the major port of Cyprus from the late thirteenth century onwards and one of the chief trading *entrepôts* of the Eastern Mediterranean, had a considerable number of taverns. The notarial deeds of the fourteenth and fifteenth centuries afford interesting information concerning the proprietors of these taverns. Most of those mentioned in the documents originate from Italy – Genoa, Venice, Milan and elsewhere – something perhaps due to the fact that the majority of deeds were drawn up by Genoese and, to a lesser extent, Venetian notaries, hence this bias. In some instances the tavern keepers simply appear as witnesses to a commercial transaction, but on other occasions they are alluded to as lenders or borrowers of money, while in particular and extremely interesting instances they and their taverns are mentioned in connection with some dispute.

It is unfortunate that the extant sources on taverns in Famagusta and even Cyprus in general tell us little concerning the types of persons frequenting such establishments, the food and drink sold there and on their urban distribution, whether they were concentrated in specific neighbourhoods or scattered throughout the city. Given that most people frequenting the taverns and those supplying the victuals sold there would have been locals, they would not normally find mention in the Genoese notarial deeds forming the vast majority of primary source material. For the same reason, non-Latin owners of taverns, Greek, Armenians and Syrians, are likewise not mentioned, due once again to the Latin bias of the extant Genoese notarial deeds. On a more positive note it is significant that the Genoese notarial deeds and other documents mention women on various occasions among those maintaining taverns, indicating their active participation in the social and commercial life of what by 1300 was Cyprus's premier port city.

The first tavern keeper mentioned in these documents is Bonosiurnus Lupus and his wife Fernia, who on 30 November 1296 confirmed the receipt of certain goods to a certain Allegro Fateinanti, promising to pay him 136 white bezants for them before the next Mardi Gras.[1] On 2 September 1300 the Genoese Guglielmo de Quarto acknowledged in writing the repayment of a debt of 35 gold pieces from the tavern keeper Antonio Nigro, a resident of either Caffa or of Candia in Crete. Antonio had borrowed this money on 15 July, promising to repay Guglielmo or his representative in Constantinople by mid-September or even earlier should the ship he was journeying on arrive sooner.[2] On 10 November 1300 Barbarino, a judicial officer of Famagusta, borrowed five white bezants from the tavern keeper Bennato, promising to repay the loan whenever Bennato saw fit and putting forward Lambert of Tyre and his guarantor, the name of the latter indicating that he was a refugee in Famagusta following the Muslim capture of Tyre in 1291. Tavern keepers also appear as witnesses. On 1 August 1300 the tavern keeper Bartholomew, described as a resident of Famagusta, witnessed the repayment of 220 bezants and some articles that the Catalan Bernard de Rose, also resident in Cyprus, had borrowed from Bernard Arnaldus of Barcelona. In December 1300 the Genoese tavern keeper Bongiorno appeared as a witness when the will of one of his deceased fellow citizens, Bernardo Zotardo, was read out, while in April 1301 two Genoese agreed on a commercial venture in the location 'in front of the house of the tavern keeper Garinus'.[3] Clearly this house was a well known urban landmark. Garinus, a tavern keeper of Venetian origin, is also alluded to in other notarial deeds of this period.

The tavern keeper James of Ancona, a town on Italy's Adriatic littoral, is mentioned in a notarial deed of 7 April 1301, according to which he submitted the sum of 17.5 white bezants as a guarantee and fine for the sailor Bolgarino, who had made his escape from the galley where he was employed. Bonaggiunta de Savio, the scribe on board the galley, acknowledged payment of this fine, and the relevant deed describes the tavern keeper James as the resident of the neighbourhood of Tortosa in Famagusta, a district inhabited by refugees from the Syrian town of the same name, captured by the Muslims at the close of the thirteenth century. In the same month the Genoese tavern keeper Perretino Carbonerio and his wife Alota acknowledged before their fellow citizen Nolasco de Nigro the receipt of a quantity of goods, regarding which they undertook to pay 92 white bezants by instalments and in full before the end of the coming October. In June 1301 the Genoese Peter Roberti nominated the tavern keeper Guirardino as one of his executors when making

---

1 *Notai Genovesi in Oltremare: Atti rogati a Cipro da Lamberto di Sambuceto (11 Ottobre 1296–23 Giugno 1299)*, ed. M. Balard, Collana Storica Fonti e Studi (henceforth CSFS) 39 (Genoa, 1983), no. 19.

2 'Actes génois de Famagouste', ed. C. Desimoni, *Archives de l'Orient latin*, 2 (1884), 3–120, no. 181; *Notai Genovesi in Oltremare: Atti rogati da Lamberto di Sambuceto (3 Luglio 1300–3 Agosto 1301)*, ed. V. Polonio, CSFS 31 (Genoa, 1982), no. 2. The tavern keeper Antonio Nigro, mentioned as originating from Caffa in the deed of 15 July 1300 and from Candia in that of 2 September 1300 is clearly the same person, a scribal error having occurred in one of the documents.

3 CSFS 31, nos 106, 176 and 306.

his will.[4] Furthermore, the above-mentioned tavern keepers Garinus and Bennato are mentioned as witnesses in a deed of September 1301 recording the sale of a Turkish slave girl, as well as in another deed recording the import of Indian aromatic herbs in Alexandretta.[5]

There are a number of references to tavern keepers in Famagusta for the year 1302. In January the tavern keeper Bennato together with Bertolino lent the sum of 25 white bezants to the Genoese Paschal de Sagona, with the latter promising to invest the money in the best possible manner during the course of a sea voyage the three of them were planning. In the same month the above-mentioned tavern keeper Guirardino appeared as a witness to a loan transaction, while in February the tavern keeper Veneticus, possibly also originating from Venice, likewise appeared as a witness to a commercial transaction. In April 1302 the Venetian tavern keeper Garinus appears in a commercial transaction as the purchaser of textiles worth 112 white bezants from the Genoese Ansaldo Lavagio. Garinus had paid for these textiles in kind and Ansaldo was acting on behalf of another fellow citizen of his, Guirardo of St Pancras. On Ansaldo's death Guirardo nominated Allegro Fateinanti as his procurator for the recovery of those goods. In June 1302 the above-mentioned Genoese tavern keeper Bongiorno gave the considerable sum of 400 white bezants to his future son-in-law, John Xarrache of Beirut, by way of a dowry for his daughter Catherine. Raymond, a tavern keeper already mentioned, was included among the witnesses to this transaction.[6] The tavern keepers in the flourishing commercial port of Famagusta were manifestly wealthy and also socially connected, even if their profession was not completely respectable, as will be seen below.

Tavern keepers in Famagusta are mentioned in subsequent notarial deeds of the period 1307–10. In March 1307 the Genoese tavern keeper Peter Anselm likewise made a will, nominating his wife Maria as his executor and stipulating that were he to predecease her she would be entrusted with his burial and the attendant expenses. Peter Anselm, moreover, bequeathed various sums of money to the churches of Famagusta, to the Dominican and Franciscan friars of the city and to the chapel of St George of the Genoese, located in the area of the loggia of the Genoese community. His wife inherited the greater part of his estate, while all the witnesses present were Genoese. There is no mention of any children. The first mention of a female tavern keeper, Marinaria, appears in January 1310, when she acknowledged the loan of a sum of 200 white bezants from the Genoese Pagano di Porta Sancti Andree, advanced to her the previous year. As she herself admitted, she had borrowed this sum 'for the purchase and sale of wine in the tavern', promising to repay him the whole sum including interest 'in good faith and without

---

4 CSFS 31, nos 313, 345 and 418.

5 *Notai Genovesi in Oltremare: Atti rogati a Cipro da Lamberto di Sambuceto (6 Luglio–27 Ottobre 1301)*, ed. R. Pavoni, CSFS 32 (Genoa, 1982), nos 168 and 173.

6 *Notai Genovesi in Oltremare: Atti rogati da Cipro da Lamberto di Sambuceto (Gennaio–Agosto 1302)*, ed. R. Pavoni, CSFS 49 (Genoa, 1987), nos 41, 52, 65, 177 and 231–4.

deception'. In February 1310 the Milanese tavern keeper John was present in a loan transaction involving, appropriately enough, the export of beer to the kingdom of Cilician Armenia.[7] There is no mention of tavern keepers in the extant Venetian notarial deeds for Famagusta dating to the middle of the fourteenth century, except for one dated 1362, in which the tavern keeper Bartholomew Furlano is simply mentioned as being witness to a will drawn up by the Venetian merchant Nicholas Contareno.[8]

Interesting references to the taverns and tavern keepers of Famagusta are to be found in notarial deeds of the fifteenth century drawn up in the town, as well as in the written depositions submitted in the course of the judicial inquests conducted against two Genoese captains of Famagusta, which the Genoese captured during their invasion of Cyprus in 1373 and held until 1464. In 1428 an especially interesting incident regarding a cleric visiting a tavern together with friends took place. This cleric, named Anthony Mansour the son of Abraham from Pera, happened to be in the tavern with his friends in October 1428 to eat and drink. A resident of Famagusta named Bisarra was in the same tavern with his own party and at some point the two parties came together and started carousing. The cleric Anthony, who happened to be holding a knife in order to cut the bread and pasta which all of them were eating, to his misfortune, struck Bisarra by accident, neither premeditatedly nor in jest, wounding him so badly in the chest so as to cause his death. Consequently the captain of Famagusta or his officers arrested Antonio, initially gaoling him and then handing him over to the Latin bishop of Famagusta, once they had realized that he was a cleric. The bishop likewise had him placed in custody, but at some point Anthony managed to escape and make his way to Rome where he sought absolution for his offence, given that it had not been premeditated. Racello de Auro de Bononia, a Hospitaller and the papal representative, granted him the absolution requested so as to enable him to return to Famagusta in his former official capacity and to recover his former honours and privileges, without having to undergo trial there before a secular court. His advocate conveyed his request to the doge and senate of Genoa, who accepted it and decreed him absolved from all accusations levelled against him.[9] This incident does to some degree explain the prohibitions on clerics frequenting taverns to be found in the councils and the decrees emanating from them promulgated by the Latin Church of Cyprus in the course of the thirteenth and fourteenth centuries.[10]

---

7 *Notai Genovesi in Oltremare: Atti rogati a Cipro da Lamberto di Sambuceto (31 Marzo 1304–19 Luglio 1305, 4 Gennaio–12 Luglio 1307) e Giovanni de Rocha (3 Agosto 1308–14 Marzo 1310)*, ed. M. Balard, CSFS 43 (Genoa, 1984), no. 82 (di Sambuceto), 38 and 75 (de Rocha).

8 C. Otten-Froux, 'Un notaire vénitien à Famagouste au XIVe siècle: Les actes de Simeone, prêtre de San Giacomo dell'Orio (1362–1371)', *Θησαυρίσματα* 33 (2003), no. 181.

9 S. Blijnyuk, *Die Genuesen auf Zypern ende 14. und im.15. Jahrhundert*, Studien und Texte zur Byzantinistik 6, ed. P. Schreiner (Frankfurt 2005), no. 8.

10 *The Synodicum Nicosiense and other documents of the Latin Church of Cyprus, 1196–1373*, ed. and trans. C. Schabel (Nicosia, 2001), 92–3, 214–15, 232–3.

The allusion to bread and pasta being served at the tavern is interesting. It constitutes one of the all too scarce references to types of food served at these establishments in Famagusta. Given that both these victuals are made from wheat it highlights, albeit indirectly, the importance of the grain supply for this Genoese enclave within the Lusignan kingdom of Cyprus. The registers of the two Genoese treasurers, the *massari*, of the city, although incomplete for the period of Genoese occupation of Famagusta, afford important information in this regard. Kept according to the double-entry accounting system practised in Genoa since the 1340s, the entries on the left consisted of the *exitus* or outgoings while those on the right were the *introitus* or revenues. The purchase of grain, for instance, was registered as an outgoing, but the grain itself was registered on the right as something coming in, in the revenues section. The Genoese imported grain into Cyprus from Sicily, and one of the towers on the ramparts of the walls circling Genoese Famagusta was called the grain tower in the treasurers' accounting records, the *massaria*. Besides, by the end of the fourteenth century, by which time urban expansion had become a thing of the past, mills had been constructed within Famagusta, and more specifically within the neighbourhoods or *contrade* of the hairdressers, St Cosmas, St Mary of Mount Carmel and Limassol.[11]

As mentioned above concerning Marinaria, a female tavern keeper in Famagusta around 1310, this profession was by no means exclusive to men. A second recorded instance of a female tavern keeper is encountered in the year 1448, the person concerned being a certain Marossa Pansana. Appearing before the judges in the course of the judicial inquest being held over the charges brought against Pietro di Marco, the former Genoese captain of Famagusta, she submitted two specific accusations against him. According to the first of these, during his term of office a Catalan named John de Letta had stolen from her a gold vessel worth 30 ducats. When she denounced him before the captain the latter had the accused taken to the torture chamber. Marossa, who was present there, demanded that he be tortured so that in his terror he would return the gold vessel, but the captain showed himself to be highly unwilling to take such a step. According to the second accusation Marossa levelled against the captain, a certain Antonio de Alba owed her 15 white bezants together with a quantity of silver worth 25 white bezants. The said Anthony was placed in custody on his return to Famagusta and the relevant receipt was impounded by Giustiniano Fatinanti. Following this, however, Captain Pietro di Marco instructed Giustiniano to relinquish this receipt despite Marossa's objections, and as a result Antonio departed without paying her what he owed her.[12]

---

11 M. Balard, 'La *massaria* génoise de Famagouste', in *Diplomatics in the Eastern Mediterranean 1000–1500: Aspects of Cross-Cultural Communication*, ed. A. Beihammer, M.G. Parani and C.D. Schabel (Leiden, 2008), 237–41; Blijnyuk, *Die Genuesen*, nos 2–4, 6-7 and 17–18.

12 *Genova e Cipro: L'inchiesta su Pietro di Marco capitano di Genova in Famagosta (1448–1449)*, ed. S. Fossati Raiteri, CSFS 41 (Genoa, 1984), no. 17.

In his defence apropos of the first accusation the former captain Pietro di Marco declared that he had indeed subjected the accused to torture but that on ascertaining that no incriminating evidence resulted he was unwilling to continue. Regarding the second accusation, he stated that he had indeed given Giustiniano orders to relinquish the receipt in his possession. The final outcome of this case is not known, even though Marossa brought forward two witnesses who upheld the veracity of her accusations in their testimonies.[13] In February 1455, however, Marossa Panssana is mentioned once again, this time as the purchaser of a house with a tavern attached to it from a certain Barnabas Ternatio. This establishment was located on a street extending from the area of the marketplace to the customs house of Famagusta. The document recording her purchase is invaluable not only for stating the general vicinity in which the tavern was located, clearly a central artery of Famagusta, but also for recording how a house was attached to the tavern, proof that as elsewhere in Europe and the Mediterranean houses had commercial premises attached to them, serving in architectural terms the dual purpose of residence and workplace. Furthermore, in June 1455 Marossa is referred to once again as the employer of a certain man named Losa from Nicosia, who owed her the sum of four ducats, the price 'for his supper and for a bed'. In addition, Marossa is recorded in the register of debts submitted during the term of office of the Genoese captain Bartholomew de Levanto during the years 1455–57, twice as a creditor and once as a debtor.[14] Another tavern keeper recorded in Genoese state archives of the mid fifteenth century was Serini Cachotripitri, who ran a tavern in a house owed by a Genoese. Her name was perhaps a corruption of Eirini Kakotripiti, in which case this tavern keeper would have been female and ethnically Greek.[15]

Another interesting charge brought against Pietro di Marco in connection with taverns in Famagusta was that of Azar de Caffa, who seems to have originated from the Genoese possession of this name in the Crimea. During Pietro di Marco's term of office he entered the tavern of a certain Antonio Cogio, who at that time was arguing heatedly with a man named Bartholomew from Pera, the Genoese colony opposite Constantinople. In the course of this altercation Antonio at some point seized a pitcher of wine with which to strike Bartholomew and Azar, observing these developments, went over to separate them, whereupon Antonio in a fit of anger struck Azar upon the head so hard with the pitcher that he fractured his skull. As a result of this mishap Azar was compelled to stay in bed for a whole month and a further 17 days before he was fit enough to go out and work again and sustained a financial loss of over 80 bezants. He was, moreover, a man subsisting by his daily wages, having

13 CSFS 41, nos 18–25.

14 *Un enquête à Chypre au XVe siècle: Le sindicamentum de Napoleone Lomellini,capitaine Génois de Famaguste (1459)*, ed. C. Otten-Froux (Nicosia, 2000), 242.

15 L. Balletto, 'Ethnic groups, cross social and cross cultural contacts on fifteenth century Cyprus', in *Intercultural Contacts in the Medieval Mediterranean*, ed. B. Arbel (London 1996) 42 and n. 27.

nothing to live on other than by the sweat of his brow. On account of this he presented himself before the captain as soon as he was able to get about, asking him to dispense justice as regarded the blow he had received from Antonio, but the captain was unwilling to help him. He had also requested the captain to reimburse him for the medical and hairdressing expenses he had had to pay.[16]

In his defence Captain Pietro di Marco maintained Azar's declarations to be mendacious, also stating that he had assigned the resolution of the matter to his deputy, Laurence de Armorinis, so that the latter might dispense justice to Azar in his capacity as a judge in the criminal court.[17] The final outcome of the case is unknown, but clearly such incidents gave taverns and those frequenting them a bad name. It should be mentioned in connection with the taverns of fifteenth century Genoese Famagusta that during the judicial inquest that took place in 1459 against Napoleone Lomellini, a former captain of the city, one of his accusers, the above mentioned Giovanni Fatinanti, asserted that whenever this captain permitted pirates to enter the city with their stolen wares, which Napoleone and his son Luca bought from then and then resold, thereby acting as receivers of stolen goods, the same pirates on occasion frequented the taverns of the city, and Luca often had to compel them to leave these establishments in order to induce them to depart from the city.[18]

Further possible allusions to taverns in Famagusta are found under King James II, the penultimate king of Cyprus who finally recaptured Famagusta from the Genoese, restoring it to the Lusignan realm, in 1464. In a document of 21 May 1468 the king granted a tax exemption to Marco Gabriel, a Genoese burgess of Famagusta in his service, of 49 bezants in taxes due from the incomes he received from houses and five *canutes* he owned in Famagusta. This word, perhaps of Armenian origin, can refer to either small shops or taverns, and perhaps some of the five establishments describes as *canutes* were in fact taverns. The same argument applies as regards another document of 1 June 1468, in which the king in a similar fashion granted the abbey of St Symeon of Famagusta an exemption from paying 12 bezants in taxes normally due from the incomes it received from four *canutes* located in Famagusta and adjoining the royal palace.[19]

The taverns of late medieval Cyprus, also called *canutes* in the language of this period, also existed in Nicosia, the capital of Lusignan and Venetian Cyprus, and even in the suburbs of the city, and these should be discussed briefly for purposes of comparison. An incident recounted in the chronicle of George Boustronios, which gives an account of the civil war between 1460 and 1464 between Queen Charlotte and her illegitimate half-brother James, who

16 CSFS 41, no. 136.

17 CSFS 41, no. 138.

18 Otten-Froux, *Une enquête*, pp. 59, 164–5.

19 *Le livre des remembrances de la secrete du royaume de Chypre (1468–1469)*, ed. J. Richard (Nicosia, 1983), nos 159-60 and no. 159, n. 3.

eventually won and ruled Cyprus as King James II until 1473, whereupon the Venetians annexed the island, shows the relatively low social standing but also the opportunities for wealth attendant on persons maintaining taverns in Cyprus. In narrating the rise of his enemy James of Malta during the civil war Boustronios states that initially he arrived in Cyprus a poor man. He was nonetheless astute enough to marry the daughter of a tavern keeper named Nicholas of Palermo, who prior to his emancipation had been a serf belonging to the count of Tripoli but afterwards opened a tavern and made a great deal of money.[20] The overall picture given is that of a person of humble birth and foreign extraction who nonetheless managed to acquire wealth from the tavern he had opened up. Clearly taverns in Cyprus could be lucrative enterprises, even if maintaining them was not considered a respectable occupation. Until 1474 there were five *canutes* in the suburbs around Nicosia, and because they were outside the city their owners were considered exempt from the payment of the municipal tax on consumables entering the city, the so-called *gabelle*. During the Venetian period the local authorities granted permission for the opening of seven additional *canutes* from 1531 onwards, but following their establishment a fierce competition ensued resulting in the decline of certain *canutes* within the city. Such establishments acquired a reputation as centres of extravagance and moral laxity on account of the drink they sold to their clients, and were regarded as discouraging Christians from the observance of the divine offices.[21] Yet despite their nefarious reputation they continued to function throughout the Lusignan and Venetian periods of Cypriot history, being attested both in Nicosia, the capital of Cyprus, and Famagusta, the island's principal port.

---

[20] Τζώρτζης (Μ)πουστρούς (Γεώργιος Βο(σ)τρ(υ)νός ή Βουστρώνιος, *Διήγησις Κρονίκας Κύπρου*, ed. G. Kehayioglou (Nicosia, 1997), σσ. 140–41, George Boustronios, *A Narrative of the Chronicle of Cyprus 1456–1489*, ed. and trans. by N. Coureas (Nicosia, 2006), § 93.

[21] N. Coureas, G. Grivaud and C. Schabel, 'The Capital of the Sweet Land of Cyprus: Frankish and Venetian Nicosia', in *A History of Nicosia*, Rimal Publications (in press).

Part II: Art and Architecture

5

St Nicholas in Famagusta: A New Approach to the Dating, Chronology and Sources of Architectural Language

Arne Franke

Introduction

We know of hundreds of buildings on the island of Cyprus constructed during the Frankish regime, many of which have survived and bear witnesses to the development of an architectural culture at that time. Thanks to its coherence and architectural beauty, St Nicholas in Famagusta in particular demands the art historian's attention (Plate 1, and see also Figures 7.6 and 7.7). Its architectural value is now even more important than ever, since the original Gothic masonry of the majority of European cathedrals of this period has been altered and restored to the point where the original elements are difficult to identify. But although the ravages of time have taken their toll, St Nicholas has remained almost untouched.[1]

With the notable exception of Camille Enlart's celebrated publication of 1899,[2] studies of St Nicholas have been neither extensive nor thorough. On the one hand this is understandable, as it is hard to better Enlart's scholarship; but on the other, it is sad to see this stagnation. Indeed, there has never been any critical review of Enlart's late nineteenth-century premises and scientific background. That is why, after a lapse of over a century, a fresh analysis of this building in the light of our current thinking is necessary.

Since the publication of *L'art gothique* there have been developments in at least three key areas, while at the same time our understanding of Gothic art in central Europe has moved on. In the first place Enlart's nationalistic interpretation has given way to a more international approach to European

---

1 A. Franke, *Die Kathedrale in Famagusta und die gotische Architektur auf Zypern* (Magisterabeit: Ludwig-Maximilians-Universität München, Munich, 2006). Unpublished.

2 C. Enlart, *L'Art Gothique et la Renaissance en Chypre* (2 vols, Paris, 1899); English translation: *Gothic Art and the Renaissance in Cyprus*, trans. and ed. D. Hunt (London, 1987).

Gothic. This approach is essential for identifying the origins of the architecture to be found in Cyprus and the influences that bore upon it. Secondly, since 1899 fresh documentary sources have come to light that relate to the cathedral, and which in some cases promote new interpretations. Thirdly, a new and more accurate approach towards the building itself which involves a detailed study of the structure instead of relying on the secondary art-historical literature, has given rise to an analysis that provides some surprisingly clear conclusions.

There are two important areas of investigation to be addressed in this chapter, drawing on both the written sources and – where the documentary material is deficient – the building itself. The first area concerns the chronology of its construction. When and why did the construction work start? Can the phases of the building process be identified? Did the different stages of construction result in a building that was complete in itself? The second area of investigation sets out to clarify the historical circumstances and will include a consideration of patrons, commissions, donations and the identity of the architect(s) and masons. As a consequence of the scarcity of surviving information, only a combination of approaches can hope to answer these questions. But when all is said and done, the evidence of the written sources, the general historical developments in Famagusta, the structure of the building and the stylistic identification of architectural forms prove to be complementary.

Sources and Historical Background

Hitherto three sources have been consulted in identifying and defining the dates for the construction of St Nicholas. First of all, an inscription on the building with the date August/September 1311 provides the information that six vaults had already been completed before an interruption,[3] and it may be assumed that this break had come about as the result of the political conflict between King Henry II and the lord of Tyre (1306–10).[4] Work was

3 +.LAN . DE . M . E. TROI CENS . ET . XI .
D' . CHRIST . A. IIII . IORS . DAOUST . FU .
DESPENDUE . LAMONEE . ORDENE
E . POR . LELABOUR . D'. LIGLISE . D' . FAM
AG' . E . COMESA . LELABOUR . LEVESQ' .
BAUDUIN . LE . DIT . AN . LEPRE
MIER(P?) . IOR . D' . SEPTEMBRE . DO
U . QUEL . LABOUR . VI . VOTES . D'
DEUS . HELES . ESTOIENT . FAIT(ES . E. ?)
.X. VOTES . DES . HELES . AVE . VIII . VOTS. D'.
LA. NAVE. D'.
LIGLISE . E
STOIT. A . FA
IRE.

4 P.W. Edbury, *The Kingdom of Cyprus and the Crusades, 1191–1374* (Cambridge, 1991), 115–40.

resumed under Bishop Baldwin in 1311 after King Henry's return from exile and the re-establishment of normality. Secondly, I have counted 17 separate legacies to the workshop or requests for burial in or next to the cathedral from notarial registers in the period 27 December 1296–19 August 1301.[5] Finally, in addition to these contemporary sources, the later Frankish chronicles, 'Amadi', Strambali,[6] Bustron[7] and Makhairas,[8] make reference to the construction.

In view of the paucity of these sources, the recent use of two papal letters of 1313[9] and 1318[10] that relate to the construction of the cathedral of St Nicholas has added significantly to the materials at our disposal.[11] These documents from the papal court in Avignon announce indulgences for donors contributing to the building costs and call on the faithful to give money. Thanks to these sources it has now become possible to prove the hypothesis that there was an earlier cathedral, perhaps constructed in the first half of the thirteenth century, on the same site.[12]

---

[5] Lamberto di Sambuceto, *Notai genovesi in Oltremare. Atti rogati a Cipro da Lamberto di Sambuceto (11 ottobre 1296–23 giugno 1299)*, ed. M. Balard, Collana storica di fonti e studi (Genoa, 1983); 'Actes passés à Famagouste de 1299 à 1301 par devant le notaire génois Lamberto di Sambuceto', ed. C. Desimoni, *Archives de l'Orient Latin*, 2 (1884): 3–120.

[6] *Chroniques d'Amadi et de Strambaldi*, ed. R. de Mas Latrie (2 vols, Paris, 1891–93).

[7] Florio Bustron, 'Chronique de l'île de Chypre', ed. R. de Mas Latrie, *Collection des documents inédits sur l'histoire de France: Mélanges historiques*, 5 (Paris, 1886).

[8] Leontios Makhairas, *Recital concerning the Sweet Land of Cyprus entitled 'Chronicle'*, ed. and trans. R.M. Dawkins (2 vols, Oxford, 1932).

[9] Omnibus vere poenitentibus et confessis, qui ad consummationem ecclesiae Famagustan., quam Balduinus episcopus Famagustan. propter augmentum populi civitatis eiusdem, ad quem recipiendum non sufficit ecclesia cathedralis antiqua, a suo praedecessore inceptam sub vocabulo beati Nicolai confessoris construi facit, eidem episcopo vel eius nuntius pius elemosynas vel alia subisdia erogaverint, concedit usque ad decennium centum dierum indulgentiam. Universis Christi fidelibus presentes littlera inpecunis. Ecclesiarum fabricis ... Pope Clement V, *Regestum Clementis papae V.*, ed. cura et studio monachorum Ordinis S. Benedicti (8 vols, Rome, 1885–92), 8: 38, no. 8998.

[10] Indulg. c dierum ad decennium illis qui manum porrexerint adjutricem fabricæ eccl. Famagustan., quæ nimis angusta est ex eo quod post depopulationem civit. Actonen. et amissionem totalem ac lugubrem Terræ Sanctæ, civitas Famagustan. facta fuit ex diversarum nationum habitatoribus, qui ad ipsam recursum habuere de ipsius terræ partibus, valde populosa. Pope John XXII, *Lettres communes*, ed. G. Mollat and G. de Lesquen, Bibliothèque de l'Écoles françaises d'Athènes et de Rome (16 vols, Paris, 1904–47), 2: 306, no. 8686.

[11] P. Plagnieux and T. Soulard, 'La cathédrale Saint-Nicolas', in J.-B. de Vaivre and P. Plagnieux (eds), *L' art gothique en Chypre* (Paris, 2006), 219–23; A. Franke, *Die Kathedrale in Famagusta und die gotische Architektur auf Zypern* (Magisterarbeit: Ludwig-Maximilians-Universität München, Munich, 2006), 17–18.

[12] P.W. Edbury, 'Famagusta in 1300', in N. Coureas and J. Riley-Smith (eds), *Cyprus and the Crusades* (Nicosia, 1995), 342.

Scattered through the published literature we find no less than six different dates for the start of work on the new cathedral: 1296,[13] 1298,[14] 1300,[15] 1301, 1308[16] and finally 1311.[17] I agree with those who regard the bequests of the years 1296 or 1298 as relating to the earlier church,[18] and I take the view that construction began no earlier than 1300 or 1301. It is only in 1300 that a bequest specifically mentions a workshop for St Nicholas.[19] It seems unlikely that in the chaos following the fall of Acre in 1291 the church authorities would have been sufficiently organized to start such a project – at least, not until around the year 1300.

Whatever the exact date for the laying of the foundation stone, scholars, when describing the origins of the construction process, have hitherto emphasized the idea that this was to be the coronation cathedral for the kingdom of Jerusalem. In this context, however, the importance of the two papal letters cannot be overestimated. In the first document one learns that the building was begun by Bishop Guy but that Bishop Baldwin was then supervising the work, and that all benefactions should be given to the bishop in person or to his trustees. Only one explanation is given for needing a new cathedral in Famagusta: the increased population. The second document, from 1318, elaborates on this and reiterates the need for the new building thanks to the 'depopulation of Acre and total loss of Jerusalem', thus rendering the cathedral too 'narrow' for all the inhabitants 'from very different nations' who live in Famagusta. The offer of indulgence was extended to everyone who should give 'a hand' for the cathedral, although whether this phrase was intended to be understood metaphorically or literally remains open to conjecture. However enticing it may be to believe otherwise, we must observe that not one of the sources even so much as hints that the new church was to serve as the place of coronation for the king of Jerusalem; indeed there is no mention of the king at all, and no direct proof that the Lusignans were involved in its building. We should therefore treat the idea that the cathedral was planned from the outset as the dynasty's coronation church with circumspection: it might simply be that,

---

13 M. Balard, 'Famagouste au début du XIVe siècle', in J. Heers (ed.), *Fortifications, portes de villes, places publiques, dans le monde méditerranéen* (Paris, 1985), 283.

14 R.C. Severis and L. Bonato (eds), *Along the most beautiful path in the world. Edmond Duthoit and Cyprus* (Nicosia, 1999), 57.

15 Enlart, *Gothic Art*, pp. 222–3.

16 Florio Bustron, p. 172; *Chronique d'Amadi*, p. 291; S. Béraud, *La culture française dans l'éspace chypriote* (Nicosia, 1990), 51.

17 M. de Vogüé, *Les Églises de la Terre Sainte* (Paris, 1860), 378.

18 Edbury, 'Famagusta', p. 342.

19 In nomine Domini, amen. Ego Isabella de Antiochia, uxor quondam Salvi de Antiochia [...]. In primis si me mori contingerit, lego corpus meum sepelliri apud ecclesiam Sancti Nicolai Famaguste. Item lego pro processione albos bissantios viginti quinque. Item laborerio dicte ecclesie Sancti Nicolai bissantios quinque. Item magistero capellano dicte ecclesie bissantio quinque. Item clerico ipsius bissantios undecim. Item pro missis capendis pro anima mea bissantios sex. Lamberto di Sambuceto, 'Actes', p. 108.

with the rapid growth of Famagusta after the fall of Acre, there was a need for a bigger church.

The dedication of the cathedral also casts doubt on the idea of royal sponsorship. Many coronation churches in Europe such as Notre Dame in Reims were dedicated to the Virgin Mary,[20] and the Frankish settlers in Cyprus could well have followed their lead. Is the identification as St Nicholas therefore mistaken? Contemporary writers suggest otherwise, particularly the report that in 1362 an icon of St Nicholas was brought from Myra to Famagusta,[21] and Conrad Grünemberg, who provides information about reliquaries in 1486.[22] The dedication to St Nicholas, we may conclude, is correct: what is missing is a high-ranking *patrocinium* for a coronation church for the kings of Jerusalem.

Instead of the Lusignans, it was the bishop of Famagusta, as the most influential person in the city, who, as the sources indicate, took the lead in the construction process. The great sums available prove that there was no lack of money: thus Bishop Guy, who began the work, donated 70,000 bezants for its construction[23] – at that time a truly immense sum.[24] Several bishops of Famagusta were royal counsellors and members of the mendicant orders. The Dominicans and Franciscans both had houses in Famagusta before the close of the thirteenth century, and it is possible that these organizations acted as the conduits for the transfer of architectural styles from central Europe. Though nothing is known about the role of the chapter in Famagusta, we may usefully observe that there were a lot of other clerics who had fled to Famagusta when the Mamluks conquered the remaining crusader strongholds in Syria. In 1295 the Pope proclaimed the amalgamation of the dioceses of Famagusta and Tortosa;[25] the presence of refugee canons of Tortosa in Famagusta and the fact that Guy was bishop of Famagusta and Tortosa could have provided a further impulse for rebuilding the cathedral in the years that followed.[26] Above all, it was the citizens who were to benefit from the new cathedral, which served not only as the seat of the bishop but also as the parish church for the city.[27] In short, there could in theory have been three groups involved in the construction: the royal court, the bishop and chapter, and the citizens or merchants of the city, who donated money. Evidence is

---

20 H. Sedlmayr, *Die gotische Kathedrale Frankreichs als europäische Königskirche* (Vienna, 1950), 408.

21 Leontios Makhairas, 1: 113.

22 *Excerpta Cypria Nova: Voyageurs occidentaux á Chypre au XVème siècle*, ed. G. Grivaud (Nicosia, 1990), 1: 124–7.

23 *Chronique d'Amadi*, p. 291; Florio Bustron, p. 172.

24 H.E. Mayer, *Geschichte der Kreuzzüge* (Stuttgart, 1995), 151, 213.

25 Edbury, *The Kingdom of Cyprus*, p. 109.

26 N. Coureas, *The Latin Church in Cyprus. 1195–1312* (Aldershot, 1997), 67. W.H. Rudt de Collenberg, 'Etat et origine du haut clergé de Chypre avant le Grand Schisme d'après les Registres des Papes du XIIIe et du XIVe siècle', *Mélanges de l'École française de Rome*, 91 (1979): 197–332.

27 Mayer, *Geschichte der Kreuzzüge*, p. 212.

lacking for the involvement of the first of these groups, and that would point to the conclusion that this was not a royal cathedral, but one financed and commissioned by the bishop, possibly in conjunction with the chapter and the diocese, and supported by the local inhabitants. It would be better, therefore, to consider the rebuilding of Famagusta cathedral as a project sponsored by the ecclesiastical authorities in the context, paralleled in many major cities in Europe, of far-reaching urban transformation.[28]

Many scholars, most recently Plagnieux and Soulard writing in 2006, have claimed that St Nicholas was already finished by 1324 when it was used for the coronation of Hugh IV.[29] I have not been able to find any proof for this thesis, as St Nicholas is not mentioned in the sources. It is well known that there was a coronation in Famagusta in 1324,[30] but either another church was used, or the ceremony took place in a construction site, using the already finished eastern parts. The first instance of a coronation of a king of Jerusalem when we are explicitly told that it took place in St Nicholas was Peter I's in 1360,[31] followed by another ceremony in 1372 for Peter II.[32]

In the light of the information for the time needed to construct the first six vaults, the date of 1324 for the completion of the building is too early. It seems more likely that the work was spread over at least five decades, before the plague of 1348.[33]

Technique, Architect and Masons

We can read the cathedral like a written source. The masons evidently adopted a European style, and this is to be explained by fashion, image and style transfer. But the fact that they also used the same techniques is more than surprising, as the demands of the patron concerning design and the abilities of the workshop could have been out of tune – although, as it happens, they were not.[34]

When we compare the roughly-built, later parts in the upper storey with the main parts of the cathedral, we get a feeling for the different ways of constructing a building. Generally in Famagusta, the styles, the abilities of the masons and the design concepts are commensurate. The masons cut the standardized ashlars of limestone with exact accuracy on every side. These

28 Balard, 'Famagouste', pp. 279–300.

29 Plagnieux and Soulard, 'La cathédrale Saint-Nicolas', pp. 223, 237. Cuneo supposed that the cathedral was already finished in 1315. P. Cuneo: 'Famagosta', in *Enciclopedia dell'arte medievale* (12 vols, Rome, 1991–2002), 6: 78–83.

30 *Chronique d'Amadi*, pp. 402–3; Edbury, *The Kingdom of Cyprus*, p. 141.

31 Leontios Makhairas, 1: 93; Strambaldi, *Chronique*, pp. 36–40.

32 *Chronique d'Amadi*, p. 432; Leontios Makhairas, 1: 309.

33 Edbury, *The Kingdom of Cyprus*, pp. 15, 153.

34 R. Ousterhout, 'The French Connection? Construction of Vaults and Cultural Identity in Crusader Architecture', in D.H. Weiss and L.J. Mahoney (eds), *France and the Holy Land. Frankish Culture at the End of the Crusades* (Baltimore, 2004), 77–94.

stones were laid on each other with a thin layer of mortar of standardized thickness, and no use was made of *spolia* or other previously used stones. An important criterion is the positioning of the stones.[35] An analysis can reveal much about the organization of the workshop. The further we move into the period of high Gothic, the more the architects responsible organized the work rationale and devised a serial production of stones whose forms could be used more than once. It can be argued that only a well-organized production-line made the Famagusta buildings possible, and that, in the case of St Nicholas, for the carved masonry used in shafts or pinnacles, the masons used patterns.

There is a scholarly consensus that over the centuries of Gothic construction the method of cutting and positioning stones changed. By analysing the horizontal and vertical joins a building can be dated, although in the case of St Nicholas more research is necessary because in the interior all the masonry has been painted. But from an examination of the rhythmical masonry courses on the exterior, it can be established that in the cathedral workshop the masons' technical skills were really up to date, and that they employed an efficient division of labour. This modern manner of production shows that it would have been necessary for an architect to have designed the cathedral. In turning to the question of the plans, we come to a *crux* of art historical research. Did the building techniques and distinctive European style reach the Famagusta masons only in the form of drawings? Or did the architects themselves come from Europe, carrying in their heads the building plans and drawings?

Earlier generations of scholars who have studied St Nicholas questioned whether local craftsmen would have been able to construct this building. There were even several attempts to identify an architect who came to Cyprus from France. Enlart took the view that it was no coincidence that the supposed master of Saint-Urbain in Troyes, Jean Langlois, came to the Holy Land in 1266.[36] Louis Gillet was confident that the Saint-Urbain master came to Famagusta.[37] St Nicholas, however, does not possess any distinguishing attributes that, when set alongside any particular building in Europe, would lead one to suppose that the European master responsible for it had then come to Famagusta. Indeed, it is not even possible to identify the regional characteristics of the 'Famagusta master', which might indicate that the architect had come from, say, the area of Champagne or Paris. I would go so far as to say that it is impossible to define the personality of the master, only his abilities.

---

35 D. Kimpel, 'Le développement de la taille en série dans l'architecture médiévale et son rôle dans l'histoire économique', *Bulletin monumental*, 135 (1977): 195–222; *idem*, 'Die Entfaltung der gotischen Baubetriebe, ihre sozio-ökonomischen Grundlange und ihre ästhetisch-künstlerischen Auswirkungen', in F. Möbius and E. Schubert (eds), *Architektur des Mittelalters* (Weimar, 1983), 246–72.

36 C. Enlart, *Villes mortes du Moyen Age* (Paris, 1920), 137.

37 L. Gillet, 'Les architectes des cathédrales', in J. Cosse (ed.), *Initiation à l'art des cathédrales* (Paris, 1999), 49.

The construction methods employed at St Nicholas point definitely to a European tradition – but, in its distinctive appearance, this is not a western European church. That is why it is wrong to attribute a 'national' French identity to the architect, as was presumed by Enlart and, more recently, by de Vaivre.[38] Whether this architectural tradition came to the workshop through travelling European craftsmen born 2,000 kilometres away or through plans and advice in writing for use by Frankish or even Cypriot masons, is not a key issue. It may even be impossible to make that distinction. What we can be certain of is that the cathedral represents an example of the transfer of architectural skills to Cyprus, which resulted in a building with a regional identity in Famagusta all of its own.

Chronology

At first sight the cathedral appears to be stylistically homogeneous, but there are small irregularities that make it possible to identify different phases and thereby create a relative chronology for the building where data for an absolute chronology is lacking. Until recently it was generally believed that the construction started at the east end with the apses and extended as far as the bay that bears the inscription. After the interruption mentioned already, the other bays followed. In 2006 Plagnieux and Soulard put forward a new thesis, which claimed that the cathedral was begun at the eastern and western ends simultaneously with the apses, the first three western bays and the lower parts of the nave; there then followed after an interruption by the upper parts of the nave.[39] They explained this new idea by drawing attention to the apparently more rudimentary masonry and design of the upper parts, while the first bays in the west and east do not differ. However, these irregularities are to be explained by the destruction of the upper parts and their subsequent restoration under Ottoman rule.[40]

I disagree with Plagnieux and Soulard's revised chronology and reiterate that the building shows clear evidence of different phases of construction, moving chronologically from the apse to the west façade:

1. In the interior the masons employed two different types of profile for the bases of the shafts: type A1 in the three apses, which differ from those in the nave (type A2). Type A2 seems to be slightly more irregular as if the serial production in the workshop was not that well established at this point.

---

38 Enlart, *Gothic Art*, pp. 508–9; J.-B. de Vaivre, 'Chronique archéologique de Chypre', *Bulletin monumental*, 158 (2000): 349–56.

39 Plagnieux and Soulard, 'La cathédrale Saint-Nicolas', pp. 227–36.

40 N. Coldstream, 'Famagusta', in *The Dictionary of Art*, ed. J. Turner (34 vols, London, 1996), 10: 774; A.J. Boas, *Crusader Archaeology* (London, 1999), pp. 134–5.

2. The bases of the exterior walls are also different. Type B1, employed in the area of the three apses, presents a profile that differs from that of the bases in use everywhere else. The first buttress close to the apse is built using type B1, while the architect used the other type, B2, for the nave. Here, it is clear, are two bays dating from before the interruption mentioned in the 1311 inscription.
3. The pinnacles of the buttresses are decorated with blind tracery. Here again we find two different types. Type C1 is in use in the lower parts of the apses, and so is commensurate with the information from the inscription. The nave and the area below the towers are totally homogeneous (type C2). Because of this homogeneity I do not believe the building was begun from east and west simultaneously, for otherwise we would expect to find another appearance of the pinnacles as in the apse. Instead, what we see is evidence indicating that the building was begun at the east end and then proceeded step by step to the west façade.
4. The archivolts of the southern and western portals differ in their design, an indication that the western portals postdate the nave.
5. The archivolt of the window of the first western bay differs from all other window archivolts. The one below the towers was constructed later, when the patterns of the archivolts were changed.
6. Much of our understanding of dating clearly relies on stylistic differences in the tracery, where we can see a clear, linear development as we move from east to west. The designs at the western extremity are the most recent; those in the apse, the oldest.
7. It can be deduced from these findings, that there were four distinct phases of construction: The lower part of the three apses is the oldest component in the cathedral, as can be seen in the profile of the shaft bases and the bases of the exterior wall. Then (phase 2) there was a change of design after the first buttress, as the architect began work on the nave. The construction continued as described in the inscription: before September 1311 the side apses and the first two bays of the side aisles were vaulted, while the nave was not yet complete, although perhaps begun in the lower parts. Then (phase 3) the nave was vaulted, and finally (phase 4) the tower bay and the west façade were completed. The side chapels were later additions and not part of the original architectural concept.

Sources of Architectural Language

If one were to go by the stylistic origins as identified in the art historical literature, one would gain the impression that St Nicholas was 'beamed up' from Western Europe to the island of Cyprus. Older writers have suggested a variety of sources. The French *style rayonnant* is often mentioned, and there have been attempts to identify Saint-Urbain in Troyes as the model for the elevation and ground plan, as well as the French coronation church at Reims for its west façade. This approach would tend to reinforce the notion that St Nicholas was intended a coronation church from the very beginning.[41] From the point of view of both art-historical study and historical influences, the stylistic sources for the cathedral are interesting, but the art-historical facts should not be obscured by historical preconceptions. The hypothesis that the style of the cathedral is a part of French architecture has had a long tradition and has not changed dramatically in the current academic mainstream. For the most part we read about an essentially French cathedral, built in Cyprus by French masons, and this necessitates a closer look at the historiography.

From the start, in the writings of Louis de Mas Latrie in 1847[42] and Melchior de Vogüé in 1860,[43] Cyprus has been regarded as an art-historical province of France. As already mentioned, Enlart was most influential by stressing that Cypriot Gothic 'is French colonial art. ... these styles came to the island direct from their original source at the moment when they reached their highest perfection ...'.[44] As a region he identifies the Champagne and stresses a *rayonnant*-influence under the patronage of King Louis IX of France. Nineteenth-century English research did not contribute much, except the magnificent drawings by Vacher and I'Anson for the Royal Institute of Architects.[45]

The next 80 years saw no significant advances in scholarship relating to the church, only much repetition. That may explain why Georg Dehio's hypothesis of 1901, that tracery and the buttresses were rooted in Cologne and Oppenheim,[46] found no echo in art-historical research until 1987, when Nicola Coldstream identified a strong influence from Strasbourg, Cologne and Freiburg-im-Breisgau. She concluded that 'in all major aspects Famagusta owes its appearance to the Rhineland' and that parts of Famagusta cathedral were a 'faithful provincial version of such Rhineland buildings'.[47] Nevertheless,

---

[41] For example, Enlart, *Gothic Art*, pp. 50–51, 221, 224, 509; de Vaivre, 'Chronique archéologique', p. 353; J.-B. de Vaivre, 'Sculpteurs parisiens en Chypre autour de 1300', in M. Balard, B.Z. Kedar and J. Riley-Smith (eds), *Dei gesta per Francos: études sur les croisades dédiées à Jean Richard* (Aldershot, 2001), 373–88; Béraud, *La culture francaise*, pp. 50–52; L. Bonato and M. Emery, 'L'architecture rayonnante à Chypre: La cathédrale Saint-Nicolas de Famagouste', *Cahier du Centre d'Études Chypriotes*, 29 (1999): 97–106; L. Bonato and M. Emery, 'Chypre au moyen-âge – Les cathédrales: L'influence française', *Mediaevalia*, 24 (2003): 245–78; J.M. Andrews, 'Santa Sophia in Nicosia: the Sculpture of the Western Portals and its Reception', *Comitatus*, 30 (1999): 63–80.

[42] L. de Mas Latrie, 'Monuments français de l'île de Chypre', *Le Magasin pittoresque*, 15 (1847): 145–7, 219–24.

[43] De Vogüé, *Les Églises*, pp. 378–9.

[44] Enlart, *Gothic Art*, p. 509.

[45] E. I'Anson and S. Vacher, 'Mediaeval and other buildings in the Island of Cyprus', *Transactions of the Royal Institute of British Architects London* (1882–83): 1–20.

[46] G. Dehio and G. von Bezold, *Die kirchliche Baukunst des Abendlandes* (Stuttgart, 1887–1901), 2: 438.

[47] Coldstream introduced this new interpretation of the Gothic architecture in

Jean-Bernard de Vaivre has cast doubt on the Rhenish influences and favours Enlart's Champagne thesis.[48] In 1999 Bonato and Emery also came out in support of this connection, when they wrote 'ce monument unique est devenu un des exemples les plus purs de l'architecture rayonnante française hors de frontières'.[49]

We need to clarify what is being debated here. In art-historical terminology *rayonnant* is a well-defined style, used especially in chapels and churches closely connected to the court in Paris and which peaked under Louis IX in the third quarter of the thirteenth century. As a result we see an exquisite architecture that is very slender and fragile, dominated in the interior by windows and shafts, of which the Sainte-Chapelle in Paris is the most famous example. For a *rayonnant* building, Famagusta is evidently 50 years too late and exhibits tracery of a later era. The roots of St Nicholas may very well lie in the *rayonnant* style, but Famagusta does not exemplify it. We shall therefore broaden the search for comparators and try to identify parallels in central Europe and in Cyprus as well as in Latin Syria. In so doing, it is possible to identify the major stylistic sources for each architectural element, and observe how they converged into the eclecticism which characterizes Famagusta cathedral.

Ground Plan

The ground plan takes the form of a basilica, characteristics of which can also be found in cathedrals in France and the Rhineland. The nave is divided into seven bays, and the width of the central nave and the side aisles is in the ratio of 2:1, an arrangement that was quite common in the thirteenth century. What is surprising in a cathedral church is that are no transepts, no radiating chapels and no ambulatory in the central apse. Even the cathedral in Nicosia has these features, while Famagusta shows a staggered choir with a polygonal main apse. That is presumably why scholars found Saint-Urbain so interesting as a source of comparison. However, other contemporaneous churches, including the cathedrals at Vienna and Ratisbon which share similar apse plans, inexplicably get overlooked in preference for Troyes. One has to ask critically why a Gothic architect should make a connection with Troyes; there is no iconological reason for this, and medieval architects were sensitive to the political impact of architectural quotations.

Basilicas without transepts and featuring a staggered choir are to be found elsewhere in the Latin East. Nearly all the cathedrals built by the crusaders – for example at Caesarea, Beirut, and Lydda – and probably also the earlier

her prefatory essay, 'Camille Enlart and the Gothic architecture of Cyprus', in Camille Enlart, *Gothic Art and the Renaissance in Cyprus*, trans. and ed. D. Hunt (London, 1987), 1–10; Coldstream, 'Famagusta', p. 774.

48 De Vaivre, 'Chronique archéologique', p. 353.

49 Bonato and Emery, 'L'architecture rayonnante a Chypre', p. 105.

cathedral at Famagusta had this ground plan. There is no need to search for examples far off in Europe when the Latin East can provide an architectural tradition.

West Façade

Ever since the basilicas in Caen, Saint-Denis or Senlis were conceived, it was normal for the west façade to be characterized by two towers, and this tradition continued in the more recent examples at Chartres, Laon, Paris and Amiens. Why then must we jump to the conclusion that the workshop in Famagusta originated in Reims? Simply because it was a coronation church? The façade with its three portals and baldachins, the tracery in the *tympana*, the rose window and towers was widespread throughout Europe. While the parallels to Reims are very close, it remains true that there are many other cathedrals in Europe with these same architectural features, and therefore there is no specific reason for seeing Famagusta as a copy of Reims. While it is possible that the architect might have 'quoted' Reims due to Famagusta's regal function, that is not necessarily so; in the absence of royal patronage, such a 'quotation' seems even less possible.

Exterior

Next to the decorated west façade there are different features of the *exterior* of St Nicholas which mark a 'change of style'[50] in Cypriot architecture: the beautiful arrangement of the buttresses, decorated by pinnacles and blind tracery; the flying buttresses formed by tracery with leaf decoration that link the buttresses to the wall; the large windows with their tracery; the big gables, and the idea of connecting all parts of the building visually by the use of blind tracery, following an innovation of the second half of the thirteenth century. Gables in this high Gothic form *par excellence* had been in use from *ca* 1240: the Sainte-Chapelle in Paris is a point of reference for this style, followed by Saint-Germer-de-Fly, Tournais, Cologne and Ratisbon. But it is hard to find a building from the same period that resembles St Nicholas in all its different aspects in the structure of the exterior walls: only the destroyed church of Saint-Louis in Poissy comes to mind.[51] But more important than the identification of a specific source for the design is, as I have emphasized already, the context of the cathedral within contemporary European architecture.

---

[50] N. Coldstream, 'Gothic Architecture in the Lusignan Kingdom', in *Byzantine Medieval Cyprus*, ed. D. Papanikola-Bakirtzis and M. Iacovou (Nicosia, 1998), 55.

[51] A. Erlande-Brandenburg, 'La Priorale Saint-Louis de Poissy', *Bulletin Monumental*, 129 (1971): 85–112.

Interior

The interior of the cathedral is the other side of the coin, being neither particularly advanced nor modern. Normally at this time we find an elevation comprising three elements: the arcading, the triforium and the clerestory. In Famagusta there is no triforium, and, although this absence can also be seen elsewhere in Europe, the probable explanation is simply that there was no roof to hide. By comparison with the architecture of central Europe, St Nicholas is not that delicate or elegant, with more wall and fewer windows. Normally the wall is framed by vertically linked shafts, which lead upwards to the vaults where they are continued by ribs, directing the gaze to the apex. Neither the profiles of the shafts, nor those of the ribs in the vaulting, are comparable with contemporary buildings in Europe. Instead, in Famagusta, the shafts only rise from the plinths of the columns and are massive, with no division between the principal and secondary shafts. They seem to be very conservative, resembling those of the second half of the twelfth century. There are examples of monastic churches from around 1300 with these features, such as those at Altenberg or Essen. Columns of this type, dating to the same era, have also been identified in southern France, in Carcassonne and Rodez, in the Netherlands at s'Hertogenbosch, and in churches in other regions well away from central France with a special connection to the monastic orders. I would argue for a regional Cypriot note for the interior where fashionable elements are missing, but where either the traditional appearance of older churches in the crusader countries or of a monastic church design is emphasized. Apparently in Cyprus these motifs seem to have been traditional in interior design with a currency that lasted for about 200 years.

Tracery

A crucial, and informative, element in any stylistic analysis is the tracery, which can be used as a fingerprint for the time, offering clues as to when the building was planned and constructed. In St Nicholas it can confidently be attributed to the late thirteenth century. A clear, linear development of tracery, from Chartres to Reims and Amiens and later the Rhineland, has been identified. Where on this time line can Famagusta be located? Various suggestions have been offered. Enlart[52] – and also a fourteenth-century pilgrim[53] – looked to Amiens. Coldstream, like Dehio before her, identified different types from the Rhineland, while others subscribed to the typical *rayonnant*-form. In characteristic British fashion, Boase thought he saw the so-called 'geometrical' tracery.[54] In my opinion the generic identification

---

52 Enlart, *Gothic Art*, p. 233.

53 T.A.H. Mogabgab, *Supplementary excerpts on Cyprus* (Nicosia, 1941), 58.

54 T.S.R. Boase, 'The Arts in Cyprus, Ecclesiastical Art', in K.M. Setton (ed.),

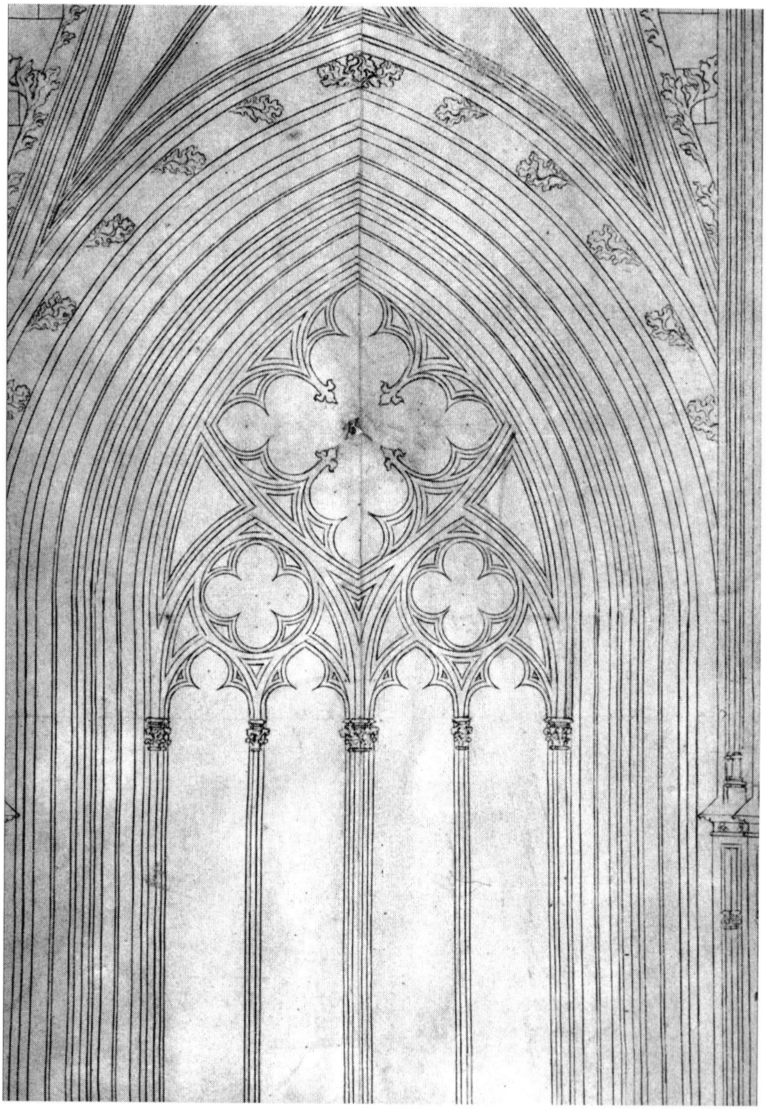

Fig. 5.1 Design drawing of window tracery for the west-façade of Cologne Cathedral, detail of '*Riss* F' (reproduced in Steinmann, M., *Die Westfassade des Kölner Domes* (Cologne, [2003]), © Dombauarchiv Köln, M. Steinmann)

with Amiens and the Rhineland is correct, but we can also see developments within the tracery – and these forms can be categorized as falling into three groups.

The least complex forms are those the windows of the side apse. Here the trefoil, a form in use from the first half of the thirteenth century, appears in combination with an ogee arch, originating between 1260 and 1300, to create a so-called 'protoflamboyante' form. The second group of forms comprise all the windows in the lower and upper storeys of the nave, and they might have been designed by the architect in a single unit. The forms of

A History of the Crusades (6 vols, Madison, 1955–89), 4: 173.

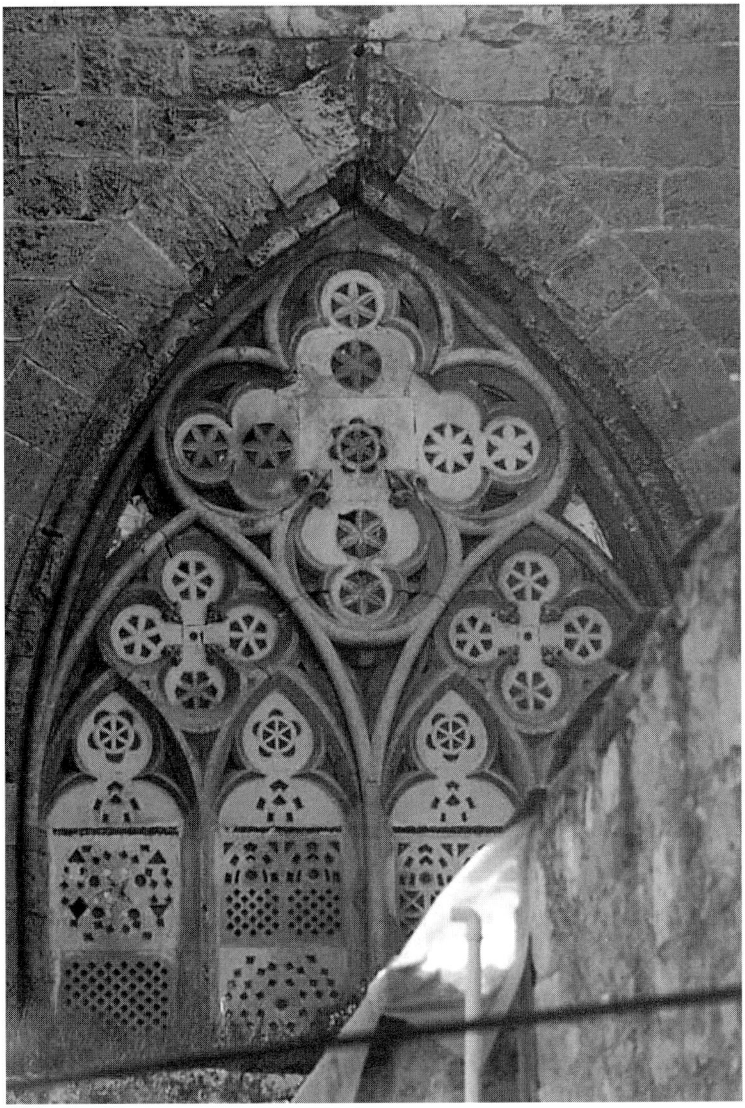

Fig. 5.2
Window tracery of St Nicholas, nave, upper storey, north (photograph: Arne Franke)

the *couronnement* are remarkably similar to those of Amiens, especially with the employment and appearance of the multicusped *oculus*. Presumably created as one of the latest forms of Amiens Cathedral in the period 1258 to *ca* 1269[55] we have an undeniable stylistic link; but there the correspondence with Amiens ends.

The third category deflects our attention to the slightly later traceries at Cologne cathedral, the multiple use of which can be seen in Famagusta. The windows from the clerestory in Cologne were built between 1270 and

[55] S. Murray, *Notre-Dame, Cathedral of Amiens. The Power of Change in Gothic* (Cambridge, 1996), 72–4.

1285,[56] absorbing Amiens' patterns, but creating new forms that were in use in Famagusta as well. A comparison between the Famagusta tracery and the drawings made in the workshop at Cologne Cathedral provides the most impressive explanation. The new tracery forms from Cologne were copied by masons throughout Europe and could certainly have made their way to Famagusta too.

In my opinion the famous so-called '*Riss* F' seems to represent a compendium for the architect of Famagusta (Figure 5.1). The '*Riss* F' was created *ca* 1280 in Cologne for use in designing the cathedral and can be regarded as one of the most complex tracery drawings of the time.[57] There are many parallels with the various windows and blind traceries at Famagusta. That in itself does not mean that the Famagusta masons necessarily possessed a copy of the '*Riss* F', but they do point to a close connection with the Rhineland and especially the workshop of Cologne. As the '*Riss* F' was drawn *ca* 1280 and the first windows in Famagusta were completed after 1300, we can see how close the contacts between the workshop at Famagusta and the cathedral workshops of central Europe and especially Cologne would have been (Figure 5.2). The source, we would argue, is thus Cologne, and only its more distant origins lay in Amiens. Oppenheim would appear as an example of a parallel phenomenon.[58] As the dating of '*Riss* F' and the upper storeys of Cologne is not known precisely, it could have taken any time from a few months to 20 years for these designs to have been brought to Famagusta.

It has been necessary to postulate this third group as representing a later stage to account for the tracery in the towers and the west façade. The important difference is that here we find spherical polygons, often used as frames for smaller traceries. This constitutes a later development and can be seen only in the most westerly bay. Taken together with the different frames for the windows, they serve as proof for a conceptual change at the workshop. Whether a different architect was responsible; whether the construction was interrupted, and this represents a later completion; or whether it was just a reception of more modern forms, is difficult so say.

To conclude this part: It now becomes clear why the three different categories of tracery cannot be identified as being in the *rayonnant* style or as coming entirely from the Rhineland. The tracery of the side apse is the earliest form. The largest section shows a strong link with Cologne and, in particular, the '*Riss* F'. Definitely later are the spherical forms in the west façade and last bay. All the styles originate from 1280 or earlier. Furthermore they provide additional evidence that the construction of the cathedral began with the apses and progressed to the west façade.

Taken together these architectural motifs would, in Europe, date to the beginning of the last quarter of the thirteenth century. That is why the

56 M. Lüpnitz, 'Der mittelalterliche Ringanker in den Chorobergadenfenstern des Kölner Domes', *Kölner Domblatt*, 62 (1997): 65–84.

57 M. Steinmann, *Die Westfassade des Kölner Domes* (Cologne, 2003), 254.

58 B. Schütz, *Die Katharinenkirche in Oppenheim* (Berlin and New York, 1982), 141–3.

cathedral, begun in 1300/1301, was somewhat behind the times; even so, considering the geographical isolation from its stylistic and theoretical origins, the architecture was still remarkably fashionable.

Conclusion

The new cathedral in Famagusta was part of the urban transformation that took place after the fall of Acre and reflects the immense increase of its population and wealth. In my opinion it was not initially intended as a place of coronation and so under royal patronage of the Lusignans, but was financed by the bishop, probably by the clergy, and by donors who lived in the city.

We shall not try to search for a simple explanation for the choice of style. It was not a French building on Cypriot soil, as would have been built in the West. The architecture incorporated different elements from different places, and their combination would have been unthinkable for a high-status cathedral in France or, indeed, anywhere else in Europe. St Nicholas has no direct antecedents in Europe.

The ground plan has its origins in crusader architecture. The exterior and interior design, however, give the impression that they were derived from two quite different buildings: a conservative interior influenced by older buildings in the crusader region or by monastic architecture, and a fashionable exterior, that stands comparison with contemporary buildings in Europe. The tracery imitates not the French *style rayonnant* but is influenced by Cologne cathedral. In Famagusta they could have used tracery drawings and plans by architects who had been in contact with the workshop in Cologne and the famous '*Riss* F'. That seems likely because we know of many drawings which in medieval times were taken from one construction site to another. The architecture may very well be rooted in France and the European Gothic tradition, but, taken as a whole, St Nicholas is a Cypriot building.

My hypothesis for a chronology of the construction process in the light of the documentary sources and an examination of the building itself and its stylistic variations goes as follows:

1. First phase: the construction of the lower parts of all three apses under Bishop Guy (after 1300 or 1301).
2. Second phase: the vaulting of the side apses and the two most eastern bays of the side aisles (before 1306 or 1308); there then followed an interruption due to political conflicts.
3. Third phase: the completion of the nave after 1 September 1311 under Bishop Baldwin.
4. The last phase: the construction of the most westerly bay, with the west façade and the towers continuing into the middle of the fourteenth century.

Notes on the Marginal Sculpture of the Cathedral of St Nicholas

Allan Langdale

> After that we first went out to find the church and came into the Cathedral of Saint Nicholas, a church as incredibly magnificent as any could be. For it is like a monstrance, decorated throughout with gold leaf and finials and sculptures of stone, not lacking in any possible splendor or ornamentation. And there are also two bell towers there, rendered through and through with such artistic construction as is mentioned above. Each of these towers has an octagonal spiral, which one ascends up to the bells, also created with great artistry. Also, that the church together with its towers and incredible treasures is to be more admired than all other art and splendor which one can admire and talk about.[1]
>
> Conrad Grunemberg, 1486

The fourteenth-century cathedral of St Nicholas in Famagusta (Plate 1) looms like a lighthouse at the edge of the sea, its towering and richly gabled corona serving solemn watch towards the shores of the Holy Land. Emphatically European, perhaps, because of its dramatic geographical isolation from the Western centres of Christianity and its ideology of crusader conquest, the church is a statement of imperium at the edge of empire. St Nicholas embodied only one of several institutional elements in the urban heart of

1 'Darnach gingen wir zuerst die Kirche aufzusuchen und kamen in das Stift Sant Nicolas, eine Kirche, so wunderprächtig, als eine nur sein kann. Denn sie ist gleich einer Monstranz ganz mit Blattwerk un Fialen und Bildern von Stein durch und durch geschmücht, keiner Pracht noch Zierde mangelnd. Und sind auch da zwei Glockentürm, ganz durchsichtig von solchem genannten Bauwerk kunstvoll aufgeführt. Dieser Türme hat jeglicher eine achteckige Schnecke, darin man aufsteigt bis zu den Glocken, auch durchsichtig und mit grosser Kunst gemacht. Also dass die Kirche mit sampt den Türmen mit der grossen Kunst mehr zu bewundern ist denn alle Kunst und Pracht, die einer noch so bewundern und erzählen mag.' It continues with a description of the tomb of King James II, 'In der Kirche liegt der letzt vergangne König Jacob neben dem Fronaltar gar in schönem Marmelstein. Man zeigte uns da die Reliquien und Kleinode der Kirche' [trans. Beverly Freeland-Clajus]. From *Excerpta Cypria Nova. Voyageurs Occidentaux a Chypre au XV Siècle*, ed. G. Grivaud (Nicosia, 1990), 1: 126.

Famagusta that conveyed Eurocentric codes of architectural expression and social organization. Surrounding the cathedral square was the palace of the Lusignan kings, the bishop's palace and the church of the Franciscans. These and other structures comprised the city's monumental civic core, to which all streets led. The architecture resonated in an urban context which was a powerful statement of Lusignan, and Latin, hegemony. Famagusta may have been a very cosmopolitan city, with Jewish, Greek, Syrian, and Latin quarters, but St Nicholas was decidedly the most monumental expression of Latin domination, eloquently marking the Latin quadrant as central and the other quarters as peripheral. Without question, it is the most important architectural monument of the city's rich and illustrious history.

This is an introductory chapter on the marginal sculpture of St Nicholas cathedral. No one has yet dealt with this aspect of the structure even though sculpture has long been seen as an important feature of Gothic cathedrals and a crucial element in their symbolism and design.[2] As a disregarded aspect of the building's heritage, we are encouraged to consider how examining the sculptures might broaden our knowledge of this important example of crusader architecture. Comparative work on the sculptures could, for example, provide new information about the origins of the masons who built the cathedral. While scholars have done this kind of work in considering the purely architectural elements of the building, the sculpture has not been utilized as a critical component of St Nicholas's history. This chapter includes an extensive section on the various interpretations of marginal sculpture, which will provide the reader with a perspective on the issues surrounding this specific classification. Some provisional hypotheses are forwarded regarding the meaning the St Nicholas sculptures may have had in the context that produced them. Part of the impetus for this study is to supply readers with a photographic record of the more significant examples of St Nicholas's figural sculpture, since a dearth of published documentation has hampered academic interaction on the subject.[3]

Preliminary observations suggest a few functions of the sculptures over and above the purely decorative. Representations of roses, lions, and dragons, for example, could be considered Lusignan symbols, motifs, or heraldic elements. Other sculptures may have had apotropaic functions, such as the winged angels found in the upper reaches of the south tower. We also find several images of hunting animals killing their prey, the significance of which we can only guess. They may act as metaphors for the military power of the dynasty or perhaps a more generalized notion such as good triumphing over evil. Certainly, at the very least, they were dynamic displays of the sculptors'

2 One exception is J.-B. de Vaivre, who has considered some figural fragments in Famagusta and their possible relation to St Nicholas in his 'Sculpteurs parisiens en Chypre autour de 1300', in M. Balard, B.Z. Kedar, J. Riley-Smith (eds), *Dei gesta per Francos. Crusade Studies in Honour of Jean Richard* (Aldershot, 2001), 373–88.

3 I would like to thank my friend Wilbert 'Skip' Norman who assisted me in my efforts to document these sculptures.

skills and provocative decorations – perhaps inspired by textile designs – that animated and accented architectural nodes of form and function (corbels, water drains, etc). There are also ancillary figures, some identifiable and others not, where meanings are difficult to determine. Taken as a whole, the sculptures do not seem to be organized into any sophisticated iconographic programme.

Much of St Nicholas's sculpture was severely damaged when the Ottomans converted the cathedral into a mosque after their conquest of Famagusta in 1571.[4] As part of the purification of the building almost all of the sculptures were beheaded in a flurry of iconoclasm. Those that survive have lost attributes which would have helped determine their subjects. Seven centuries of erosion have also taken their toll.[5] This is especially true for the works on the towers which have been exposed to rain, wind, and the sea air. Some of these figures appear as if they are melting away, such as a statue from the north face of the south tower. Even so, we can still make out the beak of an eagle-like bird with feathered wings and talons which grasp a small four-legged animal (Figure 6.1).[6]

The sculptures of St Nicholas cathedral have never been systematically documented or discussed by art historians. The otherwise thorough Camille Enlart largely ignored them, although he did pay some attention to the sculptures on other ecclesiastical monuments in Famagusta such as St George of the Latins.[7] Other early visitors who studied the city's historical edifices, such as Edward I'Anson and Sydney Vacher, were similarly blind to the myriad figures which populated the structure. They too focused exclusively on architectural features, as do more recent studies. Nonetheless, such studies

---

4 St Nicholas is known locally as the Lala Mustafa Pasha Cami, after the Ottoman general who conquered Famagusta in 1571.

5 Having made these observations it should be added that the Gothic cathedrals of Europe have also suffered many instances of destruction, especially during the French Revolution and numerous wars. Much of what can be seen on French buildings today are reconstructions, original medieval fragments often having been destroyed or relegated to museums. St Nicholas is exceptional in that it would appear that much of its sculpture is 'original'. However, there are caveats. We do not know, for example, whether there may have been any replacement of statuary as part of the restoration work carried out during the period of British rule on Cyprus. Greater scrutiny needs to be given to one of the most important resources for the historical architecture of the eastern part of Cyprus, the Mogabgab Archive, which is a vast photographic record of conservation projects undertaken by the Department of Antiquities from the 1930s until the early 1960s. It is not known for certain whether all the negatives in the collection have been printed. The original negatives are kept in archivally insecure conditions in the antiquities department offices in Famagusta.

6 The four gargoyles which extended from the horizontal moulding above the façade's portals have completely disappeared. Only their ragged footings remain. They may have resembled those surviving gargoyles from the church of St George of the Latins in Famagusta or those on the cathedral of the Holy Wisdom in Nicosia.

7 C. Enlart, *Gothic Art and the Renaissance in Cyprus*, trans. David Hunt (London, 1987), 258–62. First published 1899. See also C. Enlart, 'Fouilles dans les Eglises de Famagouste de Chypre', *Archaeological Journal*, 62 (1905): 195–217.

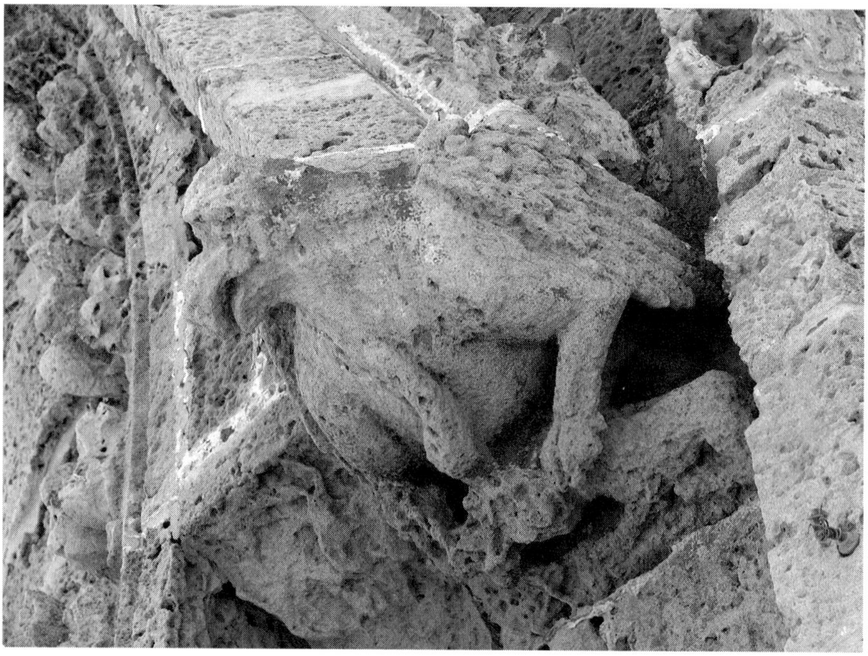

Fig. 6.1 Sculpture of winged figure on the north face of the south tower of St Nicholas (photograph: Allan Langdale)

could be useful guideposts for scholars tracing the iconographic and stylistic sources for St Nicholas's sculptures.[8]

The eliding of this aspect of the church's decoration is not surprising since the only sculpture that can be found on St Nicholas may be classified as 'marginal', depicting strange creatures and hybrid figures rather than the type of sculpture which represents characters from religious narratives and which might provisionally be called 'official' sculpture. There have been many attempts to solve the iconographic mysteries of marginal sculptures, but it was only in the late 1980s that art historians began to develop methodologies to contend with the social functions of this ubiquitous but rarely studied genre of sculpture that adorns the cathedrals, churches and even the public buildings of the Romanesque and Gothic periods.[9]

---

8 E. I'Anson and S. Vacher, 'Medieval and Other Buildings in the Island of Cyprus', *Transactions of the Royal Institute of British Architects*, 33 (1883): 33–52. See also M.J.K. Walsh, 'A Gothic Masterpiece in the Levant: St Nicholas Cathedral, Famagusta, North Cyprus', *Journal of Cultural Heritage*, 6 (2004): 1–6; N. Coldstream's introduction in Enlart, *Gothic Art and the Renaissance in Cyprus*, pp. 9–10; A. Franke's essay in this volume as well as his thesis on St Nicholas, *Die Kathedrale in Famagusta und die gotische Architektur auf Zypern*, Ludwig-Maximilians-Universität, München, 2006; P. Plagnieux and T. Soulard, 'La Cathedrale Saint Nicolas de Famagouste', in J.-B. de Vaivre and P. Plagnieux (eds), *L'Art Gothique de Chypre* (Paris, 2006), 218–37. Coldstream and Franke argue that the origins of St Nicholas's architectural style can be found in the Rhineland, though they disagree about which churches served as primary exemplars. Their hypotheses challenge Enlart's belief that St Nicholas's architectural progenitors lay in the Champagne region of France.

9 The primary works are A. Woodcock, *Liminal Images. Aspects of Medieval*

Disdain for such sculpture was recorded early with St Bernard of Clairvaux's (1090–1153) well-known denunciation of them in Romanesque monastic architecture:

> What profit is there in those ridiculous monsters, in the marvelous and deformed comeliness, that comely deformity? To what purpose are those unclean apes, those fierce lions, those monstrous centaurs, those half-men, those striped tigers, those fighting knights, those hunters? ... For God's sake, if men are not ashamed of these follies, why at least do they not shrink from the expense?

Following his lead, the few other medieval commentators who made any mention of marginal sculptures were similarly contemptuous. Eight centuries later, the great French historian of medieval art, Emil Mâle, had barely diverged from Bernard's evaluation, dismissing such sculptures as meaningless. Indeed, in his famous work *The Gothic Image,* Mâle used the quotation from St Bernard as proof of the sculptures' lack of significance, projecting his disdain into the later centuries of the Gothic period.[10] But it is not surprising that Mâle would align himself with St Bernard as his own views were profoundly scholastic and intellectual. Mâle proposed that, 'The countless statues, disposed in scholarly design, were a symbol of the marvelous order that through the genius of St Thomas Aquinas reigned in the world of thought.'[11] Marginal sculptures did not, however, fit easily into this 'marvelous order'. Yet Mâle by no means ignored these myriad strange forms. In some instances he identified what he thought were legitimate symbolic meanings gleaned from medieval bestiaries such as the *Physiologus* and works such as the *Speculum Ecclesiae.*[12] But for the more unruly instances Mâle chided those who tried to force symbolic or iconographic significance upon them. Thus, while he could happily claim that the Middle Ages saw the world as a symbol, he also believed that scholars wasted their efforts in trying to find symbolism in all cases:

> In their point of departure, however, they were right; they perceived that for the great minds of the Middle Ages the world was a symbol. But they were mistaken in their belief that a symbolic meaning was concealed in even the least important work of art.[13]

Architectural Sculpture in the South of England from the Eleventh to the Sixteenth Centuries (British Archaeological Reports 386, Oxford, 2005); N. Kenaan-Kedar, *Marginal Sculpture in Medieval France: Towards the deciphering of an enigmatic pictorial language* (Aldershot, 1995). Other studies include J.R. Benton, *Holy Terrors. Gargoyles on Medieval Buildings* (New York and London, 1997); A. Weir and J. Jerman, *Images of Lust. Sexual Carvings on Medieval Churches* (London, 1986); R. Sheridan and A. Ross, *Gargoyles and Grotesques. Paganism in the Medieval Church* (Boston and New York, 1975).

[10] E. Mâle, *The Gothic Image. Religious Art in France of the Thirteenth Century,* trans. D. Nussey (New York, 1958), 48–9. First published in 1913.

[11] Ibid., p. vii.

[12] Ibid., pp. 33–46. See also Woodcock, *Liminal Images,* pp. 25–6.

[13] Mâle, *The Gothic Image,* p. 48.

And later:

> True symbolism holds too large a place in medieval art to make it necessary to look for it where it does not exist.[14]

A shift in the scholarly consideration of the marginal has occurred only more recently, prompted by Michael Camille's books such as *The Gothic Idol* of 1989 (intentionally echoing Mâle's *The Gothic Image*) and *Images at the Edge* of 1993, which provided a theoretical framework for addressing not only marginal sculpture but also other instances of the marginal in medieval art.[15] Nevertheless, one proceeds to study such material mindful of Mâle's dispiriting warning that 'all attempts at explanation must be foredoomed to failure'.[16]

Mâle established that the significance of some enigmatic sculptures could be traced to local origins. Citing the instance of the oxen in the towers of the cathedral at Laon and their relationship with a native Laonese story, he saw that meanings could be found in depictions which otherwise, and elsewhere, would have variant, or no, meaning.[17] Thus specific context was vital to determining significance and valid meanings could be revealed through indigenous or highly localized mythologies. In recent publications Nurith Kenaan-Kedar and Alex Woodcock have refined this approach, thereby reframing the issues surrounding the marginal sculpture of the middle ages.[18]

The architectural sculptures that can be found on most Gothic cathedrals and churches can be roughly parsed into the two aforementioned general categories, official and marginal, about which more should be said.[19] Official sculpture refers to that sculpture which depicts biblical and religious narratives or personages and images of the saints, their lives, martyrdoms or miracles. Official sculpture is largely didactic, and it is the plentitude of such representations (along with similar kinds of imagery in stained glass, wall and panel paintings, as well as metal- and woodwork) that has given Gothic churches the reputation of being visual Bibles for the illiterate masses, providing encyclopedic representations of Biblical and hagiographic narratives and, further, extensive development of typologies and moral and religious themes.[20] Marginal sculpture, on the other hand, depicts strange gargoyles, fantastic mythical or hybrid creatures, themes from vernacular culture, and grotesques of various kinds. Even sculptures representing sexually lewd figures are common. While the elite sacred sculpture, the official sculpture, is characterized by its grandeur, solemnity, restraint and dignity, marginal sculpture is its converse: offensive, violent, bestial and

14 Ibid., p. 51.

15 M. Camille, *The Gothic Idol. Ideology and Image-making in Medieval Art* (Cambridge, 1989); *idem.*, *Images on the Edge. The Margins of Medieval Art* (London, 1992).

16 Mâle, *The Gothic Image*, p. 61.

17 Ibid., pp. 55–6.

18 See above, note 9.

19 These terms are also used by Kenaan-Kedar, *Marginal Sculpture in Medieval France*.

20 See, however, the informed discussion in Woodcock, *Liminal Images*, pp. 7–9.

perverse. Their fabulous figures are often contorted, gesticulating wildly, glaring, pulling orifices open and displaying genitals. It is as if the cast of the hell portion of a Last Judgement scene has escaped the confines of the tympanum and colonized the whole cathedral, allowing sin to roam about unfettered on the consecrated structure.

The binary categorization of official and marginal, though, is in many instances a misleading opposition which might direct us away from more useful and inclusive parameters. Indeed, there is a substantial amount of Gothic sculpture that straddles this opposition armature. Even themes and imagery from popular culture could be reinterpreted through theological prisms and given religious significance. A marginal type could jump over and have a quasi-official or didactic status. There was thus a substantial grey zone where the distinction between marginal and official was shifting and pliable. Among the many examples, mention can be made of the popular notion of the lion breathing life into its cubs reconfigured as a symbol of the resurrection, or the pelican as a symbol of Christ. Astrological symbols, too, were common subjects in the archivolts of portals, where they hinted at the celestial scope of the created universe. These, accompanied by the labours of the months, indicated the sacred time of heaven equated with the annual seasonal cycles experienced by humans. An argument might be made that the sculpture we often refer to as marginal was, in fact, quite central to the lives of the medieval people who viewed it. One could propose that such sculpture is not so much marginal, but, rather, has been marginalized through history by the hierarchy inherent in the classical intellectual tradition, and, later, by the similarly exclusive nature of high iconography in art history.[21] Yet in the present case, the marginal/official classification helps define categorical boundaries germane to our study, since all of St Nicholas's surviving sculpture can be counted among the former. We are obliged, in this context, to give close consideration to the leaven of the marginal at St Nicholas.

Official sculpture normally occupied the most visible locations on the church or cathedral (the portals, in particular, the liminal zones between interior and exterior). Marginal sculptures, conversely, usually populated the less visible upper portions of the structures.[22] Because of this the marginal sculptures had a different relationship with spectators. As worshippers entered the church they were embraced by the sacred figures in the tympana, archivolts, and jambs of the recessed portals. These official sculptures defined

---

21 Woodcock, *Liminal Images*, pp. xvii–xix. See also N. Kenaan-Kedar, 'Interaction of Marginal and Official Iconography: The West Facade of St Hilaire in Foussais – Its Oral, Visual and Literary Sources', in N. Kenaan-Kedar and A. Ovadiah (eds), *The Metamorphosis of Marginal Images: From Antiquity to Present Time* (Tel Aviv, 2002), 159–75.

22 Mâle also believed that this fact also supported the idea that the sculptures had no important meanings, noting that one can only see them with a good pair of binoculars, a tool obviously not available to medieval people. See also Kenaan-Kedar, *Marginal Sculpture in Medieval France*, p. 2, and Kenaan-Kedar, 'Sculpture High Up: The Forgotten Meanings of Monumental Sculpture on Churches' Roofs and Towers', in A.W. Reinick and J. Stumpel (eds), *Memory and Oblivion* (Amsterdam, 1997), 719–26.

the threshold of the sacred and were dramatic signifiers of the transition from a secular exterior to a sacral interior.[23] These sculptures confronted believers and reminded them of religious hierarchy and prepared them for the decorum and *ordo* of the mass. Marginal sculptures, on the other hand, were more likely to be seen while standing back from the cathedral, passing by it, admiring it as an object, a production of the secular world and an edifice connoting various notions that might include very worldly ones such as civic pride or the wealth of a city and the skill of its masons. St Nicholas is somewhat distinctive in that substantial marginal sculptures are found not only in the upper reaches but around the main entrances as well. The numerous dragons, leonine figures and contorted and attacking animals which surround the western portals dominate the façade with a forceful presence never overshadowed by the monumental human figures of Christ, Mary and the Saints that might otherwise have commanded devotional, alternative gazes.

Whatever official sculpture may have been planned for St Nicholas, there is no evidence that it was ever executed or put in place. The only part of the cathedral where there appears to have been architectural accommodations for official sculptures is around the central doorway (Figure 6.2).[24] These accommodations were for monumental statues of sacred figures (seven of them) about three-quarters life size and very slender in proportion, one of which was almost certainly Christ or St Nicholas in the trumeau and, perhaps, another being John the Baptist in one of the jambs as there is a well preserved boss in one of the canopies which depicts the *Agnus Dei*, a symbol associated with John (Figure 6.3).[25] As for the other five statues, we have no clues. However, we might at least make an educated guess. Since St Nicholas, like the cathedral of the Holy Wisdom in Nicosia, functioned as a coronation cathedral (in Nicosia, the Lusignan kings were crowned as kings of Cyprus, while at St Nicholas they were crowned kings of Jerusalem), some references to virtuous kings from the Old Testament – Solomon or David, for example – might have been iconographically appropriate and worked in a fashion similar to the royal imagery in the Nicosia cathedral.[26] However, more

---

23 Woodcock challenges this dichotomy of the internal and external and provides examples of highly secular activities which could take place in church interiors. Woodcock, *Liminal Images*, p. 78.

24 There is perhaps one exception. At the apex of the arch of the central portal, at the crest of the archivolts, are the much damaged remnants of an angel which once held a scroll and pointed to a text once painted on it. Enough of this figure survives for us to compare it with a much better preserved example in the same location above the portal of the Carmelite Church in Famagusta. This fragment is discussed in de Vaivre, 'Sculpteurs parisiens en Chypre autour de 1300'. See note 2.

25 But since the *Agnus Dei* was a fairly common boss or capstone decoration in Lusignan architecture – indeed, another exists in one of the other canopies – we cannot press this very strongly.

26 Arne Franke has suggested, however, that St Nicholas was not originally intended as a coronation cathedral even though it took up that function at a later date. See Franke, *Die Kathedrale in Famagusta*, pp. 22–5. For the sculpture of the cathedral of the Holy Wisdom ('Santa Sophia') in Nicosia, see J.M. Andrews, 'Santa Sophia in

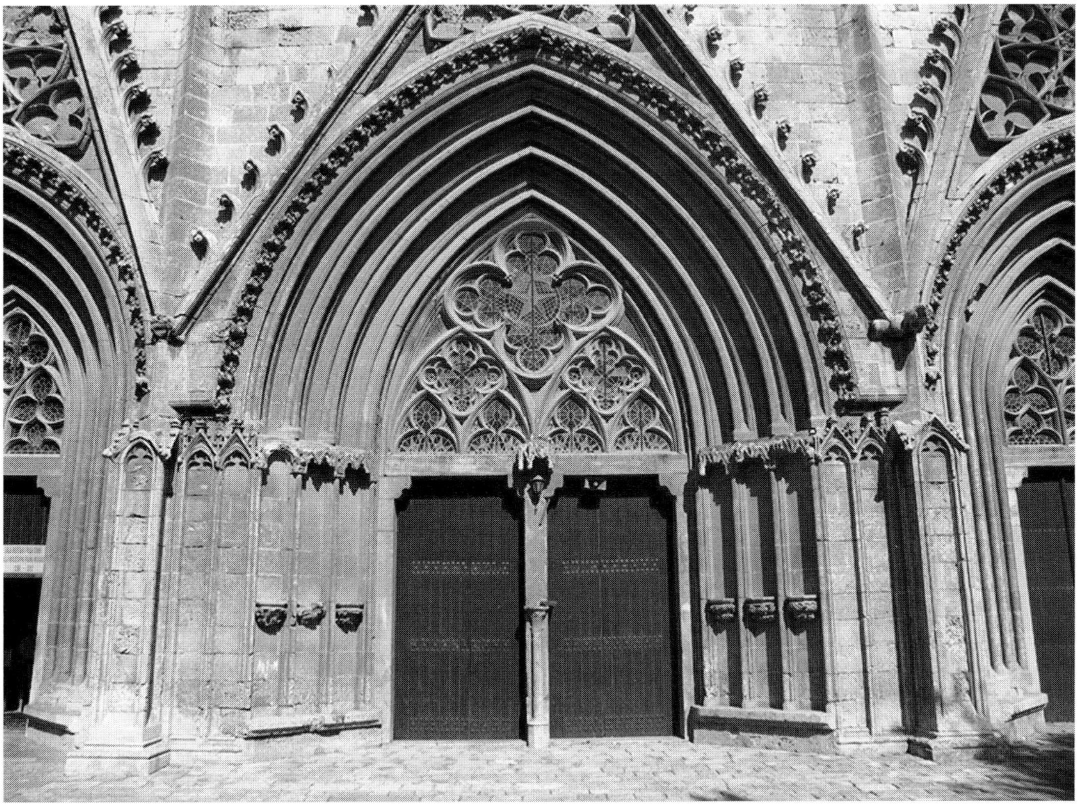

Fig. 6.2 Central portal of St Nicholas (photograph: Allan Langdale)

certainty about such intentions awaits additional confirmation, either textual or archaeological.

Only one lifesize figure from Famagusta survives, though without a head (Figure 6.4), depicting an ecclesiast wearing a chasuble. The back side of the statue is not carved, indicating that it was to be seen only frontally. We do not know what church it came from, or what kind of monument it decorated, but it gives us some idea of the high quality of the works which have been lost.[27]

The interpretive work dealing with marginal sculpture is made more challenging by the paucity of textual information around which to gather interpretations, which is why modern theories abound as to their significance. One school emphasizes the pagan heritage of many of the characters and hybrids. Griffons, for example, are seen as survivals from antiquity, representing an unbroken link to the pagan past as guardian figures. The Green Man, too, an antique visage who survived the centuries after the decline of Rome (his earliest manifestations are of a male face amongst the acanthus leaves of Corinthian-style capitals) enjoyed a long metamorphosis. He is the

Nicosia: the Sculpture of the Western Portals and its Reception', *Comitatus*, 30 (1999): 63–80.

27 This statue is discussed in de Vaivre, 'Sculpteurs parisiens en Chypre autour de 1300'. See note 2.

Fig. 6.3 Boss of the *Agnus Dei* from one of the canopies of the central portal of St Nicholas (photograph: Allan Langdale)

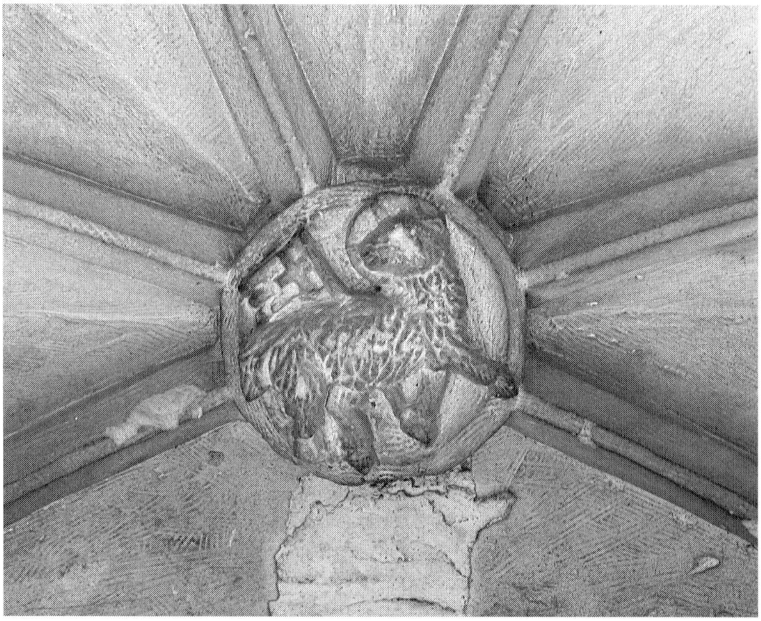

most ubiquitous of all the marginal types in Cypriot Gothic architecture, and he appears at least three times on St Nicholas. He may be a type of apotropaic figure or connote resurrection with his breath of life emanating from his mouth and nostrils.[28] Many of the scholars who think that such figures represent pagan survivals emphasize their protective nature, where they ward off evil rather than being embodiments of it. And while such a function may have accrued to some such forms in antiquity, the attribution may seem incongruent for the Middle Ages and the context of cathedrals.[29] The towers of St Nicholas are populated mostly by winged creatures, but these include angels as well as monsters. Perhaps there is some logic in having such figures in the upper reaches: it may well be that the angels, griffons and eagle-like creatures had a protective function, guarding the cathedral from evil, keeping watch over the island and eyeing the nearby coast of the Holy Land, a locus of both desire and dread for the Lusignans who still cherished their lost kingdoms but also feared the Muslim threat to their island realm.

Emil Mâle supported the idea that marginal sculptures were the masons' inventions and demonstrations of skill. He characterizes the medieval masons as creative craftsmen, too naïve to be called artists. In characterizing the work of the sculptors, he wrote:

[28] Woodcock, *Liminal Images*, pp. 54–61. Woodcock also cites the green man's numerous appearances in funerary contexts. However, while this might be the case in England it does not seem to be the case in Cypriot medieval architecture. See also K. Basford, *The Green Man* (Ipswich, 1978), and Lady Raglan, 'The Green Man in Church Architecture', *Folklore*, 50 (1939): 45–57.

[29] Woodcock, *Liminal Images*, pp. 13–14.

> But for the most part they were content to be craftsmen who delighted in nature for its own sake, sometimes lovingly copying the living forms, sometimes playing with them, combining and contorting them as they were led by their own caprice.[30]

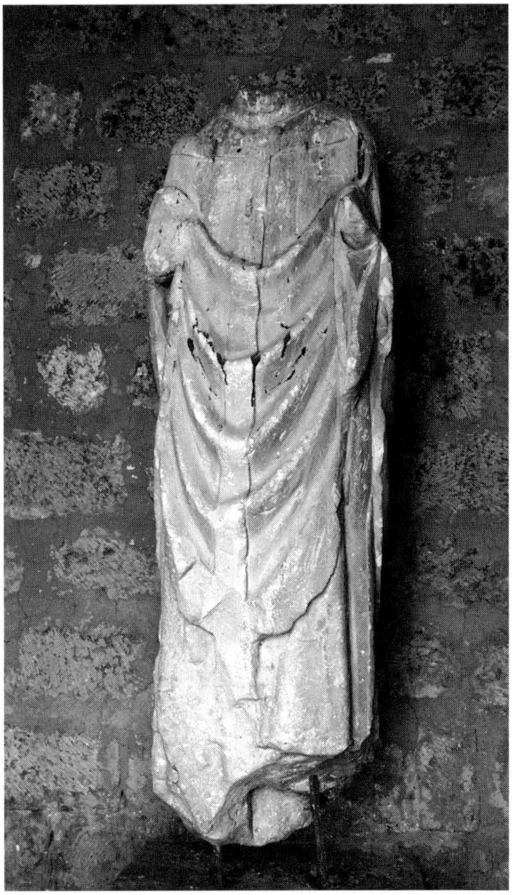

Fig. 6.4 Statue of an ecclesiast or saint, limestone, ht. 56 in. Kept in the 'Chimney Mansion' Museum, Famagusta (photograph: Michael Walsh)

But, more than their own caprice, the sculptors had not only bestiaries but model books and eastern textiles to provide a corpus of strange and hybrid creatures.[31] Yet Mâle, so focused as he was on 'high culture', used this naiveté of the sculptors to once more dismiss the sculptures as meaningless. A currently more accepted variation on this theory is that the gargoyles and monsters of marginal sculpture represent popular cultural elements which found their way onto the cathedrals as part of the vernacular repertory of the masons. In this formulation the masons' sculptures are unthreatening drolleries designed for the popular tastes and imaginations of ordinary medieval people who appreciate their playfulness, capriciousness, vulgarity and, at times, their references to fables from folk culture.

For some contemporary theorists the marginal menageries are complementary to the festivals of inversion and disorder that punctuated the medieval calendar. Examples include the Feast of the Ass (or Feast of the Fool) where the public enjoyed the inversion of the lower and higher, complete with parodies of the mass and other religious institutions.[32] The marginal sculptures are equated with the carnivalesque instances when the world was turned upside down and the divine order was turned into chaos, where the clerical and the common traded places in the chain of being. They are moments when the folkloric and the popular competed with the canonical text and the law. While the hierarchical and sacred human figural sculptures of the Biblical personages and saints offered order, edification and salvation, the grotesques offered distractions and relief from the heavy didacticism of the official sculptures. Given the rich and varied popular and folk culture of the middle-ages, there is much to recommend this position.

Kenaan-Kedar suggests that the poses and gestures of some marginal sculptures were part of a vernacular language derived from stereotyped

30 Mâle, *The Gothic Image*, p. 48.

31 Ibid., pp. 49–50.

32 Woodcock, *Liminal Images*, pp. 28–9.

characters from street theatre (jongleurs, acrobats, drunkards, prostitutes, fools) where there was a great deal of improvisation and variations on themes that were well known in specific locales.[33] Kenaan-Kedar's notion of the improvisational nature of marginal sculpture points to the myriad nuances of meanings that types could have had in specific contexts. Indeed, this is why she has undertaken analysis of a number of particularized case studies. Meanings of popular types were fluid and ever being altered in creative ways in response to local circumstances, even while their general codification had certain consistencies. Such circumstances could have had profound influences on the expression and readings of specific marginal sculptures. That the functions of some marginal sculptures may be intimately related to local or regional visual dialects might explain why we find it so challenging to deal with them today. One of the projects yet to be realized is a further fleshing out of a Lusignan, Cypriot 'dialect' to provide a lens through which to evaluate St Nicholas's sculptures. Such a visual-cultural dialect would be complex indeed, given the cosmopolitan nature of medieval Cyprus.

There is another inflection to consider. The fantastic hybrid beasts and strange human figures may also represent the evil which is a moral antithesis to the sacred figures. In this interpretation, the marginal sculptures are far from fun or playful. Working as potent opposites to the sacred images, they caution the viewer about the evil which lurks in every shadow, ready to take advantage of moral weakness. The panoply of creatures is in this sense as didactic as the Biblical scenes to which they were normally pendant. They provide a dichotomy to official sculpture and thus they represent the choice to attend to virtue or vice, or sanctity or sin. The cathedral itself, a sacred edifice bound to the earth but aspiring to heaven, becomes a liminal structure caught in the battle between the earthly and the heavenly, a great psychomachia of good versus evil. It is the type of relation frequently found in medieval art, literature and philosophy, where good opposes evil in diverse situations.

Another issue germane to our consideration of the St Nicholas's sculptures is the issue of realism (or naturalism) in Gothic sculpture. In the Gothic period, people were still at a relatively early stage as regards the reintroduction of monumental sculpture in the West. In the centuries after the decline of Rome the tradition of monumental representational sculpture was interrupted. Viewing images, especially three-dimensional ones, was a rare experience for most people. Thus the impact of any image, and especially three-dimensional images, must have been very powerful. Freud noted that the uncanny is best exemplified in experiences when one mistakes an inanimate representation for an actual living thing. Medieval people may have had just such uncanny experiences when viewing realistic sculptures. It is just such a possibility, of course, which hastened theologians to warn against idolatry. But while idols may have indeed elicited misdirected devotion with their quasi-living fascination, depictions of creatures or grotesque humanoid figures may have also instilled real fear, real belief and uncertainty as to their reality. It may

[33] Kenaan-Kedar, *Marginal Sculpture in Medieval France*, pp. 62, 70.

well be that the doubly uncanny nature of these haunting marginal works functioned as potent incentives to obedience and devotion for fear of their malign influences. This issue becomes even more relevant when considering the high degree of realism in Gothic sculptures as opposed to their more abstract and, often, more two-dimensional Romanesque predecessors. The Gothic sculpted image seemed more alive because of its naturalism and volume, and the sculpture of St Nicholas partakes of this degree of naturalism, even if the figures are of 'fantastic' beings or creatures. This is also an issue for any scholars wishing to undertake comparative analyses of St Nicholas's sculptures. They are the products of a well trained master and workshop (or group of workshops). Though much damaged, what remains indicates a high degree of skill and an ability to convey a striking level of naturalistic and expressive detail, especially in the animal figures.

The numerical superiority of animal figures on St Nicholas is also a subject of some interest: for Europeans the carvings of strange and fabulous creatures signified the regions beyond the 'civilized' world; in the same way that the depictions of strange peoples sometimes indicated exotic lands well beyond Europe or the Middle East, as in the depiction of foreign peoples in the Pentecost tympanum at Vézelay.[34] Many medieval people believed that strange creatures, such as griffons, actually did exist.[35] Thus the preponderance of fantastic animals on a cathedral at the eastern edge of Christianity may have engendered certain inflections having to do with periphery or exotic hinterlands.

Kenaan-Kedar has observed that the fabulous creatures that were very common in Romanesque architectural sculpture became much less pervasive in the Gothic era. She observes that, 'In addition, the virtual disappearance of Romanesque images of monstrous creatures points perhaps to an urban society that was increasingly rational and less in thrall to fears of the unknown.'[36] This interpretation could certainly be qualified, but it is nonetheless intriguing since the prevalence of animal figures at St Nicholas might in this light be seen to be somewhat anachronistic. Perhaps, in the spirit of Kenaan-Kedar's observation, the Lusignans were acutely aware of their position at the margins of Christianity and thus rather more 'in thrall to fears of the unknown'.

---

34 A. Katzenellenbogen, 'The Central Tympanum at Vézelay: Its Encyclopedic Meaning and its Relation to the First Crusade', *Art Bulletin*, 26 (1944): 141–51.

35 The Dominican Felix Faber, from Ulm, made two pilgrimages to the Holy Land, in 1480 and 1483, and visited Cyprus on both occasions. He tells a story involving 'gryphons' and, even in the late fifteenth century, seems to believe that they existed. *Excerpta Cypria. Materials for a History of Cyprus*, trans. and ed. by C.D. Cobham (Cambridge, 1908; repr. New York, 1969), 42.

36 Kenaan-Kedar, *Marginal Sculpture in Medieval France*, p. 78. Her study focuses almost completely on those sculptures that represent human figures. Such anachronism is common on Cyprus. For example, a Venetian renaissance period house in Nicosia (now the Lapidary Museum) is decorated with corbels with reliefs of figures very much derived from a Romanesque repertoire.

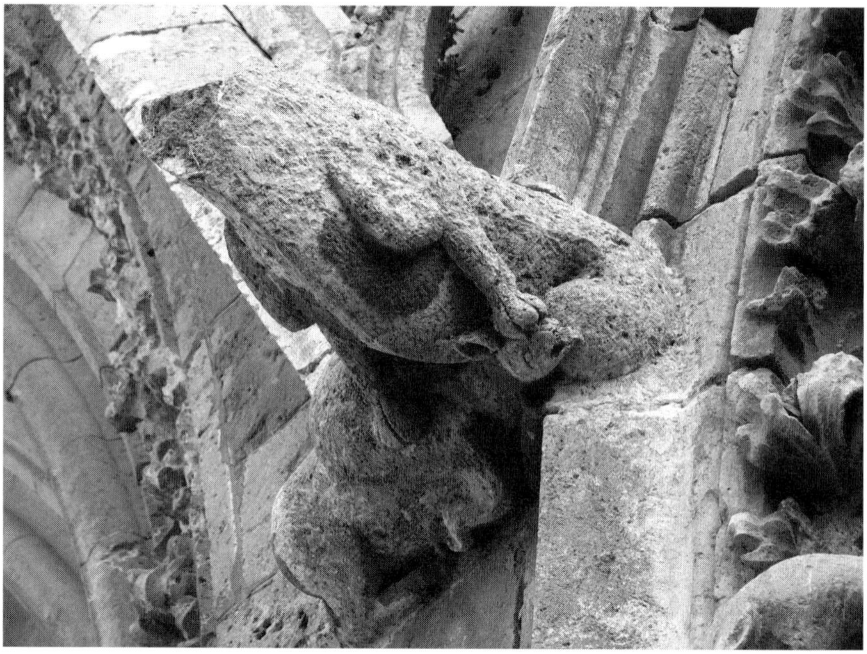

Fig. 6.5 A gargoyle water spout from St Nicholas (photograph: Allan Langdale)

Although no clear programmatic organization or complex symbolism seems to present itself in St Nicholas's sculpture, a synopsis of the major subjects can at least give some sense of the range of representations. Most of the marginal sculpture can be found on the façade of the cathedral and on the two towers, though several small dog-like creatures dot the upper reaches of the apses. Some are gargoyles that functioned as waterspouts (Figure 6.5), though most are corbel figures at the bases of gables and hood mouldings (Plate 2, and Figures 6.6–6.7). Several small sculptures, mostly of dragons and lions (or strange hybrids with serpentine and leonine body parts – many are too damaged to be clearly identified) – can be found populating the canopies of the jambs of the central portal (Figure 6.8). One small dragon, well concealed, is the only whole survivor of the vagaries of time (Figure 6.9). It gives us a good idea of what the other fragmentary dragons originally looked like. It is here where we might propose some degree of iconographic consistency, for if there was indeed some regal imagery intended around the central portal, both the lions and dragons would have been appropriate representations of Lusignan royalty, since lions appear in the Lusignan coat of arms and the dragons may have alluded to Melusine, a central figure in Lusignan mythology. The story revolves around the legendary love between Raymondin (or in some versions, Guy) de Lusignan, count of Poitou, and Melusine, who, unbeknownst to Raymondin, is a part serpent, mermaid-like creature. She agrees to marry Raymondin but, wanting her true identity to remain a secret, exacts a promise: that he will never gaze upon her while she bathes. However, the temptation becomes too great and Raymondin peeks while she is bathing. She turns into a dragon and flies away, never to return.

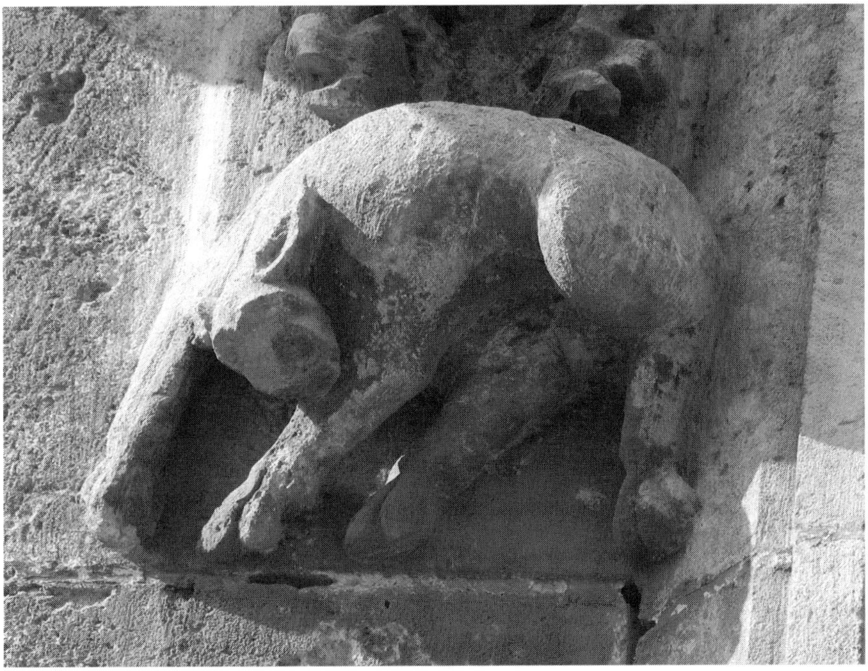

Fig. 6.6 Corbel figure from St Nicholas (photograph: Allan Langdale)

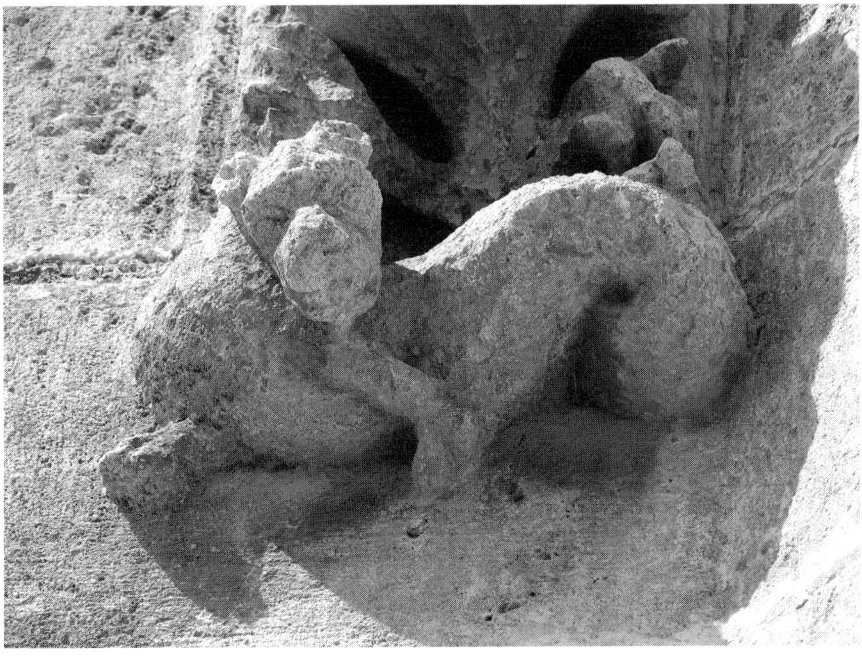

Fig. 6.7 Corbel figure from St Nicholas (photograph: Allan Langdale)

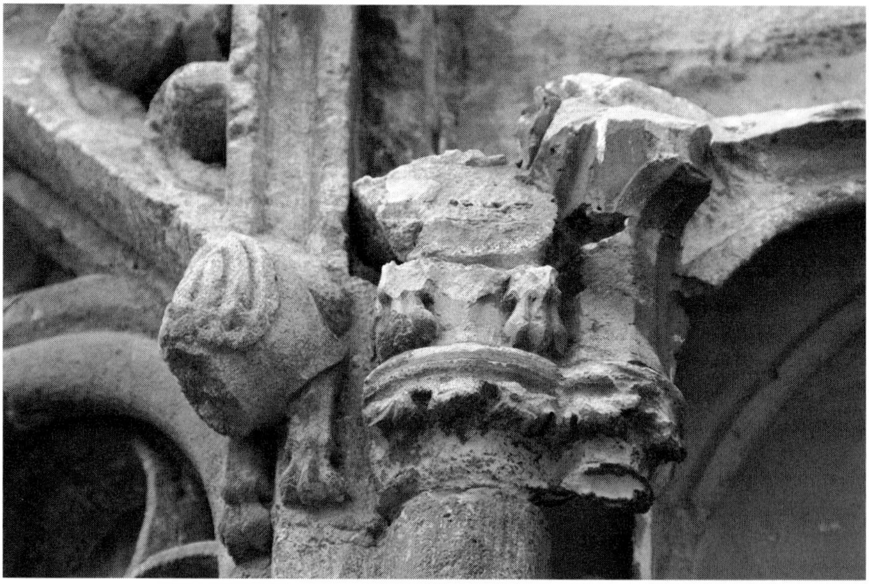

Fig. 6.8 Fragments of leonine animals on the canopies of the central portal jambs of St Nicholas (photograph: Allan Langdale)

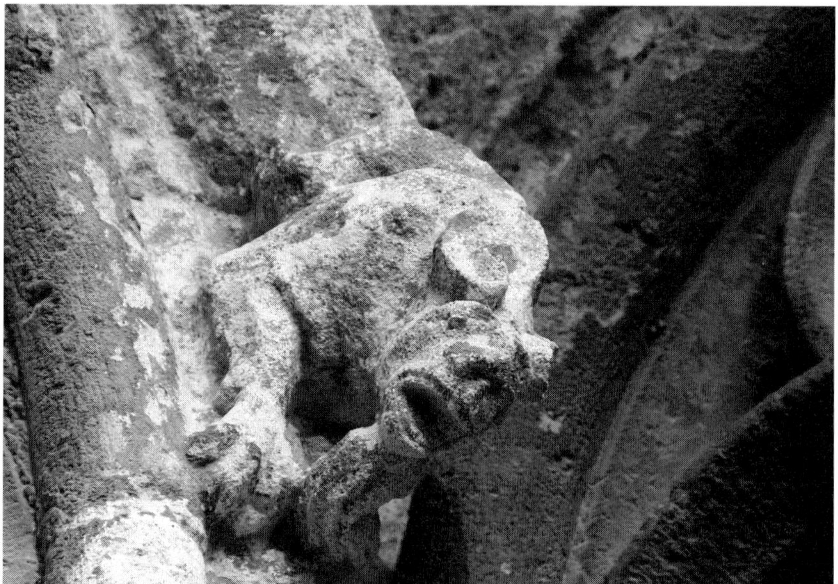

Fig. 6.9 Dragon near the canopies on the façade of St Nicholas (photograph: Allan Langdale)

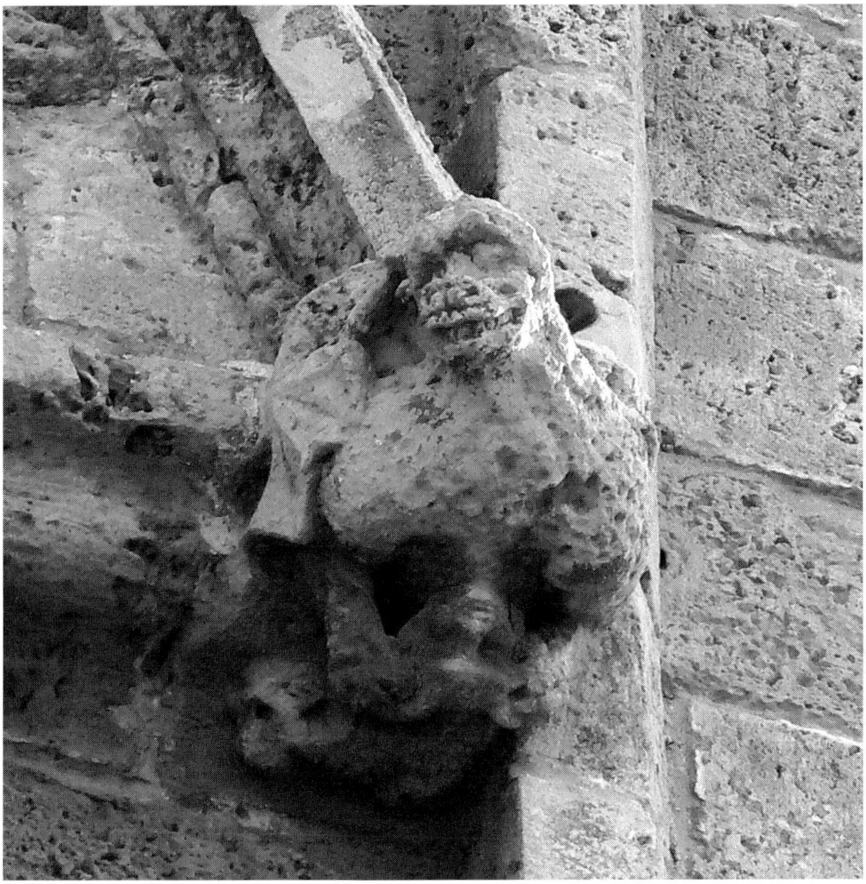

Fig. 6.10 Dragon figure from the façade of St Nicholas, south tower (photograph: Wilbert 'Skip' Norman)

It is possible that another allusion to the Melusine myth might be found in the tower sculptures, where the northernmost figure on the façade has what seems like a long, scaled tail. On the opposite, southernmost side is a dragon that holds some weaker beast in its talons (Figure 6.10). Could it be Melusine as mermaid balanced with her dragon counterpart? The notion of dragons being protectors of the cathedral is supported by this myth, since the dragon Melusine was considered to be the protector of the Lusignan castle in Poitou.[37] She makes an appearance hovering over the Lusignan castle in the March page of the Duc de Berry's *Très Riches Heures*. The dragon imagery on St Nicholas provides a case illustrative of the problems of interpretation. While it may be attractive to juxtapose these sculptures with a Lusignan myth, it is far from certain that such a reference was either intended or read in this manner. At least in the case of the lion figures and the roses, we have a more

[37] See C. Naud, *Le dragon dans l' art roman du Poitou-Charentes* (Poitiers, 1972). In some descriptions of Melusine the lower part of her body is described as serpentine. Snakes also figure in Lusignan heraldry where they are shown twining around swords, as in the well-preserved marble coat of arms mounted in the ravelin of Famagusta.

definite link to Lusignan heraldic iconography. But to venture beyond we find interpretation is beset with uncertainties.

The rose, which appears in the bosses of a couple of the canopies of the central portal (it is a motif that appears frequently in Lusignan architectural decoration), is also found in bouquets held by some of the figures which decorate the tower. One, who seems to be dressed in mail like a knight, on the west face of the north tower, carries such a bouquet (Figure 6.11). The Dominican monk, Felix Faber, recounted the tradition where knights would present themselves to the king or queen of Cyprus and pledge to support the island realm. For their promise they received a dagger decorated with a rose.[38] Perhaps the sculpture alludes to the virtue of chivalry and the knights who swore to defend Cyprus if it was ever attacked. Chivalry was certainly a fundamental component of Lusignan culture: the youthful and tragic King Peter I of Cyprus (1328–69) was seen in his day to be an embodiment of this medieval virtue so definitive of the crusader mentality.

Another compelling figure, on the west face of the south tower, is one of St Nicholas's most recognizable generic types: the figure of a nude man suffering in hell (Figure 6.12). Figures like him appear in many instances in medieval Last Judgement scenes. He is most frequently naked with his genitals clearly visible, holding his head in despair as he contemplates the eternal pain he will suffer for his adulterous life.[39] A number of other figures on the towers seem to hold pots, with the mouths of the pots perhaps functioning as actual drain spouts. Since figures with spouting pots often signified the personifications and sources of rivers in Christian art there may be some references here to the Jordan River or the Four Rivers of Paradise. Of course, like the gargoyles out of whose mouths rainwater would flow, the pots would similarly be animated by draining water and the logic of the representation would be evident.

Another figure, which seems to be a harpy with a gaping mouth, decorates the eastern face of the south tower (Figure 6.13). The harpy exchanges looks with a figure of a man with crossed legs who seems to gaze back with a worried expression. Since the harpy was a decidedly negative creature emblematic of temptation and sin, the concerned visage of the man might be read as an appropriate reaction. The naked suffering man appears on the same tower as a reminder of the wages of sin. Famagusta was infamous for its moral decrepitude and descent into luxury. St Brigit, addressing the people of the city at the height of their wealth c. 1370, gave an accounting of Famagusta's innumerable sins, calling it a modern day Sodom and Gomorrah. Could she see, as she gave her sermon in the square in front of St Nicholas, those beasts looking down from the city's most sacred edifice? They may have offered eloquent illustrative material for her dire warnings. Indeed, although marginal sculpture may never have been intended to function in this way, it seems likely that the medieval preachers who often delivered their fiery

---

[38] See *Excerpta Cypria. Materials for a History of Cyprus*, p. 37.

[39] Kenaan-Kedar publishes a similar figure from Ste Radegonde, Poitiers, in *Marginal Sculpture in Medieval France*, p. 109, fig. 3.33.

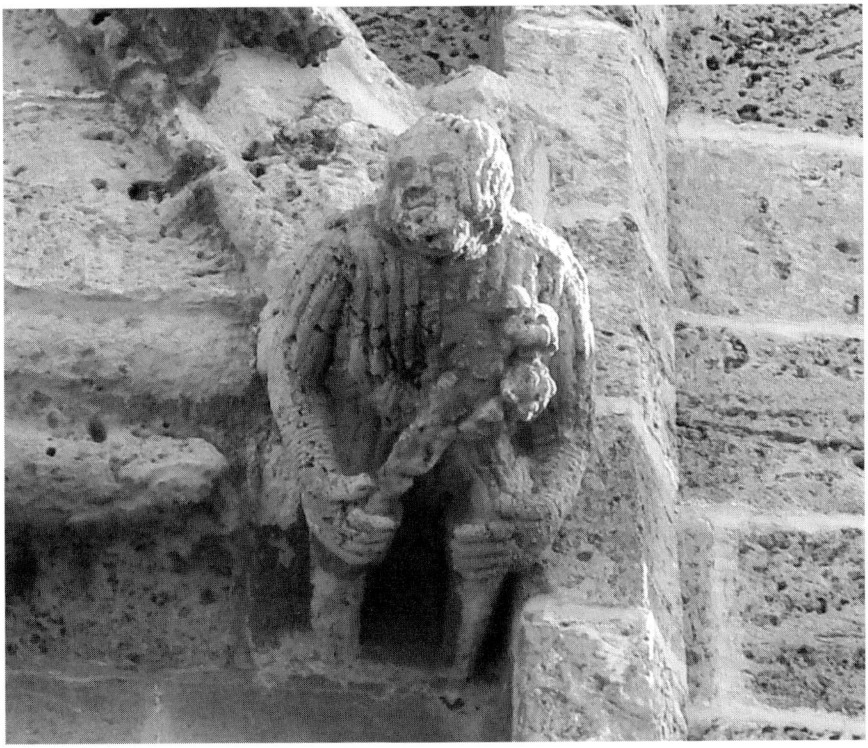

Fig. 6.11 Knight (?) figure from the façade of St Nicholas, north tower (photograph: Wilbert 'Skip' Norman)

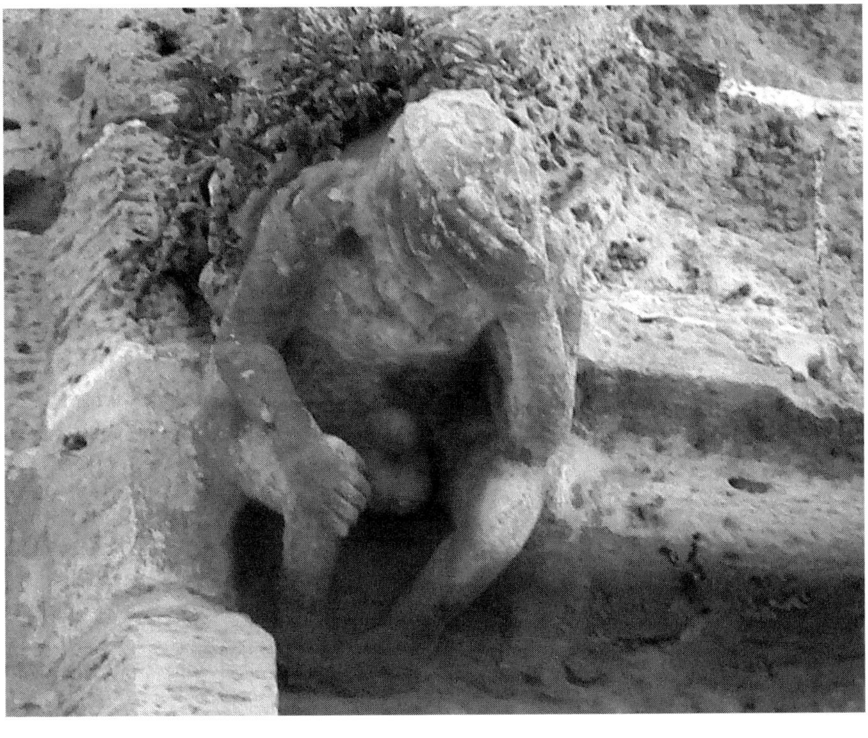

Fig. 6.12 Nude man suffering, from the façade of St Nicholas, south tower (photograph: Wilbert 'Skip' Norman)

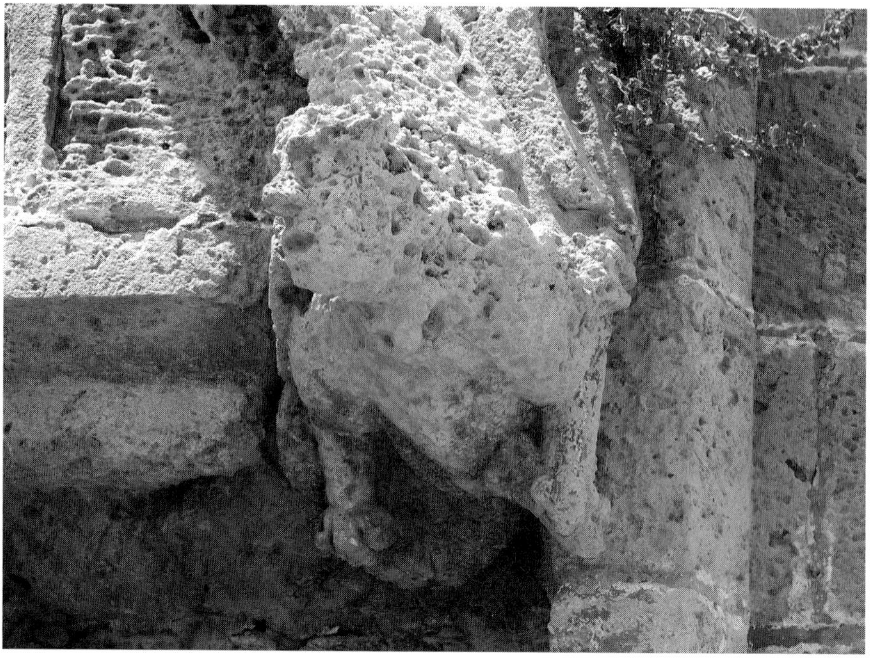

Fig. 6.13 Figure of a harpy (?), St Nicholas, east face, south tower (photograph: Allan Langdale)

sermons in cathedral squares would have, at least on some occasions, made effective rhetorical use of this convenient and powerful imagery to emphasize their dire warnings.

In Famagusta, metaphors of marginality find an uncommonly rich context. St Nicholas teetered for centuries at the far eastern edge of Christianity, on the seaboard demarking Orient and Occident, Christian and Muslim, 'betwixt Greek and Saracen' as St Willibald noted of the island when he passed through Cyprus in the early eighth century. Thus the building's liminal locus is strangely complemented by the marginal sculptures that ornament it. Metaphors of margin and edge, centrality and periphery are, however, complicated, for where, exactly, was the centre for the Lusignans? Was Jerusalem the *axis mundi* for the crusaders or their ancestral homes in France? Did they consider themselves to be at the periphery – the furthest outpost of Catholicism, or tantalizingly close to the centre, Jerusalem? What inflections might the marginal sculpture have had in the rarified context of Lusignan Cyprus? Thus, one of the key problems in any consideration of the context of St Nicholas is to define, in as much as it is possible, how the Lusignans saw themselves. There is evidence that at least a few of them really did see themselves as representatives of Christianity on the edge of its range, on a borderland where threat lurked just a day's sail away.

The work of producing detailed photographic documentation of the sculpture of St Nicholas still confronts us. A comprehensive archive would assist greatly in encouraging scholarly research. Work needs to be done by those art historians equipped to attend to the iconographic and formal details of the sculptures with an aim to determining any consistencies with sculptures in France or Germany. Similarities in the depictions of subjects or in the hands of artists might support or weaken either Enlart's claim that St Nicholas was constructed by masons from the Champagne or more contemporary ideas that trace the building's origins to the Rhineland. Such analysis might also bring to light new, alternative theories about the masons and workshops associated with the cathedral. Crusader era sculptures from the Holy Land might also provide tantalizing information about St Nicholas.[40]

[40] More studies of crusader era marginal sculptures from the Holy Land would assist research, such as in N. Kenaan-Kedar's essays, 'A Neglected Series of Crusader Sculpture: The Ninety-Six Corbels of the Church of the Holy Sepulchre', *Israel Exploration Journal*, 42 (1992): 103–14; 'The Two Lintels of the Church of the Holy Sepulchre in Jerusalem', in *Knights of the Holy Land. The Crusader Kingdom of Jerusalem*, ed. S. Rosenberg (Jerusalem, 1999), 176–86; and 'The Role and Meanings of Crusader Architectural Decoration: From Local Romanesque Traditions to Gothic Hegemony', *Schriften des Historischen Kolleges Kolloquien*, 37 (1997): 165–78. Numerous illustrations of capitals and sculptural fragments appear in J. Folda's *Crusader Art in the Holy Land: from the Third Crusade to the Fall of Acre, 1187–1291* (Cambridge, 2005).

Les Ordres mendiants à Famagouste: une référence spirituelle et architecturale

Thierry Soulard

L'implantation des ordres mendiants à Famagouste aux XIIIe et XIVe siècles

Dominicains et Franciscains avaient établi très tôt des couvents à Nicosie. Ils sont en effet attestés vers 1226 dans la capitale du royaume latin de Chypre.[1] A cette époque, les premiers couvents des Prêcheurs étaient fondés dans le sud de la France, à la suite de celui de Toulouse, le premier de l'ordre (1215).[2] De même, les frères mineurs commençaient leur extension partie d'Assise en 1209, et les premiers couvents étaient fondés autour des années 1220 hors d'Italie.[3] La date précise de l'installation à Famagouste de ces deux ordres n'est pas connue, mais elle est consécutive à la perte progressive des dernières places fortes latines de Terre sainte.[4] La position du port, face aux côtes syriennes, explique le remarquable développement de la ville (Figure 7.1) dans la dernière décennie du XIIIe siècle: au fur et à mesure de l'avancée des Mamelouks et de la chute des derniers vestiges du royaume de Jérusalem, on assiste à un afflux de population, réfugiés et marchands. Ce sont surtout ces derniers qui vont faire de Famagouste une grande place commerciale durant un siècle et assurer la richesse de la ville, devenue la nouvelle Acre. Famagouste connut alors un essor économique considérable, la plaçant parmi les principales places de commerce des Latins en Orient,

1 N. Coureas, *The Latin Church in Cyprus, 1195–1312* (Aldershot, 1997): 205–15.

2 M.-H. Vicaire, 'Le développement de la province dominicaine de Provence (1215–1295)', *Les Mendiants en pays d'Oc au XIIIe siècle, Cahiers de Fanjeaux*, 8 (1973): 35–77.

3 F.-R. Durieux, 'Approches de l'histoire franciscaine du Languedoc au XIIIe siècle', ibid., pp. 79–100.

4 M. Balard, 'Famagouste au début du XIVe siècle' in J. Heers (ed.), *Fortifications, portes de ville, places publiques dans le monde méditerranéen* (Paris, 1985): 279–99; P.W. Edbury, 'Famagusta in 1300', *Cyprus and the Crusades*, ed. N. Coureas et J. Riley Smith (Nicosia, 1995): 337–53.

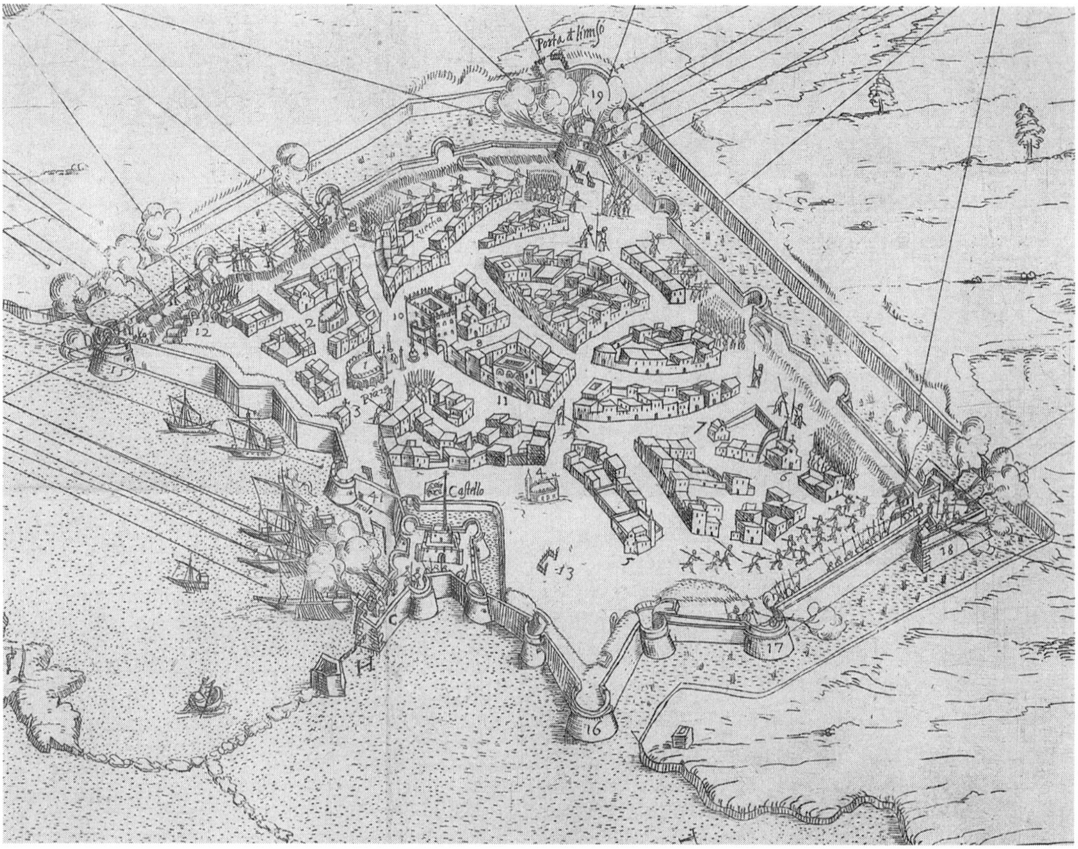

Fig. 7.1 Stephano Gibellino, *Gravure représentant le siège de Famagouste* (Brescia, 1571), cl. BNF, détail représentant la ville

« le rendez-vous de toutes les nations de l'occident » jusqu'à sa prise par les Génois en 1373.[5]

Les frères mineurs sont mentionnés les premiers dans les actes notariés génois. Deux actes datés d'octobre 1296 citent le frère Philippe d'Antioche, gardien de l'église Saint-François de Famagouste, ainsi qu'un autre frère, témoignant alors de l'existence du couvent avec son église.[6] L'édifice attesté à cette date est celui qui subsiste encore sous forme de ruines (Figure 7.2), comme le démontre l'analyse du monument.[7] Il accueille de nombreuses

5 L. de Sudheim, 'De itinere Terre Sancte', cité par M. Balard, 'La place de Famagouste génoise dans le royaume des Lusignan (1374–1464)', *Les Lusignans et l'Outre-Mer*, ed. C. Mutafian (Poitiers, 1993): 17.

6 *Notai genovesi in oltremare: Atti rogati a Cipro da Lamberto di Sambuceto (11 ottobre 1296–23 giugno 1299)*, ed. M. Balard, CSFS 39 (Genova, 1983), n° 11, pp. 15–16, 22 octobre 1296: « *Frater Philipus de Antiocia de ordine fratrum minorum ecclesie sancti Francisci de Famagosta, guardianus dicte ecclesie* … ». Le frère déclare avoir reçu 100 besants blancs laissés en legs aux Franciscains par Léonard de Bonigracia. Dans un autre acte lié au même testament (n° 5, pp. 7–8, 15 octobre 1296), il est aussi fait mention de Jacques de Tripoli, frère mineur de Famagouste.

7 P. Plagnieux et T. Soulard, 'Famagouste, l'église des Franciscains', dans J.-B. de Vaivre et P. Plagnieux (ed.), *L'art gothique en Chypre* (Paris, 2006): 238–42.

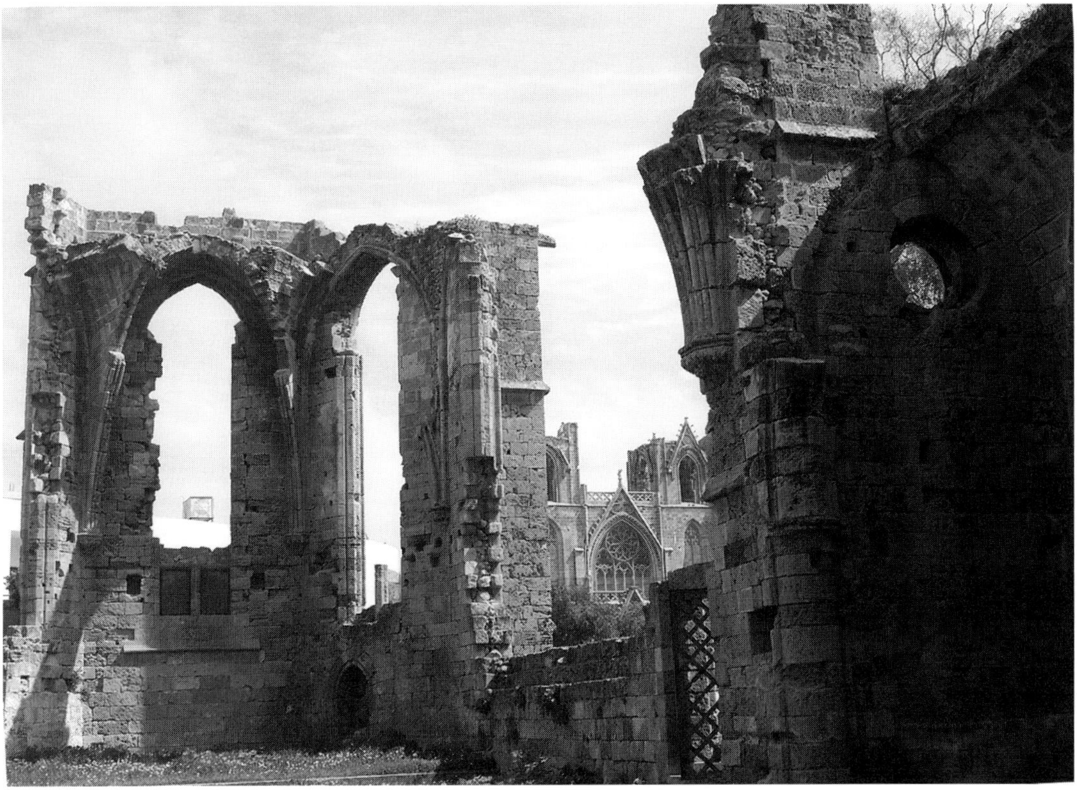

Fig. 7.2 Eglise des Franciscains, vue générale (photograph: Justine Andrews)

sépultures qui apparaissent dans les testaments: le 3 juillet 1300, celle de Giovanni Zacharias;[8] le 27 juillet, celle de Nicolas de Raynaldo;[9] le 22 septembre de la même année, celle de Pierre de Marffi;[10] celle de Jacques de Pergame en juillet 1301;[11] celle de Payen de Fellino le 15 août 1301.[12] Enfin, un acte est instrumenté le 23 juin 1302 à côté de l'église.[13]

Les frères pêcheurs semblent s'être établis presque en même temps que les Franciscains à Famagouste. Comme l'a démontré Nicolas Coureas, le couvent des Dominicains de Famagouste n'est pas cité par Bernard Gui en 1277 parmi les établissements de l'Orient latin, alors qu'il apparaît dans une liste de 1303.[14] C'est aussi dans les actes du notaire génois Lamberto di

8 *Notai genovesi in oltremare: Atti rogati a Cipro da Lamberto di Sambuceto (3 lulio 1300–3 agosto 1301)*, ed. V. Polonio, CSFS 31(Genova, 1982), n° 12, pp. 12–14.

9 'Actes passés à Famagouste de 1299 à 1301 par devant le notaire génois Lamberto di Sanbucto', ed. C. Desimoni, *Archives de l'Orient latin*, 2 (1884), n° 187, p. 99.

10 Polonio, *Notai genovesi in oltremare*, n° 23, pp. 26–7.

11 *Notai genovesi in oltremare: Atti rogati a Cipro da Lamberto di Sambuceto (6 lulio 1301–27 ottobre 1301)*, ed. R. Pavoni, CSFS 32 (Genova, 1982), n° 5, pp. 4–5.

12 Ibid., n° 46, pp. 59–62.

13 *Notai genovesi in oltremare: Atti rogati a Cipro da Lamberto di Sambuceto (gennaio–agosto 1302)*, ed. R. Pavoni, CSFS 49 (Genova, 1987), n° 239, p. 287: « *juxta sive ante ecclesiam Fratrum minorum* ».

14 Coureas, pp. 212–13.

Sambuceto qu'apparaissent les premières mentions du couvent et de l'église Saint-Dominique à partir de 1300, à l'occasion de legs.[15] Le 19 septembre 1300, le génois Januinus Ralla établit par testament sa sépulture dans l'église des prêcheurs, et fait un legs pour la construction de l'édifice, qui était donc en chantier à ce moment.[16] De même, le riche marchand de Narbonne Bernard Faxit, par testament en date du 5 décembre 1300, choisit aussi l'église des Dominicains pour dernière demeure, léguant 50 besants pour le chantier, toujours en activité.[17] Dans le même acte, il cite le cimetière des frères prêcheurs de Famagouste, témoignant d'une institution déjà bien établie.[18] Enfin, le testament de Payen de Fellino, du 15 août 1301, mentionne la construction d'un des bâtiments claustraux, le *laboratorium* –la salle de travail et d'étude probablement.[19] A partir de 1301, les legs faits aux Dominicains se multiplient, témoignant de l'importance prise par le couvent, dont il ne subsiste rien aujourd'hui, mais dont l'emplacement est connu.[20]

En 1300, seuls les Franciscains et les Dominicains sont établis à Famagouste, comme en témoigne le testament de Bernard Faxit.[21] En effet, le Narbonnais prévoit des legs pour toutes les communautés des trois villes auxquelles il est attaché. Ainsi, il dote les trois couvents mendiants de Nicosie, les frères prêcheurs, les frères mineurs et les frères de Sainte-Marie du Carmel, sans oublier les dames du couvent de Sainte-Claire; en revanche, les frères ermites de Saint-Augustin sont absents. A Narbonne, les quatre ordres mendiants bénéficient de ses largesses. Il ne mentionne en revanche à Famagouste que deux des quatre ordres mendiants. En effet, les Carmes et les Augustins sont arrivés plus tard. Les frères de Sainte-Marie du Carmel, déjà présents à Nicosie, reçurent l'autorisation de s'installer à Famagouste en mars 1311, par lettre du pape Clément V.[22] Comme le démontre l'étude du bâtiment subsistant (Figure 7.3), l'église a été édifiée immédiatement

15 Desimoni, 'Actes passés à Famagouste', n° 189, p. 101, 25 juillet 1300: testament d'Obertus de Vintimilio. Polonio, *Notai genovesi in oltremare*, n° 12, pp. 12–14, 3 juillet 1300: testament de Giovanni Zacharias.

16 Polonio, *Notai genovesi in oltremare*, n° 22, p. 24: « ... *lego corpus meum sepelliri apud ecclesiam fratrum Predicatorum Famagoste ... Item lego dicte ecclesie fratrum Predicatorum, pro opera dicte ecclesie, bisancios albos quinque* ».

17 Ibid., n° 145, pp. 162-3: « *Item lego... operi dicte ecclesie fratrum Predicatorum, bisancios L...* »

18 Ibid., p. 163: « *Item, in pane calido qui dari debeat ad cimeterium fratrum Predicatorum Famagoste pauperibus bisancios XXV.* »

19 Pavoni, *Notai genovesi in oltremare* (CSFS 32), n° 46, pp. 59–62: « *Item lego, pro anima mea, laboratorio fratrum Predicatorum Famagoste,bisancios albos quinque.* »

20 Plagnieux et Soulard, 'Famagouste, l'église Saint-Pierre Saint-Paul', dans de Vaivre et Plagnieux, pp. 273–4. On ne saurait retenir l'identification de Saint-Pierre Saint-Paul avec l'église des Dominicains, clairement située près du port et du château (cf. *infra*, Une nouvelle Acre: le grand dessin de Henri II).

21 Polonio. *Notai genovesi in oltremare*, n° 145, pp. 162–3.

22 *Registrum Clementis papae V*, ed. cura et studio monachorum ordini S. Benedicti, 8 vols. (Rome, 1885–92), 6, n° 6751, p. 116, 13 mars 1311. D'après cette bulle, Famagouste ne faisait pas partie jusqu'alors des lieux d'implantation du Carmel, qui s'était pourtant établi en Chypre dès le milieu du XIIIe siècle. Cf. Coureas, pp. 215–19.

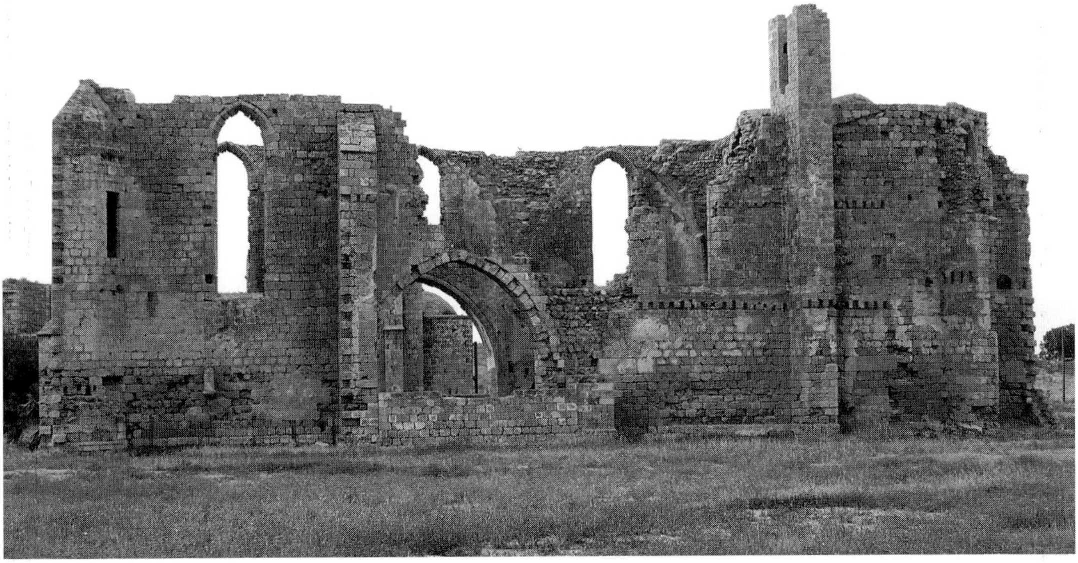

Fig. 7.3 Eglise des Carmes, vue générale extérieure, flanc sud (photograph: Thierry Soulard)

après cette autorisation.[23] C'est donc peu après les Franciscains et les Dominicains que les Carmes se sont implantés à Famagouste, sous le règne du roi Henri II (1285–1324), durant la vague de repli des Latins venus de Terre sainte.

L'établissement de l'ordre des ermites de Saint-Augustin à Famagouste est en revanche beaucoup moins bien connu, de même qu'on ignore tout de l'emplacement de leur couvent. L'ordre n'est jamais mentionné dans les testaments conservés entre 1296 et 1310, ce qui tend à prouver qu'ils n'étaient pas encore présents dans la ville. Ce n'est qu'en 1361 qu'apparaît la première mention de l'église Saint-Augustin, de l'ordre des ermites, dans les actes d'un notaire vénitien: le testateur prévoit sa sépulture dans cet édifice.[24] La même année, un Vénitien demande à être enterré dans le monastère Saint-Antoine, de l'ordre des ermites.[25] Il existait donc un autre couvent, Saint-Antoine, dépendant des ermites de Saint-Augustin. Il ne saurait s'agir d'une erreur du notaire (Saint-Antoine à la place de Saint-Augustin), puisque cet établissement est cité à d'autres reprises comme appartenant aux ermites.[26]

23 Plagnieux et Soulard, 'Famagouste, l'église Sainte-Marie du Carmel', dans de Vaivre et Plagnieux, pp. 251–6.

24 *Nicola de Boateriis, notaio in Famagosta e Venezia (1355-1365)*, ed. A. Lombardo (Venise, 1973), n° 157, pp. 161–5, 24 février 1361, testament de Jacques de Bochasiis de Ferrare: « *In primis volo et iubeo quod corpus meum cum ab huius mundi luce fuerit, Deo iubente, privatum sepeliatur apud ecclesiam Sancti Augustini fratrum Heremitarum Famagoste…* ». Le couvent est aussi cité dans le même acte: « *…dimitto conventui fratrum Heremitarum Sancti Augustini de Famagusta bisancios centum albos…* ».

25 Ibid., n° 168, pp. 179–82, 29 juillet 1361, testament de Bartholomée Gritti, vénitien, habitant de Famagouste: « *In primis volo et iubeo quod corpus meum … sepeliatur apud monasterium Sancti Antonii ordinis Heremitarum Famagoste …* ».

26 W.H. Rudt de Collenberg, 'Les grâces papales autres que les dispenses

On ne peut identifier cette église avec celle de l'hôpital Saint-Antoine, connue par ailleurs,[27] qui dépendait de l'ordre hospitalier des chanoines réguliers de Saint-Antoine-en-Viennois, et donc sans rapport avec les ermites de Saint-Augustin. Plusieurs testaments postérieurs à 1361 citent aussi les Augustins.[28] L'installation de l'ordre à Famagouste a donc dû intervenir entre 1310 et 1361, mais les lacunes des sources actuellement connues ne permettent pas plus de précision. On peut toutefois noter que l'ordre avait été organisé en 1256, après les trois autres ordres mendiants; il est mentionné à Nicosie seulement en 1299.[29]

Concernant les ordres féminins, les Clarisses semblent s'être installées à Famagouste vers 1330, bien après les Franciscains, puisque leur couvent était en construction en 1333.[30] Rien n'indique leur présence avant cette date, elles sont en revanche mentionnées par la suite dans les testaments.[31] Enfin, une lettre pontificale de 1371 cite, sans plus de précisions, une chapelle du couvent des Dominicaines de Famagouste dédiée à Saint-Augustin.[32]

Une nouvelle Acre: le grand dessin d'Henri II (1285–1324)

L'implantation des Franciscains et des Dominicains dans la dernière décennie du XIIIe siècle, puis des Carmes à partir de 1311 s'inscrit dans la restructuration de Famagouste voulue par le roi Henri II (1285–1324) à la suite de l'essor économique et démographique de la ville. Seul le monarque

matrimoniales accordées à Chypre de 1305 à 1378', *Epeteris tou Kentrou Epistemonikon Ereunon*, 8 (Nicosia, 1975–77): 252: 17 juin 1371, *Indulgentia pro capella SS Petri et Pauli prope ecclesia Sancti Antonii, Famaguste (O. Aug. Erem.), et fundata a domini Roberti de Cosentia, clerico de Famagusta.*

27 Plagnieux et Soulard, 'Famagouste, l'hôpital Saint-Antoine', dans de Vaivre et Plagnieux, pp. 248–50.

28 C. Otten-Froux, 'Un notaire vénitien à Famagouste au XIVe siècle, Les actes de Simeone, prêtre de San Giacomo dell'Orio (1362-1371)', *Thesaurismata*, 33 (2003): 98–101, entre 1362 et 1364, testament de Jean de Chastel; pp. 105–10, 8 novembre 1369, testament de Jean Contareno.

29 Coureas, pp. 242–3. Le testament de Bernard Faxit (Polonio, *Notai genovesi in oltremare*, n° 145, pp. 162–3) ne le citant pas en 1300, alors qu'il semble exhaustif, donne à penser que le couvent des Augustins de Nicosie n'était pas encore vraiment construit, ce que confirme l'analyse du bâtiment subsistant, qui permet une datation des premières décennies du XIVe siècle (Plagnieux et Soulard, 'Nicosie, l'église des Augustins', dans de Vaivre et Plagnieux, pp. 178–80).

30 C. Otten-Froux, 'Notes sur quelques monuments de Famagouste à la fin du Moyen Age', dans J. Herrin, M. Mullett, C. Otten-Froux (ed.), *Mosaic, Byzantine and Cypriot Studies in honour of A. H. S. Megaw*, British School at Athens Studies, suppl. vol. 8 (Nottingham, 2001): 148, 154 n. 62: testament du Pisan Giovanni de Rau qui laisse 100 besants blancs « *monialibus et monasterio monialium Sancte Clare de Famagusta pro fabrica eiusdem ecclesie* ».

31 Otten-Froux, 'Un notaire vénitien à Famagouste au XIVe siècle', pp. 98–101, entre 1362 et 1364, testament de Jean de Chastel; pp. 105–10, 8 novembre 1369, testament de Jean Contareno.

32 W.H. Rudt de Collenberg, p. 252, 7 mars 1371

avait l'autorité nécessaire pour décider du remodelage complet de la cité, considérablement agrandie, en construisant une enceinte, englobant un périmètre beaucoup plus vaste que celui de l'ancienne agglomération byzantine.[33] L'étude des plans anciens de la ville, en particulier celui de Gibellino de 1571[34] (Figure 7.1), montre qu'il existe deux types de tissu urbain à l'intérieur même des remparts, délimités selon une ligne est-ouest partant du château. L'un, dense, caractérise la partie sud de Famagouste et comprend les quartiers du port, de la cathédrale Saint-Nicolas et de la cathédrale grecque Saint-Georges. Il correspond au noyau primitif. L'autre, dans la partie nord de la ville, plus restreinte, apparaît sur le plan de 1571 beaucoup moins densément urbanisée. Cette extension décidée par le roi a presque exclusivement accueilli des communautés religieuses. La prise de la ville en 1373 par les Génois, qui a stoppé l'essor de Famagouste, a probablement mis fin au lotissement de cette zone, qui est encore aujourd'hui quelque peu délaissée.

La partie ancienne de la ville, au sud, a été restructurée lors de ces grands travaux. La cathédrale Saint-Nicolas fut reconstruite à partir de la dernière décennie du XIIIe siècle, sur un plan beaucoup plus vaste.[35] Elle remplaçait un édifice qui datait de moins d'un siècle, devenu beaucoup trop petit, comme le relatent les actes pontificaux.[36] De surcroît, la cathédrale était destinée à accueillir le couronnement des rois de Chypre comme rois de Jérusalem, qui avait lieu jusque là à Tyr, où Henri II avait été couronné en 1285.[37] Après la perte de cette cité, Famagouste la remplaça dans cette fonction: le couronnement d'Hugues IV eut lieu en 1324 dans la nouvelle cathédrale Saint-Nicolas.[38] Face

33 N. Faucherre, 'L'enceinte urbaine de Famagouste', dans de Vaivre et Plagnieux, pp. 307–9.

34 S. Gibellino, *Gravure représentant le siège de Famagouste* (Brescia, 1571).

35 Plagnieux et Soulard, 'Famagouste, la cathédrale Saint-Nicolas', dans de Vaivre et Plagnieux, pp. 218–37.

36 Ibid., p. 219, n. 18: lettre de Jean XXII, 24 novembre 1318.

37 La participation royale ne fait guère de doutes pour la construction de la cathédrale, et nous ne pouvons souscrire aux thèses d'A. Franke, 'Saint Nicholas in Famagusta: A new approach to the dating, chronology and sources of architectural language' dans le présent ouvrage. En effet, si l'évêque et les chanoines ont financé les chantiers de construction des cathédrales en Occident, le cas de Chypre est particulier: l'évêché de Famagouste avait été créé en 1196, et c'est le roi qui avait concédé les possessions temporelles de l'évêque et des chanoines; celles-ci n'étaient pas suffisantes pour financer un tel chantier. Même si le prélat a sûrement été le maître d'ouvrage de l'édifice, la construction, commencée en même temps que la restructuration de la ville, s'insère dans le grand projet d'Henri II pour Famagouste. Enfin, il n'y a pas de raison sérieuse de douter que la nouvelle cathédrale devait accueillir le couronnement des rois de Chypre comme rois de Jérusalem, puisque Tyr était tombé en 1291 en même temps qu'Acre, peu de temps avant le début des travaux. Tout le projet d'Henri II visait à faire de Famagouste la nouvelle Acre et la nouvelle Tyr, comme le relève Etienne de Lusignan. Le couronnement comme roi de Jérusalem du successeur d'Henri II, Hugues IV, des mains de l'évêque de Beyrouth, n'a pu avoir lieu que là. Il n'y avait d'ailleurs pas d'autre édifice suffisamment important à ce moment pour accueillir une telle cérémonis.

38 Florio Bustron, 'Chronique de l'île de Chypre', ed. R. de Mas Latrie, *Collection de Documents inédits sur l'histoire de France: Mélanges historiques*, 5 (Paris, 1886): 253.

à cet édifice, Henri II fit ériger un palais urbain (*hospitium*), aujourd'hui disparu, conformément à la mode des hôtels royaux urbains. L'implantation de ce palais a dû être conçue en même temps que celle du couvent des Franciscains, qu'Henri II appréciait tout particulièrement.[39] Un passage, par une porte au seul usage du roi, lui permettait de se rendre directement de son hôtel au couvent mitoyen, pour y prier de jour comme de nuit.[40] Ainsi, la cathédrale, le palais royal et le couvent des frères mineurs, qui constituaient désormais le chœur de la cité, appartiennent à un même projet émanant du monarque.

C'est dans la partie nord nouvellement constituée que furent installés sous Henri II les Dominicains et les Carmes, puis sans doute peu après les religieuses bénédictines de Sainte-Anne de Jérusalem (Figure 7.4), ainsi que des communautés orientales telle celle des Arméniens. Le couvent des Dominicains avait été établi près du château, réédifié durant le même règne.[41] Il était ainsi tourné vers le port, zone importante pour la mission évangélisatrice des Prêcheurs. Bien qu'il ne subsiste aucun élément clairement identifiable du couvent, l'emplacement ne fait aucun doute, comme le montre le plan de 1571 qui situe l'église Saint-Dominique au fond d'une grande place la séparant du château (Figure 7.1). Il paraît impossible en revanche d'identifier l'église Saint-Pierre-Saint-Paul comme siège des Prêcheurs à Famagouste. Cette hypothèse les situerait près du palais royal, comme à Nicosie.[42] Elle repose sur l'interprétation des chroniques d'Amadi et de Bustron qui exposent que l'usurpateur Amaury avait fait déplacer en 1310 la place existant en avant de la cour royale pour la transférer devant le monastère des Prêcheurs,[43] dans un contexte de travaux autour du château.[44] L'expression « cour royale » désigne en fait le château, siège des institutions, et non le palais. Par ailleurs, le terme de cour est employé dans les actes des années 1300 comme lié au château.[45]

---

39 L. de Mas Latrie, *Histoire de l'île de Chypre* (Paris, 1852–61), 3: 693–4, acte du 25 septembre 1313: le confesseur d'Henri II est le frère mineur Rodulphus; p. 705, le frère mineur Aymeric, de l'entourage royal, est mentionné à Famagouste dans une lettre de François de Forn au roi Jacques II d'Aragon du 29 mai 1316. Le seul indice fiable sur la date de la construction du palais est fourni par l'édification simultanée du couvent des frères mineurs. En revanche, la mention en 1300 de la « *loggia regis* » ne correspond pas forcément au palais, même si c'est cependant envisageable (Balard, 'Famagouste au début du XIVe siècle', p. 282).

40 Mas Latrie, *Histoire de l'île de Chypre*, 2: 187, 1340: mémoire confidentiel adressé par l'infant Fernand de Majorque au roi de Majorque: « *de hospicio autem regis itur ad fratres minores per quoddam hostium secretum, quare inter hospicium dicti domini regis et ipsos fratres minores predictos non est nisi paries in medio, sicut dominus rex Enricus, bone memorie … ordinaverat et transiebat per dictum locum ad fratres minores de nocte et de die* ».

41 C. Corvisier, 'Le château de Famagouste', dans de Vaivre et Plagnieux, pp. 351–66. Si les chroniques attribuent sa réédification à Amaury, prince de Tyr, qui s'était proclamé régent du royaume sous Henri II entre 1306 et 1310, il est probable que la reconstruction avait été lancée par le souverain dès la fin du XIIIe siècle (p. 365).

42 Edbury, p. 343.

43 Bustron, pp. 193–4, 1310: « *…fece mutar la piazza ch'era avanti la corte regal, et metterla drio al monasterio de predicatori* ».

44 Plagnieux, Soulard, 'Famagouste, église Saint-Pierre-Saint-Paul', pp. 273–4.

45 Balard, *Notai genovesi in oltremare*, n° 13, pp. 17–19, 28 octobre 1296, testament de

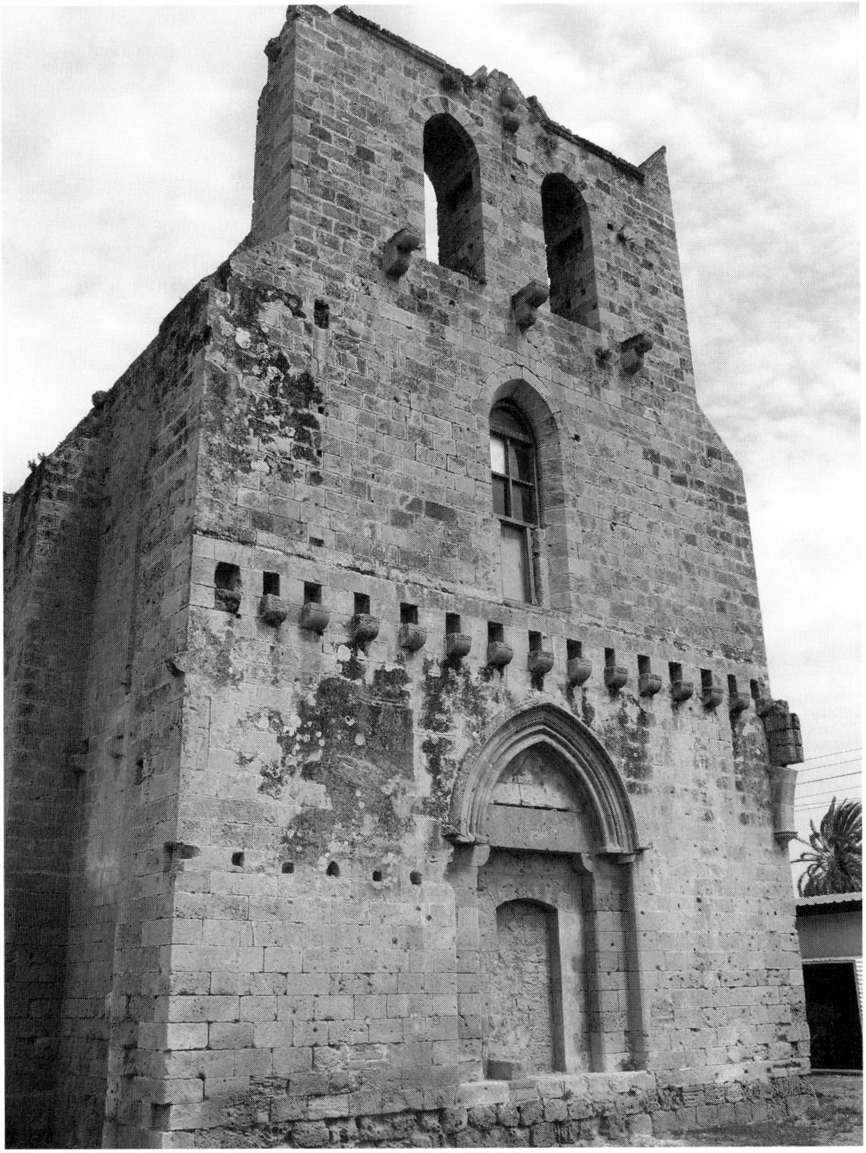

Fig. 7.4 Eglise Sainte-Anne, vue générale extérieure (photograph: Allan Langdale)

Enfin, les indications topographiques de la documentation génoise permettent aussi de situer le couvent des Prêcheurs dans cette zone proche du château.[46]

Les Carmes furent implantés à partir de 1311 dans cette partie nouvellement lotie de la ville, au nord-ouest, près de l'actuel bastion Martinengo, le long

Pierre Pilosus: « … *in presencia domini Michaelis vicecomitis Famagoste pro domino rege Cipri et juratorum curie dicti domini regis de Famagoste.* »; Pavoni, *Notai genovesi in oltremare* (CSFS 32), n° 122, pp. 153–5, 15 septembre 1301, « …*ante castellanum Famagoste… recepi a iuratis eiusdem curie* ». Le terme latin de *curia* correspond à la *corte* de la chronique de Bustron.

[46] Otten-Froux, 'Notes sur quelques monuments de Famagouste à la fin du Moyen Age', pp. 147–8.

de la rue longeant les remparts. Les bâtiments conventuels s'élevaient au sud de l'église, mais ils ont disparu: il ne subsiste que des traces de leur implantation sur le flanc de l'édifice, conservée (Figure 7.3). Le souverain a choisi l'emplacement, mais il a certainement aussi participé à la construction, puisqu'une des trois clefs de voûte gisant encore à terre porte la croix de Jérusalem, emblème royal que l'on retrouve sur la façade, associé au lion des armes personnelles des Lusignans. Une frise héraldique peinte dans l'abside représente aussi les écartelés de 'Chypre ancien' et le lion des Lusignans. Le couvent était mitoyen de celui des Arméniens, implantés exactement en même temps, et voisin de ceux d'autres communautés orientales avec lesquelles les Carmes entretenaient traditionnellement un dialogue religieux.[47] Cette organisation témoigne d'une implantation réfléchie de tout un groupe d'établissements conventuels.

L'implication des laïcs

Comme en témoignent les nombreux legs testamentaires en faveur des ordres mendiants, la vocation des frères d'encadrer spirituellement la population urbaine a été pleinement réalisée.[48] Nobles et bourgeois choisissent d'ailleurs fréquemment leurs églises pour dernière demeure. Les deux édifices subsistants, des Franciscains et des Carmes, témoignent dans leur structure même de cette nouvelle participation des laïcs. Ainsi l'église des frères mineurs présente les restes de deux emmarchements marquant les espaces liturgiques. L'un, à l'entrée de l'abside, délimitait le sanctuaire, dont la clef, aujourd'hui à terre, était placée au-dessus de l'autel et sculptée de l'*Agnus Dei*. L'autre, en marbre, séparait la travée contiguë à l'abside -le chœur des frères-des deux premières travées réservées aux laïcs, dont l'entrée se faisait par la façade. Dans ce dernier espace, trois enfeus sont encore visibles dans les restes du mur de la première travée. Les parois latérales de la deuxième travée ont été percées entre les deux contreforts, de chaque côté, afin d'insérer deux chapelles. Seule la chapelle sud subsiste, en assez bon état, avec les restes d'un autel (celle du nord n'est plus qu'à l'état de fondations). Comme les enfeus, les fonctions des chapelles étaient funéraires. Leur adjonction dans la première moitié du XIVe siècle[49] et les nombreuses dalles funéraires, retrouvées par

47 La Vie de saint Pierre Thomas, mentionne en 1365-1366 la proximité du Carmel avec les couvents des Arméniens, des Grecs et d'autres communautés « schismatiques » ainsi que des Latins, appuyant l'hypothèse que cette zone nouvellement lotie avait été dévolue aux communautés religieuses. Philippe de Mézières, 'Vita sancti Petri Thomasii', *Acta Sanctorum*, janvier, 2: 1005. « *Et eisdem horis, quibus sic in orationibus prostratus erat, ignis de coelo super cameram ipsius per Armenos et alios ibi vicinos et confines visus est quampluries descendere. Quod miraculum non solum per praefatos Armenos et Graecos, verum etiam per schismaticos et fidei Catholicae alienos, et qui hoc, ut dictum est, viderant, est indubitanter approbatum* ».

48 Coureas, pp. 226–9.

49 Plagnieux et Soulard, 'Famagouste, l'église des Franciscains', p. 242.

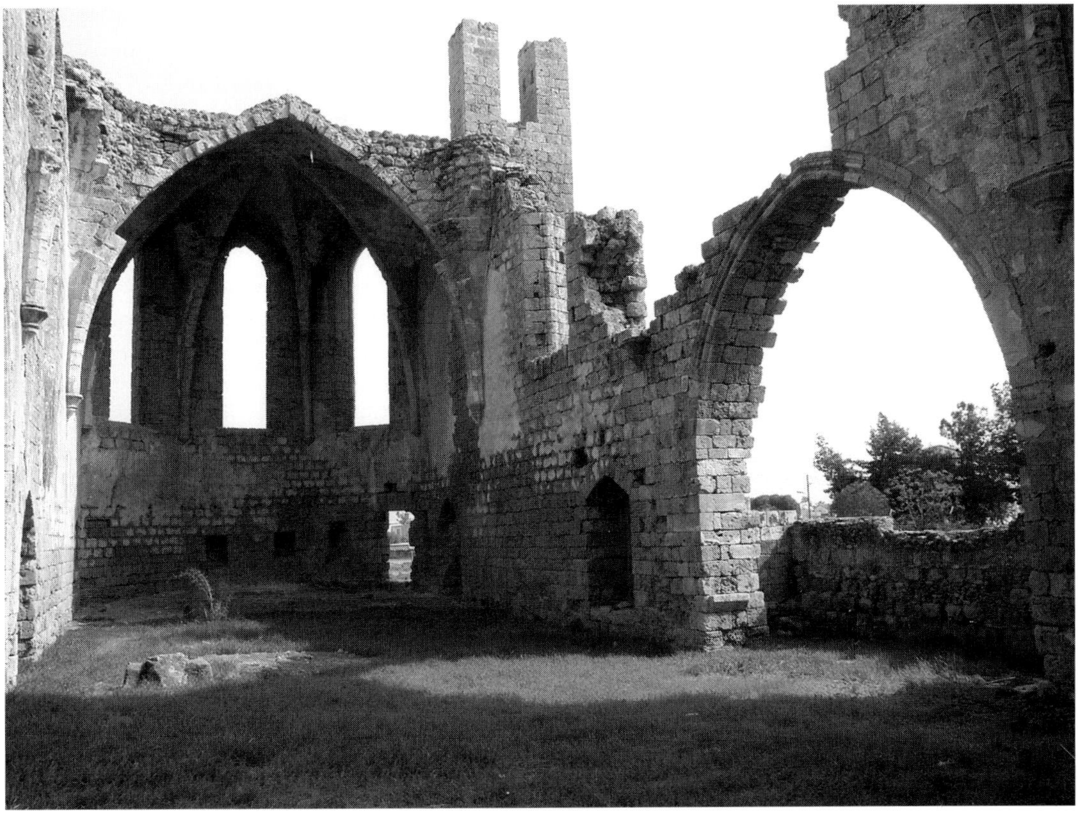

Fig. 7.5 Eglise des Carmes, vue intérieure vers l'abside (photograph: Thomas Kaffenberger)

Camille Enlart lors de ses fouilles en 1901,[50] témoignent du succès grandissant des Mendiants auprès des laïcs.

L'église des Carmes (les figures 7.3 et 7.5; voir aussi les figures 15.7 et 15.8), en ruines elle-aussi mais mieux conservée, offre le même type de répartition des espaces, ménageant une place importante pour les laïcs. Le sanctuaire, limité à l'abside, était aussi matérialisé par un emmarchement. Sur l'un des pans coupés de l'abside, côté sud, à côté du lavabo lié à l'autel, une porte donnait accès à une sacristie, détruite. Une autre porte percée dans le mur droit de l'abside communiquait avec le bâtiment des religieux et le dortoir, dont il ne subsiste plus que l'empreinte sur le flanc de l'édifice. La troisième travée de l'église, contiguë à l'abside, abritait le chœur des Carmes: une porte ouvrait sur le cloître, dont on perçoit les arrachements à l'extérieur. Comme à Saint-François, dont le plan est très proche, les deux premières travées occidentales étaient destinées aux laïcs. Sans passage vers les bâtiments conventuels, cet espace ouvrait sur la ville par le portail percée dans la façade occidentale. Cette dernière, ouvrant vers la ville par la rue adjacente, est d'ailleurs la seule partie de l'édifice ayant reçu une ornementation.

50 C. Enlart, 'Fouilles dans les églises de Famagouste de Chypre', *The Archaeological Journal* (déc. 1905): 7–23.

Cinq enfeus ont été ménagés dans les murs, dont quatre dans la première travée, et deux chapelles peu profondes ont été ouvertes ultérieurement entre les contreforts de la seconde travées, évoquant le même aménagement que dans l'église des frères mineurs. La majorité des sépultures se trouvait donc dans l'espace des laïcs. Une pierre tombale de marbre blanc, retrouvée au milieu du chœur des religieux par Camille Enlart, à une place particulièrement honorifique, présente un intérêt particulier. Représentant un chevalier en armure, elle avait été « écrasée par la chute d'une clef de voûte, armoriée du même blason que le tombeau ».[51] L'épitaphe montre qu'il s'agissait de Gui Babin, mort en 1363, appartenant à un haut lignage qui joua un grand rôle dans l'histoire de Chypre. L'emplacement de la tombe ainsi que les armes sur la clef de voûte prouvent que le personnage, et probablement avant lui sa famille, avaient été des bienfaiteurs de l'abbaye. Ce lignage avait sûrement participé au financement du chantier. Enfin, la présence d'une clef de voûte avec une figure héraldique d'aigle pourrait être mise en relation avec les armes de l'archevêque de Nicosie, Jean de Conti, présent à Chypre entre 1319 et 1332, qui aurait alors appuyé la construction.

Questions de style

Deux églises des ordres mendiants subsistent aujourd'hui, à l'état de ruines, il ne reste rien des autres, pas plus que des bâtiments conventuels. Elles offrent cependant suffisamment d'éléments architecturaux pour caractériser un style qui tranche délibérément avec celui, richement orné, du gothique rayonnant adopté dans la première phase de construction de la cathédrale (Figure 7.6 and Plate 1) ainsi qu' à l'église Saint-Georges des Latins (see also Figure 17.3 and Figure 15.10).[52] L'austérité des constructions des Mendiants revêt une dimension spirituelle essentielle, en conférant au dépouillement et à la pauvreté des bâtiments un caractère emblématique.[53] Les églises Saint-François et Sainte Marie du Carmel offrent des plans similaires constitués d'une seule nef terminée par une abside à pans coupés. En élévation les murs sont percés d'étroites fenêtres, contrastant avec les larges baies à remplages des édifices rayonnants. Enfin, les ogives supportant les voûtes reposent sur des consoles et non sur des faisceaux de colonnettes.

L'église des Franciscains[54] (Figure 7.2) est totalement en ruines, et plus rien ne subsiste des bâtiments conventuels, qu'il est même impossible de situer précisément.[55] Il est probable que le couvent a été abandonné dès la période

51 Ibid., pp. 2–4.

52 T. Soulard, 'La diffusion de l'architecture gothique à Chypre', *Cahiers du Centre d'Études chypriotes*, 36 (2006): 73–124.

53 T. Soulard, 'Une spiritualité renouvelée dans la pierre. L'architecture des ordres mendiants', *Dossiers de l'archéologie, L'architecture religieuse médiévale, art roman et art gothique, une nouvelle vision*, 319 (janvier–février 2007): 92–9.

54 Plagnieux et Soulard, 'Famagouste, l'église des Franciscains', pp. 238–42.

55 Le voyageur Nicolas Martoni louait en 1395 la beauté des lieux, tout en

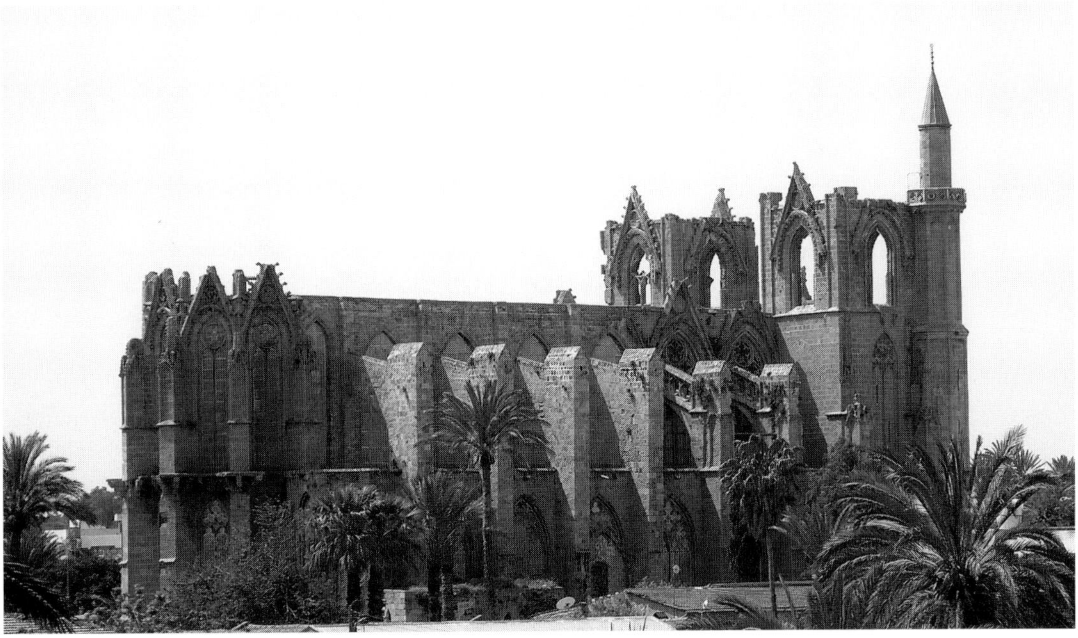

Fig. 7.6 Cathédrale Saint-Nicolas, vue générale du flanc nord (photograph: Thierry Soulard)

vénitienne, puisque Pierre Mésange ne le mentionne pas lors de son passage en 1507,[56] et surtout il ne figure pas sur le plan de Gibellino de 1571, pourtant fort exhaustif. Seule une partie du flanc sud de l'église, avec une chapelle ajoutée ultérieurement -relativement bien conservée-, ainsi que les murs de l'abside et une partie de la façade ont subsisté. On peut cependant en restituer facilement la structure. Les trois grandes travées de nef sont de plan carré, voûtées d'ogives quadripartites, et comportent des arcs formerets, qu'on ne retrouve pas dans les autres églises conservées de Famagouste. L'abside à pans coupés est couverte d'une voûte à six branches. Le profil de ces dernières, constitué de trois tores, diffère des nervures de la nef, au profil comportant deux tores séparés par un méplat, témoignant ainsi de la volonté de différencier le sanctuaire abritant l'autel. Les ogives reposent sur des consoles ornées de longues feuilles en forme de languettes à l'aspect métallique. Elles présentent le même type que celles des chapiteaux de la cathédrale. Chaque travée est percée de fenêtres étroites et allongées qui ménagent de larges surfaces murales. Bien que les remplages aient totalement disparu, les arrachements permettent d'affirmer que les baies étaient subdivisées en deux lancettes. Extérieurement, de puissants contreforts épaulent le bâtiment. La façade est

remarquant la pauvreté du couvent: *Relation du pèlerinage à Jérusalem de Nicolas de Martoni, notaire italien (1394–1395)*, ed. L. Le Grand, *Revue de l'Orient latin* 3 (1895). Le dernier témoignage d'acticité de cet établissement est la pierre tombale retrouvée par Enlart lors de fouilles, datée 1476: C. Enlart, 'Fouilles dans les églises de Famagouste de Chypre', p. 21. La transformation de l'église en bain par les Ottomans après 1571 a achevé de ruiner l'édifice.

[56] *Journal de pèlerinage au Saint-Sépulcre de Pierre Mésenge* ..., Bibliothèque municipale d'Amiens, manuscrit, fonds. Lescalopier 98, fol. 89.

empreinte de la même austérité, une simple porte surmontée d'une baie. Deux chapelles ont été ajoutées ultérieurement, greffées entre les contreforts de la deuxième travée. Celle du sud, la seule conservée, présente des caractères comparables à ceux des chapelles ajoutées sur le flanc sud de la cathédrale ainsi qu'à ceux des églises Saint-Pierre-Saint-Paul et Saint-Georges des Grecs vers le milieu du XIVe siècle: arc d'entrée au profil assez lourd, bases décorées de modillons de plinthe, chapiteaux et ogives.

Malgré son austérité, en fonction des préceptes de l'ordre fixés après le chapitre général de Narbonne de 1260, l'église montre quelques éléments communs avec la cathédrale, comme les ornements végétaux des consoles. En effet, l'édifice remonte à l'extrême fin du XIIIe siècle, alors que débutait le chantier de la cathédrale. Le maître d'œuvre avait parfaitement assimilé l'architecture des églises des ordres mendiants, mais les équipes de tailleurs de pierre n'avaient sans doute pas la même familiarité avec l'architecture gothique. En effet, les ogives ne sont pas solidaires des voûtains: ce sont de simples éléments plaqués sur l'arête des voûtains, appareillés en dents de scie.[57] Cette particularité existait déjà en Terre sainte, dans la salle des chevaliers du Krak où une ogive plaquée s'est intégralement détachée alors que les autres subsistent. Elle se retrouve sur d'autres monuments chypriotes, en particulier dans l'église des Carmes.

Du couvent des Carmes il ne reste que l'église, un peu moins ruinée que celle des frères mineurs.[58] Le voyageur Nicolas de Martoni décrit ainsi les lieux en 1394:[59] « Il y a dans la cité un monastère de Sainte-Marie du Carmel. L'église est très belle et très digne, voûtée, avec des chapelles latérales, avec de très belles scènes peintes; il y a un très beau cloître avec des oranges et d'autres fruits, il existe un dortoir et plusieurs autres bâtiments pour l'usage des frères. Dans cette église, j'ai vu les saintes reliques suivantes: le chef de sainte Ursule dans un très beau reliquaire d'argent, un tibia de saint Léon pape, le chef de saint Cufinus et celui de saint Sosius, et du bois de la sainte Croix du Seigneur ». Les bâtiments conventuels s'élevaient sur le flanc sud de l'église. S'ils ont entièrement disparu, ils ont cependant laissé une empreinte qui permet d'en comprendre l'organisation. Contre la travée droite aveugle de l'abside, il existait un bâtiment à étage dont subsistent seulement les traces d'encastrement de poutres sur deux niveaux: il comprenait probablement une salle capitulaire surmontée d'un dortoir. Un campanile s'élève d'ailleurs sur le contrefort voisin. Comme le prouve cette empreinte, le bâtiment des religieux était donc en matériau léger, probablement en bois, selon les usages de l'ordre. Le dortoir communiquait à l'étage avec l'église par un arc dont il reste les quelques assises. Plus à l'est, contre le pan coupé de l'abside, se trouvait probablement une sacristie, dont on peut encore voir l'arrachement.

57 On observe le même type d'ogives plaquées sur certains monuments du sud de la France, par exemple, sur les ruines de l'église du monastère cistercien Saint-Félix de Montceau, de l'extrême fin du XIIIe siècle

58 Plagnieux et Soulard, 'Famagouste, l'église Sainte-Marie du Carmel', pp. 251–6.

59 Cité par C. Enlart, *L'art gothique et de la renaissance en Chypre* (Paris, 1899): 337.

Le départ du mur de clôture est visible à l'arrière de cette sacristie. Le long des travées occidentales de la nef s'élevait sans doute le cloître cité par Martoni, comme le montre l'amorce d'un arc. L'escalier en vis pris dans le contrefort sud de la façade ouvrait sur le couvent, au-dessus de la galerie du cloître, par une porte qui donne aujourd'hui dans le vide. Dans le prolongement de la façade, on observe le départ du mur de clôture côté occidental.

Le plan de l'église, de trois travées terminées par une abside à pans coupés, avec l'adjonction ultérieure de deux chapelles latérales au niveau de la deuxième travée –citées par Martoni-, correspond à celui des Franciscains. Toutefois, l'élévation de l'église Sainte-Marie du Carmel est encore plus austère et dépouillée. De grands contreforts épaulent la paroi nue, sans animation plastique ni décor, lui conférant une rigueur extrême. Les baies, constituées d'étroites lancettes, ne comportent ni remplage, ni archivolte, ni aucune mouluration; elles semblent percées à l'emporte-pièce. L'édifice devait recevoir un éclairage parcimonieux, d'autant plus que la travée droite de l'abside est aveugle, mettant en valeur les trois fenêtres du fond, pour moduler l'éclairage autour de l'autel. L'abside était couverte par six branches d'ogives, aujourd'hui détachées des voûtains, et la nef par trois voûtes quadripartites. Le profil des nervures est extrêmement simple, une section carrée à angles abattu, d'un type identique à celui de l'hôpital Saint-Antoine et des parties basses du château de Famagouste. Elles retombaient sur des consoles sans décor, en forme de pyramide renversée. La simplicité de ces éléments n'empêche pas une exécution très soignée, à la stéréotomie parfaite. Seule la façade tranche par son décor sur le dépouillement du reste de l'édifice. Elle est encadrée par deux grands contreforts polygonaux –celui du sud renferme l'escalier en vis lié aux bâtiments du cloître. Un porche a été ajouté ultérieurement, coupant les sculptures à mi-hauteur. Une grande baie à trois lancettes surmonte le portail:[60] elle s'inspire du décor rayonnant de la cathédrale. Enfin, entre les deux niveaux, trois écus sculptés présentent les armes royales. Cette façade relativement ornée, comme nous l'avons vu, ouvrait sur la ville et le monde des laïcs, ce qui explique ce choix stylistique contrastant avec le reste du monument.

Le décor peint, observé par Camille Enlart qui y avait relevé plusieurs phases de réalisation,[61] est aujourd'hui en grande partie détruit ou effacé. Enlart avait identifié sur la travée droite de l'abside côté sud sainte Hélène, représentation probablement en rapport avec les reliques de la sainte Croix conservées dans l'église d'après Martoni. De saints évêques en habits sacerdotaux latins et grecs, parmi lesquels on peut identifier encore saint Nicolas, sont aussi peints dans l'abside, et font peut-être écho à la préoccupation particulière des Carmes de promouvoir l'union des Eglises. Côté nord, saint Georges est encore visible. Sur le revers de la façade, Enlart a pu distinguer des religieux en habit de Carmes, aujourd'hui presque totalement effacés. Cette iconographie vient à

---

60 Ces éléments ont fait l'objet d'importantes restaurations, mais la structure originelle en a été respectée.

61 Enlart, *L'art gothique,* pp. 342-7.

l'appui de l'identification du couvent, par ailleurs bien établie par les sources historiques et le plan de Gibellino.

Le style gothique rayonnant adopté à la cathédrale Saint-Nicolas et à l'église Saint-Georges des Latins qui s'en inspire n'est pas une transposition directe de modèles de l'Ile-de-France, mais puise à un fonds ornemental véhiculé par des carnets de modèles dont l'existence a été prouvée (Figure 7.7). Il dénote en outre une certaine influence des ordres mendiants, peut-être déjà diffusée en Terre sainte. Le plan de la cathédrale, avec une large nef flanquée d'étroits collatéraux, sans transept, et un chevet formé de trois absides polygonales, reprend celui de la cathédrale d'Acre étudié par Denis Pringle. L'élévation est simplifiée avec deux niveaux, grandes arcades et fenêtres hautes, sans triforium. Ce type de plan et d'élévation simplifiés se retrouve au sud de la France à la fin du XIIIe siècle, dans une zone où les couvents mendiants se sont implantés très tôt. Ainsi, parmi de nombreux exemples, l'église de Montagnac en Languedoc (vers 1300) présente ce même type de plan à trois vaisseaux sans transept fermés par des absides à pans coupés ainsi qu'une élévation à deux niveaux, synthétisant la double influence rayonnante et mendiante. La diffusion de ce style, au-delà du Midi de la France, s'est étendue à toute l'Europe et probablement à la Terre sainte (l'absence de monument conservé interdisant toute véritable comparaison). Le prédécesseur de Guy, l'évêque qui a lancé les travaux de Saint-Nicolas, était un dominicain, Mancellus.

Comme nous l'avons démontré, c'est très probablement sous ce prélat que le projet a été élaboré et les choix stylistiques effectués. Les travaux ont en effet débuté dès l'accession de Guy à l'épiscopat en 1298, comme le laissent supposer les emprunts contractés à cet effet, le chantier étant en pleine activité en 1300.[62] L'art gothique rayonnant introduit à Chypre avait déjà été quelque peu modulé sous l'influence des ordres mendiants. Quant à la seconde campagne de la cathédrale (les travées centrales), elle a marqué l'adoption d'un style dépouillé directement tiré de l'architecture des églises de Mendiants. Nous restons convaincus que la pierre indiquant la reprise des travaux en 1311 après une interruption de quelques années due aux troubles politiques n'a pas été placée par hasard sur le troisième contrefort du flanc ouest: elle est exactement à l'emplacement du changement de parti entre les trois travées occidentales avec leurs six voûtes et le nouveau style simplifié. Sans revenir précisément dans le cadre de cette publication sur les arguments que nous avons déjà exposé en détail dans un précédent ouvrage, nous ne pouvons être d'accord avec les thèses d'Arne Franke, qui revient à la chronologie de Camille Enlart, avec quelques nouveaux arguments mais qui nous semblent tout autant discutables. La netteté de la reprise, au nord et au sud, au même emplacement des fenêtres hautes, exclut l'hypothèse d'une large reconstruction de l'époque ottomane. Plus encore, les arcs boutants constitués d'une volée simple et de culées dépourvue de tout ornement et, dans une certaine mesure, les fenêtres sans remplages ont servi de référence

---

62 Plagnieux et Soulard, 'Famagouste, la cathédrale Saint-Nicolas', p. 219.

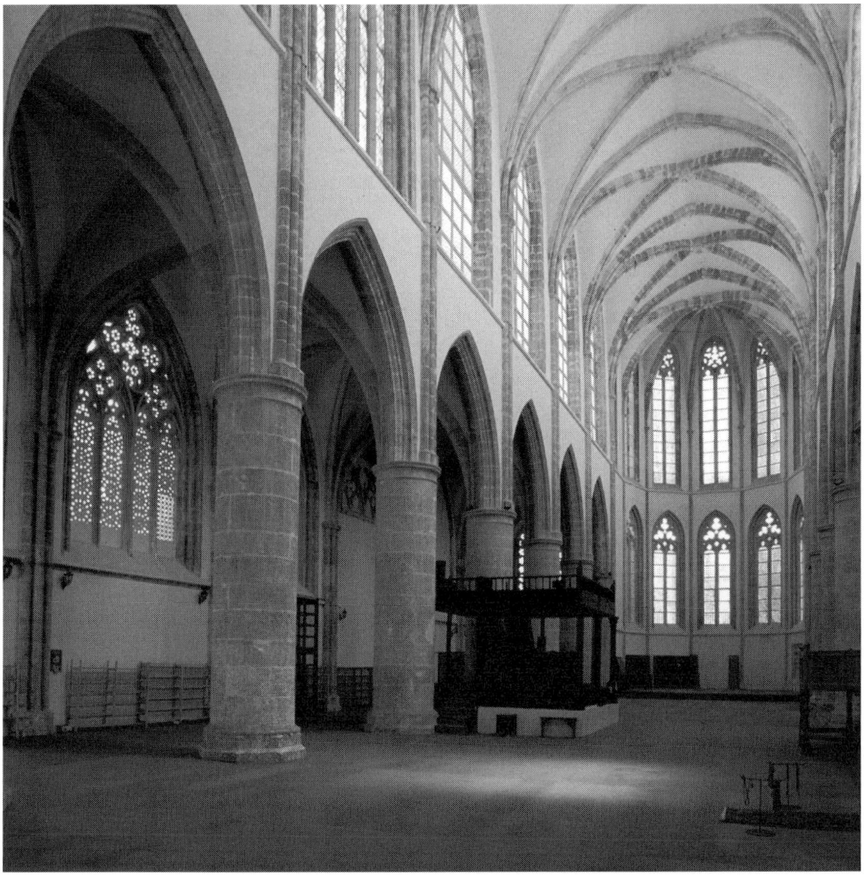

Fig. 7.7 Cathédrale Saint-Nicolas de Famagouste, élévation intérieure (photograph: Thierry Soulard)

à des édifices postérieurs de Famagouste, comme Saint-Pierre-Saint-Paul et Saint-Georges-des-Grecs vers le milieu du XIVe siècle.

Le cas de l'église Sainte-Anne est plus simple. Comme nous l'avons démontré, elle appartenait à un monastère de Bénédictines, à la suite de Sainte-Anne de Nicosie, en référence au monastère Sainte-Anne de Jérusalem.[63] L'identification de l'édifice n'est pas douteuse, grâce au plan de Gibellino. L'église (Figure 7.4), datable du deuxième quart du XIVe siècle, est constituée d'une nef de deux travées fermée par une abside polygonale, reprenant le plan de Saint-François et du Carmel. Son élévation (see Figure 12.6) est percée d'étroites fenêtres qui évoquent aussi le Carmel. L'abside est voûtée d'ogives qui reposent sur des consoles, la nef étant couverte de voûtes d'arêtes –cette différence marquant probablement les espaces liturgiques. Cette esthétique austère traduit l'adoption presque complète du style des ordres Mendiants, en particulier du Carmel voisin, à l'exception des voûtes d'arêtes qui font plutôt référence aux constructions romanes de Terre sainte, d'où était originaire la congrégation. Cette forte attraction architecturale exercée sur les autres

63 Plagnieux, Soulard, 'Famagouste, l'église Sainte-Anne', pp. 261–5.

communautés monastiques par les Mendiants se retrouve partout en Occident à la même époque. Par exemple, dès la fin du XIIIe siècle, la cathédrale d'Albi, dont l'évêque était fortement marqué par la spiritualité franciscaine, reflète ces idéaux de pauvreté et de dépouillement. A partir des années 1345, l'église du monastère bénédictin de La Chaise-Dieu, reconstruite par le pape Clément VI qui y avait prévu sa sépulture, s'inspire totalement de cette esthétique (unité spatiale, fenêtres étroites mettant en valeur les murs nus et sévères, ogives puissantes avec des éléments de modénature à angles vifs). On peut encore citer, parmi bien d'autres références, la collégiale Saint-Didier d'Avignon fondée en 1355 par le cardinal Bertrand de Déaux.

L'architecture des ordres mendiants, en phase avec la spiritualité du moment, est devenue une véritable référence pour les églises de Famagouste dès le second quart du XIVe siècle, y compris pour les communautés non latines pour lesquelles elle était facilement adaptable. Son esthétique austère, s'exprimant par des volumes simples, des surfaces murales dépouillées percées d'étroites fenêtres, se retrouve par exemple à l'église des Arméniens, à Saint-Pierre-Saint-Paul, à Saint-Georges des Grecs ou dans les églises jumelles.[64] Toutefois, elle se combine avec des formes léguées par la Terre sainte romane, telles les absides voûtées en cul-de-four ou les voûtes d'arêtes, engendrant ainsi un style original.

---

64 Soulard, 'La diffusion de l'architecture gothique à Chypre'; T. Soulard, 'L'architecture gothique grecque du royaume des Lusignan', *Identités croisées en un milieu méditerranéen: Le cas de Chypre (Antiquité-Moyen Age)*, ed. S. Fourrier et G. Grivaud (Rouen, 2006): 359–88.

The Holy Mother of God Armenian Church in Famagusta

Dickran Kouymjian

In the spring of 1974, shortly before the events that resulted in the division of the island, my wife and I were able to visit and quickly photograph the Armenian Church known as St Mary in Famagusta (Plate 3). A family we assumed was Turkish inhabited the church. The parents were at work and the children, a boy and girl who were both very young adolescents, let us enter and examine the interior (Figure 8.1). The slides and photographs were taken without extra lighting or a tripod. Upon our return to Lebanon, someone at the Catholicosate of the Great House of Cilicia in Antelias, under whose jurisdiction the diocese of Cyprus falls, informed us that the family was in fact probably Armenian. This I could not verify. I was unable to devote time to the study of the church and the medieval frescoes that covered its walls until two years later when I presented a paper on it to the XVth International Byzantine Congress in Athens.[1] A second paper followed some years later at the 25th Spring Symposium of Byzantine Studies at the University of Birmingham.[2] Neither paper was published, and the texts or drafts of them appear to have been lost. It is only lately through conferences in Montpellier and Antelias that my interest in this material has been reawakened thanks to Michael Walsh, Nicolas Coureas and Brunehilde Imhaus. More recent work on Famagusta and on the Armenian Church makes me doubt whether my documentation, once interesting because of the timing of our visit, is of much scientific importance. Nevertheless, it seems to me that presenting some of this material, augmented by a survey of the sources and literature in Armenian on the church, might in some small way contribute to the interest in preserving and restoring this monument along with others in Famagusta and elsewhere in Cyprus.

There are no specific records relating to the circumstances or the date of the church's construction in Armenian sources. Latin documents, however, are quite explicit. According to a papal bull of 1311, the church's construction

1 Athens, 5–11 September 1976: 'The Frescoes of the Armenian Church in Famagusta, Cyprus: Preliminary Report'.

2 Birmingham, 25–28 March 1991: 'Armenian Art in Cyprus in the 14th Century'.

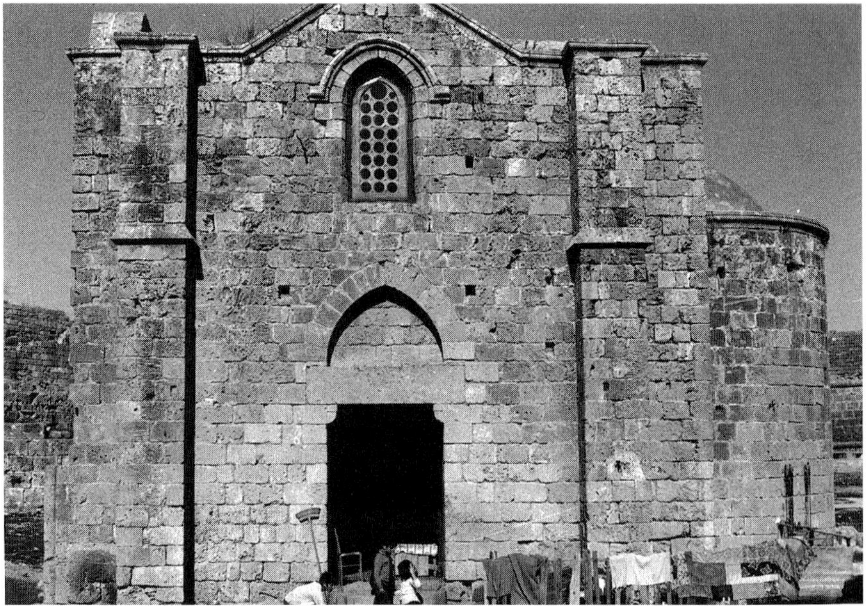

Fig. 8.1 Armenian Church with residents in 1974 (photograph: Dickran Kouymjian)

had recently started,[3] and a further papal letter indicates that it had been completed by 1317.[4] The stone church lacks inscriptions of any sort. The principal western authors, Camille Enlart, George Jeffery, Jean-Bernard de Vaivre and Philippe Plagnieux,[5] concur that the church of St Mary is datable to the fourteenth century, some like Enlart placing it late in the century.

3 *Regestum Clementis V*, ed. cura et studio monachorum Ordinis S. Benedicti, 8 vols (Rome, 1885–92), no. 7209 (10 August 1311): '... in civitate Famagustane ad honorem ipsius Virginis quandam ecclesiam vocatam beate Marie de Vert, de licentia venerabilis fratris nostri episcopi Famagustane, in qua presbyteri Armeni habentur inibi Domino servientes, de novo edificare inceperit'. Quoted in part in P. Plagnieux and T. Soulard, 'Famagouste. L'Église des Arméniens (Sainte-Marie-de-Vert)', in J.-B. de Vaivre and P. Plagnieux, *L'Art Gothique en Chypre* (Paris, 2006), 258, n. 6, cf p. 260 for the dates.

4 *Lettre communes de Jean XXII*, ed. G. Mollat, 16 vols (Paris, 1904–47), no. 6022 (13 December 1317): 'Episcopo et capitulo Famagustan mandatur ut de tertia parte reddituum ecclesie Famagustane, juxta antiquam consuetudinem regni Cypri pauperibus erogari solita, 200 argenti bisantios annis singulis usque ad quinquennium cleribus pauperibus Armenis commorantibus in ecclesia S. M. Viridis Famagustan assignari faciant.' Quoted by Plagnieux and Soulard, 'Famagouste', p. 258, n. 7. This is confirmed in a letter of 13 April 1318. Mollat, no. 6958; Plagnieux and Soulard, p. 258, n. 8. 'Episcopo et capitulo Famagustan mandatur ut de tertia parte reddituum ecclesie Famagustane, juxta antiquam consuetudinem regni Cypri pauperibus erogari solita, 200 argenti bisantios aniis singulis usque ad quinquennium cleribus pauperibus Armenis commorantibus in ecclesia S. M. Viridis Famamagustan assignari faciant.'

5 C. Enlart, *L'art gothique et la Renaissance en Chypre*, 2 vols (Paris, 1899); English trans. by D. Hunt, *Gothic Art and the Renaissance in Cyprus* (London, 1987), 286–8; G. Jeffery, *A Description of the Historic Monuments of Cyprus: Studies in the Archaeology and Architecture of the Island* (Nicosia, 1918, repr. London, 1983), 143; Plagnieux and Soulard, op. cit., pp. 257–60.

The major Armenian studies by Vahan Kurkjian, Arshak Alpoyachian, Babgén Gulesserian, Ghevond Ch'épéyan,[6] while providing primary source references from the first quarter of the fourteenth century, postulate an earlier foundation going back in some cases to the late twelfth century, during the time of Nersés of Lambron (1153–98).

Armenians have been in Cyprus since early Byzantine times. Several Byzantine governors of the island were of Armenian origin, but relations between Armenians and Cyprus became close during the period of the Crusades, which corresponds to the establishment of an Armenian presence, and eventually in 1198 a kingdom, in Cilicia. In the latter twelfth century there was already a prelate, a certain T'adéos, bishop of Cyprus, who signed a declaration of faith in 1179 prepared by Catholicos Grigor IV (1173–93) at the request of Emperor Manuel I Comnenus (1143–80).[7] Later, in 1307, Catholicos Grigor VII convoked a church council in Sis and among those present was the Prelate of Cyprus, Bishop Nikoghayos.[8] In the early fourteenth century the Cilician Armenian nobility was very active in Cyprus. In 1308 after the renovation by Henry II of a convent attached to the Latin church of Notre Dame de Tyr in Nicosia, Princess Euphemia (Armenian, Fimi), daughter of the Armenian king Het'um I, was appointed Mother Superior.[9] Earlier in 1305 her cousin Het'um the historian, known as Hayton in the Latin sources, author of the famous *Fleur des histoires de la terre d'Orient*, and himself the son of Oshin, brother of King Het'um I, came to Cyprus. He was back in Cyprus in 1308 after a sojourn in Europe.[10]

It is in this context that we first hear of the Armenian Church in Famagusta of the Holy Mother of God, in Armenian, *Surb Astuvacacin*, a literal translation of Theotokos. Our information comes entirely from colophons of Armenian manuscripts copied in Cyprus. The earliest reference to such a church is the colophon of a Gospel manuscript dated 1280: 'I, Petros of Cilicia, came to … the island of Cyprus, at [the church] of the Holy Mother of God (*i dur'n Srbuhoy Astuacacnin*) … [and] completed the copying of these Gospels.'[11] Although no locality on the island is mentioned the reference is most probably to Famagusta.

6 Bakuran (Vahan M. K'iwrkchian/Kurkjian), *Kipros kghzin* (*The Island of Cyprus*) (Nicosia, 1903), 51; A. Alpoyachian, 'Kipros kghzin (Ir ants'ealn u hnerkan)' ('The Island of Cyprus (Its Past and Present)'), *T'eodik Yearbook* (1927), 192–239; BAK (Babgen Archbishop Kiwleserian/Gulesserian), *Hay Kiprose* (*Armenian Cyprus*) (Antelias, 1936), 46, 53, 71; Bishop Ghevond (Ch'épéyan), *Yishadakaran kiprahay gaghut'i* (*Memorial on the Cypriot-Armenian Community*) (Antelias, 1955), 2.

7 M. Ch'amch'ian, *Hayots' patmutiwn* (*Armenian History*), vol. 3 (Venice, 1786), 132: 'T'adéos epis. Kiprosi'. See also Gulesserian, *Armenian Cyprus*, p. 53.

8 Bishop Ghevond, *Cypriot-Armenian Community*, p. 2.

9 Ibid.

10 But in the same year he was forced to return to Cilician Armenia when his son-in-law, Oshin, became king. See A. Kapoïan-Kouymjian, *L'Égypte vue par des Arméniens (XIe–XVIIe siècle)* (Paris, 1988), 55–6.

11 New Julfa, Armenian Prelacy, manuscript no. 33, fo. 335. See also A. Mat'evosyan, *Hayeren jer'agreri hishatakaranner. XIII dar* (*Colophons of Armenian Manuscripts: Thirteenth Century*) (Erevan, 1984), no. 408, p. 510.

The only other church that might have been so designated by the Armenians was that of Notre Dame de Tyr in Nicosia, but that was a Latin church despite such converts as the later Armenian head of the convent, Euphemia. The church was only given to the Armenians shortly after the Ottoman conquest of Cyprus in 1570. Slightly later, in 1287, the scribe Khach'atur, along with other scribes, copied another Gospel book in Cyprus under the protection of SS Var'var'a and Sargis the General, again without mentioning a specific locality.[12]

The first direct reference to Famagusta is from 1305 in a colophon that Jacobus Dashian found in a codex of 1773, a collation of Old Testament manuscripts. It was in the collection of the Mekhitarist fathers of Vienna and copied an older colophon from a manuscript in the Armenian Patriarchate of Jerusalem.[13] Unfortunately, a search through the Jerusalem catalogue has failed to find the precise manuscript.[14] The colophon is by Yohannés the scribe: in 1305 '... at Maghuayn of Cyprus, ... remember Yohannés the writer'. Bishop Ghevond corrects the reading to Maghu[s]ayn, that is to say Maghusa/Famagusta. In 1306 and again in 1308, Levon the priest copied two psalters in Cyprus, both of which are now in the Jerusalem collection; the first at a village called Cips/Djips (today Kornokipos/Kornodjipos) under the protection of the archangels, Mikayel and Gabriel, and the second at Maghusa, but without a reference to the church of St Mary.[15] Colophons of 1308 and 1309 by Yohannés with Step'anos the priest as patron in an Old Testament manuscript, mention Maghusa but again without reference to the church of the Holy Mother of God.[16]

The earliest reference to both Famagusta/Maghusa and the church of the Holy Mother of God is in a manuscript containing the Acts of the Apostles and the Gospel of St John copied by a well-known scribe who was important in Cilician royal circles, the priest Step'annos Goynerits'ants' in 1310–12. 'Written in 1310 ... with the intercession of the Holy Mother of God'; and further along, 'written by Step'annos Goynerits'ants' for Lady Alic (Alice), wife of the seneschal of Cyprus ... on 29 December 1312 on the Island of Cyprus at Maghusa under the protection of the Holy Mother of God.'[17]

---

12 Erevan, Matenadaran (henceforth M), ms 6845, fo. 280, cf. Mat'evosyan, *Colophons. Thirteenth Century*, no. 495, pp. 609–10. Perhaps Famagusta as suggested by Gulesserian, *Armenian Cyprus*, p. 53.

13 J. Dashian, *Catalog den armenischen handscriften in der Mechitaristen-bibliothek zu Wien* (in Armenian with German title and *résumé*) (Vienna, 1895), no. 244, p. 632. See also Bishop Ghevond, *Cypriot-Armenian Community*, p. 56.

14 N. Bogharian, *Grand Catalogue of St. James Manuscripts*, 11 vols., in Armenian with English title, (Jerusalem, 1966–91). It was not included in L. Khach'ikyan, *XIV dari Hayeren jer'agreri hishatakaranner* (*Fourteenth-Century Armenian Manuscript Colophons*) (Erevan, 1950).

15 J1033, fo. 685 and J1926, fo. 648, Bogharian, *Jerusalem Catalogue*, 4: 45 ff. and 6: 22. The patron of the later manuscript was a certain T'oros the priest. (J = the Armenian Patriarchate of Jerusalem manuscript collection.)

16 J1926, fos 268v and 426v, Bogharian, *Catalogue*, 6: 417.

17 The original manuscript seems not to have survived. An eighteenth-century Commentary on the Acts of the Apostles copies the earlier colophon of 1310. Bogharian, *Catalogue*, 3: no. 700, p. 145. Khach'ikyan, *Fourteenth Century Colophons*, no. 92, pp. 68–9,

By this date, according to the papal bull of 1311, the church was probably under construction. Shortly afterwards in 1314, Step'annos copied another manuscript, a collection of religious texts, again for Alic, in Maghusa, Cyprus, under the protection of the Holy Mother of God and St John the Evangelist.[18]

Only in a colophon of 1317 do we read for the first time in Armenian sources that the Holy Mother of God was a monastery and that it was called Kanch'uor, pronounced Kanch'vor, translated in Latin as green.[19] As we saw above (notes 3–4) in the Latin documents, the church, referred to as 'Marie de Vert', was begun in 1311 and completed in this year 1317. The original is a colophon in a manuscript of the *Commentary on Chronology and the Liturgy* by Khosrov Anjevatsʿi and Nersés Lambronatsʿi by the scribe (also the patron and editor), Yovhanés Vardapet; it was recopied in two later manuscripts. The part of the colophon that relates to the Famagusta church is as follows: 'This book was written by the insignificant sinner Yohanés, servant of the word of God, in the year of the Armenian race 766 [=1317] on the Island of Cyprus, at the church (*tachar*) of the Mother of God (*Astucoy mor*), Theotokos (*Astuacacnin*), which is a monastery (*vank'*), and is called Kanch'uor (Kanch'vor) in this city Famagusta (*Maghusa*).'[20]

This is the first and only time, according to my records, that the Holy Mother of God in Famagusta is referred to as a monastery and is said to be called Kanch'vor, rendered in the secondary literature as 'Green'. The word *kanch'vor* is otherwise lexically unattested, but it is assumed that it is derived somehow from *kanach'*, the colour green, rather than *kanch'*, a cry, scream or lament. Yet if an Armenian wanted to say green, one would expect *kanach'avor* or the grammatically incorrect *kanch'avor*. This is a very rare appellation for the Virgin, perhaps referring to fertility of fields or a painting or fresco with a green background or showing Mary dressed in green. The only medieval church with such a name is St Mary the Green in Ascalon, itself associated

extracted from a published collection from Gherla in Transylvania, presents a slightly different version.

18 J265, fo. 300v, Bogharian, *Catalogue*, 2: 61. On Step'annos Goynerits'ants' and his relationship to the royalty of Cilician Armenia and Cyprus see H. Achar'ian, *Hayots' anjnanunneri par'aran* (*Armenian First Name Dictionary*), vol. 4 (Erevan, 1948), 635–6.

19 Gulesserian suggests that the term was already in use in 1307, even perhaps in 1179: 'It seems to us that the residence of Bishop T'adéos of Cyprus who participated in the Council of Hromkla in 1179 was Kanch'avor as was that of Bishop Nikoghayos who participated in the Council of Sis in 1307', *Hay Kipros*, p. 53. But as far as I can tell, this is projecting back from the colophon of 1317; in the acts of the Council of 1179 no specific place in Cyprus is mentioned.

20 J1142, fo. 664, Bogharian, *Catalogue*, vol. 4, p. 226 (re-copied at St. James in Jerusalem in a manuscript of the Commentary on the Liturgy by Anjevats'i in 1840. J2254, fo. 100; Bogharian, *Catalogue*, 7: 349). Khach'ikyan, *Fourteenth Century Colophons*, no. 175, p. 135, takes his information from M6273, vol. 1 of *Nshkhark'patmut'ean Hayots'* (*Fragments of the History of the Armenians*) by Ghevond P'irghalémian. The emendations by Khach'ikyan must be ignored and P'irghalémian incorrectly copied the word Kanch'uor as Kanch'ut.

with the early crusaders.[21] Perhaps another interpretation would be the monastery of the weeping or lamenting Virgin, from Armenian *kanch'*, cry, scream, shriek.

I know of no further textual references to the Famagusta church until modern times, though I have collected some 16 colophonic citations from Armenian manuscripts copied in Cyprus between 1318 and 1679. Seven of these refer to Levk῾osia (variant spellings: Levk῾usieay, Lôk῾oshia, Lôk῾ôshay, Lôk῾och῾a, Lôk῾ashé) and one to Nicosia (1679); those of the seventeenth century (six) consistently refer to the church of the Holy Mother of God in Levk῾oia/Nicosia.

I think it reasonable to suggest that after the first quarter of the fourteenth century the church was in decline and perhaps soon neglected. It was built sometime from the late thirteenth century to the first quarter of the fourteenth century; its frescoes must date from that latter period. It is curious that there are no references in Armenian sources to the church in the mid-fourteenth century or immediately after, when we are told by James of Verona that in 1335 there was an influx of some 1500 Armenian refugees from Cilicia.[22] In any case, when these refugees arrived in Famagusta there was an Armenian monastery, clearly attested 18 years earlier.

The modern history of St Mary suggests it was not used in the nineteenth century. In 1907 the holes in the church's walls were repaired and the main doorway was fitted with a strong gate;[23] this work was intended to protect the wall paintings inside as much as possible.[24] Babgen Gulesserian reports in 1936 that 30 years earlier, in 1906, Bishop Petros (later catholicos) of the Cilician Catholicosate upon visiting the church made a formal request to the government for the restoration of the church and its return to the Armenians. He pursued this request upon his return to Sis (today Kozan), the Holy See. The church was restored and eventually, in a letter dated 20 January 1936, given over to the Armenians for 90 years with an annual charge of five pounds sterling.[25] From the 1940s onwards an itinerant priest administered to the Armenian faithful in Limassol and Famagusta.[26] There was a school in Famagusta in the house where the teacher lived, with 17 students in 1955.[27] Church services were sometimes held there, the church being too far during

---

21 'The small church, which is built against the eastern wall of Ascalon near the Gate of Jerusalem, is thought to be St Mary the Green (Maria Viridis). It remounts to the Byzantine era, but was rebuilt anew by the Crusaders.' M. Gil, *A History of Palestine, 634–1099*, trans. E. Broido (Cambridge, 1997). For an alternative interpretation see D. Pringle , *The Churches of the Crusader Kingdom of Jerusalem: a Corpus* (Cambridge, 1993–2009), 1: 63–4.

22 C.B. Cobham, ed. and trans., *Excerpta Cypria* (Cambridge, 1908; repr. 1969), 17.

23 Jeffery, *Description*, p. 144.

24 R. Gunnis, *Historic Cyprus* (London, 1936), 40.

25 Gulesserian, *Armenian Cyprus*, pp. 73–4. He had visited the church in 1934.

26 Alexander-Michael Hadjilyra suggests it would probably have been Fr Khoren Kouligian.

27 Bishop Ghevond, *Cypriot-Armenian Community*, pp. 86–7.

inclement weather. The Armenian community in Cyprus in 1955 numbered over 4,000.[28] His Holiness Karekin I Hovsepian, catholicos of the Great House of Cilicia, made pastoral visits to Cyprus, including Famagusta, in 1946, 1947 and 1948.[29]

The Frescoes of the Church of the Holy Mother of God[30]

Architecturally Camille Enlart adequately and carefully described the church of St Mary. More recently Plagneiux and Soulard, as well as Langdale and Walsh, have repeated and augmented this information.[31] The stone church is rectangular, resembling the simple hall church or mono-nave popular in Armenia from the fifth-century conversion to Christianity until late medieval times, although the great majority of Armenian churches including such single nave affairs were domed.

All the walls of the church were frescoed, an unusual rather than usual practice. Many Armenian churches dateable to the fifth or sixth centuries were decorated with frescoes, but these, though often spectacular, represent a small minority compared to the thousands without wall paintings. Among those with cycles of paintings from the life of Christ are the tenth century churches of the Holy Cross on the island of Aght'amar[32] and SS Peter and Paul at Tat'ev. The Church of St Gregory built at Ani under the patronage of the rich merchant Tigran Honents' in 1215 has a large fresco cycle of the conversion of the Armenians to Christianity, but also liturgical scenes in the now exposed narthex. Finally, there is an important and large series of frescoes in a Byzantine-Georgian style in the northern church of Ahlata in Lori. However, iconographic parallels to the church in Famagusta must be sought primarily in miniature cycles of the abundant Armenian Gospel manuscripts from the thirteenth and fourteenth centuries and earlier.

---

28 According to the registration census of October 1956 there were 4,549 Armenians in Cyprus; I would like to thank Alexander Hadjilyra for this information.

29 Bishop Ghevond, *Cypriot-Armenian Community, passim.* Today (2007–2008) there are approximately 2,500 Armenians living in Cyprus, in addition to some 1,000 non-Cypriot Armenians working on the island.

30 Since this chapter was written the very interesting iconographic study and contextualization of the Armenian frescoes within the artistic tradition of Cyprus was published by Michele Bacci, 'The Armenian Church in Famagusta and Its Mural Decoration: Some Iconographic Remarks', *Hask hayagitakan taregirk'*, vol. XI (2007–2008, published 2009), pp. 489–508.

31 Enlart, *L'art gothique,* pp. 366–8; Plagnieux and Soulard, 'Famagouste', pp. 257–60; A. Langdale and M.J.K. Walsh, 'The Architecture, Conservation History, and Future of the Armenian Church of Famagusta, Cyprus', *Chronos* (2009), pp. 7–40.

32 N. Thierry, 'Les peintures de l'Eglise de la Sainte-Croix d'Aghtamar (915–921)', *The Second International Symposium on Armenian Art, Erevan, 1978*, vol. 3 (Erevan, 1981), 182–90.

Since 1974 much of the lower register of the frescoes in St Mary Church have been covered with whitewash.[33] Below is a listing of the scenes represented in the frescoes and details about them from traditional sources. Camille Enlart was the first to describe them at the end of the nineteenth century, but at times the positioning of the scenes is confused. G. Jeffery made a summary description of the frescoes commenting on what was still visible in his time (1918).[34] Bishop Babgen Gulesserian lamented the deterioration of the frescoes, covered with graffiti in many languages, including Armenian (Plate 5); and noted that the Armenian inscriptions were essentially unreadable, but saw the words 'St. Barbara (?), this is Abka(r) (*Surb [Var'var'é?], Abka(r)in é*)'.[35] Monica Bardswell's unpublished description of 1937 is more systematic and at times furnishes better details.

East Wall and Apse

The dome of the apse once had a *Christ in Majesty*, according to Bardswell 'probably a Majesty', although since the church is dedicated to the Mother of God, it may well have been the Virgin. Nothing was discernable in 1974. On the south side of the vault of the apse there was, so Enlart recorded, a kneeling figure with a white robe, probably a donor, with a large coat of arms above to the left. Although both Enlart and Jeffery referred to this figure, in Bardwell's time the head was missing; in 1974 nothing discernable appears on my photos, and Langdale and Walsh report nothing but bare stones at the spot. Below Enlart saw the Apostles seated with Armenian inscriptions and Bardswell referred to them as nimbed on a dark blue background; under them Enlart identified full length standing figures as the patriarchs of the Eastern church under arches, which Bardswell called canopies and Jeffery, niches. In 1934 Gulesserian was able to make the identifying Armenian inscriptions for the Apostles Thaddeus and Bartholomew.[36] Enlart saw a similar, but larger, figure on the vertical pilaster of the apse to the north. According to the latter only two of these were visible: a patriarch or ecclesiastic on the left/north side and a figure with a red cloak blessing, with a small kneeling donor to the right. On the 1974 photo of the apse, there is only the slightest glimmer of what appears as a row of seated figures just above the string course that divides the vault from the lower cylindrical back of the altar area.

---

33 Reported by Langdale and Walsh, 'Armenian Church of Famagusta', pp. 7–40.

34 Jeffery, *Description*, pp. 143–4.

35 Gulesserian, *Armenian Cyprus*, p. 73.

36 'T'adéos and Bart'ogheméos', ibid. These two are always included among the 12 in Armenian artistic and literary traditions, see Dickran Kouymjian, 'Identifying the Apostles in Armenian Narrative Miniatures', *From Byzantium to Iran: Armenian Studies in Honour of Nina G. Garsoïan*, Jean-Pierre Mahé and Robert W. Thomson (eds) (Atlanta: 1997), 453–74.

South Wall

There are two subjects, one on each side of the central doorway. Enlart spoke of a large figure of St John the Baptist with 16 associated scenes framing it and the Death of the Virgin. Mrs Bardswell (see Appendix) is more precise, though she was unable to determine the number of scenes from the St John's life: 'Very large figure of St John the Baptist surrounded by square compartments arranged perpendicularly on either side, containing ? [sic] scenes from his life (all perished) within yellow frame. To left and to right, a strip of ornament containing shields of arms, one of them bearing a mitre and crosier on white shield.' Additionally, she describes in some detail a large Dormition of the Virgin on the east end of the south wall: 'Death of Virgin, she lies on a couch, above is the figure of Our Lord who receives her soul, as a swaddled infant. Our Lord in a white mandorla, and around Him a red glory filled with angels who bear candlesticks, censers, etc. All painted in red and white. Below, left and right Apostles weeping. Above to the right, there are angels in adoration on a green background.' Langdale and Walsh report that St John is covered by whitewash, which is probably the case with the Dormition as well.

A photo of 1974 shows 12 rectangles placed vertically, six on each side of the portrait of the standing St John, who has a golden halo and long curled hair falling to the right. His bare right arm, bent at the elbow, holds an object at his breast. At first glance it looks like a hand cross, but closer examination shows it as a knife like object. His left shoulder is covered with his red-brown garment and in his hand he holds an object that looks very much like a serpent winding down to ankle level (Plate 5). None of the 12 panels reveals any clear sense of what scene was originally depicted. The left hand band of heraldic emblems is totally effaced; the right band includes two shields, one with perhaps a spear and the lower one with what might be an eagle. Below it is graffiti: 'L. Bon 1898.' Another example of graffiti on the saint's lower garment has the date 1828. To the upper right, above the figure's head the reading of Armenian SB, S[ur]b, saint, is possible. No trace of the Dormition was seen or photographed.

West Wall

Enlart identified the two standing figures to the north or right of the door as the Virgin and St Helena. Bardswell offers more details: 'To the north of door, two figures of saints, under arched ornamental canopies, green backgrounds. On the left a female saint in cloak, who holds a head of our Lord within a medallion. Inscription on the background in Armenian. On right, a royal personage, nimbed, crowned, wearing much jewellery. Armenian inscription.' In 1974 the figures were still visible. Individual Armenian letters can be made out here and there on each of the two panels, but there are not enough letters to offer the names of the two female figures. Though Bardswell did not offer names for the saints, Enlart was able to read or have read the Armenian inscriptions and one must assume the identifications are correct. The figure represented as St Helena has a white kerchief attached to the right side of her waist and her crown is very pointed. The other figure has all the characteristics of the Virgin, but the head or figure in a halo itself within a large circle seemingly held at her chest is difficult to visually decipher. Is it intended to be the Virgin of Wisdom, with the Christ Child in a round mandorla of light, a theme popular in early Christian but also Armenian art?[37]

To the left of the door is a large framed, nearly square portrait of St George killing the dragon (see Figure 12.9). The horse is galloping to the left with St George, whose cape flows right and is turned frontally while he is looking back and stabbing the serpent's head under the hind feet of his mount with his long spear. He has a shield attached to his left upper arm. The frame is yellow, the background grey, the horse red and the dragon green. In the 1974 photographs the colours are faded but the image is still visible even though much diminished. Bardswell has left a photograph of the fresco as it was in 1937, as well as a copy that she executed.[38] It has completely disappeared today.

North Wall

The Life of Christ cycle, including the Passion, is painted on the north wall. The scenes are in two parallel bands, the subjects more or less in chronological order, but with the lower band starting with a large and full Nativity including the washing of the infant below the main scene, followed rather than preceded by the Annunciation in the centre in a smaller panel sandwiched between the door and a window, and followed by the Baptism. To the right of this on the same level is an ogival niche, in the spandrels of which is crowded the naked torso of Christ with His arms crossed on His chest. The upper band continues the cycle with the Flagellation to the left followed by Christ before Pilate. An arched window with the parallel vertical rows of circular openings interrupts the series. The paintings continue with the Crucifixion, the Deposition or Descent from the Cross, and the Entombment, which abuts the east wall.

Camille Enlart simply lists the scenes, discussing only the Nativity in detail; Mrs Bardswell is more detailed on this important north wall (see Figure 12.8). Following the chronological order of Christological cycle, the Annunciation in 1974 was virtually unidentifiable with most of the paint in the middle of the scene dropped off. But in 2007 the outlines in cobalt blue of the Virgin's head

37 The enthroned Virgin and Child in the Presentation of the Magi, Etchmiadzin Gospels, final miniatures, c. 600, fo. 229, N. Kotanjian, *The Etchmiadzin Gospels* (Erevan, 2000: text in Armenian, Russian, English), 64; Bible Syriac, BnF, ms. Syr. 341, see S. Der Nersessian, 'Le peinture arménienne au VIIe siècle et les miniatures de l'Évangile d'Etchmiadzin', reprinted in S. Der Nersessian, *Byzantine and Armenian Studies* (Lisbon, 1973), 1: 529, 2, fig. 277.

38 These were communicated to me from the Courtauld Institute at the same time as her typed notes.

are still apparent in a detailed close-up.[39] Both Enlart and Bardswell found strong affinities with Italian style paintings, the latter adding that the plaster was tinted buff with green backgrounds. Unfortunately, her photographs of the north wall lack this section, but she describes the Annunciation as 'very fragmentary. To left St Gabriel. To right the Blessed Virgin Mary. Centre, pot of lilies. (Vase with two handles).' The Nativity, the first scene on the lowest register at the west, is the largest and iconographically the most complete scene among the frescoes. The Virgin is reclining to the left, next to and parallel to the manger in the form of a sarcophagus-like rectangle (Figure 8.2). Above to each side are five angels, the first one on the right extending a hand toward the Child, who lies in swaddling clothes and has a halo. To the left, at the height of Mary's head, are the three magi drawn in miniature size. Enlart pointed out that the Virgin's name was inscribed in Armenian on her purple robe, that the head of the ox and the ass are visible next to the manger, and that there are 13 angels. In Bardswell's photograph only nine angel heads and ten halos can be counted; the animals have disappeared though perhaps their hooves or their ears or horns are apparent. In 1974 the angels on the right have almost faded away, with the first angel being the clearest; the Virgin and Jesus are still easy to identify though diminished. The magi are quite clear, in file with hands extended and bearing gifts towards the Mother and Child. Their costumes and their peculiar hats, like little folded cards pinned at the top of their hair, are reminiscent of those in Cilician Armenian Nativity miniatures from the second half of the thirteenth century.[40] Below as an extension of the episode is pictured the washing of the child by midwives, a popular iconographic element in the same Cilician manuscript illustrations. Enlart observed two women, as did Bardswell, but her photograph lacks them. In 1974 the one on the left was quite clear seemingly holding the child, while in the centre is a large rectangular basin with a tablet on which is a spouted urn for water and a basin. The woman on the right is faded away and partly fallen off. By 2007 virtually all of the Nativity had disappeared or was whitewashed over.[41]

The Baptism is to the right of the door and on the same level as the Nativity. Bardswell's photographs lack this scene, but her description traces most of the elements and offers some idea of the colour.[42] Our 1974 photograph in black and white shows the elements rather clearly: John the Baptist to the left, Christ

---

39 Photograph by Wilbert 'Skip' Norman. See Langdale and Walsh, 'Armenian Church of Famagusta', fig. 17.

40 T'oros Roslin painted the scene many times, but usually with the Magi entering from the right, while others had them as in the fresco on the left. See S. Der Nersessian, *Miniature Painting in the Armenian Kingdom of Cilicia*, 2 vols (Washington, 1993), 2: figs 183–4, 212–13, 378–80.

41 Photograph by Wilbert 'Skip' Norman. Langdale and Walsh, 'Armenian Church of Famagusta', fig. 10.

42 Bardwell's description: 'Green background. To left St. John … stands on the bank … and pours water on head of Christ, who stands … naked, water up to middle (not heaped up water). To right two angels stand on the bank. Of most of this subject only the under-painting remains; the outline sketched in red.'

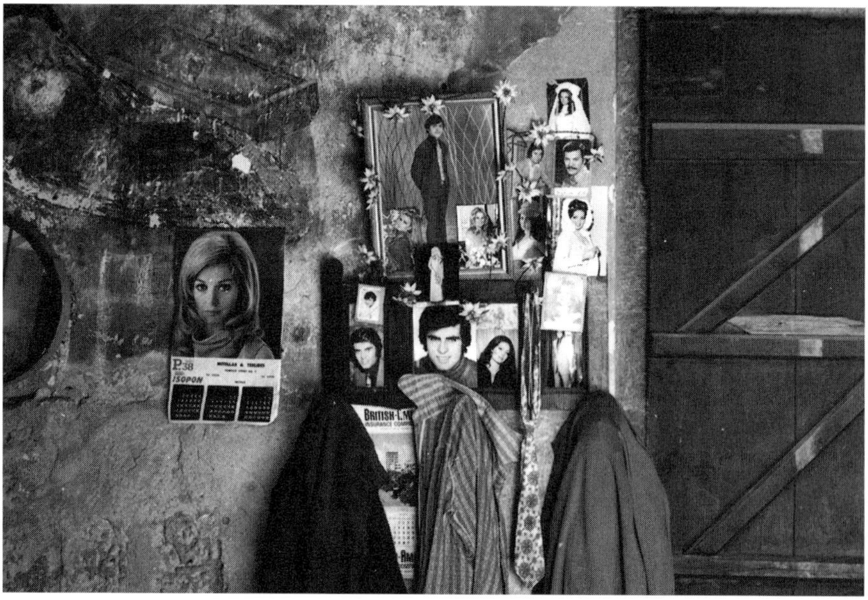

Fig. 8.2 Detail from *Nativity* in 1974 (photograph: Dickran Kouymjian)

naked with halo standing in the Jordan, with a ray of light perpendicularly descending from the orb of heaven and with the dove evident. To the right two angels are holding their garments. The lower parts are already deteriorated. There is only a vague sense of the garments flowing down on each side. The photos taken by Wilbert Norman in 2007 seem to show clearly and in good colour the head of the furthest angel and the feet of John with graffiti in various languages carved over it.[43]

The series then moves to another band devoted to the Passion except for the Annunciation, in the middle directly above the north entry and under the window. Enlart saw above the doorway, in or above the tympanum, Christ with extended arms.[44] There was no trace of such a fresco in 1974; Bardswell does not speak of it but moves directly to the Annunciation. Perhaps Enlart confused it with the *Pieta* above the piscine arch at the eastern extremity of the north wall next to the Baptism. In my 1974 photograph of the top of the doorway and in the photograph of 2007 there simply seems to be no room for a painting.[45]

The five scenes in the top band (excluding the Annunciation) according to Enlart are the Flagellation, Christ Bearing the Cross, the Crucifixion, the Descent from the Cross, and the Entombment, but he offers no details.[46] Bardswell's account is more substantial. She hesitatingly thought the second scene was Christ before Pilate. Here is the section from her notes:

---

43 Langdale and Walsh, 'Armenian Church of Famagusta', figs. 18–19.

44 Enlart, p. 367: '*Dessus du portail nord.* Tympan, buste du Christ, les bras étendus'.

45 Langdale and Walsh, 'Armenian Church of Famagusta', fig. 10.

46 Jeffery, *Description*, p. 144, sees the same 'Carrying of the Cross' after the Flagellation rather than Christ before Pilate.

(A) Series more Italian in style than the rest of the paintings. Plaster tinted buff, green backgrounds.

(1) The Scourging. Christ in centre, bound to pillar. An executioner to the right and to left with whip of knotted thongs. A building top left.

(2) ? Christ before Pilate. Mostly, perished. Christ centre left faces right, hands bound before Him. Right part of picture missing.

(3) Crucifixion. Skull of Adam under the cross. Left, Virgin fainting in the arms of the two Maries, to right, St John. All the upper part gone.

(4) ? Deposition (very faint). Several figures to right.

(5) Entombment, or Pieta. Several figures carry the body of Christ wrapped in winding sheet and laid across the lap of the Virgin. A female figure stands behind.

In 1974 as well as in 2007 (Langdale and Walsh, fig. 11) many of the frescoes were still visible, probably protected through being high up on the wall. The Flagellation is quite clear with Christ facing right in three quarter profile, hands tied to the pillar and feet apart as though walking to the right (Plate 16). In the upper left a building with a pitched roof is evident, but those scourging Christ are not easily visible (even on the left, very clear in Bardswell's photo), in part because a large part of the upper right of the panel shows either the naked wall or the plaster repair near a square recess or window. A single very faint figure of the following episode did not allow any help in determining the scene.

The cross of the Crucifixion was still apparent in the 1974 photographs as was the silhouette of St John and very vaguely a mass, which could represent the fainted Virgin. Of the Descent from the Cross, again a faint trace of the cross is visible with a figure on the right perhaps removing a nail. The last of the cycle, the Entombment, is the best preserved today as it was in 1974. Christ in his burial shroud is being moved toward the right by two figures (perhaps Joseph of Arimathea in the foreground) with another figure close by on the rear part of the body, which seems to be lying or passing over the Virgin, since her bended knees are very clear. To the extreme right is a third male figure, with bare legs seemingly guiding the corpse into the tomb. Such a representation of the burial is known in late thirteenth- and early fourteenth-century Armenian manuscripts.[47] In the case of the Lectionary of Het'um, it is combined with the removal from the cross as in the fresco.

There remains one more scene found at the east end of the lower band above the arch of the piscine (the basin used to dispose of water from various liturgical rites). Bardwell's photograph is very clear, showing Christ naked from the waist up, perhaps in the tomb, with his hands crossed on his waist. The

---

[47] Der Nersessian, *Miniature Painting in the Armenian Kingdom of Cilicia*, fig. 473, Mat. 979, Lectionary of Het'um II, 1286, fo. 194; fig. 472, Mat. 7651, Gospels of the seven painters, late thirteenth century to 1320, fo. 81.

figure was still clear in 1974, but it was hard to make out the two instruments of the passion Bardswell had seen. The image of the 'Pity' as Bardswell calls it or in the case of Enlart, 'Christ ressuscitant' is a symbol of the Resurrection appearing in the fourteenth century in western art, sometimes with the Holy Women near the body or as a *Pieta*. It is essentially foreign to the Armenian tradition. This essentially completes the cycle but it was probably added after the original cycle; the painting looks fresher in the earlier photos. Technically, the cycle continues on the south wall with the Dormition of the Virgin, but that too is a late subject in Armenian iconography essentially borrowed from the Byzantine or Western tradition.

The history of the Life of Christ cycle in Armenian painting is complex.[48] In the early Christian period the first such cycles contained the Annunciation, the Nativity and ended with the Baptism. By the eleventh century a larger cycle of from seven to 15 scenes was used in Gospels manuscripts. Armenian churches were not systematically graced with wall paintings as in the Byzantine tradition. The earliest surviving fresco cycle at the Church of the Holy Cross on the island of Aght'amar (915–21) with 25 scenes is unique in its extent.[49] Yet, it too lacked the Flagellation, the Descent from the Cross, the Entombment, the Dormition, and the *Piéta,* while incorporating the other scenes we find at Famagusta including the Judgement of Pilate.

The frescoes themselves were, at least initially, probably painted by an Armenian artist from Cilicia in the first half of the fourteenth century. The Armenian inscriptions and the refined style of many of the figures and their garments underline an eclectic court art prevalent in Cilician Armenian manuscripts. Perhaps with the planned or at least projected restoration of the church and its paintings, a clearer notion of the style and the iconographic details of the scenes will allow future art historians to more conclusively evaluate the history, style, and influences at work in what is a unique witness to Armenian wall painting of the late medieval period associated with Cilicia and its Latin tendencies.

---

48 D. Kouymjian, 'The Evolution of Armenian Gospel Illumination: The Formative Period (9th–11th Centuries)', *Armenian and the Bible*, ed. C. Burchard (Atlanta, 1993), 125–42; idem, 'Armenian Miniature Painting in Asia Minor in the Eleventh Century: The Melitene Group', *The Armenian Communities of the Region of Kesaria (Gesaria/Caesarea)*, proceedings of the conference, UCLA, May 17, 2003, ed. R. Hovannisian, in preparation.

49 N. Thierry, 'Les peintures de l'Eglise de la Sainte-Croix d'Aghtamar', pp. 182–90.

Gothic and Byzantine in the Monumental Arts of Famagusta: Diversity, Permeability and Power

Justine M. Andrews

The image that Famagusta presents today is but a shadow of the city's visual presence in the fourteenth century. From only the skeletons and ghosts of the monuments and their decoration we draw conclusions regarding the identities and origins of Famagusta's patrons, painters, and architects. Our conclusions and assumptions are driven by the dramatic scale and elaboration of the Gothic vocabulary used in so many of the churches of the city. Our curiosity is piqued by the very fragmentary and faded nature of the paintings within the churches. Immediate associations are made with the painted Byzantine churches of the Troodos mountain range and other Orthodox monuments of Cyprus. But this binary dialogue between Gothic and Byzantine is familiar to almost all studies of art in the eastern Mediterranean, and particularly examples produced within the crusading environment. The conflicts and co-existence of the Orthodox and the Latin communities of the island have been the foundation of much research.[1]

Famagusta is one city that insists on a different approach. Emerging as a commercial centre only in the late thirteenth century, Famagusta's dramatic rise in economic power allowed it a unique position in the kingdom of Cyprus. The city's fortunes during the fourteenth century shifted between an extravagantly wealthy merchant class, an increasingly debt-ridden king, and finally a usurping foreign power that rode out the city's somewhat inevitable wave of affluence. The monumental arts of Famagusta must be seen within these confusing circumstances. While the city of Famagusta may present itself

1 Peter W. Edbury, 'Latins and Greeks on Crusader Cyprus', in D. Abulafia and N. Berend (eds), *Medieval Frontiers: Concepts and Practices* (Aldershot, 2002), 133–42; A. Nicolaou-Konnari, 'The Encounter of Greeks and Franks in Cyprus in the late twelfth and thirteenth centuries. Phenomena of acculturation and ethnic awareness', Ph.D. Diss. (University of Wales: Cardiff, 1999); N. Coureas, *The Latin Church in Cyprus, 1195–1312* (Aldershot, 1997); M. Efthimiou, *Greeks and Latins on Cyprus in the Thirteenth Century* (Brookline, MA, 1987).

as an artistic centre dominated by two distinct vocabularies, Latin Gothic in architecture and Orthodox Byzantine in painting, ultimately we will find the selection and choice of artistic styles and motifs dependent on a complex array of needs and drawn from a much broader array of sources. In this way I believe Famagusta becomes a case study for much of Cypriot art in the fourteenth century. Cyprus at this time was not a simple *mélange* of components that can be catalogued. It was a distinctive culture that had proven itself flexible and permeable. The ability of the island's artists, patrons and audiences to blur the lines between what we continually come back to as cultural monoliths (Gothic, Byzantine, etc) is what ultimately makes the island's artistic heritage unique. Recent studies have grappled with the multiplicity of the island's art and audience and opened the discussion to embrace this cultural mixing.[2] Rather than list the various components of this intermingling of cultures and artistic forms, this chapter will expand the initial binary schema of art in Famagusta, but continue to probe the nature, character and mingling that determined the distinctiveness of the late medieval culture of Cyprus.

Gothic

The most powerful category of description for the visible monuments of Famagusta today is Gothic. The many remains of churches and some domestic structures truly dominate the old city: tall stone structures that thrust skyward, with pointing arches and gables, flying arches of buttressing, and elegant narrow windows dressed with curving tracery. But indeed the term Gothic itself needs some exploration for the fourteenth century. At this time in northern Europe the architectural styles that had been developing from the late twelfth century flourished in forms that were highly stylized and decorative. Often the term flamboyant is used to describe the flame-like traceries, the dramatically perforated façades, and unified interiors of the churches adorned in this style. At the same time there are elements of late medieval architectural forms present in Cyprus that fall under the category 'Gothic' but are drawn from sources in Italy or Germany. While Gothic may happen to be the overriding form of architecture chosen by many communities in Famagusta during the fourteenth century, it is worthwhile exploring some of the distinctions and similarities among these monuments. The following is not a comprehensive study of the monuments of Famagusta and their

---

2 A.W. Carr, 'Art', in A. Nicolaou-Konnari and C. Schabel (eds), *Cyprus Society and Culture 1191–1374* (Leiden and Boston, 2005), 285–328; T.C. Papacostas, 'Gothic in the East: Western Architecture in Byzantine Lands', in C. Rudolph (ed.), *A Companion to Medieval Art: Romanesque and Gothic in Northern Europe* (Malden, MA, 2006), 510–29; J.G. Schryver, 'Monuments of Identity: Latin, Greek, Frank and Cypriot?' in S. Fourrier and G. Grivaud (eds), *Identités croisées en un milieu méditerranéen: le cas de Chypre (Antiquité – Moyen Âge)* (Rouen, 2006), 385–405.

relationship to the Gothic, but a selection of monuments and their details which will reveal the inherent diversity of architectural production in Famagusta.

Perhaps the earliest adoption of a pronounced Gothic form in architecture is the Franciscan Church in Famagusta (see also Figure 7.2).[3] This church is located adjacent to the royal palace and near to the cathedral. It exhibits a simplified plan that was typical of Italian mendicant churches of the thirteenth century. Three square bays in the nave have no aisles and terminate in a fourth bay which incorporates a three-sided apse. There are carved brackets with deep foliate ornament and elegant ribbed vaults that are anchored by carved bosses. The springing of the bifurcated ribs of the vaults from thickly carved crockets together with several arched niches along the western end of the nave walls are elements that we find repeated in several of the Famagustan churches of the fourteenth century. It was described by the chronicler Nicolà de Martoni in the end of the thirteenth century as a much larger complex with particularly beautiful gardens and cloister.[4]

As Famagusta was transformed into an international centre after the fall of the last crusader cities in the Holy Land, so did the positions of the bishop and cathedral of the city change. From 1291 the bishops took a more active role in the political life of the kingdom. There was a particular connection between the bishop and the king during the rule of Henry II (1285–1324).[5] Both the king and bishop must have been conscious of the new need of a coronation site for Henry's heir to the crown of Jerusalem.[6] In addition, the pope also recognized that the current cathedral, possibly built under the Latin archbishop Eustorge in the first half of the thirteenth century, was insufficient for the many emigrants from the Holy Land.[7] Thus a new cathedral project was conceived in the late thirteenth century.

Hugh IV was crowned king of Cyprus in Nicosia in 1324, and according to the author of the *Chronique d'Amadi*, he was crowned king of Jerusalem in Famagusta one month later.[8] According to the inscription on the church from 1311, the apsidal chapels and two adjoining bays were complete at that

---

3 *L'art gothique en Chypre*, eds J.-B. de Vaivre and P. Plagnieux (Paris, 2006), 238–42. Michalis Olympios has recently shown that this is the earliest surviving Gothic church in Famagusta and should be dated to the 1290s. (International Cyprological Congress, Nicosia, Cyprus, May 2008).

4 de Vaivre and Plagnieux, p. 240.

5 Bishop Baldwin Lambert of Famagusta was instrumental in retrieving Henry II from exile in Armenia. C. Schabel, 'The Latin Bishops of Cyprus, 1255–1313, with a note on Bishop Neophytos of Solea', *Epeterida*, 30 (2004): 75–111.

6 Henry II had only five years earlier been crowned king of Jerusalem in Tyre. 'Chronique d'Amadi' in *Chroniques d'Amadi et de Strambaldi*, ed. R. de Mas Latrie (Paris, 1891), 1: 217.

7 Florio Bustron, *Chronique de l'île de Chypre*, ed. R. de Mas Latrie in *Collection de documents inédits sur l'histoire de France: Mélanges historiques* (Paris 1886), 5: 56, 128; de Vaivre and Plagnieux, p. 218; P.W. Edbury, 'Famagusta in 1300' in N. Coureas and J. Riley-Smith (eds), *Cyprus and the Crusades* (Nicosia, 1995), 342.

8 P.W. Edbury, *The Kingdom of Cyprus and the Crusades 1191–1374* (Cambridge, 1991), 141.

date, and we may assume that by 1324 there was sufficient progress on the new cathedral to warrant Hugh's coronation there.[9] These changes in function allowed for a stronger embrace of a contemporary Gothic vocabulary in the new cathedral of St Nicholas in Famagusta. Its façade and exterior east end in particular express a distinctly French style that reflected the international position of the city and function of the monument[10] (Plate 1).

The façade of the cathedral in some details evokes the powerful image of the French coronation cathedral at Reims. The same sharply gabled portals and glazed tympana in quatrefoil tracery, and deep niches for sculpture, leave no room for Byzantine-style panel paintings or other incorporations of local imagery found in the cathedral of Nicosia (see also Figure 6.2). Although only the smallest fragments of the sculptural programme at St Nicholas survive, it is clear that the façade was meant to be teeming with fantastic beasts, angels, and even representations of monks or clergy, positioned in the interstices, angles and joins.[11] While literally crumbling today, the chevet also presents a striking visual display of intricate finial projections and tall lancet windows that immediately evoke the words 'Gothic' or 'French' (Figure 9.1). The picture is complicated however by the tracery within the windows of St Nicholas which has been convincingly compared to Cologne cathedral and a set of drawings of similar windows dated to the late thirteenth/early fourteenth century and now in Cologne.[12]

On careful viewing, the façade of St Nicholas is less perforated than the Gothic architecture of France to which it is repeatedly compared. The windows in the second story are blind and there is a distinct horizontality to the façade emphasized by the balustrade of the second story balcony. Balconies and viewing platforms appear repeatedly in later Famagustan churches, suggesting that exterior rituals or presentations were performed. The interior of the cathedral is even more discordant (see also Figure 7.7). There are no slender composite piers but large, thick, cylindrical ones. The nave arcade is capped by the horizontal course beneath the large windows. There is no triforium or gallery. The east end terminates in three apses without an ambulatory. In its overall appearance, St Nicholas cathedral must have suggested primarily the grandeur of Gothic architectural principles, yet it was in fact made up of many elements that were likely as not understood as only vaguely indicative of the Latin Church and held possible royal associations. For the ecclesiastical patrons and royalty who were crowned kings of

[9] In contrast to his brief description of the coronation in the cathedral of Santa Sophia in Nicosia, the chronicler of the Amadi text does not give the name the church in Famagusta. 'Chronique d'Amadi', pp. 402–3.

[10] de Vaivre and Plagnieux, pp. 225–37.

[11] For a further discussion of the sculpture of the façade, see Allan Langdale's chapter in this volume.

[12] See A. Franke in this volume. N. Coldstream also mentions the connection between Cologne and the Latin cathedral in Famagusta, in her introduction to Camille Enlart, *Gothic Art and the Renaissance in Cyprus*, trans. and ed. P. Hunt (London, 1987), p. 9.

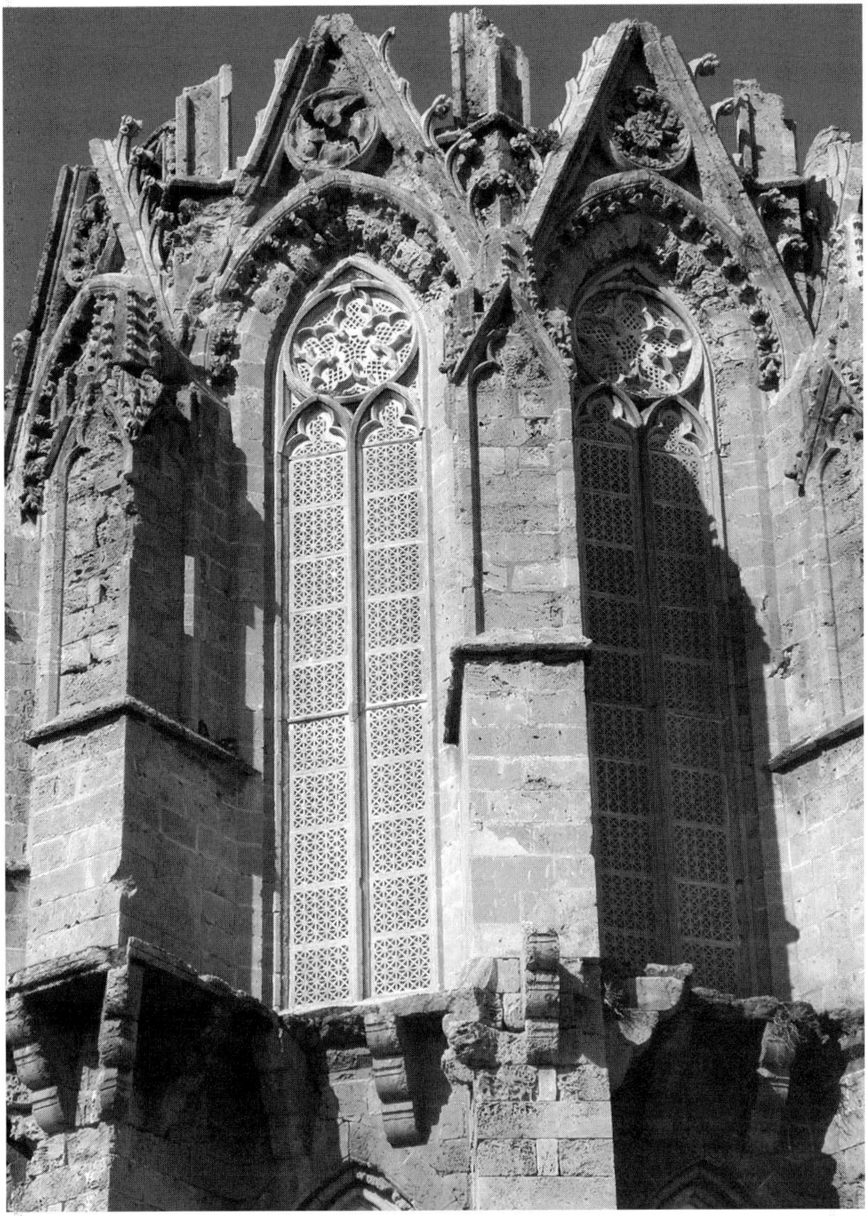

Fig. 9.1 Cathedral of St Nicholas, detail of chevet (photograph: Thomas Kaffenberger)

Jerusalem at St Nicholas, the cathedral was an attempt to make a sharp break with local architectural examples as well as examples from the Holy Land. While the cathedral expressed this distinct Western presence, the individual components of its 'Gothic' image were not burdened with this static meaning.[13]

The Orthodox cathedral church dedicated to St George draws from the powerful model of the Latin cathedral of St Nicholas, and is also related to the

[13] Schryver, p. 392.

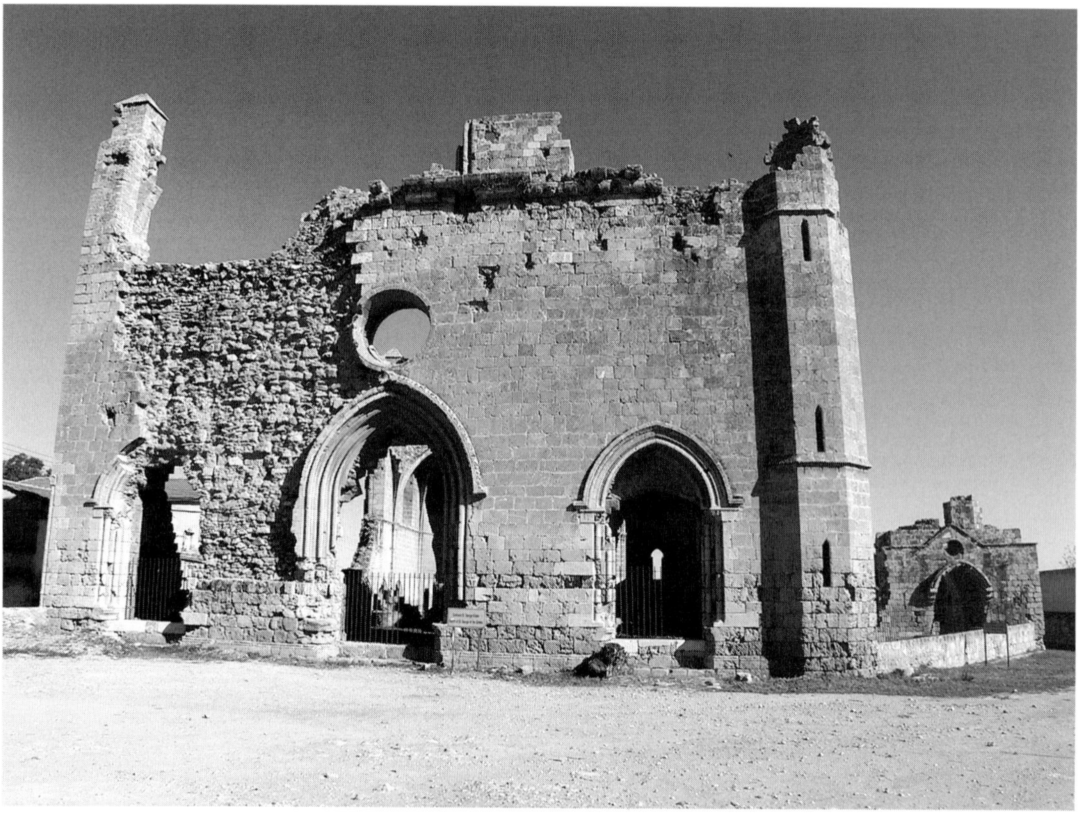

Fig. 9.2 Cathedral of St George of the Greeks, west façade (photograph: Wilbert 'Skip' Norman)

church of SS Peter and Paul and the Church of St Mary of Carmel (Plate 3).[14] Its western end is distinct from the Latin cathedral and presents a flat screen-like façade broken by three doorways. The central door has no sharp gables filled with tracery, but continuous moulding around the archivolts into the jambs, and a drip moulding of thickly carved leaves surmounts the pointed archway. The side doors have more simplified moulding but include colonettes with foliate capitals. Above the central door is a circular window (Figure 9.2). The tall vaults are missing, but the east end stands with evidence of flying buttresses that were positioned over the aisles, as also seen in SS Peter and Paul. The interior holds the remains of large rounded piers of the nave arcade. Few of the windows still carry fragments of trilobed and quatrefoil tracery. The east end is made up of three apses with no ambulatory as in the cathedral of St Nicholas. The Gothic elements in this Orthodox cathedral are remarkable, but come from a modified form of the Latin cathedral of St Nicholas, rather than from a direct model in northern Europe. The choice of the Gothic architectural forms is only mitigated by the inclusion of a templon, traces of which can still

14 T. Soulard, 'L'architecture gothique grecque du royaume des Lusignan: les cathédrales de Famagouste et Nicosie', in S. Fourrier and G. Grivaud (eds), *Identités croisées en un milieu méditerranéen: le cas de Chypre (Antiquité – Moyen Âge)* (Rouen, 2006), 358–9.

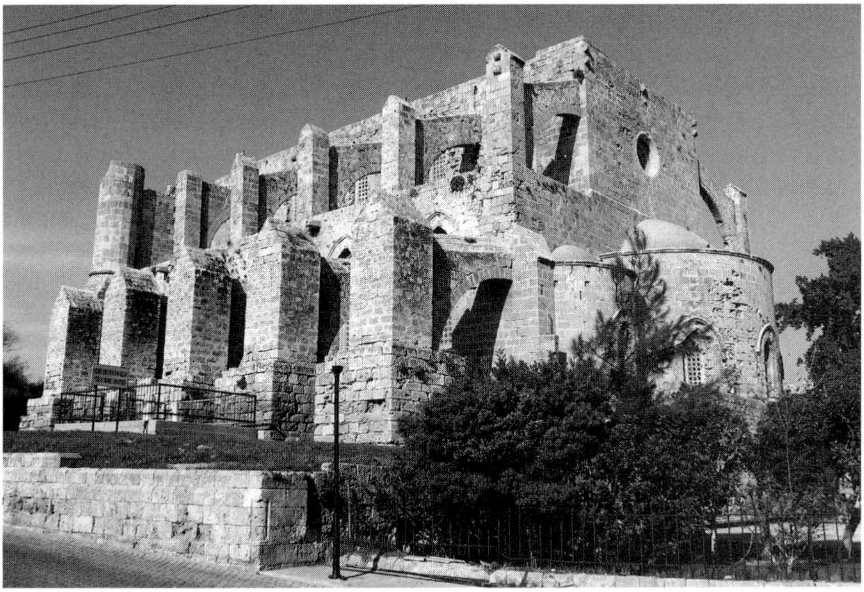

Fig. 9.3 Church of SS Peter and Paul (photograph: Allan Langdale)

be found between the fourth and fifth bay, and the prominent synthronos or platform in the east end, typical of Orthodox basilicas.[15]

Although we know little of the foundation and patronage of this monument, we can suggest that an Orthodox cathedral could only have been erected after the re-installment of the Greek bishops sometime after 1340.[16] It is fascinating that these patrons took up the Gothic architectural forms of flying buttress, traceried windows, and ribbed vaults. Perhaps this was due to a choice of local or available masons. In addition it is likely that the Orthodox community wished to display their increasing status within the Lusignan kingdom by presenting their prominent church in the architectural vocabulary as powerfully as possible and laden with the most explicit message of their community's position. On account of the monument's clear associations with two nearby edifices, the Latin cathedral and SS Peter and Paul, the Orthodox community shares the visual stage of Famagusta with the patrons of these churches. However, there is very little in the broad, unpenetrated façade, thick piers and heavy buttresses suggesting a strong northern European Gothic here. The church harkens to earlier crusader structures, although on a larger scale, and possibly to Italian examples of the Gothic.

The church called SS Peter and Paul stands across the plaza from the Latin cathedral to the west and is on the south side of the Lusignan palace complex (Figure 9.3). One of the few large churches in Famagusta to retain its vaults, the church is a beautiful example of the height and light that was the goal

---

15 de Vaivre and Plagnieux, p. 293.

16 Soulard, p. 357; de Vaivre and Plagnieux, p. 288; E. Constantinides, 'Monumental Painting in Cyprus during the Venetian Period, 1489–1570', in N.P. Sevcenko and C. Moss (eds), *Medieval Cyprus, Studies in Art, Architecture, and History in Memory of Doula Mouriki* (Princeton, 1999), 265.

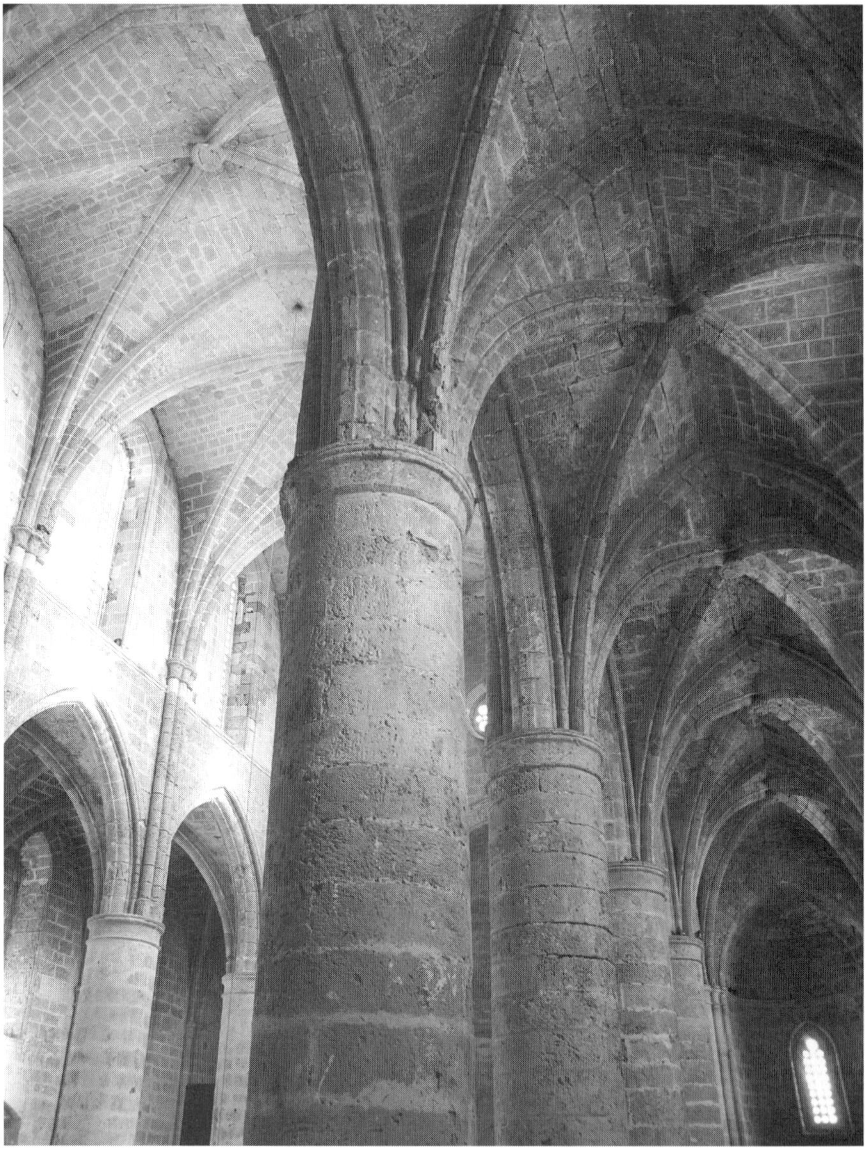

Fig. 9.4 Church of SS Peter and Paul, interior (photograph: Allan Langdale)

for these fourteenth-century architects. There is considerable controversy over exactly when the church was built and to whom its patronage can be ascribed.[17] The structure most likely dates to the mid-fourteenth century. Several chroniclers repeat the story that the church was paid for by a merchant, from just a fraction of his profits from one transaction in Syria. It has also been speculated that this patron was Syrian Christian, perhaps a Nestorian.[18] Recently, however Plagnieux and Soulard have discounted these

[17] de Vaivre and Plagnieux, pp. 272–4.

[18] de Vaivre and Plagnieux, p. 272; M. Walsh, 'The Re-emergence of The Forty

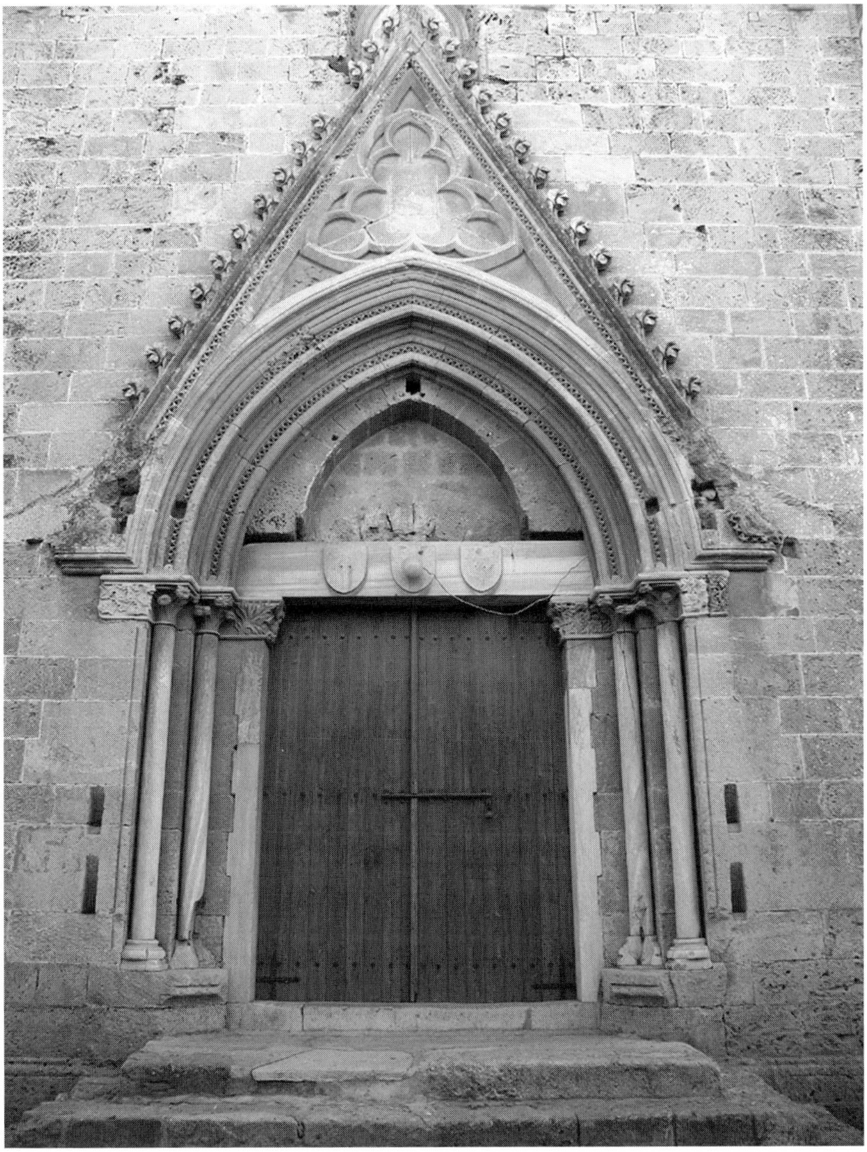

Fig. 9.5 Church of SS Peter and Paul, north door (photograph: Michael Walsh)

earlier accounts and reported that the church was for the Latin rite, and was under the control of the royal family.[19] They speculate that the connection to the royal Lusignan family explains the church's neglect during the period of Genoese control (1373–1464), and then again under the Venetians, who exercised suzerainty over Cyprus from 1473 and whose direct rule began

Martyrs of Sebaste in the Church of Saint Peter and Paul, Famagusta, Northern Cyprus', *Journal of Cultural Heritage* 8 (2007): 82–3.

[19] de Vaivre and Plagnieux, p. 284.

in 1489. The chronicler François Attar reports that the church was in use for grain storage by 1520.[20]

In elevation and plan it is very similar to the cathedral of St Nicholas (Figure 9.4). Its large round piers support four-part ribbed vaults terminating in bosses carved with the arms of the Lusignan family (lion rampant) or kingdom of Jerusalem (five crosses). The semi-circular apse is preceded by a pointed arch and the vaults are supported by flying buttresses that spring from the roofs of the side aisles. A set of supporting flying-buttresses was added to the lower exterior of the south aisle at a later date.[21] The portals on the western façade are relatively plain, and adorn a flat, wide western end.

Perhaps the most distinctive feature of the church is the north door that faces the royal palace (Figure 9.5). It was clearly sculpted with attention, suggesting a relationship between SS Peter and Paul and the royal palace. A sharp gable of foliate ornament frames blind poly-lobed tracery, and originally terminated in sculpted figures. Slender marble colonettes grace the jambs and support foliate capitals. The marble pilasters that immediately flank the doors are capped with carved capitals, depicting two angels, one censing and the other presenting a holy object, perhaps the symbols of the Passion, or the elevation of the soul (these have been hammered off). The sculpture is similar in style to the small figures found in the central doorway of Santa Sophia in Nicosia. The style of the sculpture and its correspondence to other programmes in Cyprus can be dated to the mid-fourteenth century.[22] The church of SS Peter and Paul is similar to the preceding two churches discussed. It shows elegance in its height and light, yet it is balanced by heaviness in the interior piers, the lack of a triforium, as well as the broad façade. It begins to show a predilection in Famagustan churches for selectively chosen elements from the Latin cathedral, primarily in sculpted decoration. It also shows a repetition in the heavy structural elements and large expanses of wall space on the exterior and interior of the buildings.

The Church of St Mary of Carmel was a large monastic establishment patronized by the royal house of Lusignan (see also Figures 7.3 and 7.5). Located in the north-west quadrant of the city, it was also noted by Martoni in 1394 as a large and beautiful complex.[23] The church also adopted the plan of the mendicant orders. Its Italianate plan incorporated three bays in its wide nave without aisles. A five-part apse encompassed the fourth bay. Although the vaults have fallen, the ribs of the apse remain and evidence of the brackets that held the ribs of the nave is present. Fragments of delicate poly-lobed tracery still hang in some of the windows.

The western façade is again wide and flanked by two strong square buttresses at each corner. Although it only includes a single central door, the

---

20 de Vaivre and Plagnieux, p. 274; L. de Mas Latrie, *Histoire de l'île de Chypre* (Paris, 1852–61), 3: 524.

21 de Vaivre and Plagnieux, p. 277.

22 de Vaivre and Plagnieux, p. 282; Enlart, pp. 262, 267.

23 de Vaivre and Plagnieux, pp. 251–2, 259.

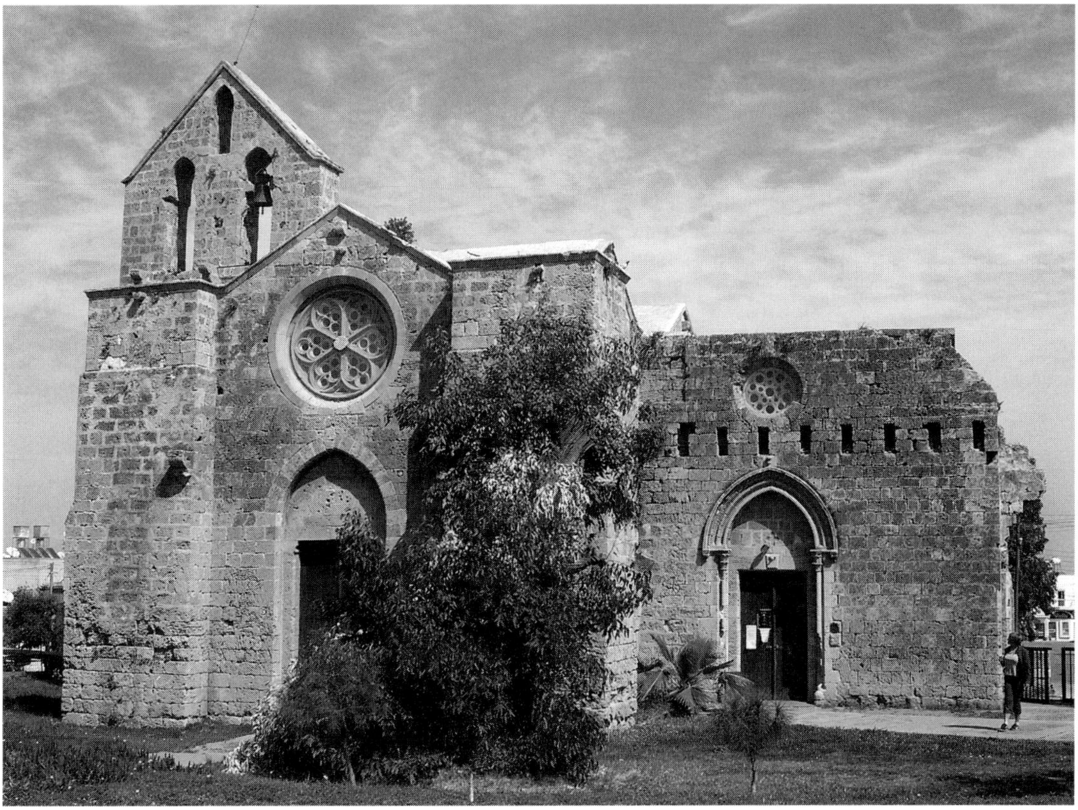

Fig. 9.6 Nestorian Church (photograph: Justine Andrews)

west end also has a large pointed window above the door that until recently retained much of its tracery. The remains of figural sculpture appear at the apex of the door and window. Between the door and window runs a plain course dressed by three heraldic shields.[24] The central shield appears to have the arms of Jerusalem and the flanking ones the arms of the Lusignan dynasty. Just under these elements is a series of post-holes which suggest the presence of a projecting porch or balcony structure.

Again, this church, part of a larger complex but probably completed in the middle of the fourteenth century, shows a combination of Gothic elements from northern and southern Europe. It also presents architectural elements that are repeated in Famagustan churches. In particular, the use of temporary wooden porches or balconies over the main doorway of the church shows a continued interest in exterior gatherings or ceremonies. The repeated presence of post-holes around the church also suggests that the patrons included other means of extending the shelter and connection of the church to further outbuildings.

Apart from the Carmelite Church, a group of churches in the north-west quarter of the city of Famagusta are interesting for their similarities to

---

24 de Vaivre and Plagnieux, pp. 251–6, 267–74; Enlart, pp. 268–72.

one another and the liberties they take with the Gothic architectural forms developing in the city. The architecture of the Nestorian Church has recently been dated by Michele Bacci to the late thirteenth century with an enlargement in the early fourteenth century (Figure 9.6).[25] The church is a single aisle church with groin vaulting. The westernmost bay projects into a vestibule. The exterior doors are rather plain. There are gables above each façade and there is a gabled bell tower with three pierced lancet openings on the north side of the church. Many of the decorative motifs, such as the zig-zag moulding of an arch that protrudes from the exterior of the south side, as well as the shafts of the interior which project at right angles to support the vaulting, suggest earlier precedents from the crusader kingdoms. Bacci compares the plan and details of the church specifically to examples from the county of Tripoli.[26] The western elements of this church therefore are filtered through examples already present in the East.

At the small church called St Anne, the single aisle retains its groin vaults with an elegant ribbed apse (see also Figures 7.4 and 12.6).[27] It includes tomb niches on the interior, but the exterior has a variety of distinct elements. On the north-east side there is a staircase and an unusual aperture which suggest that the church was connected to another (now lost) nearby building. Around the entire exterior are pronounced post-holes with projecting supports, again giving evidence of a porch structure or balcony that in this instance surrounded the entire structure. The bell tower is flush with the façade and rises above the single doorway that is surmounted by a simple molded arch. Enlart associated all of the architectural elements with southern France and dated the church to the early fourteenth century.[28] Without patron or documentation it is difficult to determine the date and circumstance of construction. However, St Anne is similar to several of the churches in this quarter of the city, including its prominent use of flagpost holders along the roof line of the church. This is similar to the structure called the Tanner's Mosque, only a few yards away.

By the end of the century a small Armenian church was erected immediately to the north of the Carmelite monastery, in the north-west corner of the city (Plate 4).[29] Enlart dates it to the late fourteenth century following further instalments of refugees in Famagusta in 1335 and 1346.[30] Later an apse was added to the north east of the structure and the entire church was painted on the interior with frescoes. The very small church includes only a single bay and apse. The bay is constructed of a groin vault. Much of the structure has been reconstructed since the time of Enlart. Today there are three simple doors on the north, south and west flanks. Gables project from each roofline and surmount small windows with drip mouldings. The pointed archways,

---

25 M. Bacci, 'Syrian, Palaiologan, and Gothic Murals in the "'Nestorian" Church of Famagusta', *Deltion tes christianikes archaiologikes Hetaireias*, ser. IV, 27 (2006): 209.

26 Bacci, pp. 209–10.

27 de Vaivre and Plagnieux, pp. 260–65.

28 Enlart, pp. 273–5.

29 de Vaivre and Plagnieux, pp. 257–60.

30 Enlart, p. 286.

drip mouldings and gabled façades suggest at least some connection with the broader development of Gothic architectural forms in the city of Famagusta. The selection and use of certain elements is seen clearly to depend on financial resources and number of the community.

Although hindered by vague or non-existent historical data as to patron and building processes, the details of many of the major ecclesiastical monuments remaining in the old city of Famagusta remind us of the complex nature of the sources and historical environment in the city. The city itself rose from the scattered ashes of the kingdom of Jerusalem, particularly the loss of Acre in 1291. Famagusta took the mantle of commercial *entrêpot* from Acre and with it the economic advantages as well as a variety of groups including monastic communities and merchants of diverse religious affiliations. The financial resources and new patrons contributed to the building of many churches such as the Nestorian church, and added to the royal support of the large monastic foundations of the Carmelites and Franciscans. The rising importance of bishops, both Latin and Greek, in the fourteenth century allowed for the construction of new cathedrals. While it is difficult to cite specific models and artists for these monuments, this brief look at the selected churches allows us to question the 'purity' of the Gothic as expressed in fourteenth-century Famagusta. The city drew from a variety of patron groups such as the royal family, Latin bishops, Syrian, Greek Orthodox and Armenian Christians, including monastic communities. These patrons appear to have drawn from a body of architectural sources and models that while chosen with some eclecticism, coalesce into a 'Gothic' form that is unique to Cyprus at this time. It is hard to imagine that the patrons, artists or audiences found meanings of specific identities, or outside cultures such as Gothic or Byzantine, western or eastern in these architectural monuments. The messages here are more reflective of the immediate impulses of economic or local political prowess as reflected in the size, selection of motifs and relationships of the monuments to one another.

Byzantine

The complex and eclectic choices of patrons of architecture in fourteenth-century Famagusta produced one commonality in their church structures: wall space. The broad, flat façades of the monuments are reflected on the interiors by large amounts of flat, unobstructed wall space. Many of the churches are without aisles and have even more prominent areas to be given over to painting. There is ample evidence of the soft local limestone having been plastered over, and once plastered the surface would logically be the perfect one for fresco. Indeed, although emerging like ghostly shadows from the walls of the open churches and peeking up behind the whitewash of converted monuments, the elaborate new monuments of the fourteenth century in Famagusta were clearly adorned with large cycles of fresco painting.

Of all the arts on Cyprus perhaps wall painting is the most famous. Ten churches of the island are today listed by UNESCO for their importance to cultural heritage. For most art historians the heart of Cypriot art beats deep within the Troodos Mountains. In contrast to the large monuments of the urban centres it is in the small Orthodox churches in rural areas like the Troodos and their extensive fresco interiors that painting survives. It is clear now that despite the disruption of the island's political and religious hierarchy in 1191 with the advent of Latin crusader rule, painting continued within the Orthodox churches of Cyprus. This early painting was characterized by its close adherence to the current imperial Komnenian styles of Byzantine painting.[31] By the late thirteenth century and fourteenth century, a time parallel to the construction of the Famagusta monuments outlined above, painting within Orthodox churches began to express elements of hybridity, incorporating western iconography and style in select scenes. Images of the Life of the Virgin in the church of the Holy Cross at Pelendri are examples that incorporate western motifs, but they are drawn from Latin sources in the East, namely the manuscript tradition established in the crusader kingdoms.[32] It is easy to assume that this strong and continuous tradition in painted church interiors might have an immediate correspondence with the painted churches in Famagusta. Nonetheless, it would be a mistake to oversimplify the complex artistic environment in Famagusta and categorize painting as exclusively Byzantine. Painted churches were common throughout Europe and the East in the fourteenth century. Italy is perhaps the most prominent example and with the variety of Italian merchant communities resident in Famagusta it is very likely some of the influence and patronage came from these groups. Therefore the elaborate decoration of the interiors of these new Famagustan churches did not entirely spring from a local Byzantine past.

What is distinct to the Orthodox churches and Byzantine frescos is the expression of a coherent programme of imagery. Among the churches of Famagusta this kind of planned programme is rarely present. Michele Bacci has noted that the frescoes of the (so-called) Nestorian church date to three distinct periods and are painted in Syrian, Gothic and Palaeologan styles. This latest campaign of painting from 1350–70, of which the St Philip on the western side of the north west pier of the bay is one example, is very high in quality and appears to be the work of Palaeologan painters from Thessaloniki or another large centre of Byzantine art.[33] The church was originally identified

---

[31] A. Papageorgiou, 'Crusader Influence on the Byzantine Art of Cyprus', in N. Coureas and J. Riley-Smith (eds), *Cyprus and the Crusades* (Nicosia, 1995), 275; A. Stylianou and J.A. Stylianou, *Painted Churches of Cyprus. Treasures of Byzantine Art* (2nd edn, Nicosia, 1997).

[32] Papageorgiou, p. 279; I. Christoforaki, 'Cyprus between Byzantium and the Levant: Eclecticism and Interchange in the Cycle of the Life of the Virgin in the Church of the Holy Cross at Pelendri', *Epeterida*, 22 (1996): 215–55.

[33] Bacci, p. 217.

by Enlart as a Nestorian church and often remarked upon for its Syriac inscriptions.[34] Most interesting is that the decoration of the church includes the arms of a Genoese ruling family in Jubail, the Embriaco-Gibelet. With this evidence Bacci concludes that the patrons of the church were refugees from the Levant. Given the inclusion of images of St Anne together with the Virgin and St Menas, Bacci suggests that the imagery was created under a Syrian Orthodox patron.[35] This is one fascinating example of the complexity of categorization of art in Famagusta. While not entirely drawing upon a local tradition of programmatic Byzantine fresco painting, the artists and patrons can directly express the most sophisticated and status-laden styles from prominent artistic centres, including, but not exclusively those of Byzantium.

The lack of traditional Byzantine programmes of painting could also be the effect of the large and longitudinal format of the churches. St Mary of Carmel for example has a variety of painted images in fragmentary states. Some of the images appear associated with individual tomb niches or possibly private altars/chapels. Others suggest painted icons of saints, such as St Nicholas (Plates 8, 17, 19). Even in its ruined state these images are somewhat dwarfed by the architectural space and it is hard to imagine a coherent narrative programme filling the walls. This may be true of the Orthodox cathedral of St George as well, for surprisingly, the massive basilica-plan church does not appear to have a single programme of imagery.

The cathedral of St George of the Greeks is impressive for its size as well as its painted imagery that is still exposed today. Most agree that the paintings date later than the church itself which was likely constructed after 1340 when a Greek bishop was reinstated in Famagusta.[36] The fragments of fresco that are visible appear to be from several different campaigns of artistic production. Some images show remarkable affinity to Italian painting, such as the Cimabuesque Crucifixion scene on the interior west wall (Plate 7). Others show a strong correspondence with contemporary Palaeologan style, particularly in the south apse image of the Betrayal (see also Figure 12.11). Other details suggest more generic western elements, such as the borders of quatrefoils which could be associated with Italian fresco painting as well as manuscript painting from the Latin East. Annemarie Weyl Carr suggests the paintings at St George are similar to the Italo-Byzantine murals at the Panagia Podithou church in Galata, Cyprus, although she believes the Podithou master may have in fact copied the frescoes at St George. She also attributes several of the frescoes to the Palaeologan style and asserts that this correspondence shows an importation of cosmopolitan painting that in the later fourteenth century displaced locally specific forms of art and became expressly the voice of the newly-assertive Orthodox community.[37]

---

34 Enlart, p. 280.
35 Bacci, pp. 214, 217.
36 Enlart, p. 257; Carr, pp. 316-18.
37 Carr, p. 318.

The later and much smaller Armenian church is one example of programmatic painting. Enlart characterized the paintings of the Armenian Church as a poor Byzantine style.[38] Although excruciatingly difficult to make out under layers of soot and whitewash (which did not impede Enlart's view), the frescoes do appear to be of a late type with Italian influences. The format is typical of many programmes within Orthodox churches on Cyprus; the scenes of Christ's life are divided by thick red frames (Plate 16, and see also Figures 12.8 and 12.9). The choice of scenes and inclusion of the Man of Sorrows above a niche on the north east wall before the apse are unusual for a Byzantine programme. The image of the Man of Sorrows does appear in late Orthodox churches such as the sixteenth-century image at the church of the Archangel or Panagia Theotokos, Galata, a church which itself includes a selection of western iconographic elements.[39] In addition, the decorative treatment of the painted architecture suggests some Italian influence. Since the Armenians appeared to have a good relationship with the Genoese, given their associations in the early fourteenth century and later privileges in the middle of the fifteenth century, it is possible that this community flourished under the Genoese rule of Famagusta and it is from this period that the painting cycle dates.

The frescoes that remain in the medieval churches of Famagusta present an intensely complex puzzle that has only very recently become the subject of scholarly attention.[40] Their painful fragmentary and faded appearance makes their study exceptionally difficult, yet even more worthwhile. There are many aspects to the paintings that should be considered including the few inscriptions that are left, as well as the iconography, figural style, and ornament. Leaving the question of inscriptions for another publication, a look at the complexity of figural style and iconography in only a few examples underlines the complexity here.

Camille Enlart recorded the remains of a fresco (now lost) in the earliest Gothic church of the city, the Church of the Franciscan monastery. The fresco, according to Enlart, appeared thoroughly western, specifically Italian in style from the fourteenth or fifteenth century. It showed a knight standing next to his horse holding a banner and wearing a grey hooded tunic with red sleeves.[41] Enlart suggests that this may have been an image of a patron of one chapel within the church. Like many of the paintings in Famagusta, this lost example suggests that Italian style and possibly iconography were powerfully present among the artistic choices in Famagusta and would be perfectly appropriate within a church that had the newest forms of northern European Gothic vaulting, windows and sculpted decoration.

The Church of St Mary of Carmel had powerful patrons among the Latin aristocracy and clergy (Peter Thomas and John del Conti both contributed to

38 Enlart, p. 287.
39 Stylianou, p. 96.
40 See Carr and Bacci.
41 Enlart, pp. 266-7 and note 41.

the church), yet the frescoes cannot strictly be seen as a western production. Images of standing saints include an image of St Nicholas, dressed as a Latin bishop (Plate 8). The painted icon also includes small scenes from the saint's life along the sides of the figure. The iconography appears to be the appropriate choice for these Carmelite patrons, yet the style of the figure in its facial features, hair, beard and drapery folds, are closest to the mid-fourteenth century figures found in the so-called Nestorian church, particularly those that are allied with the Palaeologan styles of Thessaloniki.[42] Within one image, iconography and style could be drawn from two different cultures.

A fragment of a sinopia is all that is left of what once must have been an extensive fresco cycle in the Church of SS Peter and Paul (Plate 9). The image is much damaged and appears to show a fragment of the image of the Forty Martyrs of Sebaste.[43] There are several men shown wearing only cloths around their waists. Some have their arms crossed over their upper bodies. One falls forward, while he is supported by another. The iconography of the Forty Martyrs of Sebaste is unusual for a Latin-rite church but finds some similarity to the image in the Panagia Phorbiotissa of Asinou. The style has been associated with either the Genoese period (late fourteenth–early fifteenth century) or the Venetian period, specifically the early sixteenth century.[44] In this example, a somewhat Byzantine iconographic image is paired with a distinctly Italian figural style. While not a comprehensive study by any means, these few examples do show the difficulties inherent in the categorization of monumental painting in Famagusta.

Even more difficult is the question of who would and could have painted these images. We do not have signed works or documents that offer artists' names. The origin of the artists in this environment seems like a fruitless question. There were so many cultural and religious affiliations in Famagusta during this period, the assignment of ethnicity by language, religion or cultural traditions may or may not have any bearing on one's artistic practice. A more worthwhile, yet still elusive, avenue of pursuit is the exploration of artists' training. Given the intricacy of the sculptural ornament, and the similarity to traceries in Germany, it seems likely that in the late thirteenth and early fourteenth century, master craftsmen from northern Europe were available in Famagusta. The adaptation of the architecture and sculpture to local materials and labour also suggests the employment of locals with specific knowledge and resources. Following the already distinct workshop development of the Latin East, painters could equally have experienced a mixed background of training. Even the painting that clearly depicts the most current Palaeologan styles could arrive from a source outside of Constantinople. The transmission

---

42 Bacci, p. 216.

43 Walsh, pp. 81–6.

44 Walsh attributes the fresco to the Genoese period (late fourteenth century or early fifteenth century). P. Plagnieux and T. Soulard attribute the painting to the early sixteenth century in J.-B. de Vaivre and P. Plagnieux (eds), *L'art gothique en Chypre* (Paris, 2006), p. 275.

of the most current Byzantine styles could also come to Cyprus from its close connections to Mystras in the Greek Peloponnese. In the late fourteenth century the Despot of Mystras, Manuel Kantakouzenos (1348–80) was married to a Lusignan from Cyprus, Isabella. This couple was an important patron of painted churches in Mystras including the katholikon of the Perivleptos Monastery in that city. They hosted the king of Cyprus, Peter II in 1371, and Isabella also visited Cyprus.[45] This relationship between Cypriot painting in the late fourteenth century and Mystras is a fruitful area for further research. It is very possible that the Byzantine artists brought the current Palaeologan styles to Cyprus by way of Greece. Ultimately, in an environment such as Famagusta, the question of who seems less important than the questions of why certain artistic expressions were chosen, and how these elements were received when their juxtapositions suggest to our modern eyes some kind of discord or dichotomy.

Diversity, Permeability and Power

Famagusta only began to emerge as an important port and urban centre after the fall of Acre in 1291. While the events of 1291 did not entirely turn the ruling class, and thus the majority of patrons, away from models and traditions of the lost crusader kingdoms of the mainland, they did force a reconsideration of Cyprus's role in international politics. Cyprus became the largest eastern Latin kingdom in Christendom, and the image of the kingdom needed to be from this point in time not just international, but of the highest courtly caliber. In the late thirteenth and early fourteenth century King Henry II developed a new relationship with the emerging city. He established a palace, directly across from the site of the Latin cathedral. This alone suggests a type of dialogue or relationship between the Latin bishops of Famagusta and the king. The Franciscan church was patronized by Henry II and situated very close to the palace.[46] The church of SS Peter and Paul, while having a less clearly defined relationship with the royal house, also flanks the palace on the other side and presents its most elaborately decorated doorway facing the royal residence. The royal family also contributed to large building programmes such as the church of St Mary of Carmel. For the first several decades of the city's development, the Lusignans were deeply involved in the development of visual culture in Famagusta.

Unique to Famagusta however was an additional set of resources and patrons that vied with the monarchy for influence in the visual culture of the city. The economy of Famagusta was fairly distinct in Cyprus, in that it included a large amount of expendable wealth. This wealth was not held by the Lusignan rulers, the aristocratic fief-holders, or the indigenous Orthodox

[45] Carr, pp. 318–20; S. Runciman, *Mistra. Byzantine Capital of the Peloponnese* (London, 1980), 56.

[46] Enlart, p. 263; de Vaivre and Plagnieux, p. 240.

community, but was the privilege of the primarily foreign merchants and bankers in the city. The growing Italian communities were thick with merchants, and their numbers were added to by refugees arriving after the loss of Christian cities in the Holy Land. These populations quickly became prominent patron groups who wanted to express their wealth and status within Famagusta by visual means, which often included their own church. Although we cannot truly determine the church referred to in the story of the Lachas brothers, it is likely that their story or one like it is true. One family could have made enough profit through trade to sponsor the building of their own church.[47] Perhaps there was even more opportunity for sponsoring the building and decoration of monuments in Famagusta as the king fell increasingly into debt during the latter half of the fourteenth century and ultimately lost the city to the Genoese in 1373.[48] It is likely that the merchant classes and the Genoese continued the patronage of painted decoration in many of the newly erected churches in Famagusta.

As this chapter has shown, there were many choices available for the visual expression of these diverse groups of patrons. One can imagine that if a royal patron wanted to express himself as the dominant Christian king in the East, he might choose the most innovative and contemporary image that would associate him with Latin Christendom, namely Gothic architecture. The sculptural decoration and scale of the Franciscan church, SS Peter and Paul and also the Latin cathedral of St Nicholas are markedly different from building programmes in the Latin East and show a close correspondence to western visual culture. A merchant living in Famagusta, however, may also have wished to express his status, wealth and piety through church building. His choices may have been drawn from the royally-sponsored monuments, as well as monuments from his native land in Syria, or Italy. A newly instated Greek bishop may also have wanted to build a structure that would compete visually with the Latin cathedral and he chose selective elements from that model. The architecture and its painting in Famagusta throw into sharp relief the relationship between identity and the arts. Does art espouse a specific identity based on its style or iconography? The examples from fourteenth-century Famagusta suggest that one choice of style or iconography is not enough to categorize the identity of its patron or audience. Art in the particular context of late medieval Cyprus functioned independently of other, more static, indicators of identity, such as specific rights and privileges which did distinguish and divide communities even in the multi-cultural commercial centre of Famagusta.[49]

While acknowledging this flexibility and permeability among the arts of Famagusta, we also acknowledge the distinct culture of late medieval Cyprus. The most important function of these churches is directly dependent on the

---

47 de Vaivre and Plagnieux, p. 272; Walsh, pp. 82–3. Enlart (pp. 211, 280) cites Machaeras, Bustron and Strambaldi.

48 L. Balletto, 'Les Génois dans l'île de Chypre au bas moyen age', in *Lusignan et l'outre-mer. Actes du Colloque: Poitiers-Lusignan 20–24 octobre 1993* (Poitiers, 1994), 31.

49 Schryver, p. 390.

unique economy and political position of Famagusta. All of the churches in both their architecture and painted decoration appear to be the expression of each patron group's status or ideal of status. Outside of inscriptions, the figural style and iconography seems less married to a cultural identity as it is to the production of beautiful and timely artworks. The sculpted portals and dramatic ribbed vaulting may have had a general association with the West, and certainly in the combined effect of the façade of the Latin cathedral of St Nicholas it may have been identified as such. However, in the adoption of these elements in the Orthodox cathedral and monuments of Armenian and Syrian Christians, it seems likely that these visual motifs were quickly accepted as indicators of power and wealth, rather than cultural identity, religion or politics. It is interesting that as she preached in the presence of several of these monuments in the 'main square' of Famagusta in 1372, St Bridget of Sweden chose not to rail against the various non-Latin communities (which she did later at the Lusignan court). In this public space, she did not frame her comments in terms of distinct identities, but preached against the decadent morals of the inhabitants and nobility.[50] Arguably it is these decadent morals, expendable wealth, and public expression of status, that distinguished Famagusta as noted by the pilgrims James of Verona and Ludolf of Sudheim, who described the extravagant wedding ceremonies of Famagustan brides.[51]

The architecture and monumental painting in Famagusta in the fourteenth century blurs the lines between distinct categories of imagery. These examples confound the modern viewer by suggesting a powerful Gothic vocabulary from northern Europe, and simultaneously a possible Byzantine tradition of painting. As we explore more deeply the available evidence in this complex city, it becomes clearer that the selection of styles and iconographies cannot be fitted into one or even two categories. More importantly, the imagery in Famagusta also reveals the flexible and permeable function that art was able to have within a city of unique economic and political status. The expansion of the arts of Famagusta beyond a binary framework of Gothic and Byzantine also shows the ability of the inhabitants of Famagusta, as well as Cypriots as a whole, to accept a variety of artistic styles and iconographies without simplifying these into distinct categories of cultural identity. Cypriots could absorb art already culturally mixed from the Holy Land, art distinctly imperial in its Palaeologan expression, as well as art indicative of the Latin Christian monarchies of the West in Gothic architecture and sculpture. They could view these all simultaneously as indicators of the status, wealth and power of the patrons of these monuments and perhaps of the glimmering city of Famagusta itself.

---

50 E. Piltz, 'Saint Bridget and Byzantium – in view of her Cyprian revelations', *Praktika tou Deuterou Diethnous Kypriologikou Synedriou* (Nicosia, 20–25 April 1982) (Nicosia, 1986), 2: 50.

51 Enlart, p. 211 (citing 'Le pèlinerage du moine augustin Jacques de Vérone (1335)', ed. R. Röhricht, *Revue de L'Orient Latin* (1895) 3: 177–8, and Ludolf of Sudheim, 'De itinere Terre Sancte', ed. G.A. Naumann, *Archives de L'Orient latin* (1884), 2/2: 336).

Famagusta from a Latin Perspective: Venetian Heraldic Shields and Other Fragmentary Remains

Vincenzo Lucchese

Since antiquity, the islands of the Mediterranean basin have attracted settlers and formed centres of commercial activity for peoples of various ethnic and cultural backgrounds.[1] During the later Middle Ages and the Renaissance two islands in particular were of primary importance in the commercial and cultural exchanges between East and West, between the Christian and the Islamic worlds: the first of these was Sicily, and the second, the more self-contained Cyprus. Both were located at commercial crossroads, something which had adverse repercussions on their political stability. Sicily was considered the pearl of the Tyrrhenian Sea, coveted by both France and Spain. Meanwhile Cyprus, situated in an area that witnessed a new surge of Ottoman expansion in the early sixteenth century, experienced political volatility, and found itself the object of the conflicting ambitions of the Genoese, Catalans and Venetians. Within this broader historical context the Lusignan kings sought to maintain a precarious equilibrium by containing the ambitions of these competing powers, something that they were increasingly less able to achieve.

The impressive history of Cyprus finds visual expression in the buildings on the island. An examination of their structures and external decoration shows how the Gothic-Renaissance *Ars Aedificandi* is enriched by sculpted handiwork and fragments of painted frescoes. The extant examples of civic

---

1 Thanks are due in particular to arch. Dario Zanverdiani for his research and support since our first study tour to Cyprus in the 1990s. I must also thank my Turkish Cypriot colleague, the architect Umit Inatci, who proved to be an amiable and generous guide in Famagusta, and my faithful friends and Greek Cypriots colleagues, Eftychia and Nedi Ioannou, Chryso Elefteriou, Constantinos Konteatis, Giannis Teloudis, Koula Ioannou and George Phaltis. In addition, I should mention other members of the Cyprus Italy Association: Leonardo da Vinci, Petros Stamataris, Christos Nikos, Lauris Andreas, Pantelis Orfanidis and Loizos Christodoulou. The English translation was undertaken by Dr Adelina Modesti (La Trobe University, Australia), whose support in the past and in this present study has been invaluable.

and religious architecture, even if they amount to only a small fraction of the artistic and architectural accomplishments that once existed, enjoy wide-ranging and deserved renown: one need only witness the fine masonry that seems to have been executed by the most highly skilled European master builders and craftsmen, some of whom possibly accompanied King Louis IX of France to Cyprus in 1248. Some superb decorative displays survive, not least those to be found on the lintels of the portals and windows of the existing buildings. After the Ottoman conquest, Cyprus remained in the spotlight of public opinion in western Europe on account of the numerous publications emanating from printing presses in Venice, as well as those of other centres such as Paris and Nuremberg that appeared in the following century. One of the most avid exponents of this form of historical propaganda was Fr Stefano Lusignano (Etienne de Lusignan), a Dominican lector already actively engaged in this mission in the Neapolitan monastery of Santa Catherina di Formello in 1570. Lusignano dedicated his initial work, entitled *Chorograffia et breve Historia Universale dell'Isola de Cipro, principiando al tempo di Noè per in sino al 1572* to King Charles IX of France and to King Henry of Poland. The volume first appeared in 1573, courtesy of the famous Bolognese publisher Alessandro Benaccio. In his description of 'the many sectors into which the island of Cyprus was divided', Lusignan provided a catalogue of the principal Cypriot and Venetian noble families that had formerly resided in the island. The catalogue he compiled forms to this day an invaluable historical tool for the dating and study of the heraldic insignia that is either still *in situ* or has been collected and placed in the museums that house lapidary inscriptions and other forms of epigraphic evidence. Another important book eventually appeared in print over a century later. This was Monsignor Antonio Maria Gratiani's *Histoire de la Guerre de Chypre*, published in Paris in 1685. In this work, the author described the daily life of the besieged Cypriots, citing episodes and naming the persons and families who played a prominent part in the defence of Nicosia, examples being the Rochas and the Podocataro. In addition, the author highlighted the rivalries existing between the Venetian captains of the walled city of Nicosia and those of Famagusta.

In the course of my visits and sojourns on the island, everyone has extended a warm welcome to me, allowing me unimpeded access to the urban sites in search of the older forms of architecture in existence prior to the Ottoman conquest. Assisted by my Greek Cypriot former students, I also availed myself of the opportunity to undertake architectural measurements in order to arrive at a more precise documentation of the sites. My first study visit took place in Nicosia in 1991, accompanied by the professor of architecture, Corrado Balistreri, within the context of a cultural exchange celebrating the links between the Veneto Region and Cyprus going back several centuries. The material gathered was also utilized by my colleague Dario Zanverdiani, who has commenced an in-depth archival study to confirm the close relationship between Cyprus and the Serenissima. In the course of a visit to the old city of Nicosia on that particular occasion various measurements of buildings were taken and details noted. Among the buildings visited was the former Byzantine church known as Stavros tou Misericou, transformed into a mosque after 1571 and thenceforth known as the Arablar Mosque. It is located in the 28 October Square within the Greek sector of Nicosia, a short distance from the Orthodox church of Phaneromene. The exterior is notable on account of its stylistically contrasting elements, such as a rich crowning continuous phytomorphic cornice, with faced volutes, and the underlying structure of buttresses, in typical French Gothic scheme with angles formed by stone drops. These buttresses are comparable to those on a number of monuments situated within the Turkish sector of Nicosia, two examples being the former church of St George of the Latins, now the Büyük Hamam, and the thirteenth-century cathedral of St Sophia. In addition, they are comparable to those found in Famagusta on the exteriors of the churches of St George of the Greeks (fourteenth century) and St George of the Latins (thirteenth/ fourteenth centuries). The interior of the Arablar Mosque is divided into three aisles, with a central apse enclosed by Gothic columns. Also of interest are two tombstones embedded in the stone floor, both of which contain an image of a recumbent figure fashionably dressed in sixteenth-century Venetian style, with breeches [brache]. Unfortunately the inscriptions have been abraded, but I hope to expand this important collection of data in the immediate future, taking advantage of the more hospitable atmosphere conducive to the conduct of field-work in the Turkish quarters of Nicosia and Famagusta.

This conference on Famagusta and its historic centre creates additional opportunities for studying the historical sites in the town, not only as evidence for history and society in the periods of Lusignan and Venetian rule, but also by way of creating a platform for discussion with respect to their conservation and the most appropriate *modus operandi* for their restoration and possible re-utilization. A number of different interpretations as to what elements constitute the historic centre of the city and how it should be treated with a view to ensuring its future preservation can be advanced. These can then be expounded within an international forum in a way that will encourage the provision of the financial resources needed to facilitate further conservation and restoration. My own contribution, inspired by a short visit to this city – so famous and yet previously unknown to me – focuses attention on the splendour of the masonry structures and the importance of the remaining sculptural decorations. As a heraldry expert and a member of the *Istituto Araldico Genealogico Italiano*, I have paid particular attention to buildings, as well as to the associated heraldic emblems of the Venetian period. The latter, according to the administration's use of the practices prevailing throughout the Serenissima, were an essential prerequisite for recording the dates of the initial construction of edifices or their subsequent renovation. At present they form a necessary element in attempting to establish dates and define chronologies.

The city of Famagusta possesses a remarkable historic town centre enclosed within a complete *enceinte*. At its centre stands the noble and imposing early fourteenth-century cathedral of St Nicholas (since the Ottoman conquest the Lala Mustafa Pasha mosque). There exist, however, many other buildings of major historical interest, the importance of which is manifest despite their obvious state of disrepair. These edifices as a whole are sending out a loud and clear signal to all members of the international community of scholars and conservators to perpetuate their legacy as monuments of a civilization famed for its universal values.

An example of this is afforded by the interesting rectangular building located to the right of the façade of the cathedral (Figure 10.1). Here two circular rose windows frame a magnificent main portal. This richly decorated entrance is crowned by Venetian heraldic emblems: to be precise, two escutcheons of the Bembo family, which claimed familial connections with Queen Caterina Cornaro. The first, enshrined in a Renaissance *accartocciato* shield, is set in the wall above the right window just under the cornice – a crowning frieze, in which the first band is composed of an order of double leaves with a channelled upper band in classical Renaissance style above (Figure 10.2). The second blazon is on the ground, carved into the side of an antique marble frieze and composed within a *sannitico* shield, typically Venetian with its two upper volutes (Figure 10.3). The two pairs of three columns of compact white limestone, which support the carved arches of the portal, have extremely stylized capitals reminiscent of an archaic Byzantine form which are out of harmony with the overhanging Gothic cornices (Figure 10.4). Between these and the capitals is a band of coussinet [*pulvini*] decorated with rosettes, and inserted in the median capital are two emblems, also of the Bembo family, which confirm their fifteenth-century origin (Figure 10.5). The keystone in the interior room, which displays the lion of the Serenissima, in the form known as *moeca* [crab], reaffirms this. The fourth ring of the arches has a mixtilineal undulation, which recalls Sicilian *Chiaramontani* buildings used in Cyprus and throughout the Mediterranean area. Numerous Sicilians during the era in which the Chiaramonte family enjoyed prominence cultivated links with Cyprus, sailing to the island as well as trading and acquiring properties there. Economic ties with Cyprus were maintained even in later periods when the island came under the dominion of Venice.[2] In view of these contacts it is no surprise that their architecture also travelled to Cyprus.

Continuing with the description of the imposing building adjacent to the Cathedral of St Nicholas, commonly named the Loggia Bembo, one observes that the outermost arch is decorated with Hercules locked in combat with a lion; the second by a winged dragon, while the third has suffered too much from wind erosion (due to the current passing through the two portals) for its decorations to be identified. The French art historian Camille Enlart put forward the suggestion that this building housed the cathedral school, but the lack of religious symbolism argues against this idea. The splendour of the

---

2 See N. Coureas, *Taverns in Medieval Famagusta* (this volume), and his mention of Nicholas of Palermo, a rich owner of a tavern and houses, politically tied to the Count of Tripoli and recorded in the chronicle (1460–64) of George Boustronios.

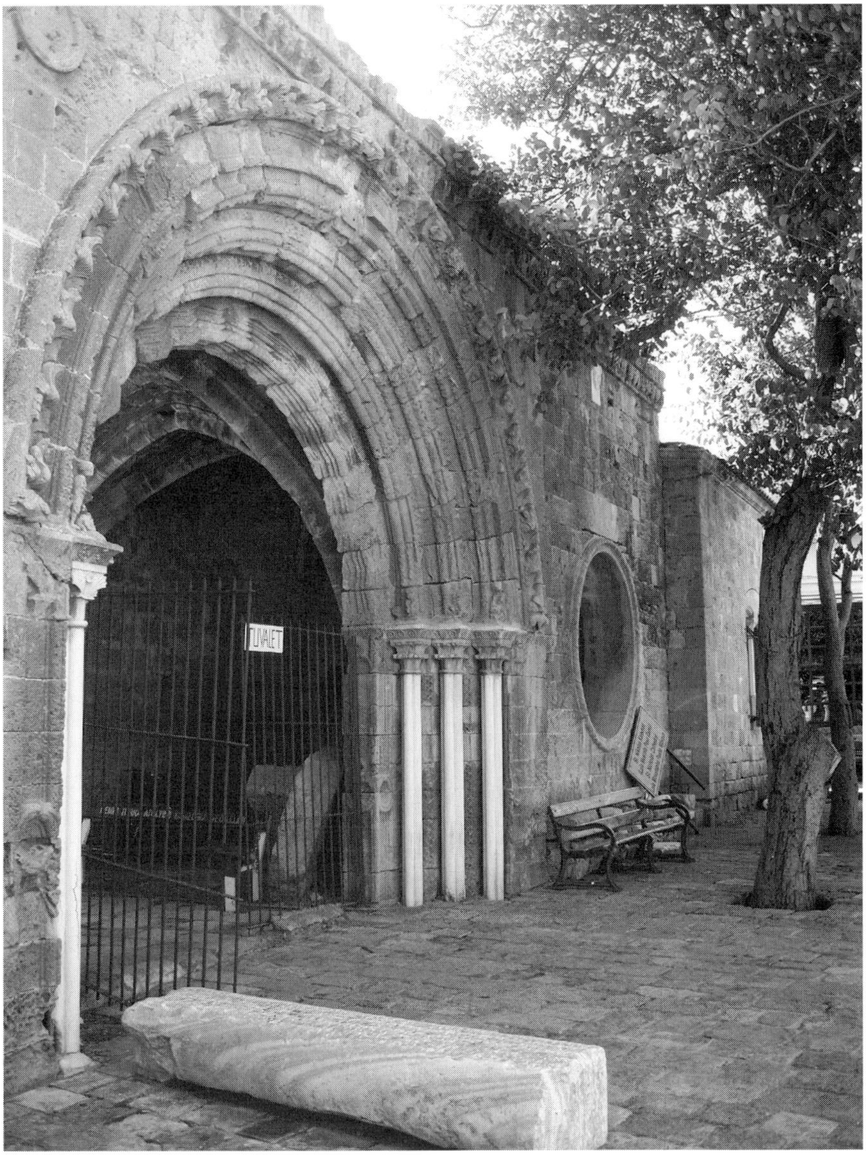

Fig. 10.1 Portal of Loggia Bembo, near Cathedral of St Nicholas (photograph: Vincenzo Lucchese)

internal structure, with its ribbed cross vaults linked to a simple rectangular plan, indicates that it functioned as a place for public gatherings (Plate 10). This idea finds support in the positioning of the two portals in the centre of the building's frontage, thereby permitting free access and exit. Indeed, the unusual size of the large circular windows, now missing the floral tracery that once radiated from their centres, and the fact that they are placed at a relatively low level with respect to the former level of the churchyard, offers an indication. Can this be interpreted as an attempt at visual and noise control by the ruling elite, which would have held meetings, restricted to noblemen, behind closed doors? Use of a building of this sort for such a purpose was

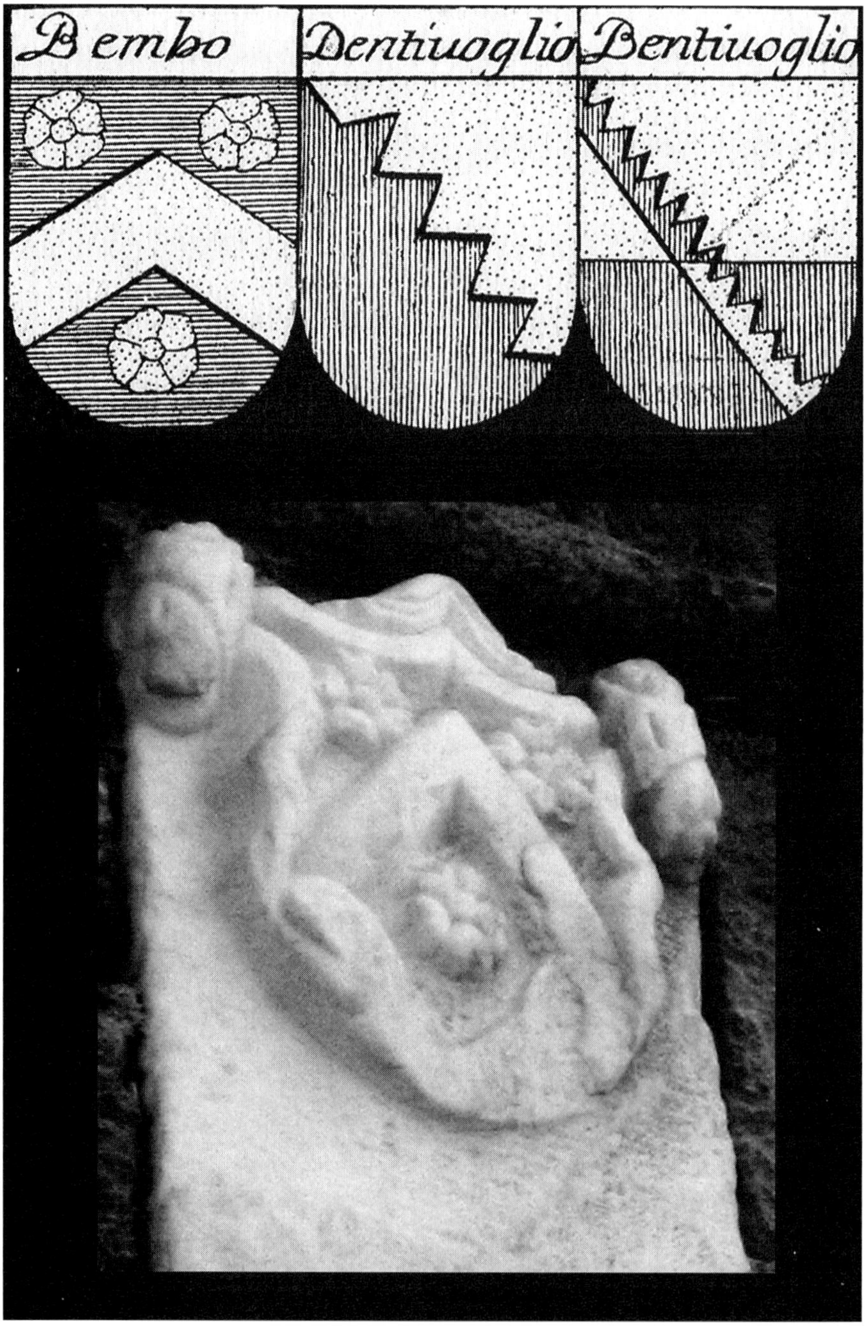

Fig. 10.2 Comparison with Bembo blazon, engraved by V. Coronelli (1706) (photomontage: Vincenzo Lucchese) and convolute shield of Bembo, walled above a window of Loggia Bembo (photograph: Vincenzo Lucchese)

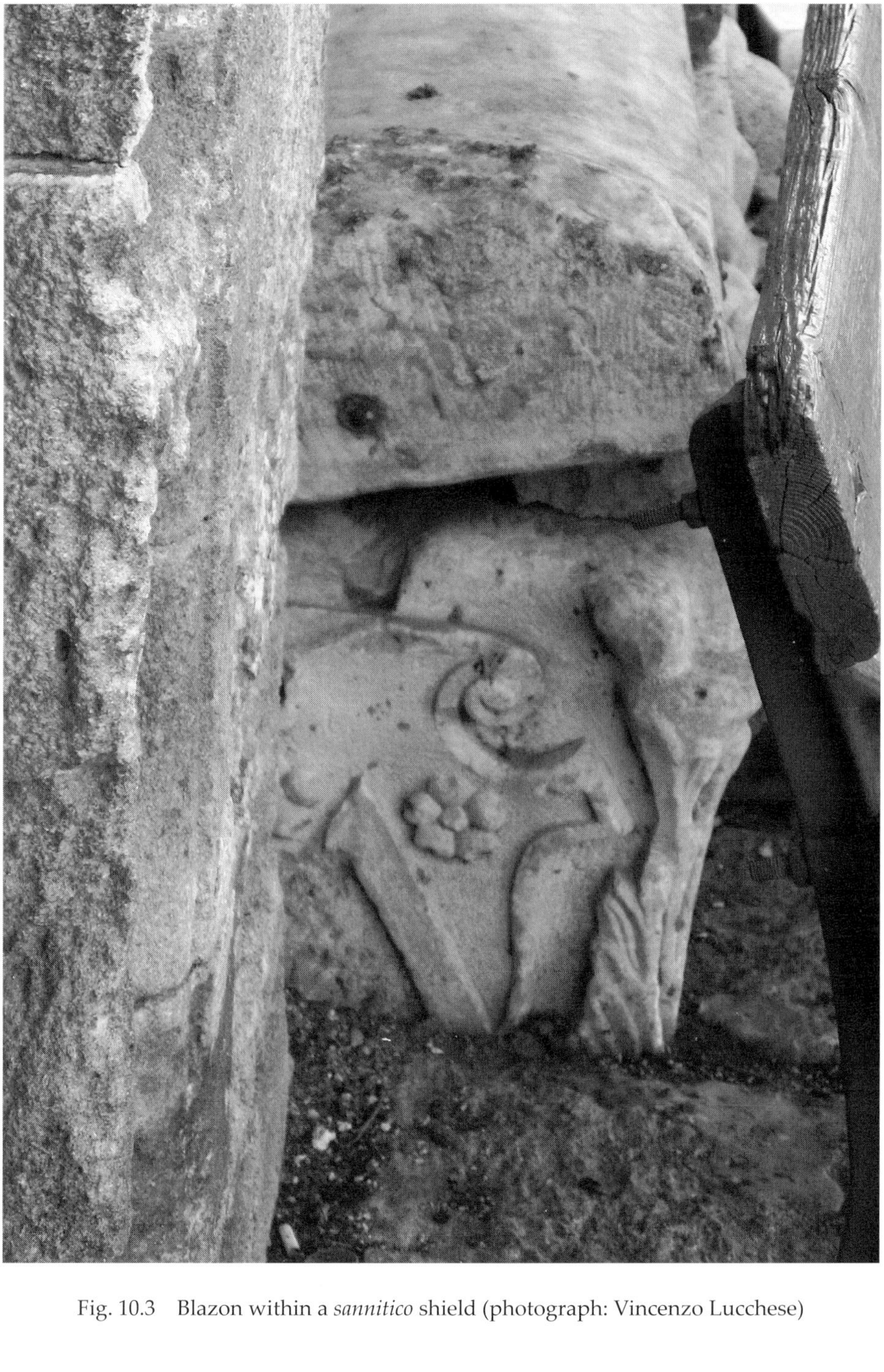

Fig. 10.3 Blazon within a *sannitico* shield (photograph: Vincenzo Lucchese)

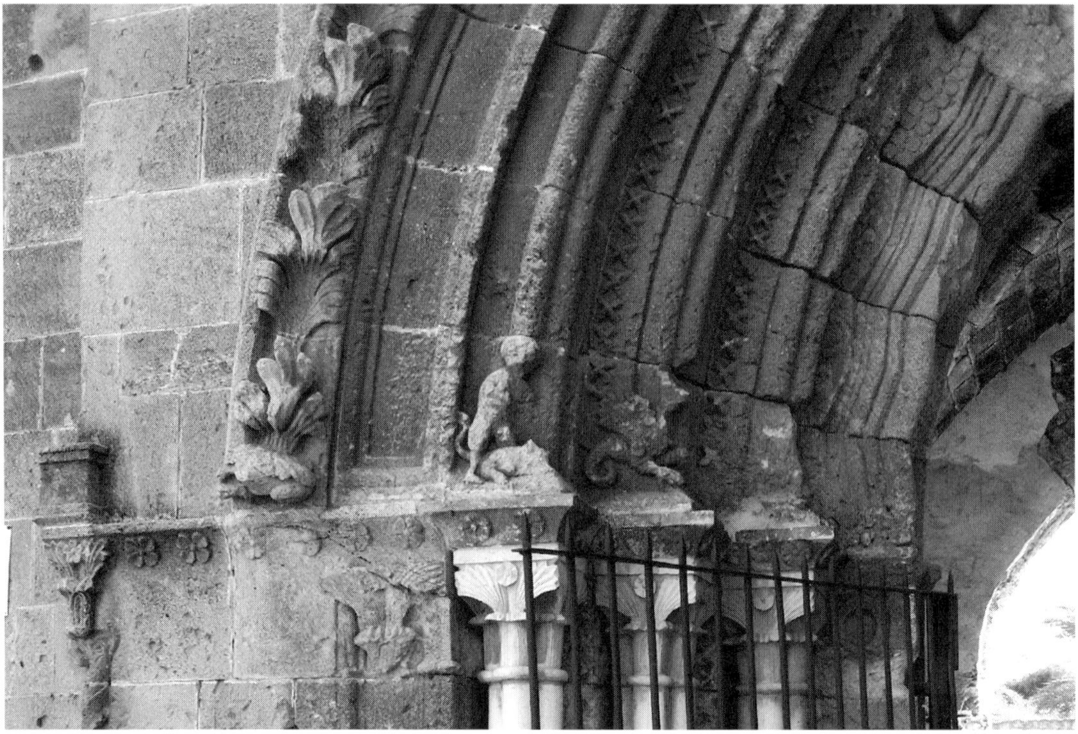

Fig. 10.4 Arch with mixtilineal undulation, in portal of House of Assemblies (photograph: Vincenzo Lucchese)

a long-established tradition in Italy. For example, at the town of Nicosia in Sicily (province of Enna), regular gatherings were held in a loggia which was at the base of the great bell-tower of the Gothic cathedral (St Nicholas, c. 1302–40). There the building dates from the same era and has a similarly rich architectural style. The corresponding edifice in Famagusta underwent repeated modifications on account of maintenance work and reconstruction. The most recent alterations were most probably executed during the period of office of the Venetian captain Daniele Bembo (1485–88), who thereby availed himself of the opportunity to reveal his antiquarian sensibilities and his appreciation of the grandeur of Greco-Roman art. The Bembo family maintained its connections with Cyprus throughout the sixteenth century, providing the island with two captains: Gian Matteo (1546–48) and Lorenzo (1564–66). Beside the large doorway there are two friezes, probably *spolia* from the classical site of Salamis, that function here as a bench. The one on the right side is richly decorated with acanthus leaves. It is pendant to the frieze, to the left, that was raised up to the elevation of a chair and placed on different geometric frames made of local stone. Its interior is carved with *girali* containing animals on the move, making this particular sculptural relief comparable to an antique frieze made of polychrome mosaic.[3] A similar type of iconography is to be found in Venice in the Romanesque-

[3] Roman mosaic in House of Dionysos, Paphos: M. Campagnolo, C. Courtois, M. Martiniani-Reber, L. Michaelidou, *Chypre – D'Aphrodite à Mèlusine* (Geneva, 2006), p. 86.

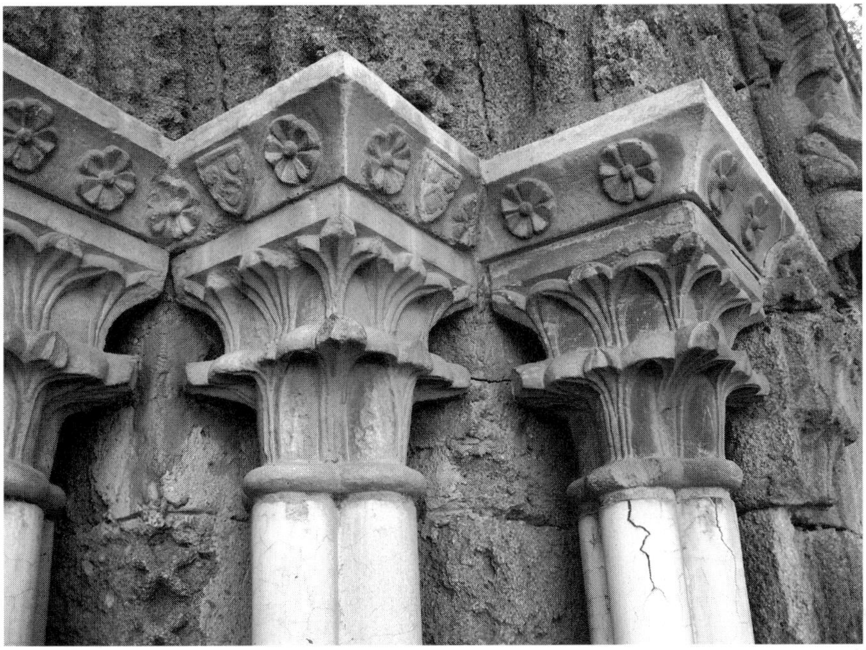

Fig. 10.5 Portal capitals of Loggia Bembo (photograph: Vincenzo Lucchese)

Byzantine friezes, such as those present in the access to the famous Palazzo Contarini[4] *dalla Porta di Ferro* (*Sestiere* of *Castello*). The ring of the raised arch (thirteenth century)[5] within the area of access is carved in low relief with *girali* that contain animals on the move (Plate 11). These are quadrupeds and birds which also include types of the late Roman imperial period. Furthermore, the arch is inscribed in a frame, also carved in low relief, where there is a continuous form of rosettes with four petals, recalling precisely the ones already mentioned and placed on the band of coussinet of the Loggia Bembo.

A similar example of architectural renewal employed in order to celebrate the Venetian administration through the reuse of ancient stonework is to be seen directly opposite St Nicholas's Cathedral. The Doric porch (1552–59) of the palace of the Provveditore utilizes four reused monolithic drums of Egyptian granite in a manner which recalls the typology of a tripartite Roman triumphal arch (Figure 10.6). The lexicon is clearly Vignolesque, displaying an awareness of the latest Sansovino-inspired architectural trends current in Venice and thereby confirming the rich variety of the styles diffused by the Serenissima. On the keystone of the central arch is the bi-chrome marble emblem of Giovanni Renier, captain in the years 1552–54 and then lieutenant 1557–59, within a foiled shield, dominated, in accordance with a Renaissance tradition, by a lion's head with *svolazzi* (Figure 10.7). Two other columns stand

4 From 1473 a branch of the family Contarini bore the title 'del Zaffo', on account of the investiture of the county of Jaffa and the lordship of Ascalon by Caterina Cornaro.

5 E. Arslan, *Venezia Gotica* (Milan, 1970), p. 17.

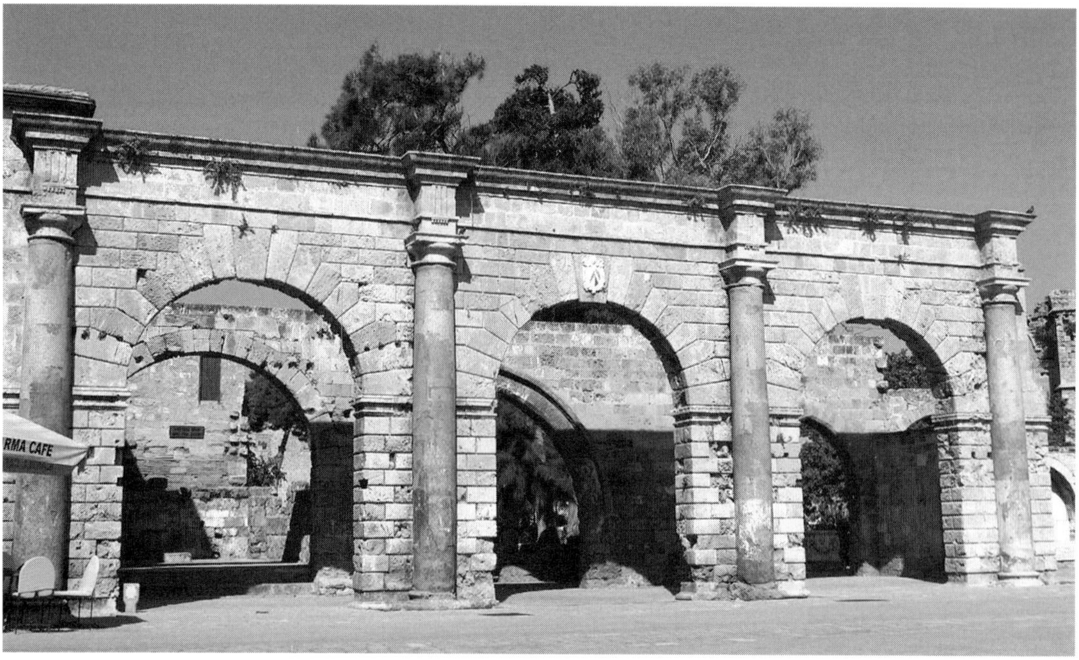

Fig. 10.6 Palace of Provveditore, with coat of arms of Giovanni Renier, Famagusta (photograph: Allan Langdale)

in isolation to the left of the cathedral, one built with an identical monolith of stone material, recalling the famous twin columns of St Mark and St Theodore in the Piazetta San Marco at Venice.

It should be stressed that, despite the poor state of preservation of many of the historic buildings in Cyprus, the Lusignan era was a particularly rich and imaginative period in the field of architecture. Concentrated in Famagusta and Nicosia is a wealth of architectural detail, with few parallels in Europe, and a considerable variety of imaginative decoration. The architectural features found there are considered rare even in Venice, regarded in the fourteenth and fifteenth centuries as being the wealthiest city of Europe after Constantinople. The lintels of some of the doorways in Cyprus for instance present full bodied sets of carving, employing geometric and phytomorphic elements reminiscent of the most beautiful forms of Flemish Gothic and exhibiting a striking similarity to the carved wooden pelmets in the altarpieces of Vivarini.

That which exists in the centre of Famagusta is an assemblage of historic monuments of inestimable value that urgently require conservation, as do the ruins of the nearby church of St George of the Greeks (Figure 10.8). Hopefully their preservation will serve as a tangible example of international collaboration. The church of St George, now reduced to its still imposing apses and its partially surviving outer walls, was once adorned by frescos by talented artists who were themselves perhaps influenced by the school of Giotto. This can be seen, in particular, from the little that remains of the fresco of the Crucifixion on the rear wall above the right portal near the spiral staircase that led to the upper floors (Plate 7). The figurative painting gives the appearance of a bi-chromatic colour scheme, similar to a photographic

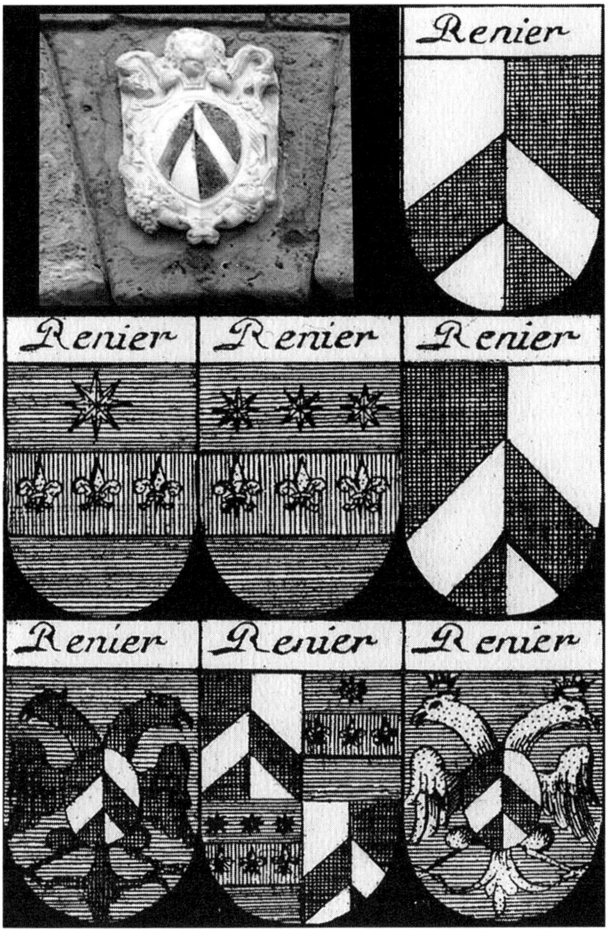

Fig. 10.7 Comparison with Renier blazon, engraved by V. Coronelli (1706) (photomontage: Vincenzo Lucchese)

negative in which the figures appear dark when compared to the background. This effect is almost certainly due to the lack of protection from the weather and has led to a consequent chemical-chromatic variation which fortunately can be restored in some cases to its original state. The grieving figures below the Cross and the angels, high in the fresco, descending alongside the Crucifix are comparable to analogous instances found in fourteenth-century Italian art.

Relations between Byzantine and Italian art have been studied in depth by Joannes A. Eliades,[6] citing in particular the Crucifixions from the Church of St Luke in Nicosia and the Church of St Domenico Maggiore in Naples. The circular symbols of the sun and moon, formerly of Roman origin, can be compared usefully to others in the Göreme region in central Cappadocia, especially the beautiful and well preserved Crucifixion in the Karanlık Kilise (Dark Church). This depiction of the Crucifixion located in the famous valley

[6] I.A. Eliades, 'Cultural Interactions in Cyprus 1191–1571: Byzantine and Italian Art', in A. Cimdina and J. Osmond (eds), *Power and culture – Hegemony, interaction and dissent*, Cliohres.net (Pisa, 2006), p. 18.

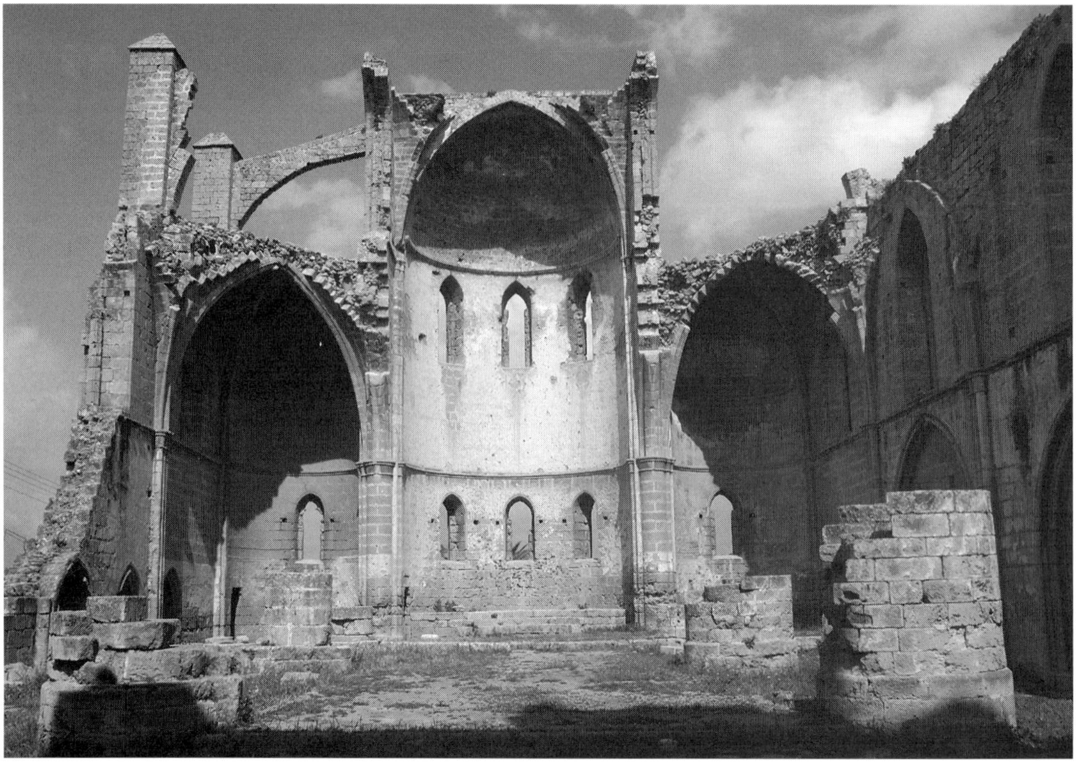

Fig. 10.8 St George of the Greeks, Famagusta (photograph: Thomas Kaffenberger)

formerly known as Korama is still considered one of the archaeological wonders of the world. In this particular instance the style illustrates Syrian influence from ancient Palestine and Armenia, with an admixture of early Christian and Byzantine art forms. All these decorative cycles probably began in the second half of the ninth century, continuing until around 1250. The main churches in the valley are known as the 'churches of the columns': the Karanlık Kilise together with the Elmani Kilise and the Çarıklı Kilise contain frescos with rich decorative supports that are datable to the eleventh century, a period witnessing a considerable upsurge in religious Byzantine art. This can be put forward as a plausible artistic influence, given its origin from a location near the island of Cyprus and adjacent to the realm of Cilician Armenia. By 1342 a member of the Cypriot Lusignan royal family, Guy, had been crowned king of Cilician Armenia, a development marking the culmination of a long history of relations between the two kingdoms fostered by a series dynastic marriages harking back to the beginning of the thirteenth century. Cilicia was overrun by the Muslims in the 1370s and following the death of the last of the Armenian Lusignans in 1393 the Cypriot royal house claimed the titular kingship of Cilician Armenia; it was for that reason that the lion rampant of Armenia appears henceforth on the arms of the Lusignan royal house, quartered with the emblems of Jerusalem and Lusignan. This quartered shield appears on some examples of the silver coinage minted in

Cyprus during the reigns of Queen Charlotte (1458–60), as well as on certain coins minted under Caterina Cornaro (1473–89).[7]

Enough survives of the church of St George of the Greeks, to permit an examination of the essential architectural features: among these are included the nave and two side aisles, where circular columns of well-drafted stones supported ogival arches, enriched by tracery-contours, that delimited the vaults upwards, then came back down in the side walls, and hid, in their trilobal section, the buttresses which provide the outer structural support. Those pilaster strips are interrupted, at the level of the top horizontal frame, by stone elements in the shape of a truncated cone, which act as capitals. These, in turn, become elements supporting the overhead rib structure. The main apse, below its semi dome, is lit by three large single ogival windows, doubled into two orders, the upper being almost double the height of the lower. The lateral apses are lit on the other hand by a single opening placed in the centre. The pictorial cycles were arranged around the walls, with the sequences of saints and episodes in the life of Christ limited by the vertical cording, as well as by the window openings themselves. In the left-hand apse schematic drawings of Venetian or European ships were etched by pious persons into the plaster, a phenomenon that probably occurred during the period of the siege, with such etchings serving as tangible expressions of the prayers given for the arrival of the Christian fleet.[8] Furthermore, there are notches that were likewise etched into the plaster, representing these painfully agonizing days of waiting (Plate 12).

Originally the columns of the nave were the same size and height, and bore the same capitals as the semi-columns that define the great apse where the clergy could be seated in the course of religious ceremonies. An examination of a cross-section of the plinths of the columns in the nave reveals that at some point they were reinforced by an outer ring of more coarsely cut masonry.

---

7 Campagnolo et al., n. 179. In Venice itself a Lusignan coat of arms was designed by John Ruskin: V. Lucchese, D. Zanverdiani, '*Da Venezia al Levante Architettura e il retaggio di una civiltà*', in F. Labelli and S. Marini (eds), *L'architettura e le sue declinazioni* (Verona, 2008), p. 64.

8 The shapes of ships and notches, which indicated the number of ships or days of travel (round trip), is very old tradition in the Mediterranean, especially in coastal villages. This very old tradition was used in temples and sacred enclosures by sailors and children. Among the many examples from the first century AD, are in the Vesuvius area, especially the villa of San Marco, near Castellammare di Stabia (vessels of different sizes and notches). In the Renaissance period, the custom of *ex voto* images for ships and sailors can be witnessed even in Venetian painting of the Crucifix and The Apparition of Mount Ararat in the Church of Sant'Antonio di Castello (Gallerie dell'Accademia), painted by Vittore Carpaccio in 1515. This church, located near the Hospital of Sailors, is filled with votive wax, coloured flags used in the navy and miniature models of galleons and galleys (see D. Zanverdiani, 'Navi' in C. Balestieri-Trincanato and D. Zanverdiani (eds), *Jacopo De Barbari – Il racconto di una città* (Mestre-Venezia, 2000); also M. Walsh, '"On of the princypalle Havenes of the See": The Port of Famagusta and the Ship Graffiti of its Ruined Churches', *International Journal of Nautical Archaeology*, 2007).

These repairs indicate the need for structural consolidation, resulting most probably from the fear of a possible collapse as a result of an earthquake or widening cracks in the upper walls of the nave. The left aisle is the only one possessing the feature of *arcosolium* tombs, with the lateral springers supporting the tombstone and showing heraldic or phitomorphic decorations forming a frame for a sculpted full-length portrait of the deceased sleeping (*gissant*). The side walls of the arches are the only walls that retain images of patron saints. The back walls, on which images of the Madonna or Christ were once visible, now reveal solely the ashlars of which they are built. This funerary typology is paralleled throughout Europe and is to be found concurrently in Italy. To rebuild the image of the splendour of decorative painting, an in-depth knowledge of the major European churches is necessary; more specifically, one has to refer to the work of the historian Camille Enlart, himself an admirer of Viollet le Duc.[9]

Scholars have noted previously the particular structural characteristics of the roof vaults. Indeed, this is possible because the condition of architectural remains permits an observation of the techniques of construction. It is as though an assonometric section was in existence – rather like those *Trecento* Giottesque frescos in which the ecclesiastic, or in some instances the donor, presents a model to the patron saint – so that this architectural complex can be read usefully by experts in the techniques of restoration. In this instance, as in the vaults of other religious buildings, we find amphorae or pitchers being

---

[9] In Venice, a city of economic and artistic importance, I wish to cite a few examples of funerary monuments of the *arcosolia* type which may correspond. In the Basilica of the Frari, the tomb of Doge Francesco Dandolo (1329–39) and his wife Elizabeth Contarini, is a masterpiece. The noble and rich family had economic interests in Cyprus and gave to the administration of the island a governor and several captains. The tomb consists of an ark, with two side shelves, which support a carved Gothic arch, in polychrome with the presence of gilding. These architectural elements surrounded a beautiful and valuable painting by Paolo da Venezia. Following the fashion of the time, the dead are presented by two patron saints to the Virgin enthroned with Child. The tomb of Duccio Alberti, the Florentine ambassador (died 1336), is engraved with the deceased sleeping (*gissant*). The space between sculpture and arches was designed for religious images accompanied by patron saints of the deceased. Another monument is that of Scipione Bon, called Friar Pacific (died 1362), where the arch is decorated by a ring of foliage and figures, sculpted and painted in polychrome with gilding. A blue sky is sprinkled with gold stars. Equally beautiful is the solemn memorial, in the form of *arcosolia*, for the Doge Morosini Michele (died 1332), in the basilica of SS John and Paul. Above the tombstone, with *gissant* in Doge dress and horn, the polychrome mosaic triumphs with crucifixion and patron saints. The bas-reliefs, statuettes and the foliage of architectural decoration can be attributed to sculptors from Masegne.

Examples of graves to *arcosolia*, are also found in other Italian cities, for example in Bologna, seat of the oldest university in Europe, where professors and those belonging to the noble families, erected these, not only within churches but under the arcades of buildings. Many are painted and to be found in Zamboni street and along the perimeter of the Basilica of San Giacomo (e.g. the Salaroli family). In Florence, the succession of medieval tombs to *arcosolia* forms the perimeter wall of the church, and the cemetery, of Santa Maria Novella, for celebrated families such as: Medici, Mazzinghi, Martelli, Guicciardini, Cerchi-Arbizi. Under the Gothic arches were painted religious images.

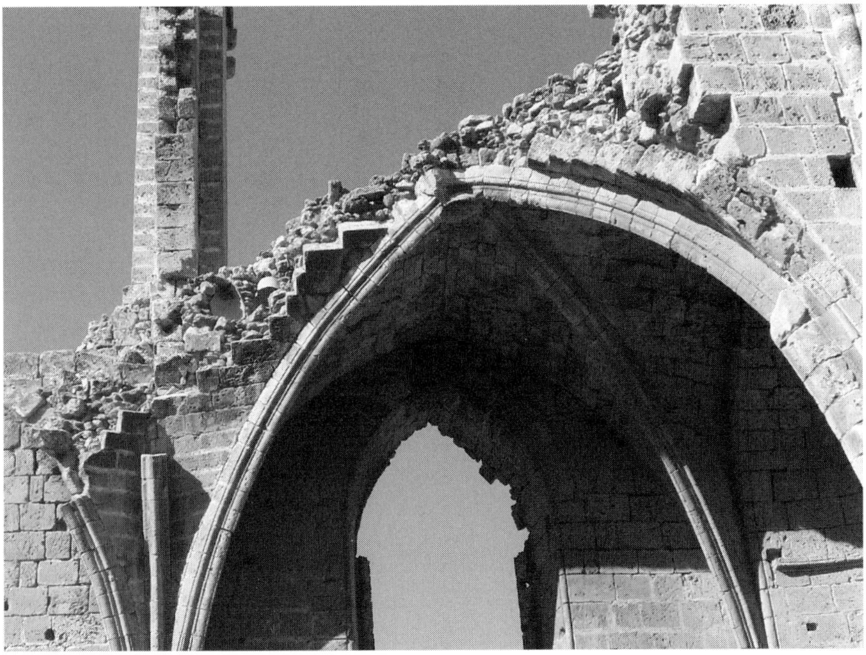

Fig. 10.9 Structure of vaults, including amphorae or pitchers, St George of the Greeks (photograph: Vincenzo Lucchese)

used to reduce the weight of the vaults in accordance with the techniques of the Roman *Ars Aedificandi* (Figure 10.9). Thus, as can be also seen in the Byzantine territories in Italy, especially the Exarchate of Ravenna, a sequence of wine amphorae, their necks broken off, were placed one within the other and made to follow the curvilinear construction of the vault, relying on the effect of gravity to hold them in place. The gaps between them were then filled and then they were plastered over. This construction technique is observable even in the case of load-bearing walls. On the exterior, the great apse flanked by the two smaller ones is reminiscent of the architectural arrangement found in Norman churches in Sicily, suggesting cultural exchange and the transmission of building techniques from various parts of Italy and Sicily to a number of locations in the eastern Mediterranean.

The west façade of St George of the Greeks was enriched by a well-carved lattice rose window, although regrettably only a few curvilinear elements now remain. Among the surviving windows of the single right aisle, only one has retained the stone mullioned open-work. Fortunately some pieces of the stonework are to be found lying on the ground and are therefore recoverable. The third span on the right and perhaps the fourth before the presbytery has direct access to a more ancient church in Famagusta constructed in the Byzantine style, this being the church of St Symeon. In this as in previous instances, the remains deserve a more detailed study so that the beauty of its proportions can be fully appreciated. Although in ruins, the church nevertheless retains its architectural interest and the ancient skills of building in stone that it exemplifies afford considerable pleasure. One is entitled to speculate on whether this architectural ensemble could be transformed into a

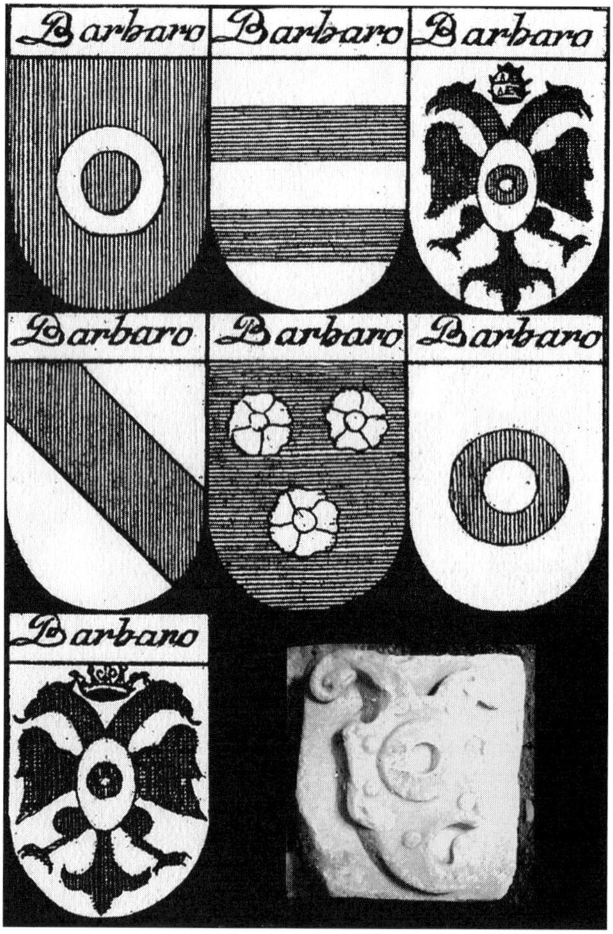

Fig. 10.10 Barbaro shield in Vaulted Chambers of Famagusta Castle. Comparison with blazon engraved by V. Coronelli (1706) (photomontage: Vincenzo Lucchese)

lapidary museum for Famagusta, serving as a point of concentration for the numerous examples of carved stones that are scattered throughout the town. At some point in the future, with the nearby church of St George of the Greeks restored by experts and provided with walk-ways and floodlights, it would form a striking setting, worthy of Famagusta's architectural heritage.

A similar programme of restoration and reuse could also be realized at the citadel commonly known as Othello's Tower, with the recovery and display of the carvings there that are currently subject to sad neglect. These carvings urgently need to be catalogued and dated; heraldic emblems must be identified firstly and subsequently must be put on display with sufficient information to explain their contexts. The sort of examples springing to mind are the two quartered coats of arms with the Lusignan lion rampant and the radiant sun, one of which is in the Museum of Archbishop's Palace in Nicosia. An additional example is furnished by the coats of arms with the *ciclamoro* [annular symbol in heraldry] of the Barbaro family in the vaulted chambers at the Castle of Famagusta, near the *San Michele* Bastion (Figure 10.10). Another

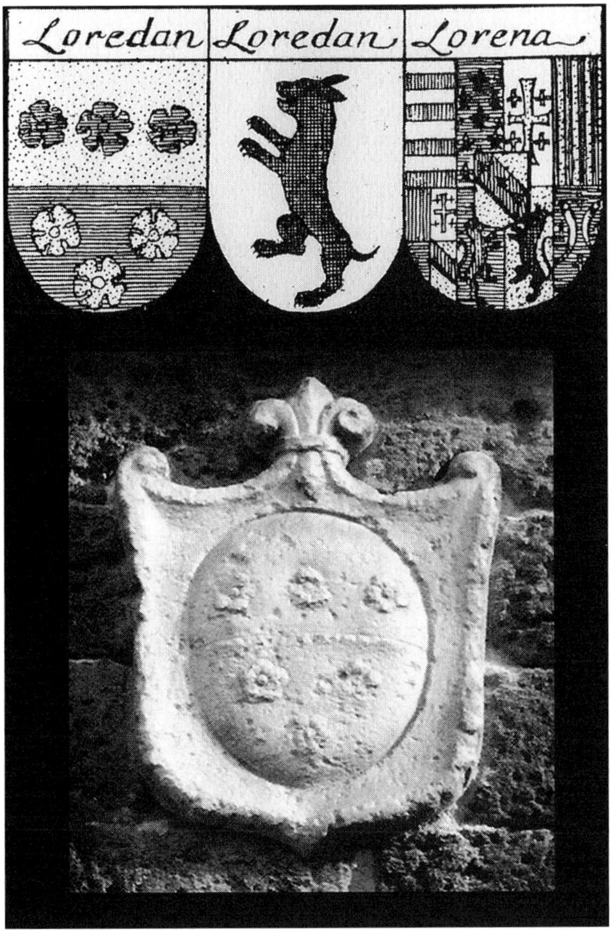

Fig. 10.11 Loredan shield on right parastas of Famagusta Gate in Nicosia. Comparison with blazon engraved by V. Coronelli (1706) (photomontage: Vincenzo Lucchese)

Barbaro coat of arms, in white stone, is embedded in the wall on the right pillar of the inward façade of the *Porta Giuliana*, now Famagusta Gate in Nicosia, above those of the Civran family. Mounted on angular parastas, however, on the extreme right of the gate, a shield of the Loredan family is to be found instead (Figure 10.11).

Those visiting the magnificent defensive structure of Famagusta cannot fail to notice the remarkable winged lion (*guardant* lion), above the main entrance of Othello's Tower, rebuilt by Venetian Captain Nicolò Foscarini (1492) (Figure 10.12). Its archaic muzzle is comparable to that of bronze lion in the Piazetta San Marco in Venice. Similar elements are the scowling visage, the protruding, stylized eyes and the mane carved as the heraldic symbol 'sun in splendour' emblazoned with special, wavy rays. These characteristics are typically present in images of the lion of Saint Mark and are dateable to the end of the fifteenth century.

This similarity shows that the sculptor had copied a drawing which almost certainly originated from Venice and served as an icon of the emblematic lion

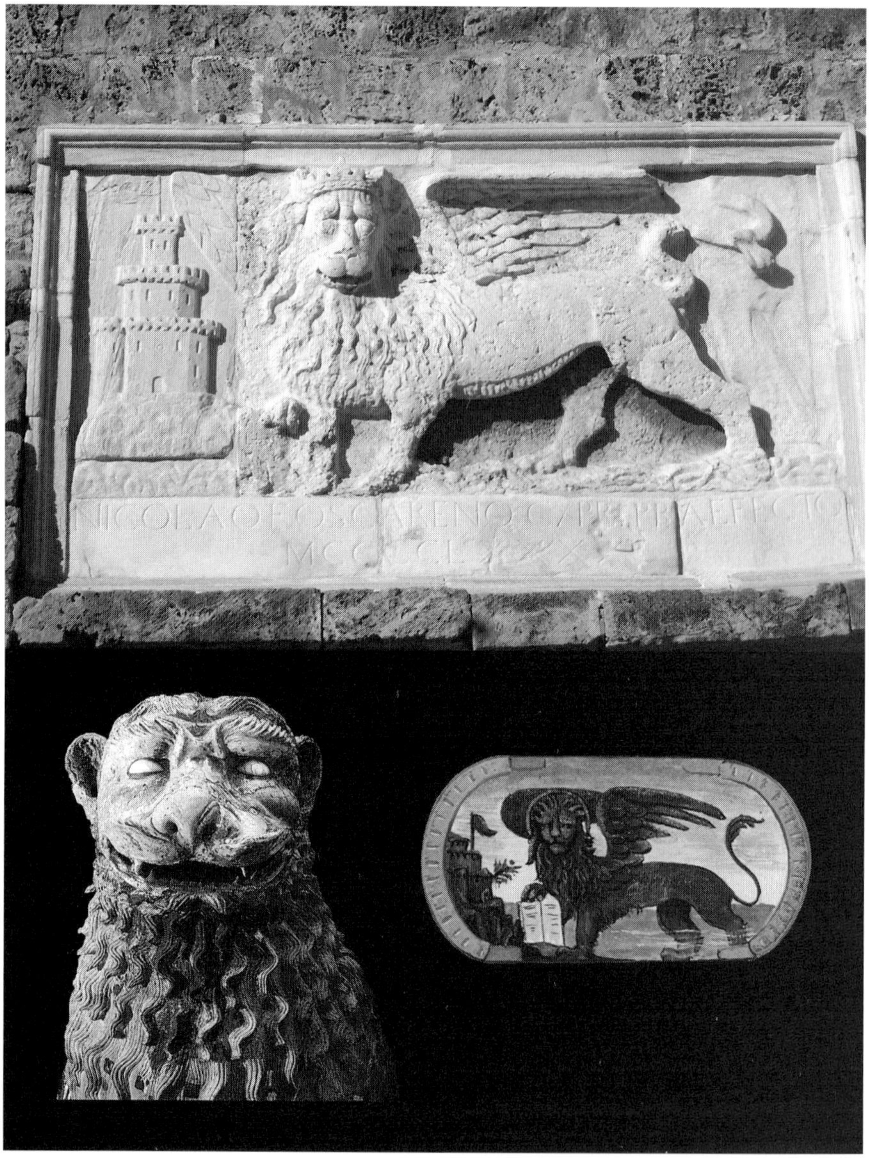

Fig. 10.12 Winged lion above main entrance of Othello's Tower, Famagusta. Comparison with lion of Piazzetta San Marco in Venice and a miniature (early 16th century) (photomontage: Vincenzo Lucchese)

of St Mark. This lion, located in the *Piazza* of Venice, was visible to everyone, including foreign visitors. In the field of painting, however, the symbol of the Serenissima Republic is representing in a more realistic manner. An example of this could be furnished by the beautiful image of 1516 executed by Vittore Carpaccio and now known as the Lion of *San Marco di Palazzo Ducale*. The two hind legs are planted firmly in the sea, the front left reposes on the ground and the front right leg supports the open Gospel. Even if the muzzle is viewed in profile and appears more realistic, however, the mane exhibits a tendency to maintain the symbolic wavy ray. The heraldic composition on the stone panel exhibits a lion *passant*, with its front paws placed on a rocky coast and both of

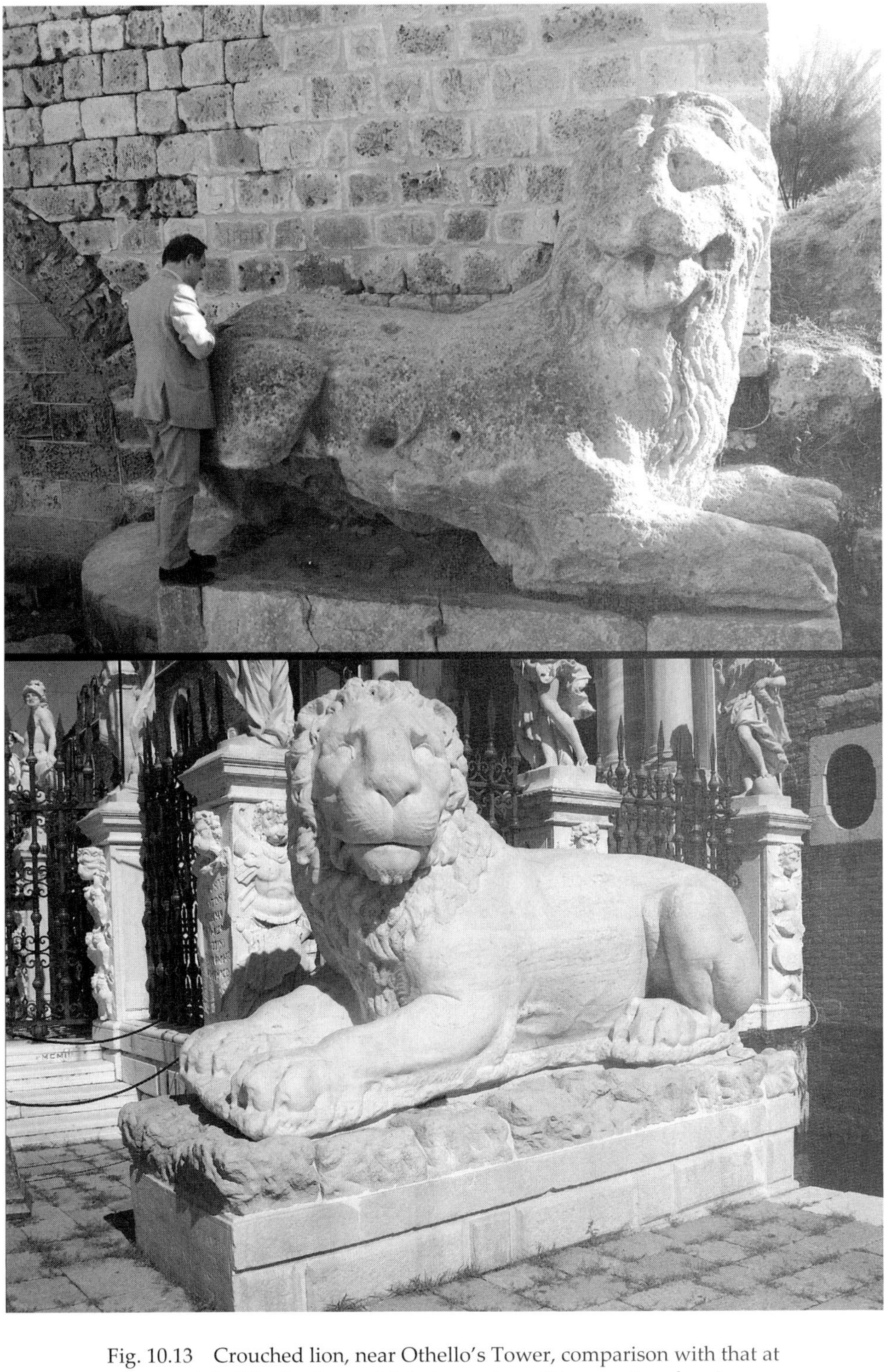

Fig. 10.13 Crouched lion, near Othello's Tower, comparison with that at portal of Venice Arsenal (photomontage: Vincenzo Lucchese)

the rear ones planted in the sea, as depicted in that painting. On a symbolic rock, included as a sign of strength, stands a castle with a crenellated tower from which an undulating banner is visible. Throughout all the territories under the dominion of Venice this heraldic composition is evocative of the *Stato da Tera* and the *Stato da Mar* [the domains of land and sea], as can be seen for example in a miniature of Doge Leonardo Loredan (1501–21).

The panel of Famagusta is similarly composite, for the figure of the lion appears older and is constructed from a type of stone different to that of the frame. Colour, degradation rates and sculptural work all differ with regard to their style. An illustration of this is the summary execution of pens on the right wing of the lion, next to the symbolic stronghold.[10] The inscription in memory of Foscarini is now only partially legible, while the date is virtually illegible (in Roman characters … XII). On the head of the lion is an ancient crown that does not appear in official iconography in those instances when it was placed on public monuments in Italy erected on dry land. In fact a halo is generally present, as attribute of the sanctity of Mark the Evangelist.

The crouched lion found at the base of the harbour walls of Famagusta is sculpted on all sides, located near the Sea Gate and is virtually *pendant* of a marble one to be found at the portal of the Venice Arsenal in 1687 (Figure 10.13). In heraldic classification this position is defined as a lion *couchant*, drawn in an alert posture. Given that the Venetian lion originates from Greece (Lepsina, Athens) and has an origin dating to the period of antiquity, by the same token the sculpted lion of Famagusta may have a similar history.

This is simply one among a multitude of avenues of research offered to us by the ruins of Famagusta. Despite despoliation, looting and abandonment, these stones continue to speak and studies undertaken in the past have chartered guidelines for a deeper appreciation of them. At this moment in time it is necessary to approach the ancient artefacts more closely, to rediscover the spirit and values of the mélange of civilizations forming its cultural context, as well as the work and life of the successive generations of craftsmen, artists, and clients. It constitutes a living, shared and inalienable heritage. Precisely for this reason, as an architect who deals with the recovery of historic architecture, combining principles of conservative restoration and the use of innovative technologies and materials, I express the hope that these buildings, even though reduced to ruins with the passage of time, will continue to communicate their message through their art and architecture.

---

10 This recalls the castle *da Mar* of Modone, on the Ionian coast of the Peloponnese: P. Marchesi, *Fortezze veneziane* (Milan, 1984), pp. 111–15; E. Molteni and S. Moretti, *Fortezze veneziane nel Levante* (Venice, 1999), pp. 33–4.

11

The Military Architecture of Venetian Famagusta

Gianni Perbellini

Introduction

The island of Cyprus has been fated to be a hostage to history from medieval times until the present. From the end of the Roman Empire onwards it has alternated between being at the forefront of either eastern or western Mediterranean expansion to or from the coasts of Asia and Africa. Athwart the routes taken by the crusaders, it was not only involved in fighting between Muslims and Christians but also in the struggles among the western maritime republics and the military orders for supremacy in the Mediterranean (Figure 11.1). In this context Famagusta represents the *antipode* to the capital Nicosia and the rest of the island. The foreign city, in which the refugees arrived in 1291 from Holy Land and fixed their residence and in which the Genoese *maona* organized their southern harbour in 1383, was finally annexed in 1473 by the Venetians. Famagusta continued to have a special relationship with Venice after 1489, when, following the abdication of Queen Caterina Cornaro, the whole of Cyprus came under the dominion of the Serene Republic.

Cyprus passed into Venetian hands on the eve of events that were to have profound political and military consequences for centuries to come. The crisis of the first half of the sixteenth century involved Venice in the struggles that were consuming the northern Italian powers with suspicion and discord. Thus, beginning in 1508, the wars started by the League of Cambrai under the leadership of Pope Julius II embroiled Italy in bloodshed for the next 20 years and placed the lands under Venetian sovereignty at risk. At that time the Mediterranean Sea was practically under the control of the Spanish Empire, with only the Gulf of Venice and the routes around the coasts of Greece to Constantinople and Alexandria constituting some semblance of a maritime buffer zone between the Spanish and Ottoman empires. The temporary, or rather symbolic, peace treaty between Venice and the Ottomans so laboriously concluded in 1479 failed to stop the Turks' bellicose preparations or conceal their intentions; nor did it curb Catalan designs on Famagusta. Just a year

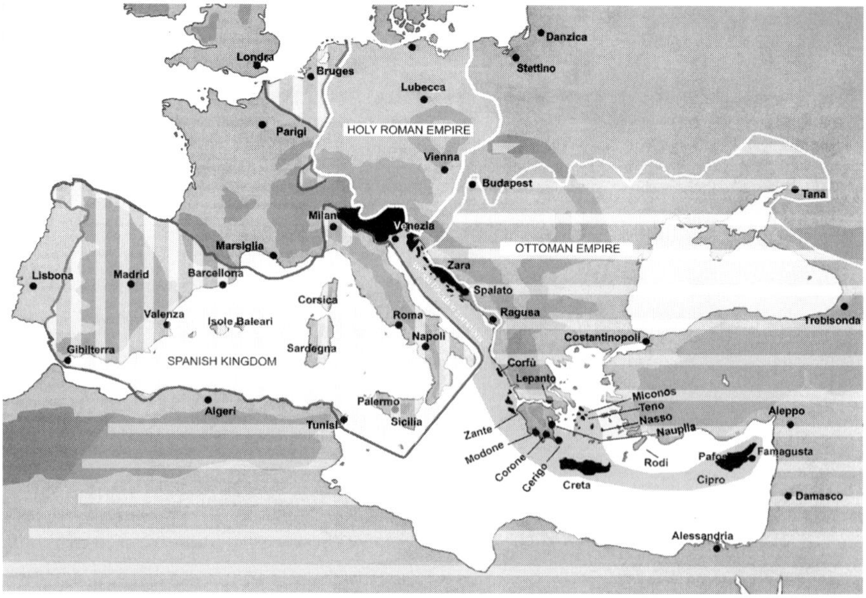

Fig. 11.1 The dynamics of power in the Mediterranean 1558–1570

later in fact, the Ottoman armies fell upon Styria and Carinthia and also seized Vallona and Otranto. Then in 1503 they invaded the Venetian possessions in the Morea and, having easily dispersed a poorly commanded Venetian fleet, imposed a peace which allowed the Serene Republic sovereignty over only Nauplia, Patras and Monemvasia.

In Famagusta the disturbances stirred up by the Catalans against Venetian dominion in 1473 had led to the assassination of the queen's uncle, Andrea Cornaro, and his nephew, Matteo Bembo, and the situation was only resolved after the formal annexation of Cyprus by Venice in 1489.[1] The island of Cyprus paid the price of its geographical position with the Ottoman occupation of 1570, and Famagusta suffered the ferocious siege which led to its capitulation in 1571. Despite Venetian efforts, the town was to all intents and purposes abandoned by the navy of the Holy League; thereafter its fate was remembered both as an infamous example of Turkish barbarity and as the stimulus for the victory achieved by the navy of the Holy League at Lepanto a few weeks later. Memories of the conquest of Famagusta remained an obstacle to any possibility of a European rapprochement with the Ottomans.[2]

The Military Architecture

From an architectural point of view, the defences of Cyprus in general and of Nicosia and Famagusta in particular, hold a central place in the struggle for supremacy in the Mediterranean and provide some of the best examples of the

1 G. Perbellini, 'The Venetian defences of Cyprus', *Fort*, 16 (1988): 10–15.

2 N. Capponi, *Lepanto 1571* (Milan, 2008), 215–59.

development from medieval defences to Renaissance military architecture. The origin of fortified bastions is ascribed to the modern era and is considered, perhaps simplistically, in relation to the struggle between western and eastern civilizations as if they came about as a direct consequence of the need to block the Ottoman expansion after the fall of Constantinople in 1453. In fact the first use of firearms mounted on ships was in a naval engagement at Zierikzee in 1304, and firearms mounted on wagons were employed in the pitched battle of Crécy in 1364. In 1397 the Della Scala family were operating three large wagons, each of which carried 144 small mortars mounted in tiers, a formidable weapon.[3] Finally, Charles VIII's invasion of Italy in 1494 demonstrated the real impact of gunpowder on warfare.

It was, however, events in Italy in the first ten years of the sixteenth century that gave the Serene Republic an unlooked-for political lesson that did much to usher in the birth of the Venetian school of bastion design. The pitched battles at Ravenna, Bicocca, Marignano and Pavia rudely brought home, at a military level, the effects of firearms with which defence and offence would have to contend from that time onwards. With the advent of artillery, the infantry was destined to become the nucleus of national armies. In Italy the uncertainties of military technique induced the most learned to return to models from the past, judging them, in antithesis to reality, to be perfect. The Vitruvian manuals as highlighted by Vegezio, Cesare Cesariano and Valturio, and which in some respects had also inspired Leonardo, now became the new architectural bible.[4] The new firearms obliged the Venetian State, made up as it was of a limited hinterland but encompassing an incredibly large number of ports, quays and docks around the coasts of the Adriatic and the Mediterranean, to introduce a systematic building programme of extensive and burdensome defence works that could only be accomplished by its own men and resources.[5] Venice retained the rigorous standardization of armaments from the medieval tradition which, thanks to the organization of its Arsenal, constituted its strength.[6] Even though the rediscovered manual by Vitruvius provided a permanent cultural underpinning, from now on the 'firing platforms' would decide the military architectural forms.

Experience in warfare would determine the model for the perfect fortified town to be chosen from among the large number of proposals put forward by the writers of treatises. The Serene Republic would be the first to build such a town, having first experimented in the course of the sixteenth century

---

3 Q. Hughes, *Military architecture* (Liphook, 1991), pp. 58–63.

4 For the transcription of the work of Vitruvius consult H. Rosenau, 'Historical aspects of the Vitruvian tradition in town planning', *R.I.B.A. Journal* (1955); M. Morini, *Atlante di Storia dell'Urbanistica* (Milan, 1963), 181–96; T. Scalesse, 'Giovan Giacomo Lonardi, Libro delle fortificazioni dei giorni nostri', *Quaderni dell'Istituto di Storia dell'Architettura*, 20–21/115–26 (Rome, 1975).

5 L. Puppi, *Architettura e utopia nella Venezia del' 500* (Milan, 1980); M. Tafuri, *Renovatio Urbis, Venezia nell'età di A. Gritti 1523–1528* (Venice, 1984); J. Bury, 'Early writing on fortifications and siege crafts: 1502–1554', *Fort*, 13 (1985): 5–48.

6 E. Concina, *L'Arsenale della Repubblica di Venezia* (Venice, 1984).

with various defensive elements and aspects of town planning in numerous projects scattered throughout almost the whole of its territories. Indeed the sixteenth century was a time of renewal in military architecture with the gradual modernization of particular features. The first adaptations of Venetian fortifications to firearms began with the round towers erected as part of the redesigned defences of Legnago between 1451 and 1454[7]; there then followed the five round towers of the larger enceinte for Vicenza by Basilio della Scola and Bartolomeo d'Alviano in 1507–1508, and, after the sieges by the League of Cambrai, the first reconstruction of the walls of Padua and Treviso in 1510–15. In these two towns the new defences were planned by Bartolomeo d'Alviano and Fra Giocondo, men who at the same period were also at work in Venice's eastern possessions. The last example of this type of artillery round tower, the Boccare bulwark, was built by Michele Leoni on the north-western walls of Verona around 1520–22; it immediately turned out to be unsuitable because of the smoke and the deafening noise produced by the artillery inside the dome of the large central gunroom. Five years later Michele Sanmicheli, who began his career in Tuscany and who was therefore acquainted with the studies and fortification works of Di Giorgio Martini, Francione, Pontelli and the two Sangallos, planned and built the pentagonal bastions for the walls of the city of Verona. Vasari later credited him with the invention of this new type of defence, which in effect was to remain in use until the end of the nineteenth century. The Renaissance architects concerned with civil and military buildings, plumbing and ballistics, such as Di Giorgio Martini, from now on would leave the work to career operatives who learned their jobs on the battlefield where, as in the case of Ferramolino or Maggi, they might even lose their lives.

The struggles between East and West were merely one facet of the events that stimulated, albeit haphazardly, developments in European military engineering, tested and diversified as they were in the course of numerous local, regional and national wars. Though apparently motivated in certain cases by the desire to resist the 'Turks', their real object was to guarantee the safety of an essentially urban civilization whose towns represented a fundamental hub in its structure.[8] In Renaissance history, events such as the capture of Otranto (1480) by the Turks or the sack of Rome by the Imperial forces, comprised episodes of conflict in which it was the urban population, both then as now the victims of war, who suffered the consequences. Nevertheless both popular and official historiography obscured or reassessed any reference to European barbarity in the struggles of this period and put in sharp relief only that of

[7] The defences in 1551 had become so obsolete that it was decided to build (1554–57) a new bastioned *enceinte*. This was planned by Michele Sanmicheli, executed by Giangirolamo Sanmicheli, and unfortunately completely destroyed during the Second World War.

[8] G. Perbellini, 'Verona da Fortezza Veneta a Piazzaforte principale del quadrilatero', in *Verona: La Piazzaforte Ottocentesca Nella Cultura Europea,* eds G. Perbellini and V. Bozzetto (Verona, 1990), 22–41.

the 'Turks'. The Renaissance reports of the conquest of Famagusta and of the sixteenth-century War of Cyprus continued to be published or re-written.[9]

In conclusion, the 'Modern Age' developments in fortification are the result of a series of continual interventions rendered necessary by improvements in artillery which had been introduced more than a century earlier and which dominated the bloody conflicts that afflicted Europe from the fifteenth to the nineteenth centuries. That is the reality, although, for the sake of convenience, official historiography has considered the transition period as being from the second half of the fourteenth century to the start of the sixteenth. We have seen how experimenting and testing went on constantly for the whole period during which the round artillery tower, the bulwark, the bastion and the *tanaille* system were employed in turn.

In the framework of Renaissance military history, Famagusta reflects, from a typological standpoint, the whole transition period: from the medieval defences (the Genoese Othello tower) to the smaller flanking round towers (Diocare, Moratto, Pulacazaro, St Luca ….), the bulwark (Arsenal, Seigneury) and finally the Martinengo Bastion, which was repeatedly used as a model for fortifications throughout Europe and Spanish America until the end of the nineteenth century[10] (Figure 11.2; see also Figures 7.1 and 12.1).

In Famagusta the first element of medieval military architecture was represented by the Lusignan-Genoese castle enclosed within the Venetian reinforcement of the citadel. Under Venetian domination, the fortifications of the town became an endless problem involving various people including Giacometto da Novello (1520), Cav. Orologi (1536), Ercole Martinengo (1555), Michele Sanmicheli, his nephew Giangirolamo (who died there in 1558) with his brother-in-law Luigi Brugnoli, Agostino Chisone, Gian Battista Zanchi (1561) and Ascanio and Giulio Savorgnano with Giovanni Magagnati (1562).[11]

---

9 G. Monello, *Accadde a Famagosta* (Cagliari, 2005).

10 G. Perbellini, *The Fortress of Nicosia: Prototype of European Renaissance Military Architecture* (Nicosia, 1994), 16–18, 22–7.

11 Venice, State Archive, P.F. 11: Catalogo delli modelli e disegni delle piazze della Seren.ma Repu.ca di Venezia e di quelli due regni Cipro e Candia; Del Regno di Cipro (Catalogue of models and drawings of the Serene Republic of Venice; strongholds on the mainland and in the two kingdoms of Cyprus and Candia.) Kingdom of Cyprus – Rodolo I (Scroll 1):

Pianta di Famagosta, con li progetti, onde ridur li suoi recinti in una regolar diffesa, del Kav.[r] Orologgi, con scala, denominazione delli respettivi posti, e varie annotazioni.

Pianta di detta con li proggetti, secondo l'idea del Co. Giulio Savorgnan de 1562. Con particolari annotazione ne' piani all'intorno, di livellazioni formate; nonché di alcuni scandagli nell'attinente Littorale, in cui vi scorge figurato un recinto circoscrivendo un Porto contiguo alla Piazza, con scala e Bussola, con varie diligenti osservazioni relativa a que' pensamenti.

Pianta di detta con varie idee intorno a quel recinto, del Coll.o Cluson, Comandante dell'Artiglieria del 1562, con scala.

Piciola pianta di detta, con scala e Bussola.

Pianta del recinto di d.a Piazza, con le varie idee del Sig.r Sforza Governator Generale, presentato del 1561, con Scala, senza Bussola.

Pianta in grande del recinto di detta, con alcuni proggetti di auttor anonimo.

The consequent defences of Famagusta consisted of an *enceinte* with a moat on the three landward sides and the harbour on the front facing the sea. This is dated 1496,[12] but the defences were still late medieval. The initial series of lowered cylindrical flanking towers, even if conceived to hold four pieces of artillery on two levels, proved inadequate. In due course, and with this realization, towers of larger dimensions were adopted in the most significant vertices, even if their shape and layout were still the same as the others. Approximately half-way along the *enceinte* on the seaward side, the citadel, a large castle with four cylindrical towers at the corners, controlled the port and blocked the access to a fortified quay, closed by the chain tower. The port, in fact, was unanimously considered the safest place and the most accessible from both the castle and the town.

In connection with the defensive capabilities of Famagusta, Ascanio Savorgnano, in his 1562 report to the Venetian Senate, pointed out that:

> the structure of the port, closed by a rock dam, is very favourable. By contrast, the enceinte is out-of-date. The twelve bulwarks are only four paces thick so they cannot resist modern artillery nor contain it on their *banquette*. The curtain walls are more or less the same thickness but too low, rising only seven paces from the depth of the ditch which is twenty paces wide.[13]

Espresse le Dimensioni delle linee con numeri; mancante di Scala, e Bussola.

Pianta d'un nuovo Bastione di d.a Piazza, fatto dall'Ingeg.re Zuanne Magagnati del 1562, con alcune annotazioni, e scala.

Detta della città, e Porto di Famagosta, con qualche idea di proggetto, sl intorno al recinto, che al Porto Medesimo, d'auttore anonimo,. con Scala e Bussola.

Pianta in grande di detta Piazza, con proggetti di Fortificazione moderna verso il Porto, del Co: Ercole Martinengo, con Scala e Bussola.

Altra pianta in grande di detta, con proggetti sl d'ingrandire la Città, che per chiudere il Porto ver Scirocco , con opere di Fortificazione, con Scala, e Bussola senza Veruna denominazione. Opera diligente, che può credersi appunto, dalla manifattura, di Girolamo s.n Michiel.

Altra detta del recinto di detta Piazza, e parte delle adiacenze esterne, con proggetti sul intorno al recinto medesimo, che per chiudere il Porto come sopra, con opere di Fortificazione moderna, d'auttore anonimo, ma che può credersi del sumentovato s.n Michiel, con Scala e Bussola.

Omissis.

Rodolo XX.

Pianta di FAMAGOST A, con varij grandiosi proggetti del Kav.r Orologgi.

Altra detta, con progetto dello Sforza Gov.r G rale del 1562.

Altra detta, con progetti, d'autore anonimo.

Altra detta, con altro progetto, pure d'auttore anonimo.

Altra detta, con varie aggiunte proposte a mag.r diffesa, d'auttore anonimo.

12 The inscription inserted in Moratto tower reads 'Nicolao De Priolis Regni Cypri prefecto MCCCCLXXXXVI', but in the headstone the number 'XXXX' seems to have been added afterwards.

13 Verona, Municipal Library, Ms 677: Ascanio Savorgnano, *Breve informazion et resoluzion delle cose più importanti di Cipro et delle provisioni necessarie per quel regno, Paphos, 7 d'Ottobre 1562.*

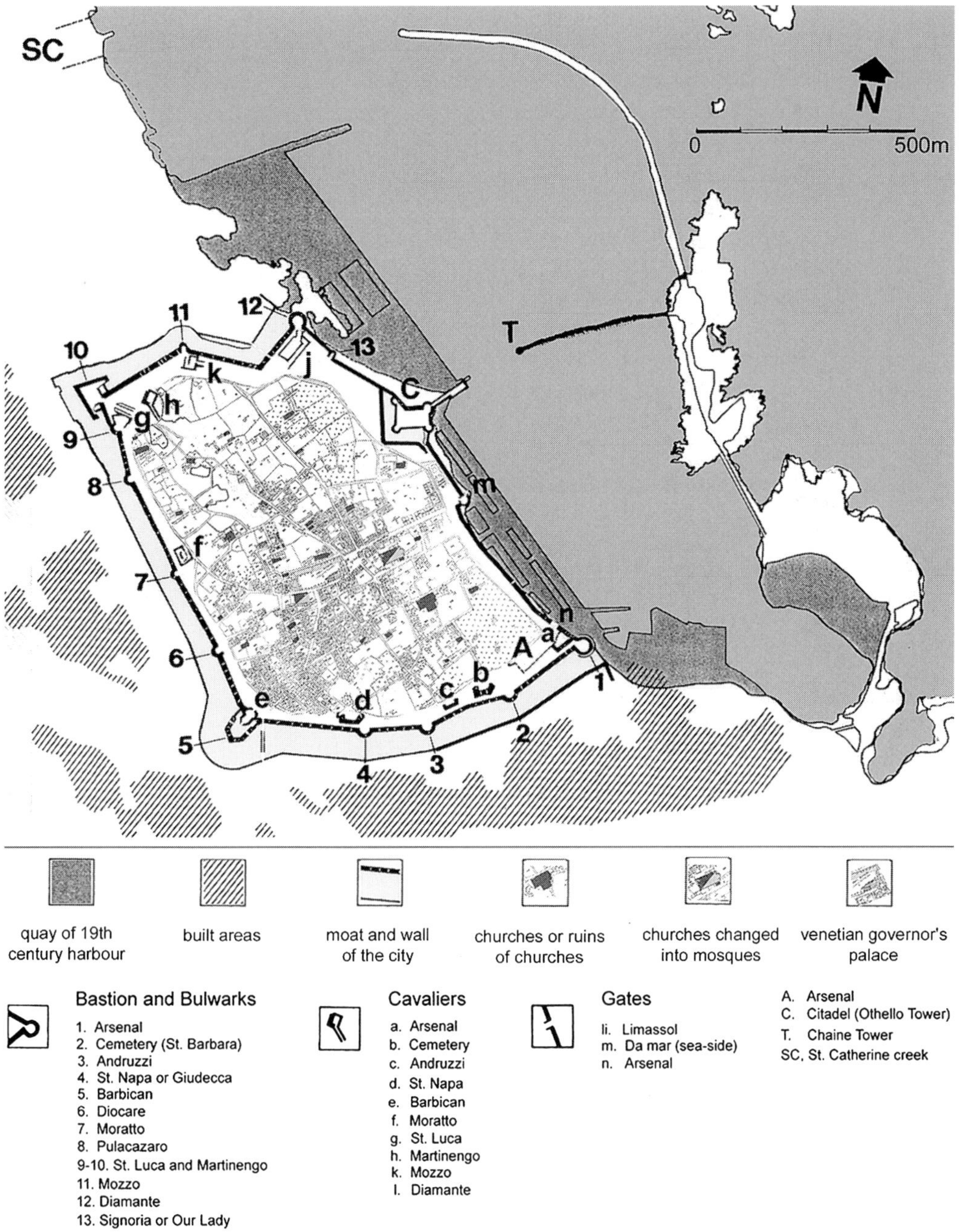

Fig. 11.2 The historic monuments of Famagusta

Evidently this defence had become obsolete within a few years and so the Ravelin and the Martinengo Bastion were added, thus completing the evolutionary process.

The Ravelin

With regard to this building, if we consider the octagonal keep to have been Venetian originally, we cannot say the same about the added bulwark which performs the function of a Ravelin, the reason being the Ottomans' incursion into the town and their subsequent reconstruction (the faithfulness of which to the original is not known) of this section after the siege. The answer, in so far as it is possible to judge, could be the one proposed in the treatise of Francesco di Giorgio Martini,[14] or the influence of the bulwarks designed by Basilio della Scola in Rhodes to strengthen the towers of St George, St John and others. Chronological considerations, however, mean that in Famagusta this possible inspiration applies equally to the initial Venetian work, and to the later Turkish reconstructions, the latter having conquered Rhodes in 1522 and so having become acquainted with the fortifications built by the Hospitallers.[15]

In fact the pseudo-octagonal heavy keep, the original land gate, was protected by the *demi lune*, or bulwark, on the flanks of which two external gates faced each other, linked to the counter-scarp by drawbridges. Structurally this bulwark was made by a double *casamate* ring with over-lapping chambers of which the lower one should have had the function of an anti-mine tunnel. Unfortunately the collapse of the vaults connecting this structure to the main one on the one hand does not permit a deep analysis of the defensive system, and on the other introduces a risky situation thanks to its high wall and also the gates. Even if less used in the Venetian repertory, the *demi lune*-shaped bulwark, built for the protection of nodal towers in the urban defence, belongs to that phase of the transition noticeable in the beginning of 1500 in defence systems at Padova and Treviso.[16]

The fact that we meet this typology before 1522 in Rhodes, where since 1520 Basilio della Scola from the Venetian school had been at work, can also clarify its adoption in Cyprus. The project of the models for the defences of Treviso and Candia by Cav. Orologgi and some plans for Famagusta made in 1536 are catalogued in the Venetian archives. Even though stratigraphical analysis of the construction phases would show that the existing structures

---

14 Francesco di Giorgio Martini, *Trattati*, ed. C. Maltese (2 vols, Milan, 1967), fols 53v, 67v, 77, 79.

15 K. Manoussou-Della, *Medieval Town of Rhodes* (Rhodes, 2001), 130–31, 156–7, 162–3.

16 L. Olivato, 'La teoria dell'arte militare nel Rinascimento veneto', in *Architettura Militare Veneta del Cinquecento* (Milan, 1988); G. Perbellini, 'La difesa delle frontiere Centro Occidentali: Orzinuovi, Legnago, Peschiera', ibid.

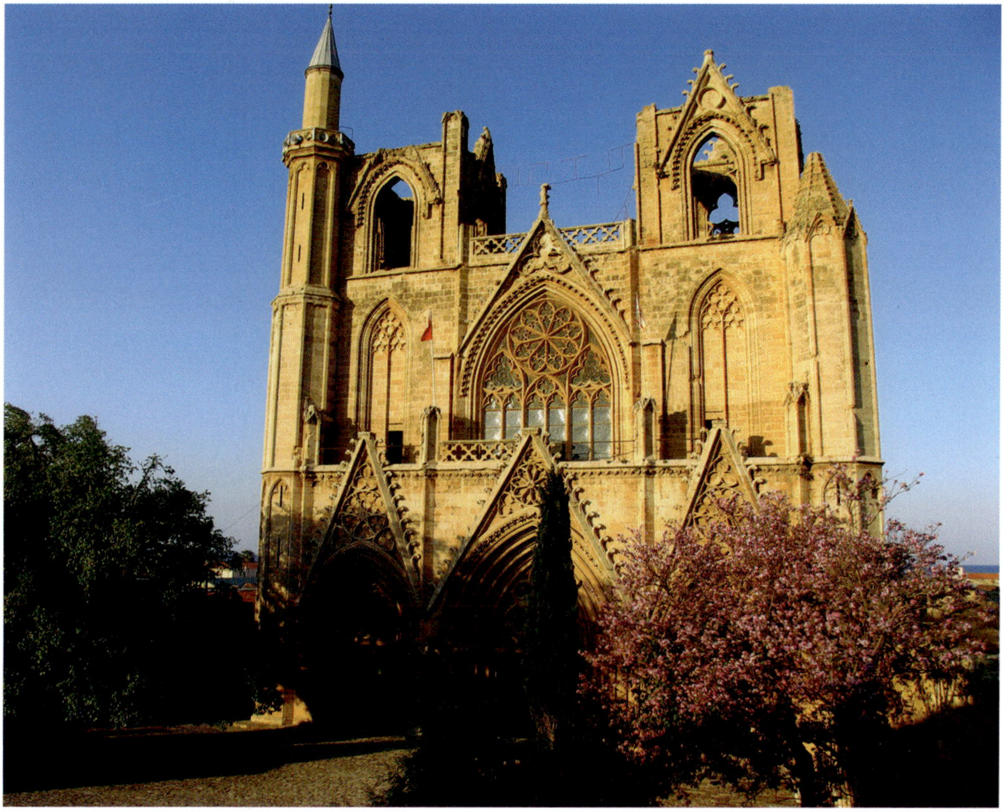

Plate 1 Façade of Cathedral of St Nicholas (photograph: Allan Langdale)

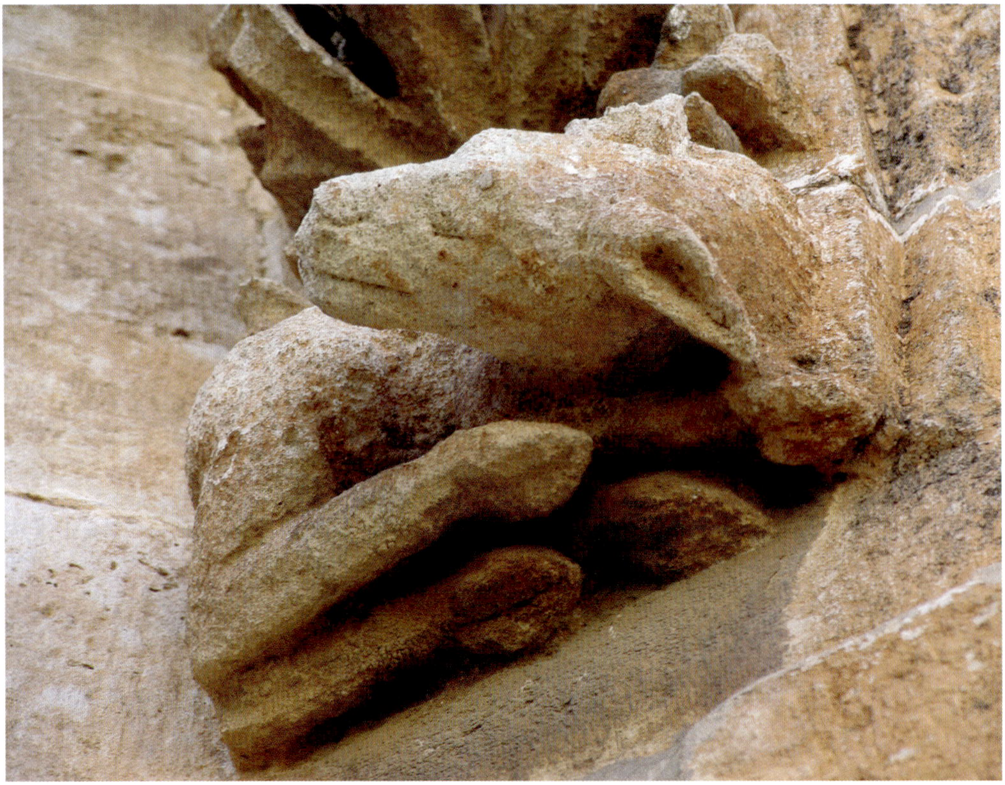

Plate 2 Corbel figure from Cathedral of St Nicholas (photograph: Allan Langdale)

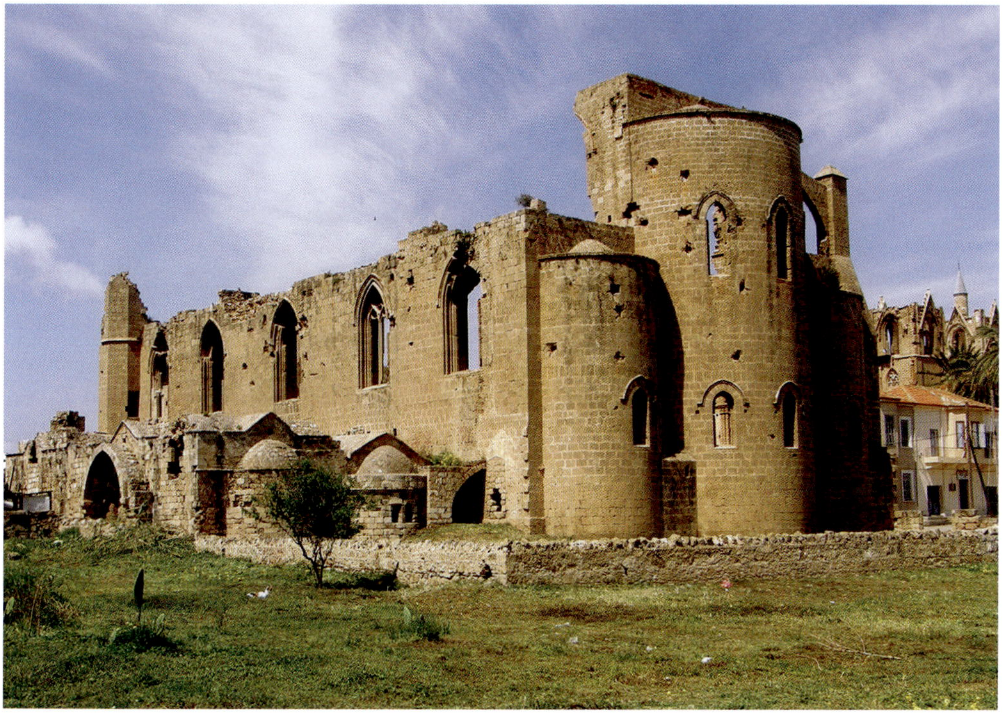

Plate 3 Cathedral of St George of the Greeks (photograph: Thomas Kaffenberger)

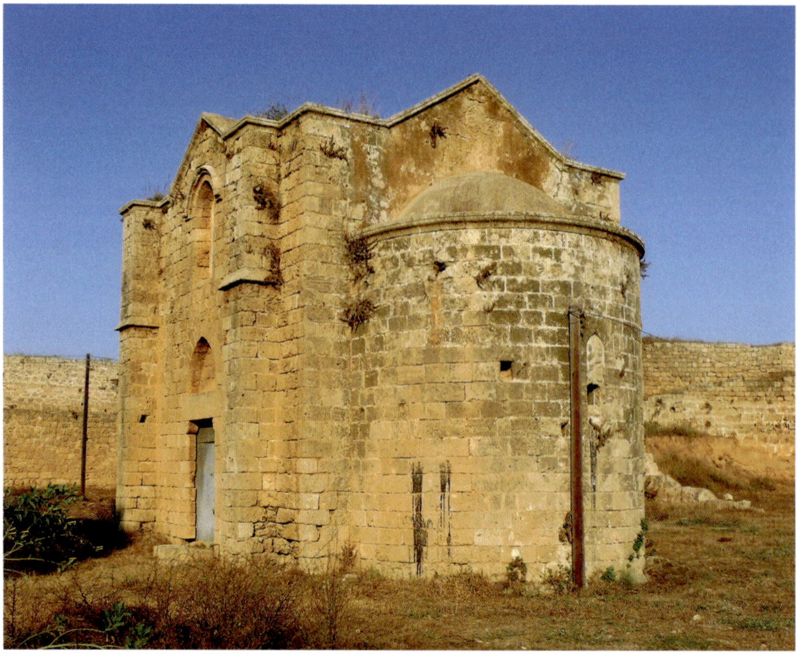

Plate 4 Armenian Church (photograph: Wilbert 'Skip' Norman)

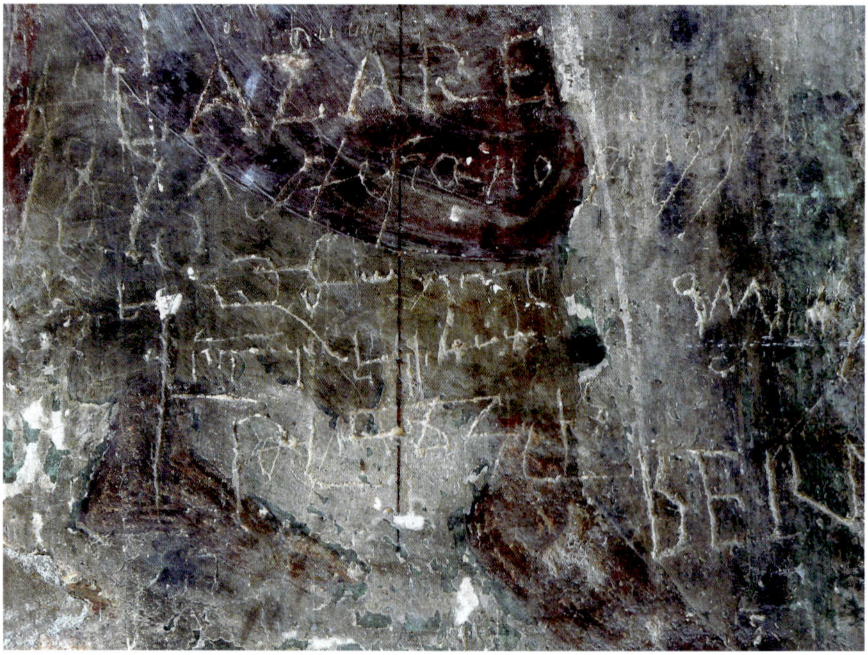

Plate 5 Historic graffiti in the Armenian Church, in Armenian, Ottoman, French, English and Italian (photograph: Michael Walsh)

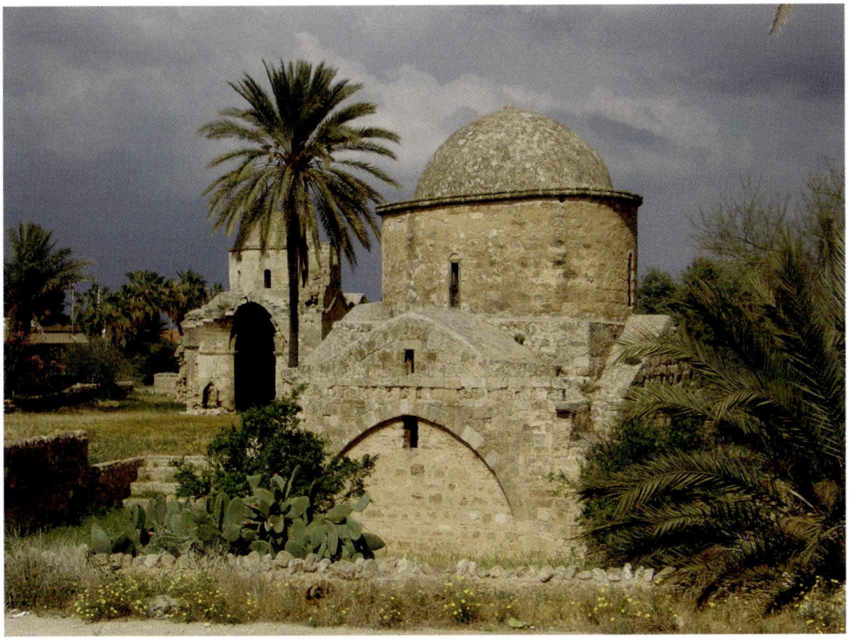

Plate 6 Byzantine churches of SS Zoni and Nikolaos in the Greek Quarter (photograph: Michael Walsh)

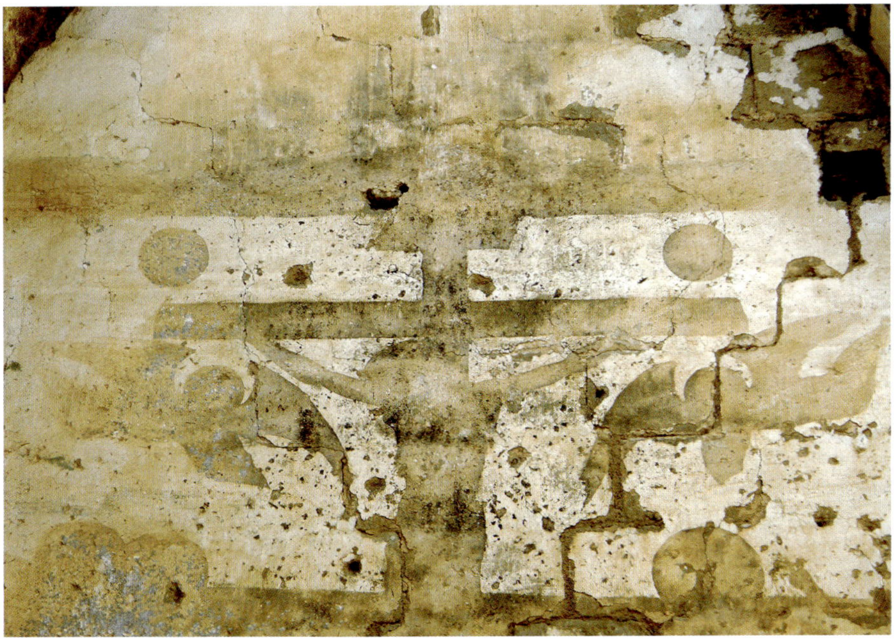

Plate 7 Cathedral of St George of the Greeks, fresco of the Crucifixion (photograph: Thomas Kaffenberger)

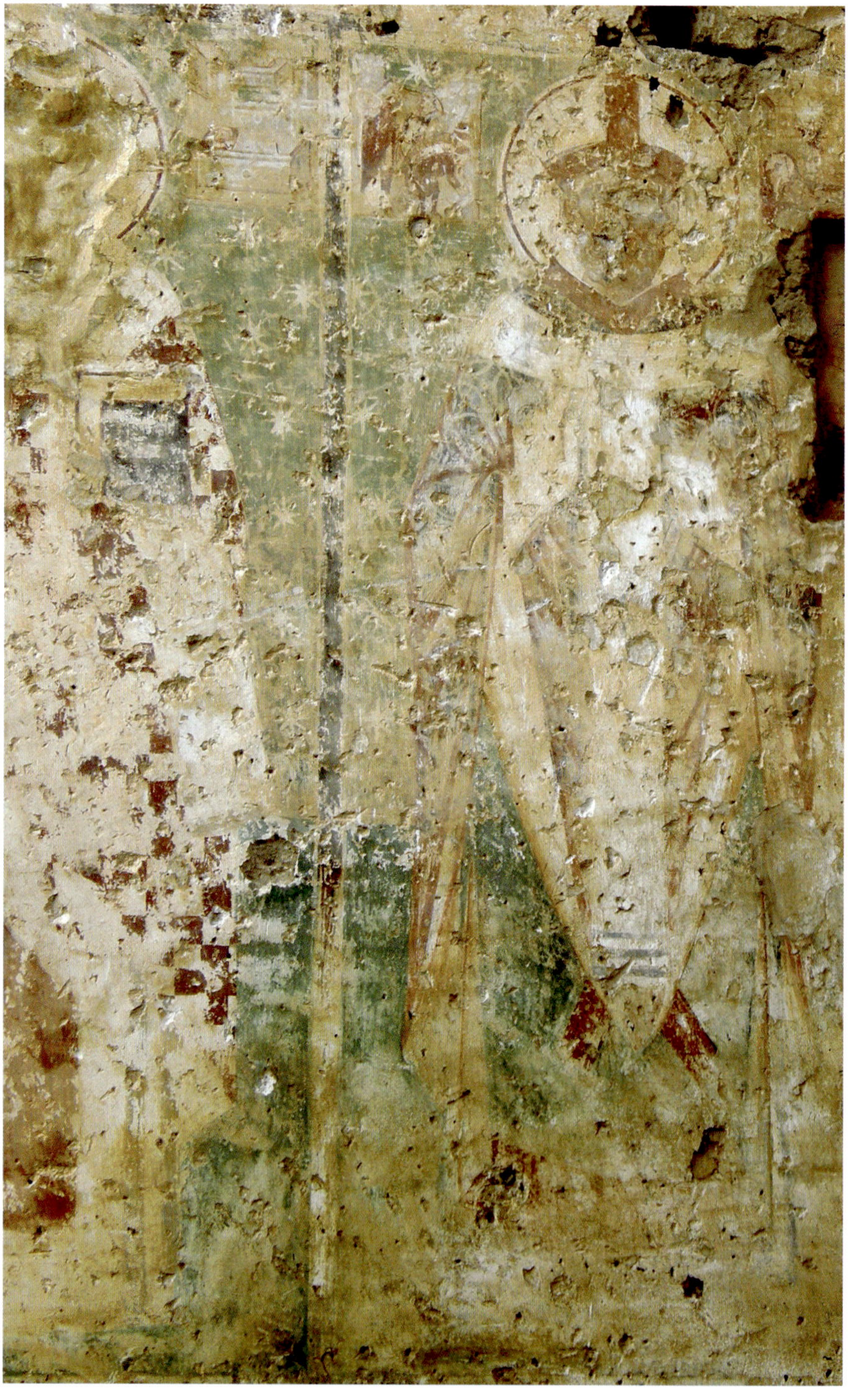

Plate 8 Church of St Mary of Carmel, fresco of St Nicholas (right) (photograph: Thomas Kaffenberger)

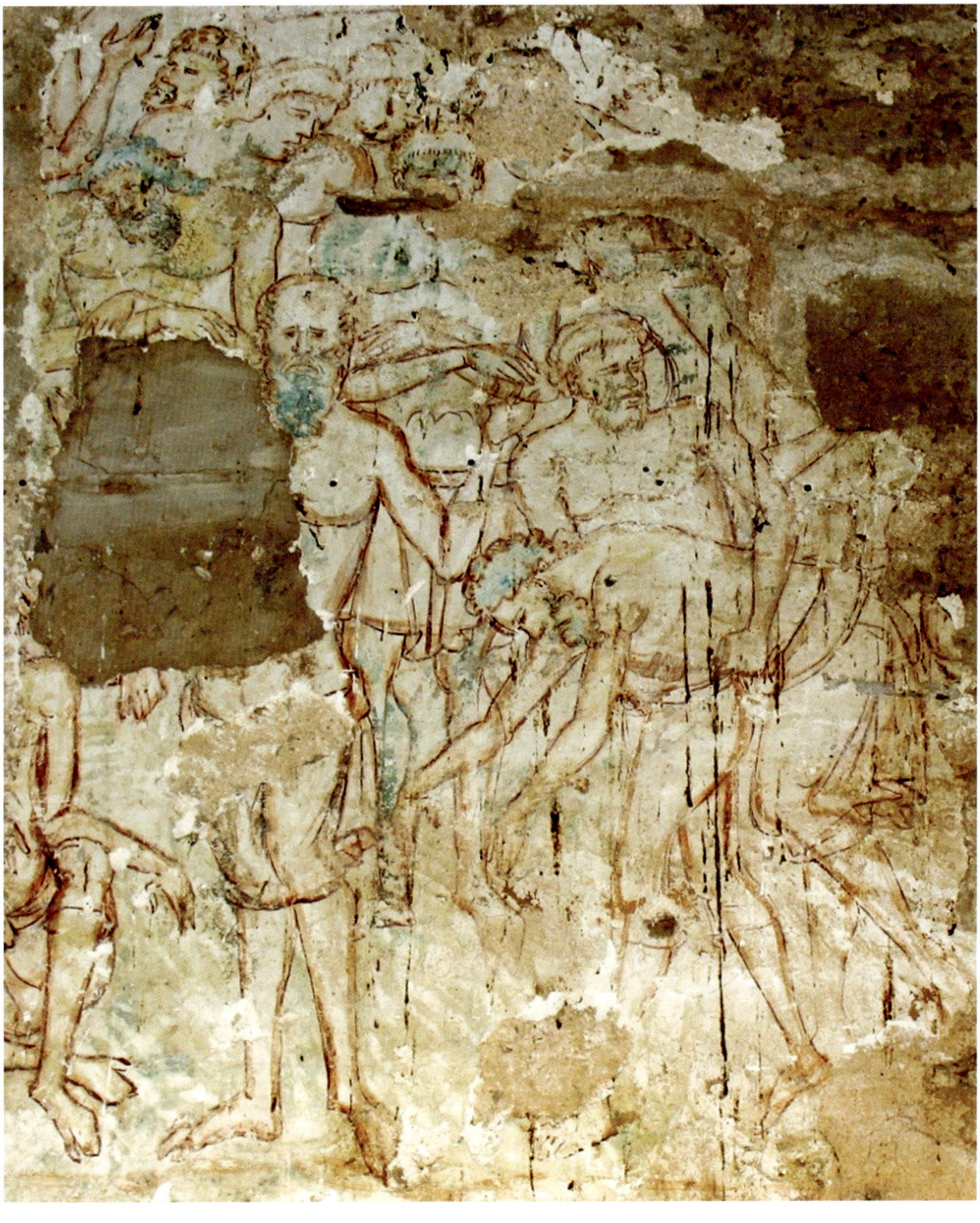

Plate 9 SS Peter and Paul, Sinopia *The Forty Martyrs of Sebaste* (photograph: Allan Langdale)

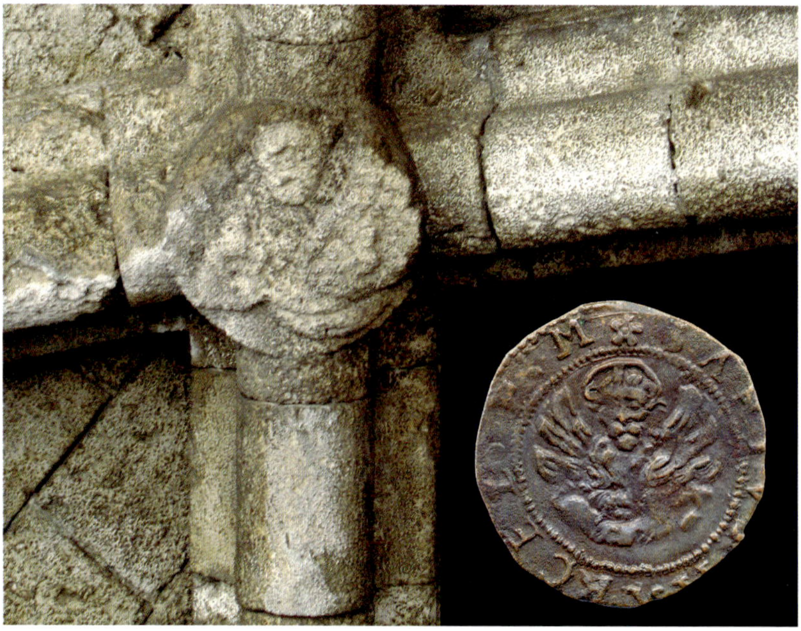

Plate 10 Keystone in Loggia Bembo, comparison with Venetian coin (photomontage: Vincenzo Lucchese)

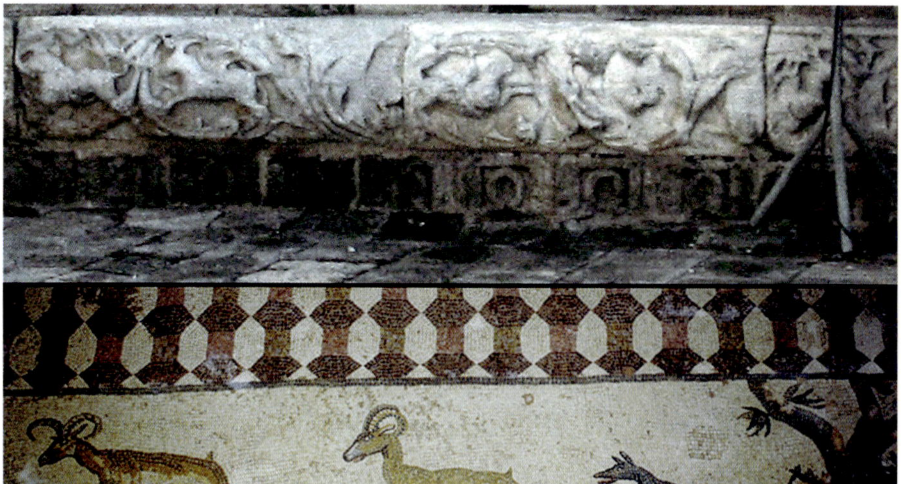

Plate 11 The frieze-pew, probably from Salamis, near Loggia Bembo. Comparison with a Roman mosaic in *House of Dionysos*, Paphos (photomontage: Vincenzo Lucchese)

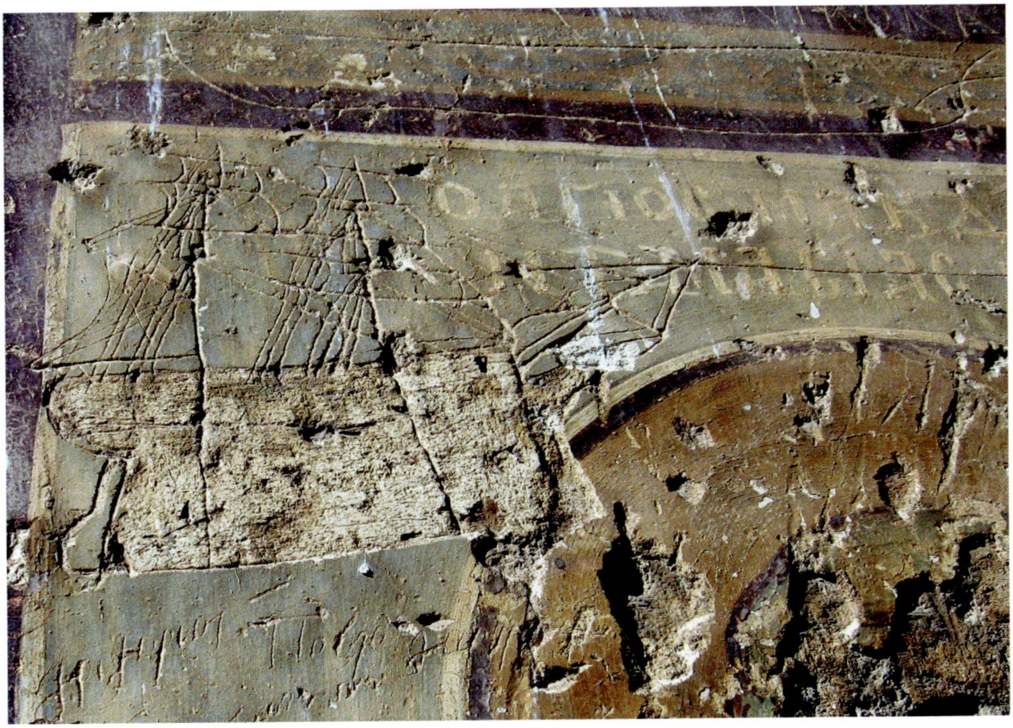

Plate 12 Drawing of galleon beside halo of a saint, left apse, St George of the Greeks (photograph: Vincenzo Lucchese)

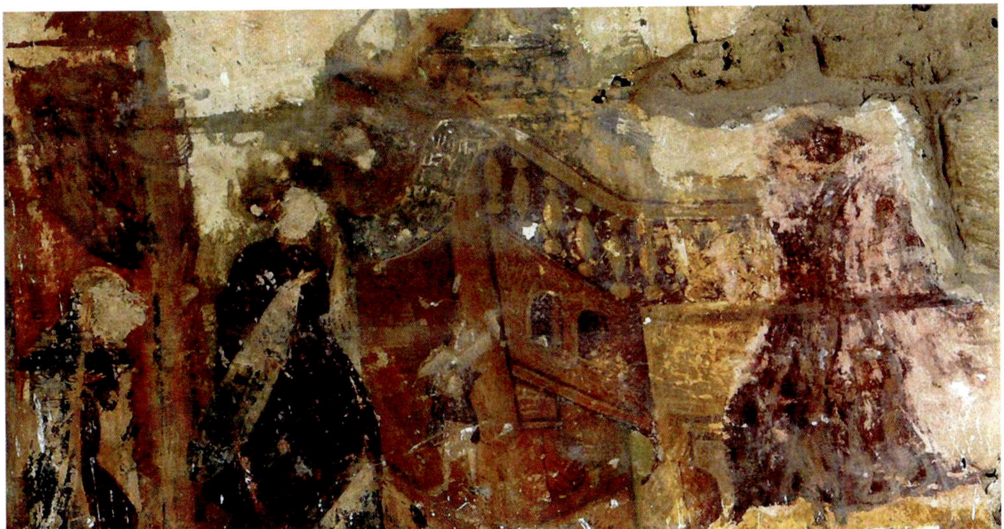

Plate 13 St Anne Church, painted fragment with scroll (photograph: Wilbert 'Skip' Norman)

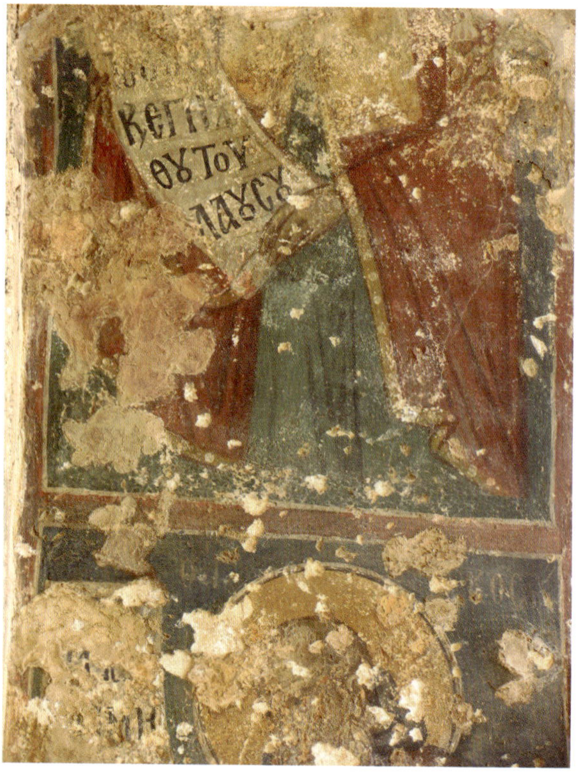

Plate 14 St Symeon Church, inscription (photograph: Allan Langdale)

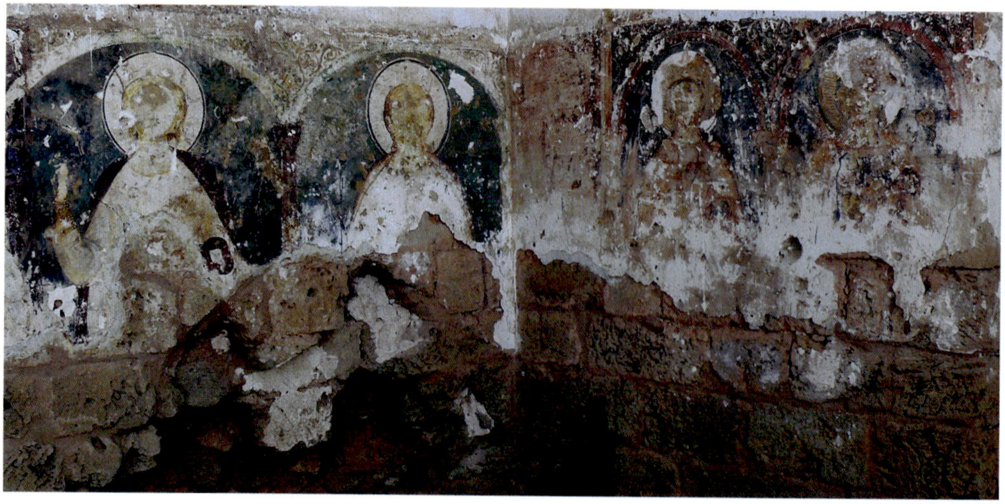

Plate 15 St Anne Church, *Four Saints* (photograph: Wilbert 'Skip' Norman)

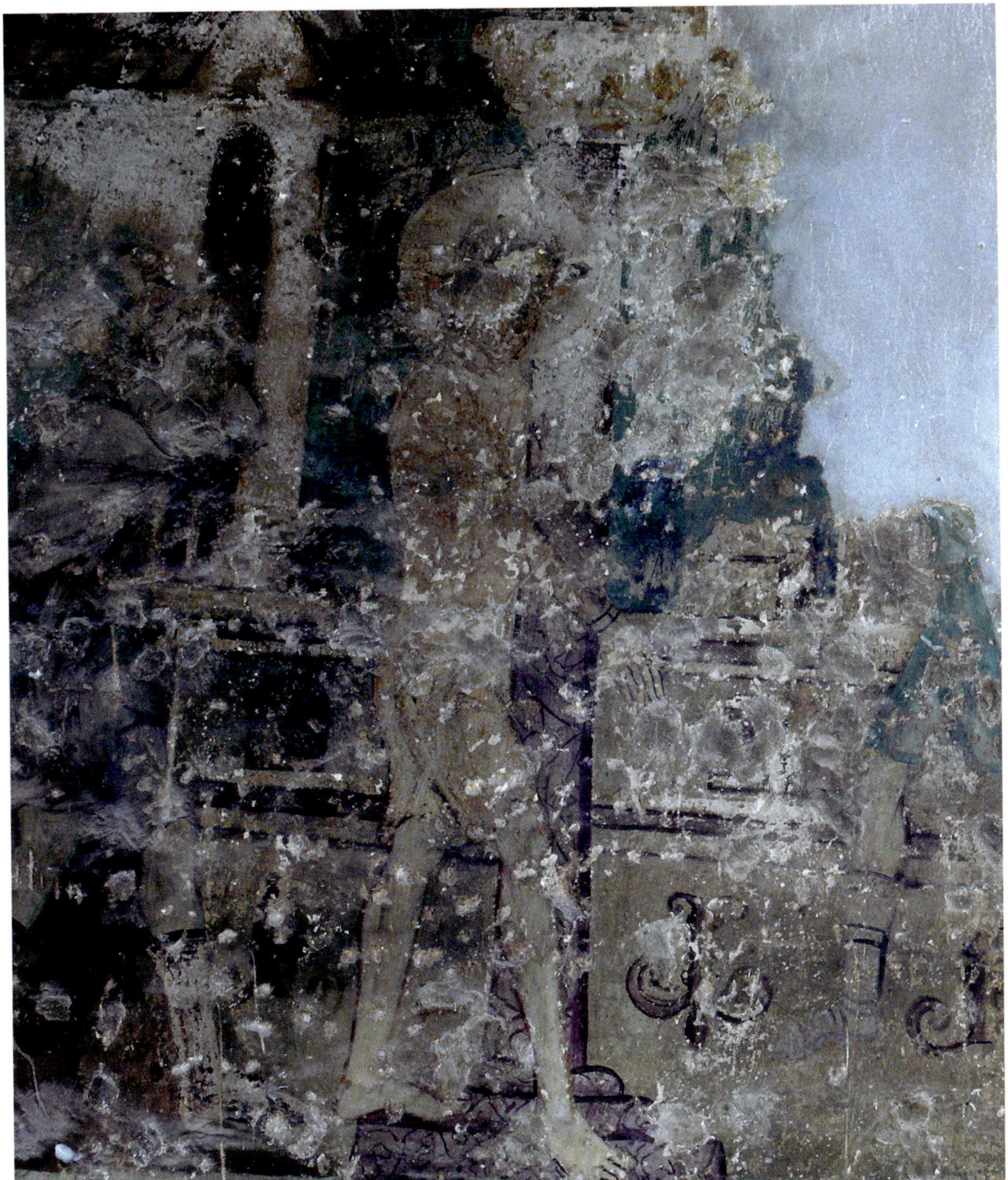

Plate 16 Armenian Church, *Flagellation* (photograph: Wilbert 'Skip' Norman)

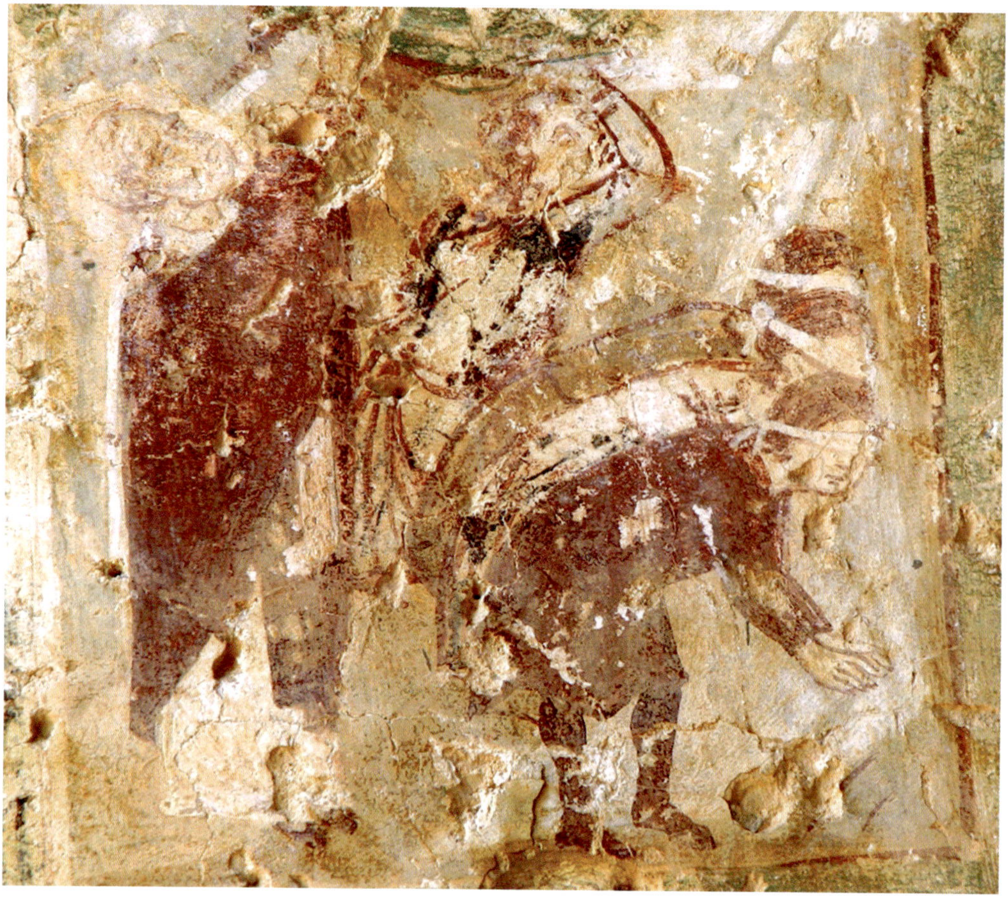

Plate 17 St Mary of Carmel, *Nepotian, Ursyn, and Apollyn* (photograph: Allan Langdale)

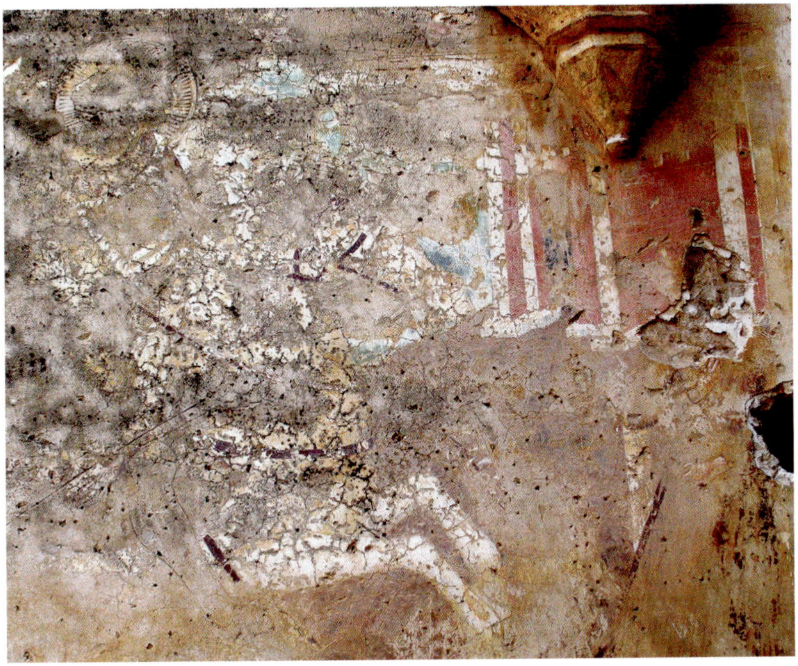

Plate 18 St Mary of Carmel, *St George and Dragon* (photograph: Wilbert 'Skip' Norman)

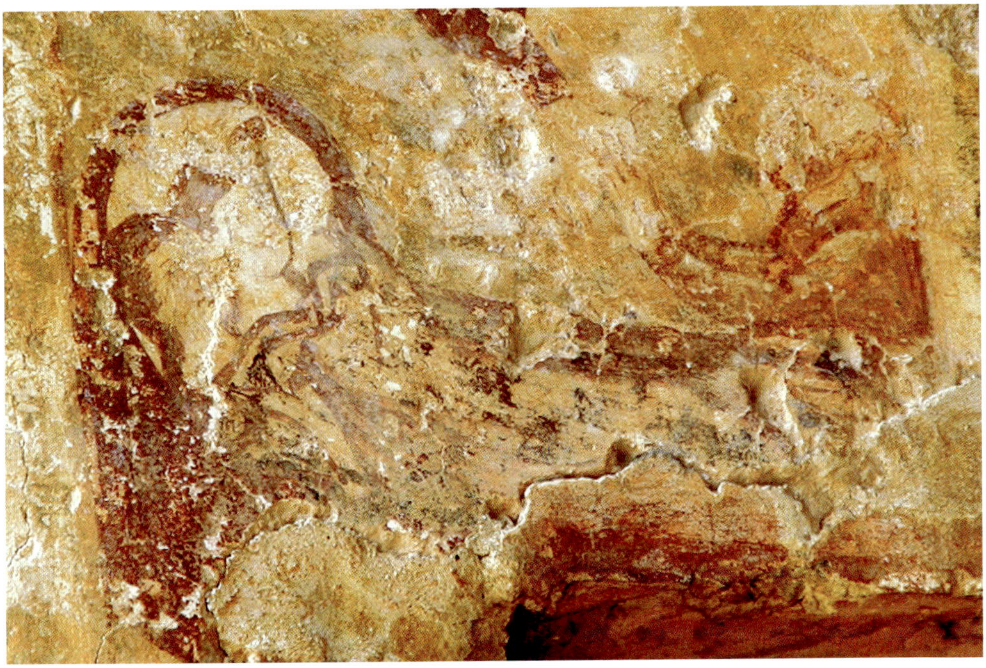

Plate 19 St Mary of Carmel, *The Sisters* (photograph: Allan Langdale)

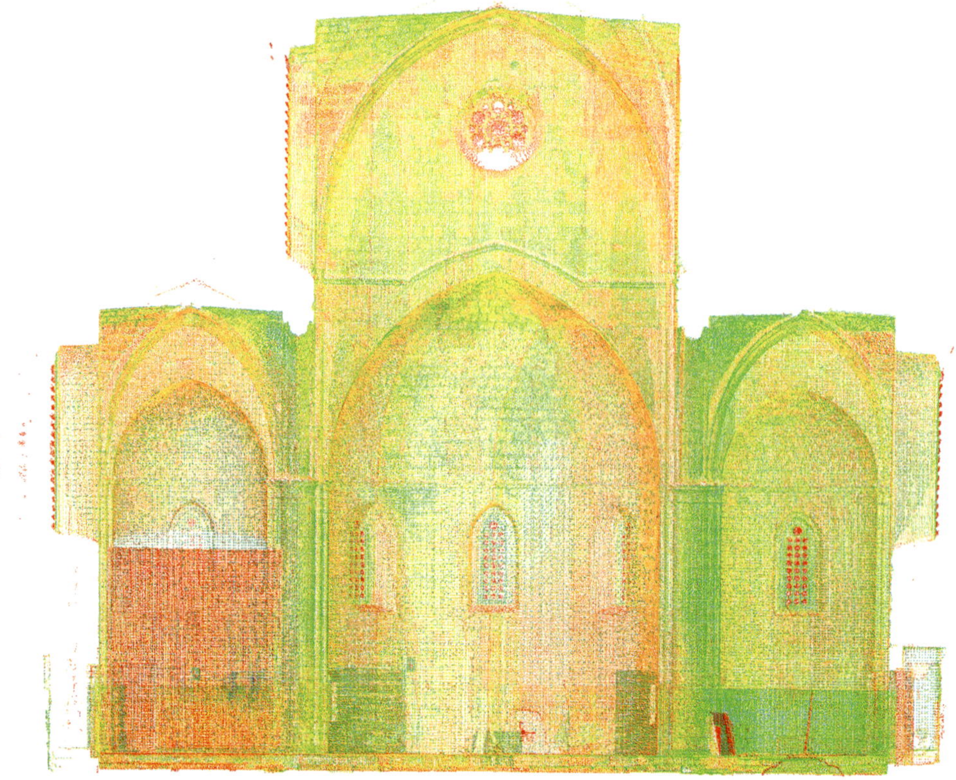

Plate 20 SS Peter & Paul, section (photograph: Kemp & Ballard)

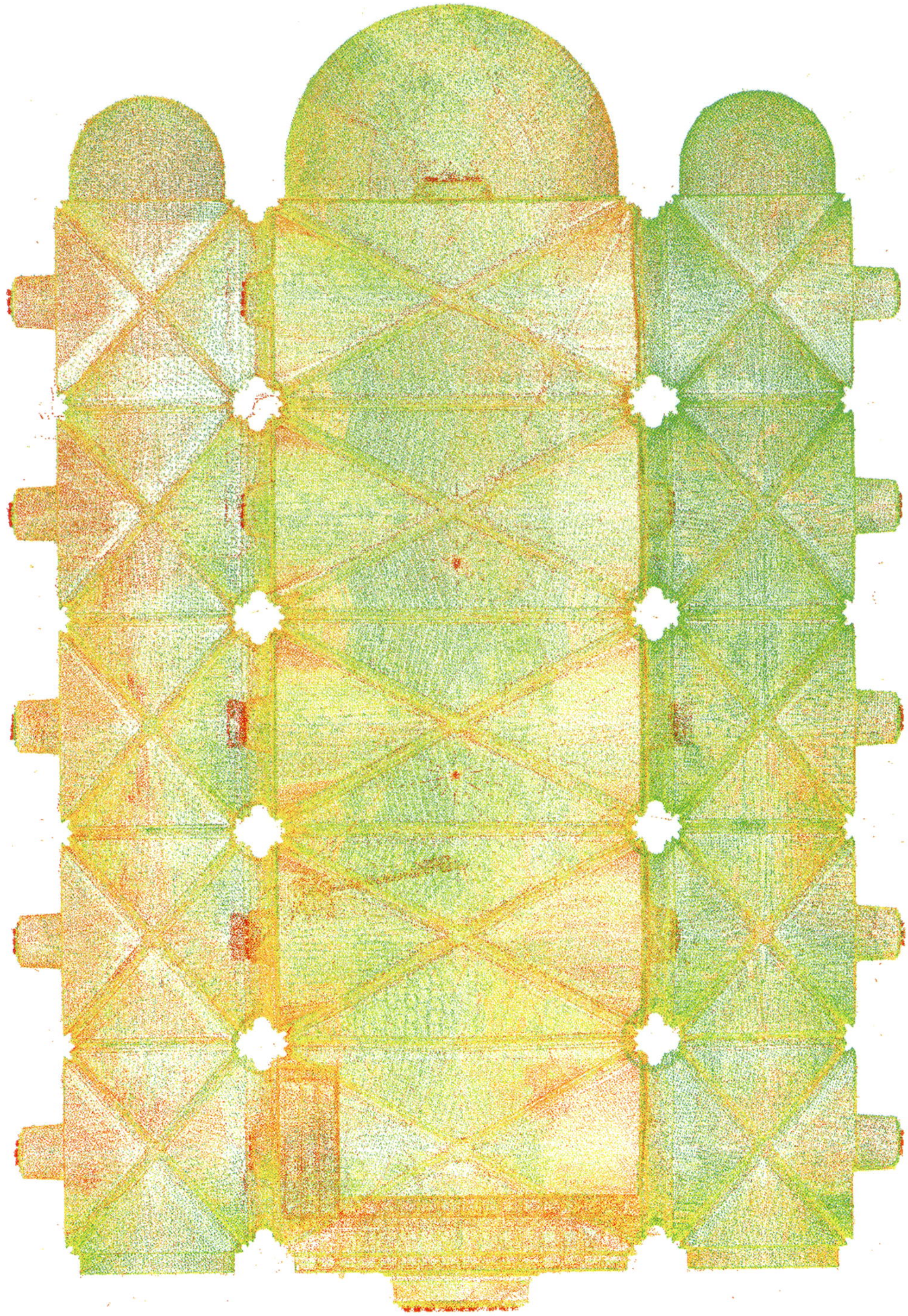

Plate 21 SS Peter & Paul, ceiling plan (photograph: Kemp & Ballard)

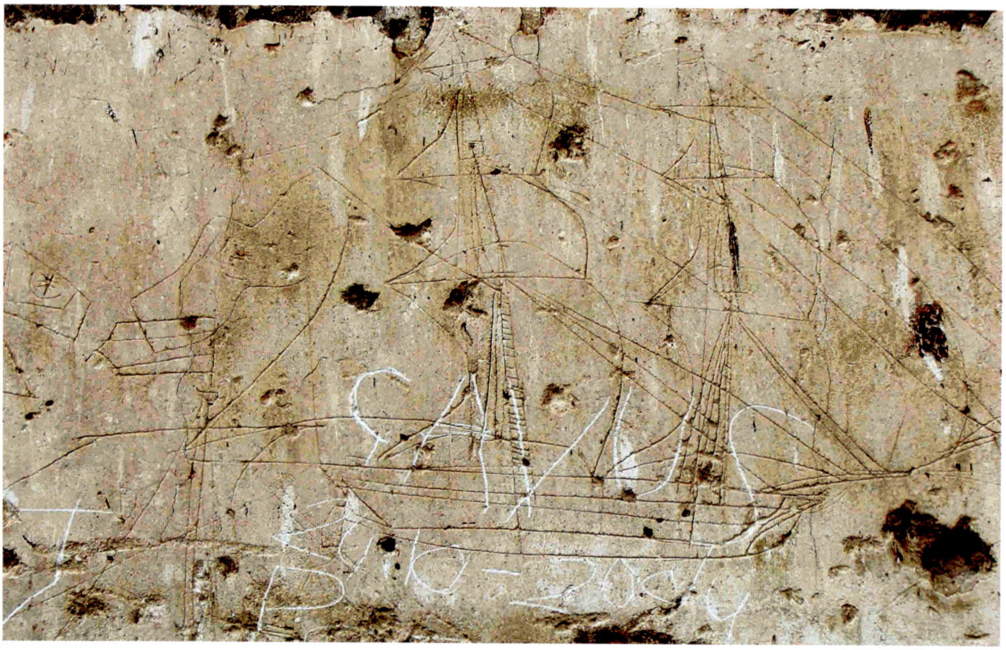

Plate 22 Recent vandalism of ship graffiti in St George of the Greeks (photograph: Silman & Severson)

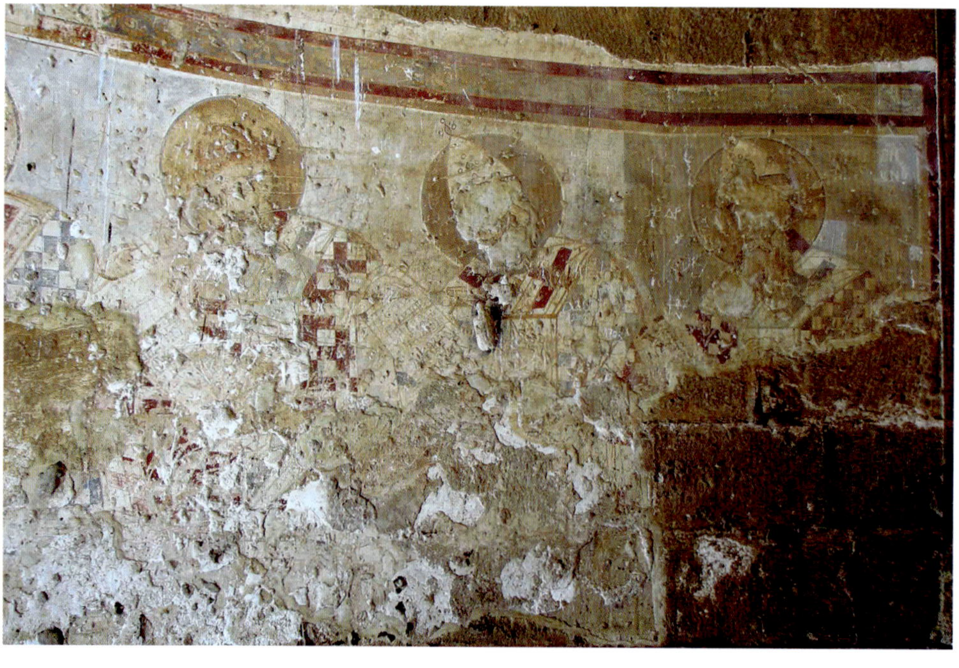

Plate 23 Cleaning samples, St George of the Greeks (photograph: Silman & Severson)

were built by Turks after 1571, the possible influence exercised by the Rhodes bulwarks and thus a linkage, even if indirect, to the Venetian school, remains to be confirmed.

The Martinengo Bastion

The idea of the pentagonal bastion was introduced in Venetian military architecture in about the second decade of the fifteenth century, mainly by Francesco Maria and Guidobaldo Della Rovere, Captain Generals of the Venetian army, and by Michele Sammicheli 'Inzegner' head of the fortifications in the Venetian Lagoon and Mainland, in Dalmatia and the Levant.[17] The shape of the spur or pentagonal bastion was optimal. It was necessary to shape it for the necessities of modern artillery that required appropriate positions for barrage fire, supporting fire and flanking fire. The flanking fire had the purpose of preventing the assailants gaining the ditch and the walls, as well as guaranteeing the protection of the guns and the artillerymen in the final stage of the battle. The bastion, as a platform for the artillery, proved to be unsafe, and moreover the *casamate* for guns, hitherto experimental, gave completely unsatisfactory results.

Vasari attributed to Michele Sanmicheli the final conception of the modern bastion in which the three forms of artillery action found adequate operating possibilities through the construction at the rear position on the flanks of the bastion, or on the half curtains, of raised positions for barrage fire.[18] This left the apical platform of the same bastion for supporting fire and also a wide space for infantry. Finally the scheme of a bomb-proof gun room, opening towards a small bailey and protected by strong *merlons* aligned on the flanking trajectory, solved the matter under the typological profile to the extent that this solution was to be repeated until the nineteenth century.[19] The existence of covered artillery positions during enemy bombardment, as well as permitting a safe use, made it possible for the artillerymen, and the cannons giving flanking fire, to prevent the besiegers from scaling the walls as so often followed the bombardment of a city.

Ascanio Savorgnano in his (perhaps for family reasons) hypercritical report wrote (1562) with reference to the defences of Famagusta and in particular to the Martinengo bastion:

> the sole ill-placed bastion cannot strike a large enough area in front of it. Its solid wall has too many 'gaps' which are a sign of its weakness. The

---

[17] G. Gerola, *I monumenti Veneti dell'Isola di Creta* (4 vols, Venice, 1905–32); T. Scalesse, 'Senigallia e Peschiera nuovi dati', *Quaderni dell'Istituto di Storia dell'Architettura,* 22/127–32 (1976): 55–74.

[18] Giorgio Vasari, *Le vite,* eds P. Della Pergola et al. (9 vols, Novara, 1967), 6: 231–66; E. Langenskiöld, *Michele Sanmicheli the architect of Verona* (Uppsala, 1938); *Michele Sanmicheli,* ed. Piero Gazzola (Venice, 1960).

[19] Perbellini, *The fortress of Nicosia,* pp. 18–19.

> counterscarp in some places is higher than the curtain wall which the enemy could approach without being seen in time. Eight thousand inhabitants, of poor nobility and quality, and 500 soldiers, as well as six companies of 50 men each, defend the town. There is plenty of ammunition but it is badly divided, the balls for the large pieces which are rarely used continue to pile up, whereas there is a shortage of the commonly used ammunition.[20]

The siege, when it came, did not go as predicted: for 11 months the town resisted the ferocious attacks of the Ottoman army, which lost about 50,000 men, despite the fact that their force was about ten times greater.[21]

Rebuilt in the Ottoman period – probably following the former Venetian building – the Ravelin can be considered the compromise solution between the round tower and the bastioned defences. The Martinengo represents the perfect model of the bastion. The victory of 1571 was so important for the Ottoman Army that the walls of Famagusta were conserved and restored, and in later centuries they came to represent a symbol of the pride and esteem of Venetian building.

---

[20] Savorgnano, *Breve informazion*.

[21] Even during more recent troubles, from 1972–74, the casamate inside the perimeter of the walls were utilized by local people as bomb proof shelters.

Part III: Conservation

What Lies Beneath: A Contemporary Survey of the Surviving Frescoes of the Churches in the Syrian Quarter of Famagusta

Michael J. K. Walsh

Introduction

This spectacular image taken by a German aviator during the Great War demonstrates clearly the abandonment of Famagusta in the opening years of the twentieth century (Figure 12.1). Outside the walls there was no development at all, and even within the city great swathes remained entirely unpopulated. The Syrian Quarter, which can be seen at top left, behind the unmistakable Martinengo Bastion, was no exception. In another photograph taken 20 years later we are offered a closer look at the same quarter and in particular, from foreground to background, the Armenian Church (with extensive foundations, now disappeared), the Carmelite Church, the Tanner's Mosque and St Anne's Church (Figure 12.2). Both images powerfully convey the result of four and a half centuries of neglect. What they cannot show, however, is the interiors of these ruins in which a breathtaking array of paintings cling doggedly to the walls in the most inhospitable of environments. They continue to do so today.

In the months and years during which artists toiled in the half-light of Famagusta's churches to apply their colourful pigments to the freshly plastered walls, the fortunes of the city soared.[1] In addition to economic wealth, the city was characterized by a cultural and ecclesiastical diversity, observed by James of Verona in 1335:

> Also in the same city are several sects, which have their own worship and their own churches. First, true Christians; secondly the Greeks, who

[1] For a fuller understanding of the rise of Famagusta at this time, see D. Jacoby, 'The Rise of a New Emporium in the Eastern Mediterranean: Famagusta in the Late Thirteenth Century', in *Studies on the Crusader States and on Venetian Expansion* (Northampton, 1989), VIII; P. Edbury, 'Famagusta in 1300', *Kingdoms of the Crusaders: From Jerusalem to Cyprus* (Aldershot, 1999) XVI.

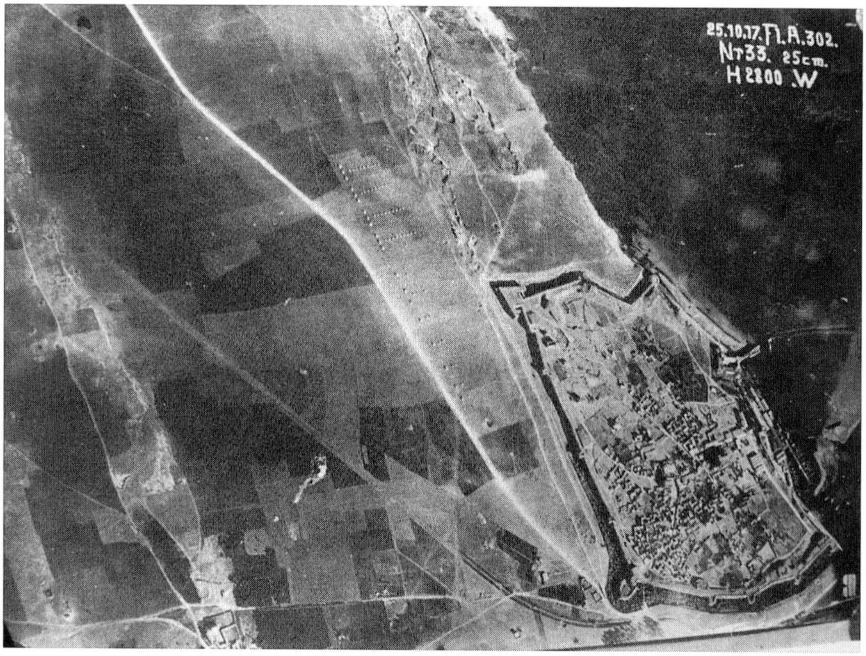

Fig. 12.1 Aerial view of Famagusta, 1917 (photographer unknown)

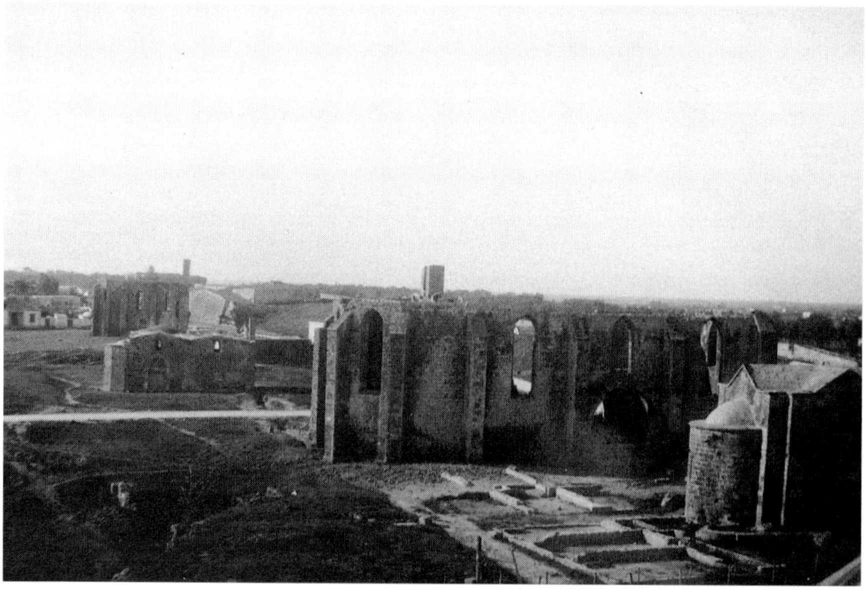

Fig. 12.2 The Syrian Quarter of Famagusta in the 1930s (photograph: Theophilus Mogabgab)

> consecrate not with unleavened wafers, but with leavened bread; they do not elevate the Body of Christ, nor do they believe that the Spirits proceeds from the Son. There are also Jacobites, who are circumcised, and are baptised with the Greek rite. There are also Armenians, who perform their worship like true Christians, but say the service in the Greek tongue, also Georgians and Maronites. Those two sects are baptised like Christians, but use the Greek service. Also Nestorians, so called from the faithless heretic Nestor, who say that Christ was only a mere man, and perform their services in Greek, but do not follow the Greeks but have a service of their own.[2]

Ludolf von Suchen, also in the fourteenth century, marvelled at how such cosmopolitanism was not only tolerated, but actually nurtured in Famagusta, when he recorded 'the tongues of every nation under heaven are heard and read and talked: and all are taught in special schools'.[3] The resultant art of Famagusta, far from being regional, and hermetically sealed from developments further afield, embodied 'a culture that [found] its identity in its ability to manage multiplicity, to admit varied languages at a high level of both quality and integrity'.[4] The paintings, in consequence, were those of a sophisticated 'multicultural and multi-confessional society'.[5] Today, read correctly, they act as a unique lens through which to observe and analyse cultural spheres of contact (often overlapping) in Famagusta and through which insights into patterns of assimilation, confrontation and segregation within the societal models of the island can be attempted.[6] They yield information on how these communities identified themselves, and offer the scholar a chance to understand the amalgam of influences that led to something greater than the mere superimposition of other cultures onto those of Cyprus. Of course, this is a complex task in a port city like Famagusta, to the point that Rupert Gunnis suggested that familiarity with Byzanto-Italian traditions, the influences from the Caucasus and Armenian, and the method of arrival through Constantinople, Salonica, Crete, Genoa or Venice, all had to be borne firmly in mind. S. Hatfield Young stressed this too, and in so doing emphasized the importance of appreciating how the 'western' influences passed through the culturally diverse filters of Syria, Palestine and Lebanon, before making landfall in Cyprus.[7] All of this, juxtaposed with the dominance of an indigenous visual vocabulary, led Carr to ask:

---

2 James of Verona in *Excerpta Cypria*, ed. C.D. Cobham (Cambridge, 1908), 17.

3 Ludolf von Suchen in *Excerpta Cypria*, p. 20.

4 A.W. Carr, 'Art in the Court of the Lusignan Kings', in *Cyprus and the Crusades*, ed. N. Coureas and J. Riley-Smith (Nicosia, 1995), 251.

5 M. Bacci 'Syrian, Palaiologan, and Gothic Murals in the "Nestorian" Church of Famagusta', *Deltion tes christianikes archaiologikes Hetaireias* (2006), 209.

6 J.G. Schryver, 'Spheres of Contact and Instances of Interaction in the Art and Archaeology of Frankish Cyprus, 1191–1359' (unpublished PhD diss., Cornell University, 2005), 178–9.

7 S. Hatfield Young, 'Byzantine Painting in Cyprus During the Early Lusignan Period' (unpublished PhD diss., Pennsylvania State University, 1983), 11.

> what was the art of the western minority: how much was it the product of western Europe directly; how much was it the product of an eastern Mediterranean cultural mélange; how much did it respond to the local, Orthodox artistic production?[8]

The neglected paintings of the churches of the Syrian Quarter, and elsewhere throughout Famagusta, might yet offer a key to such an understanding.

A Short History of Neglect

Famagusta's halcyon days were not to last for long. Indeed, from the beginning, there were those lamenting the foul morality which accompanied such wealth and prestige, and warning that no society, as corrupt and self-satisfied as that of Famagusta's, could have anything other than a wretched future. St Bridget of Sweden preached of grim consequences in the cathedral square; Dante's *Paradiso* anticipated the final judgement with 'Wailings and groanings in Famagusta's streets';[9] and Leontios Makhairas recorded Famagusta's fatal 'sin of pride'.[10] The more tangible fiscal decline began as early as 1344, with the lifting of a papal prohibition on direct trade between western merchants and Muslims, which damaged Famagusta's lucrative role as a middleman.[11] In 1394 Niccolò da Martoni could observe that up to one quarter of the city was already deserted,[12] while Pero Tafur noted in the 1430s that the city was severely depopulated through bad air and bad water, and that this had led to widespread illness and ophthalmic problems amongst the dwindling number of residents.[13] Fortunes rallied somewhat under the Venetians, but then spiralled again shortly after the sighting of 'The Sword of God' comet in 1569 which, it was believed, augured doom.[14] The 1571 Ottoman siege realized that prophecy, and was followed, in an almost biblical manner, with locust infestations, earthquakes, plagues and even a whirlwind. The port silted up and pestilential air gave Famagusta a deadly reputation amongst travellers. Not only forgotten, but consciously avoided, Famagusta, with its art and architecture, receded into a history of neglect. By 1750, Hasselquist tells us, only 300 people inhabited the city,[15] and in 1779 an anonymous author wrote that it was 'entirely neglected'.[16] When curious travellers eventually did venture into the city again at the end of the nineteenth century, armed with

---

8 Carr, 'Art in the Court of the Lusignan Kings', p. 240.

9 Dante Alighieri in *Excerpta Cypria*, p. 15.

10 Leontios Makhairas, *Recital concerning the Sweet Land of Cyprus entitled 'Chronicle'* ed. R.M. Dawkins, 2 vols. (Oxford, 1932), 1: 465.

11 See P. Edbury, *The Kingdom of Cyprus and the Crusades* (Cambridge, 1991), 151–6, 171.

12 Niccolò da Martoni in *Excerpta Cypria*, p. 20.

13 Pero Tafur in *Excerpta Cypria*, p. 31.

14 A. Calepio in *Excerpta Cypria*, p. 143.

15 Hasselquist in *Excerpta Cypria*, p. 307.

16 *Excerpta Cypria*, p. 323.

clumsy cameras, the images they captured were haunting. Some churches had collapsed, others were reused and most had had cut stone removed for other building projects on the island and further afield. The cityscape was one of desolation, devoid of living tenants, and silent.

The most significant respite for the churches of Famagusta, and their art, began at the end of the Ottoman era when a preliminary antiquity law was set in place. This was followed by the British 'Law on Famagusta Stones' in 1891[17] which was in turn superseded by more comprehensive legislation in 1905. In the interwar years a small group of committed individuals filed scathing reports on the state of the historic monuments of Cyprus, and of the consequent loss of British prestige internationally as a result.[18] The *Times* even published a letter to name and shame those parsimonious government individuals who were choosing not to see the urgent heritage needs of Cyprus.[19] It was with the private intervention of Lord Mersey, and the establishment of the Committee on Cyprus Monuments (which included the Archbishop of Canterbury, the Director of the British Museum and other notables), that help for Famagusta's churches finally arrived.[20] Simultaneously, on 1 January 1935 a new Department of Antiquities came into being, under the directorship of J.R. Hilton, followed by A.H.S. Megaw, with the Assistant Director of Antiquities for Famagusta being Theophilus Mogabgab M.B.E. (1888–1965).[21] Remembered as a 'short man, wearing an ancient three-piece drill suit and a hat of which the brim was pulled down all round', Mogabgab's achievements in stabilizing Famagusta's historic monuments were remarkable.[22] The paintings received their first

17 This law 'To Provide for the Preservation of Ancient Buildings in the Town of Famagusta' was passed on 18 May 1891 and included specifically protection of Ottoman heritage. See: M. Walsh, '"The Vile Embroidery of Ruin": Historic Famagusta between Ottoman and British Empires in *fin de siècle* Cyprus: 1878–1901' *Journal of Intercultural Studies* (2010).

18 This fact was made more embarrassing when the French appeared willing to make a substantial bequest to the government of Cyprus in 1933 to look after the medieval monuments there. See C. Roueché, 'The Prehistory of the Cyprus Department of Antiquities', in *Mosaic: Festschrift for A.H.S. Megaw*, eds J. Herrin, M. Mullett and C. Otten-Froux (London, 1996), 155–66.

19 W. Buckler et al., 'The Antiquities of Cyprus: Byzantine Culture', *Times* (22 September 1933).

20 Additional funding was received from the Carnegie Corporation in New York City and also the Leverhulme Trustees. The Government provided salaries and additional small grants for specific projects. See Roueché, 'Cyprus Department of Antiquities', pp. 162–3.

21 See E.U. Tumer, 'Twentieth-Century Restorations to the Medieval and Renaissance Monuments of Famagusta' (this volume).

22 C. Hurst, *The View from King Street: An Essay in Autobiography* (London, 1997), 133. Hurst asserts that for Mogabgab to work under A.H.S. (Peter) Megaw was a source of some discomfort, and that his relationship with Rupert Gunnis (the secretary at Government House and sometime Inspector of Antiquities) was worse again. The same account tells of how a recently discovered cache of Venetian weapons was taken out to sea and dropped overboard on the orders of the Police Commissioner, and how further losses happened with the destruction of Government House in 1931 during political unrest.

attention in centuries too via his colleague Mrs Monica Bardswell of the Courtauld Institute in London, who worked voluntarily alongside him for 18 months (Figure 12.3). Her efforts were concentrated on the frescoes of the Land Gate shrine, the Armenian Church, St George of the Greeks, Ayia Zoni, the Nestorian Church, St Anne's, the Carmelite Church, St Symeon and the 'rock cut church' outside the Martinengo Bastion. The contemporary art historian owes a great deal to her. Bardswell, by stabilizing the edges of the images and waxing their surfaces, secured time in the inexorable process of decay. Work was slowed down again by the Second World War (when Famagusta was actually bombed) and then restarted for a while before finally coming to a halt completely in 1956. Towards the end of the 1950s and during the early years of independence, the churches of the Syrian Quarter were used, and misused: sometimes as homes for refugees fleeing from political turmoil outside the walls, and at other times, as storage sheds. Some were simply abandoned.

The Painted Churches of the Syrian Quarter

The Conway Library at the Courtauld Institute in London houses a priceless black and white photograph taken of the interior of St Anne's Church by Mrs Bardswell (Figure 12.4). In it, over two registers, and divided into six distinct panels (there were more, but six are all that fit in Bardswell's frame) we can see elaborate scenes of: *The Descent from the Cross, The Entombment, The Death of the Virgin, A Bishop, The Presentation of Christ at the Temple* and *The Baptism of Christ*, as they appeared in the 1930s. A detail of *The Descent from the Cross* (Figure 12.5) allows us a closer look at the style which had led Enlart to make an attribution of an Italo-Byzantine 'school' of painting, not dissimilar to that in the chapel at Pyrga dating to 1421.[23] Though it is undoubtedly tempting to commit to a cross referencing with the school of Giotto and fourteenth-century Italy, especially through the background landscape, and the mourning principal characters, Annmarie Weyl Carr advocates caution, and a much more guarded provenance, whereby 'a criss-crossing of religious and ethnic backgrounds, [but] all reflect an Italianate component in their taste'.[24] Anne Derbes tightened the focus further to specify the type of interaction, to Tuscany in particular, which she believed to be ecclesiastical rather than commercial.[25] Enlart commented that often the work was 'clumsily drawn and

[23] This Italo-Byzantine style is further explored in E. Constantinides, 'Monumental Painting in Cyprus during the Venetian Period, 1489–1570', in *Medieval Cyprus: Studies in Art, Architecture and History in Memory of Doula Mouriki*, eds N. Ševčenko and C. Moss (Princeton, 1999).

[24] See: A.W. Carr, 'Byzantines and Italians on Cyprus: Images from Art', *Dumbarton Oaks Papers*, 49 (1995): 343. I should point out that she was not talking about the art of Famagusta when she made this assessment.

[25] A. Derbes, 'Siena and the Levant in the Later Duegento', *Gesta*, 28 (1989): 190–204.

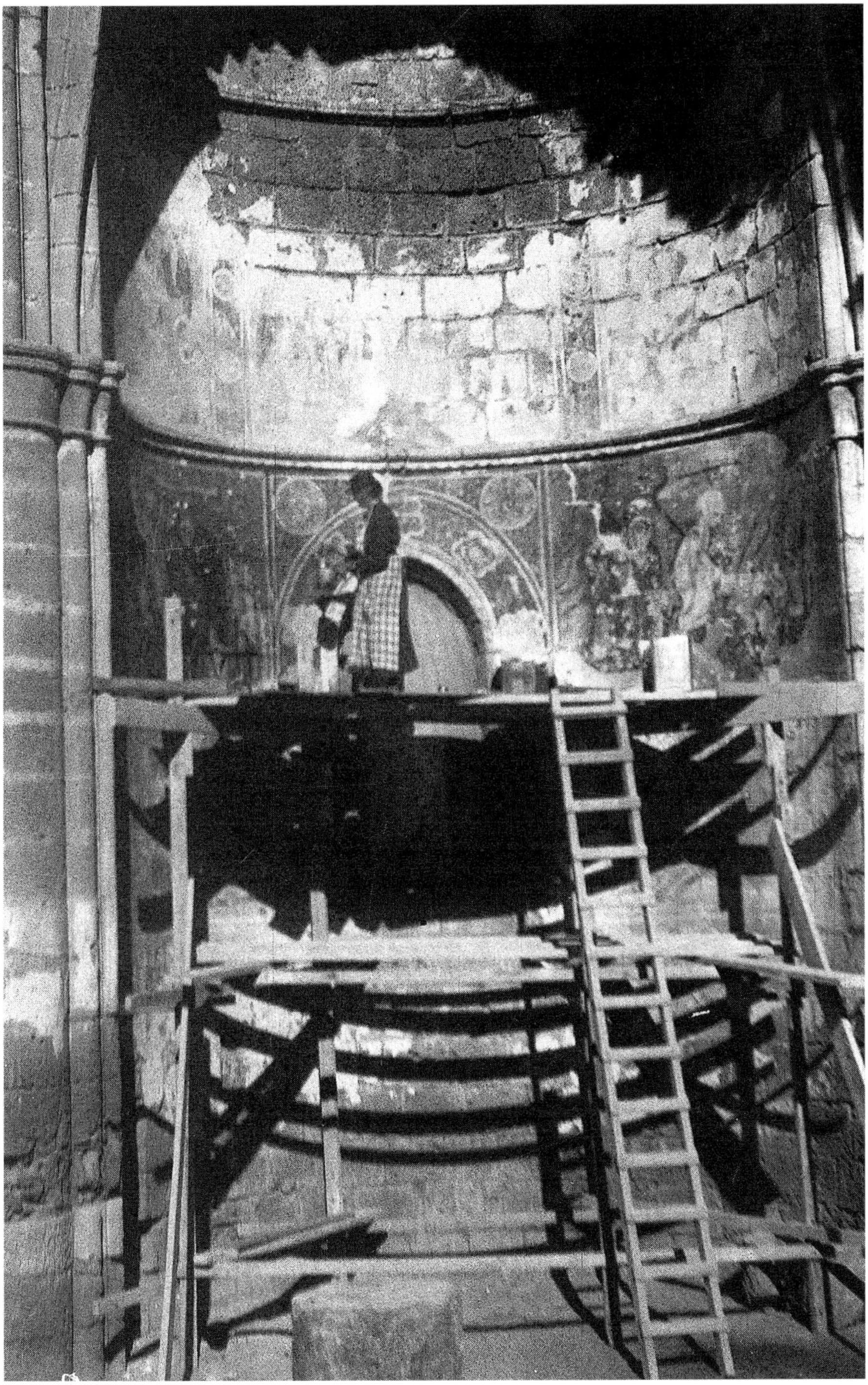

Fig. 12.3 Mrs Monica Bardswell at work in the 1930s on St George of the Greeks (Conway Library, Courtauld Institute)

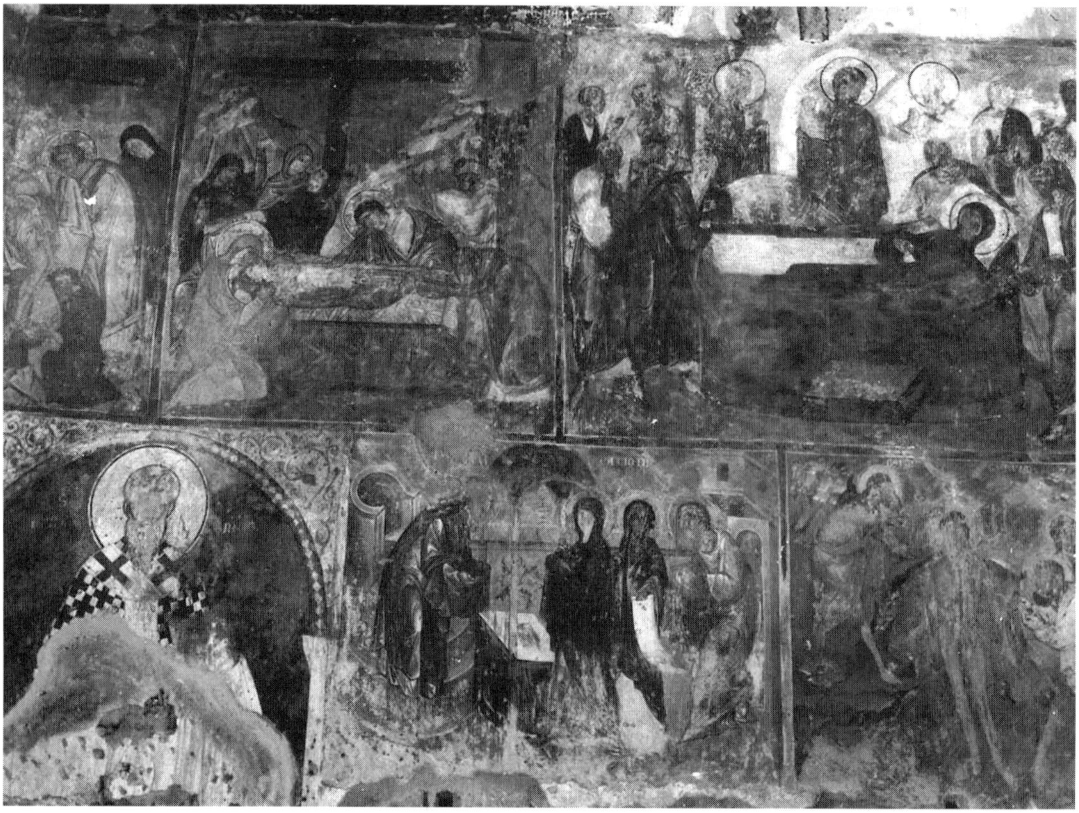

Fig. 12.4 St Anne Church, frescoes of the south wall (photograph: Monica Bardswell, Conway Library, Courtauld Institute)

drably coloured',[26] but noted interestingly that principal characters tended to be depicted according to a 'western inspiration', whereas supporting, or peripheral, characters tended to gravitate more towards a Byzantine feel. Some hint of the colours used can yet be seen in this fragment on the eastern section of the south wall (Plate 13), and an architectural detail may create a further visual link to the *Flagellation* in the Armenian Church.[27] In this image too, and in *The Presentation of Christ at the Temple*, there are barely legible inscriptions which might be similar to the much clearer inscription at St Symeon Church – *ke gas thou tou laou sou* (Plate 14). The 'slate grey' River Jordan, the hairy legged 'wild man' (St John the Baptist) and the sharp toothed fish, symbolizing demons, and intent on tormenting Christ, spill off the edge of Mrs Bardswell's negative and are lost to us. This is a shame, as almost all of the paintings in the photograph have since been covered with white paint (Figure 12.6). In the western portion of the southern wall, and on the interior of the western wall on either side of the door, other images of saints survive. Clearest of all is the southern panel, within two arches decorated with floral designs (for similarities see saint/bishop in Figure 12.4), divided

26 C. Enlart, *L'art gothique et la renaissance en Chypre*, 2 vols. (Paris, 1899); translated as *Gothic Art and the Renaissance in Cyprus*, ed. D. Hunt (London, 1987), 277.

27 Enlart, *Gothic Art*, p. 278, n. 239.

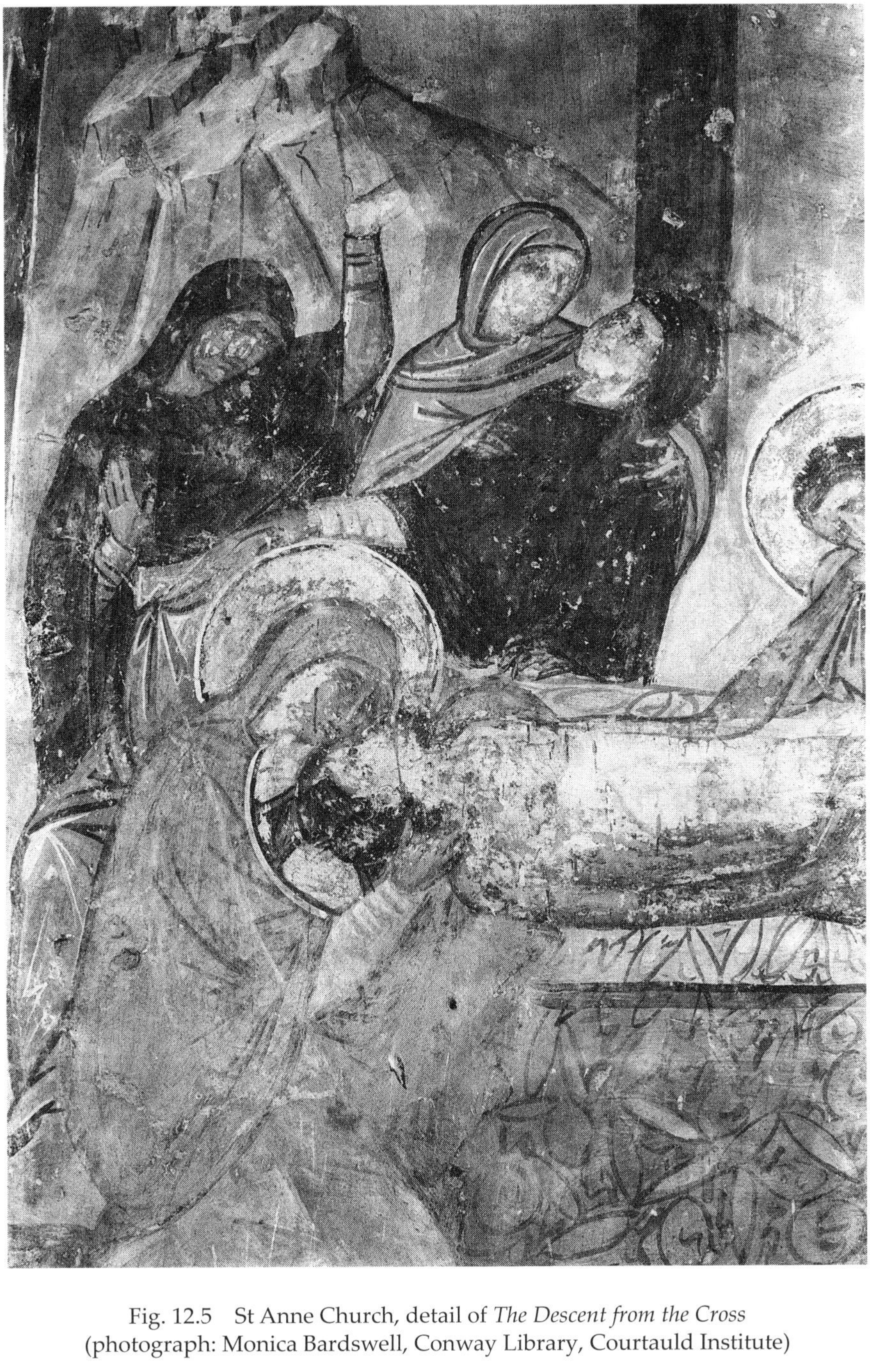

Fig. 12.5 St Anne Church, detail of *The Descent from the Cross* (photograph: Monica Bardswell, Conway Library, Courtauld Institute)

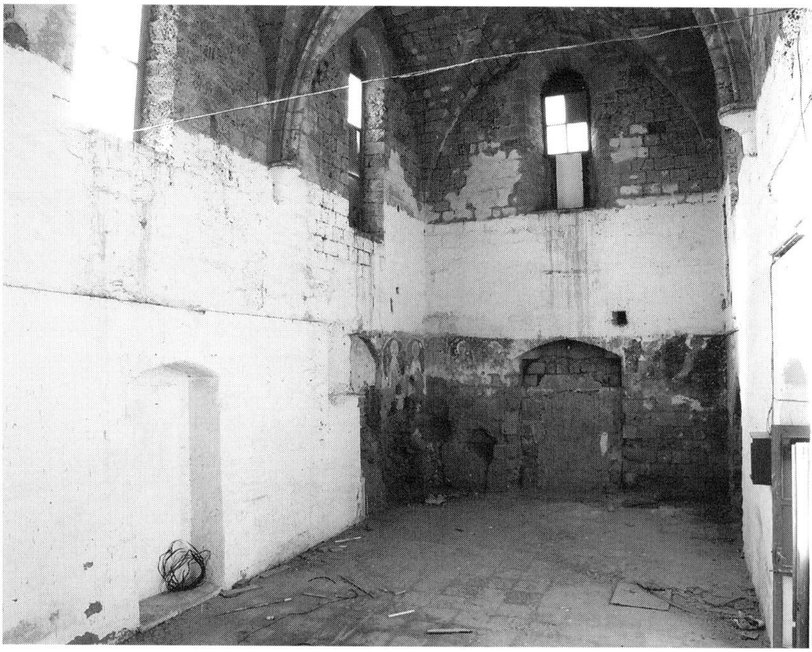

Fig. 12.6
St. Anne Church, Interior 2008 (photograph: Wilbert 'Skip' Norman)

by an undecorated column and capital. Over the scar of a now missing tomb are the SS Catherine and Ursula, beside whom, on the interior of the west wall to the south of the door, two male saints are also visible with scratched halos in relief, similar to that of *St George* in the nearby Armenian Church, and on the figures on the north wall of St Mary of Carmel (Plate 15). Experts have suggested that solubility tests be conducted as there is yet a chance that the white paint can be removed to expose what Bardswell photographed, and what Enlart (1896), and Jeffery (1917), had seen and described.

The first register, at ground level, has experienced a much more drastic fate however, having been cemented over. The first impression is that whatever once lay beneath the cement layer must now be gone for good. On closer inspection, however, several reasons for optimism emerge. It seems that the original walls were roughly tiled, or breeze blocked, before the cement layer was applied; in short, the concrete does not lie directly on the painted surface. Elsewhere, on the western section of the northern wall, wood and a layer of masonite-like fibreboard was installed, before cement was applied. *The Assumption*, over the founder's tomb on the north wall, has a clearly visible and crudely applied wooden 'frame' which bisects the halo of the virgin (Figure 12.7). To the right of the image one can observe the cardboard disappearing beneath the concrete. The important point here is that all of this western section was once behind a similar cement 'wall', as traces of cement all along the floor indicate. This wall has been removed (or collapsed) to reveal what we see today and so can therefore be removed in the rest of the church as well. It seems certain that under the right conditions much of the painted interior of St Anne's Church can be recovered, although Philippe Plagnieux

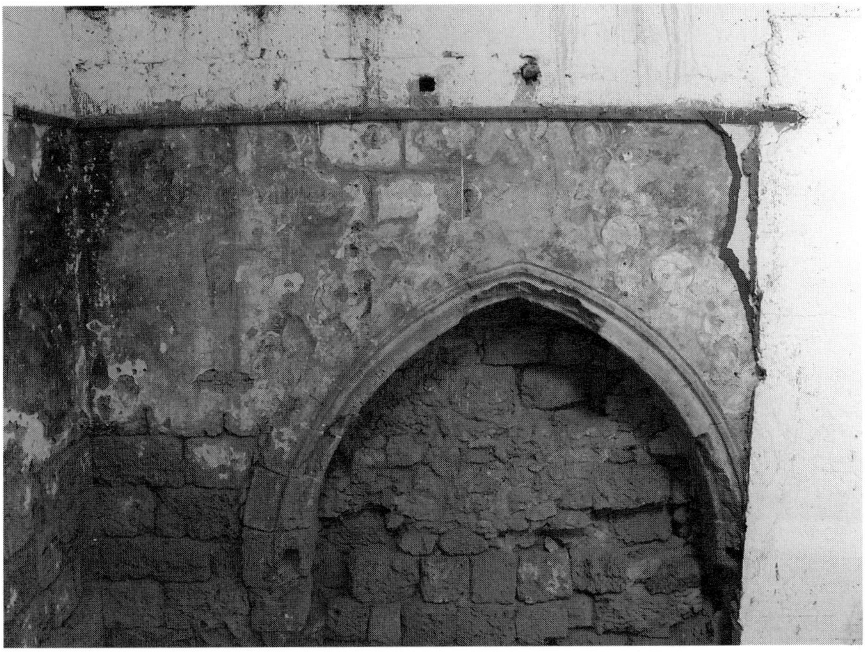

Fig. 12.7
St Anne Church, *The Assumption* (photograph: Wilbert 'Skip' Norman)

and Thierry Soulard temper their optimism with a warning 'On peut espérer retrouver un jour les fresques d'origine sous la peinture, mais des moyens techniques importants seraient nécessaires pour cette opération.'[28] The World Monuments Fund inspectors concluded 'By delicately separating the cement from the edges, it may be possible to remove the cement covers with only minimal damage to the painting.'[29] In the meantime, urgent consolidation is required as empty edgings indicate some recent losses at St Anne's Church, the Armenian Church and in the similarly executed, though desperately faint, images of *St Michael, St George*, the *Raising of Lazarus*, the *Last Supper* and *Washing of the Feet* in the nearby Tanner's Mosque.

Similarly important are the fragmentary remains in the Armenian Church where, in 1934, a French report insisted 'C'est dans cette église arménienne, comme dans la cathédrale des Grecs, que nous rencontrons les plus intéressants vestiges de peintures murales conserves à Famagouste.'[30] Much of the painting had already been lost before the church's roof was fixed by Mogabgab, and then further problems resulted when much of what remained

28 P. Plagnieux and T. Soulard, 'L'Église Sainte-Anne', in *L'Art Gothique en Chypre*, eds J.B. de Vaivre and P. Plagnieux (Paris, 2006), 261–5.

29 K. Severson and R. Silman, *The Historic Walled City of Famagusta* (Report for the World Monuments Fund, 2008. See this volume).

30 A. Carlier, *Les Villes Françaises de Chypre* (Paris, 1934), 30. The writer says the images are Byzantine in flavour, reminiscent of Mistra and replete with Armenian inscriptions which made the identification of the church possible in the first place. See also A. Langdale and M.J.K. Walsh, 'The Architecture, Conservation History, and Future of the Armenian Church of Famagusta', *Chronos* (2009).

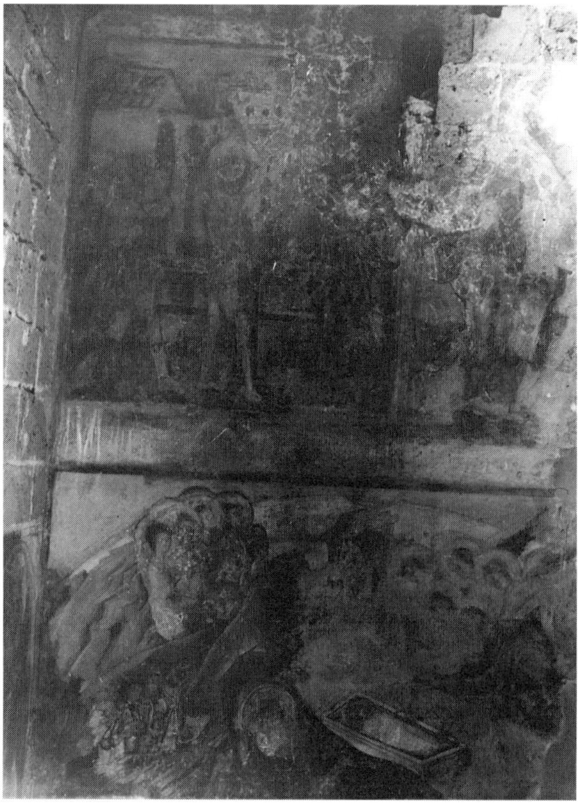

Fig. 12.8 Armenian Church, *Flagellation* and *Nativity* (photograph: Monica Bardswell, Conway Library, Courtauld Institute)

was whitewashed over when it was used as a temporary home during the interethnic problems of the early 1970s and after.[31] Only the upper registers escaped whitewash, and even these have suffered from smoke and other damage. Where hope might lie is in the fact that these frescoes were waxed in the 1930s and in so doing were bequeathed a protective layer against smoke, dirt and other atmospheric threats. Today they still feel somewhat greasy to the touch and so 'If the waxy layer is sufficiently thick, it may act as a release layer, greatly facilitating the safe removal of the white paint.'[32] It seems, therefore, that smoke damage and the whitewash may come off should the wax layer on which they sit be removed too.

Mercifully, there are three photographs of the Armenian Church frescoes housed at the Conway Library at the Courtauld Institute, London. The scene of the *Flagellation of Christ* is quite clear even today (Plate 16, and Figure 12.8).

31 The church had been leased to the local Armenian community who wished to use it. Apparently they provided the funds to undertake the restoration. See A.H.S. Megaw in 'Shorter Reports', *Report of the Department of Antiquities Cyprus 1937–1939* (Nicosia, 1951), 176; A Langdale and M.J.K. Walsh, 'A Short Report on Three Newly Accessible Churches in the Syrian Quarter of Famagusta', *Journal of Cyprus Studies*, 13/33 (2007), 105–27; M. Bacci, 'The Armenian Church in Famagusta and Its Mural Decoration', *Culture of Cilician Armenia* (2009), 489–508.

32 Severson and Silman, *The Historic Walled City of Famagusta* (as note 29).

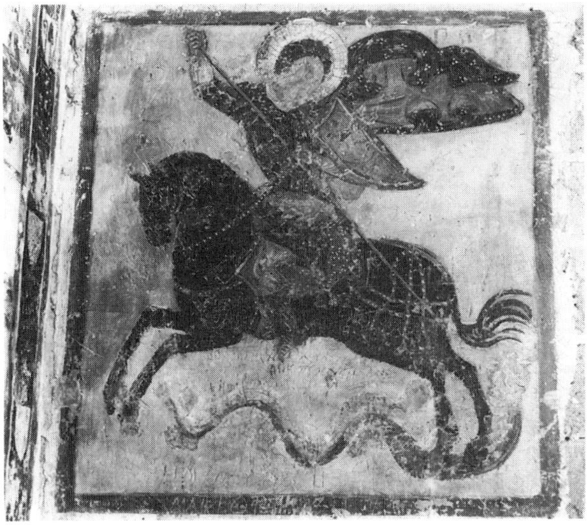

Fig. 12.9 Armenian Church, *St George and the Dragon* (photograph: Monica Bardswell, Conway Library, Courtauld Institute)

Both the figure of Christ and that of the deliverer of the punishment are legible though extensively chipped. The panel, depicting the *Nativity*, beneath it however, is covered in whitewash with only some of the halos of the 13 worshipping angels protruding. The Armenian inscription, the Christ child in the sarcophagus-like crib, the ox and ass, St Helena and the Virgin, all observed by Enlart, and partially captured in this 1974 photograph (see also Figure 8.2), are now gone.[33] The mounted figure of *St George* on the west interior represents significant potential for future conservation work, given that today only the ghostly fluted incisions of the radiating halo emerge from behind the white paint, despite its enviable condition in the 1930s (Figure 12.9).

Both St Anne's and the Armenian Church are roofed.[34] Elsewhere, in churches where the vaults have succumbed to the ravages of history and seismic activity, paintings are exposed to 'airborne particulates' and 'are seriously impacted by biological growth in addition to erosion'.[35] Only when they are located in a protective niche, sheltered from the wind, sun and rain, have they survived. St George of the Greeks is an obvious example where even a cursory glance at the images from the 1930s shows the deterioration from

---

33 Enlart felt that this painting closely resembled a similar composition in Mistra. See Enlart, *Gothic Art*, p. 288 note.

34 See also M. Bacci, 'Syrian, Palaiologan, and Gothic Murals in the "Nestorian" Church of Famagusta', *Deltion tes christianikes archaiologikes Hetaireias* (2006); M.J.K. Walsh 'The Re-emergence of the *Forty Martyrs of Sebaste*', *Journal of Cultural Heritage* (2007).

35 Severson and Silman, *The Historic Walled City of Famagusta*. Camille Enlart also noted some interesting frescoes in St Francis Church and recorded the following intriguing comment concerning their destruction: 'Mâites de Famagouste, les génois avaient usé de procédés analogues, car dans les peintures murales de l'église des Carmes, les armes des Lusignan furent alors partout grattées avec soin. On en peignit d'autres lorsque Jacques II eut repris la ville un siècle plus tard.' See: C. Enlart, 'Fouilles dans les églises de Famagouste de Chypre', *Archaeological Journal* Vol. 62 (1905), p. 216.

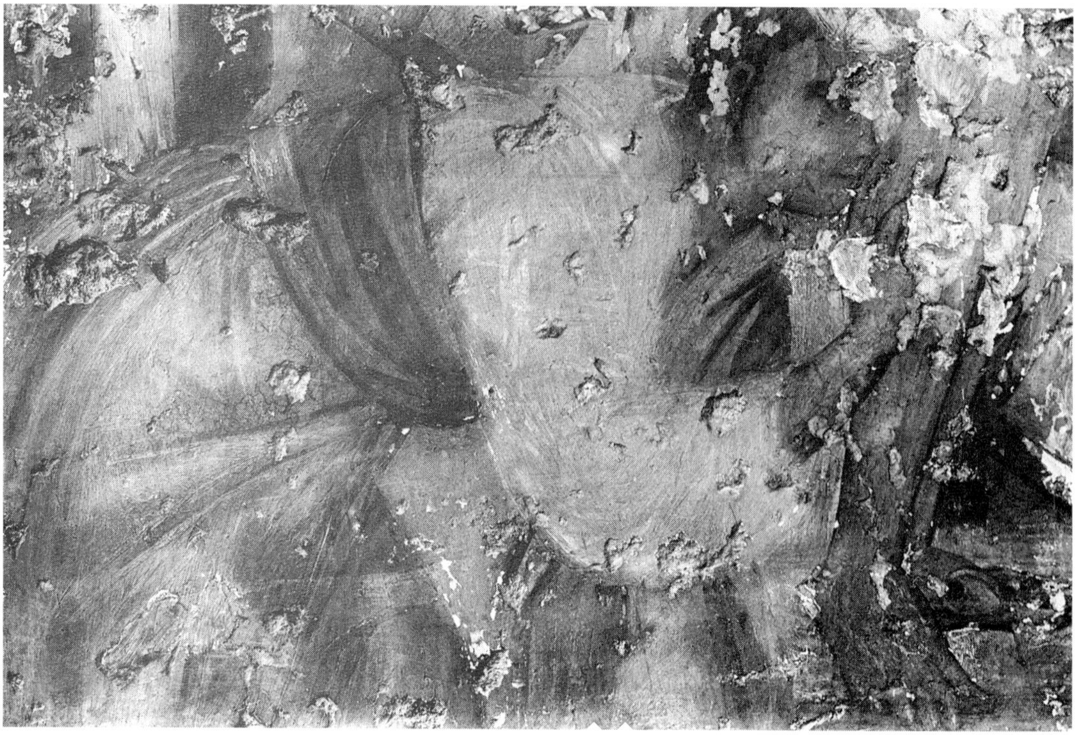

Fig. 12.10 St George of the Greeks, apse of south aisle (photograph: Monica Bardswell, Conway Library, Courtauld Institute)

the descriptions that Enlart offered less than a half a century before. Further comparisons with what is visible today speak for themselves. Nowhere is this more marked than in the southern apse where four images frame the window. The *Descent from the Cross*, the *Entombment*, the *Resurrection of Jesus and the Just* and the *Holy Woman at the Sepulchre*, no longer atop the row of apostles and doctors of the church, offer the conservationist one last great hope of safeguarding a virtually unstudied fragment of Cypriot art history before it is finally too late (Figures 12.10 and 12.11).[36] The Carmelite Friary of St Mary is another fine example of what is yet at risk.

The Carmelite Order arrived in Cyprus before the great expulsion from Acre in 1291 and stayed on the island throughout the Lusignan and Venetian periods. The friary, authorized in 1311, therefore had an extremely long and grand history, at the heart of which was its art. When Niccolò da Martoni visited Famagusta in 1394 he observed in *De monasterio S. Marie de Carmine*, 'very beautiful scenes and pictures';[37] Edward I'Anson reported in 1882 that 'the frescoes still remain wonderfully preserved', especially one of *St George and the Dragon*;[38] Enlart called them 'perhaps the most interesting of all those

[36] M.J.K. Walsh, 'On of the princypalle Havenes of the See': The Port of Famagusta and the Ship Graffiti of its Ruined Churches', *International Journal of Nautical Archaeology* Vol. 37, No. 1 (2008).

[37] Cited in R. Gunnis, *Historic Cyprus* (London, 1936), 100.

[38] E. I'Anson and S. Vacher, 'Mediaeval and Other Buildings in the Island of

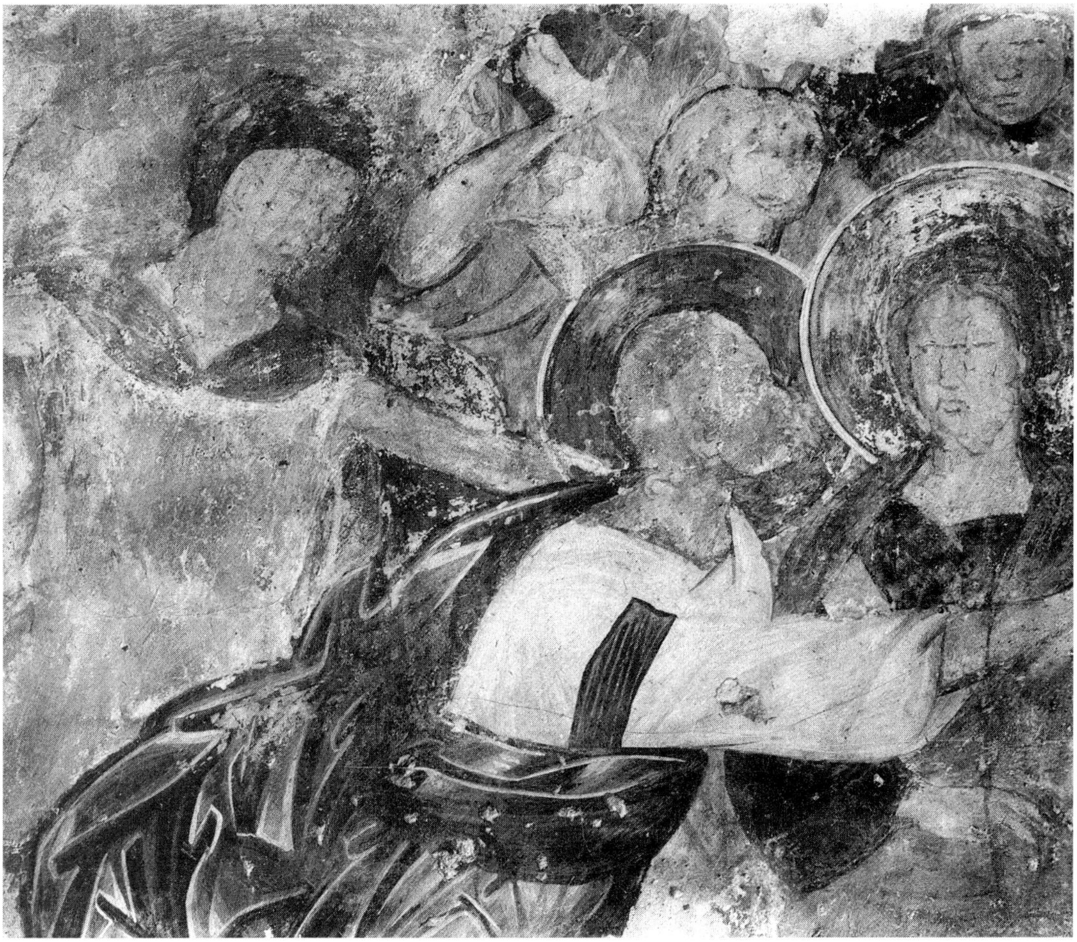

Fig. 12.11 St George of the Greeks, apse of south aisle (photograph: Monica Bardswell, Conway Library, Courtauld Institute)

[paintings] among the ruins of Famagusta', then went on to describe many images which he believed to be fourteenth- and fifteenth-century Italian, but which have disappeared since.[39] Thankfully, he took the time and care to sketch principal figures and scenes such as: *St Catherine of Alexandria* (and flanking scenes), *St George and the Dragon*, *Kneeling Donors*, *Carrying the Cross*, and heraldry in the apse. George Jeffery also reported on these images at the Society of Antiquaries, London, in 1916, in particular a painted representation of drapery on a rod, which bore various heraldic devices, and which he felt might be the work of a Tuscan hand.[40] Albert Kammerer in 1925 observed 'Au fond du choeur Sainte-Marie du Carmel, de belles fresques dans le style Italien, avec des armoires bien conserves achèvent de mourir sous le ciel

Cyprus', *Transactions of the Royal Institute of British Architects* (1882–83), 18.

[39] Enlart, *Gothic Art*, p. 278, n. 239.

[40] G.E. Jeffery, 'Report on the Carmelite Church', *Proceedings of the Society of Antiquaries* (1916), 106–11.

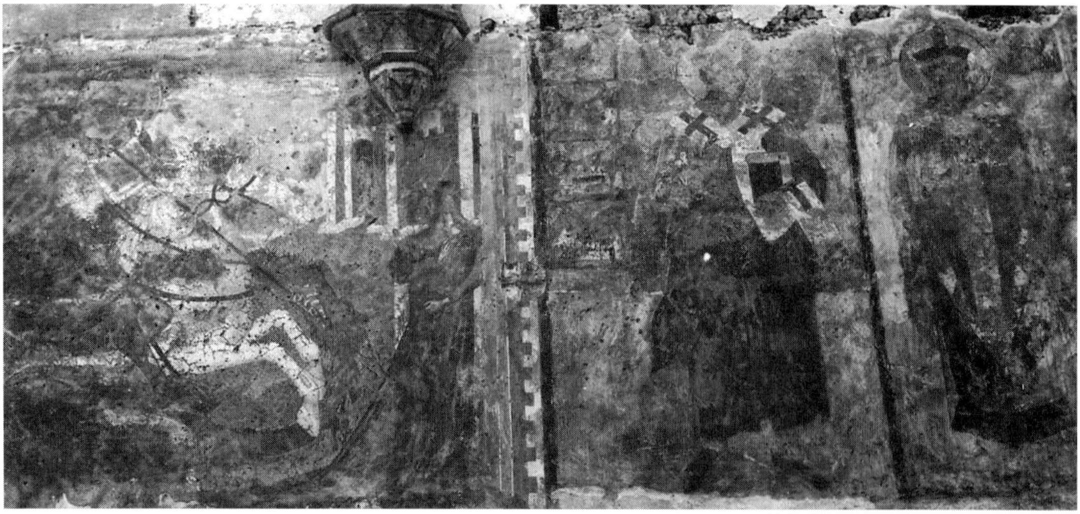

Fig. 12.12 St Mary of Carmel, *St George and Dragon* (photograph: Monica Bardswell, Conway Library, Courtauld Institute)

éclatant.'[41] Bardswell's images from the 1937 and 1938 certainly show that the images, although in an advanced state of disrepair, were significantly clearer then than they are today, especially when we compare *St George and the Dragon* (Figure 12.12 and Plate 18).

Beside St Nicholas, in vertical registers, there are scenes from his life and the miracles he performed.[42] Typically these depict 'episodes' including: scenes from the monastery in Myra in Lycia, heading the monastery table, as the archimandrite, consecration as Bishop, in prison conversing with three generals, and various miraculous sea journeys.[43] The clearest image of these in the Carmelite Church is a moment of execution, where three blindfolded boys bend over, while two figures raise their arms behind them (Plate 12). Enlart suggested that the grey bearded figure was the saint himself, arresting the sword which had been raised for execution, even if this was not entirely consistent with the story of the Salting Tub that he simultaneously suggested. The correct literary reference is in fact to the same work, that of the Genoese Dominican friar, Jacobus de Voragine, and his *Golden Legend* of 1266, but more particularly to the near execution of the three princes Nepotian, Ursyn, and Apollyn, which is described as follows:

> And whilst they were at dinner, the consul, corrupt by money, had commanded three innocent knights to be beheaded. And when the blessed Nicholas knew this, he prayed these three princes that they would much hastily go with him. And when they were come where they should be beheaded, he found them on their knees, and blindfold, and the righter brandished his sword over their heads. Then S. Nicholas embraced with the love of God, set him hardily against the righter, and took the sword out

41 A. Kammerer, *A Chypre: L'ile d'Aphrodite* (Paris, 1925), 33.

42 N. Ševčenko, *The Life of St Nicholas in Byzantine Art* (Turin, 1983).

43 Constantinides, 'Monumental Painting in Cyprus during the Venetian Period', p . 271.

> of his hand, and threw it from him, and unbound the innocents, and led them with him all safe.[44]

In another scene, to the right of the saint's head, there is an extremely faint image of two sisters lying in bed while St Nicholas's hand reaches money through a window to a distraught, now grateful, father, who had been contemplating the desperately needed money that could be made by an illicit and immoral transaction concerning his girls.[45] Nicholas continued to pass, or throw, gold through the window anonymously so that there could be no chance that the sisters would be required to forfeit their virginity unwillingly (Plate 19).

While the literary references are perfectly clear, the art historian cannot help but wonder whether donors' portraits would have been included in these scenes.[46] One also wonders if these flanking scenes were conducted by other artists/apprentices from a particular 'school', or by the hand of the master himself. If so, these faded and fragmentary pictures, small in scale and almost inaccessibly high on the wall, are offering us a collective portrait not only of a saint, but of a patron and indeed of a school of art – a priceless vignette for the historian of medieval and renaissance art in Cyprus!

For some the shattered remnants of Famagusta's art history are as heartbreaking as they are irreparable. For others, it is precisely this fact that makes the few surviving fragments so priceless. That they are still uncared for is a source of deep concern as, when they are gone completely, a unique chance to observe 'the larger constellation of communities' that made up fourteenth- and fifteenth-century Famagusta will have been lost.[47] Achille Carlier was hardly exaggerating when he reflected on the importance and the beauty of 'l'art roman qui se mit à refleuris sur le sol de Chypre au XV siècle'.[48] Although theirs is a history of neglect, these images are perhaps Famagusta's most treasured, yet most endangered, asset.

---

44 W.G. Ryan (trans.), *The Golden Legend: Readings on the Saints* (Princeton, 1993), 21–7.

45 My thanks to Colum Hourihane at the Index of Christian Art, Princeton University, for confirming this subject attribution.

46 This is seen in icon painting much more so that in wall painting.

47 See A.W. Carr, 'Perspectives on Visual Culture in Early Lusignan Cyprus', *Archaeology and the Crusades (Proceedings of the Round Table, Nicosia, 1 February 2005)*, eds P. Edbury and S. Kalopissi-Verti (Athens, 2007), 83–110.

48 Carlier, *Les Villes Françaises de Chypre*, p. 30.

13

Twentieth-Century Restorations to the Medieval and Renaissance Monuments of Famagusta

Ege Uluca Tümer

Introduction

The British period in Cyprus was extremely important for the medieval and renaissance monuments of the island. Contrary to the Ottoman period which preceded it, there now arose an increasing interest in Cyprus's ancient monuments, leading scholars and travellers to produce many books and articles. The British government itself also demonstrated a willingness to assist with the maintenance and restoration of monuments, not least in the historic city of Famagusta. This study incorporates the years from 1878, as a prelude, to the vital period from 1935–1956 when the principal programmes of restoration were undertaken. Though the conservation practices were handled as professionally (financially and technically) as possible, and although all the restoration works were photographed in detail, they were not sufficiently published. Two reports of the Department of Antiquities, Cyprus, dated 1936 and 1951, offer only tantalizing summaries of the activities in Famagusta in 1936 and between 1937 and 1939.

This chapter aims to make the twentieth-century restorations to the medieval and renaissance monuments of Famagusta clearer, and offer an evaluation of these works. In order to do this, the necessary data on photographs and accessed written documents has been categorized in tables under certain titles and subtitles. The restoration and conservation works have been categorized chronologically. In assessing the quality of the work in the city, I have cited at length the Venice Charter of 1964, which is the universal charter for the development of scientific restoration approaches, signed by more than 70 countries. The Venice Charter is especially significant as it was signed just eight years after the completion of works in Famagusta and has recently been validated by ICOMOS, without alteration.

Monuments in Famagusta between 1878 and 1935

Appreciating the importance of both the port and the city of Famagusta, the British administration on Cyprus put into operation several projects. This began in 1878 with the passing of the Famagusta Improvement Law under the supervision of an 'Eastern Divisional Engineer'. By its terms, the town was divided into streets, open spaces and tenements to ensure proper rebuilding and the introduction of an effective sanitation system. The harbour was cleared to make way for a return of shipping, facilitated by a railway terminal which in turn gave access to the rest of the island. These two projects were unsurpassed in importance.[1] The Famagusta harbour development projects were implemented in two phases: 1903–1905 and 1931–33.[2] In 1904, after the construction of a 36-mile long railway between Famagusta and Nicosia, there was now access to the port from outside the city walls, and from 1933, during the second phase of harbour development works, a road from south of the city led to the port.[3] The draining of the marshes on the north side of the city and improvements to the moats was another significant project for Famagusta. In these areas, the excess water was pumped out and eucalyptus trees were planted in 1900.[4] In so doing, the age-old scourge of malaria was finally removed from Famagusta.

During the first 50 years of British rule in Cyprus, Famagusta was valued more for its economic capacity as a port (even if it did not fulfil expectations),[5] than for its architectural and historical heritage. This was exemplified by the construction of three gates (Figure 13.1) through the harbour wall, between the citadel and the Sea Gate, in 1903 during the development of the harbour and the related commercial buildings along the north-eastern side of the city and the Piazza-Sea Gate axis. These, I would argue, are examples of early disharmonious interferences with the urban pattern and monuments of Famagusta.

Some demolitions and the relocation of some important monuments during this 50-year period should also be highlighted. In the last decade of the nineteenth century, the Konak, the Ottoman governmental building next to Palace, on the site of the old prison, was demolished,[6] as was the Ottoman Palace in Nicosia, which had been originally the Lusignan Palace.[7] Similarly,

---

1 Ş. Hafızoğlu, 'Stone use in British Domestic Architecture in North Cyprus' (unpublished Masters Thesis: Famagusta, 2000), 55–6. Cf. W.H. Dixon, *British Cyprus* (London, 1879), 279.

2 K.K. Keshishian, *Famagusta Town and District: Cyprus: A survey of its people and places from ancient times* (Limassol, 1985), 86.

3 C.W.J. Orr, *Cyprus under British Rule* (London, 1972), 15–16; Keshishian, p. 86.

4 B. Stewart, *My Experiences of Cyprus* (London, 1908), 57.

5 Orr, p. 154.

6 C. Enlart, *Gothic Art and the Renaissance in Cyprus*, ed. and trans. D. Hunt (London, 1987), 466. The existing building was constructed in 1899.

7 R. Hanworth, *The Heritage of North Cyprus* (Nicosia: 1990), 109. This author states that the building was unnecessarily demolished in 1904. H. Luke, *Cyprus under the Turks (1571–1878): A Record based on the Archives of the English Consulate in Cyprus under the Levant Company and After* (London, 1921), 1.

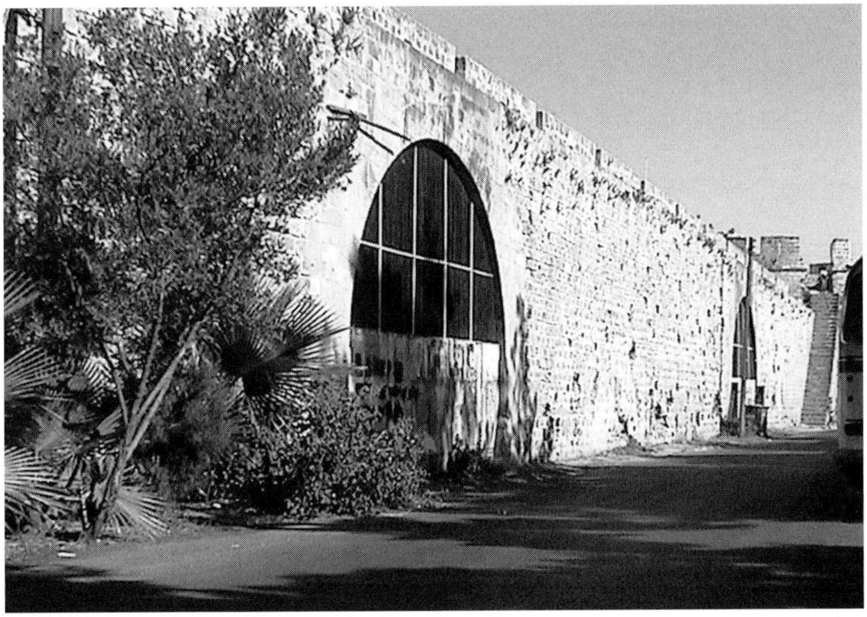

Fig. 13.1 British period entrances in the curtain wall at the port (photograph: Ege Tümer)

two ancient columns, and a sarcophagus in the middle of the Piazza, indicated on the Gibellino engraving of 1571 (see also Figure 7.1),[8] were relocated in 1878. The columns were moved next to the Madrasa building,[9] and the sarcophagus was taken to the Protestant cemetery and used as a tomb for an English official.[10] A further loss to Famagusta's historic monuments in this period came with the demolition of the building opposite the churches commonly ascribed to the Templars and Hospitallers. In 1903 Enlart had photographed this monument which he identified as the 'Genoese Loggia' (Figure 13.2) on the strength of historical documents.[11] This building, however, is remarkably close to that numbered 11 and marked as 'Palazzo della Regina' on the 1571 Gibellino engraving. Enlart's images, and notes on the structure in 1903, were the last made before Mogabgab photographed its remaining foundations in the 1930s.

8 C. Enlart, *L'Art gothique et la Renaissance en Chypre* (Paris, 1899), plate xxi.

9 Supposition for the relocation of the columns is based on their location in the Gibellino engraving, and Drummond's definition in 1750 as 'Two granite pillars in front of the church, upon the right, between them stand a sarcophagus adored with festoons.' in C.D. Cobham, *Excerpta Cypria: Materials for a History of Cyprus* (New York: Kraus Reprint Co., 1969), 274.

10 Mrs Lewis, *A Lady's impressions of Cyprus* (London, 1893), 282–3; C. Enlart, *Villes Mortes du Moyen Age* (Paris, 1920), 142.

11 Enlart, *Villes Mortes*, p. 152; Enlart, *Gothic Art*, p. 456. Cf. P.W. Edbury, 'Famagusta in 1300', in N. Coureas and J. Riley-Smith (eds), *Cyprus and the Crusades* (Nicosia, 1995), 340; M. Balard, 'Famagouste au début du XIVe siècle', in J. Heers (ed.), *Fortifications, portes de villes, places publiques dans le monde méditerranéen* (Paris, 1985), 283, 286.

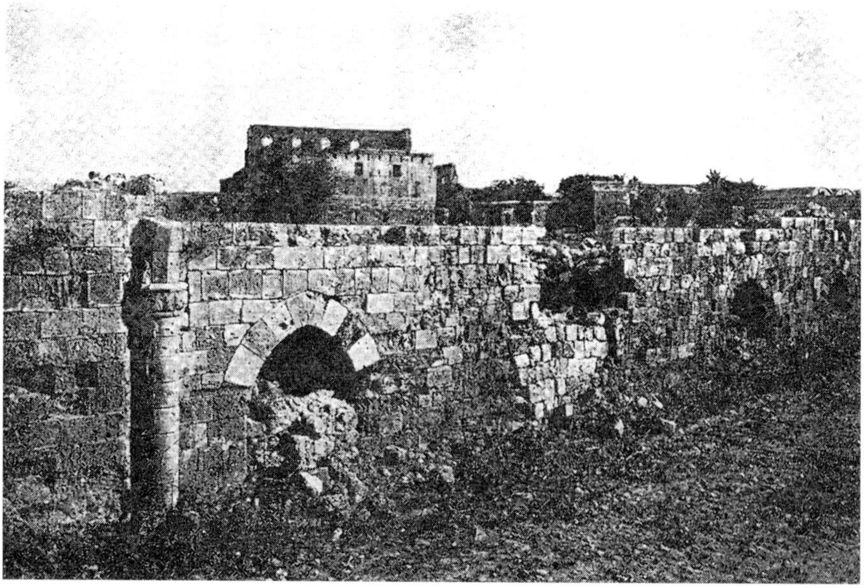

Fig. 13.2 The Genoese loggia, as identified by Enlart but today disappeared (C. Enlart, *Villes Mortes du Moyen Age* [Paris, 1920], p. 152)

Restoration Work between 1935 and 1956

At the beginning of the twentieth century, a project was launched for the conservation and restoration of monuments throughout the island to be financed by the revenues remaining in the 'Locust Destruction Fund'.[12] Additional funding was supplied by the New York Carnegie Corporation in 1938, in addition to the funds collected in the United Kingdom through the Mersey Committee for Cyprus Monuments Fund. By 1938, at the height of their activity, 71 workmen, including 20 masons, were hired to work with the assistance of local prisoners. Mrs M. Bardswell, a painting restoration specialist, volunteered her services, and over a period of 18 months in 1937 and 1938 restored many church frescoes. Mr J.R. Bowler supervised all the restoration work from 1935 to February 1939, after which trained Cypriot foremen took over, except at Famagusta. Here, Theophilus A.H. Mogabgab, architect and officer of the Department of Antiquities in Famagusta, who had previously exercised local supervision, assumed responsibility for the restoration work.[13]

Between 1935 and 1956 the most comprehensive rehabilitation and restoration work took place in Famagusta, which was where the majority of the island's Medieval and Renaissance buildings were located. Mogabgab's remarkable concern for environmental conditions, as well as for the integrity of the monuments within their socio-historical context, ensured that individual

12 G. Chacalli, *Cyprus under British Rule* (Nicosia, 1902), 147–8.

13 *Report of the Department of Antiquities Cyprus, 1937–39* (Nicosia, 1951), 171 (henceforth *RDAC*, 1951).

projects were subsumed within a wider urban rehabilitation and conservation scheme. Few of Famagusta's historic monuments went untouched. However, Mogabgab produced only one report on his excavations and research in Famagusta between 1937 and 1939, published as a part of the *Report of the Department of Antiquities Cyprus* in 1951.[14] He did, however, fastidiously record every step of each project by taking, labelling and cataloguing thousands of black and white photographs which, in the absence of significant written reports, must serve as the principal archive for the architectural historian.

Restoration work in Famagusta began in 1935 with the opening of the entrance to a secret passage in the south-west section of the moat.[15] In 1936 work at the Ravelin, the church of St George of the Greeks and the Venetian Palace, and excavations in the 'Nameless Church V' (Plot 83)[16] got underway. At this early stage, the efforts were directed in general towards limited excavations, clearance and the lowering of the roads around these monuments to their original levels (Tables 13.1–13.3).

In these early years restoration work included, in varying measures, plastering, strengthening, excavation and clearance. Using the techniques current at that time, there was widespread consolidation of masonry. Most of the sites were excavated and cleared, and their security increased by building enclosing walls. After the completion of the first phase of the work between 1937 and 1939, excavations and clearance continued on and around the city walls. At the same time inappropriate additions from the Ottoman period such as walls, blocked doors and window openings, and modern roofs were mostly removed, while the demolition of some houses in close proximity to the monuments was also deemed necessary.

Classification and Distribution of Restoration Works

A detailed and comprehensive study of Mogabgab's sole report and his impressive photographic archive allows us to identify four main types of work carried out on 56 separate buildings or sites between 1935 and 1956. These four types of work were: 1) excavation and clearance, 2) attention to later intrusions, 3) restoration, and 4) rehabilitation of the environment. The buildings themselves can also be categorized in three main groups: 1) fortifications (Table 13.1); 2) churches (Table 13.2); and 3) palaces and houses (Table 13.3). (For further sub-categorizations, see the fortifications group for 'citadels', 'bastions and cavaliers', 'moats' and 'walls'.) Furthermore, an

14 *RDAC*, 1951, pp. 181–90.

15 *RDAC*, 1951, p. 183.

16 These plot numbers are stated by T. Mogabgab in his notes. Locations of nameless churches I–V are sequentially on Piyale Pasa Street, on the North-East of St George the Greeks, on south of Ali Paşa Street, on north of Ali Pasa Street, on north-west end of Kislayolu Street. *RDAC*, 1951, p. 175.

Name of the Monument		Works on the Monuments									
		Excavations and clearance	Refinement of latter day interventions			Restorations			Rehabilitation of environment		
		Excavations and clearance	Demolition (demolition of modern buildings/ attachements)	Blocking up	Removal of accretions (opening blocked door, window e.g.)	Simple repairs (plaster, stone e.g. repairs on wall surfaces)	Restoration of architectural elements and paintings (windows, doors, sills e.g)	Reintegration, restoration of structural elements (grouting, inserting r.c. e.g.)	Lowering ground (road, parcel, approaches eg.)	Rehabilitation of close buildings	Building / lowering / raising enclosing wall
	Citadel (Ic Kale)	X	X		X	X	X	X			
Bastions and Cavaliers	Ravelin (Akkule Tabya)	X			X	X	X	X			
Bastions and Cavaliers	Torion del Arsenale (Canbulat Tabya)		X			X					
Bastions and Cavaliers	Martinengo Bastion (Tobhane Tabya)		X			X					
Bastions and Cavaliers	Diamante Bastion and Cavalier (Karpaz Tabya)	X			X	X		X			
Bastions and Cavaliers	Santa Napa Bastion (Altın Burcu)		X								
Bastions and Cavaliers	Andruzzi Bastion (Su Burcu)	X			X				X		
Bastions and Cavaliers	Campo Santo Bastion and Cavalier (Halkalı Burcu)	X				X		X			
Bastions and Cavaliers	Del Mozzo Bastion (Kopuk Burcu)	X				X					
Bastions and Cavaliers	San Luca Bastion (Altıparmak Burcu)	X			X						
Bastions and Cavaliers	Moratto Bastion and Cavalier	X			X	X		X			
Bastions and Cavaliers	Diocare Bastion	X			X	X		X	X		
Bastions and Cavaliers	Land Gate Cavalier	X	X		X	X		X			
Moats	West Moat	X									
Moats	South-West Moat	X			X						
Moats	South Moat	X			X	X					
Moats	North Moat	X									
Walls	Land Gate Approaches	X	X			X		X	X		
Walls	Curtain between Diamate and Signoria Towers				X	X		X			
Walls	Sea Walls							X			
Walls	Counterscarp					X		X			X

Table 13.1 Twentieth-century restorations on fortifications

Name of the Monument		Works on the Monuments: Excavations and clearance	Refinement of later day interventions			Restorations			Rehabilitation of environment		
		Excavations and clearance	Demolition (demolition of modern buildings / attachments)	Blocking up	Removal of accretions (opening blocked door, window e.g.)	Simple repairs (plaster, stone e.g. repairs on wall surfaces)	Restoration of architectural elements and paintings (windows, doors, sills e.g)	Reintegration, restoration of structural elements (grouting, inserting r.c. e.g.)	Lowering ground (road, parcel, approaches eg.)	Rehabilitation of close buildings	Building / lowering / raising enclosing wall
St.Nicholas and Environs	St.Nicholas Church (NE of cathedral bombed in 1941)	■	■	■	■	■	■	■	■		■
St.Nicholas and Environs	Bishop's Chapel	■				■		■	■		
St.Nicholas and Environs	Ragazzione Annexe					■	■	■			■
St.Nicholas and Environs	Cells	■				■		■			■
St.Nicholas and Environs	Stationes						■	■			
St.Nicholas and Environs	Fountain and Columns in Piazza	■									■
	St.George of the Latins Church	■	■					■	■		
	St.George of the Greeks Church	■	■			■	■	■	■		■
	SS. Peter and Paul Church (Planned to be used as museum)	■	■		■	■	■	■	■	■	■
	Franciscan Church	■	■		■	■	■	■	■		■
	Carmelite Church	■			■	■	■	■	■		
	Templar Church	■			■	■	■	■	■		■
	Hospitalier Church	■	■	■	■	■	■	■	■		■
	St.Anne Church (war time army church)					■	■	■			
	San Antonio Church	■				■	■	■			
	Ayios Yeorghios Xorinos Church (Building in Service in 1941)	■			■	■	■	■	■		
	Armenian Church (Building in Service in 1945)	■				■	■	■	■		
	St.Symeon Church (N semi dome bombed out in 1941)	■					■		■		
	Ayios Nicolas Church					■	■	■	■		
	Ay. Zoni Church	■				■					■
	Ayia Photou Church	■				■	■				
	Lala Mustafa Pasa Mosque	■		■	■	■	■				■
	Tabakhane Mosque		■			■	■	■			
	Nameless Church I (Plot 240)	■				■			■		
	Nameless Church II (Plot 241)	■									
	Nameless Church III (Plot 354)	■	■			■		■	■	■	■
	Nameless Church IV (Plot 356)	■	■			■	■				■
	Nameless Church V (Plot 18)	■						■			

Table 13.2 Twentieth-century restorations on churches

Name of the Monument		Works on the Monuments									
		Excavations and clearance	Refinement of latter day interventions			Restorations			Rehabilitation of environment		
		Excavations and clearance	Demolition (demolition of modern buildings / attachements)	Blocking up	Removal of accretions (opening blocked door, window e.g.)	Simple repairs (plaster, stone e.g. repairs on wall surfaces)	Restoration of architectural elements and paintings (windows, doors, sills e.g)	Reintegration, restoration of structural elements (grouting, inserting r.c. e.g.)	Lowering ground (road, parcel, approaches eg.)	Rehabilitation of close buildings	Building/ lowering/ raising enclosing wall
Palace and Environs	Venetian Palace	■	■		■	■	■	■	■		■
	Armoury (West part of palace)	■	■			■	■	■	■	■	■
	Chapel (Lapidary Museum)	■	■		■	■		■	■		
	Bedestan (Palazzo)	■			■	■	■	■	■	■	
	Genoese Loggia (Demolished btw 1903-35)	■									■
	Biddulph Arch	■							■		
	Pointed Arch of a House (Mehmet Ali S)					■	■				

Table 13.3 Twentieth-century restorations on palace and environs

amalgam of 'churches' and 'palaces and houses', saw two other geographical distinctions of 'St. Nicholas and environs' and 'Palace and environs'.

In 44 of the 56 building projects undertaken, 'excavation and clearance' of both interiors and exteriors, to reveal the original floors and surrounding levels of the site, was the principal objective. In a few cases more comprehensive excavations were done and remains were found in or around: the Piazza, the Palace, the Ravelin, the Citadel, the Armenian Church, the church of SS Peter and Paul and the Templar and Hospitaller Churches. It might be observed through the photographic records and the fragmentary notes that Mogabgab made, that these excavations were not scientifically or systematically carried out. Indeed, Mogabgab, appointed director of the Antiquities Office in Famagusta, was in fact an architect. He was the only professional appointed for the work, and no archaeologists directed the excavations. Similarly, due to budgetary constraints, prisoners were used for excavations instead of experienced workmen. It was only when unexpected discoveries came to light that more comprehensive excavations were undertaken (Figures 13.3–13.5). 'Excavations and clearance' work was also noted in all parts of the city's fortifications, except at the Canbulat Tower, the Martinengo Bastion, and the

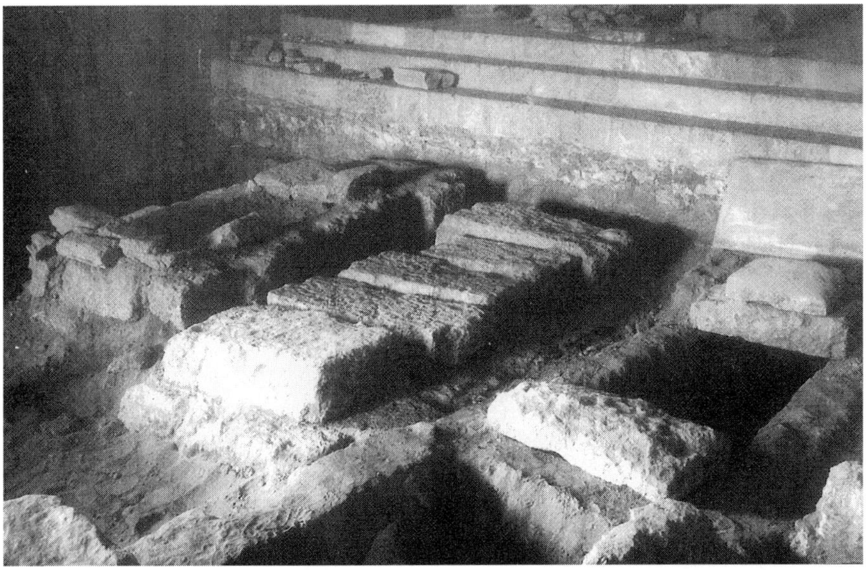

Fig. 13.3 Grave excavations in the Templars' Church, 1941 (Mogabgab Archive, unpublished)

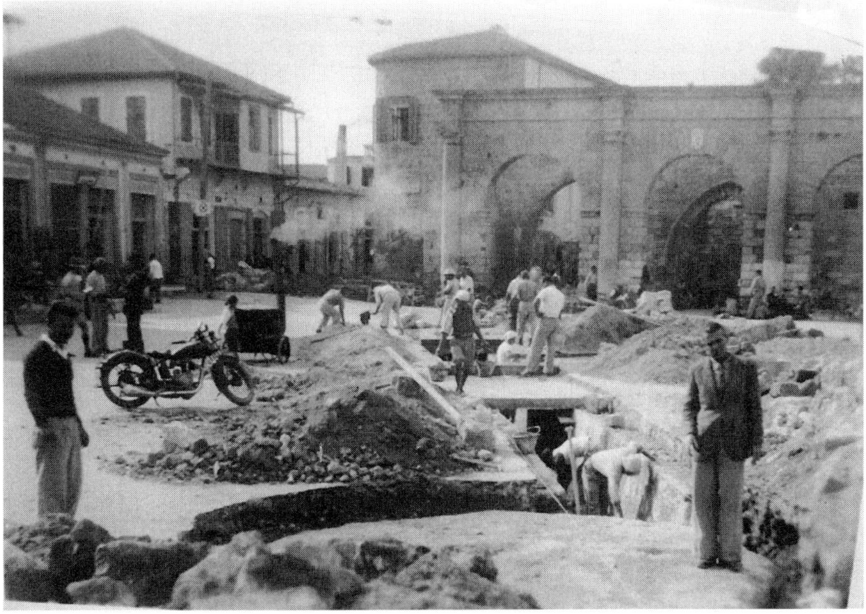

Fig. 13.4 Accidental discovery of Venetian fountain in 1947 (Mogabgab Archive, unpublished)

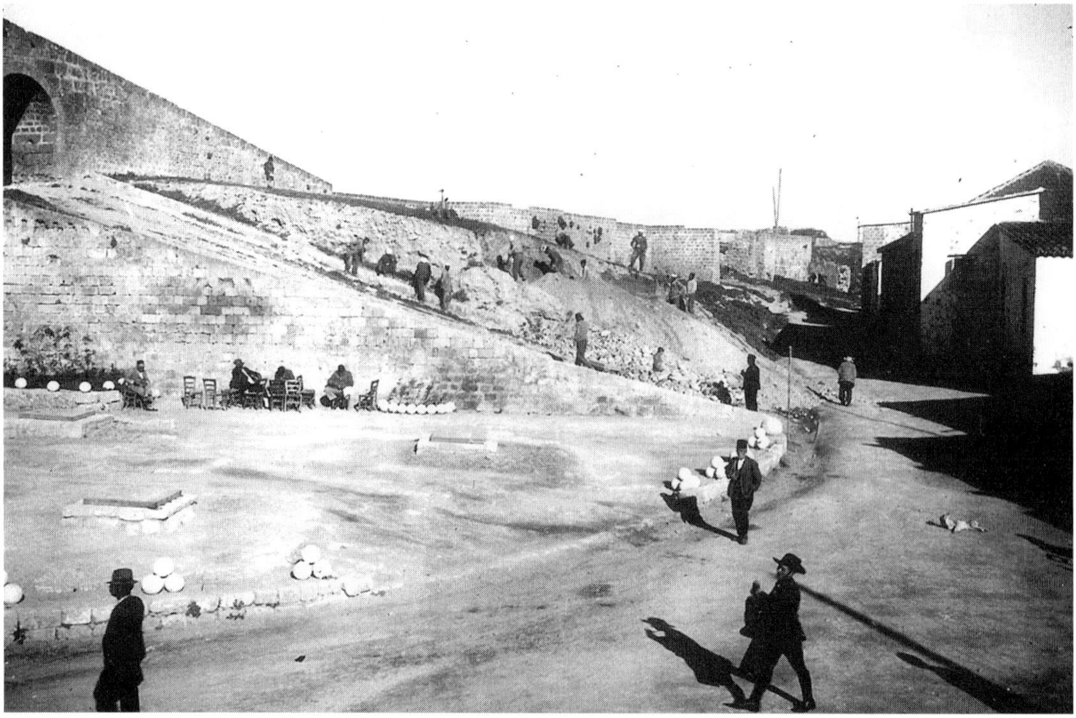

Fig. 13.5 Land gate approaches, excavation and clearance, 1937 (Mogabgab Archive, unpublished)

sea walls between the Diamante and the Signoria Bastions. Of the 28 buildings in the 'churches' group, 'excavations and clearance' was not recorded in any of the following: the Ragazzione Annexe, Staciones,[17] St Anne, St Nicholas and the Tabakhane Mosque. In the 'palaces and houses' category, 'excavations and clearance' was carried out in all seven buildings except at a house on Mehmet Ali Gormus Street where a pointed arch was repaired.

'Attention to later intrusions' can be grouped under three subtitles: 1) demolition, 2) blocking up, and 3) removal of accretions. Demolition of modern buildings, remains, later additions, or buildings built too close (or attached to) historic monuments, are counted under group 1. Removals of later architectural elements, opening blocked doors and windows, demolishing later roofs or walls, come in the 'removal of accretions' category. These activities were undertaken in 22 of the 56 cases, while demolition was deemed necessary in 18 cases. Blocking up was employed in the Mustafa Pasha Mosque and the churches of St Nicholas Cathedral and the Hospitallers. The 'removal of accretions' was applied to each building category, but especially to fortifications and to about one third of the churches. Demolition also took place in approximately one third of the fortification and church projects. Of

---

17 These are the shops in St Nicholas Cathedral's plot, along Liman Yolu. Enlart used the term 'staciones' for vaulted cellars in the lower part of Bishop's palace. Enlart, *Gothic Art*, p. 459. Mogabgab's definition for this work was 'restoration of arch of mediaeval n. entry to Parvis'.

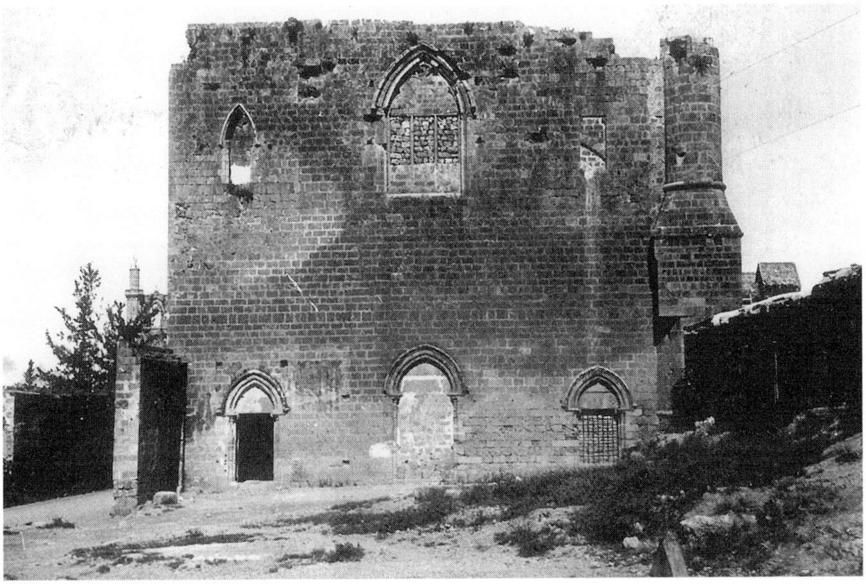

Fig. 13.6
SS Peter and Paul before opening of windows and doors, 1938 (Mogabgab Archive, unpublished)

the seven listed buildings in the 'palaces and houses' group, three demolitions and three removals of accretions were carried out. (Figure 13.6).

'Restorations' were evaluated according to the extent of the work required. The first group involved small-scale projects, such as plastering, re-pointing and minimal repairs on masonry, and as such was titled 'simple repairs'. The second group was 'restoration of architectural elements and paintings', and the third group was 'reintegration and restoration of structural elements'. This third group comprised comprehensive interventions, such as completing or rebuilding a lost and/or collapsed part of a monument. 'Simple repairs' were done on 41 buildings, 'Restoration of architectural elements and paintings' totalled 26 cases, since it was not normally applicable for the fortifications, while 'Reintegration and restoration of structural elements' was carried out on 35 buildings. 'Simple repairs' and 'restorations of architectural elements and paintings', were very common for churches and palaces-houses, with a rate of approximately 66 per cent, while 'Reintegration and restoration of structural elements' was 68 per cent. Among the fortifications' restorations, simple repairs and reintegration, as well as restoration of structural elements, were recorded in half the buildings, while 'restoration of architectural elements and paintings' occurred only in the Citadel, the Ravelin and the Land Gate (Figure 13.7).

The final group of works carried out in Famagusta between 1935 and 1956 can be categorized under the heading 'rehabilitation of environment', with further subsections: 'lowering ground', 'rehabilitation of nearby buildings' and 'building, lowering and raising enclosing walls'. These were rarely practised on fortifications, because neither 'rehabilitation of nearby buildings', nor 'building, lowering and raising enclosing wall' were suitable approaches. Only in around three areas of the fortifications was the ground lowered and

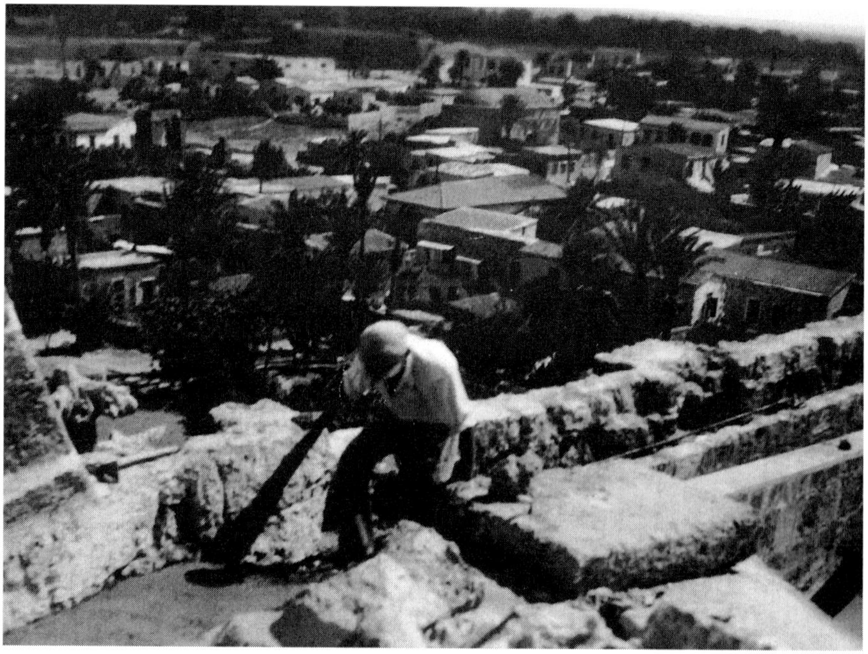

Fig. 13.7 Restoration of the city walls, 1939 (Mogabgab Archive, unpublished)

barriers constructed in the western part of counterscarp. In complete contrast to the fortifications, 'rehabilitation of environment' was one of the foremost issues for the 'churches' and the 'houses and palaces' groups (Figure 13.8).

Almost half of the churches of Famagusta had the ground lowered and enclosing walls built around them. 'Rehabilitation of nearby buildings' was not as common. On only a few private houses facing the church of SS Peter and Paul, as well as on another such house facing the Nameless Church III (plot 546), was such work carried out. In the 'houses and palaces' group, ground lowering took place around five buildings out of the seven, while 'Building, lowering and raising enclosing walls' was carried out on three buildings. 'Rehabilitation of nearby buildings' was not that common in this group either, although the construction of a new fountain to the south west of the Palace (which was not really rehabilitation work), underpinning houses on the right, and constructing steps to houses after lowering the level of the road in front of the Bedestan, were all completed.

Some of the monuments underwent long-term, intense and diverse restoration projects in this period, in particular: (Table 13.4) the Citadel, the Ravelin, St Nicholas Cathedral and the Venetian Palace, which were then followed by: St George of the Greeks, SS Peter and Paul, Ayios Yeorghios Xorinos, the Armenian Church, the Carmelite Church, the Templar and Hospitaller Churches and the Bedestan. In churches, restoration work was more extensive, especially on structures in use, or planned for re-use in the near future. 'Rehabilitation of environment' also seemed to be prioritized in churches, palaces and houses, in addition to widespread ground lowering, road construction and wall building. This was not the case for fortifications

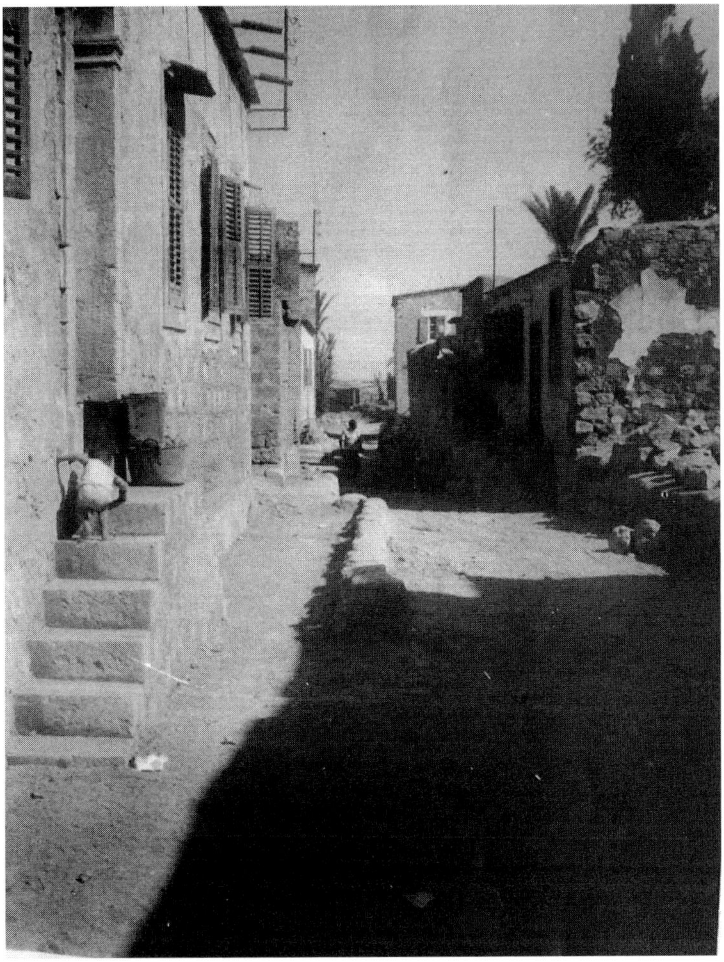

Fig. 13.8 Bedestan Street in 1946 (Mogabgab Archive, unpublished)

where excavations and clearance were the main forms of activity, alongside the 'removal of accretions' and 'demolition of nearby buildings'. Probably the extensive use, and continued maintenance, of Famagusta's fortifications during the Ottoman Period,[18] not true of the majority of churches, explains the additions and alterations to be seen there.[19]

It is clear that between 1937 and 1939 restoration work, including the painting restoration by Mrs Bardswell between 1937 and 1938,[20] was wide-ranging and comprehensive. Almost 30 buildings were, at one time or another, under restoration in the three years up to 1940, when, as a result of the Second World War, work slowed. By 1944 only three buildings were

18 N. Çevikel, *Kıbrıs Eyaleti, Yönetim, Klise, Ayan ve Halk (1750–1800)* (Famagusta, 2000), 107.

19 During the Ottoman Period, most of the closed sections of the fortifications were used as barracks or prisons, and the strength of city walls was valued until the nineteenth century.

20 *RDAC*, 1951, p. 178.

Name of the Monument			1935	1936	1937	1938	1939	1940	1941	1942	1943	1944	1945	1946	1947	1948	1949	1950	1951	1952	1953	1954	1955	1956
Fortifications	Citadel					■			■	■		■			■	■	■	■	■	■				
	Bastions and Cavaliers	Ravelin		■	■	■	■	■	■							■	■	■	■	■	■		■	■
		Arsenal Bastion												■		■	■							
		Martinengo Bastion									■		■			■	■		■					
		Diamante Bastion and Cavalier			■	■	■																	
		Santa Napa Bastion				■																		
		Andruzzi Bastion				■	■																	
		Campo Santo Bastion and Cavalier					■											■						
		Del Mozzo Bastion			■	■	■									■								
		San Luca Bastion			■		■																	
		Moratto Bastion and Cavalier			■	■	■		■					■										
		Diocare Bastion			■										■	■								
		Land Gate Cavalier			■		■	■			■				■		■							
	Moats	West Moat				■														■				
		South-West Moat	■					■											■		■			
		South Moat														■				■	■			
		North Moat																			■			
	Land Gate Approaches				■	■	■	■	■										■					■
	Curtain btw Diamante and Signoria Towers					■	■									■		■						
	Sea Walls				■																			
	Counterscarp																■	■	■					
Churches	St. Nicholas and Environs	St. Nicholas Church				■	■	■	■	■	■		■		■		■		■		■		■	
		Bishop's Chapel						■	■	■	■		■		■									
		Ragazzione Annexe														■		■	■		■			
		Cells											■				■		■					
		Staciones												■				■						
		Fountain and Columns (Piazza)					■								■						■			
	St. George of the Latins Church				■	■	■																■	■
	St. George of the Greeks Church			■	■	■	■		■						■									
	SS. Peter and Paul Church				■	■		■			■	■	■											
	Franciscan Church				■		■		■												■			■
	Carmelite Church				■	■	■	■	■	■								■						
	Templar Church						■	■	■	■	■						■	■			■			
	Hospitaller Church				■		■	■	■	■								■						
	St. Anne Church				■	■										■								
	San Antonio Church							■																
	Ayios Yeorghios Xorinos Church				■	■	■		■		■		■	■	■	■								
	Armenian Church				■	■		■	■	■	■		■											
	St. Symeon Church				■	■	■		■															
	Ayios Nicolas Church						■	■	■	■														
	Ay. Zoni Church									■	■							■						
	Ayia Photou Church				■	■	■						■											
	Lala Mustafa Pasha Mosque						■						■	■	■									
	Tabakhane Mosque					■		■								■								
	Nameless Church I (Pl.716)					■				■	■						■							
	Nameless Church II (Pl.754)																■							
	Nameless Church III (Pl.546)				■	■		■										■	■					
	Nameless Church IV (Pl.548)				■	■			■				■						■					
	Nameless Church V (Pl.83)			■		■	■			■								■						

Table 13.4 Distribution of restoration works on monuments through the years

under restoration. After the war the number of projects began to regain momentum so that between 1947 and 1951 between ten and 15 buildings were under restoration in any one year. It remained, nonetheless, only half of the number of active projects in the halcyon years of 1937 and 1939.

After 1951 the number of buildings under restoration remained at a steady four to five per year until 1956.[21] After 1952 we find mostly the excavation and clearance of moats, the completion of other excavations, the lowering of the approaches to monuments to their original levels, the construction of enclosing walls in and around the Ravelin, the Citadel, the Venetian Palace, the cathedral of St Nicholas, the Franciscan and Templar Churches, and the demolition of a storehouse next to St George of the Latins. From this examination of the progress of work through the years under consideration (Table 13.4), we see that most of the churches were dealt with between 1937 and 1942, while more than half of the work on fortifications came after 1942. This, in large part, was necessary thanks to the military activities at these buildings and the bomb damage during the Second World War. Mogabgab recorded the bomb damage to Famagusta in 1941[22] both in his notes and in his photographic collection, including the south range of the Citadel, the north east of the church of St Nicholas, the northern apse of the church of St Symeon, the south chapel of the Franciscan Church and the Hospitaller Church. He also documented war damage to the restorations in the north-western corner of western moat, the south-west bastion and parapets of the Citadel, to the gap in the curtain and parapets of the walls between the Diamante and Signoria Bastions, the parapets of the Diamante Bastion, Martinengo Bastion, Del Mozzo Bastion, Diocare Bastion, and Canbulat Tower, the parapets and arched entry on top of the Land Gate cavalier, the east wing of Campo Santo Bastion and the eastern part of the south counterscarp. It was not, however, just bomb damage that the war brought, and in time work began on removing the wartime additions to monuments. This was a significant operation which involved the removal of machine gun emplacements on top of the Martinengo Bastion in 1943, the wartime screen of the Diocare Bastion in 1947, the wartime huts in the counterscarp in 1948, sand bags from around the façade of the Palace and Diocare Bastion in 1948, the cisterns at the west of the main entry of the Citadel in 1948, the wartime accretions on top of the south-western bastion of the Citadel in 1949, traces of a lean-to roof on war store sheds in the south moat in 1952, dismantling the petrol tank in the Martinengo Bastion in 1948, and a storehouse abutting the west of St George of the Latins as late as 1955–56.

---

21 Except for the year 1953 for which Mogabgab's notes document the restoration of 11 buildings.

22 The island was threatened from the Italian naval base in the Dodecanese about 200 miles away. Serious attacks however did not develop until 1941, when the evacuation of Greece and then of Crete, 350 miles to the west, brought Cyprus into the main Middle East defence line. K. Kyriakides, *Cyprus and Projection of British Sea Power since 1878*, 2nd Mediterranean Maritime History Network Conference, Messina/Taormina, Sicily, 4–7 May 2006. (http://home.um.edu.mt/medinst/mmhn/klearchos_kyriakides.pdf) (accessed 21.08.2009).

Evaluation of the Works on Monuments in Famagusta

Mogabgab's detailed notes and his extensive collection of photographic records allow a comprehensive evaluation of the work executed between 1935 and 1956. Undoubtedly, the restoration work that continued for over 20 years during the first half of the twentieth century was greatly beneficial to Famagusta and its monuments. Not only were most of the monuments strengthened, excavated, cleaned, restored and surrounded by fences, but public awareness of the significance of the town was considerably heightened. Re-functioning also had a very positive effect on monuments. The Armenian Church and Ayios Yeorghios Xorinos Church were re-opened for worship and thoroughly maintained continuously until 1963.[23] Though the plans for using the church of SS Peter and Paul as a museum could not be implemented, it started being used for various cultural activities, and, in any case, it was rescued from being used as a granary. The Citadel became a multi-functional hall for cultural activities and the Palace was used as an open-air museum after excavations and restorations.

In the fifth article of the 1964 Venice Charter, which remains the international reference point for the conservation and restoration of monuments and sites, it is stated that the conservation of monuments is often facilitated by re-use, while modifications demanded by such a change of function, should be limited. The re-functioning in the monuments of Famagusta was successfully done by following this principle. On the other hand, there were also some negative consequences that must be considered, especially when seen through the subsequent lens of Venice Charter.[24] From this perspective, and in particular in the light of article 12 of the charter, the restoration work in Famagusta can be criticized for not being distinguishable from the original, and so falsifying the artistic and historical evidence.[25] In the ninth article of the Venice Charter, an emphasis is placed upon the aesthetic and historic value of the monument and restoration based on respect for original material and authentic documents.[26] It implies that restoration must stop at the point

23 After 1955 the war for independence began in earnest, and three years after the establishment of the Republic of Cyprus in 1960, conflict between Cypriot Turks and Cypriot Greeks began. These struggles caused the restoration work to stop in Famagusta.

24 C. Erder, *Tarihi Çevre Bilinci* (Ankara, 2007), 240–43. The Venice Charter can be found at: http://www.international.icomos.org/charters/venice_e.htm (accessed 21.08.2009).

25 Article 12: *Replacements of missing parts must integrate harmoniously with the whole, but at the same time must be distinguishable from the original so that restoration does not falsify the artistic or historic evidence.*

26 Article 9: *The process of restoration is a highly specialized operation. Its aim is to preserve and reveal the aesthetic and historic value of the monument and is based on respect for original material and authentic documents. It must stop at the point where conjecture begins, and in this case moreover any extra work which is indispensable must be distinct from the architectural composition and must bear a contemporary stamp. The restoration in any case must be preceded and followed by an archaeological and historical study of the monument.*

where conjecture begins and any extra work which is indispensable must be distinct from the architectural composition and bear a contemporary stamp. Most of the reconstruction at Famagusta was not based on documents, and few bore a contemporary stamp. The use of reinforced concrete, especially for strengthening the vaults of monuments, also seems (in retrospect) to have been inappropriate. Although article ten of the charter endorses its widespread use for consolidation, the harmful effects of concrete are now apparent, due principally to the incompatibility of the material with the original porous stone. Moreover, insertion of reinforced concrete channels on top of vaults created an excess weight on roofs which they had not been designed to bear.

One might argue too that there was a lack of respect for the Ottoman heritage and contributions in this work. Although most of these later additions were crude, their removal is certainly open to criticism, and in direct contradiction to the eleventh article which states: 'The valid contributions of all periods to the building of a monument must be respected, since unity of style is not the aim of a restoration.' Similarly, the demolition of houses and khans, many of which were in reasonable condition and some of which were worthwhile buildings in their own right (as can be seen on the photographic record) during the cleaning of monuments, is dubious. Before the Venice Charter it was common to sacrifice houses for the sake of historic monuments, but in its sixth article it introduced that idea that conservation implied preserving not only the monument but also its traditional setting. The demolition which took place between 1935 and 1960 has caused irreversible changes to the city's old fabric. Similarly, the unjustifiable replacement and dislocation of Ottoman fountains situated in front of Akkule Masjid and the Palace must also be criticized. The seventh article emphasizes the prevention of moving monuments from the setting in which they occur, as they are inseparable from their history. The sixteenth article, which demands precise documentation and analytical and critical reports, as well as full written and visual resources relating to preservation, restoration and excavation, was not adhered to in Mogabgab's work, notwithstanding the survival of his priceless photographic archive from which we work today.

In conclusion, T.A.H. Mogabgab's undertakings in the first half of the twentieth century saved many of the historic buildings of Famagusta from collapse. In retrospect it can now be appreciated that some of the procedures were inappropriate, damaging the urban fabric, and it is also a source of regret that there was no systematic set of reports produced to accompany the work. Through excavation and clearance, however, the architectural heritage of the city became visible, while many details concerning the fortifications, architecture and urban history of Famagusta came to light. The work also improved living conditions for the inhabitants by removing a huge amount of sand and stones from the walled city.

Monumental Buildings in the Revitalization Process of Historic Urban Quarters: The Case of the Walled City of Famagusta

Naciye Doratlı

Introduction

Historic urban quarters, as places where a great diversity of historic and cultural values have accumulated, furnish memories of their own origins. As many scholars have emphasized, without such values cities would be like men without memories. They reflect the achievements of a significant sample of the varied cultures of the world, and, while some represent the efforts of indigenous tradition, others display the impact of exported or colonial activities. All mingle their diverse influences to create unique forms and patterns of use.[1] These invaluable places are increasingly threatened with destruction, not only by the normal processes of decay, but also from changing social and economic conditions.

Before the 1960s, comprehensive redevelopment was regarded as the remedy for halting the process of deterioration and for maintaining and developing these places' prosperity, survival and competitiveness. It was only later that historic urban quarters were examined and re-evaluated with regard to their positive qualities. Accordingly the concept of architectural heritage has gradually changed during the last 40 years from consisting primarily of outstanding monuments or, at least, individual buildings to a more comprehensive conception of the built environment where the most interesting elements may be the assemblage of more common buildings, the street pattern or the interaction between buildings and landscape. The architectural heritage has gradually become an integral part of the cultural heritage as a whole, with the result that 'evaluation of existing remains from the past in accordance with the contemporary needs and the singling out the

---

1 Naciye Doratlı et al., 'An Analytical Methodology for Revitalization Strategies in Historic Urban Quarters: a Case Study of the Walled City of Nicosia, North Cyprus', *Cities*, 21/4 (2004): 329–48.

components or elements which have the potential for the enhancement of the area, became fashionable'.[2]

Following this changing attitude, a number of international agreements for the protection of these values have been signed and implemented. Within the Council of Europe, the European Charter of the Architectural Heritage (1975) introduced the term 'integrated conservation', and the Granada Convention for the Protection of the Architectural Heritage of Europe (1985) laid further stress on this aspect and added as its major contribution a definition of the different forms of architectural heritage. 'Integrated conservation' comprises the requirement to include conservation as a necessary part of spatial and urban planning, establishing links between heritage protection and cultural activities, and preserving technical and traditional skills. It places emphasis on the importance of conservation through revitalization and indicates indirectly the necessity of strategic approaches towards conservation through a process of revitalization.

The process of revitalizing historic urban quarters involves the integration of the historic legacy, inheritance and sense of place with the demands of contemporary economic, political and social conditions. Accordingly, revitalization can be defined in its simplest form as a 'process through which the deterioration and decay of a historic urban quarter can be addressed, terminated or reversed'.[3] It raises complex issues that have to be approached from many different perspectives since, in the long-term, it must involve social and economic dimensions and not purely physical protection and enhancement measures. Such a process calls for joined-up thinking to relate conservation-area objectives to considerations of physical quality, social viability, economic vitality and the wider concern for sustainability. This, in turn, demands the rapid, efficient and focused conversion of new knowledge into socially, economically and environmentally acceptable solutions.[4]

In common with many other historic urban quarters, the Walled City of Famagusta (see also Figure 11.2), a unique place displaying the remains of a long sequence of previous cultures, is faced with deterioration and decay, despite the planning studies and the piecemeal implementation of conservation policies during the last two decades. The Walled City was declared a Conservation Area in 1989 under the new Town Planning Law (55/89), 249 buildings were listed in 1999 by the Department of Antiquities and Museums and in December 2005 a 'Revitalization Plan for the Walled City' was finalized. Additionally, projects such as the pedestrianization of Namık Kemal Square and İstiklal Avenue and the provision of car parking areas have been implemented. However, these efforts have, so far, not been

2 Steve Tiesdell et al., *Revitalizing Historic Urban Quarters* (Architectural Press, Oxford, 1996), p. vii.

3 Naciye Doratlı, *A Model for Conservation and Revitalization of Historic Urban Quarters in Northern Cyprus*, unpublished PhD thesis (Eastern Mediterranean University, Gazimagusa, 2000), 32.

4 Doratlı et al., 'An Analytical Methodology for Revitalization', p. 330.

sufficient to address the deterioration process, and it is as yet too early to expect any discernable impact from the new Revitalization Plan. Most recently, the Walled City has been included in the 2008 Watch List of the World Monuments Fund (WMF).

The main aim of this chapter is to assess the on-going conservation efforts and activities within the Walled City of Famagusta in line with the revitalization strategies. Firstly, a theoretical framework regarding revitalization – sustainable urban conservation – will be outlined from both conceptual and implementation perspectives. Secondly, a brief account of the evolution of the Walled City of Famagusta and its historic monuments will be presented. Finally, the Revitalization Plan for the Walled City will be summarized and assessed in the light of revitalization principles with the main emphasis placed on the historic buildings.

A Brief Introduction to Revitalizing Historic Urban Quarters

Conceptual Framework

Tiesdell and his colleagues argue that revitalizing historic urban quarters involves both the renewal of the physical fabric and the active economic utilization of buildings and spaces.[5] Accordingly, there is a need for both physical and economic revitalization. One may prefigure the other. For example, a cosmetic or 'physical' revitalization may be a short-term strategy intended to induce a deeper long-term 'economic' revitalization that will result in an attractive, well-maintained public sphere. However, in the longer perspective, economic revitalization is required because ultimately it is the productive utilization of the private sector that pays for the maintenance of the public sphere. Depending on their inherent qualities, as well as on local physical and socio-economic conditions, different comprehensive approaches, in other words different strategies – functional restructuring, functional diversification, or functional regeneration[6] – should be engaged in the revitalization of historic urban quarters.[7]

Tourism and culture-led revitalization approaches, as employed in the revitalization plan for the Walled City of Famagusta, form a strategy for restructuring the economic base.[8] This is in keeping with the proposition that if a historic urban quarter suffers severely from physical, functional and locational

5 Tiesdell et al., *Revitalizing Historic Urban Quarters*, p. 20.

6 *Functional restructuring*: changes in occupation with new uses or activities replacing the former ones; *functional diversification*: keeping the existing uses to some extend and introducing some new uses; *functional regeneration:* existing uses remain but operate more efficiently or profitably.

7 Doratlı, *A Model for Conservation*, p. 34.

8 The justification for determining of the most relevant approach does not fall within the scope of this chapter.

obsolescence, revitalization can only be realized through restructuring the economic base of the area for the sake of sustainable conservation.[9]

Framework for Implementation

Unless a rational basis for implementing strategies and policies for revitalization is provided, there is a danger that all efforts may get no further than the drawing board without any fruitful results. For a wide range of decisions and their consequent impact on physical, social, cultural and economic issues, the framework for implementation should provide a rational basis for answering the following questions:

- What should be preserved, and to what extent?
- How to do it?
- Rights and duties, responsibilities of the actors involved (Who is doing what)?
- How to involve the community in conservation activities?

All these issues are crucial for the successful implementation of conservation and revitalization policies, and require an applicable legal basis, the financial means and facilities, a sound organizational framework, and public participation.

The ground-breaking concept of 'Integrated conservation' as launched by the Council of Europe in 1975 places emphasis on the importance of these issues, while the European Charter of Architectural Heritage includes recommendations regarding the necessary amendments for the framework of implementation. Accordingly, the success of any efforts to revitalize historic urban quarters is highly dependent upon determining the most relevant strategic approach as well as providing a sound and rational basis for implementation.[10]

Famagusta

General Description and Regional Setting

Famagusta, situated on the eastern coast of the island of Cyprus, has a population of c. 35,000. Through its long, rich and turbulent history, the city has enjoyed the opportunity to acquire a great variety of outstanding monuments of historical, architectural and cultural interest. Today it boasts a large and well-equipped port, and the Eastern Mediterranean University, the largest university on the island with a student population of 15,000.

---

9 Doratlı, *A Model for Conservation*, p. 240.

10 Naciye Doratlı, 'Revitalizing Historic Urban Quarters: A Model for Determining The Most Relevant Strategic Approach', *European Planning Studies,* 13/5 (2005): 749–72.

A Brief Overview of the Evolution of the City and the Walled City of Famagusta

The historical and urban development of Famagusta dates back to the first century AD and then passes through eight identifiable periods: the Eastern Roman Empire (648–1192 – the foundation of the city); Lusignan rule (1192–1373 and 1464–89); Genoese rule (1373–1464); Venetian rule (1489–1571); Ottoman rule (1571–1878); British rule (1878–1960); the period from 1960 to 1974, and the period from 1974 to the present.

It was the Venetians who turned Famagusta into the fortified city we know today. The present walls mostly date from the fifteenth and sixteenth centuries and provide a superb example of a fortified medieval city with its bastions, citadel, rock-cut moat, and Sea and Land Gates.[11] In the two decades following the Ottoman conquest of 1571, the population was transferred from Anatolia and the existing non-Muslim population was forced out of the Walled City. Ottoman policy towards the Walled City affected social and economic life as well as the attendant physical and spatial form. The Ottomans, while engaging in some new building projects, were mainly content to keep the existing buildings and structures and make use of them with necessary modifications and transformations in order to fit the socio-economic and cultural life of the new inhabitants. Thus the cathedral was converted into a mosque – the Lala Mustafa Pasha Mosque[12] – through the addition of a minaret; a *bedesten* and *arasta* were developed to fulfil the requirements of mercantile activities; a *medrese*, baths, and fountains were built to complete the physical infrastructure and meet basic daily needs. Most people lived in the southern half of the Walled City, and the organic urban pattern was enriched through the introduction of *cul-de-sacs* which fitted well the Islamic culture and life style.

In 1878, the Ottomans leased the island to the British; in 1914 Great Britain annexed it following the outbreak of World War One, and in 1925 the island became a Crown Colony of the British Empire.[13] Urban expansion beyond the walls towards the south, which had already started during the Ottoman period, was accelerated. Thus, the two major ethnic groups were distributed around various parts of the overall city. The majority of the inhabitants within the city walls were Turkish Cypriots. The British also constructed an administrative area between the walls and Maraş (Varosha), with the intention of developing an alternative city centre which would include mainly administrative and

---

[11] Rupert Gunnis, *Historic Cyprus: A Guide to its Towns and Villages and Castles* (Nicosia, 1973), 89.

[12] Although the name Lala Mustafa Pasha Mosque is used today, in fact this name was given officially in 1954. Until then it was named as Aya Sophia. Netice Yıldız, 'Kıbrıs'ta Osmanlı Kültür Mirasına Genel Bir Bakış', in *Türkler*, eds H.C. Güzel, K. Çiçek, S. Koca (Yeni Türkiye Yayınları, 2002), Cilt 19: 966–93.

[13] Although it was under the British rule, Cyprus remained legally the property of the Ottomans until 1914. On the entry of the Ottomans in the First World War against the allies, Cyprus was annexed as the British colony. However, its formal establishment as a Crown Colony took place in 1925. Hill, 4: 285, 412–13.

commercial activities. However, the Walled City retained its significance as a traditional core as well as a residential quarter. Additionally, due to the increasing use of the harbour, a number of storage buildings were constructed both within and without the Walled City.

What characterized the British period from those that had gone before, was the construction of new buildings on empty land to meet the changing needs of Famagusta, and the demolition of others, with scant regard for the traditional pattern and urban characteristics.[14] As Jeffery noted, there had in fact been a wholesale clearance of old building stone from Famagusta during the 1880s and 1890s to assist construction work in Port Said. Much was then lost before a law was passed to prevent the practice from proceeding further.[15]

This approach of the new administration resulted in differences in the development pattern of the historical area. For example, new roads were constructed, contrasting starkly with the traditional tissue and terraced houses which had hitherto formed the urban pattern and were now interspersed by detached buildings. It is worth mentioning that 52.5 per cent of the existing buildings in the Walled City today date from the British period, especially to the period after 1946 when the 'Streets and Buildings Regulation – Cap. 96' for managing the new developments was introduced. It should also be noted however, that although the administration displayed a negligent attitude towards the traditional urban tissue during this period, it simultaneously paid considerable attention to the historic monuments. A process of 'listing' historic monuments began in accordance with the provisions of 'Cap. 31 – First and Second Schedule' (1931), this work being overseen by T.A.H. Mogabgab, an architect and later the Antiquities Officer for the District of Famagusta.

During the years 1960–74 the administration of the city was separated into two municipalities, the Turkish (predominantly within the Walled City) and the Greek (all other districts). The overall city grew in size, as did its population, and the south-east of Aşağı Maraş (Kato Varosha) towards Maraş (Varosha) acquired the role of a centre for tourism. Consequently, the walled city was overshadowed by the rapid development of Maraş, although importance was still placed on its historic structures, despite developing political difficulties. From 1974 onwards the Walled City has experienced static development dynamics, as many of the new inhabitants, many of whom are immigrants, have been located outside of the walls, thus deflecting pressure away from development within.

Despite the Walled City, together with the walls themselves and the moat, being declared a conservation area in 1989, the process of deterioration and decay has not been halted, with the result that Famagusta's vitality continues to ebb. This is because:

---

14 Harry Luke, *Cyprus, A Portrait and an Appreciation* (Nicosia, 1965), 96.

15 George Jeffery, *Historic Monuments of Cyprus* (Nicosia, 1918), 157.

- Area schemes prepared for the various parts of the historic quarter were only implemented in a piecemeal fashion by the public authorities owing to legal, financial and organizational constraints;
- Area schemes were prepared with a strong emphasis on physical revitalization; dynamics of place, obsolescence and the position of the Walled City within the overall urban context were not fully considered;
- The base of popular appeal is not strong enough, nor are there financial incentives to spur private interest and investment;
- As a result, the conservation of the area has yet to become 'a shared vision' in the community.[16]

According to the land-use survey conducted under the'Revitalization Plan', there are 811 buildings, 941 dwellings and 703 commercial units, including 247 shops of one sort of another, 17 banks and insurance or finance companies, several storage buildings, 16 professional offices, 10 administrative offices, and 7 NGO offices or centers.[17] In addition, there are a variety of communal services, such as four elementary schools, two mosques, public utilities, a police station, and a variety of recreational facilities including a library, a museum, restaurants, pubs, cafes, a sports club and a playing field. The provision for these various activities enables one to claim that the Walled City is still an attractive place to live and work. However, the high percentages of vacant houses (149 out of 941 = 15.8 per cent) and shops (217 out of 464 = 46.8 per cent) are indicative of the disturbing locational obsolescence facing the area.[18]

Monumental Buildings in the Walled City

According to the Revitalization Plan for the Walled City of Famagusta (Figure 14.1), there are 77 properties there which have been classified as historic monuments (including the fortification with its bastions, cavaliers and the moat),[19] and this accounts for 7.5 per cent of all buildings.[20] The vast majority are in public ownership and are either in public use or vacant. The high vacancy rate (not counting the fortifications with its bastions, cavaliers and

---

16 Naciye Doratlı et al., 'Revitalizing a Declining Historic Urban Quarter: The Walled City of Famagusta, North Cyprus', *Journal of Architectural and Planning Research*, 24/1 (2007): 65–88.

17 Gazimağusa Belediyesi, *Gazimağusa Surlariçi Canlandırma Planı Rapor I Mevcut Durum* (unpublished report, 2005), pp. 22–34.

18 Locational obsolescence is primarily an attribute of the functional activities within the area. When a building was originally built, its location was determined in terms of accessibility to other uses, markets, and suppliers, transportation infrastructure and the like, but in the course of time the location may become unfavourable or obsolete for the activities for which the building was constructed. Tiesdell et al., *Revitalizing Historic Urban Quarters*, p. 25.

19 All the historic monuments are listed including all those listed in 1931.

20 Gazimağusa Belediyesi, *Gazimağusa Surlariçi Canlandırma Planı Rapor I Mevcut Durum*, p. 42.

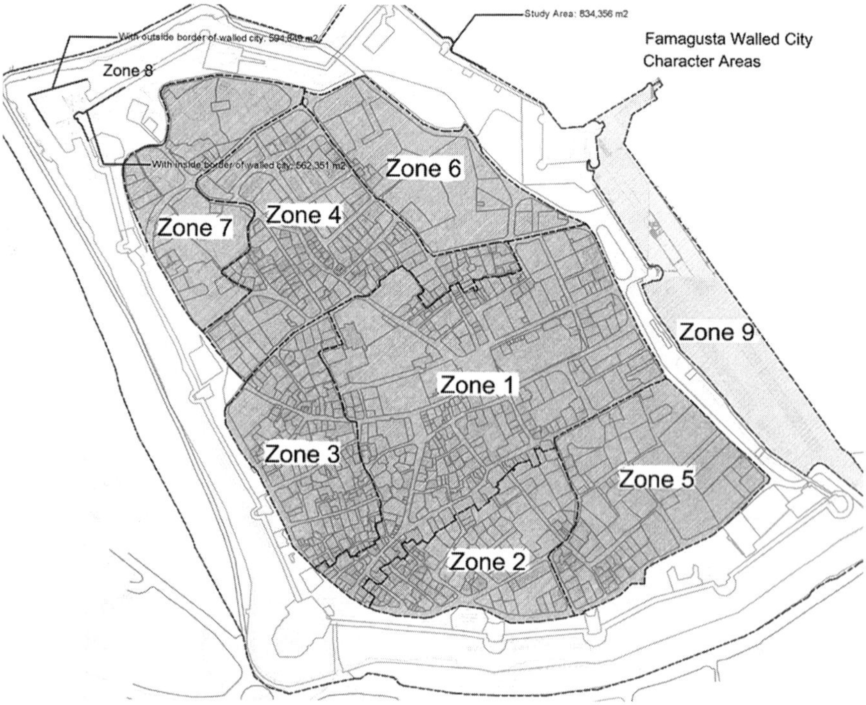

Fig. 14.1 Character areas for Famagusta (Naciye Doratlı)

the Othello Tower) – 32 per cent of all historic monuments – is clear evidence of locational obsolescence.

Chronological Presentation of the Monumental Buildings

This section will provide a summary of the listed historic monuments and sites in the Walled City of Famagusta, classified according to the period in which they were constructed. It should, however, be noted that in subsequent periods some were modified in accord with the requirements of the rulers. Thus for example, several churches built during Lusignan Period, were transformed into mosques under the Ottomans.

Lusignan Period (1192–1489)

- Cathedral of St Nicholas (Lala Mustafa Pasha Mosque – listed together with the medrese, tombs, shops and the small chapel)
- 'Monastery cells' of St Nicholas Cathedral
- Franciscan church
- Church of St George of the Latins
- Nestorian church
- Church of SS Peter and Paul (Buğday Camii/Sinan Pasha Mosque)
- Twin Churches (the Templar and Hospitaller churches)
- Church of St Anthony (ruin with hospices/loggias)

- Church of St George of the Greeks
- Church of St Anne
- Carmelite church
- Armenian church
- Tanners' church (Tabakhane Mesjit)
- Ayia Zoni
- Church of St Nicholas
- Church of Stavros (Mustafa Pasha Mesjit)
- Salt store

Venetian Period (1489–1571)

- Fortifications: Othello Tower, Martinengo Bastion, Ravelin (Akkule) Bastion, Arsenal (Canbulat) Bastion, Porta del Mare, Diamante
- Venetian Palace
- Venetian House
- Biddulph's gate

Ottoman Period (1571–1878)

- Kertikli Hamam
- Cafer Pasha Bath
- Medrese
- Tomb of 28 Celebi
- Tomb of Mehmet Efendi
- Tomb of Canbulat
- Kızıl Hamam
- Fountain

Revitalization Plan for the Walled City

Let us begin by highlighting the important features of the revitalization plan and offering a brief critique of certain key issues. The overall approach of the plan fits well with the principles of conceptual and rational integrated conservation. It may, however, experience a number of legislative and organizational limitations that lie beyond the scope of this chapter.

Important Features of the Revitalization Plan for the Walled City

The Plan has been prepared by Gazimağusa Municipality and was funded by the EU under the Partnership for Future (PFF) Programme as well as by the United Nations Office for Project Services (UNOPS). It was completed in the space of nine months, between April and December 2005, by a team of planners, architects and landscape architects, making use of wider public consultation where necessary.

Methodology

Character area and tourism and culture-led revitalization strategies have been utilized for this plan. A character area-based planning approach can be considered as an appropriate option for two reasons:

- Although the Walled City itself is a historic urban district as a whole, which is clearly defined by its surrounding fortifications, it is possible to identify nine districts (or 'character areas'), thanks to their distinctive functional and physical characteristics.
- Through a character area-based planning approach, distinctive features as well as opportunities for areas with different characters can easily be identified. Additionally, the competitive advantage of each area can be evaluated and may positively support and sustain the revitalization efforts for the whole Walled City.

The findings in the report, as well as the author's own studies,[21] suggest that it is not possible to revitalize the Walled City of Famagusta through an indigenous regeneration of the traditional activities of the locality, nor through functional diversification. The declining character of the area, which has been a result of physical, functional and locational obsolescence, reveals that it is only through a functional restructuring of its economic base that the area can be revitalized. Only with the provision of adequate finance, is the conservation, maintenance and improvement of the area possible.

Considering the potential of the Walled City as a place with rich and varied historical and cultural resources, the utilization of a 'tourism and culture-led revitalization strategy' seems to be the most appropriate decision. A strategy of this sort would provide an economic base for restructuring relevant to the needs of the Walled City and utilizing its existing strengths. So far in the planning process, the existing situation in terms of physical structure including land-use and the structural condition and density of the buildings, the townscape, the image of the city and the landscape have been defined along with an evaluation of the architecture, a façade analysis, a scrutiny of the vacant buildings, and an examination of transportation and traffic. This data has then been used to establish the character areas summarized below.

[21] Doratlı et al., 'Revitalizing the Walled City of Gazimağusa', pp. 42–59; Doratlı et al., 'Revitalizing a Declining Historic Urban Quarter', pp. 65–88.

Character Areas (Figure 14.1)

ZONE 1 – TRADITIONAL CORE

This is the most dynamic part of the Walled City. It is a fully mixed-use area, with shops, banks, offices, restaurants and cafes, a municipal covered bazaar, mosques, houses and organized car-parking lots. Historic Monuments, such as the Lala Mustafa Pasha Mosque, the Buğday Mosque, the Venetian Palace, the Twin Churches, the Venetian House as well as some other listed buildings including the Chimney House, the Gazi Elementary School and the old prison building, are located here. Namık Kemal Square, which was pedestrianized in 1998, is located at its heart. The large number of contrasting buildings in the area indicates that it has been the most attractive part of the Walled City, and, although there is a height limitation, it has attracted new developments. However, the establishment and rapid growth of the university have created a negative impact on the dynamics of this district, as they have on the Walled City as a whole.

ZONE 2 – RESIDENTIAL AREA WITH COMMERCIAL USES

This is the area in the south of the Walled City, between the traditional core and the office district and open land. It is the area in which most of the conservation problems are recognized:

- Almost all of the few remaining houses of the traditional tissue are in poor condition;
- A considerable proportion of the buildings that were built towards the end of British Period and later, are out of character with the architecture of the traditional tissue;
- Though few in number, some houses are being used for inappropriate purposes such as storage, and repair and manufacturing workshops;
- The dominant land-use is housing, but, on its fringe next to the ring road, a block, which was to a large extent developed during the last decade, is occupied by a mixture of ground-floor shops with dwellings on the upper floors.

ZONE 3 – RESIDENTIAL AREA

This is a distinguished residential area with an urban pattern and residential buildings of architectural value. Courtyard type houses with narrow organic streets are dominant in the area, as is the Kızıl Hamam, one of the two houses with an under passage dating from the Ottoman period, and a school building, currently used by an NGO.

ZONE 4 – RESIDENTIAL AREA

This is the area where the traditional tissue has been somewhat distorted, thanks to developments that took place towards the end of the British period and subsequently. Many detached or semi-detached houses interrupt the rhythm of the stylistically dominant terrace houses, while five blocks of municipal row houses, which were built late in the British period to house harbour workers, and which are out of keeping with the traditional character, dominate the townscape of the area. Two of these blocks each contain 12 dwelling units, whereas the other three have 15. They are in poor structural condition, and their sanitary facilities fail to meet contemporary standards. The ruins of the Kertikli Hamam dating from the Ottoman period are located in this area.

Zone 5 – An Open Area with Historic Buildings

This district in the northeastern part of the Walled City can be regarded as the least developed area within the walls. At first sight, there is no trace of the traditional tissue in the area, although there are several ruined churches as well as an old cemetery. Because of the presence of these ruins, which were listed under the British Antiquities Law (Cap. 31), the area was preserved from any kind of development for a long while after 1963. The New Gate, one of the four entrances into the Walled City, which was opened during the British period, is located at the northern edge of the area. The new wide road, which runs along the edge of the walls and connects this entrance with the Canbulat Gate, stands in contrast with the organic street pattern of the Walled City. A library, an elementary and a nursery school, a sports club building, a restaurant, a sports field and an orphanage are all located here. These facilities are dispersed throughout the area in a haphazard fashion, leaving a great deal of lost space in between, and displaying little respect for the traditional tissue. Two blocks of refugee houses, built to accommodate homeless families after 1963, are among the few residential buildings in the area.

Zone 6 – An Open Area with Historic Buildings

This is located on the south-eastern corner of the Walled City, and exhibits different physical and functional characteristics from those previously examined. Buildings of little artistic or architectural value, which are currently being used as offices, storage spaces to serve the harbour and veterinary services, were constructed in the British Period and form important components of the original tissue. To the rear of these buildings lies empty land and open storage belonging to a private shipping company, and this forms a contrasting visual perception against the densely built up areas of the traditional tissue. The churches of St George of the Greeks, Ayia Zoni and St Nicholas are located in this area (Plate 6).

Zone 7 – An Open Area with Historic Buildings

This is a large area in the north west of the Walled City, adjacent to the Martinengo Bastion, which until recently has been used for military purposes. Now that military use has ceased, there should be opportunity to infuse new life into the quarter. The churches of St Mary of Carmel, St Anne, the Armenian Church and Tabakhane Mesjit, are all located in this area (Plate 4).

Zone 8 – Walls and Moat and Outside Ramparts

Together these form the most high profile monumental structures of the Walled City and are an outstanding example of military architecture. In addition to its two original gates (the Land Gate and the Porta del Mare), there is the Othello Tower, the Martinengo Bastion and 13 other bastions. The walls have an almost trapezoidal ground plan, with a north-west to south-east orientation; they have a total circumference of approximately 3.5 km,[22] a maximum height of 15m and a width of 8m. The fortifications also protected the medieval harbour. What survives today mainly belongs to the sixteenth century and was constructed for the defence of the town against the expected Ottoman siege. The moat around the fortification has a minimum depth of 7.5m and a width of 24m.[23] Its excavation was a huge undertaking and was spread over at least two centuries. The rock is a soft limestone and is horizontally stratified which makes it easy to quarry into rectangular building blocks. There are also numerous man-made caves along the cliffs which were probably quarry workshops where stone cannon balls were made, or were perhaps used as dwellings.

Zone 9 – The Harbour

The centuries-old harbour is still in use to this day. There are colonial buildings in the area, which are used as customs houses and for storage and other purposes.[24]

Additional Findings and Output

In addition to the determination of physical, historic and architectural characteristics of the Walled City, the socio-economic, legal and institutional characteristics were also established through a questionnaire survey. Following the identification of the strengths, weaknesses, opportunities and threats (SWOT), an appreciation of the constraints and potential of each character area was determined. After a thorough analysis and synthesis, a vision has been identified for Famagusta as: 'A world city, where the cultural heritage is fully protected, which is a pole of attraction and lively throughout the day; which is well integrated with its citizens.' Projects for the physical and economic revitalization of the Walled City were then proposed, selected, adopted and finally transformed into an action plan. This plan includes comments on the main features, stakeholders, priorities (both short and long term), potential financial resources and constraints. Prior to the introduction of

---

22 G. Perbellini, *Le Fortificazioni di Cipro dal X al XVI Secolo* (Rome, 1975), 36.

23 Gunnis, *Historic Cyprus*, p. 89.

24 Gazimağusa Belediyesi, *Gazimağusa Surlariçi Canlandırma Planı Rapor II Potansiyeller, unpublished report* (2005), 35.

projects that emphasize the historic monuments, it highlights some important issues which might endanger the success of the plan in the long run.

A Brief Critique of the Revitalization Plan for the Walled City

An assessment of the Revitalization Plan reveals that in general terms it is comprehensive and well prepared. However, there are certain pitfalls, weaknesses and threats which should be taken into consideration, not least with regard to its bold emphasis on tourism and its attitude against the symbiotic relationship between the Walled City and the rest of the town as well as the potential of the Eastern Mediterranean University.

Emphasis on Tourism

In her book *Tourists in Historic Towns*, Aylin Orbasli points out some important issues about tourism and heritage management. She states that:

> Tourism is potentially an important catalyst for the safeguarding of historic fabric and the initiation of conservation on an urban scale. Appreciation of the historic environment by visitors not only becomes a reason for conservation but can increase local interest in the environment. Although tourism is not a direct financial resource for conservation, indirectly it opens up previously unavailable investment finances.[25]

Beside the positive contributions of tourism to the protection of cultural heritage, she calls attention to the danger of overemphasis, which may transform the urban heritage into a stage set and commercialize the precious historic environment to an unacceptable extent. Brian Graham also highlights this risk:

> If taken to the extreme, economic commodification of the past will so trivialize it that, arguably, it can result in the destruction of the heritage resources which is its raison d'être. Thus major urban heritage sites such as the medieval cities of Carcassonne or Bruges may be regarded simultaneously as either successful and profitable providers of satisfying heritage experiences, or little more than stage-sets for mock medieval displays and tawdry souvenir shops that demonstrate the primacy of economic change.[26]

In addition to this he states that the most successful heritage cities are those of sufficient size to offer numerous amenities, including heritage, but are not dominated by it.[27]

With these perspectives in mind, an assessment of the Revitalization Plan reveals that there is too much emphasis on tourism. This may very well result in some serious problems, seen elsewhere in other historic towns,

---

25 Aylin Orbasli, *Tourists in Historic Towns* (London, 2000), 42.

26 Brian Graham, 'Heritage as Knowledge: Capital or Culture', *Urban Studies*, 39 (2002): 1007.

27 Graham, 'Heritage as Knowledge', p. 1014.

such as overcrowding and over-consumption, and may actually lead to the deterioration of the cultural heritage. However, it should be stressed that the intention here is not to imply that it is entirely wrong to utilize a tourism and culture-led strategy for the revitalization of the Walled City. The Walled City is a tourist attraction, and it would be unrealistic to ignore this potential. What is being advocated instead is the importance of incorporating and utilizing this potential in conjunction with the many other strengths Famagusta possesses.

The Symbiotic Relationship between the Walled City and the Rest of the Town

One of the most striking points to bear in mind about revitalization is that historic urban quarters are only part of the economic vitality; they are rarely autonomously functioning zones and usually have a symbiotic relationship with the rest of the city.[28] They must therefore be considered within the context of the city as a whole, and so the respective needs of both historic urban quarters and newly developing quarters should be taken into account jointly.

When we evaluate the revitalization plan for the Walled City from this perspective, it becomes clear that the vital symbiotic relationship between it and the rest of the town has not been fully appreciated or explored. In fact, the competitive advantages of the newly developing areas have not been considered at all. In particular, the legislative proposals for the project are too narrowly focused on the Walled City. Suggestions should be made to the central government for introducing amendments into the legislation which are directly related to protection and enhancement of historic urban quarters; as well as the legislation, which influences, may support or hinder conservation and revitalization process.[29] It is important to provide incentives for conservation areas but at the same time to provide measures (disincentives) in the newly developing parts of the city, in order to increase the attractiveness and competitiveness of the historic area.

Potential of the Eastern Mediterranean University

The SWOT Analysis should have been conducted to generate an internal and external appraisal, in order to see the overall picture more clearly. If this

[28] Tiesdell et al., *Revitalizing Historic Urban Quarters.*

[29] According to the Amsterdam Declaration, and to the recommendation of the Council of Europe to the member governments (Council of Europe, 1977, p. 15), not only the laws and regulations related to protection of cultural heritage of monuments and sites, but also those on regional and town planning and on housing have to be revised, since most of the national legislation on regional and town planning was promulgated to serve and support economic development and the growth of the road traffic. Hence, the Integrated Conservation approach takes the protection of historical and cultural heritage from the domain of legislation directly related to or influencing conservation, to a much larger domain of much other legislation. Naciye Doratlı, 'KKTC'de Tarihi Kentsel Alanların Korunmasına İlişkin Yasal Çerçeveye Eleştirel Bakış', in Ayşegül Mengi (ed.), *Kent ve Planlama, Geçmişi Korumak Geleceği Tasarlamak, Ruşen Keleşe Armağan, II. Kitap* (İmge Kitapevi, 2007).

had been done, the potential of the Eastern Mediterranean University (EMU) would definitely not have been disregarded in the proposals. EMU, with its 15,000 students and good working relationship with the Municipality, offers a great potential which should have been taken into account, especially if one of the major goals was to address the process of obsolescence. Thus, for restructuring the economic base of the Walled City, in addition to tourism and a culture-led revitalization strategy, attracting some functions of EMU to the area should have been considered. The vibrant urban texture of the Walled City is flexible enough and has the potential to absorb the requirements and demands of certain functions of the university, or perhaps even a faculty, through adaptive reuse. Even a brief literature survey reveals that, especially in the USA, universities play a crucial role in the revitalization of neighbourhoods and population centres.[30] Robert Forrant's example of the University of Massachusetts at Lowell, demonstrates clearly how an urban university can help tackle economic and developmental problems in areas of environmental degradation.[31] EMU in Famagusta can play a much more important role than these US examples, since it has a major role in the economy of the town as a whole.[32] Considering the functionally distinctive areas within the walls, and the architectural evaluation of the buildings in these areas, it seems obvious that British storage buildings and those in the near vicinity could easily be transformed to suit this new and important function. Could they not be converted into faculty buildings, accommodation facilities for students and academicians, workshops for arts and into leisure facilities? In other words, with the conservation and revitalization of this valuable cultural and historic building stock as the primary objective, the university would make full use of the physical and spatial potential of these areas through its educational, residential and cultural activities.[33] In so doing, there would be a more balanced development within the Walled City, and the possible negative impact of tourism would be averted.

A Brief Introduction of Projects with an Emphasis on Historic Monuments

The Revitalization Plan for the Walled City includes, broadly speaking, seven groups of projects:

- Cultural and tourism projects
- Social, communal and commercial projects

30 R.L. Mullins Jr. and John I. Gilderbloom, 'Urban Revitalization Partnerships: perceptions of the university's role in Louisville, Kentucky', *Local Environment*, 7/2 (2002): 163; Robert Forrant, 'Pulling together in Lowell: The university and the regional development process', *European Planning Studies*, 9/5 (2001): 613–28.

31 Forrant, 'Pulling together in Lowell'.

32 Doratlı et al., 'Revitalizing a Declining Historic Urban Quarter', p. 85.

33 Doratlı et al., 'Revitalizing a Declining Historic Urban Quarter', p. 86.

- Accessibility and traffic projects
- Old harbour and marina projects
- Landscape projects
- Traditional Core Area Improvement projects
- Legal and administrative projects

Not surprisingly, most of the project proposals for the monumental buildings fall within the first group. Physical revitalization, it might be argued, is merely a cosmetic and short-term strategy. Economic revitalization, however, is central, being ultimately the productive utilization of the private realm which pays for the maintenance of the public sector. Accordingly, all seven project groups for Famagusta include both physical revitalization projects (proposals for refurbishment, conversion and development) and economic revitalization projects (proposals for new uses, mostly for tourism and cultural activities).

The project proposals for the historic monuments can be classified as (a) projects for improving the setting of historic monuments (physical revitalization), and (b) projects for restoration and infusing new life (economic revitalization). However, as the historic monuments are state owned, infusing new life into them is not the concern of the private sector but lies within the responsibility of the public authorities, and is therefore dependent on the availability of funds as the cost of their restoration is high. As the public authorities are responsible, it can be argued that any attention given the historic monuments would help increase the confidence in the area and result in an attractive, well maintained public realm. On the other hand, infusing new life into them brings us into the sphere of economic revitalization. The important issue is that a balance be sought between the demands of the market, the limitation of the building fabric, and the maintenance of the character and authenticity of the surrounding environment.[34]

Projects for Improving the Background Environment/Physical Revitalization – Short Term

The short-term projects within this group in the action plan would improve and enhance the public realm. Leaving aside the last two projects,[35] they can be realized much more easily than the projects in the second group for three reasons:

- Their scope and content are not complicated.
- They can be funded by local resources.
- There can be no bureaucratic obstacles to their implementation as they are directly under the responsibility of Gazimağusa Municipality.

---

[34] Orbasli, *Tourists in Historic Towns*, p. 44.

[35] Two projects (the last two in the list) call for public-private venture, which is not a frequent exercise in North Cyprus.

Projects in this group are:

- Excursion paths for monuments
- Bus stops and waiting areas
- Festival and street activities
- Accessibility
- Short- and long-term car parking
- Car parking for disabled people
- Public transportation
- Pedestrianization of the traditional core
- Modern sculpture park
- Improvement to the garden of Lala Mustafa Pasha Mosque
- PR, image and communication
- Face-lifting of contrasting buildings at Namık Kemal Square
- Rehabilitation of buildings that are out of keeping with the town silhouette

Projects for Restoration and Infusing New Life/Economic Revitalization – Long Term

- Martinengo Bastion: multi-purpose centre for arts and cultural activities
- Buğday (Sinan Pasha) Mosque: performing arts centre
- Old prison, Gazi Elementary School and Chimney House: museum complex
- Othello Tower restoration
- Sea Gate: Exhibition and concert hall
- Identification of archeological potential of the Walled City
- Inventory of the bastions and cavaliers and deciding appropriate functions for them
- Kertikli Hamam: Restoration and use as a Turkish Bath
- The Moat: leisure and recreation areas
- Martinengo Bastion: park and sports area
- Akkule (Ravelin) Bastion: observation deck
- Canbulat (Arsenal) Bastion: observation deck

All of the projects fit well with the overall scenario for the Walled City. However, great care must be taken not to overemphasize tourism. If applied inappropriately it might even harm the historic environment in the long run.

Realization of most of the second group projects will be much more troublesome and complicated than for those in the first group. Firstly, preparation of the restoration projects would take much time – almost certainly several years – and would require extensive, specialized, human resources. Secondly, the restoration of the historic monuments will require a huge amount of money and cannot be realized with only local resources.

Concluding Remarks

It is clear that owing to its multi-cultural layers, the historic Walled City of Famagusta deserves every effort for its protection and revitalization. The newly prepared 'Revitalization Plan for the Walled City' is a major step towards safeguarding the centuries-old historic buildings, be they monumental or mundane, and which collectively constitute the architectural heritage of the city. The concern of the international community, which has taken the Walled City into the World Monument Fund Watch List 2008, is also of great importance. Additionally, Europa Nostra the pan-European Federation for Cultural Heritage, both of which have shown great interest in the protection of the historic city, have formed a working group under its Scientific Council. This group has started to work focusing on the fortress of Famagusta.

Although there have been several piecemeal conservation efforts, these important developments should be considered a new and more promising beginning. The historic monuments, which are the prime constituents of the architectural heritage, should be infused with new life in order to be taken into the future. However, it should be kept in mind that their contexts also add value to these priceless remains. Destruction of the context would, in the words of Donald Appleyard, leave the historic monuments 'like mountains without foothills, Old Masters without frames'.[36] Additionally, the policy of integrated conservation, which is now accepted as normative for the protection of cultural heritage, is also shaped around the idea that architectural heritage 'means far more than just single monuments considered in isolation such as religious buildings, stately homes or castles. They also cover groups of buildings and sites or, to be more precise, landscapes and historic settings, which may consist of town centers ....'[37] Accordingly, it is vital to appreciate that, even if there is an urgent need to take steps to preserve historic monuments, the efforts for revitalization should be kept in line with the policy of integrated conservation. There is a need now for technical and financial support to initiate a detailed survey (including measured drawings) of all the historic monuments and archeological sites, as well as for the preparation of restoration projects. Local resources will never be enough to support such a tremendous duty, although there is certainly the will. In the meantime, action at home should be initiated to provide the necessary legal, organizational and administrative bases through the amendment of the current framework for implementation in line with international conventions.

Considering the universal value of the Walled City of Famagusta, it is the duty of all parties, both at local and international level, to take every action to protect and to carry it to the future as a World Heritage site without delay.

---

[36] Donald Appleyard, *The Conservation of European Cities* (Cambridge, MA, 1979), 16.

[37] Council of Europe, *Convention fort he Protection of the Architectural Heritage of Europe (Granada)*, The Council of Europe's cultural heritage conventions, (1985), http://www.coe.int/Treaty/en/Treaties/Html/121.htm (accessed 24.03.2008).

15

An Inspection of Three of Famagusta's Churches

Paulo B. Lourenço and Luís F. Ramos

Built heritage, comprising structures such as bridges, tunnels, houses and so on, is a major investment of national resources in any country. This built heritage permanently accumulates damage due to deterioration of materials, repeated loading and exceptional events. As a result, conservation, repair and strengthening, are often necessary. Within this process, inspection and diagnosis techniques, play a major role, providing information and allowing the definition of adequate remedial measures. Structures of architectural heritage, by their very nature and history (material and assembly), present a number of challenges in conservation, diagnosis, analysis, monitoring and strengthening. These limit the application of modern legal codes and building standards. The recommended methodology adopts an iterative process between the tasks of data acquisition, structural behaviour, diagnosis and safety. The latter evaluation comes in two consecutive and related stages on the basis of which the effective need for, and extent of, treatment measures are determined. If these stages are performed incorrectly, the resulting decisions will be arbitrary: poor judgement may result in either conservative and therefore heavy-handed conservation measures or inadequate safety levels. Recently, the 'Recommendations for the Analysis, Conservation and Structural Restoration of Architectural Heritage' has been approved by ICOMOS, providing a sound basis of principles and guidelines.

In Famagusta three churches were selected for advanced, non-destructive inspection, namely dynamic and sonic testing, and preliminary diagnosis. These were: St George of the Latins, St George of the Greeks and The Carmelite Church.

Visual Inspection: St George of the Latins

The Church of St George of the Latins is in a ruinous state of preservation (see also Figure 17.3). The church, however, still preserves its northern half, the lower section of the apse and part of its south side, which collectively offer enough evidence to demonstrate that it was an impressive example of Gothic architecture, with excellent masonry, compact proportions and rich stone carved decoration. The church is dated to the end of the thirteenth century and is a single-aisled building with four groin vaults which are supported by a grouping of three thin columns located in the north and south walls. A search of photographic archives indicates that the present condition of the church seems not to differ significantly from the condition around 1940. Severe deterioration of stones can be noted from drawings made in 1882, and several other stones have been replaced in the conservation work which took place around 1940. The present condition is characterized by: severe stone deterioration (Figure 15.1), loose stone elements (Figure 15.2), a highly corroded reinforced concrete lintel over the main door (Figure 15.3), inefficient buttresses due to stone deterioration (Figure 15.4), and a crack/rotation of the tower, possibly due to a previous earthquake/foundation problems (Figure 15.5).

St George of the Greeks

The Church of Saint George of the Greeks is the largest Frankish Orthodox church in Cyprus measuring 37.5 × 20.5 m^2. It is dated with some certainty to the second half of the fourteenth century. The building is an interesting example of a Greek Orthodox church with French Gothic architectural features. Unfortunately, all that is left of the building is its east end, its central and side apses with their pointed domes, the nave's south wall and the lower part of the west end (Plate 3; see also Figures 9.2 and 10.8). The church is built with square sandstone blocks and it is three-aisled with two rows of columns. The dome sat on the square space formed by the second and the third column of each row, and the building has groin vaults. In the east the three aisles end in semi-circular apses. The roof had supporting pillars that bore the weight of the building's central aisle. The church's windows are simple and pointed whilst the entrances are adorned with carved relief decoration. Attached to the church's south side is the small, ruined church dedicated to Saint Symeon. The interior of the church was adorned with wall paintings but most of them were destroyed after the dome and the upper part of the building collapsed. Some fragments survive in the apses (depicting the figures of saints) but are exposed to the elements and are severely weathered. The present condition of the church seems not to differ significantly from its condition around 1940. Still, some aspects to be considered in any future conservation project are as follows (Figure 15.6). Recorded damage/possible remedial actions: (1) doors required to prevent free access; (2) moderate cracking present, (3) need to verify if removal/consolidation of masonry/stones are needed, (4) needs protection of frescoes and engravings, (5) needs consolidation of window tracery, (6) needs consolidation of vault (roof possibly needs works to protect from rainwater), (7) needs consolidation of arch, (8) severe biological contamination; (9) needs consolidation of flying arch.

The Carmelite Church

The church of St Mary of the Carmelites is situated in the northwest corner of Famagusta. Because the Carmelites originated from the Carmel Mountains of Syria, this area became known as the Syrian quarter of the city. It was built in the fourteenth century as the church of a monastery, and has a single nave of four bays and a three-sided apse. In the second bay, two small chapels were added. The roof had ribbed vaults, and the exterior walls were supported by buttresses. The tomb of Peter Thomas, who was the Pope's representative and the Patriarch of Constantinople, who died in 1366, was in this church. The walls of the church were covered in frescoes, and some of those are still (just) visible. Outside the west door, you can also see the remains of sculptures above the entrance. Recently, the tracery added by the British above the main door around 1940 collapsed (Figure 15.7). The present condition of the church seems not to differ significantly from the condition around 1940 according to a visual comparison made with the images in the Mogabgab Archive. Some further aspects to be considered in any conservation projects are provided in (Figure 15.8). Recorded damage/possible remedial actions: (1) base of the towers exhibiting severe stone deterioration, (2) voids in the masonry, (3) possible elements to remove, (4) protection needed for frescoes and engravings.

In Situ Non-Destructive Testing

Dynamic Tests

Modal identification, or dynamic identification analysis, is a procedure that combines vibration testing techniques and analytical methods to determine modal (natural) parameters of structures. The modal parameters are frequencies, mode shapes, and damping coefficients. In other words, modal identification analysis is a diagnosis tool used to understand how a structure responds dynamically, e.g. to an earthquake, and to validate a computational representation of a structure. During the inspections on the historical constructions of Famagusta, dynamic identification tests were carried out in the same three churches: St George of the Latins, St George of the Greeks and Carmelite church. Three accelerometers with 10 V/g sensitivity, able to measure 0.07 mg (g the gravity acceleration), were used to measure accelerations. The sensors were connected to a laptop by a data acquisition system with 24-bit resolution with a USB cable connection (Figure 15.9). Here, we present only the results for St George of the Latins Church as an example of the work conducted throughout the city. The measurements were carried

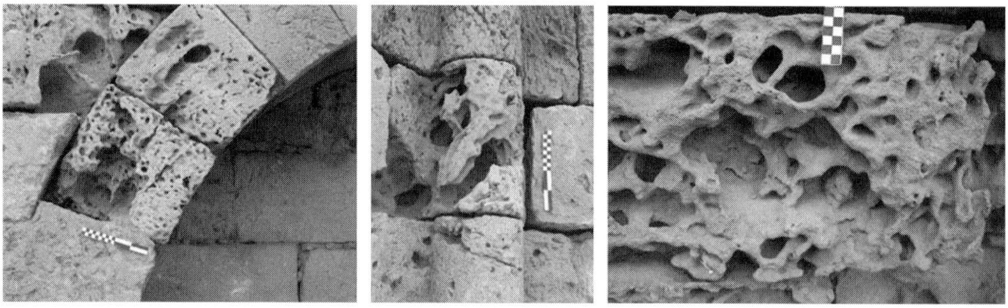

Fig. 15.1 St George of the Latins, stone deterioration (photographs: Lourenço and Ramos)

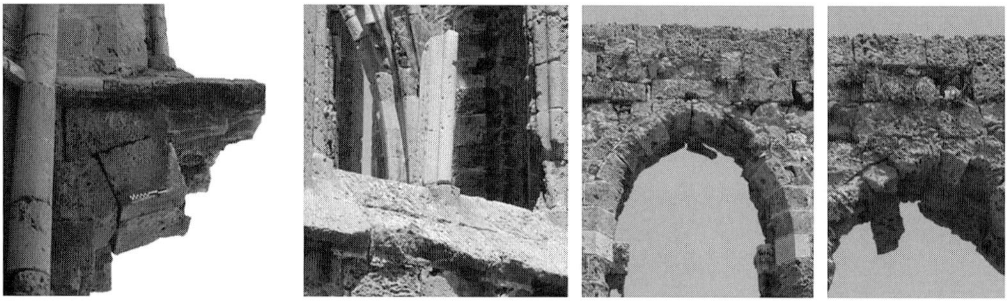

Fig. 15.2 St George of the Latins, loose stone elements (photographs: Lourenço and Ramos)

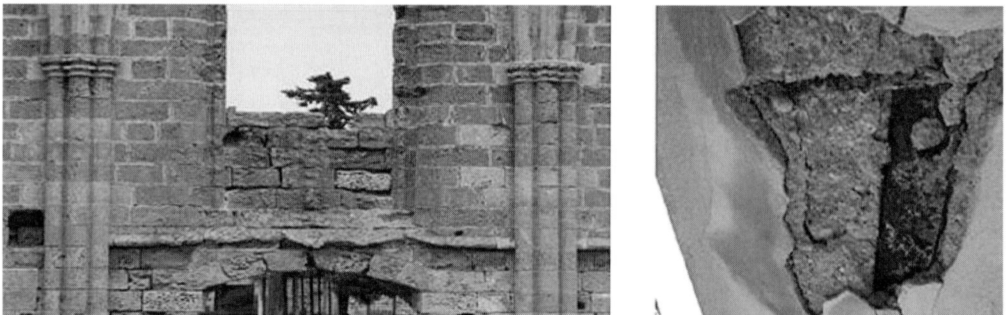

Fig. 15.3 St George of the Latins, corroded modern lintel (photographs: Lourenço and Ramos)

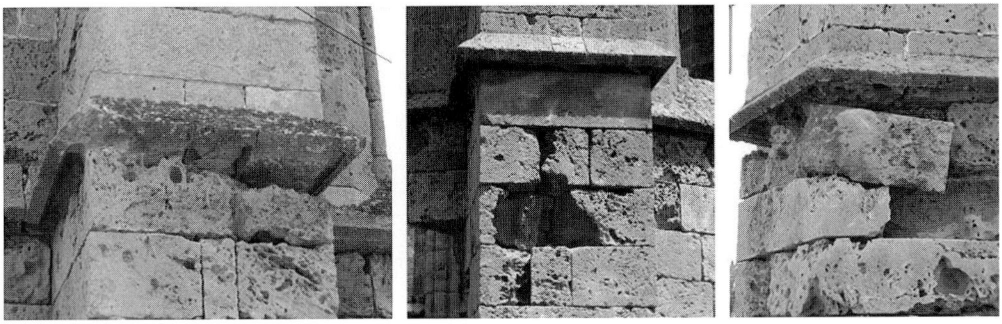

Fig. 15.4 St George of the Latins, weakened buttressing through stone deterioration (photographs: Lourenço and Ramos)

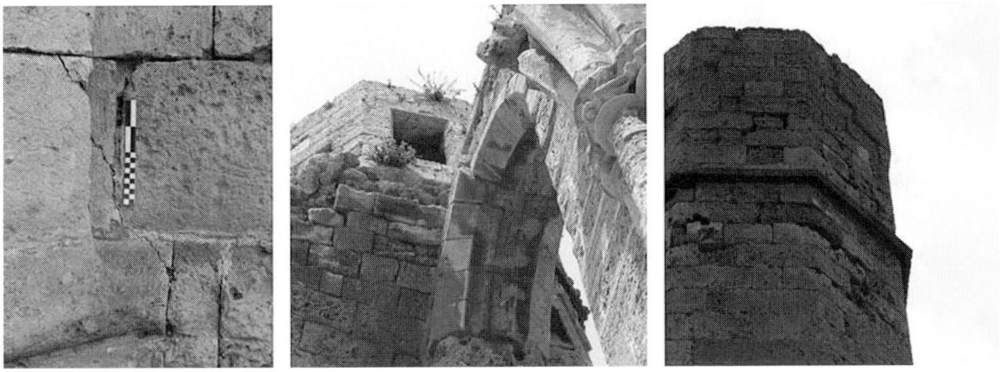

Fig. 15.5 St George of the Latins, earthquake damage and cracking (photographs: Lourenço and Ramos)

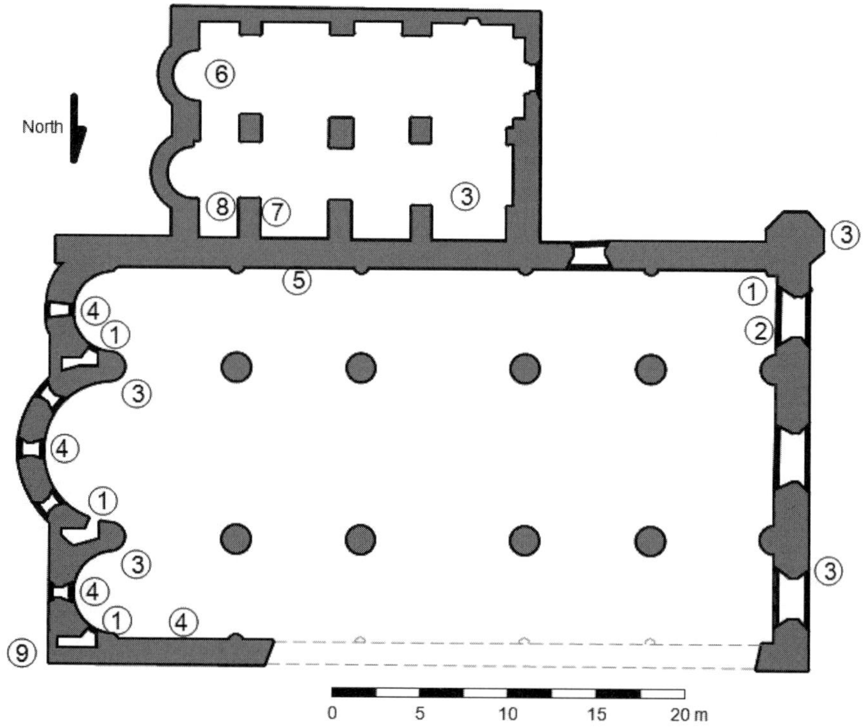

Fig. 15.6 St George of the Greeks and St Symeon with problematic areas marked. Plan (Lourenço and Ramos)

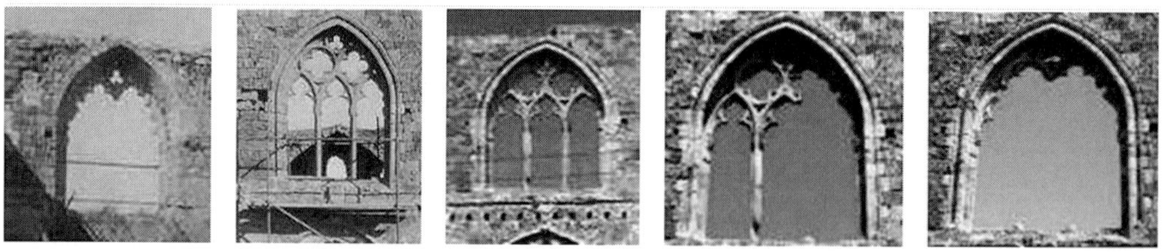

Fig. 15.7 The Carmelite Church with window tracery deterioration (photographs: Lourenço and Ramos)

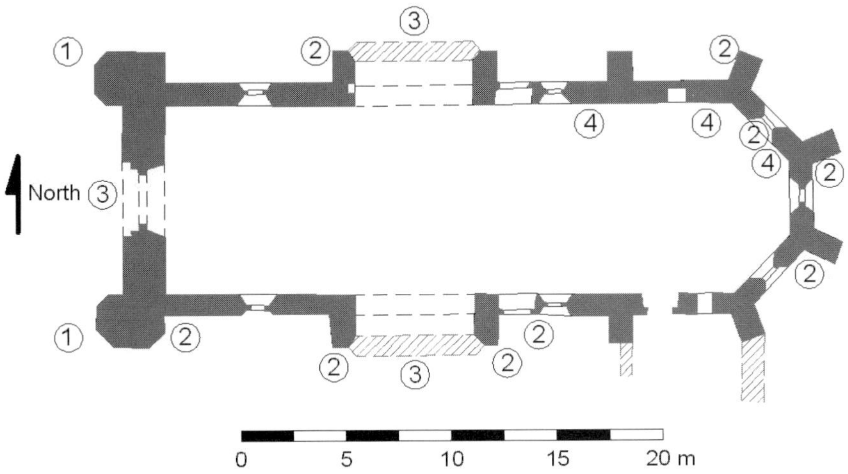

Fig. 15.8 The Carmelite Church with problematic areas marked (Lourenço and Ramos)

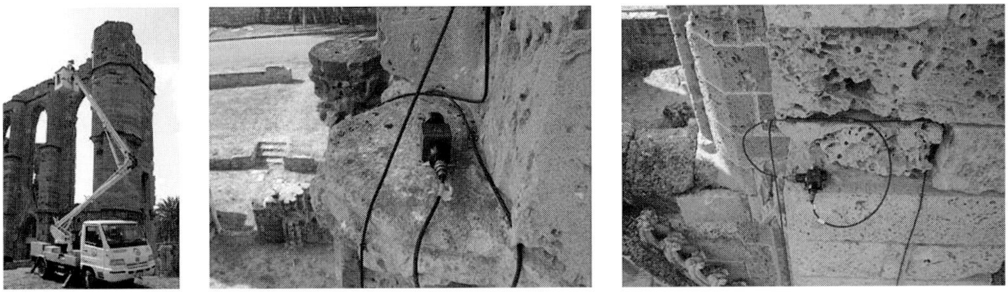

Fig. 15.9 Test planning of St George of the Latins Church (photographs: Lourenço and Ramos)

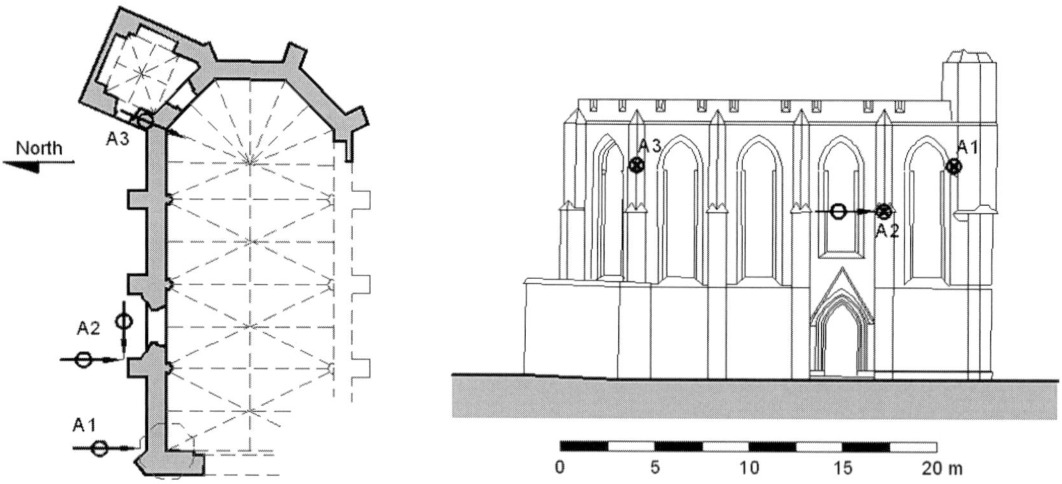

Fig. 15.10 Dynamic testing on St George of the Latins (Lourenço and Ramos)

out in three points in the North façade, close to the top of three buttresses. The measuring points are indicated in the letter A (Figure 15.10). Images of the dynamic measurements can be seen as can the stabilization diagram of the SSI method, where 17 stable columns can be observed, corresponding to 17 natural frequencies of the structure below 20 Hz. The standard deviation values for frequencies are very low, indicating that the estimation is accurate. The mode configurations are mainly out-of-plane modes, as expected due to the unconstrained walls of the church ruins.

Sonic Tests

Sonic tests are based on the propagation properties of elastic waves on a solid. By knowing the distance between two points in the wall and by measuring the travel time, it is possible to calculate the sonic velocity (the velocity of the elastic waves). For sonic tests, two types of sensors are used, the hammer for impacts transmission and the receiver, which can be an accelerometer. The sensors are connected to a data acquisition system (DAQ) that acquires at a high sampling rate. When the geometry of a body, or structure, is known (e.g. the thickness of a wall or buttress), the time lag between the impact signal and the receiver signal allows the estimation of the sonic velocity inside the body. When materials with different densities, or voids, or cracks, exist inside another material, the sonic velocity decreases. If the body/structure is tested at several points, a sonic velocity map can be computed and it will qualitatively indicate the constitution of the wall and/or the presence of voids and cracks.

Sonic tests were only carried out at St George of the Latins church on two buttresses, one on the North façade and one on the South façade. The aim was to evaluate the internal condition, mainly if there are internal voids, different density materials, or if repair works had occurred in the recent past. The tests were carried out with two accelerometers and one small hammer.

The hammer was used to hit next to one accelerometer (the transmission sensor), while the other (the receiver) was placed in an opposite side of the stone or buttress. Two vertical alignments and five horizontal alignments were tested (10 points per alignment). The results show that the sonic velocity ranges from 1400 to 2400 m/s. The average value for the alignments is 1597 and 2249 m/s, respectively. It is possible to see that the outer points of the buttress have a higher velocity than the inner points. The results indicate that the stones in the outer alignment were probably replaced by new ones in the recent past, while the internal part of the buttresses are in worse condition. In the South buttress small differences were found between the velocity values. Ranging from 1400 to 2600 m/s, the average values for the two alignments were 1923 and 1996 m/s, respectively. The values indicate that the internal condition of the buttress in the two alignments is similar, with similar distribution of voids.

The full report, including the comprehensive results of all similar tests on St George of the Greeks and St Mary of Carmel, was submitted in August 2008 (Report 08-DEC/E-11).

An Assessment of the Structural Fabric of the Church of Saints Peter and Paul: A Case Study in Historical Record and Structural Appraisal

George S. Ballard and Stephen W. Kemp

Any plan to bring back into use and conserve an ancient standing structure, which has had little or no maintenance for many years and clearly needs attention to give it both the robustness and the durability necessary to make the conversion viable and effective, is faced immediately with a problem: is the cost of achieving this object vastly more than the funds available, or is it an issue that can be taken on and delivered within a reasonable budget? The older the building and the more complex its architectural form, the harder this is to estimate without the solid base of information that must be the starting point for any preliminary study. The information base needs to record what is to be conserved of the architectural form and its impact – a primary requirement of the historic documentation so that any intervention does not alter it – at the same time as the structure itself is recorded. Structure is defined in the simple sense that any standing structure is a mechanical system that supports itself, and carries no risk of part or all falling to the ground. The intention to bring an historic structure back into use for public access brings an extra demand: it must be shown to be compliant with the codes that apply to modern structures. Sufficient reserves found within the original, or additional, strengthening must be applied to demonstrate that required factors of safety can be found. Modern buildings usually have plans and records and make use of well-defined materials, that allow their compliance to be relatively easily demonstrated, but with increasing age the records veer from being limited to being non existent. The difficulties of the task are increased when dealing with materials which may have lost some of their original strength, due to weathering, use or simple aging; the problems are made more complex when previous interventions have interrupted or hidden the original design intention. Furthermore, if the structure is subject to extraordinary and damaging forces, such a wave action or strong-motion earthquakes, then answering the question 'how much will it cost to secure this structure for the future?' becomes not only necessary but onerous. It is often necessary as well at this very early stage for that question to be answered with a method as well as a price. This is something that requires a thought-out remedial scheme that obeys both conservation needs and code compliance, while remaining achievable, simple, minimalist and sympathetic to the structure.

All these issues demand attention when addressing the conservation requirements at SS Peter and Paul in Famagusta. The mid fourteenth-century Lusignan foundation, comprising a Gothic design with a central five-bay nave and two side aisles leading to three apsidal chapels, and rising to a ribbed and vaulted roof space, is remarkably well preserved. In the course of the intervening centuries, however, it has been converted to a Mosque, has had seismic protection added by Ottoman architects, probably in the seventeenth or eighteenth century, has been allowed to fall into disrepair, has been converted into a store and then, during the period of British rule, into a library. Since then it has been converted back to a store, and it now stands empty and unused. During this period there have been at least four disastrous earthquakes, which have reduced some of the many churches of Famagusta to rubble, and the soft shelly limestone of which it is built has lost its protective render, now exposing it to wind and rain. In all probability it originally carried a timber pitched roof which has been replaced by a flat roofing system applied directly over its vaulting, probably by the Ottomans, and which itself has been replaced a number of times. At the west end, there were once additional rooms, both at ground level where there had possibly been a small narthex, and over the first bay of both the aisles, possibly two storeys high, as evidenced by put holes and brackets to support timber flooring. These rooms were probably later additions, and, judging from their architectural form, probably Venetian rather than Ottoman. On the south-west corner an original spiral stairway giving access to these upper levels was extended and altered in the Ottoman period to form a minaret which has now fallen to the ground. Much of the stone can be found on the ground around the tower, suggesting that the fall was recent, since it is unlikely that it would have gone unrepaired while the building was still in use as a mosque.

An investigation was mounted to assess the church, based on three main activities: a measured survey and historic record documenting the building as it stands, that provided a full set of drawings of the existing structural form and which recorded its data by means of a non-destructive examination of the fabric and an inspection of the hidden structure and form, which in turn allowed the structural analysis to proceed. Grouping this as a total package addressed to the issue of its economic conservability ahead of the conservation plan is a relatively unusual approach, but avoids the frequent trap of expending budget on a complex plan, only to discover well along the way that a serious unforeseen structural issue creates a budget overrun or an insuperable obstacle. The investigation was designed to take advantage of and integrate modern methods and technology, an approach regularly used in modern construction but less common in such heritage architectural work, where their use is more piecemeal. It is rare that the dimensional data assembled for historic documentation is collected with a view to an easy transfer into finite element modelling of the structural performance. It is also unusual for an instant record of the multiple historic construction of a solid roof to be added to the historic documentation without excavation through the fabric, whilst at the same time providing the structural analysis with the correct mass and layering of the system.

The core of the dimensional survey was the use of 3D laser scanning, set within a survey control framework, to allow both the interior and exterior surfaces to be mapped to an accuracy of a few millimetres, including the registration between the two. The laser as a reflectorless system thus takes its measurements directly from the architectural surfaces; it is positioned within the control framework and within minutes identifies a 'point cloud' – a set of points in space which are an accurate representation of the surface discriminating down to one or two millimetres, producing drawings. This was coupled with rectified photography, thereby ensuring that there is also an accurate metric record of the architectural surface (Plate 20). The approach has some advantages over photogrammetry in that the dimensional accuracy is achieved directly in the measurement rather than in the post process of stereo images. In addition the point cloud is a constantly accessible source of digital three dimensional values – which can be re-accessed automatically at any time. For example, in this study it became necessary, during the course of the evaluation of previous earthquake damage, to identify and map the separation of the inner and outer leaves of the walls, which themselves had moved overall out of plane, by bowing horizontally and vertically. Access to the cartesian (xyz value) location of every part of the surface, accurately registered between inner and outer, made this a task of moments, rather than a tedious evaluation. The disadvantage that mapping architectural enrichment by this approach is time consuming in both survey and process time was negated by the observation that there was very little enrichment to be found, and that the enrichment found was well resolved by the photographic data. Much of the surface is rough and weathered, and apart from noting that the whole is in need of re-pointing, and that surface roughness probably is indicative of the extent of weathering, an accurate photographic record of every rough stone is of little historic value. More importantly, particular attention could be paid by this system to generating data which translated relatively easily into finite element modelling systems. This is largely a matter of ensuring that individual elements extracted from the point cloud and 3D models were indeed single elements and not split down (by the processing to vectorial representation in the computer-aided design [CAD] systems used) into non existent sub-units. Care was also taken to include in the development of the survey control direction from the structural engineering assessment, so that the critical element dimensions were taken. The output of this phase was therefore both an historic document recording the building and fabric at the moment of survey, as well as detailed 'as built' or rather 'as received' drawings from which much of the basic structural calculations could be made. Non-destructive testing (NDT) has established itself as an important tool in conservation planning. It has the ability, without invading the fabric, to establish the arrangement of materials hidden within a structure, or else the continuity of the material at the surface to particular depths. This, together with information on its mechanical condition, increases the knowledge of the structure without any need to damage it.

In SS Peter and Paul, the basic visible construction was the soft and easily weathered local limestone, set in lime mortar, with dressed stones well coursed and bonded. Some ruined sections of wall showed that the dressed stones were external leaves, and the hearting was frequently mortared rubble. Weathering in Cyprus is largely a cycle of wind erosion following softening during the relatively infrequent rains. It was noticeable that any exposed underside of stone was more rapidly eroded by this process, thus the bottom arris of a stone where the pointing had been lost and the soffit of the external buttresses all showed more extreme erosion than surfaces that shed rain well. The stones of the ribs in the Gothic vaulting also showed damage indicative of softening – but of course without wind damage – raising concerns that the water penetrating the roof may have affected the stabilizing fill over the vaults as well as compromising the structural value of the stones and mortar.

Ground-penetrating radar (GPR) was used to establish the arrangement, and to confirm where the construction was solid stone, and where the hearting was rubble filled. It identified not only the thicknesses of the two leaves but also the location of ties across the wall between the leaves. Working from above and below the roofs, the make up of the roof was established, including the thickness of the vaulting, the fill over it, and the layering of the present lime and cement renders of the roofing system over lying that. Below ground, radar confirmed both that there were relatively few interments within the church, and the continuity of the rock head on which the structure was founded, based on calibration by physical probing through the floor, and around the outside of the church. On the buttresses it also confirmed that there was a discontinuity within the lower buttresses to the south, confirming the assumption based on observation that the original buttresses had at some point been increased in mass. This can probably be dated to the Ottoman period either after or between disastrous earthquakes of the seventeenth and eighteenth centuries, given that their architects had a proficient understanding of mass damping for seismic protection.

Variations in moisture content of the fill were also detected by the radar, beginning the process of tracking paths for moisture through the structure, to assess the extent of any damage caused (Plate 21). This tracking was then continued using thermographic imaging to identify zones where moisture had found its way through the vaulting – in places this was obvious, due to the presence of algal growth on the surface, in others apparently dry areas were shown to be concentrated water paths. As the inspection work was carried out in a period of almost no rain, the probability is that the locations found are more seriously subject to water penetration during the occasional heavy downfalls that typify the local climate. More pertinently it appeared that water entering the roof system did not pass down into the walls, probably largely because of the through stones (identified in the radar) at the impost of the groin vaults to the walls, and the presence of a cemented plug (rubble in lime) at the base of the fill. The thermography also confirmed that there was no attic space above the vaults: morning sunshine warmed the southern half of the roof with no transfer to the northern half which was in shadow, indicating direct thermal flow through the fabric, and not via an intervening airspace. Similarly, the full expanse of the walls was checked for diurnal heat flow, and no evidence of differentials was recorded that might indicate possible voided spaces within the structure.

These two methods, together with simple careful visual inspection, provided the basis for understanding the arrangement of the interior. Some indication of strength was also required which was identified using acoustics. Samples were compression tested to give a base line calibration of strength, which is the most critical parameter in a compression structure. There was some issue in testing the samples, as the surface structure of most of the stones collapses if wetted. Only samples from the interior could therefore be tested, and, with an uncertainty of the depth of weathering, any sample could be potentially unrepresentative.

The velocity of an acoustic wave in a continuous elastic medium should be approximately proportional to its density and elasticity, which to the first approximation should make estimates of strength relatively easy. However, as the strength of limestone is also proportional to density, the relationship between velocity and strength is necessarily nonlinear. Calibrating against a sample of reasonably sound material does nevertheless provide a base line value: reductions in velocity indicate a decrease in strength.

The method used was Dynamic Impedance (or Impact Echo ASTMS 1383–98), a relatively poorly understood and little used method, largely because its implementation, requires considerable skill and dexterity in achieving usable and useful results, which are based on using broad frequency band impacts to set up resonances, or standing waves, within solid elastic media. The primary response is a full thickness resonance, the wavelength of which is set by the acoustic velocity of the material. Secondary responses are also found, where resonances are set up either between the surface and discontinuities or simply between discontinuities. The data is therefore analysed in the frequency domain rather than in the time domain, as a series of discrete power spectrum peaks. This should not be confused with echo sounding, in which the time of travel of a wave of much shorter wavelength than the depth being sounded is recorded to cover the two-way distance (there and back) to and from the point measured, purely in the time domain. The frequency analysis of the Dynamic Impedance method can, however, be located in time within the signal stream; thus discrete locations for the intermediate secondary signals can be found. It is therefore possible to identify whether a stone is a single uniform elastic medium, in which case the strength can be related back to the primary calibration, or whether it separated into zones of different density, or simply cracked and lacking integrity. The information is therefore akin to that which can be derived from cores, with the lack of physical observation more than made up for by the ability to take many readings without any invasion or loss of historic fabric. This process assisted in showing that main stones of the walls were rarely weathered to a depth greater than ~40mm (in 300–450mm thickness), and were otherwise sound. More importantly, the ribs and panel stones forming the vaults were not only more generally weathered and weakened, suggesting a long history of water penetration into the fill above, but also that above the quarter point the vault stones were a continuous diaphragm rather than spanning between and keyed into the ribs. This information was of importance in defining any repairs to the ribs, which were badly damaged in a number of places by dislocation and spalling, due more to displacement and distortion of the vaulting than weathering. As they therefore carry no load beyond their self weight, replacement and remediation would not be the onerous task it would have been had they been fully loaded. Once restored the ribs would then be available as a reliable limiter of any hinging or distortion of the vault diaphragm during any strong motion earthquake.

The flat roof over the vaulting had clearly been the subject of frequent interventions. At least two major episodes of reinstatement could be identified, in that the main roof was formed in a cement mortar/concrete, but with some patches remaining around the edge of an earlier lime mortar-based roof. Local anecdote suggested that lime mortar with a prickly pear juice organic retarder/plasticizer was regularly used in the eighteenth and nineteenth centuries as roofing. The cementitious roofing contained bars running transversely directly above the centre line of the cross groins. These were corroding badly, but regularly placed links suggested additional bars, which were confirmed by radar. Linkage into steel in the parapet was sought but not found, possibly because it was too severely corroded to detect. The presence of reinforcing steel almost certainly dated from the British period, and indicated previous interest in providing tensile strength across the roof; oddly, however, the steel was formed as a bent, and thus tended to create a downward force on the crown with increasing tension. The two side aisles may also have originally been covered by a sloping timber roofing system hidden behind a low parapet, but the present form is an entirely flat largely cementitious roof, with minimal falls to scuppers through the parapet wall. The radar indicated the probability of a shallow brick or timbrel arch below this level and above damp and damaged fill over the vaulting.

These basic structural elements, forming the church, had patently survived seven centuries of weather and rain, and more significantly, a number of high-intensity seismic events, all of which have left their mark in terms of weakened, weathered stones, deteriorated mortar, distorted arches, walls out of plumb and apparently separating; there is also an alarming split in the walls at parapet level, suggesting the outer leaf might be at risk of toppling. Cracks and distortion in the wall also suggested a general outward bowing of the north and south walls. Two particularly severe earthquakes have been recorded, in the sixteenth and seventeenth centuries, but other events almost certainly occurred, one of which was probably responsible for the collapse of the minaret. A preliminary appraisal showed that the most severe loading the structure will endure is a strong motion event. Estimates of the 1724 earthquake suggest a probable magnitude of 7.5 to eight with a deep focus off shore and reported damage indicates intensities of c. 10 on the Mercalli scale in the town. Another event of this magnitude could reasonably be expected in the Famagusta region within the next 100 years, and any re-use of the church should be sufficiently robust to provide protection to this level. A structural appraisal, however, must consider at the same time the durability of a structure and assess the likelihood of deterioration over the period. The structure must, with reasonable maintenance, be as capable of withstanding such an event today as well as it would at the end of the design service life. Where components are found to be lacking then the appraisal must identify what needs to be done now to achieve the desired overall serviceability. The demands of conservation add to this, in that the structural appraiser must find ways in which any strengthening, improvement or alteration should not only be reversible, in that any addition should be readily removable in any future conservation scheme, but also minimal in its impact on the visible architectural form. Any replacement needs to be fully justified as a *sine qua non* of the restoration, either today or during the intended service life. Inevitably, the path of structural conservation must also consider how to achieve its ends as economically as possible. It is assumed that the original structural design would have been carried out by a master mason who would have fulfilled the modern roles of both architect and engineer. Design procedures were normally graphical rather than analytical and relied largely on the cumulative experience of the mason and his guild, which itself would have been acquainted with historical methodology reaching back to Vitruvius.

Applying modern methodologies and computer-based techniques can only provide an approximation of the original design, but the same principles apply to both approaches: the loads of the structure needed to be taken safely to the foundations, which themselves needed to be sufficiently stable to carry the loads imposed on them. Good factors of safety in the engineering expectations of materials to allow for variability are as important in an analysed building as they would be with a more empirical approach. Attempts to over analyse historic buildings by modern standards may ignore the success of the earlier design, merely because of the inaccuracies of assumptions about material properties, mechanical interfaces and connections which are difficult – but not impossible – to justify.

SS Peter and Paul has survived the ravages of wind, rain and earthquake, where other structures in the town have not. In this the investigation was fortunate in that within a radius of a few hundred metres there were other former churches, particularly the cathedral dedicated to St Nicholas (now a mosque) and St George of the Greeks (now a ruin) of a similar age and construction style (as opposed to architectural style, although all three are in the Gothic style with very strong similarities in both construction and architectural form). St Nicholas provides a more complete example of the original finish, and has also survived earthquakes, but St George has fallen victim to a strong-motion event in the seventeenth century, thereby revealing the style and methods of construction.

The first task at SS Peter and Paul therefore was to understand in principle how it is that the structure has worked successfully until now, but without assuming that it will necessarily carry on working in the future. The modern engineer must, when assessing a structure, apply relevant codes and standards which are in themselves based on analysis and calculation, but always with the addition of good engineering judgement where reliance cannot be placed on calculation alone.

Structurally the church is a simple set of rectangular boxes, stacked to form the traditional Gothic of a central clerestory nave supported on columns which themselves form the inner side of the two aisles; the only stiffening in the form of cross walls are the three apses in the east and the simple flat façade to the west, leaving the north and south walls to rely on the box structure to maintain rigidity. The clerestory box has no base and therefore relies on the aisle boxes. Two conditions must be considered, the building standing under its own weight (static gravitational) or responding to external applied forces (dynamic). The static vertical loads (the mass of the building) are clearly carried by the walls and columns, and a simple estimate suggests that they are adequate for this task and are far from any critical stress. Lateral loads or thrusts (generated by the roof load transmitted down into the vertical walls), together with the dynamic horizontal loads of wind pressure and ultimately seismic accelerations, are not as clearly supported. Initial calculation showed that these assumptions were correct and predicted that the building was unstable at very light horizontal loads. The boxes each with open sides appeared like a house of cards, capable of surprising vertical loads but responding catastrophically to a sideways push. This observation did not stand up to reason as the building was clearly standing. The southern side of the church is braced by two levels of buttress but the northern side has only the higher level of buttress. This arrangement appears odd but may be simply pragmatic: the location on a principal street in proximity to the later Venetian Palace probably explains the absence of a lower row of buttresses to the north. It is also possible that the southern lower buttresses were a later addition, forming a necessary part of an Ottoman seismic protection system. There was perhaps also a connection across the street to the Palace that would have provided buttressing. Note that Turkish engineering practices understood the function of a buttress for earthquake protection as a mass damper, which had no need of fixed connection to the wall: its purpose was simply to take energy out of any out of plane oscillation of the wall. Neither St Nicholas nor St George, both of which had upper clerestory level buttressing but none to ground level, have escaped severe earthquake damage. The vault of St Nicholas has had to be rebuilt; St George has been damaged beyond repair. Mass damping to the lower levels, i.e. the lower two 'boxes' of the construction, would not of itself provide stability as the upper box and the inner walls of the lower boxes remain unstable. In simple terms, without a tensile connection across the main upper roof and within the clerestory roof, the walls can set up independent oscillations, with one clerestory wall moving either out of phase or at a different frequency from the other. As one clerestory wall tilts outwards, the bottom tries to move inwards, pushing the top of the columns, which tend to lean inwards. This is a potentially highly unstable condition. If the opposing clerestory wall moves in opposing motion, the vaults are stretched and may fail, or, if moving at a different frequency, they may add an additional thrust, overturning the wall. Very little tensile strength is required to ensure that the two walls act as a single unit so that both walls sway together. Damping either side of this system will prevent energy storage in the sway, and will reduce the likelihood of an overturning condition being reached. This was easily demonstrated by finite element modelling of the structure. Understanding how this tensile strength, which has clearly been at work in the church, functions became the main difficulty in proving the building to modern codes. A re-examination of the arrangement suggested that friction in the components of the roof structure would provide the predicted restraint and tensile control sufficient to prevent independent motion of the vaults and clerestory walls; a similar reasoning provided limited but sufficient tensile strength across the aisle vaults to stabilize the motion of the columns.

Finding how the system probably works is, however, only half the story: the question is how to guarantee the system for its future service life? Modern codes cannot rely on non quantifiable friction to maintain life safety and structural integrity; justification would require some real tensile components in the structure to provide the necessary protection. Thought was given to restoring the roof to the original (and long departed) pitched form and proving tensile strength in the bottom elements of the truss. However, the wisdom of removing both the additional high level mass and windage from the stability equation, and of relying on the flat roof to protect from weather prevailed, and so the introduction of real tensile capacity into the flat roof system was selected. It appeared that the steel bar bents, introduced during the British period, may have been with the intention of providing tensile connection, but these are now well past any reliable performance, and corrosion is now corrupting the water protection offered by the roof. Removing these, and the upper most layers of render, would allow a lightweight reinforced concrete slab to replace the already leaking render roof, with no significant increase in dead load. This would provide a complete plate over the upper surface, providing both tensile strength to control out of plane motion in the walls as well as bracing to prevent the entire nave from racking, and could be continued as a remedial rationale over the aisle roofs as well. Such a solution could also be better equipped to give long-term weather protection to the interior of the church. With this strengthening, the rest of the structural conservation plan simply entails making good the weathering of the external surface and repair of internal detailing.

Although the above resolution appears remarkably simple in terms of remedial action, given the extensive work put into the investigation, it is precisely that depth of investigation that has allowed such a simple solution to what is essentially a seismic retrofit problem. It was this that lay at the heart of the process of securing the conservation of the historical architectural monument and permitting its return to the community as a fully operational and accessible building.

17

The Historic Walled City of Famagusta, 2008: A Report

Robert Silman and Kent Severson

The observations in this report are based on a three day visit to Famagusta by Robert Silman (Robert Silman Associates, Structural Engineers, New York and Washington D.C.) and Kent Severson (Conservator in Private Practice, Boston, Massachusetts) on behalf of the World Monuments Fund at the end of March 2008. A remarkable number of structures were examined in a very short time. Most of the monuments in Famagusta are open air and unrestricted to visitors. Exceptions include the churches of SS Peter and Paul, St Anne, and the Tanner's Church; access to these buildings was graciously provided through the local office of the Directorate of Ancient Buildings and Museums (Eski Eserler ve Müzeler Dairesi); the Church of St Nicholas/Lala Mustafa Camii, a working mosque, is open for public visit during the day at most times. Othello's Castle is a tourist attraction charging a modest entrance fee.

Prior to the visit, Silman and Severson were provided with a copy of the World Monuments Fund Watch® List Nomination Form for the Historic Walled City of Famagusta. The historical background, contents, legal situation, significance, and current threats to the city are thoroughly described by Dr Michael Walsh, the author of the application. To the extent that it is possible to make an assessment in such a short visit, his description appears to be accurate and thorough. Prior to the visit, Dr Walsh provided a number of recent articles on Famagusta and DVD copies of the video production *The Stones of Famagusta* were acquired. A great deal of additional material (articles, documentary papers and bibliographic material) was provided by Dr Walsh during a visit to his office at Eastern Mediterranean University. In the course of his research, Dr Walsh and his team became aware of a photographic archive made during the period of British administration of the island (the Mogabgab Archive). The images are small-scale black and white prints, from the 1930s to the 1950s, documenting (among other things) some of the repair work undertaken during this period. The prints are glued to cardboard pages with typewritten labels identifying locations, dates and work depicted. There are hundreds of these cards, stored in 12 boxes.

A second collection of photographs of the wall paintings inside the Armenian Church, the Church of St Mary of the Carmelites, and the Church of St Anne (date and source unknown, provisionally labeled 'Conway' and possibly related to the work of Mrs Bardswell in the late 1930s as described below) was also made available, as were a series of scanned nineteenth-century drawings by Duthoit.

Building Fabric and Deterioration

The historic structures of Famagusta are for the most part built from three types of local stone: a brown medium-fine grained, heterogeneous, marly limestone; a lighter, yellowish porous but homogeneous limestone with large clearly visible shell fragments; and a very fine buff limestone. Most structures (including the churches and the city walls) utilized the first type of limestone as the primary dimension stone, but also for some decorative elements. The second type of stone was used less frequently, and the third was reserved for the finest decorative elements, such as column capitals and gargoyles. Occasionally imported marble and, less frequently, granite and travertines appear in structures as columns, threshold blocks and other details; these are most likely reused ancient materials (*spolia*) probably taken from the nearby Roman city of Salamis. The ancient churches, bath buildings and domestic or commercial buildings are generally constructed of exposed wythes of ashlar dimension stone, filled with a core of mortared rubble (Figure 17.1). The mortar was not analysed but visual inspection reveals mixed sand aggregates and particles of pure white, suggesting a traditional lime mortar. Rarely, other mortars are visible, including a peculiar pure white material and grey Portland cement-based material; these appear to be associated with subsequent interventions, both ancient and modern. The city walls are likewise constructed of the first type of stone, in massive quantities of large-scale blocks, much of which is likely to have been quarried during the construction of the moat. Where the walls have been cut, it can be seen that they are likewise constructed from ashlar outer wythes, but filled with packed mixed soil and rubble, rather than mortared rubble. The most commonly used dimension stone exhibits a distinctive erosion pattern where softer, poorly bound zones are lost, resulting in deep, irregular voids. This erosion pattern occurs on both exposed and protected surfaces, both high up and lower down on structures, suggesting that it is caused primarily by wind action rather than water flow (Figure 17.2). It is postulated that these are marly zones, where the clay expands and softens with diurnal condensation and is subsequently lost to the frequent high winds. Interestingly, the material left behind is relatively hard and weather resistant, and in many cases capable of bearing some considerable load. Much of the dramatic erosion now visible probably occurred long ago and, while ongoing, it appears that the erosion is

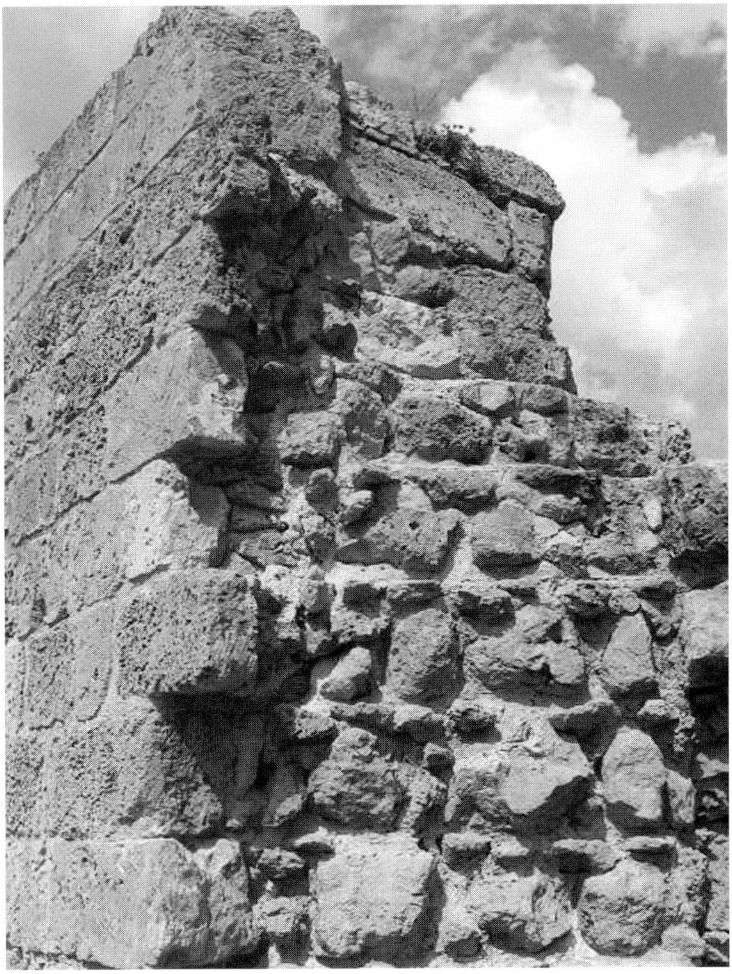

Fig. 17.1 Ashlar dimension stone, filled with a core of mortared rubble (photograph: Silman and Severson)

a relatively slow process. This erosion can be seen in the vertical faces of the living rock along cuts forming the walls of the moat around the city.

Many of the structures in Famagusta, particularly the churches, survive only as truncated ruins. The most dramatic examples of this type of ruin are St George of the Greeks (Plate 3, and see also Figure 10.8), St George of the Latins (Figure 17.3), St Mary of the Carmelites (see also Figure 12.12) and, to a lesser extent, St Francis and St Nicolas (Greek Orthodox) (Plate 6). While the climate of northeastern Cyprus is often quite dry, heavy downpours do occur in the winter and spring. Where roof structures are lost or compromised, water ingress has softened and eroded mortars between stones and in the rubble core of standing walls. The loss of mortar, together with the erosion of the dimension stone, are the two main causes of deterioration threatening the historic structures. These phenomena are observed over and over when touring the city. Salt efflorescence and rising damp does not appear to be a major factor in the deterioration of the stone as the erosion occurs at all levels

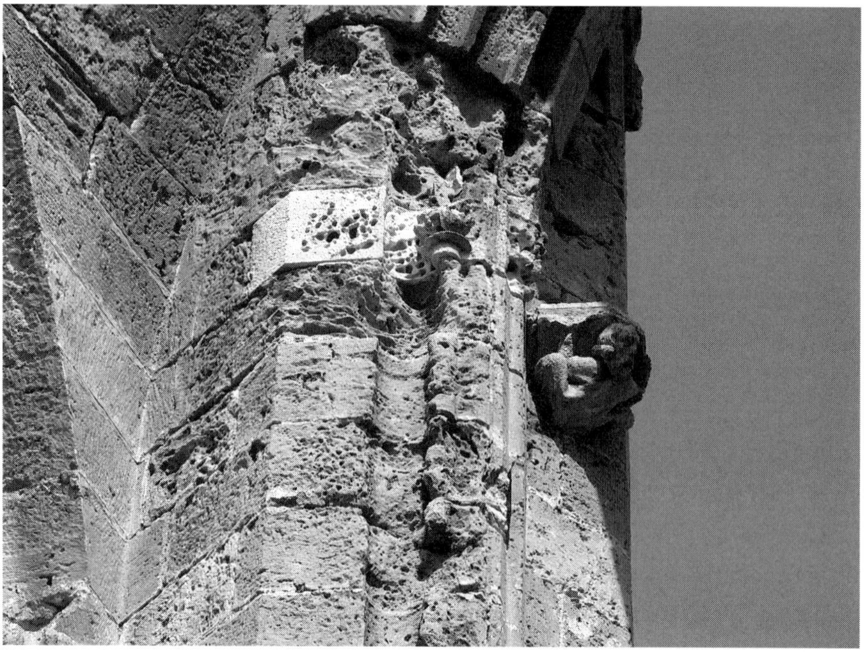

Fig. 17.2 Wind and water erosion (photograph: Silman and Severson)

in structures, there is no evidence of horizontal drying fronts, and little or no efflorescence was observed.

Where roof structures survive, they generally seem to be sound. Examples of buildings with surviving roofs include: St Nicholas Church/Lala Mustafa Camii (see also Figure 7.6), SS Peter and Paul Church (see also Figure 9.3), St Anne's Church, the Tanner's Church, Othello's Castle and the Armenian Church (Plate 4). Except for the roof over the south side of SS Peter and Paul, no roof structures were examined from the outside. Inside, most roofed buildings exhibit little to moderate evidence of water infiltration with the exception of the Tanner's Church where there is clear salt efflorescence on much of the interior surface of the roof, especially at the east end. The loss of the glass elements in the Kertikli Hammam, has left the roof structures generally perforated and open to the weather.

Although the Church of St Nicholas has been more or less maintained during the long period of its use as Lala Mustafa Camii, many of the recent repairs have been made in a haphazard fashion, often using Portland cement mortars. More significantly, much of the exterior masonry does not appear to have been pointed in decades and there are open joints throughout. The massive brackets and platforms beneath the upper windows on the east end of the building are cracked and precarious (Figure 17.4). It was reported by the attendant on duty that the interior had been painted in 1995; there is slight evidence of water infiltration visible on the ceiling.

The exterior of the roof on SS Peter and Paul (the only roof that was examined in this visit) is now covered with cement mortar; the slab is cracked in many places with plant growth emerging from the cracks. There is step

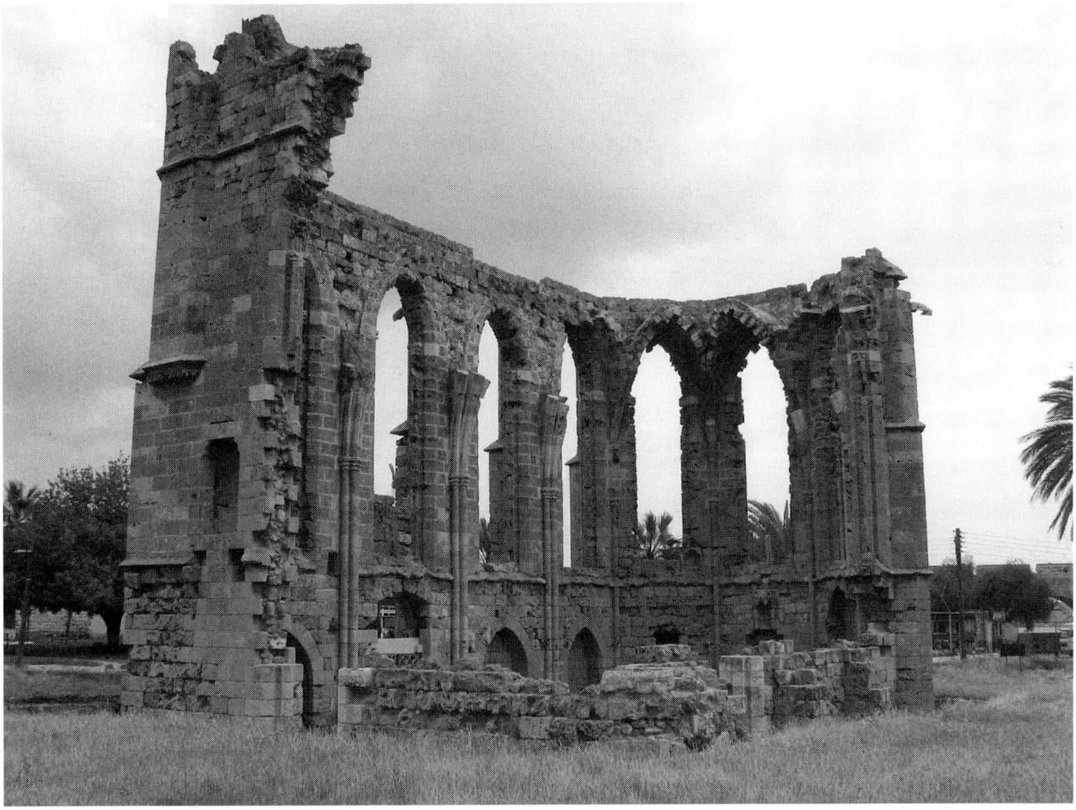

Fig. 17.3 St George of the Latins, general view (photograph: Silman and Severson)

cracking beneath the bulge in the parapet on the south side, highlighted by Dr Walsh in the Nomination Form for WMF (Section 7.3, p. 8).

The historic buildings of Famagusta are generally left unguarded and access by visitors is unrestricted. The grounds of the unrestricted monuments appear to receive at least moderate maintenance, such as occasional trash collection and the cutting of weeds and grass. Nevertheless, they tend to become collection points for trash and vulnerable to vandalism. Evidence of drinking parties (empty bottles, etc.) is seen frequently as is material left by some using the structures as shelter (bedding, etc.) While graffiti, painted or incised in plasters or stone, is not rampant, it occurs regularly. Most disturbing is the scratched-in graffiti on the wall paintings in St George of the Greeks (Plate 22).

Previous and Recent Interventions

During the time of the British administration and the Republic of Cyprus, approximately from 1935 through 1972, many of the monuments in the city were repaired and/or partially reconstructed. These interventions are briefly but comprehensively documented in the annual Reports to the Director of

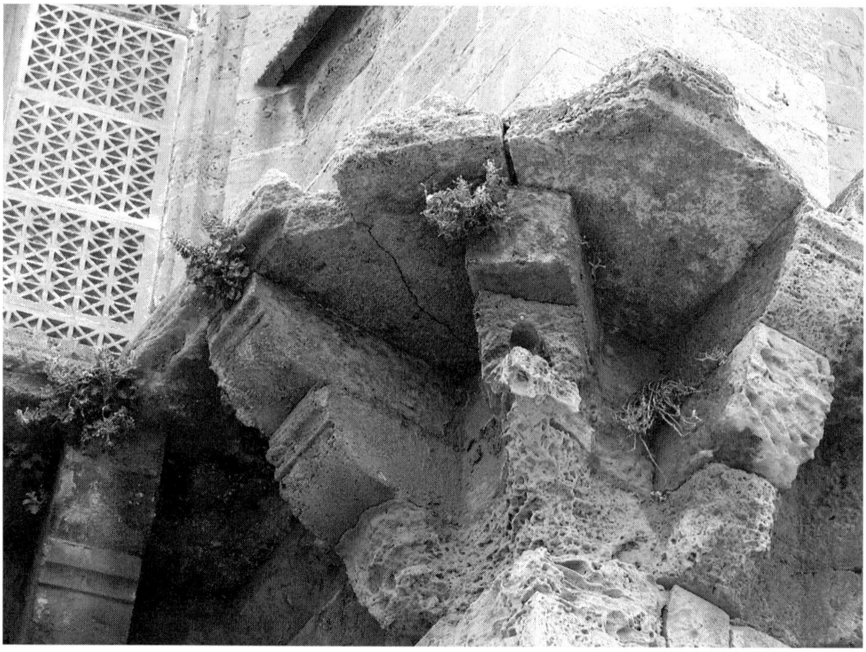

Fig. 17.4 Eroded brackets on the apse of St Nicholas Cathedral (photograph: Silman and Severson)

Antiquities of Cyprus (RDAC) and the Cyprus Annual Report of the Director of Antiquities (CARDA); photocopies of many of these entries were provided by Dr Walsh and are submitted with this report. These interventions included the reorganization of the city's central square (with the relocation of the Aga Cafer Paşa Fountain near the Venetian Palace), reinforcement of many functional structures (such as the bridge across the moat at the Land Gate) and numerous repairs and partial reconstructions. Work included insertion of many substantial infills using materials and techniques that closely resembled the original building fabric. Among these, the stabilization of the broken wall at the west end of the Church of St George of the Latins and the infill supporting the south wall of the Church of St Nicolaos are examples of aesthetically attractive interventions that have contributed greatly to the stability of the structures.

Among the interventions during this period was a campaign in 1937 and 1938 to stabilize wall paintings, undertaken by one Mrs Bardswell. The documents indicate that this work included application of edgings around the paintings and application of a coat of protective wax. These interventions have contributed greatly to the survival of much of the painted plaster and will likely have great implications for their conservation in the future (see *Wall Paintings and Plasters*, below).

Between 2004 and 2006, a programme of improvement sponsored by the European Union was undertaken to repave the Venetian Palace and the central square of the city, to redirect traffic around the north side of the square and restore the central market building on the north side of the square, known as the Bandabuliya. The latter project transformed a traditional open market structure into a sterile, 'shopping mall'-like space with a handful of cafes and restaurants but without the character typically associated with a vital, working market. Under the same auspices, a project to stabilize and restore the Sea Gate in the city wall, near the port, was begun, but work was stopped, reportedly due to dissatisfaction with the quality and character of the restorations; this structure remains closed to the public with no evidence of ongoing activity inside.

In 2006, a USAID funded capacity building project by International Resources Group (IRG), through their Supporting Activities that Value the Environment (SAVE) programme, was initiated to provide demonstration/training sessions to local participants in modern stone conservation techniques. Using the Cafer Paşa Fountain and the ancient Roman sarcophagus on the west side of the main square as a project site, the stones were cleaned, missing elements replaced with new dimension stone, and the fountain structure pointed with lime mortars (this project was directed by K. Severson). The same group has cleaned the interior of the Church of SS Peter and Paul, secured the open windows and gaps in the masonry against pigeons, and within the past 60 days, conducted a laser scanning documentation survey of the structure.

Several small-scale structures in and around the city centre have been recently converted into restaurants and taverns. These include the Monk's Inn, on a side street to the south of the St Nicholas/Lala Mustafa Camii, the Ginko Restaurant in the medrese of the Lala Mustafa Camii, on the east side of the main square, Jax Bar, on a side street off the south side of the main square, and the Hammam Inn, in the Ottoman bath building adjoining the Church of St Francis on the north west corner of the main square. These seem to be effective and sensitively done examples of adaptive re-use of historic structures. There is considerable additional historic building stock in the city that could be likewise adapted for touristic enhancement while preserving the character and historic building fabric.

Wall Paintings and Plasters

Many of the historic churches in the city, as well as some of the secular buildings, retain *in situ* fragmentary wall plasters with a considerable amount of surviving polychromy. Based on visual inspection (no sampling or field analyses undertaken during this visit) substrates consist of a single thin layer (0.5–1.5cm. thick) of traditional lime mortar. Painting appears to have been executed in a combination of *fresco bono* and *secco* technique, along with a few incised or raised elements in substrates (primarily halos). There are very few instances of multiple layers of painting; one example was spotted in the vaulting on the north side of St Simeon church, one of the oldest structures in the city. In a very few places the plasters have been scored for application of a subsequent layer of mortar, but this is rare and is likely from the period after the Ottoman conquest. One valuable feature of the plastered and painted decorations is the historical incised graffiti. These marks often depict the ships of visiting sailors, as well as inscriptions with names, dates and other texts, some dating to the sixteenth century. The graffiti are a subject of particular interest to Dr Walsh who has published an article on the subject.

In truncated ruins, wall paintings and plasters have generally survived only in protected areas, such as the undersides of vaults or under surviving roof structures, but in a few cases some have also survived on very exposed walls. Conditions of the paintings and plasters range from very well preserved fragments (such as the underside of the vaults on the south side of St George of the Greeks) to badly eroded passages where the painting only survives as a ghost and the substrates are crumbly and rough. Where mortars survive, they appear to be generally well attached to the walls, but there are invariably edges that are now crumbling and separating. Where paintings are partially exposed, there are varying degrees of loss and soiling primarily by airborne particulates. In the apse of St George of the Greeks, small cleaning tests have been undertaken (Plate 23). Where paintings are very exposed, they are seriously impacted by biological growth in addition to erosion.

The best preserved wall painting cycles are to be found inside the churches with surviving roofs: the Armenian Church and the Church of St Anne, with some surviving fragments in the Tanner's Church and a very important example of a *sinopia* in SS Peter and Paul. It is reported that the Armenian Church was used during the military actions of the 1970s for housing and it appears to have been used later for administrative purposes; it is now out of use and unsecured, with recent graffiti on some walls and numerous pigeons in the building. The lower portion of the church has been painted white up to approximately three metres, covering much wall painting (heads of saints can be seen just above the line of paint on the east wall). In places the plasters are detaching from the walls and empty edgings indicate some recent losses.

Similarly, St Anne's was used by the Turkish military but has recently been turned over to the Turkish Cypriot Educational Authorities (see Allan Langdale and Michael Walsh, 'A Short Report on Three Newly Accessible Churches in the Syrian Quarter of Famagusta', *Journal of Cyprus Studies*, 2008). The walls inside the church have been painted white up to about seven metres from the floor; however, the lower section at the east and west ends are not painted (Plate 15, and see also Figures 12.6 and 12.7) Up to a point about three and a half or four metres on the north and south walls, the painted plaster was covered before painting with a layer of cement, c. 3cm. thick. In looking at the edges of this layer it appears that a separating layer of masonite-like fibreboard was installed prior to application of the cement; traces of the fibreboard are visible in places at the edges. Examination of the junction of the modern floor (installed after the cement layer) and the walls at the east and west ends of the church reveal traces of similar covers, but these are now removed. The paintings at either end of the church are somewhat damaged, but generally survived the covering and subsequent removal process. The edges of the cement suggest that wooden strapping was nailed to the walls

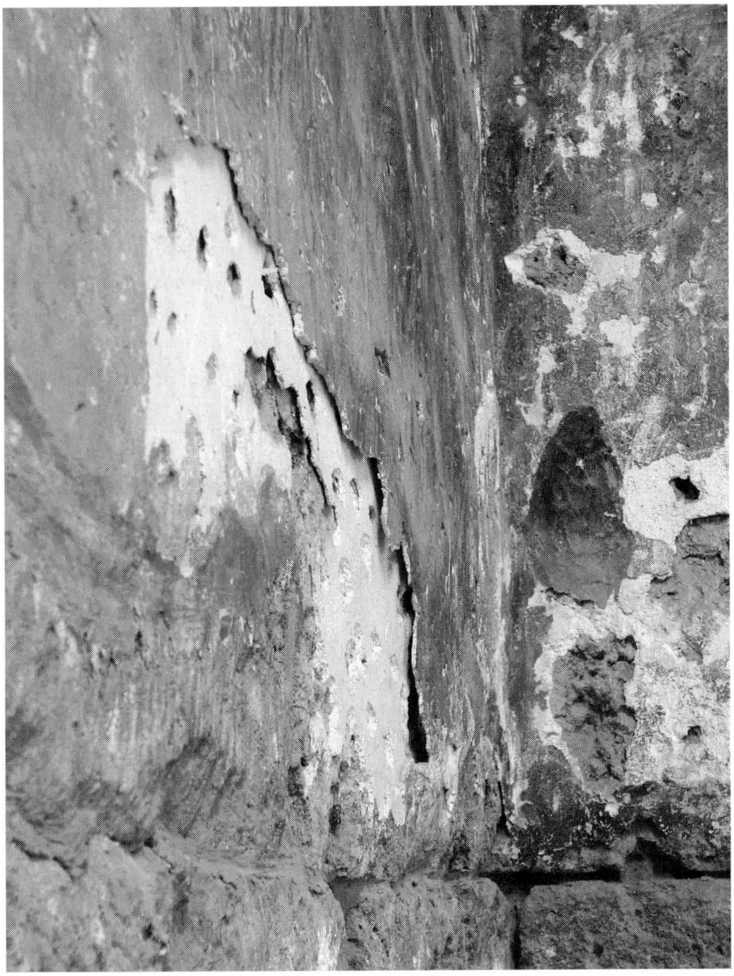

Fig. 17.5 Potential plaster loss in the Church of St Anne (photograph: Silman and Severson)

as formers and anchors for the protective mortar. Examination of the edges of the remaining cement covers reveals many areas where the cement came around the edges of the strapping and is in direct contact with the wall painting. In other areas, however, the cement cover is pulling away from the wall painting cleanly. This evidence suggests that the paintings beneath the remaining cement covers may survive. By delicately separating the cement from the edges, it may be possible to remove the cement covers with only minimal damage to the paintings. The plaster substrate at the west end of the church and returning at the corners on both the north and south sides is detaching from the wall at the bottom edge and is in immediate danger of serious loss (Figure 17.5). The stone inside a niche on the north wall is severely eroded; the void is partially filled with mortared bricks and mortared cast cement block. The masonry in the area above this niche is unstable.

None of the white paint in either of these churches was tested for solubility. The paintings are slightly waxy to the touch probably as a result of the work of Mrs Bardswell in the 1930s. If the waxy layer is sufficiently thick, it may act as a release layer, greatly facilitating the safe removal of the white paint.

The *sinopia* on the south wall of the Church of SS Peter and Paul does not appear to have been affected by the recent cleaning of the interior of the building (Plate 9). The painting is fragile, and the plaster is unsecured (without protective edgings), leaving it vulnerable to further loss. There are additional painted plasters on the south and west walls in the second storey gallery; these were not examined in this visit, but were briefly examined by Severson 2007. These, like the *sinopia*, are fragile, unsecured and separating slightly from the wall.

Political Issues

As deterioration due to natural forces continues, efforts to mitigate these conditions are hampered by the paralysis of local authorities brought on by the ongoing political situation. Although the resulting neglect of the ancient monuments has in a sense protected them from overzealous interventions, the city is growing. It is reported anecdotally that many residents are renting their residential properties inside the city walls to recent immigrants (primarily from Turkey) and relocating to newer development outside the city walls, particularly to the west and north, where there are numerous new luxury hotels and casinos, residences, and the campus of Eastern Mediterranean University.

It can be expected that with the eventual reunification of the island there will be a massive influx of attention from not only the tourism industry, but from developers and local residents seeking to capitalize on redevelopment. Reunification will also bring a dramatic upswing in traffic at the port facility, part of which is just outside the city walls to the east. Protection of both the ancient monuments and the unique environment created by the walled city during this transformation will require strong political will. All aspects relating to the ancient monuments of the area under Turkish Cypriot administration are administered by the Directorate of Ancient Buildings and Museums (Eski Eserler ve Müzeler Dairesi). This area is divided into regional offices with a director for each region and the current director of the Famagusta region is Mr Hasan Tekel. Effective preservation of the monuments in the area under Turkish Cypriot administration will depend on revitalization of this administrative apparatus (particularly with regard to conservation issues) and careful integration with the better developed equivalent institution in the Republic of Cyprus.

At the time of the visit, Dr Walsh was about to depart for a conference he organized entitled *Medieval and Renaissance Famagusta: A Workshop for the Advanced Study of History, Art & Architecture in the Historic City* (see his Nomination to the WMF, Section 8.1, p. 10). He communicated that one goal of the conference was to persuade representatives of UNESCO to develop an alternative classification for cultural heritage sites in occupied territories that would permit greater funding for preservation prior to reunification. This would be an important first step to breaking the political logjam that has paralysed preservation efforts in the northern regions of Cyprus. In April, Dr Walsh forwarded the press release from Europa Nostra detailing a joint statement by the Greek and Turkish Cypriot representatives of Famagusta stating their dedication to the preservation of the Historic City. This positive step is due largely to Dr Walsh's dedication and capable management of the sensitive political issues involved.

Basic Recommendations

The scale of preserving the remaining historic elements of Famagusta is of such enormous proportions that one almost does not know where to begin. It is quite clear that an overall preservation philosophy needs to be developed, written into a document and agreed upon by all of the stakeholders. In this document decisions must be made as to the standards that are to be adopted, which are to be saved as buildings and which as stabilized ruins, the priorities for the work, the identity of the decision makers and the regulators/enforcers of the rules – something like a master plan. Budgets will then need to be established and realistic estimates of funding sources identified. Assuming that the prioritized schedule of work will extend for many years, all emergency stabilization efforts must be highlighted and immediate threats of loss of fabric or collapse dealt with at once with the first available funds. Most of the sites are open to the public and a good deal of thought needs to be addressed to securing the sites against vandalism. Again, a prioritized security system will have to be developed as not all sites can be protected equally well. The documentation effort alone will take a huge amount of person-power, time and money. Standards of documentation must be developed as part of the master plan. Perhaps some of the latest technological tools such as computer tablet annotation and attribute systems can be used.

While each of the buildings that make up Historic Famagusta has its own unique set of problems, the similarity in building fabric and mechanisms of deterioration threatening these structures do not vary widely. These include:

- Lack of security.
- Structural instability of many of the remaining fragments.
- Instability resulting from the Ottoman bombardment.
- Erosion of primary dimension stone.
- Loss of mortar in joints and mortared rubble core due to water ingress.
- Deteriorating or inappropriate modern repairs.
- Damage to churches resulting from change in governance of the city from Christian to Muslim.

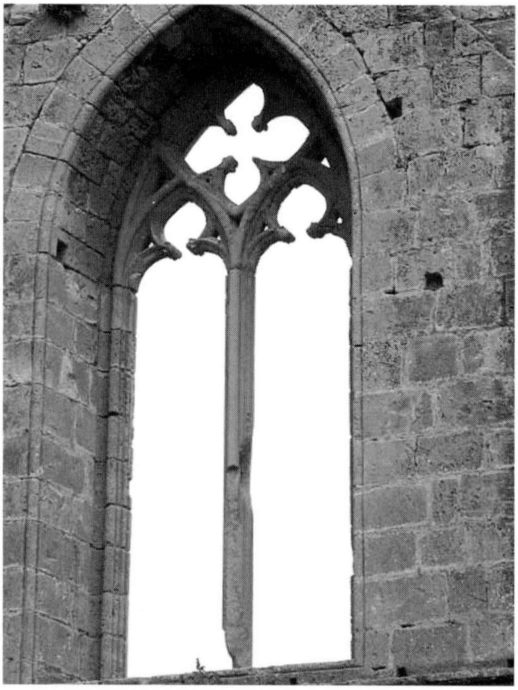

Fig. 17.6 The erosion of previous restorations, St George of the Greeks (photograph: Silman and Severson)

Immediate Interventions

In the course of this visit, several places that would benefit from immediate intervention were identified:

- St George of the Greeks: the stone tracery in the second window on the south wall of the nave was restored in 1936 (see RDAC 1936). The bottom of the central column is now split, with some loss of material (probably concrete), revealing rusting iron reinforcements. This restoration is in danger of collapse and should be provided with temporary shoring. Several walls and buttresses are totally free standing and require immediate bracing (Figure 17.6).
- St Mary of the Carmelites: This beautifully proportioned church has one very serious problem with a large Gothic arch in the north wall that is loaded so asymmetrically (a high stone wall on one half and nothing on the other half) that collapse appears imminent (see also Figure 7.3). The well-preserved ribbed vault of the apse is in somewhat less danger but the unravelling of the upper walls on both the north and south sides of the apse will eventually destabilize this element.
- St Anne: the wall paintings at the west end of the nave, where the cement covers have been removed, are extremely fragile and substantial sections could collapse with even the most casual hand contact. At minimum, a stanchion and rope barrier with warning signs

in several languages should be installed in front of this area to warn visitors not to touch the plasters. As soon as possible, a conservator with demonstrable experience in stabilization of wall plasters should be engaged to develop and execute an emergency stabilization programme.

Summary

There can be little doubt that the Historic Walled city of Famagusta is a first-rate historic site, deserving of the support of World Monuments Fund and one that ultimately should be listed as a World Heritage Site. It is hoped that a new interim status in the UNESCO designation system can be formulated, but it is likely that until the current political situation is resolved, little can be done for most of the structures. The work done at the church of SS Peter and Paul is an example of an isolated initiative, unguided by any sort of master plan or overall effort at preservation of the monuments of Famagusta. Although no harm was done to the fabric of the church (only cleaning and non-destructive testing), the city would be better served were this work integrated into a larger plan.

Threats to the structures and character of Famagusta include ongoing natural deterioration of buildings and ruins through weathering and potential seismic activity, as well as pressure from ongoing growth of the city and unrestricted development. Solutions to the natural deterioration, primarily pointing and filling voids in eroded stone, bracing unstable elements, general weatherproofing, seismic mitigation, and the stabilization and cleaning of wall paintings are relatively straightforward, requiring little additional research beyond application of generally accepted conservation methodology to the individual structures. What makes preservation of the buildings of Famagusta particularly challenging is the sheer quantity of building fabric in need of attention.

With the eventual reunification of the island will doubtless come a dramatic increase in traffic (both touristic and industrial) and developmental pressures. Meanwhile, the structures and the environment in and around the city continue to degrade. It is therefore of vital importance to increase the world's awareness of the special qualities of Famagusta and to lay the necessary ground work for an appropriate evolution of the city from an isolated gem to an accessible, well-protected historic urban site.

Appendices

Appendix I

Address delivered by Michael J. K. Walsh in Paris, 4 April 2008

In Frodsham and Langdale's film *The Stones of Famagusta* we are taken on a tour of a majestic and noble city. We are left in the closing scenes, however, with images of a setting sun and a stark warning: 'Architectural history does not repeat itself. Once gone, these monuments to the world's architectural heritage will be lost forever.' One hundred and seven years earlier, in 1901, a similar warning was issued by a distraught Englishman who pleaded:

> Famagusta is one of the most precious specimens of medieval fortification left in the world. It can never be reproduced or reborn, since the time that bred it is dead. Now in our enlightened age, when we know the value of such relics, are the remains of the old city to be wantonly destroyed before our eyes?[1]

These are the words that bring us here today. It seems that we are *not* heeding the repeated warnings – while time, for many of the structures and monuments, is running out. A Cypriot city, steeped in the art and architecture of countless other cultures, over a thousand years, is desperately in need of help. Any other city, so historically important, and so densely packed with the remnants and relics of such a rich and turbulent history, would be the destination for NGOs, grants and University research/restoration projects. The unique political climate in Cyprus has not permitted this for some time, however, and so the last significant attention received by the historic monuments of Famagusta was in the 1950s. But it would be a mistake to believe that the problems started in the twentieth century. In fact the decline, the neglect, has been going on much longer than that as we can read in the words of a travelling monk who, in the mid-eighteenth century recorded the ghostly urban spectacle:

---

1 R.H. Haggard, *A Winter Pilgrimage* (London, 1901), p. 153.

> In it [Famagusta] there are old buildings and beautiful churches ... Who having seen the beauty ... will not weep about it, or who having seen the skill and the art with which [they have] been constructed will not be amazed by it? And there is no hope or power, which can restore them or take care of them, and they will forever remain forsaken, deserted and abandoned.[2]

We are here to ensure that that prophecy is not realized. Why else would the World Monuments Fund have placed the entire walled city on their 2007 list of the world's 100 most endangered sites, and why too would ICOMOS have included a chapter called 'Famagusta: An Appeal for International Cooperation', in their 2008 publication *Heritage at Risk*? The World Monuments Fund inspectors who visited Famagusta earlier this week said that work needed to begin 'today'. The appeal this morning, therefore, is simple. Famagusta needs international expertise and funding. Something so important, so delicate, so irreplaceable, cannot be ignored any longer.

This meeting is vitally important for the city, but if we leave today and forget about Famagusta, then it has achieved nothing. Instead, this has to be the beginning of a new era of concern, cooperation and collective cultural responsibility. While the academics gather at the National Archive later to share their expertise and to work towards a book on the historical and artistic importance and fragility of Famagusta, in absolute reality the destiny of the city and its tangible remains, lie with the people in this room and the influence they can exert when they leave. Words alone can do nothing to save one of the most important urban landscapes in the entire Eastern Mediterranean.

If you could see Famagusta you would not be able to ignore it. With that in mind, I invite you to watch the following film, and to celebrate with Frodsham and Langdale the triumph that is Famagusta. I urge you, however, to heed this latest warning, so that triumph is not allowed to turn to tragedy. This *is* our responsibility.

---

2 The archive from which this passage comes, which also houses drawings of Famagusta by the travelling monk, is the Akademija Nauk in Kiev. Cited in R. Severis, *Travelling Artists in Cyprus* (London 2000), 18.

Appendix II: Press Release

PRESS RELEASE

Agreement reached by Greek and Turkish Cypriots to join forces to save their Historic Town of Famagusta

EUROPA NOSTRA

Fédération européenne du patrimoine culturel
Pan-European Federation for Cultural Heritage

Présidente / President
S.A.R. La Infanta Doña Pilar de Borbón

Président exécutif / Executive President
Andrea H. Schuler

Efforts to save Famagusta, once known as the richest city in the world, have brought together the Turkish and Greek Cypriot Representatives of this legendary town to work together on this unique and timely rescue initiative.

Paris/The Hague, 8 April 2008 - **"There is no future without the past, but the past makes no sense without the future. I am therefore here today to give whole-hearted support to our Turkish Cypriot companions in the task of safeguarding the valuable heritage of Famagusta. At the same time we ask for their support to our endeavours to ensure that promoting culture in Famagusta goes hand in hand with the respect for human rights"**, declared **Alexis Galanos**, Greek Cypriot Representative of Famagusta. Continuing in the same vein, **Oktay Kayalp**, Turkish Cypriot Representative of Famagusta, confirmed a strong desire to **"set aside political problems in order to save the heritage of Famagusta as the heritage of Europe which ought to be handed over to future generations"**. He expressed his hope that this meeting would lead to a brighter future for the citizens of both communities.

Under the guidance of Europa Nostra, the pan-European federation for cultural heritage, the highest representatives of the Greek Cypriot and the Turkish Cypriot communities of the city of Famagusta, **Alexis Galanos** and **Oktay Kayalp** made a unique joint public appearance at the Representation of the European Commission in France on Friday 4 April in the aim of saving their historic city from further decay. This important bi-communal initiative of cooperation in the field of cultural heritage follows on from the public meeting which took place in December 2007 at the Ledra Palace Hotel, in the UN Buffer Zone in Nicosia under the auspices of the United Nations.

The meeting organised by Europa Nostra aimed to raise the awareness of the international community on the urgent need for launching an major conservation programme to safeguard Famagusta's remaining cultural heritage; and to facilitate the desire of both communities in Famagusta to establish the most suitable coordinating structure through which funds may be made available for such a conservation programme without giving rise to legal or political dispute.

Denis de Kergorlay, Europa Nostra's Vice-President who moderated the meeting, stated **"It is high time that Famagusta be brought out of oblivion back into the European public consciousness. Europa Nostra is prepared to work very hard to contribute to the revival of Famagusta's unique cultural heritage and to raise awareness of the public out large on the highly significant place occupied by Famagusta in shared European history. A successful "Famagusta project" should therefore become a symbol of renewal and dialogue"**.

The meeting in Paris was also the occasion for screening the international premiere of **"The Stones of Famagusta - the Story of a Forgotten City"**, a feature length documentary which showcases the beauty and the historic importance of the city. Film-makers **Allan Langdale** (Canada) and **Dan Frodsham** (UK) were present to discuss the film and to encourage its wider distribution throughout Europe and beyond.

Michael Walsh, convenor of the international expert colloquium on Medieval Famagusta used the metaphor of the setting sun in the closing scene of the documentary film to highlight that this should serve as a stark warning that

Lange Voorhout 35
NL - 2514 EC Den Haag
tel + 31 70 302 40 50
fax + 31 70 361 78 65
office@europanostra.org
www.europanostra.org

"Time is running out for the monuments and works of art which are in dire need of international expertise and funding". He concluded by emphasising that the future of Famagusta is a shared European responsibility and issued an urgent plea for all actors to keep the momentum of this meeting and to put forward concrete proposals for joint action.

Costa Carras, Vice-President of Europa Nostra, underlined that **"culture can work as one of the creative forces in European society that brings people together, and that Europa Nostra stands ready to contribute towards making this a reality in Famagusta"**. To this end, **Gianni Perbellini**, President of Europa Nostra's Scientific Council, offered the scientific expertise of Europa Nostra to accompany any future conservation work to be carried out according to the highest international standards.

During the debate that ensued, participants concluded the need for all to take up responsibility for the shared European history and for the European spirit to prevail in a future common project to safeguard and restore Famagusta's cultural heritage. Hope was also expressed that working together in restoring common cultural heritage in Famagusta and elsewhere in Cyprus could contribute to solving other problems that are faced, conjointly and separately, by the Greek Cypriot and Turkish Cypriot communities in Cyprus.

FAMAGUSTA

The fabled city of Famagusta, located in North-East Cyprus, has been over many centuries at the crossroads between the West and the East and has played a pivotal role in the history of military, trade and cultural relations between the Christian and Islamic Worlds. The heritage treasures of this city combine medieval Christian churches, Venetian gateways, Ottoman mosques and baths and some of the most impressive city walls to be seen anywhere in the world. Famagusta, once known as the richest city in the world, was in medieval times (13th-16th centuries) ruled by the French dynasty of Lusignans. It then fell under the domination first of Genoa and then of the Venetian Republic (as a Venetian stronghold it served as the setting for Shakespeare's Othello), and eventually became an important Ottoman harbour city after 1571. There is no place like it anywhere else in the world. Threatened by earthquakes, abandonment and neglect, this beautiful historic city with the tangible remains of so many cultures is now in a severe state of deterioration and action is urgently needed to salvage this precious heritage. Famagusta was therefore recently placed on the 2008 World Monuments Watch List of 100 Most Endangered Sites. For all these reasons, the Greek Cypriot and the Turkish Cypriot representatives of Famagusta decided to join forces in an attempt to raise the awareness of the European/International community about the plight of their city and to work together in harmony for the common good.

INTERNATIONAL EXPERT COLLOQUIUM

In addition to this unique initiative between the Greek Cypriot and Turkish Cypriot Mayors of Famagusta, a two-day international colloquium was held (4-5 April 2008, National Archives of Paris) to bring together, also for the first time, the most prominent scholars from Europe and beyond to discuss the European and global significance of the history and architecture of Famagusta.

Appendix III
Chronology of Venetian Administration, for Dating the Coats of Arms of Famagusta

Part I: *Luogotenenti* [Lieutenants] (Civil Governors)

1489–1491	Francesco Barbarigo
1491–1493	Girolamo Pesaro
1493–1495	Giovanni Donato
1495–1497	Andrea Barbarigo
1497–1499	Cosimo Pasqualigo
1499/1500–1501	Andrea Venier
1501–1503	Nicola Priuli
1503–1505	Pietro Balbi
1505–1507	Cristoforo Moro
1507–1509	Lorenzo Giustiniani
1509–1511	Nicola Pesaro
1511–1514	Paolo Gradenigo
1514–1516	Donato Marcello
1516–1518	Fantino Michiel
1518–1519	Alvise d'Armer
1519–1522	Sebastiano Moro
1522–1523	Jacopo Badoer
1523–1525	Domenico Capello
1525–1527	Donato di Lezze
1527–1529	Silvestro Minio
1529–1531	Francesco Bragadin
1531–1533	Marcantonio Trevisan
1533–1535	Stefano Tiepolo
1535–1536	Giovanni Moro
1536–1539	Domenico da Mosto
1539–1541	Francesco Badoer
1541–1543	Cristoforo Capello
1543–1545	Luigi Riva
1545–1547	Carlo Capello

1547–1548	Vittorio Barbarigo
1548–1550	Salvatore Michiel
1550–1551	Alessandro Contarini
1551–1553	Francesco Capello
1553–1555	Marco Grimani
1555–1557	Gianbattista Donato
1557–1559	Giovanni Renier
1559–1561	Giovanni Barbaro
1561–1563	Pietro Navagero
1563–1565	David Trevisan
1565–1566	Pandolfo Guoro
1566–1567	Nicola Querini
1567–9 Sept. 1569	Nicola Dandolo
1569–1570	Sebastiano Venier

Part II: *Capitani* [Captains] (Military Governors)

1480–1483	Giovanni Diedo
1483–1485	Francesco Cicogna
1485–1488	Daniele Bembo
1488–1489	Matteo Barbaro
1489–1491	Baltassare Trevisan
1491–1493	Nicolò Foscarini
1493–1495	Cosimo Pasqualigo
1495–1497	Nicolo Priuli
1497–1499	Bartolomeo Minio
1499 –1501	Troilo Malipiero
1501	Girolamo Bon
1501–1503	Lorenzo Contarini
1503–1505	Paolo Antonio Marin
1505–1507	Domenico Benetti
1507–1509	Benetto Sanudo
1509–1511	Pietro Lion
1511–1514	Luigi Contarini
1514–1516	Giovanni Centani
1516–1518	Vincenzo Cappello
1518–1520	Bartolomeo da Mosto
1520–1522	Zaccaria Loredan
1522–1525	Nicolò Dolfin
1525–1526	Andrea Donato
1526–1527	Marcantonio Canale
1527–1530	Anzolo Trevisan
1530–1532	Antonio Soriano
1532–1534	Tommaso Contarini

1534–1535	Domenico Contarini
1535–1537	Lunardo Venier
1537–1538	Maffio Pisani
1538	Giovanni Gritti
1538–1540	Giovanni Contarini
1540–1542	Nicolò Giustiniani
1542–1544	Giovanni Contarini (2nd time)
1544–1546	Andrea Dandolo
1546–1548	Gian Matteo Bembo
1548–1550	Francesco Grimani
1550–1552	Marco Loredano
1552–1554	Giovanni Renier
1554–1556	Cornelio Barbaro
1556–1558	Pietro Navagero
1558–1560	Domenico Trevisan
1560–1562	Pandolfo Guoro
1562–1564	Nicolo Gabriel
1564–1566	Lorenzo Bembo
1566–1569	Marco Michiel
1569–15 Aug 1571	Marcantonio Bragadin

Appendix IV: Armenian Manuscript Colophons from Famagusta and Cyprus

Compiled by Dickran Kouymjian

DATE	PLACE	SCRIBE	PATRON	TEXT	MANUSCRIPT
1280	*Kipros, i durn Srbuhoy Astuacacnin*	Petros of Cilicia		Gospel	NJ33; Mat'evosyan, #408
1287	*Kipros: S. Var'var'a, S. Zoravarin Sargis*	Khach'atur grich' (scribe), Alidz, 3 others	Abraham	Gospel	M6845, *Mat. Cat.* II, col. 405
1305	*Kipros; Maghuayn Kiprosu*, corrected by Ghevond to *Maghu[s]ayn*, p. 56	Yōhannēs grogh (scribe), also mentions Georg vardapet		Collation of Bible, 1773, citing various earlier colophons	This from a Jer. ms. Dashian, p. 632 [not J1926 of 1308-1309]; quoted in Ghevond, p. 56; not in Xač'ikyan, *14th Colophons*
1305, 1308	Het'um/Hayton in Cyprus				Kapoïan, p. 56
1306	Famous island of *Kipros*, in the village called *Čips (Djips)* under the protection of the archangels Mikayel & Gabriel	Levon the priest		Psalm Book, f. 685	J1033, *Jer. Cat.* IV (1969), pp. 45 ff.
1308	[*Kipros*?]	Levon	Patron T'oros the priest	Psalm book, f. 648	J1714, *Jer. Cat.* VI (1972), p. 22
1308, 1309	*Kipros, i Maghusa k'aghak'*. (No mention of St. Mary)	Yovanes, Yohannēs	K'ahanay (priest) Step'anos	Old Testament, ff. 268v, 426v	J1926, *Jer. Cat.* VI (1972), p. 417
1310	*Kipros kghzi* (island)	Step'annos Goynerec'anc'anc', earlier scribe		Acts of the Apostles	J700, *Jer. Cat.* III (1968), f. 651, p. 145
pre-1311	Kipros and Akner	?		Gospel	M9450, *Mat.* II, 931
1310, 1312	Kipros, *i Maghusay, hovaneaw S. Astuacacin*	Step'anos Goynereric'anc'	Lady Alic, daughter of Baron Het'um	New Testament and Lectionary	Gherla 2(13), Xač'ikyan, *14th Cent.*, #92; K'olanjyan, pp. 436-7

1314	*Kipros, k‘. Maghusa, i vanks hayoc‘, end hov. S. Astuacacin*	Step‘anos Goy-nere[r]ic‘anc‘		Cisakan	J265, *Jer. Cat.* II (1967), pp.59-61, f.300v
1316	*Lek‘osia (Nicosia)*	Smbat	Step‘anos k‘ahanay	Psalter	M3412. *Mat.* I, col. 1006
1317	*Kipros, Maghust, dur‘n astucoy mor tačarin Astuacacnin [or e vank‘ ev koč‘i kanč‘ut],* mistaken reconstruction	Yohannēs, servant of God	Yohannēs	Commentary on Liturgy, Nersēs Lambronac‘i	Xač‘ikyan, *14th Cent.*, #175, p. 135
1317	*Kipros kghzi, i dur‘n Astucoy mór tačarin Astuacacnin, or ē vank‘, ev koč‘i kanč‘vor i k‘aghak‘is Maghusa.*	Yovhanēs vardapet, patron, scribe, editor	Same as previous	Commentary on Liturgy, Kh. Anjevac‘i & N. Lambronac‘i, f. 664	J1141, *Jer. Cat.* IV (1969), p. 226
1317	*Kipros, Kanč‘uor i k‘aghak‘is Maghusa[y] …*	Yovhan[n]ēs	Same as previous	Commentary on Liturgy, f.100, 1840, St. James,	J2254, *Jer. Cat.* VII (1974), p. 349
1317-1318	*Kipros, S. Sargis*	T‘oros	T‘oros; binder Sahag	New Testament	M242, *Mat. Cat.* I, cols. 280–81
1310 1311 1317 1318	*Kipros, S. Astuacacin, S. Varvar‘a, S. Sargis, S. Makar* Churches	Step‘annōs Goynereric‘anc, Yovhannēs, T‘oros			*Encyclopedia*, II, p. 694
1341	*Kipros, Levk‘osia* = Nicosia	Poghos		Miscellany, f. 36,	J1337, *Jer. Cat.*. IV (1969), p. 604
1379	*Kipros*		Sargis kahanay (priest)	Bible	M9116, *Mat. Cat.* II, col 873
1426	*Kipros*	Gaspar Hamt‘ec‘i		Commentary on Catholic letters, Sargis Shnorhali	M6262, Xač‘ikyan, *15th Cent.*, vol. 1, #373, p. 354

DATE	PLACE	SCRIBE	PATRON	TEXT	MANUSCRIPT
1467	*Lamōshay* =?Limassol, *i kipros kghzodj, i mayrak'aghak' Lewk'usieay* (Nicosia)		Bp. Sargis prelate	Yaysmavork'	Xač'ikyan, *15th Cent.*, vol. 2, #340, p. 266; Ghevond, pp. 99–100, text
1468	*Kipros: S. Astuacacin, S. Barseghay ekegh. yishatak or ē i Kipros*	Martiros		Gospels, f. 267	Xač'ikyan, *15th Cent.*, vol. 2 , #359, p. 279; Munich #1, *HA* (1891), p. 238
1581	*i Kipros kghzi*	Hayrapet abeghay		Hymnal	Ghevond, p.102
1636	*Kipros, Lawk'oshia* (Nicosia), *i dur'n S. Astuacacnay*			Ancient Arm mss	J3848, *Jer. Cat.* XI (1991), ms of 1912, p. 284
1641, 1648	*Kipr'un, end hovaneav S. Astuacacnis, i kghzis i Kiprun, i k'aghak'n Lōk'ōshay* (Nicosia)	Step'annos erec' (priest)		Ritual	*Encyclopedia*, II, 1641, p. 694
1650	*i yanpatē Kirposi, or S. Makar anun koč'i*	Tonapet dpir (clerk)		Psalm Book	Ghevond, p. 102
1668	*Lawk'oč'a* (Nicosia); *S. Astuacacin*			Lectionary'	Ghevond, p. 103
1670 1674	*i covoc' kghzi i Kēpros or mak anun Gheprez..k'. Lawk'óshay, katoghikē ekegh. or Astuacacnin*	Yohanēs episkopos.	Later colophon of Tēr Karapet K'ésabc'I, 1793,1795	Hymns of Yovhanēs	Ghevond, pp. 105–6; *Encyclopedia*, II, p. 694 for 1674
1671	*Kipros*	Sargis gronavor (cleric)	Cypriot vardapet	Miscellany	M2022, *Mat. Cat.* I, col.702; *Encyclopedia*. II, p. 694
1675	*Kipros, Lawk'ashé, I dur'n S. Astuacacnin*			Gospels	J1967, *Jer. Cat.* VI (1972)
1679	*Nikosioy S. Astuacacnin ekegh*	Vardan vardapet		Lectionary	Ghevond, p.103

Abbreviations

Dashian	Jacobus Dashian, *Catalog den armenischen handscriften in der Mechitaristen-bibliothek zu Wien* (in Armenian with German title and résumé), Vienna, 1895
ekegh.	*ekeghec'i*, church
Encyclopedia	*Abridged Armenian Encyclopedia*, vol. II, Erevan, 1995 (in Armenian)
Ghevond	Bishop Ghevond (C'épéyan), *Yishadakaran kiprahay gaghut'i* (Memorial on the Cypriot-Armenian Community), Antelias, 1955
HA	*Handēs Amsorya*
J	Jerusalem manuscript from the Armenian Patriarchate of St. James
Jer. Cat.	Norayr Bogharian, *Grand Catalogue of St. James Manuscripts*, 11 vols, in Armenian with English title, Jerusalem, 1966–91
k'	*k'aghak'*, city
Kapoïan	Angèle Kapoïan-Kouymjian, *L'Égypte vue par des Arméniens*, Paris, 1988
K'olanjyan	Suren K'olanjyan, "Summary Catalogue of the Armenian Manuscripts in the City of Gherla, *Banber Matenadarani*, vol. 9 (1969), pp. 433–85 (in Armenian)
M	Erevan, Mashtoc' Matenadaran Repository of Manuscripts
Mat. Cat.	*Catalogue of Manuscripts in the Mashtoc' Matenadaran*, Erevan, vol. I, 1965, vol. II, 1970 (in Armenian)
Mat'evosyan	Artashes Mat'evosyan, *Hayeren jer'agreri hishatakaranner. XIII dar* (Colophons of Armenian Manuscripts. Thirteenth Century), Erevan, 1984
NJ	New Julfa, Isfahan, manuscript in the Armenian Prelacy
S.	*Sourb*, Saint
Xač'ikyan	Levon Xač'ikyan, *XIV dari Hayeren jer'agreri hishatakaranner* (14th-Century Armenian Manuscript Colophons), Erevan, 1950; *15th Century*, vol. I, 1955, vol. II, 1958

Appendix V: Typed Notes by M[onica] Bardswell, February 1937 from Conway Library, Courtauld Institute

Reproduced by Dickran Kouymjian

Famagusta Armenian Church

14th-century church. Sacked by the Turks in the 16th century.

North Wall

Upper tier, from the west
(A) Series more Italian in style than the rest of the paintings. Plaster tinted buff, green backgrounds.
(1). The Scourging. Christ in centre, bound to pillar. An executioner to the right and to left with whip of knotted thongs. A building top left.
(2) ? Christ before Pilate. Mostly, perished. Christ centre left faces right, hands bound before Him. Right part of picture missing.
(3) Crucifixion. Skull of Adam under the cross. Left, Virgin fainting in the arms of the two Maries, to right, St John. All the upper part gone.
(4) ? Deposition. (very faint) Several figures to right.
(5) Entombment, or Pieta. Several Figures carry the body of Christ wrapped in winding sheet and laid across the lap of the Virgin. A female figure stands behind.

Lower tier below (A).
(B) Another series, more Byzantine in style and more coarsely painted. Enclosed in red frames edged white. From the west:
(1) Very large, Nativity; the Virgin reclines centre, Child in an oblong box on her left. Left at top, four nimbed figures in adoration. Right at top, a group of angels in adoration. Left centre, Magi, not nimbed, bearing gifts. Left at bottom, two midwives prepare the bath.

(2). Over arched recess, Annunciation, very fragmentary. To left St. Gabriel. To right the Blessed Virgin Mary. Centre, pot of lilies. (Vase with two handles).
(3) Baptism of Christ. Green background. To left St. John the Baptist. Stands on the bank of a stream and pours water on head of Christ, who stands in the stream naked, water up to middle. (Not heaped up water). To right two angels stand on the bank. Of most of this subject only the under-painting remains; the outline sketched in red.
(4) Image of Pity over a recess, ? Easter sepulcher. Half figure of Christ stands in tomb, hands crossed before Him, showing wounds. Cross behind and two of the Instruments of the Passion, sponge and spear. Background dark blue.

East Wall

(C) The apse and its surroundings.
(1) Respond of arch, a saint, very fragmentary.
(2) Vault of the apse, lower south side: Kneeling figure, head missing, probably the donor, large shield of arms above to left. Kneeling in adoration of ? (Probably once a Majesty on the vault of the apse) Below a string-course, remains of the figures of the Twelve Apostles surrounding the apse. Bearded, nimbed, on dark blue background.
(3) Below were figures of saints within arched canopies. Full length figures, two very fragmentary, remain. On the north side, an Ecclesiastic, Patriarch? On the south side, a figure in red cloak, blessing. Small kneeling donor to the right.

South Wall

(D) To the east. Death of Virgin, she lies on a couch, above is the figure of Our Lord who receives her soul, as a swaddled infant. Our Lord in a white mandorla, and around Him a red glory filled with angels who bear candlesticks, censers, etc. All painted in red and white. Below, left and right Apostles weeping. Above to the right, angels in adoration on a green background.
(E) To the west. Very large figure of St. John the Baptist surrounded by square compartments arranged perpendicularly on either side, containing ? [sic] scenes from his life (all perished) within yellow frame. To left and to right, a strip of ornament containing shields of arms, one of them bearing a mitre and crosier on white shield.

West Wall

(F) South of the door, within a yellow frame and a grey background: St. George on a red horse, slaying a red and green dragon. (Copy by M. Bardswell)

(G) To the north of door, two figures of saints, under arched ornamental canopies, green backgrounds.
(1) On the left a female saint in cloak, who holds a head of our Lord within a medallion. Inscription on the background in Armenian.
(2) On right, a royal personage, nimbed, crowned, wearing much jewellery. Armenian inscription.
Note: the backgrounds, whether blue or green, are put on over an undercoat of black. The under colour of the faces and hands is yellow-green, like raw sienna. Some paintings are drawn in first in red outline, others, (C2 and F) in green.
M.B. Feb. 1937.
All the paintings in the church preserved by M. Bardswell.

Bibliography

The editors elected to list only the key texts utilized in the preparation of this volume.

Original Sources

Documents and Collections of Materials

Aristeidou, A.Ch. (ed.), *Anekdota engrapha tes Kypriakes istorias apo to archeio tes Venetias, 1 (1474–1508) (Pegai kai meletai tes Kypriakas istorias*, vol 16) (Nicosia, 1990).

Balard, M. (ed.), *Notai Genovesi in Oltremare: Atti rogati a Cipro da Lamberto di Sambuceto* (11 ottobre 1296–1323 giugno 1299) (Collana Storica Fonti e Studi [henceforth CSFS] 39, Genoa, 1983).

— (ed.), *Notai Genovesi in Oltremare: Atti rogati a Cipro da Lamberto di Sambuceto* (31 Marzo 1304–19 Luglio 1305, 4 gennaio–12 luglio 1307) e Giovanni de Rocha (3 agosto 1308–14 marzo 1310) (CSFS 43, Genoa, 1984).

Bliznyuk, S. (ed.), *Die Genuesen auf Zypern ende 14. und im. 15. Jahrhundert*, Studien und Texte zur Byzantinistik 6, ed. P. Schreiner (Frankfurt 2005).

Bogharian, N., *Grand Catalogue of St. James Manuscripts*, 11 vols., in Armenian with English title (Jerusalem, 1966–91).

Carbonetti Venditelli, C. (ed.), *Il Registro della cancellaria di Federico II del 1239–1240* (Istituto Storico Italiano per il Medio Evo, Fonti per la storia dell'Italia medievale, Antiquitates, 19/1), 2 vols. (Rome, 2002).

Chazaud, A.-M. (ed.), 'Inventaire et comptes de la succession d'Eudes, comte de Nevers (Acre 1266)', *Mémoires de la Société Nationale des Antiquaires de France*, sér 4: 2 (1871).

Clement V, Pope, *Regestum Clementis papae V.*, ed. cura et studio monachorum Ordinis S. Benedicti, 8 vols (Rome, 1885–92).

Cobham, C.D. (ed. and trans.), *Excerpta Cypria* (Cambridge, 1908; repr. 1969).

Dashian, J., *Catalog den armenischen Handshcriften in der Mechitharisten-Bibliothek zu Wien* (in Armenian with German title and résumé) (Vienna, 1895).

Dehaisnes, C. (ed.), *Documents et extraits divers concernant l'histoire de l'art dans la Flandre, l'Artois et le Hainaut avant le XVe siècle*, 2 vols. (Lille, 1886).

Desimoni, C. (ed.), 'Actes passés à Famagouste de 1299 à 1301 par devant le notaire génois Lamberto di Sambuceto', *Archives de l'Orient latin*, 2, Pt. II (1884).

— (ed.), 'Actes passés à Famagouste de 1299 à 1301 devant le notaire génois Lamberto de Sambuceto', *Revue de l'Orient Latin*, 3 (1893).

Douët-d'Arcq, L. (ed.), *Nouveau recueil de comptes de l'argenterie des rois de France* (Paris, 1874).

Fossati Raiteri, S. (ed), *Genova e Cipro: L'inchiesta su Pietro di Marco capitano di Genova in Famagosta (1448–1449)* (CSFS 41, Genoa 1984).

Gilmour-Bryson, A. (trans.) *The Trial of the Templars in Cyprus. A Complete English Edition* (Leiden, Boston and Cologne, 1998).

Gual Camarena, M., *Vocabolario del comercio medieval. Collección de aranceles aduaneros de la Corona de Aragón* (Siglos XIII y XIV) (Tarragona, 1968).

Guigniaut, J.-D. et J.N. de Wailly (eds), *Recueil des Historiens des Gaules et de la France*, 21 (Paris, 1855).

Huillard-Bréholles, J.L.A. de (ed.), *Historia diplomatica Frederici secundi*, 6 vols. (Paris, 1852–61).

Khach'ikyan, L., *XIV dari Hayeren jer'agreri hishatakaranner* (Fourteenth-Century Armenian Manuscript Colophons) (Erevan, 1950).

Liagre-de Sturler, L., *Les relations commerciales entre Gênes, la Belgique et l'Outremont d'après les archives notariales génoises (1320–1400)* (Brussels-Rome, 1969).

Martène, E. and U. Durand (eds), *Veterum Scriptorum et Monumentorum ... Amplissima Collectio*, 9 vols. (Paris, 1724–33).

Mas Latrie, L. de (ed.), *Histoire de l'île de Chypre sous le règne de la maison de Lusignan*, 3 vols. (Paris, 1852–61).

— (ed.), 'Nouvelles preuves de l'histoire de l'île de Chypre sous le règne des princes de la maison de Lusignan', *Bibliothèque de l'École des Chartes*, 34 (1873).

— (ed.), 'Commerce et expéditions militaires de la France et de Venise au moyen âge', *Collection de documents inédits sur l'histoire de France, Mélanges historiques*, 3 (Paris, 1880).

— (ed.), 'Documents nouveaux servant de preuves à l'histoire de l'île de Chypre sous le règne de la maison de Lusignan', *Collection de documents inédits sur l'histoire de France, Mélanges historiques*, 4 (Paris, 1882).

Mat'evosyan, A., *Hayeren jer'agreri hishatakaranner. XIII dar* (Colophons of Armenian Manuscripts, Thirteenth Century) (Erevan, 1984).

Mogabgab, T.A.H. (ed.), *Supplementary Excerpts on Cyprus* (Nicosia, 1941).

Mogabgab Photographs Archive, Famagusta Department of Antiquities.

Mollat, G. (ed.), *Lettres communes du pape Jean XXII analysées d'après les registres dits d'Avignon et du Vatican*, 16 vols. (Paris, 1904–47).

Otten-Froux, C. (ed.), *Un enquête à Chypre au XVe siècle: Le sindicamentum de Napoleone Lomellini, capitaine Génois de Famaguste (1459)* (Nicosia, 2000).

Otten-Froux, C. (ed.), 'Un notaire vénitien à Famagouste au XIVe siècle. Les actes de Simeone, prêtre de San Giacomo dell'Orio (1362–1371)', *Thesaurismata*, 33 (2003).

Pallavicino, E. (ed.), *I Libri iurium della Repubblica di Genova*, 1/7 (Fonti per la storia della Liguria, XV; Pubblicazioni degli Archivi di Stato, Fonti, vol. 35, Genoa, 2001).

Pavoni, R. (ed.), *Notai Genovesi in Oltremare: Atti rogati a Cipro da Lamberto di Sambuceto (6 luglio–27 ottobre 1301)* (CSFS 32, Genoa, 1982).

— (ed.), *Notai Genovesi in Oltremare: Atti rogati a Cipro da Lamberto di Sambuceto (gennaio–agosto 1302)* (CSFS 49, Genoa, 1987).

Polonio, V. (ed.), *Notai Genovesi in Oltremare: Atti rogati a Cipro da Lamberto di Sambuceto (3 luglio 1300–3 agosto 1301)* (CSFS 31, Genoa, 1982).

Predelli, R. and A. Sacerdoti (eds), *Gli statuti marittimi veneziani fino al 1255* (Venice, 1903).

Richard, J. avec la collaboration de Th. Papadopoullos (eds), *Le livre des remembrances de la Secrète du royaume de Chypre (1468–1469)* (Nicosia, 1983).

Richard, J. (ed.), *Chypre sous les Lusignans. Documents chypriotes des archives du Vatican (XIVe et XVe siècles)* (Paris, 1962).

Röhricht, R., *Regesta regni Hierosolymitani (MXCVII–MCCXCI)*, 2 vols. (Innsbruck, 1893–1904).

— and H. Meissner (eds), *Deutsche Pilgerreisen nach dem Heiligen Lande* (Berlin, 1880).

Sandoli, S. de (ed.), *Itinera Hierosolymitana Crucesignatorum (saec. XII–XIII)*, 4 vols (Jérusalem, 1978–84).

Savorgnano M., *Arte militare terrestre e marittima* (Franceschini: Venezia, 1599).

Schabel, C. (trans.), *The Synodicum Nicosiense and other documents of the Latin Church of Cyprus, 1196–1373* (Nicosia 2001).

Schäfer, K.H. (ed.), *Die Ausgaben der apostolischen Kammer unter Johann XXII. nebst den Jahresbilanzen von 1316–75 mit darstellender Einleitung* (Vatikanische Quellen zur Geschichte der päpstlichen Hof- und Finanzverwaltung, 2 vols., Paderborn, 1911).

Schottmüller, K. (ed.), *Der Untergang des Templer-Ordens*, 2 vols (Berlin, 1887; repr. New York-Vaduz, 1970).

Sopracasa, A. (ed.), *I trattati con il regno armeno di Cilicia* (Pacta veneta, vol. 8, Rome, 2001).

Legal Texts and Narrative Sources

'A New Text of the Annales de Terre Sainte', ed. P.W. Edbury in I. Shagrir, R. Ellenblum and J. Riley-Smith (eds), In *Laudem Hierosolymitani: Studies in the Crusades and Medieval Culture in Honour of Benjamin Z. Kedar* (Aldershot, 2007).

'Annales de Terre Sainte', eds R. Röhricht and G. Raynaud, *Archives de l'Orient latin*, 2 (1884).

'Las cruzadas en la historiografía española de la época: traducción castellana de un redacción desconocida de los "Anales de Tierre Santa"', ed. A. Sánchez Candeira, *Hispania: Revista Española de Historia*, 20 (1960).

'Liber magistri Salmonis (1222–-1226)', ed. A. Ferretto, *Atti della Società ligure di storia patria*, 36 (1906).

Ambroise, *The History of the Holy War: Ambroise's Estoire de la Guerre Sainte*, eds M. Ailes and M. Barber (Woodbridge, 2003).

Andrea Dandolo, 'Chronicon Venetum a pontificatu Santi Marci ad annum usque MCCCXXXIX', in L.A. Muratori (ed.), *Rerum Italicarum Scriptores*, 12 (Milan, 1728).

Angelo Gatto, *Narrazione del terribile assedio e della resa di Famagosta nell'anno nell'anno 1571 da un manoscritto del capitano Angelo Gatto da Orvieto*, ed. P. Catizzani (Orvieto, 1895).

Antoine Maria Gratiani, *Histoire de la Guerre de Chypre, ecrite en latin .. ... Et traduite en Francais par monsieur Le Peletier* (Paris, 1685).

Ascanio Savorgnano, *Breve informazion et resoluzion delle cose più importanti di Cipro et delle provisioni necessarie per quel regno*, Paphos, 7 d'Ottobre 1562, Verona, Municipal Library, Ms 677.

Bartolomeo Sereno, *Commentari della Guerra di Cipro e della Lega dei Principi Cristiani contro il Turco* (Montecassino, 1845).

Bertrandon de la Broquière, *Le Voyage d'Outremer de Bertrandon de la Broquière, premier écuyer tranchant et conseiller de Philippe le Bon, duc de Bourgogne*, ed. C. Schefer (Paris, 1892).

Cesare Campana, *Volume primo, che contiene libri dieci: ne' quali diffusamente si narrano le cose auuenute dall' anno 1570 fino al 1580. Nuouamente stampate, con gli argomenti a ciascun libro. Con vna tauola de' nomi proprij, & delle materie* (Venice, 1599).

Christoforo Brenzone Silvestrini, *Vita e fatti del valorosissimo capitano Astorre Baglioni da Perugia, con la guerra di Cipro* (Verona, 1591).

Chronicles and Memorials of the reign of Richard I, ed. W. Stubbs (London, 1864—65).

Chronique d'Ernoul et de Bernard le Trésorier, ed. L. de Mas Latrie (Paris, 1871).

Chroniques d'Amadi et de Strambaldi, ed. R. de Mas Latrie, 2 vols. (Paris, 1891—93).

Crescenzio, B. *Il crudelissimo assedio, et nova presa della famosissima fortezza di Famagosta*, Milano 1571.

Cronaca del Templare di Tiro (1243—1314), ed and trans. L. Minervini (Naples, 2000).

Del successo in Famagosta, diario di un contemporaneo: Nobili nozze Gozzi – Guaita, ed. L.A. Visinoni (Venice, 1879).

Emmanuel Piloti, *Traité d'Emmanuel Piloti sur le Passage en Terre Sainte* (1420), ed. P.-H. Dopp (Louvain-Paris, 1958).

Excerpta Cypria Nova: Voyageurs occidentaux á Chypre au XVème siècle, ed. G. Grivaud (Nicosia, 1990).

Famagosta, A. da. *La perdita di Famagosta e la gloriosa morte di M.A. Bragadino*, ed. A. Morosini (Venice, 1891).

Florio Bustron, 'Chronique de l'île de Chypre', ed. R. de Mas Latrie, *Collection de Documents inédits sur l'histoire de France: Mélanges historiques*, 5 (Paris, 1886).

Francesco Balducci Pegolotti, *La pratica della mercatura*, ed. A. Evans (Cambridge Mass., 1936).

Francis Altomira, *Narrazione della Guerra di Nicosia, fatta nel Regno di Cipro, da' da' turchi l'anno l'anno 1570* (Bologna, 1571).

George Boustronios, *A Narrative of the Chronicle of Cyprus 1456—1489*, trans. N. Coureas (*Texts and Studies in the History of Cyprus*, vol. 51, Nicosia, 2005).

George Boustronios/Τζώρτζης (Μ)πουστρούς (Γεώργιος Βο(σ)τρ(υ)νός ή Βουστρώνιος), Διήγησις Κρονίκας Κύπρου, ed. G. Kehayioglou (Nicosia 1997).

Georgio Vasari, *Le vite*, eds P. Della Pergola et al. 9 vols. (Novara, 1967).

Giacomo Badoer, *Il libro dei conti di Giacomo Badoer* (Costantinopoli, 1436--1440), eds U. Dorini and T. Bertelè (Rome, 1956).

Giovanni Pietro Contarini, *Historia delle cose successe dal principio della guerra mossa da Selim Ottomano a' a' Venetiani, fino al dì della gran giornata vittoriosa contra Turchi* (Francesco Rampazetto: Venezia, 1572).

Giovanni Sagredo, *Memorie istoriche de Monarchi Ottomani* (Venice, 1677).

Girart d'Amiens, *Escanor: roman arthurien en vers de la fin du XIIIe siècle*, ed. R. Trachsler (Geneva, 1994).

Il Compasso de Navegare. Opera italiana della metà del secolo XIII, ed. B.R. Motzo (Cagliari, 1947).

Jean sire de Joinville, *Histoire de Saint Louis. Credo et lettre à Louis X*, ed. N. de Wailly (Paris, 1874).

John Anthony Guarnerius, *De Bello Ciprio* (Bergamo, 1602).

La continuation de Guillaume de Tyre (1184--1197), ed. M.R. Morgan (Paris, 1982).

La règle du Temple, ed. H. de Curzon (Paris, 1886).

Leontios Makhairas, *Recital concerning the Sweet Land of Cyprus entitled 'Chronicle'*, ed. R.M. Dawkins, 2 vols. (Oxford, 1932).

Leontiou Makhaira, *Khroniko tes Kyprou: Parallele diplomatike ekdose ton kheirographon*, eds A. Nikolaou-Konnari and M. Pieris (Nicosia, 2003).

Marco Polo, *Il Milione*, ed. L. F. Benedetto (Florence, 1928).

Marino Sanudo, 'Liber Secretorum fidelium crucis', in J. Bongars (ed.), *Gesta Dei per Francos* (Hanau, 1611; repr. Jerusalem, 1972).

Memorie Veronesi della guerra di Cipro e della battaglia di Lepanto, ed. A. Avena (Venice, 1912).

Nicholas de Martoni, 'Relation du pèlerinage à Jérusalem de Nicolas de Martoni, notaire italien (1394-1395)', ed. L. Le Grand, *Revue de l'Orient latin*, 3 (1895).

Paolo Paruta, *Storia della guerra di Cipro, libri tre di .. …* (Siena, 1827).

Peregrinationes medii aevi quatuor: Burchardus de Monte Sion, Ricoldus de Monte Crucis, Odoricus de Foro Julii, Wilbrandus de Oldenborg, ed. J.C.M. Laurent (Leipzig, 1864).

Pero Tafur, *Andanças é viajes de Pero Tafur por diversas partes del mundo avidos (1435--1439)*, ed. M. Jiménez de La Espada (Madrid, 1874).

Philip of Novara (Filippo da Novara), *Guerra di Federico II in Oriente (1223--1242)*, ed. and trans. S. Melani (Naples, 1994).

Philip of Novara, *The Wars of Frederick the Second against the Ibelins in Syria and Cyprus by Philip of Novara*, trans. J. La Monte and M.J. Hubert (New York, 1936).

Pietro Bizarus, *Cyprivm Bellvm, inter Venetos, et Selymvm Tvrcarvm Imperatorem gestum, Petro Bizaro* (Basilea, 1573).

Recueil des historiens des croisades, Lois, ed. A. Beugnot, 2 vols (Paris, 1841--43).

Ritter Grünembergs, *Pilgerfahrt ins Heilige Land 1486*, eds J. Goldfriedrich and W. Fränzel (Leipzig 1912).

Steffano di Lusignano, *Chorograffia et breue historia uniuersale dell' isola de Cipro principiando al tempo di Noè per in fino al 1572* (Bologna, 1573).

Taki-Eddin-Ahmed Makrizi, *Histoire des sultans mamelouks de l'Égypte*, ed. and trans. É. Quatremère, 2 vols. (Paris, 1837–-1845).

The 'Templar of Tyre': Part III of the 'Deeds of the Cypriots', trans. P. Crawford (Aldershot, 2003).

Voyage de la Saincte Cyté de Hierusalem, ed. C. Schefer (Paris, 1882).

Wilbrand of Oldenburg, 'Itinerarium Terrae Sanctae' in S. de Sandoli (ed.), *Itinera Hierosolymitani Crucesignatorum*,, 4 vols. (Jerusalem, 1978–-84), 3.

Zeebout, A., *Tvoyage van Mher Joos van Ghistele*, ed. R.J.G.A.A. Gaspar (Hilversum, 1998).

Zibaldone da Canal. *Manoscritto mercantile del sec. XIV*, ed. A. Stussi (Fonti per la storia di Venezia, Fonti vari, Venice, 1967).

Secondary Works

Abbasoğlu, M.S., 'Historical Analysis of Medieval Famagusta', unpublished MA thesis (Eastern Mediterranean University, Famagusta, 2003).

Achar'ian, H., *Hayots' anjnanunneri par'aran* (Armenian First Name Dictionary), 4 vols (Erevan, 1948).

Allsen, T.T., *Commodity and Exchange in the Mongol Empire. A Cultural History of Islamic Textiles* (Cambridge, 1997).

Alpoyachian, A., 'Kipros kghzin (Ir ants'ealn u hnerkan)' ('The Island of Cyprus [Its Past and Present]'), *T'eodik Yearbook* (1927).

Andrews, J.M., 'Santa Sophia in Nicosia: the Sculpture of the Western Portals and its Reception', *Comitatus*, 30 (1999).

Appleyard, D. (ed.), *The Conservation of European Cities* (Cambridge, MA, 1979).

Arbel, B., 'Venetian Cyprus and the Muslim Levant, 1473–1570', in N. Coureas and J. Riley-Smith (eds), *Cyprus and the Crusades* (Nicosia, 1995).

—, *Cyprus, the Franks and Venice, 13th–16th Centuries* (Aldershot, 2000).

Arslan, E., *Venezia Gotica* (Milan, 1970).

Ashtor, E., 'Il commercio levantino di Ancona nel basso Medioevo', *Rivista Storica Italiana*, 88 (1976).

—, *Levant Trade in the Later Middle Ages* (Princeton, N. J., 1983).

Bacci, M., 'Syrian, Palaiologan, and Gothic Murals in the "Nestorian" Church of Famagusta', *Deltion tes christianikes archaiologikes Hetaireias* (2006).

BAK (Babgen Catholicos Kiwleserian/Gulesserian), *Hay Kiprose* (*Armenian Cyprus*) (Antelias, 1936).

Bakuran (Vahan M. K'iwrkchian/Kurkjian), *Kipros kghzin* (*The Island of Cyprus*) (Nicosia, 1903).

Balard, M., 'Famagouste au début du XIVe siècle', in J. Heers (ed.), *Fortifications, portes de villes, places publiques, dans le monde méditerranéen* (Paris, 1985).

—, *Les marchands italiens à Chypre* (Cyprus Research Centre, Collected Studies, II: Nicosia, 2007).

—, 'La *massaria* génoise de Famagouste', in A. Beihammer, M.G. Parani and C.D. Schabel (eds), *Diplomatics in the Eastern Mediterranean 1000–1500: Aspects of Cross-Cultural Communication* (Leiden, 2008).

Balistreri, C. (ed.), *Costruire insieme per la pace – Costruttori e rilevatori di pace (progetto Cipro)*, Regione Veneto, *Dipartimento per le Politiche e la Promozione dei Diritti Civili*, 2 vols (Milan, 1992–94).

Balistreri-Trincanato, C. and D. Zanverdiani, *Jacopo De Barbari – Il racconto di una città* (Mestre-Venice, 2000).

Balletto, L., *Piemontesi del Quattrocento nel Vicino Oriente* (Biblioteca della Società di Storia, Arte e Archeologia per le provincie di Alessandria e Asti, 26) (Alessandria, 1992).

—, 'Les Génois dans l'île de Chypre au bas moyen âge', in C. Mutafian (ed.), *Les Lusignans et l'Outre-Mer* (Actes du Colloque de Poitiers-Lusignan [20–24 October 1993]) (Poitiers, 1995).

—, 'Ethnic groups, cross social and cross cultural contacts on fifteenth century Cyprus', in B. Arbel (ed.), *Intercultural Contacts in the Medieval Mediterranean* (London 1996).

Basford, K., *The Green Man* (Ipswich, 1978).

Bautier, R.-H., 'La place de la draperie brabançonne et plus particulièrement bruxelloise dans l'industrie textile du Moyen Age', *Annales de la Société royale d'archéologie de Bruxelles, volume jubilaire* (Brussels, 1962).

—, 'Les relations économiques des Occidentaux avec les pays d'Orient au Moyen Age. Points de vue et documents', in M. Mollat (ed.), *Sociétés et compagnies de commerce en Orient et dans l'Océan indien* (Actes du Huitième colloque international d'histoire maritime, Beyrouth, 1966) (Paris, 1970).

—, *Sur l'histoire économique de la France médiévale. La route, le fleuve, la foire* (London, 1991).

—, *Commerce méditerranéen et banquiers italiens au Moyen Age* (Aldershot, 1992).

Belgrano, L.T. (ed.), 'Prima serie di documenti riguardanti la colonia di Pera', *Atti della Società ligure di storia patria*, 13 (1877–84).

Benton, J.R., *Holy Terrors. Gargoyles on Medieval Buildings* (New York and London, 1997).

Béraud, S., *La culture française dans l'éspace chypriote* (Nicosia, 1990).

Bettinelli, G., *Famiglie patrizie venete* (Giuseppe Bettinelli stampatore: Venezia, 1774).

Bianchi, F. and D. Howard, 'Life and Death in Damascus. The Material Culture of Venetians in the Syrian Capital in the Mid-Fifteenth Century', *Studi Veneziani*, N.S. 46 (2003).

Bliznyuk, S., 'Il commercio alla veneziana tra Cipro e Damasco', in Ch. A. Maltezou and P. Schreiner (eds), *Bisanzio, Venezia e il mondo franco-greco (XIII–XV secolo)* (Atti del Colloquio Internazionale organizzato nel centenario della nascita di Raymond – J. Loenertz o. p., Venezia, 1–2 dicembre 2000) (Venice, 2002).

Boas, A. J., *Crusader Archaeology* (London, 1999).

Boase, T.S.R., 'The Arts in Cyprus, Ecclesiastical Art', in K.M. Setton (ed.), *A History of the Crusades*, 6 vols (Madison, 1955–89).

Bonato, L. and M. Emery, 'L'architecture rayonnante à Chypre: La cathédrale Saint-Nicolas de Famagouste', *Cahier du Centre d'Études Chypriotes*, 29 (1999).

—, 'Chypre au moyen-âge – Les cathédrales: L'influence française', *Mediaevalia*, 24 (2003).

Bowen, H., 'Nizām al- Mulk', *Encyclopaedia of Islam*, 2nd edn, 12 vols (Leiden, 1960–2004).

Brand, C.M., *Byzantium confronts the West 1180–1204* (Cambridge, Massachusetts, 1968).

Bromily, G.N., 'Philippe de Novare: Another Epic Historian?', *Neophilologus*, 82 (1998).

Buckler, W. et al., 'The Antiquities of Cyprus: Byzantine Culture', *Times* (22 September 1933).

Bury, J., 'Early writing on fortifications and siege crafts: 1502–1554', *Fort*, 13 (1985).

Camille, M., *The Gothic Idol. Ideology and Image-making in Medieval Art* (Cambridge, 1989).

—, *Images on the Edge. The Margins of Medieval Art* (London, 1992).

Campagnolo, M., C. Courtois, M. Martiniani-Reber and L. Michaelidou, *Chypre – D'Aphrodite à Mèlusine* (Geneva, 2006).

Campana, C., *Delle Historie del Mondo* (Pavia, 1602).

Capponi, N., *Lepanto 1571 – La Lega Santa contro l' impero ottomano* (Milan, 2006).

Carbonell-Lamothe, Y., 'Les monuments gothiques des Lusignan', in J. Charles-Gaffiot (ed.), *La France aux Portes de l'Orient. Chypre, XIIe-XVe siècle* (Paris, 1991).

Carlier, A., *Les Villes Françaises de Chypre* (Paris, 1934).

Carr, A.W., 'Art in the Court of the Lusignan Kings', in N. Coureas and J. Riley-Smith (eds), *Cyprus and the Crusades* (Nicosia, 1995).

—, 'Byzantines and Italians on Cyprus: Images from Art', *Dumbarton Oaks Papers*, 49 (1995).

—, 'Art', in A. Nicolaou-Konnari and C. Schabel (eds), *Cyprus Society and Culture 1191–1374* (Leiden and Boston, 2005).

—, 'Perspectives on Visual Culture in Early Lusignan Cyprus', in P. Edbury and S. Kalopissi-Verti (eds), *Archaeology and the Crusades (Proceedings of the Round Table, Nicosia, 1 February 2005)* (Athens, 2007).

Cecchetti, B., *La vita dei Veneziani nel 1300. Le vesti* (Venice, 1886), repr. in B. Cecchetti, *La vita dei Veneziani nel 1300*, introduction by U. Stefanutti (Bologna, 1980).

Çevikel, N., *Kıbrıs Eyaleti, Yönetim, Klise, Ayan ve Halk (1750–1800)* (Famagusta, 2000).

Ch'amch'ian, M., *Hayots' patmutiwn* (*Armenian History*), vol. 3 (Venice, 1786).

Chacalli, G., *Cyprus under British Rule* (Nicosia, 1902).

Christoforaki, I., 'Cyprus between Byzantium and the Levant: Eclecticism and Interchange in the Cycle of the Life of the Virgin in the Church of the Holy Cross at Pelendri,' *Epeterida tou Kentrou Epistemonikon Erevnon*, 22 (1996).

Claverie, P.-V., '"*La cristiandat en mayor peril*" ou la perception de la question d'Orient dans la Catalogne de la fin du XIIIe siècle', in *Les templiers en Pays catalan* (Perpignan, 1998).

—, 'L'ordre du Temple au cœur d'une crise politique majeure: la *Querela Cypri* des années 1279–1285', *Le Moyen Age*, 104 (1998).

—, *L'ordre du Temple en Terre sainte et à Chypre au XIIIe siècle*, 3 vols (Nicosia, 2005).

—, E. et J.-P. Grélois, '*Apud Ciprum Nicossiam*: notes sur les relations cyprio-auvergnates au XIIIe siècle', *Epeterida tou Kentrou Epistemonikon Erevnon*, 31 (2005).

Coldstream, N., 'Famagusta', in J. Turner (ed.), *The Dictionary of Art*, 34 vols. (London, 1996).

—, 'Gothic Architecture in the Lusignan Kingdom', in D. Papanikola-Bakirtzis and M. Iacovou (eds), *Byzantine Medieval Cyprus* (Nicosia, 1998).

Concina, E., *L'Arsenale della Repubblica di Venezia* (Venice, 1984).

Constantinides, E., 'Monumental Painting in Cyprus during the Venetian Period, 1489–1570', in N.P. Sevcenko and C. Moss (eds), *Medieval Cyprus, Studies in Art, Architecture, and History in Memory of Doula Mouriki* (Princeton, 1999).

Coronelli V., *Blasone Veneto* (Venice, 1706).

Coulon, D., et al. (eds), *Chemins d'outre-mer. Études sur la Méditerranée médiévale offertes à M. Balard* (Paris, 2004).

Council of Europe, *A Future for Our Past, European Architectural Heritage* (Strasbourg, 1977).

—, *Convention for the Protection of the Architectural Heritage of Europe* (Granada, 1985). For the Council of Europe's cultural heritage conventions, see http://www.coe.int/Treaty/en/Treaties/Html/-121.htm (24.03.2008).

Coureas, N., *The Latin Church in Cyprus 1195–1312* (Aldershot, 1997).

—, 'The role of the Templars and the Hospitallers in the movement of commodities involving Cyprus, 1291–1312', in P. Edbury and J. Phillips (eds), *The Experience of Crusading*, 2 vols (Cambridge, 2003), 2.

—, 'Economy', in A. Nicolaou-Konnari and C. Schabel (eds), *Cyprus. Society and Culture 1191–1374* (Leiden, 2005).

—, G. Grivaud and C. Schabel, 'The Capital of the Sweet Land of Cyprus: Frankish and Venetian Nicosia', in *A History of Nicosia* (Rimal Publications: in press).

Cuneo, P., 'Famagosta', in *Enciclopedia dell'arte medievale*, 12 vols (Rome, 1991–2002).

Da Lezze, D., *Historia turchesca* (Bucharest 1910).

Day, J. (ed.), *Les douanes de Gênes, 1376–1377* (Paris, 1963).

Dehio, G. and G. von Bezold, *Die kirchliche Baukunst des Abendlandes* (Stuttgart, 1887–1901).

Demurger, A., *Jacques de Molay: Le crépuscule des templiers* (Paris, 2002).

Derbes, A., 'Siena and the Levant in the Later Duegento', *Gesta*, 28 (1989).

Desimoni, C., 'Notes et observations sur actes du notaire génois Lamberto di Sambuceto', *Revue de l'Orient Latin*, 2 (1894).

—, 'Observations sur les monnaies, les poids et les mesures cités dans les actes du notaire génois Lamberto di Sambuceto', *Revue de l'Orient Latin*, 3 (1895).

Dixon, W.H., *British Cyprus* (London: Chapman and Hall, 1879).

Doratlı, N., 'A Model for Conservation and Revitalization of Historic Urban Quarters in Northern Cyprus', unpublished PhD thesis (Eastern Mediterranean University, Famagusta, 2000).

—, 'KKTC'de Tarihi Kentsel Alanların Korunmasına İlişkin Yasal Çerçeveye Eleştirel Bakış', in Ayşegül Mengi (ed.), *Kent ve Planlama, Geçmişi Korumak Geleceği Tasarlamak, Ruşen Keleşe Armağan, II. Kitap* (İmge Kitapevi, 2007).

— et al., 'Revitalizing the Walled City of Gazimağusa (Famagusta)', *Open House International*, 26/1 (2001).

— et al., 'An Analytical Methodology for Revitalization Strategies in Historic Urban Quarters: A Case Study of the Walled City of Nicosia, North Cyprus', *Cities*, 21/4 (2004).

— et al., 'Revitalizing a Declining Historic Urban Quarter: The Walled City of Famagusta, North Cyprus', *Journal of Architectural and Planning Research*, 24/1 (2007).

Douët-d'Arcq, L., 'Tarif des marchandises qui se vendaient à Paris à la fin du XIIIe siècle', *Revue archéologique*, 9 (1852).

Edbury, P.W., *The Kingdom of Cyprus and the Crusades* (Cambridge, 1991).

—, 'The Templars in Cyprus', in M.C. Barber (ed.), *The Military Orders: Fighting for the Faith and Caring for the Sick* (Aldershot, 1994).

—, 'Famagusta in 1300' in N. Coureas and J. Riley-Smith (eds), *Cyprus and the Crusades* (Nicosia, 1995).

—, *The Conquest of Jerusalem and the Third Crusade* (Aldershot, 1996).

—, 'The Lyons *Eracles* and the Old French Continuations of William of Tyre' in B.Z. Kedar, J. Riley-Smith and R. Hiestand (eds), *Montjoie. Studies in Crusade History in Honour of Hans Eberhard Mayer* (Aldershot, 1997).

—, 'Latins and Greeks on Crusader Cyprus', in D. Abulafia and N. Berend (eds), *Medieval Frontiers: Concepts and Practices* (Aldershot, 2002).

Efthimiou, M., *Greeks and Latins on Cyprus in the Thirteenth Century* (Brookline, Mass., 1987).

Eliades, I.A., 'Cultural Interactions in Cyprus 1191–1571: Byzantine and Italian Art', in A. Cimdina and J. Osmond (eds), *Power and culture – Hegemony, interaction and dissent* (Pisa, 2006).

Emmanuel, M., 'Monumental Painting in Cyprus During the Last Phase of the Lusignan Dynasty, 1374–1489', in N.P. Ševčenko and C. Moss (eds), *Medieval Cyprus: Studies in Art, Architecture and History in Memory of Doula Mouriki* (Princeton, 1999).

Enlart, C., *L'Art gothique et la Renaissance en Chypre* (2 vols, Paris, 1899); English translation: *Gothic Art and the Renaissance in Cyprus*, ed. and trans. D. Hunt (London, 1987).

—, 'Fouilles dans les Eglises de Famagouste de Chypre', *Archaeological Journal*, 62 (1905).

—, *Villes Mortes du Moyen Age* (Paris, 1920).

Erder, C., *Tarihi Çevre Bilinci* (Ankara, 2007).

Erlande-Brandenburg, A. 'La Priorale Saint-Louis de Poissy', *Bulletin Monumental*, 129 (1971).

Folda, J., *Crusader Art in the Holy Land: from the Third Crusade to the Fall of Acre, 1187–1291* (Cambridge, 2005).

Forrant, R. 'Pulling together in Lowell: The University and the Regional Development Process', *European Planning Studies*, 9/5 (2001).

Franke, A, 'Die Kathedrale in Famagusta und die gotische Architektur auf Zypern' (MA Thesis, Ludwig-Maximilians-Universität München: Munich, 2006).

French, D. 'A Sixteenth Century English Merchant in Ankara?', *Anatolian Studies*, 22 (1972).

Fresne du Cange, C. du., *Glossarium ad scriptores mediae et infimae latinitatis*, 10 vols (Paris, 1883–87).

Fuess, A., *Verbranntes Ufer. Auswirkungen mamlukischer Seepolitik auf Beirut und die syro-palästinensische Küste (1250–1517)* (Leiden, 2001).

Gattoni, M., 'La spada della croce: la difficile alleanza ispano-veneta-pontificia nella Guerra di Cipro. Politica estera e teoremi filosofici nei documenti politici', *Ricerche storiche*, 29, 3 (1999).

Gay, V., *Glossaire archéologique du Moyen Âge et de la Renaissance*, texte revu par H. Stein, 2 vols. (Paris, 1887–1928).

Gazimağusa Belediyesi, *Gazimağusa Surlariçi Canlandırma Planı Rapor I Mevcut Durum*, unpublished report (2005).

—, *Gazimağusa Surlariçi Canlandırma Planı Rapor II Potansiyeller*, unpublished report (2005).

—, *Gazimağusa Surlariçi Canlandırma Planı Rapor III Öneri Raporu*, unpublished report (2005).

Gazzola, P. (ed.), *Michele Sanmicheli* (Venice, 1960).

Gerola, G., *I monumenti Veneti dell'Isola di Creta*, 4 vols (Venice, 1905–32).

Bishop Ghevond (Ch'épéyan), *Yishadakaran kiprahay gaghut'i* (Memorial on the Cypriot-Armenian Community) (Antelias, 1955).

Gil, M., *A History of Palestine, 634–1099*, trans. E. Broido (Cambridge, 1997).

Gillet, L., 'Les architectes des cathédrales', in J. Cosse (ed.), *Initiation à l'art des cathédrales* (Paris, 1999).

Ginanni, M'A., *L'arte del blasone dichiarata per alfabeto* (Venice, 1756).

Giorgio Martini, F. di, *Trattati*, ed. C. Maltese, 2 vols (Milan, 1967).

Gkioles, N., *He Khristianike Tekhne sten* Kypro (Christian Art in Cyprus) (Nicosia, 2003).

Graboïs, A., 'Christian Pilgrims in the Thirteenth Century and the Kingdom of Jerusalem: Burchard of Mount Sion', in B.Z. Kedar, H.E. Mayer, R.C. Smail (eds), *Outremer. Studies in the History of the Crusading Kingdom of Jerusalem, presented to Joshua Prawer* (Jerusalem, 1982).

Graham, B., 'Heritage as Knowledge: Capital or Culture', *Urban Studies*, 39/5–6 (2002).

Guglielmotti, P.A., *La guerra dei pirati e la marina pontificia dal 1500 al 1560* (Florence, 1876).

Gunnis, R., *Historic Cyprus: A Guide to its Towns and Villages and Castles* (London, 1936, repr. Nicosia, 1973).

Hadjigavriel, L.L. (ed.), *Venice Cyprus* (Nicosia, 2006).

Hafızoğlu, Ş., 'Stone use in British Domestic Architecture in North Cyprus', Unpublished M.A. thesis (Famagusta, 2000).

Hanworth, R., *The Heritage of North Cyprus* (Nicosia, 1990).

Hatfield Young, S., 'Byzantine Painting in Cyprus during the Early Lusignan Period' (unpublished PhD diss., Pennsylvania State University, 1983).

Heers, J., *Gênes au XVe siècle. Activité économique et problèmes sociaux* (Paris, 1961).

Heyd, W., *Histoire du commerce du Levant au moyen-âge*, 2 vols (Leipzig, 1885–86).

Hill, G., *A History of Cyprus*, 4 vols (Cambridge, 1940–52).

Hughes, Q., *Military architecture* (Liphook, 1991).

Hurst, C., *The View from King Street: An Essay in Autobiography* (London, 1997).

I'Anson, E. and S. Vacher, 'Mediaeval and Other Buildings in the Island of Cyprus,' *Transactions of the Royal Institute of British Architects* (1882–83).

Iorga, N., 'Notes et extraits pour servir à l'histoire des croisades au XVe siècle', *Revue de l'Orient latin*, 6 (1898).

Jacoby, D., 'Citoyens, sujets et protégés de Venise et de Gênes en Chypre du XIIe au XVe siècle', *Byzantinische Forschungen*, 5 (1977): repr. in D. Jacoby, *Recherches sur la Méditerranée orientale du XIIe au XVe siècle. Peuples, sociétés, économies* (London, 1979).

—, 'The Rise of a New Emporium in the Eastern Mediterranean: Famagusta in the Late Thirteenth Century', *Meletai kai hypomnemata* (Hidryma Archiepiskopou Makariou III), 1 (1984): repr. in D. Jacoby, *Studies on the Crusader States and on Venetian Expansion* (Northampton, 1989).

—, 'Silk in Western Byzantium before the Fourth Crusade', *Byzantinische Zeitschrift*, 84/85 (1991/92) repr. in idem., *Trade, commodities and Shipping in the Medieval Mediterranean* (Aldershot, 1997).

—, 'To emporio kai he oikonomia tes Kyprou (1191–1489)', in Th. Papadopoullos (ed.), *Historia tes Kyprou*, vol. 4/1, *Mesaionikon Basileion, Enetokratia* (Nicosia, 1995).

—, 'Silk Economics and Cross-Cultural Artistic Interaction: Byzantium, the Muslim World and the Christian West', *Dumbarton Oaks Papers*, 58 (2004).

—, 'The Economic Function of the Crusader States of the Levant: a New Approach', in S. Cavaciocchi (ed.), *Relazioni economiche tra Europa e mondo islamico. Secc.* XIII–XVIII (Istituto Internazionale di Storia Economica 'F. Datini', Atti delle Settimane di Studi e altri convegni, vol. 38) (Florence, 2007).

—, 'The Venetians in Byzantine and Lusignan Cyprus: Trade, Settlement, and Politics', in A. Nicolaou-Konnari (ed.), La Serenissima *and* la Nobilissima: *Venice in Cyprus and Cyprus in Venice* (Nicosia, 2009).

Jeffery, G.E., 'Report on the Carmelite Church', *Proceedings of the Society of Antiquaries* (1916).

Jeffery, G., *A Description of the Historic Monuments of Cyprus: Studies in the Archaeology and Architecture of the Island* (Nicosia, 1918, repr. London, 1983).

Kaffenberger, T., *Hagios Georgios in Famagusta – ein Beispiel des Kulturtransfers. Baugeschichtliche Untersuchungen* (unpubl. MA Thesis, Johannes Gutenberg-Universität Mainz, 2010).

Kammerer, A., *A Chypre: L'ile d'Aphrodite* (Paris, 1925).

Kaoulla, C. and C. Schabel, 'The Inquisition against P. de Castro, Vicar of the Dominican Province of the Holy Land in Nicosia, Cyprus, 1330', *Archivum Fratrum Praedicatorum*, 77 (2007).

Kapoïan-Kouymjian, A., *L'Égypte vue par des Arméniens* (XIe–XVIIe siècle) (Paris, 1988).

Karageorghis, V., L. Loizou-Hadjigavriel L. and C. Maltezou (eds), *Cyprus Jewel in the Crown of Venice* (Nicosia, 2003).

Katzenellenbogen, A., 'The Central Tympanum at Vézelay: Its Encyclopedic Meaning and its Relation to the First Crusade', *Art Bulletin*, 26 (1944).

Kedar, B.Z., 'Jerusalemite Jews in Genoese Famagusta, 1388', in B.Z. Kedar (ed.), *Jerusalem in the Middle Ages. Selected Papers* (Jerusalem, 1979).

—, J. Riley-Smith and R. Hiestand (eds) *Montjoie: Studies in Crusade History in Honour of Hans Eberhard Mayer* (Aldershot, 1997).

Kenaan-Kedar, N., 'A Neglected Series of Crusader Sculpture: The Ninety-Six Corbels of the Church of the Holy Sepulchre', *Israel Exploration Journal*, 42 (1992).

—, *Marginal Sculpture in Medieval France: Towards the deciphering of an enigmatic pictorial language* (Aldershot, 1995).

—, 'Sculpture High Up: The Forgotten Meanings of Monumental Sculpture on Churches' Roofs and Towers', in A.W. Reinick and J. Stumpel (eds), *Memory and Oblivion* (Amsterdam, 1997).

—, 'The Role and Meanings of Crusader Architectural Decoration: From Local Romanesque Traditions to Gothic Hegemony,' *Schriften des Historischen Kolleges Kolloquien*, 37 (1997).

—, 'The Two Lintels of the Church of the Holy Sepulchre in Jerusalem,' in S. Rosenberg (ed.), *Knights of the Holy Land: The Crusader Kingdom of Jerusalem* (Jerusalem, 1999).

—, 'Interaction of Marginal and Official Iconography: The West Facade of St Hilaire in Foussais – Its Oral, Visual and Literary Sources', in N. Kenaan-Kedar and A. Ovadiah (eds), *The Metamorphosis of Marginal Images: From Antiquity to Present Time* (Tel Aviv, 2002).

Keshishian, K.K., *Famagusta Town and District: Cyprus: A survey of its people and places from ancient times* (Limassol, 1985).

Kimpel, D., 'Le développement de la taille en série dans l'architecture médiévale et son rôle dans l'histoire économique', *Bulletin monumental*, 135 (1977).

—, 'Die Entfaltung der gotischen Baubetriebe, ihre sozio-ökonomischen Grundlange und ihre ästhetisch-künstlerischen Auswirkungen', in F. Möbius and E. Schubert (eds), *Architektur des Mittelalters* (Weimar, 1983).

King, D. and M., 'Silk Weaves of Lucca in 1376', in I. Estham and M. Nockert (eds), *Opera Textilia Variorum Temporum, To honour Agnes Geijer on her Ninetieth Birthday 26th October 1988* (Stockholm, 1988).

Kouymjian, D., 'The Evolution of Armenian Gospel Illumination: The Formative Period (9th–11th Centuries)', in C. Burchard (ed.) *Armenian and the Bible* (Atlanta, 1993).

—, 'Identifying the Apostles in Armenian Narrative Miniatures', in J.-P. Mahé and R.W. Thomson (eds), *From Byzantium to Iran: Armenian Studies in Honour of Nina G. Garsoïan* (Atlanta, 1997).

Kyriakides, K., 'Cyprus and Projection of British Sea Power since 1878', 2nd Mediterranean Maritime History Network Conference, Messina/Taormina, Sicily, 4–7 May 2006 (http://home.um.edu.mt/medinst/mmhn/klearchos_kyriakides.pdf).

La Graviere, J. and J.-P. de Edmond, *La Guerre de Chypre et la Bataille de Lepante*, 2 vols (Paris, 1888).

Langdale, A. and M.J.K. Walsh, 'A Short Report on Three Newly Accessible Churches in the Syrian Quarter of Famagusta', *Journal of Cyprus Studies*, 13/33 (2007).

—, 'The Architecture, Conservation History, and Future of the Armenian Church of Famagusta', *Chronos* (2009).

Langenskiöld, E., *Michele Sanmicheli the architect of Verona* (Uppsala, 1938).

Latham, R.E., *Dictionary of Medieval Latin from British Sources* (London, 1975).

Lewis, Mrs. *A Lady's Impressions of Cyprus* (London, 1893).

Lombard, M. *Les textiles dans le monde musulman, VIIe–XIIe siècles* (Paris, 1978).

Lopez, R. and G. Airaldi, 'Il più antico manuale italiano di pratica della mercatura', in *Miscellanea di studi storici*, 2 (Collana storica di fonti e studi diretta da Geo Pistarino, vol. 38) (Genoa, 1983).

Lucchese, V., 'Antico portale in Anastasias Toufexi Street, Da un quaderno d'appunti: Nicosia Nord', idem (with S. Fassini), 'La chiesa – moschea Arablar', in C. Balistreri (ed.), *Costruire insieme per la pace* (Milan, 1992), 1.

— and Zanverdiani D., 'Da Venezia al Levante. Architettura e il retaggio di una civiltà', in F. Labelli and S. Marini (eds), *L'architettura e le sue declinazioni* (Verona, 2008).

Luke, H., *Cyprus under the Turks (1571–1878): A Record based on the Archives of the English Consulate in Cyprus under the Levant Company and After* (London, 1921).

—, *Cyprus, A Portrait and an Appreciation* (Nicosia, 1965).

Lüpnitz, M., 'Der mittelalterliche Ringanker in den Chorobergadenfenstern des Kölner Domes', *Kölner Domblatt*, 62 (1997).

Mâle, E., *The Gothic Image. Religious Art in France of the Thirteenth Century*, trans. D. Nussey (New York, 1958).

Manoussou-Della, K., *Medieval Town of Rhodes* (Rhodes, 2001).

Marchesi, P., *Fortezze veneziane 1508–1797* (Milan, 1984).

Mas Latrie, L. de, 'Monuments français de l'île de Chypre', *Le Magasin pittoresque*, 15 (1847).

Mayer, H.E., *Geschichte der Kreuzzüge* (Stuttgart, 1995).

Mazzaoui, M.F., *The Italian Cotton Industry in the Later Middle Ages, 1100–1600* (Cambridge, 1981).

Meersseman, G.-G., 'Etudes sur les anciennes confréries dominicaines, I: Les confréries de saint Dominique', *Archivum Fratrum Praedicatorum*, 20 (1950).

Megaw, A.H.S., 'Shorter Reports', Report of the Department of Antiquities Cyprus 1937–1939 (Nicosia, 1951).

Monello, G., *Accadde a Famagosta* (Cagliari, 2005).

Monnas, L., 'Silk Cloths Purchased for the Great Wardrobe of the Kings of England, 1325–1462', *Textile History*, 20 (1989).

—, 'Textiles for the Coronation of Edward III', *Textile History*, 32 (2001).

Morini, M., *Atlante di Storia dell'Urbanistica* (Milan, 1963).

Morton, A.H., 'The letters of Rashid al-Din: Ilkhanid Fact or Timurid fiction?', in R. Amitai-Preiss and D.O. Morgan (eds), *The Mongol Empire and its Legacy* (Leiden, 1999).

Mullins, R.L. Jr and J.I. Gilderbloom, 'Urban revitalization partnerships: perceptions of the university's role in Louisville, Kentucky', *Local Environment*, 7/2 (2002).

Munro, J.H., 'The Medieval Scarlet and the Economics of Sartorial Splendour', in N.B. Harte and K.G. Ponting (eds), *Cloth and Clothing in Medieval Europe: Essays in Memory of Professor E.M. Carus-Wilson* (London, 1983).

Murray, S., *Notre-Dame, Cathedral of Amiens: The Power of Change in Gothic* (Cambridge, 1996).

Nam, Jong-Kuk, *Le commerce du coton en Méditerranée à la fin du Moyen Âge* (Leiden, 2007).

Naud, C., *Le dragon dans l' art roman du Poitou-Charentes* (Poitiers, 1972).

Nersessian, S.D., 'Le peinture arménienne au VIIe siècle et les miniatures de l'Évangile d'Etchmiadzin', reprinted in S. Der Nersessian, *Byzantine and Armenian Studies* (Lisbon, 1973).

—, *Miniature Painting in the Armenian Kingdom of Cilicia*, 2 vols (Washington, 1993).

Nicol, D.M., *Byzantium and Venice: A Study in Diplomatic and Cultural Relations* (Cambridge, 1988).

Nicolaou-Konnari, A., 'The Encounter of Greeks and Franks in Cyprus in the Late Twelfth and Thirteenth Centuries: Phenomena of Acculturation and Ethnic Awareness' (unpublished PhD diss., University of Wales: Cardiff, 1999).

Nicosia Municipality and Italian Embassy (catalogue eds), *Caterina Cornaro – L'ultima regina di Cipro 1473–1489* (Nicosia, 1995).

Olivato, L., 'La teoria dell'arte militare nel Rinascimento veneto', in *Architettura Militare Veneta del Cinquecento* (Milan, 1988).

Orbasli, A., *Tourists in Historic Towns* (London, 2000).

Orr, C.W.J., *Cyprus under British Rule* (London, 1972).

Ouerfelli, M., *Le sucre. Production, commerciation et usages dans la Méditerranée médiévale* (Leiden, 2008).

Ousterhout, R., 'The French Connection? Construction of Vaults and Cultural Identity in Crusader Architecture', in D.H. Weiss and L.J. Mahoney (eds), *France and the Holy Land: Frankish Culture at the End of the Crusades* (Baltimore, 2004).

P.A., 'A Note on *Suf* or Camlet', *Bulletin of the American Institute for Iranian Art and Archaeology*, 5 (1938) [author's surname not identified, See Jacoby chapter note 18].

Papacostas, T.C., 'Gothic in the East: Western Architecture in Byzantine Lands', in C. Rudolph (ed.), *A Companion to Medieval Art: Romanesque and Gothic in Northern Europe* (Malden, Mass., 2006).

Papageorgiou, A., 'Crusader Influence on the Byzantine Art of Cyprus', in N. Coureas and J. Riley-Smith (eds), *Cyprus and the Crusades* (Nicosia, 1995).

Parker, R., *Aphrodite's realm, An illustrated guide and handbook to Cyprus* (Nicosia, 1962).

Pasero, C. *La partecipazione bresciana alla guerra di Cipro e alla battaglia di Lepanto (1570–1573)* (Brescia, 1954).

Perbellini, G., 'Le fortificazioni di Cipro', *Castellum*, 17 (1973).

—, *Le Fortificazioni di Cipro dal X al XVI Secolo* (Rome, 1975).

—, 'La difesa delle frontiere Centro Occidentali: Orzinuovi, Legnago, Peschiera' in *Architettura Militare Veneta del Cinquecento* (Milan, 1988).

—, 'The Venetian defences of Cyprus', *Fort*, 16 (1988).

—, 'Verona da Fortezza Veneta a Piazzaforte principale del quadrilatero', in G. Perbellini and V. Bozzetto (eds), *Verona: La Piazzaforte Ottocentesca Nella Cultura Europea* (Verona, 1990).

—, *The Fortress of Nicosia: Prototype of European Renaissance Military Architecture* (Nicosia, 1994).

Piltz, E., 'Saint Bridget and Byzantium – in view of her Cyprian revelations,' *Praktika tou Deuterou Diethnous Kypriologikou Synedriou* (Nicosia, 20–25 April 1982), 3 vols. (Nicosia, 1985–87), 2.

Piponnier, F. 'À propos de textiles anciens, principalement médiévaux', *Annales. Économies, Sociétés, Civilisations*, 22 (1967).

Plagnieux, P. and T. Soulard, 'Famagouste. L'Église des Arméniens (Sainte-Marie-de-Vert)', in J.-B. de Vaivre and P. Plagnieux (eds), *L'art gothique en Chypre* (Paris, 2006).

—, 'L'Église Sainte-Anne' in J.-B. de Vaivre and P. Plagnieux (eds), *L'art gothique en Chypre* (Paris, 2006).

—, 'La cathédrale Saint-Nicolas', in J.-B. de Vaivre and P. Plagnieux (eds), *L'art gothique en Chypre* (Paris, 2006).

—, 'Famagouste. L'Hôpital Saint-Antoine', in J.-B. de Vaivre and P. Plagnieux (eds), *L'art gothique en Chypre* (Paris, 2006).

Podocataro, A., *Relazione dei successi di Famagosta* (Theiner: Venezia, 1876).

Pringle, D., *The Churches of the Crusader Kingdom of Jerusalem: a Corpus*, 4 vols (Cambridge, 1993–2009).

Puppi, L., *Architettura e utopia nella Venezia del' 500* (Milan, 1980).

Quarti, G. A., *La guerra contro il Turco in Cipro ed a Lepanto (1570–71)* (Venice, 1935).

Raglan, Lady, 'The Green Man in Church Architecture', *Folklore*, 50 (1939).

Report of the Department of Antiquities Cyprus, 1937–39 (Nicosia, 1951).

Richard, J., 'Guy d'Ibelin, O. P., évêque de Limassol et l'inventaire de ses biens (1367)', *Bulletin de correspondance hellénique*, 74 (1950), repr. in J. Richard, *Les relations entre l'Orient et l'Occident au Moyen Âge. Études et documents* (London, 1977).

—, 'Le peuplement latin et syrien en Chypre au XIIIe siècle', *Byzantinische Forschungen*, 7 (1979), repr. in J. Richard, *Croisés, missionnaires et voyageurs. Les perspectives orientales du monde latin médiéval* (London, 1983).

—, 'Une famille de "Vénitiens blancs" dans le royaume de Chypre au milieu du XVème siècle: les Audeth et la seigneurie du Marethasse', *Rivista di Studi bizantini e slavi*, 1 (1981).

—, 'Les comtes de Tripoli et leurs vassaux sous la dynastie antiochénienne', in P.W. Edbury (ed.), *Crusade and Settlement* (Cardiff, 1985).

Richard, J.-M., *Une petite nièce de Saint-Louis Mahaut, comtesse d'Artois et de Bourgogne* (1302–1329). *Étude sur la vie privée, les arts et l'industrie, en Artois et à Paris au commencement du XIVe siècle* (Paris, 1887).

Roccatagliata, A., 'Aspetti di storia economica cipriota alla fine del Trecento', *La storia dei Genovesi*, 9 (1989).

Rosenau, H., 'Historical aspects of the Vitruvian tradition in town planning', *R.I.B.A. Journal* (1955).

Roueché, C., 'The Prehistory of the Cyprus Department of Antiquities', in J. Herrin, M. Mullett and C. Otten-Froux (eds), *Mosaic: Festschrift for A.H.S. Megaw* (London, 1996).

Rudt de Collenberg, W.H., 'Etat et origine du haut clergé de Chypre avant le Grand Schisme d'après les Registres des Papes du XIIIe et du XIVe siècle', *Mélanges de l'École française de Rome*, 91 (1979).

Runciman, S., *Mistra: Byzantine Capital of the Peloponnese* (London, 1980).

Ryan, W.G. (trans.), *The Golden Legend: Readings on the Saints* (Princeton, 1993).

Saraceni, C. *I fatti d'armi famosi, successi fra tutte le nationi del mondo* (Venice, 1600).

Scalesse, T., 'Giovan Giacomo Lonardi, Libro delle fortificazioni dei giorni nostri', *Quaderni dell'Istituto di Storia dell'Architettura*, 20–21/115–26 (Rome, 1975).

—, 'Senigallia e Peschiera nuovi dati', *Quaderni dell'Istituto di Storia dell'Architettura*, 22/127–32 (1976).

Scarfi, B.M. (ed.), *Il leone di Venezia* (Venice, 1990).

Schabel, C., 'Hugh the Just: The Further Rehabilitation of King Hugh IV Lusignan of Cyprus', *Epeterida Kentrou Epistemonikon Erevnon*, 30 (2004).

—, 'The Latin Bishops of Cyprus, 1255–1313, with a note on Bishop Neophytos of Solea,' *Epeterida Kentrou Epistemonikon Erevnon*, 30 (2004).

Schilbach, E., *Byzantinische Metrologie* (Handbuch des Altertumswissenschaft, vol. 12/4 = Byzantinisches Handbuch, vol. 4) (Munich, 1970).

Schryver, J.G., 'Spheres of Contact and Instances of Interaction in the Art and Archaeology of Frankish Cyprus, 1191–1359' (unpublished PhD diss., Cornell University, 2005).

Schryver, J.G., 'Monuments of Identity: Latin, Greek, Frank and Cypriot?', in S. Fourrier and G. Grivaud (eds), *Identités croisées en un milieu méditerranéen: le cas de Chypre (Antiquité – Moyen Âge)* (Rouen, 2006).

Schütz, B., *Die Katharinenkirche in Oppenheim* (Berlin and New York, 1982).

Sedlmayr, H., *Die gotische Kathedrale Frankreichs als europäische Königskirche* (Vienna, 1950).

Sella, P., *Glossario latino italiano: Stato della Chiesa – Veneto, Abruzzi* (City of the Vatican, 1944).

Ševčenko, N., *The Life of St Nicholas in Byzantine Art* (Turin, 1983).

Severis, R. C. and Bonato L. (eds), *Along the most beautiful path in the world: Edmond Duthoit and Cyprus* (Nicosia, 1999).

Sheridan, R. and Ross, A. *Gargoyles and Grotesques. Paganism in the Medieval Church* (Boston and New York, 1975).

Solalinde, J. Alfau de, *Nomenclatura de los tejidos espanoles del siglo XIII* (Madrid, 1969).

Soulard, T., 'L'architecture gothique grecque du royaume des Lusignan: les cathédrales de Famagouste et Nicosie', in S. Fourrier and G. Grivaud (eds), *Identités croisées en un milieu méditerranéen: le cas de Chypre (Antiquité – Moyen Âge)* (Rouen, 2006).

Steinmann, M., *Die Westfassade des Kölner Domes* (Cologne, 2003).

Stewart, B., *My Experiences of Cyprus* (London, 1908).

Stylianou, A. and J.A. Stylianou, *The Painted Churches of Cyprus* (London 1985).

—, *Painted Churches of Cyprus. Treasures of Byzantine Art*, 2nd edn (Nicosia, 1997).

—, *The History of the Cartography of Nicosia* (Nicosia, 2006).

Tafuri, M., *Renovatio Urbis, Venezia nell'età di A. Gritti 1523–1528* (Venice, 1984).

Thierry, N., 'Les peintures de l'Eglise de la Sainte-Croix d'Aghtamar (915–921)', *The Second International Symposium on Armenian Art, Erevan, 1978*, vol. 3 (Erevan, 1981).

Tiesdell, S. et al., *Revitalizing Historic Urban Quarters* (Oxford, 1996).

Tomitano, B., *Resa di Famagosta e fine lagrimevole di Bragadino e di Astorre Baglioni. Per le faustissime nozze Marcello Zon* (Venice, 1858).

Vaivre, J.-B. de, 'Chronique archéologique de Chypre', *Bulletin monumental*, 158 (2000).

—, 'Sculpteurs parisiens en Chypre autour de 1300', in M. Balard, B.Z. Kedar and J. Riley-Smith (eds), *Dei gesta per Francos. Crusade Studies in Honour of Jean Richard* (Aldershot, 2001).

—, 'Les églises jumelles de Famagouste', *Monuments et mémoires de la fondation Eugène Piot*, 82 (2003).

Valente, G., *Vita di Occhiali: da schiavo a re di Tunisi, Tripoli e Algeri* (Catanzaro, 1994).

Verlinden, C., 'Marchands chrétiens et juifs dans l'État mamelouk au début du XVe siècle d'après un notaire vénitien', *Bulletin de l'Institut historique belge de Rome*, 51 (1981).

Vogüé, M. de, *Les Églises de la Terre Sainte* (Paris, 1860).

Walsh, M.J.K., 'A Gothic Masterpiece in the Levant: St Nicholas Cathedral, Famagusta, North Cyprus', *Journal of Cultural Heritage*, 6 (2004).

—, 'The Re-emergence of The Forty Martyrs of Sebaste in the Church of Saint Peter and Paul, Famagusta, Northern Cyprus', *Journal of Cultural Heritage* 8 (2007).

—, 'On of the princypalle Havenes of the See': The Port of Famagusta and the Ship Graffiti of its Ruined Churches', *International Journal of Nautical Archaeology*, Vol. 37, No. 1 (2008).

—, '"The Vile Embroidery of Ruin": Historic Famagusta between Ottoman and British Empires in *fin de siècle* Cyprus: 1878–1901', *Journal of Intercultural Studies* (2010).

Weir, A. and J. Jerman, *Images of Lust: Sexual Carvings on Medieval Churches* (London, 1986).

Wilber, D.N. and M. Minovi, 'Notes on the Rab'-i-Rashidi', *Bulletin of the American Institute for Iranian Art and Archaeology*, 5 (1938).

Woodcock, A., *Liminal Images: Aspects of Medieval Architectural Sculpture in the South of England from the 11th to the 16th Centuries* (British Archaeological Reports 386, Oxford, 2005).

Yıldız, N., 'Kıbrıs'ta Osmanlı Kültür Mirasına Genel Bir Bakış', in H.C. Güzel, K. Çiçek, S. Koca (eds), *Türkler* (Yeni Türkiye Yayınları, 2002).

Zangger, K., *Contribution à la terminologie des tissus en ancien français attestés dans des textes français, provençaux, italiens, espagnols, allemands et latins* (Bienne, 1945).

Ziada, M.M., 'The Mamluk Conquest of Cyprus in the Fifteenth Century', *The Bulletin of the Faculty of Arts, Fouad I University* (Cairo), 2/1 (1934).

Index

Abbreviations: abb. = abbot; abp. = archbishop; Arm. = Armenian; Aug. = Augustinian; Ben. = Benedictine; bp. = bishop; bro. = brother; Byz. =Byzantine; can. = canon; capt.– captain; Carm. = Carmelite; Cat. = Catalan; cd. = cardinal; chr. = Chronicle/Chronicler; Cist. = Cistercian; cpl. = chaplain; C.ple. =Constantinople; cst =constable; ct. = count; Cyp. = Cypriot; d. = daughter; Dom. = Dominican; emp. = emperor; fam. = family; Fran. = Franciscan; Gen. = Genoese; Gk. = Greek; hb. = husband; Hosp. = Hospitaller; hist. = historian; hse. = house; intpr. =interpreter; k. = king; Lat. = Latin; lg. = legate; Mar. = Maronite; mon. = monastery; Nst. = Nestorian; np. = nephew; Ott. – Ottoman; pr. = prince; prov. =province; ptr. = patriarch; q. = queen; s. = sister/son; Tpl. = Templar; Turk. = Turkish; vct. = viscount; Ven. = Venetian.

Abraham from Pera, 68
Acre, 2, 20–21, 27, 48–9, 57, 59–62, 78–9, 91, 115, 120, 130, 159, 210
Adriatic, 66, 189
Aegean Sea, 26, 61
Africa, 187
Aght 'amar, 139
Akkule Masjid, 233
Alba, Antonio de, 69
Albergati, Domenico, 56
Albi, 132
Alerio, Pietro, 57, 63
Alexandretta (Iskanderun), 25, 67
Alexandria, 3, 25, 27, 31–2, 187
Alice (d' Ibelin), 136–7
Almeria, 21
Alota, wife of Carbonerio, Gen., 66
Alp Aslan, Seljuk ruler, 21
Alphonse ct. of Poitiers, 18–19
Alpoyachian, Arsak, 135
Altenberg, 87
Altoluogo/Theologo (Ephesus), 26
Alviano, Bartolomeo d', 190
Amadi, Chronique d', 43–6, 48–51, 53–4, 63, 77, 122, 149
Amadi, Francesco, Cyp. chr., 7, 43
Amiens, 86–90
Anatolia, 239
Ancona, 32
Andruzzi Bastion, Fig. 11.2, Tables 13.1, 13.4
Angora, 16
Ani, 139
Anjevats 'I, Khosrov, Arm., 137
Annales de Terre Sainte, 44–6
Annan Plan, 5
Anselm, Peter, Gen., 67
Antelias, 133
Antioch, 25
Aphrodite, island of, 59
Appleyard, Donald, 253
Apulia (Pouille), 63
Arablar Mosque, 169
Aragon, 58
Armenia, 21, 178, 201
Armenians, 65, 122, 124, 133–46, 159, 162, 166, 201
Armorinis, Lawrence de, Gen., 71
Armoury, Table 13.3
Arnaldus, Bernard, Cat., 66
Arsenal (Famagusta), 7, 49, 51, 191, Fig. 11.2

Arsenal Bastion, 224, 231, 243, 252, Fig. 11.2, Tables 13.1, 13.4
Arsenal Gate, 246, Fig. 11.2
Ascalon, 49, 137
Asia, 16, 23, 25, 187
Asia Minor, 21, 23, 26, 32
Asinou, 163
Assisi, 115
Athens, 133, 186
Attar, François, 156
Audeth, Anton, 35
Augustinian Hermits, 118–20
Avignon, 77, 132
Ayas, 2, 20–22, 25, 27, 48
Aydin, Turk. Emirate, 26
Aynal, Al-Malik Al-Ashraf, Mamluk sultan, 34
Azar de Caffa, 70–71

Babin, Guy, 126
Bacci, Michele, 158, 160–61
Badoer, Giacomo, Ven., 33
Bagnese, Branca, Ven., 17
Balbo, Giovanni, 56
Baldwin bp. of Famagusta, 77–8, 91
Balistreri, Corrado
Bandabuliya, 280
Bandes, Guy de, 60
Barbarino, 66
Barbaro, fam., 182–3, Fig. 10.10
Barbican, Fig. 11.2
Barcelona, 40, 58–9
Bardi, Florentine banking hse., 16
Bardswell, Monica, 140–46, 204, 206, 208, 214, 220, 229, 276, 280, 284, 307–9 (App. V), Figs.12.3–12.5, 12.8–12.12
Barsbay, Mamluk sultan, 33
Bartholomew
Bartholomew of Pera, 70
Beaujeu, Guillaume de, Tpl., 54
Bedestan Street, Fig. 13.8
Bedestan: see Palazzo del Provedittore
Beirut, 2, 25, 27, 31, 85
Bellapais, mon., 53
Bembo Daniele, Ven. capt., 174, App. III
Bembo, Gian Matteo, Ven. capt., 174, App. III
Bembo, Lorenzo, Ven. capt., 174, App. III
Bembo, Matteo, 188
Bembo, Ven. fam., 9, 170, Fig. 10.2
Benaccio, Alessandro, 168
Benedictines, 122, 131
Bennato, 66–7
Bernardin, Andrea, Ven., 32
Bertolino, 67
Bethsan, Ague de, 63
Biblia de Alba, 16
Bicocca, 189
Biddulph's Gate, 243, Table 13.3
Binelli, Niccolò, 56
Birmingham, 133
Bisarra, 68
Black Death (Peste), 2, 55, 80
Black Sea, 25, 33, 61
Boase, Thomas S.R., 87
Boccare Bastion, 190
Bolgarino, 66
Bonato, Lucie, 85
Bongiorno, Gen., 66–7
Bononia, Racello de Auro de, Hosp., 68
Boston, 275
Boussat, André, Ven., 59–60
Boustronios, George, Cyp. chr., 71–2
Bowler, J.R., 220
braccio, bras, unit of measurement, 39–41
British Empire, 239
Broquière, Bertrandon de la, 32
Bruges, 248
Brugnoli, Luigi, 191
Bugday (Sinan Pasha) Mosque: see Church of SS Peter and Paul
Burchard of Mt Sion, 19
Bustron, Florio, Cyp. chr., 43, 54, 77, 122
Büyük Hamam, 169
Byzantium, Byz. Empire, 21

Cachotripitri, Serini, Gk?, 70
Caen, 86
Caesarea, 85
Cafer Pasha Bath, 243
Cafer Pasha Fountain, 243, 280
Caffa, 26, 66
Cairo, 25, 31, 33–6, 61
Calabria, 30
Cambrai, League of, 187, 190
Camille, Michael, 98
Campo Santo Bastion, 231, Tables 13.1, 13.4
Canbulat, Tomb of, 243
Canbulat: see Arsenal
Candelor (Alanya), 25
Candia, 66, 194

canna, unit of measurement, 39
canutes, 71–2
Cappadocia, 177
Carbonell-Lamothe, Yvette, 56
Carbonerio, Perretino, Gen., 66
Carcassone, 87, 248
Cardona, Berenguer de, Tpl., 58
Carinthia, 188
Carlier, Achille, 215
Carmelites, 118–20, 122–5, 129, 159, 212
Caromb, Raimbaud II de, Tpl., 61
Carpaccio, Vittore, 184
Carras, Costas, 6
Catalonia, Catalans, 58, 167, 187–88
Catherine Cornaro, q. of Cyprus, 3, 170, 179, 187
Catherine d. of John Xarrache, 67
Caucasus, 201
Cavaliers
  Andruzzi, Fig. 11.2
  Arsenal, Fig. 11.2
  Barbican, Fig. 11.2
  Campo Santo, Tables 13.1, 13.4
  Cemetery, Fig. 11.2
  Diamante, Fig. 11.2, Tables 13.1, 13.4
  Land Gate, 231, Tables 13.1, 13.4
  Martinengo, Fig. 11.2
  Moratto, Fig. 11.2, Tables 13.1, 13.4
  Mozzo, Fig. 11.2
  St. Luca, Fig. 11.2
  St Napa, Fig. 11.2
Celebi 28, Tomb of, 243
Cells, Tables 13.2, 13.4
Cesariano Cesare, 189
Ch'épéyan, Ghevond, 135
Chain Tower, Fig. 11.2
Champagne, 81, 84–5, 113
Charles IX, k. of France
Charles VIII, k. of France, 189
Charlotte, q. of Cyprus, 35, 71, 179
Chartres, 86–7
Chiaramonte, Sicilian fam., 9, 170
Chieti, Gualterio da, ct., 54
Chimney House, 245, 252
Chisone, Agostino, 191
Chronique d'Ernoul et de Bernard le Trésorier, 44, 47
Churches
  Ahlata (Lori), Arm., 139
  Armenian Church: see St Mary Vert
  Ayia Photou (St Claire), Gk., Tables 13.2, 3.4
  Ayios Georgios Xorinos, Nst., 158–61, 163, 204, 228, 232, 242; Fig. 9.6, Tables 13.2, 13.4
  Ayia Zoni, Gk, 204, 243, 246, Plate 6, Tables 13.2, 13.4
  Bishop's Chapel, Tables 13.2, 13.4
  Carikli Kilise (Cappadocia), Gk., 178
  Elmani Kilise (Cappadocia), Gk., 178
  Holy Cross (Aght 'amar), Arm., 139
  Holy Cross (Pelendri), Gk., 160
  Holy Wisdom (Nicosia), Lat., 100, 150, 156, 169
  Holy Saviour of Kubba (Lebanon), 55
  Karanlik Kilise (Cappadocia), Gk., 177–8
  Nestorian Church: see Ayios Georgios Xorinos
  'Nameless Church', Nos. I–V, 221, 228, Tables 13.2, 13.4
  Notre Dame (Reims)
  Panayia Phaneromene (Nicosia), Gk., 169
  Panayia Phorbiotissa (Asinou), Gk., 163
  Panayia Podithou (Galata), Gk., 161
  Panayia Theotokos (Galata), Gk., 162
  SS Peter and Paul (Tat'ev), Arm., 139
  SS Peter and Paul, Lat., 2, 4, 6, 10, 122, 128, 131–2, 152–3, 156, 163–5, 224, 228, 232, 242, 245, 252, 265–75, 278, 281–2, 284, 287, Plates 9 and 20–21, Figs. 9.3 to 9.5, 13.6, Tables 13.2, 13.4
  St Anne, Lat., 9, 122, 131, 158, 199, 204, 208–9, 211, 226, 243, 247, 275–6, 278, 282, 286; Figs.7.4, 12.2, 12.4 to 12.7, 17.5, Plates 12–13 and 15, Table 13.2
  St Anthony, Aug., 119, 242, Tables 13.2, 13.4
  St Anthony, Tpl., 8, 53, 55–6
  St Augustine, Aug., 119
  St Augustine, Dom. Chapel
  St Catherine d'Enfé (Lebanon), 55
  St Claire, Lat. St Didier (Avignon), 132
  St Domenico Maggiore (Naples), Lat., 177
  St Dominic, Lat., 118, 122

St Francis, Lat., 4, 116, 125–6, 131, 149, 162, 164–5, 231, 242, 277, 281, Fig. 7.2, Tables 13.2, 13.4
St George, Gen. chapel, 67
St George of the Greeks, 2, 10, 121, 128, 131–2, 151–3, 161, 169, 176, 179, 181–2, 204, 209, 211, 221, 228, 243, 246, 255–7, 263, 272–3, 277, 279, 282, 286, Figs. 9.2, 10.8, 10.9, 12.3, 12.10, 12.11, 15.6, Plates 3, 7, 12, 22–3, Tables 13.2, 13.4
St George of the Latins, 10, 95, 126, 130, 169, 231, 242, 255–7, 262, 277, 280, Figs. 15.1 to 15.5, 15.9 to 15.10, 17.3, Tables 13.2, 13.4
St George of the Latins (Nicosia), Lat., 169
St Gregory (Ani), Arm., 139
St Luke (Nicosia), Gk., 177
St Mary, Carm., 10, 126, 128–9, 131, 152, 156–8, 161–2, 164, 199, 204, 208, 212–14, 228, 243, 247, 255, 257, 263, 276–7, 286, Figs. 7.3, 7.5, 12.12, 15.7 to 15.8, Plates 8 and 17–19, Tables 13.2, 13.4
St Mary of Tyre (Nicosia), Lat., 135–6
St Mary the Green (Ascalon), 137
St Mary Vert (Green), Arm., 8, 10, 132–46, 158, 162, 199, 204, 206, 208–11, 224, 228, 232, 243, 247, 276, 278, 282, Figs. 8.1, 8.2, 12.8; Plates 4–5 and 16, Tables 13.2, 13.4
St Nicholas, Lat. Cathedral, 1–2, 4–5, 8–9, 75–113, 121, 130, 150–53, 156, 161, 164–6, 170, 175, 224, 226, 228, 231, 239, 242, 245, 252, 272–3, 275, 278, 281, Figs. 5.2 to 6.13, 7.6, 9.1, 17.4, Plates 1–2, Tables 13.2, 13.4
St Nicholas, Lat. Cathedral (Nicosia, Sicily), 174
St Nicholas, Lat., NE of Cathedral, Table 13.2
St Nicholas, Gk., 243, 246, 277, 280, Plate 6, Tables 13.2, 13.4
St Simeon/Symeon, Gk., 71, 181, 204, 206, 231, 256, 281, Plate 14, Tables 13.2, 13.4
St Sophia (Nicosia): see Holy Wisdom
St Urbain (Troyes)
Saint-Chapelle (Paris)
Stavros tou Misericou, Gk., 169
Twin (Templar and Hospitaller?) Churches, Lat., 132, 219, 224, 226, 228, 231, 242, 245; Fig. 13.3; Tables 13.2, 13.4
Cibo, Sorleone, 60
Cilicia, Arm. kingdom, 9, 20, 24, 26, 28, 68, 135, 138, 146, 178
Cips/Djips: see Kornokipos
Citadel (Castle) of Famagusta, 182, 224, 227–8, 231–2, Fig. 11.2, Table 13.1
Civran, fam., 183
Clarisses, 118, 120
Clemence, q. of France, 27
Clement V, pope, 118
Clement VI, pope, 132
Cogio, Antonio, 70–71
Cologne, 8, 84, 86, 89–91, 150
Constance of Aragon, 49
Constantinople, 26, 29, 32–3, 66, 70, 163, 176, 187, 189, 201, 257
Contareno, Nicholas, Ven., 68
Conti, John del, abp. of Nicosia, 49, 126, 162
Conway Library, 204, 210, 276, Figs. 12.3 to 12.5, 12.8 to 12.12
Cornaro, Andrea, Ven., 188
Corner, Lodovico, Ven., 28
Council of Europe, 236, 238
Courtauld Institute, 204, 210, Figs. 12.3 to 12.5, 12.8 to 12.12
Crécy, battle of, 189
Crete, 59, 66, 201
Crimea, 26, 70
Curzola, war of, 48

daktyloi, unit of measurement, 39
Dalmatia, 195
Damascus, 25, 27, 31–2
Damietta, 25
Dante (Alighieri), 202
Dardanelles, 29
Dashian, Jacobus, 136
Déaux, Bertrand de, cd., 132
Dehio, George, 84, 87
Del Mozzo Bastion, 231, Fig. 11.2, Tables 13.1, 13.4
Della Scala, fam., 189
Demurger, Alain, 62
Derbes, Anne, 204
Desimoni, Cornelius, 39

Diamante Bastion, 226, 231, 243, Fig. 11.2, Tables 13.1, 13.4
Diocare Bastion, 231, Fig. 11.2, Tables 13.1, 13.4
  flanking tower, 191
Dominicans, 67, 79, 115, 117–20, 122–123
Dommarien, Jacques de, Tpl., 60, 63
Don River, 26
Duc de Berry, 109
Duthoit, 276

Egypt, 1–2, 15, 21, 25–6, 28, 30, 34–6, 38, 51
Eleanor of Aragon
Eleanor of Sicily
Eliades, Johannes, 177
Embriaco, Gen. fam., 161
Emery, Maryse, 85
Enlart, Camille, 10, 55–6, 75, 81–2, 84–5, 87, 95, 113, 125–6, 129–30, 134, 139–44 146, 158, 161–2, 170, 180, 204, 208, 211–12, 219, Fig. 13.2
Enna, Sicilian province, 174
Entença, Bernat Guillem d', Cat. ct., 58, 62
Eschiva of Ibelin, lady of Beirut, 49
Essen, 87
Eudes, ct. of Nevers, 20
Euphemia (Fimi) Arm. princess, 135–6
Europa Nostra, 6, 11, 253, 285
Europe, 9, 48, 51, 70, 75, 79, 81, 83, 86–9, 105, 130, 135, 148, 152, 157, 160, 163, 166, 168, 176, 180, 191, 202, 236
European Charter of Architectural Heritage, 236, 238
European Commission, 6–7, 11
European Union, 5, 280
Eustace of Neuville, 19
Eustorge, Lat. abp., 149

Faber, Felix, Dom., 110
Falcon, Tpl. Ship, 24
Famagusta (St Barbara) Cemetery, Fig. 11.2
Famagusta Gate (*Porta Giuliana*)
Fateinanti, Allegro, 65, 67
Fatinanti, Giustiniano, 69–71
Faxit, Bernard, 118
Fellino, Payen de, 117–18
Fernia, wife of Lupus, 65
Ferramolino, 190
Forrant, Robert, 250
Foscarini, Nicolò, Ven. capt., 183, 186
Four Rivers of Paradise, 110
Fra Giocondo, 190
France, 18, 20, 27, 85, 87, 91, 112–13, 115, 130, 150, 158, 167
Francione, 190
Franciscans, 19, 67, 94, 115–20, 124, 129, 159
Frederick II, German emp., 20, 45, 47, 49, 54
Freiburg-im-Breisgau, 84
Freud, Sigmund, 104
Frodsham, Dan, 6
Furlano, Bartholomew, 68

Gabriel, Marco, Gen., 71
Galanos, Alexis, 6
Galata, 161
Gamir, Berenguer, Tpl., 59
Garinus, Ven., 66–7
Gastria, 8, 54
Gavi, Luca di, Gen., 37
Gavio, Oberto de, Gen., 22
Genoa, Genoese, 2–3, 7–9, 19, 24–5, 29–30, 32, 37, 40–41, 48, 51–2, 55–6, 61–2, 65, 68–71, 116, 121, 155, 161–3, 165, 167, 191, 201, 239
Genoese loggia, 219, Figs. 13.2, 13.3
Genoese war, 45–6, 51
George of Famagusta, abb., 53
George, camlet weaver, 28, 40
Georgians, 201
Germany, 9, 113, 148, 163
Ghazan Khan, Mongol Ilkhan, 25, 58
Ghevond, Arm. bp., 136
Giangirolamo, 191
Gibelet: see Jubail
Gibellino, Stefano, 130–31, 219, Fig. 7.1
Gibellino, Stephan, 121, 127
Gillet, Louis, 81
Giotto, 176, 204
Giustinian, Jeronimo, Ven., 36
Global Heritage Fund, 6
Golden Horde, 26
Gonem, William, abp. of Nicosia, 34
Goreme/Korama region, 177, 178
Goynerits'ants', Step'annos, Arm., 136–7
Graham, Brian, 248
Granada Convention, 236

Gratiani, Antonio Maria, 168
Great Britain: see United Kingdom
Great Wall, 16
Greece, 164, 186
Greeks, 65, 94, 112, 159, 199, 201
Green Man, 101
Grigor IV, Arm. Catholicos, 135
Grigor VII, Arm. Catholicos, 135
Grünemburg, Conrad, 79, 93
Gui, Bernard, 117
Guirardino, 66
Guirardo of St Pancras, Gen., 67
Gulesserian, Babgén, Arm. bp., 135, 138, 140
Gumpenberg, Stephan von, 34
Gunnis, Rupert, 201
Guy (of Trento) bp. of Famagusta, 78–9, 91, 130
Guy of Ibelin, bp. of Limassol, 29

Hasselquist, Frederic, 202
Henry II, k. of Cyprus, 49–50, 53–4, 63, 76–7, 119–21, 135, 149, 164
Henry k. of Poland, 168
Henry of Tyre, 63
S'Hertogenbosch, 87
Het 'um I, k. of Armenia, 135
Het 'um, (Hayton) of Gorhigos, historian, 49, 135
Hilton, J. R., 203
Hohenstaufen, hse. of, 46
Holy Land, 81, 93, 102, 113, 115, 119, 128, 130–31, 149, 151, 165–6, 187
Holy League, 188
Homs, battle of, 63
Honents', Tigran, Arm., 139
Hosp. Order, Hospitallers, 30, 50, 53, 55–6, 58, 64, 194
Hugh III, k. of Cyprus, 50, 54
Hugh IV, k. of Cyprus, 46–7, 49–50, 80, 121, 149–50

I'Anson, Edward, 84, 95, 212
Ibelins, hse. of, 45, 47
Ile de France, 130
Imhaus, Brunehilde, 133
Iohannes son of Iosepe, 23
Istiklal Ave., 236
Italian maritime republics, 2, 50
Italy, Italians, 9, 25–6, 57, 65–6, 115, 148, 160, 165, 180–81, 186, 189, 204

Jacobites, 201
Jacobus de Voragine, Gen. Dom., 214
Jaffa, 57
James II, k. of Cyprus, 3, 34–5, 37, 71–2
James of Ancona, 66
James of Malta, 72
James of Verona, 138, 166, 199
Janus, k. of Cyprus, 31, 33
Jeffery, George, 134, 140, 208, 213, 240
Jerusalem, 3, 7, 50–51, 78–80, 100, 112, 115, 121, 124, 149, 156–7, 159, 178
Jerusalem, Arm. Patriarchate, 136
Jews, 37, 51, 94
John II, k. of Cyprus, 34
John of Joinville, 19
John Xarrache of Beirut, 67
John, Milanese, 68
Jordan River, 110, 206
Jubail, 161
Julien de Saint-Georges, Tpl., 59
Julius II, pope, 187

Kammerer, Albert, 213
Kanch 'uor/Kanch 'vor: see St Mary Vert
Kantakouzenos, Manuel, 164
Karekin I, Hovsepian, Arm. Katholikos, 139
Kayalp, Oktay, 6
Kenaan-Kedar, Nurith, 98, 103–5
Kertikli Hammam, 243, 246, 252, 278
Khach 'atur, Arm., 136
Khirokitia, 63
Kizil Hamam, 243, 245
Konak, 218
Konya, 32
Kornokipos, 136
Kozan: see Sis
Krak (des chevaliers), 128
Kubba, Holy Saviour of
Kurkjian, Vahan, 135
Kyrenia, 30

La Chaise-Dieu, Ben. mon., 132
Ladislas, k. of Naples, 31
Lajazzo: see Ayas
Lakha/Lachas, Nst. fam., 165
Lala Mustapha Mosque: see St Nicholas, Lat. Cathedral
Lambert of Tyre, 66
Lambronats 'i, Nerses, 137

Land Gate, 204, 227, 239, 247, 280, Fig. 13.5
Langlois, Jean, 81
Languedoc, 130
Laodicea (Latakia), 25, 27
Laon, 86, 98
Lapidary Museum (Chapel), Table 13.3
Larnaca, 35
Lavagio, Ansaldo, Gen., 67
Lebanon, 133, 201
Lefkara, 63
Legnano, 190
Leonardo, Giovan Giacomo, 189
Leoni, Michele, 190
Lepanto, 188
Lepsina, 186
Les gestes des Chiprois, 45
Lesgare, Bertrand, 31, 41
Letta, John de, Cat., 69
Levant, 19, 21–2, 38, 161, 195
Levanto, Bartholomew de, Gen. capt., 70
Leventis Foundation, 6
Levon, Arm., 136
Limassol Gate (Famagusta), Fig. 11.2
Limassol, 2, 8, 48–9, 58–60, 62–3, 69, 138
Lindahl, Ingemar, 6
Loggia Bembo, 170, 175, Plates 10–11, Figs. 10.1, 10.5
Lomellini, Luca, s. of Napoleone, 71
Lomellini, Napoleone, Gen. capt., 37, 71
London, 204, 210, 213
Loredan fam., 183, Fig. 10.11
Loredan, Leonardo, Ven. doge, 186
Lorenzo, Ven. capt.
Losa, 70
Louis II, duke of Bourbon, 31, 41
Louis IX, k. of France, 19, 49, 84, 168
Louis X, k. of France, 27
Lowell, 250
Ludolf of Sudheim (von Suchen), 166, 201
Lupus, Bonosiurnus, 65
Lusignans (general), 1–2, 37, 46, 50, 69, 71–2, 78–9, 91, 94, 100, 102, 104–6, 109–10, 112, 124, 153, 155–7, 164, 166, 169, 176, 178, 191, 212, 239, 242, 266
  Aimery de, cst., 63
  Amaury de, 45, 49–50, 63, 76, 122
  Guy de, ct. of Poitou, 106 Guy de, k. of Armenia, 178
  Guy de, k. of Jerusalem, 21
  Isabella de, 164
  Raymondin, ct. of Poitou, 106
  Stephen de, Cyp. chr., 9, 43, 168
Lycia, 214
Lydda, 85

Madrasa/Medrese, 219, 243
Magagnati, Giovanni, 191
Maggi, 190
Makhairas, Leontios, Cyp. chr., 7, 44, 46, 50–51, 77, 202
Makrizi, Arab hist., 19
Mâle, Emil, 97–8, 102–3
Malik Shah, Seljuk ruler, 21
Mamluks, 1–3, 15, 20, 22, 36, 45–6, 59, 79, 115
Mancellus, Dom. bp. of Famagusta, 130
Mansour, Anthony, 68
Manuel Comnenus, Byz. Emp., 135
Mar, Benedetto di, Gen., 61
Mar, Lanfranco di, Gen., 61
Mar, Pasquale di, Gen., 61
Mar, Percivalle di, Gen., 61
Maraclea, 61
Marco Polo, 16, 23
Marco, Pietro di, Gen. capt., 69–71
Marffi, Pierre de, 117
Maria of Bourbon, 49
Maria wife of Peter Anselm, 67
Maria, Francesco, Ven., 195
Marignano, 189
Marinaria, 67, 69
Maronites, 201
Marquet, Bernat, 58–9
Marseilles, 24–5, 61
Martin IV, pope, 54
Martinengo Bastion, 9, 123, 191, 194–6, 199, 204, 224, 231, 243, 246–7, 252, Fig. 11.2, Tables 13.1, 13.4
Martinengo, Ercole, 191
Martini, Francesco di Giorgio, 190, 194
Martoni, Nicola de, 8, 30, 38, 52, 128–9, 149, 156, 202, 212
Mary, s. of k. Janus, 31
Mas Latrie, Louis de, 44, 84
Massachusetts, 275
Matteo, Gian, Ven. capt.
Mecca, 31
Mediterranean, 1–2, 4, 16, 23, 30–31, 38, 65, 70, 147, 187–9, 292
Megaw, A. H. S. (Peter), 203
Mehmet Ali Street house, 226, Table 13.3

Mehmet Efendi, Tomb of, 243
Melusine, 106, 109
Mersey, Lord, 203, 220
Mésange, Pierre, 127
Messina, 29
Mestre, Simon, 62
Michael II, Byz. emp., 25
Midi, 130
Milan, 65
Minho, University of, 5
Moats: 252, 280
  West, 231, Tables 13.1, 13.4
  North, Tables 13.1, 13.4
  South-West, Tables 13.1, 13.4
  South, Tables 13.1, 13.4
Mogabgab, Theophilus, 203, 219–21, 231–3, 240, 275, Figs. 12.2, 13.3 to 13.8
Molay, Jacques de, Tpl., 60–61
Møller, Michael, 6
Monemvasia (Malvoisie), 56, 188
Mongols, 23, 26, 38, 57
Montagnac, 130
Montaigut, Pierre de, Tpl., 54
Monte, Oberto de, 63
Montpellier, 29, 133
Moratto Bastion, Tables 13.1, 13.4
  flanking tower, 191, Fig. 11.2
Morea: see Peloponnese
Morgan, Margaret Ruth, 44
Murcia
Muslims, 2, 51, 66, 102, 112, 178, 187, 202
Mustafa Pasha Mosque (Church of Stavros), 226, 243
Myra, 79, 214
Mystras, 164

Namik Kemal Square, 236, 245, 252
Narbonne, 118, 128
Nauplia, 188
Negroponte, Antonio da, 33
Nérses of Lampron, 135
Nestorians, 154, 201
Netherlands, 87
New Gate, 246
New York Carnegie Corporation, 220
New York, 5–6
Nicholas of Palermo, 72
Nicosia (Cyprus), 1, 3, 7, 21, 23–4, 28–30, 33–8, 40–41, 50–51, 54–5, 59, 70–72, 85, 100, 115, 122, 138, 149, 168–9, 176, 187–8, 218
Nicosia (Sicily), 9, 174
Nigro, Antonio, Gen., 66
Nigro, Nolasco de, Gen., 66
Nikoghayos, Arm. bp., 135
Nizam al-Mulk, 21
Norman, Wilbert, 144, Figs. 12.6 to 12.7
Notre Dame, 79
Novello, Giacometto da, 191
Nuremberg, 168

Oiselay, Aymon de, Tpl., 63–4
Old Testament, 16, 100, 136
Oppenheim, 84, 90
Orbasli, Aydin, 248
Orologgi, Cav., 191, 194
Oshin, bro. of k. Het 'um, 135
Othello's Tower, 9, 182–3, 191, 242–3, 247, 252, 275, 278, Figs. 10.12, 10.13
Otranto, 188, 190
Ottoman bath, 281
Ottoman Palace (Nicosia), 218
Ottoman Period, Ottomans, 3, 9–10, 82, 95, 130, 136, 167–8, 187–9, 194, 196, 202–3, 217, 221, 229, 233, 239, 242, 245–7, 266, 268, 272, 281, 285

Padua (Padova), 194
Palazzo Contarini, 175
Palazzo del Proveditore, Ven., 4, 175, 221, 228 Fig. 10.6, Table 13.3
Palestine, 1–2, 58, 178, 201
Pansana, Marossa, 69–70
papal trade embargo, 2
Paphos, 1, 8, 48, 51, 54, 63
Paris, 6, 17, 81, 86, 168
Pascal, Tpl. treasurer, 59
Patras, 188
Pavia, 189
Pedro IV, k. of Aragon, 29
Pegolotti, Francesco Balducci, 16–17, 20, 27, 33, 39–40
pekhys, pic, picco, unit of measurement, 39–40
Pelendri, 160
Peloponnese, 164, 188
Pera, 32
Pergame, Jacques de, 117
Perivleptos mon. (Mystras), Gk., 164
Persia, 25, 57
Peruzzi, Florentine banking hse., 23–5
Peter I, k. of Cyprus, 3, 29, 45–6, 50–51, 80, 110

Peter II, k. of Cyprus, 3, 29, 50–51, 80, 164
Petros of Cilicia, 135
Petros, Arm. Katholikos, 138
Petzet, Michael, 6
Philip of Antioch, Fran., 116
Philip of Novara, chr., 45, 47
Philip the Good, duke of Burgundy, 32
Philip V, k. of France, 20
Phocea, 26
Piazetta San Marco, 176, 183, Fig. 10.2
Piazza (Famagusta), 218–19, 224, Table 13.2
Pico, Giacomo, Gen., 57
Pieridis Foundation, 6
Piloti, Emmanuel, 31–2
Pisa, Pisans, 20, 24
Plagnieux, Philippe, 82, 134, 139, 154, 208
Podocataro, fam., 168
Poitou, 109
Pontelli, 190
Port Said, 240
Porta Giuliana (Famagusta Gate), 183
Porta Sancti Andree, Pagano di, Gen., 67
Porta, Iohannes de, Gen. intpr., 22, 24
Porto Bonello, 25
Pringle, Denis, 130
Processus Cypricus, 8, 59, 61
Protestant Cemetery, 219
Pulacazaro, flanking tower, 191, Fig. 11.2
Pyrga, Royal Chapel, 204

Quarto, Guglielmo de, Gen., 66
Querela Cypri, 54
Qinnasrin, Syrian prov., 25
Qutlugh Shah, Mongol general, 58

Ragazzione Annexe, 226, Tables 13.2, 13.4
Ralla, Januinus, Gen., 118
Ramleh, 27
Raoul of Nesles, cst. of France, 27
Rashid al Din, scholar, 25
Ratisbon, 85–6
Raval (Ravendel/*Ravendal*?), Gauvain de, Tpl., 61
Ravelin (Akkule), 194, 196, 221, 224, 227–8, 231, 243, 252, Tables 13.1, 13.4
Ravenna, 181, 189
Raymond of Piis, lg., 49
Raymond, Hugh, consul, 61
Raynaldo, Nicholas de, 117
Recital concerning the Sweet Land of Cyprus, 46
Reims, 17, 60, 79, 84, 86–7, 150
Renaissance, 43, 167, 170, 175, 189–91, 217
Renier, family, Fig. 10.7
Renier, Giovanni, Ven. capt., 175
Rhineland, 8, 84–5, 87–8, 90
Rhodes, 28–9, 34, 51, 194–5
Ribaldo, Antonio, 37
Richard I (Lionheart), k. of England, 49
Roberti, Peter, Gen., 66
Rocha, Giovanni da, Gen., 59
Rochas, fam., 168
Rodez, 87
Roman Empire, 187, 239
Roman sarcophagus, 281
Rome, 68, 101, 104, 190
Rose, Bernard de, 66
Rosso, Pietro, 58
Rovere, Guidobaldo della, Ven., 195
Royal (later Venetian) Palace, 156, 164, 224, 228, 231–3, 243, 245, 272, 280, Table 13.3
Ruad, 49, 58–9, 61
ruga Templi, 8, 56

St Anne, Ben. mon. in Famagusta, 131
St Anne, Ben. mon. in Jerusalem, 131
St Anne, Ben. mon. in Nicosia, 131
St Anne, Tpl. ship, 62
St Anthony, Gen. Dom. penitential order of, 55
St Anthony, hospital, 57, 120, 129
St Anthony, Tpl. commandery, 54, 56–7, 63–4
St Anthony of Vienne, order of, 120
St Bernard of Clairvaux, 8, 97
St Brigitte of Sweden, 8, 110, 166, 202
St Catherine's Creek, Fig. 11.2
St Cosmas, neighbourhood, 69
St Cufinus, 128
St George (Rhodes), tower, 194
St Helena, 128–9, 142, 211
St John (Rhodes), tower, 194
St John, Tpl. ship, 57–8
St Leo, pope, 128
St Mary of Mt Carmel, mon., 128
St Mary of Mt Carmel, neighbourhood, 69
St Napa (Giudezza) Bastion, Fig. 11.2, Tables 13.1, 13.4

St Nicholas, ship, 58
St Sebastian, 55
St Sosius, 128
St Thomas Aquinas, 97
St Ursula, 128
St Willibald, 112
Sagona, Paschal de, Gen., 67
Saint Denis, 86
Saint-Germer-de-Fly, 86
Saint Louis in Poissy, 86
Saint-Urbain in Troyes, 81, 83, 85
Sainte-Chapelle, 85–6
Salamis, 174, 276
Salines, 48
Salonica: see Thessaloniki
Salt store, 243
Sambuceto, Lamberto di, Gen., 48, 56–61, 117–18
San Apollinario, 28
Sangallo, 190
San Luca, Bastion, Table 13.4 flanking tower, 191, Fig. 11.2
San Michele Bastion, 182
Sanmicheli, Michele, Ven., 190, 195
Sunt Nicolau, ship
Santa Catherina di Formello, Lat. mon., 168
Santmartí, Sanç Pérez de, 58
Sanudo, Marino, 44
Saracens, 50, 112
Saray, 26
Satalia (Antalya), 25–7
Savio, Bonaggiunta de, 66
Savorgnao, Ascanio, 191–2, 195
Savorgnano, Giulio, 191
Schabel, Christopher, 47
Schilbach, Erich, 39
Scola, Basilio della, 190, 194
Sea Gate (Porta del Mare), 7, 218, 239, 243, 247, 252, 281, Fig. 11.2
Seattle, 5
Senlis, 86
Serralier, Raymond, 29
Sesto, Oddone del, Gen., 56
Seymun, Mansur ibn, scribe, 62
Sicily, Sicilians, 29, 69, 167, 170, 181
Signoria (Seigneury) Bastion, 191, 226, 231, Fig. 11.2
Simisso, 33
Sis, 25, 138
Sodom and Gomorrah, 110
Solaro, Giacomo da, Gen., 57
Soranzo, Lorenzo, Ven., 32
Spain, 58, 167
Spanish America, 9, 191
Spanish Empire, 187
Staciones, 226, Tables 13.2, 13.4
Step 'anos, Arm., 136
Strambaldi, Diomede, Cyp. chr., 44, 77
Strasbourg, 84
Stubbs, John, 5
Styria, 188
Syria, 1–2, 8, 15–16, 20–23, 26, 28, 30, 38, 48–9, 51, 57–8, 79, 85, 94, 165, 201, 257
Syrians, 22–3, 65, 154, 159, 166

Ta'déos, Arm. bp., 135
Tabakhane Mosque: see Tanners' Mosque
Tabriz, 25
Tafur, Pero, 33–4, 202
Tana, 26
Tangut, 16, 23
Tanners' Mosque, 158, 209, 226, 243, 247, 275, 278, 282, Tables 13.2, 13.4
Tarsus, 25
Templar Order, Templars, 8, 49, 53–64
Ternatio, Barnabas, 70
Theodore, Gk. doctor, 62
Theodore, Gk. priest, 28
Theophilus, Byz. emp., 25
Thessaloniki, 160, 163, 201
Thetis Foundation, 6
Thomas, Gk., bro. of Theodore, 62
Thomas, Peter, papal lg., 162, 257
Tibet, 23
Tiepolo, Giacomo, Ven. doge, 20
Tiesdell, Steve, 237
Tortosa, 58–9, 66, 79
Toulouse, 115
Tournais, 86
Trebizond, 33
Très Riches Heures, 109
Trevisan, Balthazar, Ven. capt., 36
Treviso, 194
Tripoli, 2, 19–21, 25, 27, 48, 58–9, 72, 158
Troodos Mts, 147, 160
Troyes, 81, 85
Turkestan, 26
Turkey, Turks, 187, 190–91, 195, 284
Tuscany, 190, 204
Tyre, 2, 48, 50, 58, 66, 121
Tyrrhenian Sea, 167

United Kingdom, 239
United States of America (USA), 250
Urgenc, 26

Vacher, Sydney, 84, 95
Vaivre, Jean-Bernard de, 55, 82, 85, 134
Vallona, 188
Valturio, 189
Vares, Pierre de, Tpl., 57
Vasari, 190, 195
Vegezio, 189
Venetian fountain, Fig. 13.4, Table 13.4
  house, 243, 245
  walls, 1, 3–4, 9, 192–6, 228, Figs. 13.1, 13.7
Veneticus, 67
Veneto region, 168
Venice, Venetians, 3, 7–8, 15, 20, 27–8, 30, 34–7, 48, 62, 65, 155, 163, 167–70, 174, 176, 178, 183, 186, 188–90, 201–2, 239, 266
Venier, Nicolò, Ven., 28
Verona, 190
Vézelay, 105
Vicenza, 190
Vienna, 85
Vindergio, Leonello da, Gen., 57
Viollet le Duc, 180
Visien, Pierre, Tpl., 57
Vitruvius, 189, 271
Vivarini, 176
Viviano de Ginnebaldo, intpr., 23
Vogüé, Melchior de, 84
Volga River

Walls (Famagusta): Fig. 13.7
  Counterscarp, 231, Tables 13.1, 13.4
  Curtain, 231, Tables 13.1, 13.4
  Land Gate Approaches, Tables 13.1, 13.4
  Sea Walls, Tables 13.1, 13.4
Washington D.C., 275
Weyl-Carr, Annemarie, 161, 201–2, 204
Wilbrand of Oldenburg, 47
William of Tyre, chr., 44
William of Tyre, continuations of, 45, 47
Woodcock, Alex, 98
World Monuments Fund (WMF), 5–6, 11, 209, 237, 253, 275, 279, 284, 287, 292

Yermasoyia, 63
Yohannés, Arm., 136
Young, S. Hatfield, 201
Yovhanés Vardapet, Arm., 137
Yumurtalik: see Ayas

Zaccaria, Matteo, 61
Zacha, widow of Anton Audeth, 35
Zacharias, Giovanni, 117
Zanchi, Gianbattista, 191
Zanverdiani, Dario, 168
Zara, 32
Zibaldone da Canal, Ven. trade manual, 27
Zierikzee, 189
Zotardo, Bernardo, 66